Frommer's®

Colorado

10th Edition

by Eric Peterson

Here's what the critics say about Frommer's:

"Amazingly easy to use. Very portable, very complete."
—BOOKLIST

"Detailed, accurate, and easy-to-read information for all price ranges."
—GLAMOUR MAGAZINE

"Hotel information is close to encyclopedic."
—DES MOINES SUNDAY REGISTER

"Frommer's Guides have a way of giving you a real feel for a place."
—KNIGHT RIDDER NEWSPAPERS

WILEY
Wiley Publishing, Inc. [redacted]

Published by:

WILEY PUBLISHING, INC.

111 River St.
Hoboken, NJ 07030-5774

ISBN 978-0-470-38229-5

Editor: Emil J. Ross
Production Editor: M. Faunette Johnston
Cartographer: Andrew Dolan
Photo Editor: Richard Fox
Production by Wiley Indianapolis Composition Services

Front cover photo: The Dead Horse Mill, outside the ghost town of Crystal
Back cover photo: Skier on Silverton Mountain, southwestern Colorado

For information on our other products and services or to obtain technical support, please contact our Customer Care Department within the U.S. at 800/762-2974, outside the U.S. at 317/572-3993 or fax 317/572-4002.

Wiley also publishes its books in a variety of electronic formats. Some content that appears in print may not be available in electronic formats.

Manufactured in the United States of America

5 4 3 2 1

CONTENTS

4 SUGGESTED COLORADO ITINERARIES 49

5 THE ACTIVE VACATION PLANNER 57

6 SETTLING INTO DENVER 69

7 WHAT TO SEE & DO IN DENVER 100

8 COLORADO SPRINGS 143

9 BOULDER 183

10 NORTHEASTERN COLORADO 214

11 THE NORTHERN ROCKIES 241

12 THE WESTERN SLOPE 333

13 SOUTHWESTERN COLORADO 367

14 THE SOUTHERN ROCKIES 403

15 SOUTHEASTERN COLORADO 427

APPENDIX: FAST FACTS, TOLL-FREE NUMBERS & WEBSITES 448

INDEX 460

LIST OF MAPS

ABOUT THE AUTHOR

A Denver-based writer, **Eric Peterson** has contributed to numerous Frommer's guides covering the American West and has authored *Frommer's Montana & Wyoming, Frommer's Yellowstone & Grand Teton National Parks,* and *Ramble California* (www.fulcrum-books.com). He also writes about travel and other topics for such publications as *ColoradoBiz, United Hemispheres, Delta Sky,* and the *New York Daily News.*

ACKNOWLEDGMENTS

The author wishes to thank for their help Rich Grant, Angela Berardino, and Carrina Junge with the Denver Metro Convention and Visitors Bureau; Kim Farin with the Boulder Convention and Visitors Bureau; Lisa Amend with the Colorado Springs Convention and Visitors Bureau; and Suzy Blackhurst with the Estes Park Convention and Visitors Bureau.

AN INVITATION TO THE READER

In researching this book, we discovered many wonderful places—hotels, restaurants, shops, and more. We're sure you'll find others. Please tell us about them, so we can share the information with your fellow travelers in upcoming editions. If you were disappointed with a recommendation, we'd love to know that, too. Please write to:

Frommer's Colorado, 10th Edition
Wiley Publishing, Inc. • 111 River St. • Hoboken, NJ 07030-5774

AN ADDITIONAL NOTE

Please be advised that travel information is subject to change at any time—and this is especially true of prices. We therefore suggest that you write or call ahead for confirmation when making your travel plans. The authors, editors, and publisher cannot be held responsible for the experiences of readers while traveling. Your safety is important to us, however, so we encourage you to stay alert and be aware of your surroundings. Keep a close eye on cameras, purses, and wallets, all favorite targets of thieves and pickpockets.

FROMMER'S STAR RATINGS, ICONS & ABBREVIATIONS

Every hotel, restaurant, and attraction listing in this guide has been ranked for quality, value, service, amenities, and special features using a **star-rating system.** In country, state, and regional guides, we also rate towns and regions to help you narrow down your choices and budget your time accordingly. Hotels and restaurants are rated on a scale of zero (recommended) to three stars (exceptional). Attractions, shopping, nightlife, towns, and regions are rated according to the following scale: zero stars (recommended), one star (highly recommended), two stars (very highly recommended), and three stars (must-see).

In addition to the star rating system, we also use **seven feature icons** that point you to the great deals, in-the-know advice, and unique experiences that separate travelers from tourists. Throughout the book, look for:

Finds	Special finds—those places only insiders know about
Fun Facts	Fun facts—details that make travelers more informed and their trips more fun
Kids	Best bets for kids, and advice for the whole family
Moments	Special moments—those experiences that memories are made of
Overrated	Places or experiences not worth your time or money
Tips	Insider tips—great ways to save time and money
Value	Great values—where to get the best deals

The following **abbreviations** are used for credit cards:

AE	American Express	DISC	Discover	V	Visa
DC	Diners Club	MC	MasterCard		

FROMMERS.COM

Now that you have this guidebook to help you plan a great trip, visit our website at **www.frommers.com** for additional travel information on more than 4,000 destinations. We update features regularly to give you instant access to the most current trip-planning information available. At Frommers.com, you'll find scoops on the best airfares, lodging rates, and car rental bargains. You can even book your travel online through our reliable travel booking partners. Other popular features include:

- Online updates of our most popular guidebooks
- Vacation sweepstakes and contest giveaways
- Newsletters highlighting the hottest travel trends
- Podcasts, interactive maps, and up-to-the-minute events listings
- Opinionated blog entries by Arthur Frommer himself
- Online travel message boards with featured travel discussions

What's New in Colorado

Colorado is a rich combination of the old and new, urban and rural, the civilized and the wild. The state's major cities lure us with their museums, galleries, performing arts, and historic sites, but just outside their boundaries awaits a vast array of outdoor recreation opportunities and some of America's most beautiful mountain scenery.

Growth, which Coloradans see as both a blessing and a curse, continues to be the main change occurring here. And for at least the next few years, those who venture into the mountains will see not only the remnants of damage from dozens of forest fires that plagued the state in 2002, but also how quickly the forests can begin to regenerate and heal themselves.

The big event in recent years was the Democratic National Convention in Denver in August 2008, where Barack Obama accepted the presidential nomination at the home of the Denver Broncos, Invesco Field at Mile High, in front of a capacity crowd. Whether the glare of the media spotlight will catalyze even more growth for the city remains to be seen.

SETTLING INTO DENVER **Southwest Airlines** has continually expanded at Denver International Airport since its first flights touched down at Denver International Airport in 2006. The light rail has expanded significantly in recent years. Four new lines have come on: The **E Line** runs along I-25 from Broadway to Lincoln Avenue in the south suburbs. The **F Line** connects 18th and California streets downtown with Lincoln Avenue. The **G Line** runs from Nine Mile in Aurora at I-225 and Parker Road to Lincoln; the **H Line** connects Nine Mile and 18th and California. Downtown Denver has a pair of new lodging options: the swank **Ritz-Carlton Denver,** 1881 Curtis St. (© **303/312-3800**), and **The Curtis,** 1405 Curtis St. (**800/525-6651** or 303/572-3300), a fun and pop-culture-loving hotel. Denver also boasts some excellent new restaurants in **Duo,** 2413 W. 32nd Ave. (© **303/820-2282**), serving terrific interpretations of American standards in a warm space in the Highlands neighborhood, and **Encore,** 2250 E. Colfax Ave. (© **303/399-5353**), a slick new Mediterranean eatery at the renovated theater complex now anchored by the Tattered Cover Book Store. See chapter 6 for details.

WHAT TO SEE & DO IN DENVER The **Museum of Contemporary Art Denver,** 1485 Delgany St. (© **303/298-7554**), opened its terrific new building in 2007, a stark, avant-garde structure that puts the artists on center stage. Six Flags sold **Elitch Gardens Theme Park,** Speer Boulevard at I-25 (© **303/595-4386**), but little has changed except for the banishment of Looney Tunes characters and Batman. New in 2009, the **Denver Museum of Nature & Science,** in City Park, 2001 Colorado Blvd. (© **303/322-7009**), will open "Expedition Health," a state-of-the-art exhibit that allows visitors an eye-opening look at the workings of their own bodies. The **Colorado Rapids** (© **303/405-1100;** www.coloradorapids.com) of Major League Soccer now play home games at the new Dick's Sporting Goods Park in Commerce City. Flying Dog bolted to Maryland, but **Great Divide Brewing Co.** opened a great new tap room at its downtown brewery, 2201 Arapahoe St. (✆ **303/296-9460,** ext. 26). See chapter 7 for details.

COLORADO SPRINGS Longtime Manitou Springs favorite **Adam's Mountain Cafe,** 934 Manitou Ave.(✆ **719/685-1430**), relocated from its longtime Cañon Avenue address to the ground floor of the restored Spa Building in 2007. Thankfully, the tasty, healthy food, and country-meets-French-Victorian vibe remain. The Hawaiian taco joint **La'au's,** 830 N. Tejon St. (✆ **719/578-5228**), is a new favorite for Colorado College students—and travelers pinching their pennies. At **Garden of the Gods,** 1805 N. 30th St. (✆ **719/634-6666**), the excellent multimedia theater presentation *How Did Those Red Rocks Get There?* was newly remade by local filmmaker John Bourbonais for 2008. A major expansion at the **Colorado Springs Fine Art Center,** 30 W. Dale St. (✆ **719/634-5581**), doubled the gallery space and won raves from critics. New in 2008 at the **Cheyenne Mountain Zoo,** 4250 Cheyenne Mountain Zoo Rd. (✆ **719/633-9925**), the $8.2-million "Rocky Mountain Wild" lets visitors get up close and personal with mountain lions, grizzly bears, moose, and other local denizens. See chapter 8 for details.

BOULDER In 2007, the stalwart Pearl Street burger joint **Tom's Tavern** shut its doors after 49 years following the passing of owner Tom Eldridge. Also closing since the last edition: **Trilogy Wine Bar** and **Rhumba.** As for openings, **Black Cat,** 1964 13th St. (✆ **303/444-5500**), sources a good deal of its ingredients from owner-chef Eric Skokan's half-acre garden. The new outdoor shopping center, **Twenty Ninth Street,** centered on the former site of the long-languishing Crossroads Mall at the intersection of Canyon Boulevard and 29th Street (✆ **303/440-0722**), is now open for business. See chapter 9 for details.

THE NORTHERN ROCKIES **Steamboat Springs** Longtime budget-oriented condominium complex **Thunderhead** had a date with a bulldozer as a base village redevelopment got underway in 2008.

Winter Park **Devil's Thumb Ranch,** Grand C.R. 83, Tabernash, 8 miles north of Winter Park (✆ **800/933-4339** or 970/726-5632), opened its terrific new lodge, as well as a spa/fitness center, in early 2008. The base village at **Winter Park Resort** is undergoing a makeover.

Breckenridge The **Arts District of Breckenridge,** Ridge Street and Washington Avenue, has blossomed into a new attraction with open studios, classes, and resident artists. **BlueSky,** 42 Snowflake Dr. (✆ **800/506-7521**), a posh new condominium lodge, opened in 2007.

Vail **Vail's New Dawn,** a multibillion-dollar makeover of Vail Village consisting of numerous hotel, residential, retail, and infrastructure projects, is almost complete. One of the latest and greatest projects to be finished was the storybook **Arrabelle at Vail Square,** 675 Lionshead Place (✆ **866/662-7625**), which opened in 2008 in Lionshead Square. West of Vail, **State Bridge Lodge and River Resort** burned to the ground in 2007.

Beaver Creek To help get you onto the mountain faster, **Beaver Creek Resort** (✆ **800/404-3535**) opened a new gondola from Avon in December 2007.

Aspen One of the longstanding affordable mom-and-pop motels, the **Limelight Lodge,** 228 E. Cooper Ave. (✆ **800/433-0832** or 970/925-3025), was bulldozed in 2006, rebuilt, and reopened in fall 2008 as a contemporary "green" motel on the same spot. Aspen's dining scene just gets better and better, with **Social,** 304 E. Hopkins Ave. (✆ **970/925-9700**), a colorful tapas eatery, one of the newest shining stars. Nearby **Snowmass Village** is in the midst of a major redevelopment, with Viceroy and Little Nell projects in the works through 2010.

See chapter 11 for more information.

THE WESTERN SLOPE **Grand Junction** The dinosaur quarry and visitor center at **Dinosaur National Monument,** 4545 E. U.S. 40, Dinosaur (✆ **970/374-3000**), has been closed indefinitely while much-needed structural repairs are made. There's still plenty to do there, though, and some spectacular scenic views as well.

Glenwood Springs **Glenwood Hot Springs Pool,** 401 N. River Rd. (✆ **800/577-7946** or 970/945-4228), opened the Spa of the Rockies in 2008. **Riviera,** 702 Grand Ave. (✆ **970/945-7692**), injected a shot of contemporary flair into the local restaurant landscape.

Paonia **Fresh and Wyld Farmhouse Inn B&B,** 1978 Harding Rd. (✆ **970/527-4389**), opened in 2008, offering a pastoral place to stay, as well as breakfasts made primarily of ingredients from the on-site garden.

See chapter 12 for more information.

SOUTHWESTERN COLORADO **Durango** **Soaring Tree Top Adventures** (✆ **970/769-2357**), accessible only by railroad, offers the most extensive zip-line course in the world. The authentic **Irish Embassy,** 900 Main Ave. (✆ **970/403-1200**), opened in summer 2008 and was an instant hit with locals and tourists alike.

Telluride **Lumière,** in Mountain Village (✆ **866/530-9466**), a LEED-certified boutique hotel, opened on the slopes in 2008.

See chapter 13 for more information.

THE SOUTHERN ROCKIES **Gunnison** There's a new observatory in Southern Colorado: The **Gunnison Valley Observatory,** Yucca Court (✆ **970/642-1111**), began hosting free star parties in 2008.

Salida Serving tasty Mexican grub and potent margaritas, the **BoatHouse Cantina,** 228 F St. (✆ **719/539-5004**), opened right on the Arkansas River in 2008.

See chapter 14 for details.

SOUTHEASTERN COLORADO In Pueblo, the **Steelworks Museum of Industry & Culture,** 1612 Abriendo Ave. (✆ **719/564-9086**), opened its doors in 2007, showcasing the history of Pueblo's industry.

See chapter 15 for details.

1

The Best of Colorado

The old and the new, the rustic and the sophisticated, the wild and the refined—all of these experiences exist practically side by side in Colorado, amid what is arguably the most breathtaking mountain scenery in America.

Colorado's booming cities—Boulder, Colorado Springs, and Denver—and its admittedly somewhat glitzy resorts—especially Vail and Aspen—offer much of the comfort and culture of New York or Los Angeles but at a slower, more relaxed pace. Throughout the state, you'll also find testaments to another time, when life was simpler but rougher and only the strong survived: historic Victorian mansions, working turn-of-the-20th-century steam trains, thousand-year-old adobe-and-stone villages, and authentic Old West towns complete with false-fronted saloons and dusty streets.

Enos Mills, an early-20th-century environmentalist and one of the driving forces behind the creation of Rocky Mountain National Park, said that knowledge of nature is the basis of wisdom. So climb on a horse or mountain bike, take a hike or a raft trip—or simply sit back and gaze at the mountains. (Atop Pikes Peak, you'll see what inspired Katharine Lee Bates to pen the lyrics to "America the Beautiful.") Whatever you do, though, don't stay indoors. Colorado truly comes alive for those who venture outdoors—to the towering Rocky Mountains, the western canyons, or the broad eastern plains.

The following are what I consider Colorado's best experiences—highlights that will help you begin planning your trip.

1 THE BEST SKI RESORTS

- **Aspen:** Not only does Aspen have predictably superior ski terrain ranging from some of the most expert runs in Colorado to what *Ski* magazine has called the best mountain in America for beginners (Buttermilk), but it's also one of the most fun, genuinely historic ski towns in Colorado. Although it might come off at first as somewhat glitzy and certainly expensive, Aspen is a real town, with longtime, year-round residents and a history that goes beyond the slopes. See chapter 11.
- **Breckenridge:** The lure of Breckenridge lies in its fabulous trails for skiers of all abilities, its location in an old gold-prospecting settlement, and its abundance of ski-in/ski-out lodging. It's also less expensive than Aspen and Vail, more rustic in feel, and appealing to families for its variety of après-ski activities. See chapter 11.
- **Telluride:** The funky historic town of Telluride at the bottom of the slopes and the posh Mountain Village at the mountain base offer the best of both worlds, as does the resort's diverse terrain, with plenty of snow for skiers of all levels. See chapter 13.
- **Vail:** This is it, the big one, America's flagship ski resort, as well as one of its largest, with 5,289 acres of skiable terrain, 193 trails, and 34 lifts. Every serious skier needs to ski Vail at least once. Its free bus system makes it easy to get around, but be prepared for steep prices, and don't look for Victorian charm—all you'll find are rows of condominiums. See chapter 11.

2 THE BEST ACTIVE VACATIONS

- **Hiking in Rocky Mountain National Park:** There's something for everyone here, from short hikes around a lovely mountain lake to the difficult 8-mile trek to the top of 14,259-foot Longs Peak. Trail heads can be accessed with the park's shuttle bus, from campgrounds, and from stops along Trail Ridge Road. However you do it, getting into the wilds is a treat in this beautiful setting. See chapter 11.
- **Cowpunching on a Cattle Drive:** To really step back into the West of the 1800s, join working cowboys on a genuine cattle drive. The **Saddleback Ranch** near Steamboat Springs (© **970/871-4697**) is a working cattle ranch, where you'll become just another cowpuncher, moving stock from one pasture to another and performing other ranch duties. See p. 267.
- **Skiing the San Juan Hut System:** Ambitious cross-country skiers who want to put a few miles behind them, as well as take in the 14,000-foot alpine peaks, love the San Juan Hut System's trail and series of shelters between Telluride and Moab, Utah. Designed for intermediate skiers, the trail can be tackled in small sections or its entirety, with overnight stays in the well-equipped huts. See chapter 13.
- **Soaring in the Treetops:** A network of 25 zip lines up to 1,400 feet long that crisscross the Animas River, **Soaring Tree Top Adventures** near Durango (© **970/769-2357**) allows visitors to get a bird's-eye view of an old-growth forest, sometimes from 100 feet above the ground. The attraction is accessible only via the Durango & Silverton Narrow Gauge Railroad. See p. 375.

3 THE BEST HIKING TRAILS

- **The Buttes Trail at Pawnee Buttes:** This easy day hike exposes you to some of the "other" Colorado: the prairie on the state's eastern plains. A 1.5-mile trail leads to Pawnee Buttes, the Rattlesnake Buttes made famous in James Michener's *Centennial.* Keep your eyes open for coyotes, a variety of birds, and other wildlife, and colorful wildflowers in the spring. See p. 231.
- **The Emerald Lake Trail at Rocky Mountain National Park:** If you like mountain lakes, this is the trail for you. Starting at Bear Lake, it's an easy .5-mile walk to Nymph Lake, then a moderate .5-mile climb to Dream Lake, and the last .8 mile brings you to Emerald Lake. Total elevation change is 605 feet over a little less than 2 miles, with spectacular scenery all along the way. See p. 259.
- **The Colorado Trail at Kenosha Pass:** This easy section of the Colorado Trail near Breckenridge is a fun day's walk or can be the starting point for a serious backpacking trip. Pick up the trail off U.S. 285 where the highway crosses 10,001-foot Kenosha Pass. This access point provides opportunities for short or long hikes through the aspen and bristlecone forest. See p. 291.
- **Hiking the Dunes in Great Sand Dunes National Monument & Preserve:** This isn't a trail at all, but an opportunity to don your best French foreign legion hat and set out into the shifting sands in search of dramatic views from the top of a 750-foot dune. See p. 422.

Colorado

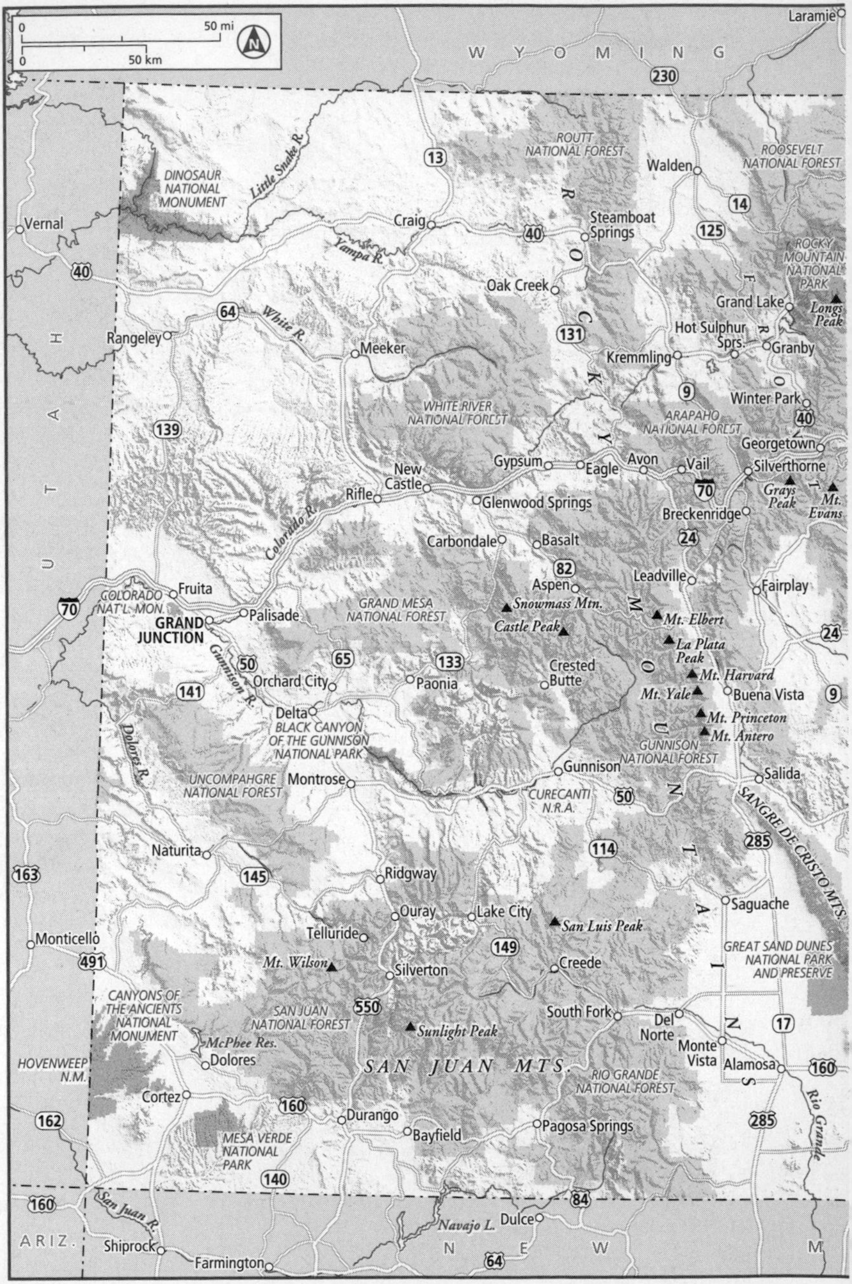

THE BEST OF COLORADO

1

THE BEST HIKING TRAILS

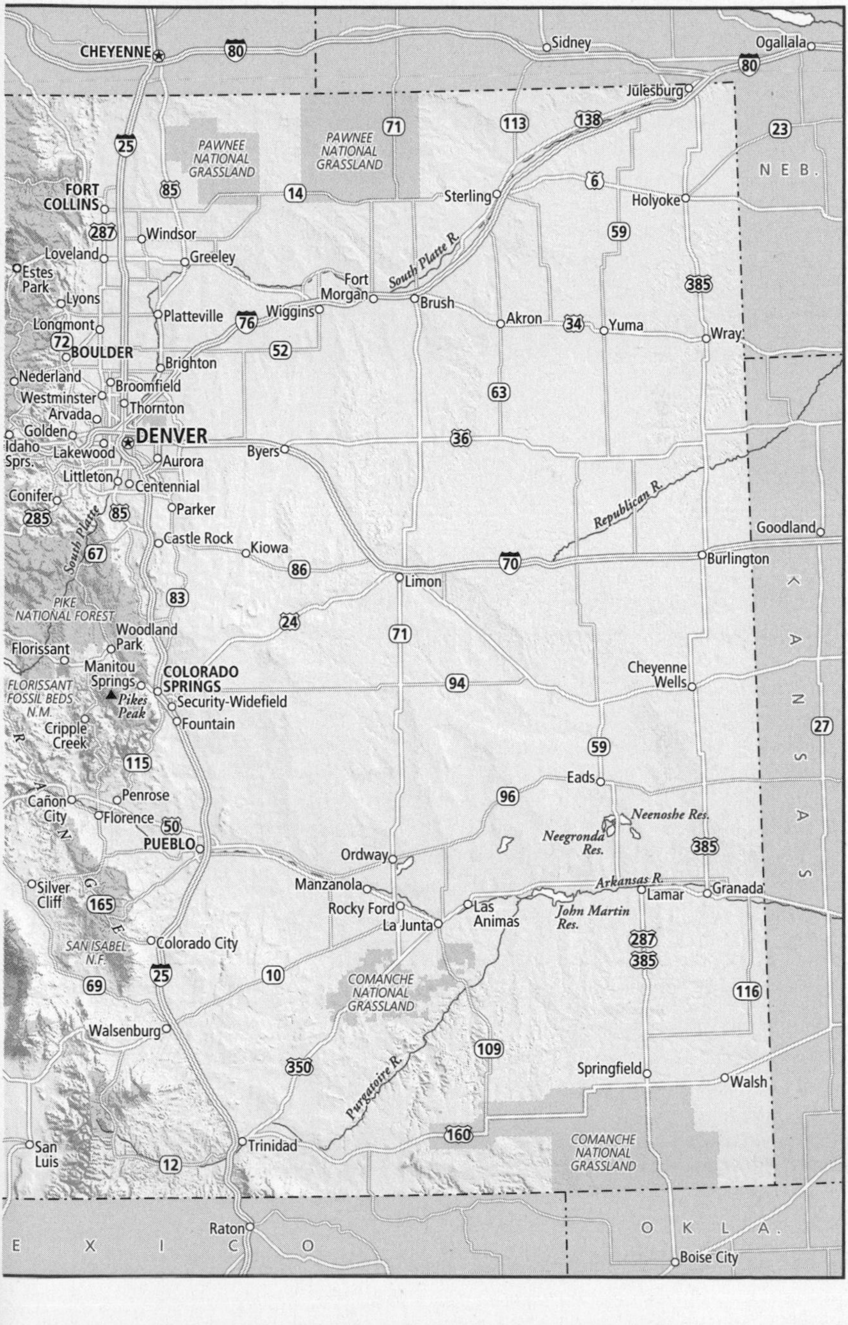
CHEYENNE
80
Sidney
Ogallala
Julesburg
71
113
138
23
25
PAWNEE NATIONAL GRASSLAND
PAWNEE NATIONAL GRASSLAND
N E B.
FORT COLLINS
85
14
Sterling
6
Holyoke
287
Windsor
59
Loveland
Greeley
South Platte R.
Estes Park
Fort Morgan
385
Lyons
Brush
Platteville
76
Wiggins
Akron
34
Yuma
Longmont
Wray
72
BOULDER
52
Brighton
Nederland
Broomfield
63
Westminster
Thornton
Arvada
Golden
DENVER
36
Idaho Sprs.
Lakewood
Aurora
Byers
Littleton
Centennial
Conifer
Republican R.
285
85
Parker
Goodland
South Platte
Castle Rock
Kiowa
1
67
86
70
Burlington
Limon
83
K
PIKE NATIONAL FOREST
24
Woodland Park
71
A
Florissant
Manitou Springs
COLORADO SPRINGS
94
Cheyenne Wells
FLORISSANT FOSSIL BEDS N.M.
Pikes Peak
Security-Widefield
N
Fountain
27
Cripple Creek
R
59
S
115
Eads
96
Cañon City
Penrose
Neenoshe Res.
Florence
Neegronda Res.
A
A
50
PUEBLO
385
N
Ordway
S
Arkansas R.
Silver Cliff
G
Manzanola
Lamar
Granada
165
Rocky Ford
Las Animas
John Martin Res.
La Junta
E
SAN ISABEL N.F.
Colorado City
287
385
69
25
10
COMANCHE NATIONAL GRASSLAND
116
Walsenburg
109
350
Purgatoire R.
Springfield
Walsh
San Luis
Trinidad
160
COMANCHE NATIONAL GRASSLAND
12
Raton
E X I C O
O K L A.
Boise City

4 THE BEST MOUNTAIN BIKING

- **Tipperary Creek Trail:** Considered by many to be Colorado's very best mountain-biking trail, this 30-mile ride from Fraser to Winter Park runs through dense forest and wildflower-covered meadows, offering views of rugged snowcapped peaks. It's also strenuous, rising from an 8,600-foot elevation to more than 10,000 feet. See p. 282.
- **Crested Butte:** Crested Butte vies with Marin County, California, as the birthplace of mountain biking. Check out the Mountain Bike Hall of Fame for a primer on the sport's history; then serious bikers should try Trail 401, a strenuous single-track loop that combines scenic beauty with steep grades and rough terrain. See p. 413.

5 THE BEST WILDERNESS EXPERIENCES

- **Hiking the Colorado Trail:** For some 500 miles, this trail winds from Denver to Durango, through some of the state's most spectacular and rugged terrain, crossing the Continental Divide, eight mountain ranges, and six wilderness areas. Just to the west of Leadville, the trail passes through the Collegiate Peaks Wilderness with a view of some of Colorado's most prominent "fourteeners" (mountains at least 14,000 ft. high) and fields of wildflowers. The hardier might take a side trip up Mount Elbert, the state's tallest peak, at 14,433 feet. See chapters 5, 7, 11, and 13.
- **Hiking in the Maroon Bells National Wilderness Area:** With a number of fourteeners, including the namesake Maroon Bells, this is one of the most scenic mountainscapes in the West. A vision of glaciated rock and lush greenery, the trails here are popular with backpackers, but there are plenty of good day hikes; if you're feeling energetic, you can hike from Aspen to Crested Butte. See p. 413.
- **Rafting Glenwood Canyon or the Arkansas River:** Running the rapids on the Colorado and Arkansas rivers is one of the best and surely most exciting ways to see one of the most beautiful canyons in the West. Although a bit too popular to provide a genuine wilderness experience, these stretches of river both have sections rated for experts during the high spring runoff, as well as quieter areas appropriate for everyone. See chapters 12 and 14.

6 THE BEST OF AMERICAN INDIAN CULTURE

- **Ute Indian Museum (Montrose):** One of Colorado's few museums dedicated to an existing Indian tribe, this excellent collection, run by the Colorado Historical Society, shows how Utes lived in the 19th century, as they were being forced to reconcile their way of life with that of the invading white pioneers. There's a particularly good exhibit of Ute ceremonial items. See p. 358.
- **Mesa Verde National Park:** Home to the most impressive prehistoric cliff dwellings in the Southwest, Mesa Verde (Spanish for "green table") overwhelms you with its size and complexity. The first national park set aside to preserve

works created by humans, it covers some 52,000 acres just outside Cortez. Among the most compelling sites are Spruce Tree House, Square Tower House, and Cliff Palace, a four-story apartment-style dwelling. See p. 386.

- **Ute Mountain Tribal Park:** These ruins differ from others in Colorado because they're located on the Ute Mountain Indian Reservation, and the only way to see them is on a guided tour conducted by members of the Ute tribe. You'll see ruins and petroglyphs similar to those in Mesa Verde, but with an informed personal guide and without the crowds. See p. 389.

7 THE BEST OF THE OLD WEST

- **Old Town (Burlington):** On Colorado's eastern plains, right next door to Kansas, is this living-history museum, containing two dozen buildings (many from the 1880s). Watch a cancan, melodrama, or gunfight in a setting more reminiscent of Dodge City than Colorado's Victorian mountain towns. See chapter 10.
- **Creede, Lake City, and Leadville:** With extensive historic districts and false-fronted buildings, these mountain towns take you back to the time when Butch Cassidy, Doc Holliday, and other infamous dudes stalked the saloons in search of the next card game. See chapters 11 and 14.
- **Bent's Old Fort National Historic Site (La Junta):** Reconstructed to the way it appeared in the 1830s and 1840s, this adobe fort shows life as it really was, when pioneers spent their time either trading peaceably with or fighting off plains warriors. See p. 444.

8 THE MOST SCENIC VIEWS

- **Garden of the Gods:** There's nothing like sunrise at Garden of the Gods in Colorado Springs, with its fantastic and sometimes fanciful red-sandstone formations sculpted by wind and water over hundreds of thousands of years. It's worth spending some foot power to get away from the crowds on one of the park's many trails, to listen to the wind and imagine the gods cavorting among the formations. See p. 162.
- **Trail Ridge Road:** Transversing Rocky Mountain National Park, Trail Ridge affords expansive and sometimes dizzying views in all directions. There are a dozen stops where you can take a short hike, possibly glimpse the unofficial mascots of the park (bighorn sheep), and get a close-up look at tundra. The drive rises above 12,000 feet and crosses the Continental Divide. See p. 255.
- **The Black Canyon of the Gunnison:** Among the steepest and most narrow canyons in North America, the Black Canyon of the Gunnison, near Montrose, offers breathtaking and sometimes eerie views into the darkness below or, for ambitious hikers, from the canyon depths to daylight above. The sheerness of its 2,500-foot-high walls, the narrowness of its 40-foot-wide base, and the resulting darkness at its core evoke a somber, almost religious mood. See p. 360.
- **Colorado National Monument:** Just west of Grand Junction are stunning vistas of red-rock canyons and sandstone monoliths. The monument's

23-mile Rim Rock Drive offers incredible views, and short walks and backcountry trails afford more solitude. You'll get the best light in the early morning or late afternoon, when the rocks glow red and shadows dance among the stone sculptures. See p. 334.

- **The San Juan Skyway:** This 233-mile circle drive that goes through Durango, Telluride, and Ouray is among the most beautiful scenic drives in America, passing through five mountain passes, historic mining camps, fields of wildflowers, stately forests, snowcapped peaks, and cascading waterfalls. It's not advisable for those who have difficulty with high elevation (Red Mountain Pass has an 11,008-ft. elevation) or steep, winding roads. Except in summer, it's wise to be sure the passes are open before heading out. See p. 382.

9 THE BEST FAMILY VACATIONS

- **Playing Cowboy at the Home Ranch and Devil's Thumb Ranch:** Nestled in the mountains near Steamboat Springs and Winter Park, respectively, these are two of the state's standout guest ranches, with luxurious perks. At the Home Ranch, expect food from an expertly trained French chef and adventurous horseback rides; at Devil's Thumb, there are all sorts of outdoor activities and geothermally heated lodge rooms and cabins. See chapter 11.
- **Riding an 1880s Narrow Gauge Steam Train:** There are two: The Durango & Silverton follows the Animas River from Durango up through the San Juan Mountains to historic Silverton; the Cumbres & Toltec chugs out of Antonito, Colorado; through the Toltec Gorge of the Los Piños River; over Cumbres Pass into Chama, New Mexico. Scenery is stupendous over both lines, and each fulfills every train buff's greatest dream of smoke in your eyes and cinders in your hair. See chapters 13 and 14.
- **Exploring Great Sand Dunes National Park and Preserve:** About 40 miles northeast of Alamosa, this huge pile of sand is a great place to explore, camp, hike, or just play in the 750-foot-tall dunes. Rangers provide guided nature walks and campfire programs in the summer, and a hiking/off-road-vehicle trail leads out the back of the monument into the national forest. See chapter 14.

10 THE BEST LUXURY HOTELS

- **Brown Palace Hotel** (Denver; ✆ **800/321-2599** or 303/297-3111): Denver's finest hotel, the Brown Palace has been open continuously since 1892, serving high society and celebrities—from President Dwight Eisenhower to the Beatles—with elegance and charm. Although most of the rooms are Victorian in decor, with Tiffany lamps and other accoutrements, my favorites are the Art Deco rooms, which have an undeniable feel of the 1920s and 1930s. See p. 79.
- **The Broadmoor** (Colorado Springs; ✆ **800/634-7711** or 719/634-7711): Colorado's top-rated resort hotel has it all—excellent dining, golf courses, pools, tennis courts, a state-of-the-art fitness center, full-service spa, and shopping, plus extraordinary service—in a magnificently restored historic building set in

immaculate grounds. Although extremely impressive, the Broadmoor is never pretentious, and it certainly knows how to pamper its guests. See p. 165.

- **The St. Regis Aspen** (Aspen; ✆ **888/454-9005** or 970/920-3300): At the base of Ajax Mountain, the St. Regis offers great views of the mountains or town, impeccable service, luxurious rooms, and all the services and amenities you'd expect in a fine hotel. Although a bit pricey, especially at Christmas, the hotel is supremely elegant in a comfortable, cozy way. See p. 328.
- **Ritz-Carlton, Bachelor Gulch** (Avon; ✆ **800/241-3333** or 970/748-6200): A stunning structure modeled after the grand national park lodges, the rock-and-log "parkitechture" exterior sheaths one of the most luxurious hotels in the West. The rooms are also studies in "New West" glitz, complete with mountain and earth tones, decor inspired by wildlife and forests, and jaw-dropping views. See p. 308.

11 THE BEST MODERATELY PRICED LODGINGS

- **Alpine Trail Ridge Inn** (Estes Park; ✆ **800/233-5023** or 970/586-4585): This is a top-notch independent motel, right next to the entrance to Rocky Mountain National Park. Proprietors Jay and Fran Grooters are also great sources for hiking advice. See p. 248.
- **Boulder Outlook** (Boulder; ✆ **800/542-0304** or 303/443-3322): The Outlook is fun, fresh, and definitively Boulder, with two bouldering rocks, a huge dog run, and discounts on bike rentals and other activities. The rooms are larger than average and the indoor pool is superb, complete with a waterfall and a mural of a cloud-speckled sky. See p. 192.
- **Siesta Motel** (Durango; ✆ **877/314-0741** or 970/247-0741): A vintage 1950s-era roadside motel owned and operated by the same family since 1975, the Siesta Motel is the best value in Durango, featuring clean, well-kept motel rooms with a king bed or two queens or doubles and a hot tub in the courtyard gazebo. See p. 378.

12 THE BEST BED & BREAKFASTS

- **Two Sisters Inn** (Manitou Springs; ✆ **800/274-7466** or 719/685-9684): Built by two sisters in 1919 as a boarding house, this splendid bed-and-breakfast has been owned and operated by Wendy Goldstein and Sharon Smith, sisters in spirit if not in blood. The four bedrooms and separate honeymoon cottage are furnished with family heirlooms and photographs, in a style best described as informal elegance. See p. 153.
- **The Leland House Bed & Breakfast Suites** (Durango; ✆ **800/664-1920** or 970/385-1920): Built as an apartment house in 1927 and handsomely restored in 1993, the Leland House offers an intriguing mix of lodging types in a comfortable inn with early-20th-century decor. Breakfast is served in the historic Rochester Hotel across the street, another restored gem under the same ownership. See p. 377.

- **The Bradley** (Boulder; ✆ **800/858-5811** or 303/545-5200): Built as an upscale inn in 1994, the Bradley nicely blends into the surrounding historic neighborhood, just northeast of the Pearl Street Mall. The striking Great Room and uniquely decorated guest rooms are all adorned with bold contemporary art from local galleries. See p. 191.

Colorado in Depth

2

The Rocky Mountains are the backbone of North America, and with more than 50 peaks that soar above 14,000 feet—more mountains of such a magnitude than are present in the rest of the lower 48 states combined—Colorado is their heart. This dazzling constellation of high points, with its evergreen and aspen forests, racing streams and rivers, and wealth of wildlife, is perfect for recreation year-round—from summer hiking, mountain-biking, and rafting to superlative winter skiing and snowboarding through deep and dry powder snow.

But Colorado isn't just mountains. It's also the wheat and cornfields of the vast eastern prairies, the high plateau country of the Western Slope, the numerous historic towns and American Indian communities, and the increasingly sophisticated cities of the Front Range.

1 COLORADO TODAY

Ask any Coloradan what makes the state unique, and the response most likely will be its mountains. It is almost impossible to exaggerate the spectacular beauty here, or the influence it has had on the development and present-day character of the state. Colorado has been a prime tourist destination practically since the day the first pioneers arrived. Particularly in the 19th century, those attracted to this rugged land tended to be independent types—sometimes downright ornery and antisocial—who sought wide-open spaces, untamed wilderness, and plenty of elbow room. Of course, the dream of riches from gold and silver mines helped, too.

These early transplants established the state's image as the domain of rugged individualists—solitary cowboys, prospectors, and others—who just wanted to be left alone. Much of that feeling still survives, and today's Coloradans have a deserved reputation as a feisty, independent lot. Colorado has the distinction of being home to some of the most politically active liberals and conservatives in the country. They don't follow trends; they make them. It's where some of the country's first municipal gay-rights ordinances were passed, yet it's also home to the vanguard of the family-values movement: Focus on the Family, one of the most powerful lobbying organizations for the Christian right's political agenda, is based in Colorado Springs.

Somewhat understandably, such a diversity of political perspectives doesn't exactly engender accord. In the early 1990s, the rest of the country got a quick lesson in Colorado-style politics during the controversy surrounding Amendment 2, a state constitutional amendment aimed at prohibiting certain antidiscrimination laws.

Although the successful 1992 ballot measure was vaguely worded, its intent was clear: to eliminate local gay-rights ordinances that Aspen, Boulder, and Denver had passed, and to prevent other communities, or the state legislature, from creating laws that would specifically protect gays and lesbians from discrimination in employment and housing.

A high-profile nationwide boycott of the state was launched in 1993, and although it scared off some convention business and kept a few tourists away, the end result was a bit of a wash, and the 1992–93 ski season was among the best in the state's history. The boycott was called off when the amendment was declared unconstitutional by the state Supreme Court later that year. The state appealed, but the ruling was upheld by the U.S. Supreme Court in the spring of 1996.

After the controversy died down, further proof of Colorado's maverick streak came just a few months later, when former three-term governor Richard Lamm—known as "Governor Gloom" for his philosophy of fiscal conservatism and individual sacrifice—announced he would seek the presidential nomination from Ross Perot's Reform Party, virtually ensuring a showdown with the megalomaniacal Perot, but also broadening the appeal of Perot's creation. Not surprisingly, he lost to Perot, but in true Colorado spirit, he went down fighting. Lamm described the toe-to-toe experience with Perot as akin to drinking water out of a fire hydrant, but also admitted he wouldn't have missed it for the world.

An issue on which almost all Coloradans agree, pretty much regardless of other differences, is the need to control tourism. While the industry's financial benefits to the state are well understood, it's generally acknowledged that if tourism is allowed to grow unchecked, the cost to the state's natural resources will be tremendous.

To that end, town officials in Vail reached an agreement with resort management in 1995 to limit the number of skiers on the mountain and alleviate other aspects of overcrowding in the village. The word from Vail and other high-profile Colorado tourist destinations is that visitors will be given incentives, such as discounts, to visit at off-peak times. Ski-area officials also have not ruled out turning away skiers after a set number of passes are sold.

Conflicts between environmentalists and the ski industry came to a head in October 1998, when militant environmental activists set fires at a Vail resort that caused more than $12 million in damage. A group called Earth Liberation Front claimed credit for the arson, although investigators said they could not prove the group was responsible. The organization wanted to halt an expansion project at Vail that it said would harm a potential habitat for the lynx, a threatened member of the cat family that is similar to a bobcat.

Another issue that has wide support across the state is controlling growth. The rugged mountains and scenic beauty that lure tourists and outdoor recreation enthusiasts have also fueled an influx of transplants—a modern version of the gold seekers and pioneers who settled the state. Since 1990, Colorado has gained new residents at the staggering rate of three times the national average.

Many of these new residents are active, outdoorsy types who relish the idea of riding their bikes to work and escaping the pollution, crime, and overcrowding of the coasts. But perhaps inevitably, many native and long-term Coloradans have begun to complain that these newcomers are changing the character of the state and bringing with them the very problems from which they sought escape.

The challenge for Coloradans in the 21st century is to solve the twin riddles of tourism and growth that are plaguing much of the American West: How do we achieve a balance between preserving a state's unique character and spectacular natural resources for future generations, while still enjoying all it has to offer today?

2 LOOKING BACK AT COLORADO

EARLY INHABITANTS

To explore Colorado today is to step back into its history, from its dinosaur graveyards, impressive stone and mud cities of the Ancestral Puebloans, reminders of the Wild West of Doc Holliday, and elegant Victorian mansions to today's science and technology. The history of Colorado is a testimony to the human ability to adapt and flourish in a difficult environment.

The earliest people in Colorado are believed to have been nomadic hunters, who arrived some 12,000 to 20,000 years ago following the tracks of the now-extinct woolly mammoth and bison. Then, about 2,000 years ago, the ancestors of today's Pueblo people arrived, living in shallow caves in the Four Corners area, where the borders of Colorado, Utah, Arizona, and New Mexico meet.

Originally hunters, they gradually learned farming, basket making, pottery making, and the construction of pit houses. Eventually they built complex villages, such as those that can be seen at Mesa Verde National Park. For some unknown reason, possibly drought, they deserted the area by the end of the 13th century, probably moving southward into present-day New Mexico and Arizona.

EXPLORATION & SETTLEMENT

Spanish colonists, having established settlements at Santa Fe and Taos in the 16th and 17th centuries, didn't immediately find southern Colorado attractive for colonization. Not only was there a lack of financial and military support from the Spanish crown, but the freedom-loving, sometimes fierce Comanche and Ute also made it clear that they would rather be left alone.

Nevertheless, Spain still held title to southern and western Colorado in 1803, when U.S. President Thomas Jefferson paid $15 million for the vast Louisiana Territory, which included the lion's share of modern Colorado. Two years later, the Lewis and Clark expedition passed by, but the first official exploration by the U.S. government occurred when Jefferson sent Capt. Zebulon Pike to the territory. Pikes Peak, Colorado's landmark mountain and a top tourist attraction near Colorado Springs, was named for the explorer.

As the West began to open up in the 1820s, the Santa Fe Trail was established, cutting through Colorado's southeast corner. Bent's Fort was built on the Arkansas River between 1828 and 1832, and the

A BRIEF HISTORY

- **12,000 B.C.** First inhabitants of Colorado include Folsom Man.
- **3000 B.C.** Prehistoric farming communities appear.
- **A.D. 1000** Ancestral Puebloan cliff-dweller culture peaks in Four Corners region.
- **Late 1500s** Spanish explore upper Rio Grande Valley; colonize Santa Fe and Taos, New Mexico; and make forays into what is now southern Colorado.
- **1776** U.S. declares independence from England.
- **1803** The Louisiana Purchase includes most of modern Colorado.
- **1805** The Lewis and Clark expedition sights the Rocky Mountains.
- **1806–07** Capt. Zebulon Pike leads first U.S. expedition into the Colorado Rockies.
- **1822** William Becknell establishes the Santa Fe Trail.
- **1842–44** Lieut. John C. Frémont and Kit Carson explore Colorado and the American West.
- **1848** Treaty of Guadalupe-Hidalgo ends the Mexican War, adds American Southwest to the United States.
- **1858** Gold discovered in modern Denver.

reconstructed fort is a national historic site near La Junta.

Much of eastern Colorado, including what would become Denver and Colorado Springs, was then part of the Kansas Territory. It was populated almost exclusively by plains tribes until 1858, when gold seekers discovered flakes of the precious metal near the junction of Cherry Creek and the South Platte, and the city of Denver was established, named for Kansas governor James Denver.

The Cherry Creek strike was literally a flash in the gold-seeker's pan, but two strikes in the mountains just west of Denver in early 1859 were more significant: Clear Creek, near what would become Idaho Springs, and in a quartz vein at Gregory Gulch, which led to the founding of Central City.

THE TERRITORY

Abraham Lincoln was elected president of the United States in November 1860, and Congress created the Colorado Territory 3 months later. Lincoln's Homestead Act brought much of the public domain into private ownership and led to the platting of Front Range townships, including Denver.

Controlling the American Indian peoples was a priority of the territorial government. A treaty negotiated in 1851 had guaranteed the entire Pikes Peak region to the nomadic plains tribes, but that was made moot by the arrival of settlers in the late 1850s. The Fort Wise Treaty of 1861 exchanged the Pikes Peak territory for 5 million fertile acres of Arkansas Valley land, north of modern La Junta. But when the Arapaho and Cheyenne continued to roam their old hunting grounds, conflict became inevitable. Frequent rumors and rare instances of hostility against settlers led the Colorado cavalry to attack a peaceful settlement of Indians—who were flying Old Glory and a white flag—on November 29, 1864. More than 150 Cheyenne and Arapaho, two-thirds of them women and children, were killed in what has become known as the Sand Creek Massacre.

Vowing revenge, the Cheyenne and Arapaho launched a campaign to drive whites from their ancient hunting grounds. Their biggest triumph was the destruction of the northeast Colorado town of Julesburg in 1865, but the cavalry, bolstered by returning Civil War veterans, managed to force the two tribes onto reservations in Indian Territory, in what is now Oklahoma—a barren area that whites thought they would never want.

Also in 1865, a smelter was built in Black Hawk, just west of Denver, setting the stage for the large-scale spread of mining throughout Colorado in the years to come. When the first transcontinental

- **1859** Gen. William Larimer founds Denver. Major gold strikes in nearby Rockies.
- **1861** Colorado Territory proclaimed.
- **1862** Colorado cavalry wins major Civil War battle at Glorieta Pass, New Mexico. The Homestead Act is passed.
- **1863–68** Ute tribe obtains treaties guaranteeing 16 million acres of western Colorado land.
- **1864** Hundreds of Cheyenne and Arapaho killed in Sand Creek Massacre. The University of Denver becomes Colorado's first institution of higher education.
- **1871** Gen. William Palmer founds Colorado Springs.
- **1876** Colorado becomes 38th state.
- **1877** University of Colorado opens in Boulder.
- **1878** Little Pittsburg silver strike launches Leadville's mining boom, Colorado's greatest.
- **1879** Milk Creek Massacre by Ute warriors leads to tribe's removal to reservations.
- **1890** Sherman Silver Purchase Act boosts price of silver. Gold discovered at Cripple Creek, leading to state's biggest gold rush.

railroad was completed in 1869, the Union Pacific went through Cheyenne, Wyoming, 100 miles north of Denver, but 4 years later the line was linked to Denver by the Kansas City–Denver Railroad.

STATEHOOD

Colorado politicians began pressing for statehood during the Civil War, but it wasn't until August 1, 1876, that Colorado became the 38th state. Occurring less than a month after the United States' 100th birthday, it was natural that Colorado would become known as "the Centennial State."

The state's new constitution gave the vote to blacks, but not to women, despite the strong efforts of the Colorado Women's Suffrage Association. Women finally succeeded in winning the vote in 1893, 3 years after Wyoming became the first state to offer universal suffrage.

At the time of statehood, most of Colorado's vast western region was still occupied by some 3,500 members of a half-dozen Ute tribes. Unlike the plains tribes, their early relations with white explorers and settlers had been peaceful. Chief Ouray, leader of the Uncompahgre Utes, had negotiated treaties in 1863 and 1868 that guaranteed them 16 million acres—most of western Colorado. In 1873, Ouray agreed to sell the United States a quarter of that acreage in the mineral-rich San Juan Mountains in exchange for hunting rights and $25,000 in annuities.

But a mining boom that began in 1878 led to a flurry of intrusions into Ute territory and stirred up a "Utes Must Go!" sentiment. Two years later, the Utes were forced onto small reserves in southwestern Colorado and Utah, and their lands opened to white settlement in 1882.

THE MINING BOOM

Colorado's real mining boom began on April 28, 1878, when August Rische and George Hook hit a vein of silver carbonate 27 feet deep on Fryer Hill in Leadville. Perhaps the strike wouldn't have caused such excitement had not Rische and Hook, 8 days earlier, traded one-third interest in whatever they found for a basket of groceries from storekeeper Horace Tabor, the mayor of Leadville and a sharp businessman. Tabor was well acquainted with the Colorado "law of apex," which said that if an ore-bearing vein surfaced on a man's claim, he could follow it wherever it led, even out of his claim and through the claims of others.

Tabor, a legend in Colorado, typifies the "rags-to-riches" success story of a common working-class man. A native of Vermont, he mortgaged his Kansas homestead in 1859 and moved west to the mountains, where he worked as a postmaster

- **1893** Women win right to vote. Silver industry collapses following repeal of Sherman Silver Purchase Act.
- **1901–07** President Theodore Roosevelt sets aside 16 million acres of national forestland in Colorado.
- **1906** U.S. Mint built in Denver.
- **1913** Wolf Creek Pass is first highway to cross Continental Divide in Colorado.
- **1915** Rocky Mountain National Park established.
- **1934** Direct Denver–San Francisco rail travel begins. Taylor Grazing Act ends homesteading.
- **1941–45** World War II establishes Colorado as a military center.
- **1947** Aspen's first chairlift begins operation.
- **1948–58** Uranium "rush" sweeps western slope.
- **1955** Environmentalists prevent construction of Echo Park Dam in Dinosaur National Monument.
- **1967** Colorado legalizes medically necessary abortions.
- **1972** Colorado voters reject a chance to host the 1976 Winter Olympics.
- **1988** Sen. Gary Hart, a front-runner for the Democratic presidential nomination,

continues

Impressions

I spent a night in a silver mine. I dined with the men down there. . . . Poems every one of them. A complete democracy underground. I find people less rough and coarse in such places. There is no chance for roughness. The revolver is their book of etiquette.

—Oscar Wilde, quoted in the *Morning Herald*, 1882

and storekeeper in several towns before moving to Leadville. He was 46 when the silver strike was made. By age 50, he was the state's richest man and its Republican lieutenant governor. His love affair with and marriage to Elizabeth "Baby Doe" McCourt, a young divorcée for whom he left his wife, Augusta, became a national scandal, the subject of numerous books, and even an opera. Today the town of Leadville is among the best places to relive the West's mining days.

Although the silver market collapsed in 1893, gold was there to take its place. In the fall of 1890, a cowboy named Bob Womack found gold in Cripple Creek, on the southwestern slope of Pikes Peak, west of Colorado Springs. He sold his claim to Winfield Scott Stratton, a carpenter and amateur geologist, and Stratton's mine earned a tidy profit of $6 million by 1899, when he sold it to an English company for another $11 million. Cripple Creek turned out to be the richest gold field ever discovered, ultimately producing $500 million in gold.

Unlike the flamboyant Tabor, Stratton was an introvert and a neurotic. His fortune was twice the size of Tabor's, and it grew daily as the deflation of silver's value boosted that of gold. But he invested most of it back in Cripple Creek, searching for a fabulous mother lode that he never found. By the early 1900s, like silver, the overproduction of gold began to drive the price of the metal down.

ENVIRONMENTALISM & TOURISM

Another turning point for Colorado occurred just after the beginning of the 20th century. Theodore Roosevelt visited the state in September 1900 as the Republican vice-presidential nominee. Soon after he acceded the presidency in September 1901 (following the assassination of President McKinley), he began to declare large chunks of the Rockies as forest reserves. By 1907, when an act of Congress forbade the

withdraws from the race after a scandal involving a Miami model.

- **1992** Colorado voters approve Amendment 2, a controversial state constitutional amendment barring any measures to protect homosexuals from discrimination.
- **1995** The $4.2-billion state-of-the-art Denver International Airport and $2.16-million Coors Field baseball stadium open. Denver goes sports-crazy with its fourth major professional sports team, the Avalanche, a member of the National Hockey League.
- **1996** The U.S. Supreme Court strikes down Amendment 2, saying it denies gays and lesbians constitutional rights afforded to all Americans. The Avalanche win the Stanley Cup, giving Colorado its first championship in any major league.
- **1997** Weather wreaks havoc across the state: First, a summer rainstorm turns a small creek that runs through Fort Collins into a roaring river that floods parts of the town, killing five residents and causing some $200 million in damage; then, in late October, a 24-hour blizzard, the worst October storm in Denver since 1923, piles

president from creating any new reserves by proclamation, nearly a quarter of Colorado was national forestland—16 million acres in 18 forests. Another project that reached fruition during the Roosevelt administration was the establishment in 1906 of Mesa Verde National Park, the first national park to preserve the works of humans.

Tourism grew hand in hand with the setting aside of public lands. Easterners had been visiting Colorado since the 1870s, when Gen. William J. Palmer founded a Colorado Springs resort and made the mountains accessible via his Denver & Rio Grande Railroad.

Estes Park, northwest of Boulder, was among the first of the resort towns to emerge in the 20th century, spurred by a visit in 1903 by Freelan Stanley. With his brother Francis, Freelan had invented the Stanley Steamer, a steam-powered automobile, in Boston in 1899. Freelan Stanley shipped one of his steamers to Denver and drove the 40 miles to Estes Park in less than 2 hours, a remarkable speed for the day. Finding the climate conducive to his recovery from tuberculosis, he returned in 1907 with a dozen Steamers and established a shuttle service from Denver to Estes Park. Two years later he built the luxurious Stanley Hotel, still a hilltop landmark today.

Stanley developed a friendship with Enos Mills, a young innkeeper whose property was more a workshop for students of wildlife than a business. A devotee of conservationist John Muir, Mills believed tourists should spend their Colorado vacations in the natural environment, camping and hiking. As Mills gained national stature as a nature writer and lecturer, he urged that the national forestland around Longs Peak, outside Estes Park, be designated a national park. In January 1915, the 400-square-mile Rocky Mountain National Park was created by President Woodrow Wilson, and today it is one of America's leading tourist attractions, with more than 2 million visitors each year.

The 1920s ushered in expansive growth of highways and the completion of the Moffat Tunnel, a 6¼-mile passageway beneath the Continental Divide that in 1934 led to the long-sought direct Denver–San Francisco rail connection. Unfortunately, the '20s also saw the worst flood in Colorado history: The city of Pueblo, south of Colorado Springs, was devastated when the Arkansas River overflowed its banks on June 1, 1921; 100 people were killed, and the damage exceeded $16 million.

The Great Depression of the 1930s was a difficult time for many Coloradans, but it had some positive consequences. The

snow across the Front Range, virtually shutting down I-25 from Wyoming to New Mexico and stranding thousands of passengers at Denver International Airport. Gary Lee Davis, convicted of the 1986 abduction and murder of a Colorado farm wife, is executed by lethal injection, the state's first execution in 30 years.

- **1998** The Denver Broncos win the Super Bowl, defeating the Green Bay Packers (the defending champs) 31–24; the stunning victory saves the Broncos the indignity of becoming the first team to lose five Super Bowls. Militant environmental activists set fires that cause more than $12 million in damage in an effort to stop expansion at a Vail resort.
- **1999** The Broncos win the Super Bowl again, this time defeating the Atlanta Falcons. The worst school shooting in United States history takes place in suburban Denver when two students open fire inside Columbine High School, killing 13.
- **2000** Colorado ski resorts report that the 1999–2000 season was the worst in history due to poor snowfall

continues

federal government raised the price of gold from $20 to $35 an ounce, reviving Cripple Creek and other stagnant mining towns.

World War II and the subsequent cold war were responsible for many of the defense installations that are now an integral part of the Colorado economy, particularly in the Colorado Springs area. The war also indirectly caused the other single greatest boon to Colorado's late-20th-century economy: the ski industry. Soldiers in the 10th Mountain Division, on leave from Camp Hale before heading off to fight in Europe, often crossed Independence Pass to relax in the lower altitude and milder climate of the 19th-century silver-mining village of Aspen. They tested their skiing skills, which they would need in the Italian Alps, against the slopes of Ajax Mountain.

In 1945, Walter and Elizabeth Paepcke—he the founder of the Container Corporation of America, she an ardent conservationist—moved to Aspen and established the Aspen Company as a property investment firm. Skiing was already popular in New England and the Midwest, but had few devotees in the Rockies. Paepcke bought a 3-mile chairlift, the longest and fastest in the world at the time, and had it ready for operation by January 1947. Soon Easterners and Europeans were flocking to Aspen—and the rest is skiing history.

THE MODERN ERA

Colorado continued its steady growth in the 1950s, aided by tourism and the federal government. The $200-million U.S. Air Force Academy, which opened to cadets in 1958, is Colorado Springs's top tourist attraction today. There was a brief oil boom in the 1970s, followed by increasing high-tech development and even more tourism.

Weapons plants, which seemed like a good idea when they were constructed during World War II, began to haunt Denver and the state in the 1970s and 1980s. The Rocky Mountain Arsenal, originally built to produce chemical weapons, was found to be creating hazardous conditions at home by contaminating the land with deadly chemicals. A massive cleanup was begun in the early 1980s, and the arsenal is now well on its way to accomplishing its goal of converting the 27-square-mile site into a national wildlife refuge.

The story of Rocky Flats, a postwar nuclear-weapons facility spurred on by the cold war, is not so happy. Massive efforts to find a solution to contamination caused by nuclear waste have been largely unsuccessful. Although state and federal officials

and potential skiers' fears about Y2K problems.

- **2001** The Avalanche win the Stanley Cup again, beating the New Jersey Devils 3–1. A California couple give the University of Colorado $250 million, the largest gift ever to a public university in the United States.
- **2001–08** A new energy boom takes place in Colorado, with drilling for oil and gas hitting an all-time high.
- **2002** One of the worst wildfire seasons in history hits Colorado, with about 1,000 fires burning some 364,000 acres across the state; the biggest fire—considered the largest forest fire in the state's history—burns 138,000 acres and destroys 133 homes southwest of Denver; other major fires occur near Durango, in Mesa Verde National Park, near Colorado Springs, and near Glenwood Springs.
- **2003** Scandal hits the U.S. Air Force Academy in Colorado Springs when dozens of female cadets come forward claiming that they had been victims of sexual assaults by male cadets and that academy officials had mostly ignored their complaints and sometimes blamed the victims.

announced early in 1996 that they had reached agreement on the means of removing some 14 tons of plutonium, their immediate plan calls for keeping it in Denver until at least the year 2010, and Department of Energy officials don't know what they'll do with it then. In the meantime, plans are under way to build storage containers that will safely hold the plutonium for up to 50 years.

As the state enters the 21st century, thoughts have turned to controlling population growth. With a growth rate of three times the national average—the state has grown by nearly 2 million people during the 1990s and the 2000s—residents and government leaders are questioning how this unabated influx of outsiders can continue without causing serious harm to the state's air, water, and general quality of life.

3 THE LAY OF THE LAND

First-time visitors to Colorado are often awed by the looming wall of the Rocky Mountains, which come into sight from a good 100 miles away, soon after drivers cross the state line from Kansas. East of the Rockies, a 5,000-foot peak is considered high—yet Colorado has 1,143 mountains above 10,000 feet, including 54 over 14,000 feet! Highest of all is Mount Elbert, at 14,433 feet, southwest of Leadville.

The Rockies were formed some 65 million years ago by pressures that forced hard Precambrian rock to the Earth's surface, breaking through and pushing layers of earlier rock up on end. Then millions of years of erosion eliminated the soft surface material, producing the magnificent Rockies of calendar fame.

An almost-perfect rectangle, Colorado measures some 385 miles east to west and 275 miles north to south. The ridge of the Continental Divide zigzags more or less through the center of the 104,247-square-mile state, eighth largest in the nation.

You can visualize Colorado's basic topography by dividing the state into vertical thirds: The eastern part is plains, the midsection is high mountains, and the western third is mesa.

That's a broad simplification, of course. The central Rockies, though they cover six times the mountain area of Switzerland, are not a single vast highland, but consist of a series of high ranges running roughly north to south. East of the Continental Divide, the primary river systems are the South Platte, Arkansas, and Rio Grande,

- **2004** Colorado obtains its fourth national park when Great Sand Dunes gains national park status, after getting additional land with help from the Nature Conservancy.
- **2006** T-REX, the biggest road and light-rail project in Denver history, is completed.
- **2006–07** Thanks to plenty of snow, Colorado's ski industry enjoys a record year: over 12.5 million visitors, nearly a quarter of the nation's total.
- **2008** Denver hosts the 2008 Democratic National Convention.

all flowing toward the Gulf of Mexico. The westward-flowing Colorado River system dominates the western part of the state, with tributary networks including the Gunnison, Dolores, and Yampa-Green rivers. In most cases, these rivers are not broad bodies of water such as the Ohio or Columbia, but streams, heavy with spring and summer snowmelt, that shrink to mere trickles during much of the year under the demands of farm and ranch irrigation. Besides agricultural use, these rivers provide necessary water to wildlife and offer wonderful opportunities for rafting, fishing, and swimming.

The forested mountains are essential in that they retain precious water for the lowlands. Eleven national forests cover 15 million acres of land, with an additional 8 million acres controlled by the Bureau of Land Management, also open for public recreation. Another half-million acres are within national parks, monuments, and recreation areas; and there are more than 40 state parks, including about 10 within an hour's drive of Denver, Boulder, or Colorado Springs.

Colorado's name, Spanish for "red," derives from the state's red soil and rocks. Some of the sandstone agglomerates have become attractions in their own right, such as Red Rocks Amphitheatre west of Denver and the startling Garden of the Gods in Colorado Springs.

Of Colorado's 4.5 million people, some 80% live along the I-25 corridor, where the plains meet the mountains. Denver, the state capital, has a population of well over half a million, with over 3 million in the metropolitan area. Colorado Springs has the second-largest population, with almost 380,000 residents, followed by Fort Collins (125,000), Pueblo (105,000), and Boulder (100,000). Because of this large, growing population, there is concern that habitat is being diminished by continued development and the needs of so many people.

4 COLORADO IN POPULAR CULTURE

Those planning Colorado vacations can turn to a number of sources for background on the state and its major cities. Among my favorites is *A Lady's Life in the Rocky Mountains,* a fascinating compilation of Isabella L. Bird's letters to her sister; they were written in the late 1800s as she traveled alone through the Rockies, usually on horseback. Those who enjoy lengthy novels will want to get their hands on a copy of James Michener's 1,000-page *Centennial,* inspired by the northeastern plains of Colorado. For a more bohemian point of view, look no further than Jack Kerouac's classic, *On the Road.* Also engrossing is Wallace Stegner's Pulitzer Prize–winning 1971 novel, *Angle of Repose.* Horror fans will surely appreciate a pair of Stephen King classics with Colorado ties: *The Stand* is set in Boulder and *The Shining* was inspired by the writer's stay at the Stanley Hotel in Estes Park.

Travelers interested in seeing wildlife will likely be successful with help from the *Colorado Wildlife Viewing Guide,* by Mary Taylor Gray. You'll likely see a lot of historical sights here, so it's good to first get some background from the short, easy-to-read *Colorado: A History,* by Marshall Sprague.

Movies set in Colorado range from numerous westerns—mostly filmed in the state's southwestern corner—such as the John Wayne classic *The Searchers,* as well as *Butch Cassidy and the Sundance Kid* and *City Slickers.* There's also *Things to Do in Denver When You're Dead, About Schmidt,* and *WarGames.* Television shows shot in the state include *Dynasty* (Denver), *Mork*

& Mindy (Boulder), and *South Park* (50 miles southwest of Denver).

Musically speaking, the region has a rich heritage and a diverse current scene. John Denver; Judy Collins; Earth, Wind & Fire; Big Head Todd and the Monsters; and the String Cheese Incident are among the bands that broke it big with strong ties to Denver or Boulder. In parts of the world, the "Denver Sound," a roots-based genre that melds gothic and country, has been gaining notoriety, with bands like 16 Horsepower, Munly and the Lee Lewis Harlots, DeVotchKa, and Slim Cessna's Auto Club gaining an international following.

5 EATING & DRINKING IN COLORADO

In Denver, Boulder, and Colorado Springs, restaurants tend to close no later than 10pm during the week and 11pm on weekends, although there are exceptions. In the resort towns, hours tend to be a little longer in peak season—whether it's summer or winter—and close earlier (or, in many cases, entirely) in spring and fall. In the smaller towns not known for recreation, expect shorter hours year-round. Tipping is standard for the U.S. at 15% to 20%. Local delicacies include Rocky Mountain oysters (yes, they are deep-fried bull's testicles), Mexican fare, beef, and game. Boulder and Paonia are on the forefront of numerous culinary trends, namely vegetarian, localvore, and organic, as are Denver and Colorado Springs and the ski towns, although to a lesser degree. There are also quite a few microbreweries throughout the state; Denver and the surrounding area has been dubbed "the Napa Valley of beer." On the Western Slope in and around Palisade and Paonia, there are numerous vineyards and wineries, but Colorado's fresh fruits and vegetables (namely Paonia cherries, Palisade peaches, and Olathe sweet corn) are also among some of the nation's best.

3

Planning Your Trip to Colorado

The beauty of a Colorado vacation is that there's truly something for everyone. Depending on where you choose to go, you can have an affordable and fun time, or you can spend a bit more and have a truly world-class experience. The more expensive resorts—Vail, Aspen, Steamboat, and Telluride—tend to fill up quickly, especially during ski season (and even more so the holiday week of Dec 25–Jan 1); you'll want to book as far in advance as possible. The same is true for the state's most popular attractions, such as the national parks—which are especially busy over school vacations. This chapter gives you the information you need to get started.

This book is organized primarily geographically, and because this is a big state, many visitors will limit their Colorado vacation to one or two regions.

1 VISITOR INFORMATION

Start by contacting the **Colorado Tourism Office,** 1625 Broadway, Denver, CO 80202 (© **800/COLORADO** [265-6723]; www.colorado.com), for a free copy of the official state vacation guide, which includes a state map and describes attractions, activities, and lodgings throughout Colorado. Another good source for Colorado information is the website of the *Denver Post,* the state's major daily newspaper, at **www.denverpost.com**.

The **Colorado Hotel and Lodging Association,** 999 18th St., Ste. 1240, Denver, CO 80202 (© **303/297-8335;** www.coloradolodging.com), offers a free guide to lodging across the state. The nonprofit **Bed and Breakfast Innkeepers of Colorado,** P.O. Box 38416, Colorado Springs, CO 80937 (© **800/265-7696;** www.innsofcolorado.org), distributes a free directory describing about 100 B&Bs across the state, including a number of historic inns in Denver, Boulder, and Colorado Springs.

Hostelling International USA, 8401 Colesville Rd., Ste. 600, Silver Spring, MD 20910 (© **301/495-1240;** www.hiayh.org), has a computerized system for making reservations in hostels worldwide and also has a print directory of U.S. hostels.

A free copy of ***Your Guide to Outdoor Adventure,*** which contains details on the state's 40 parks, is available from state park offices at 1313 Sherman St., Ste. 618, Denver, CO 80203 (© **303/866-3437;** www.parks.state.co.us). State park offices can also provide information on boating and snowmobiling.

Destination: Colorado—Predeparture Checklist

- Are there any **special requirements** for your destination? Vaccinations? Special visas, passports, or IDs? Detailed road maps? Bug repellents? Appropriate attire? If you're flying, are you carrying a current, government-issued ID, such as a driver's license or passport?
- Did you find out your daily ATM withdrawal limit?
- Do you have your credit card PIN numbers? If you have a five- or six-digit PIN number, did you obtain a four-digit number from your bank?
- To check in at a kiosk with an e-ticket, do you have the credit card you bought your ticket with or a frequent-flier card?
- If you purchased traveler's checks, have you recorded the check numbers and stored the documentation separately from the checks?
- Did you bring your ID cards that could entitle you to discounts, such as AAA and AARP cards and student IDs?
- Did you leave a copy of your itinerary with someone at home?
- Do any theater, restaurant, or travel reservations need to be booked in advance?
- Some attractions (such as the top of the dome in the Colorado State Capitol in Denver, and the U.S. Air Force Academy and Peterson Air & Space Museum in Colorado Springs) have been closed for security reasons or have reopened with special restrictions. Call ahead for specifics.
- If you want to attend a Denver Broncos game, call early—home games sell out months ahead.
- Make lodging arrangements far in advance for the resort towns during ski season.
- Savings are often available by buying lift tickets before departure either by phone or on the resort's website. For those who are planning to ski 10 or more days, there are plenty of different season passes to shop and compare.

2 ENTRY REQUIREMENTS & CUSTOMS

ENTRY REQUIREMENTS

Passports

New regulations issued by the Department of Homeland Security now require virtually every air traveler entering the U.S. to show a passport. As of January 23, 2007, all persons, including U.S. citizens, traveling by air between the United States and Canada, Mexico, Central and South America, the Caribbean, and Bermuda are required to present a valid passport. As of January 31, 2008, U.S. and Canadian citizens entering the U.S. at land and sea ports of entry from within the Western Hemisphere will need to present government-issued proof of citizenship, such as a

Cut to the Front of the Airport Security Line as a Registered Traveler

In 2003, the **Transportation Security Administration** (**TSA;** www.tsa.gov) approved a pilot program to help ease the time spent in line for airport security screenings. In exchange for information and a fee, persons can be prescreened as registered travelers, granting them a front-of-the-line position when they fly. The program is run through private firms—the largest and most well known is Steven Brill's **Clear** (www.flyclear.com), and it works like this: Travelers complete an online application providing specific points of personal information, including name, addresses for the previous 5 years, birth date, social security number, driver's license number, and a valid credit card (you're not charged the **$99 fee** until your application is approved). Print out the completed form and take it, along with proper ID, with you to an "enrollment station" (this can be found in over 20 participating airports and in a growing number of American Express offices around the country, for example). It's at this point where it gets seemingly sci-fi. At the enrollment station, a Clear representative will record your biometrics necessary for clearance; in this case, your fingerprints and your irises will be digitally recorded.

Once your application has been screened against no-fly lists, outstanding warrants, and other security measures, you'll be issued a clear plastic card that holds a chip containing your information. Each time you fly through participating airports (and the numbers are steadily growing), go to the Clear Pass station located next to the standard TSA screening line. Here you'll insert your card into a slot and place your finger on a scanner to read your print—when the information matches up, you're cleared to cut to the front of the security line. You'll still have to follow all the procedures of the day, like removing your shoes and walking through the x-ray machine, but Clear promises to cut 30 minutes off your wait time at the airport.

On a personal note: Each time I've used my Clear Pass, my travel companions are still waiting to go through security while I'm already sitting down, reading the paper and sipping my overpriced smoothie. Granted, registered traveler programs are not for the infrequent traveler, but for those of us who fly on a regular basis, it's a perk I'm willing to pay for.

—David A. Lytle

birth certificate, along with a government-issued photo ID, such as a driver's license. A passport is not required for U.S. or Canadian citizens entering by land or sea, but it is highly encouraged to carry one.

For information on how to obtain a passport, go to **"Passports"** in the **"Fast Facts"** appendix (p. 452).

Visas

The U.S. State Department has a **Visa Waiver Program (VWP)** allowing citizens of the following countries to enter the United States without a visa for stays of up to 90 days: Andorra, Australia, Austria, Belgium, Brunei, Denmark, Finland, France, Germany, Iceland, Ireland, Italy,

Japan, Liechtenstein, Luxembourg, Monaco, the Netherlands, New Zealand, Norway, Portugal, San Marino, Singapore, Slovenia, Spain, Sweden, Switzerland, and the United Kingdom. (***Note:*** This list was accurate at press time; for the most up-to-date list of countries in the VWP, consult www.travel.state.gov/visa.) Canadian citizens may enter the United States without visas; they will need to show passports (if traveling by air) and proof of residence, however. ***Note:*** Any passport issued on or after October 26, 2006, by a VWP country must be an **e-Passport** for VWP travelers to be eligible to enter the U.S. without a visa. Citizens of these nations also need to present a round-trip air or cruise ticket upon arrival. E-Passports contain computer chips capable of storing biometric information, such as the required digital photograph of the holder. (You can identify an e-Passport by the symbol on the bottom center cover of your passport.) If your passport doesn't have this feature, you can still travel without a visa if it is a valid passport issued before October 26, 2005, and includes a machine-readable zone, or between October 26, 2005, and October 25, 2006, and includes a digital photograph. For more information, go to **www.travel.state.gov/visa**.

Citizens of all other countries must have (1) a valid passport that expires at least 6 months later than the scheduled end of their visit to the U.S., and (2) a tourist visa, which may be obtained without charge from any U.S. consulate.

As of January 2004, many international visitors traveling on visas to the United States will be photographed and fingerprinted on arrival at Customs in airports and on cruise ships in a program created by the Department of Homeland Security called **US-VISIT.** Exempt from the extra scrutiny are visitors entering by land or those (mostly in Europe; see above) that don't require a visa for short-term visits. For more information, go to the Homeland Security website at **www.dhs.gov/dhspublic**.

For specifics on how to get a visa, go to **"Visas"** in the **"Fast Facts"** appendix (p. 454).

Medical Requirements

Unless you're arriving from an area known to be suffering from an epidemic (particularly cholera or yellow fever), inoculations or vaccinations are not required for entry into the United States.

CUSTOMS

What You Can Bring into the U.S.

Every visitor more than 21 years of age may bring in, free of duty, the following: (1) 1 liter of wine or hard liquor; (2) 200 cigarettes, 100 cigars (but not from Cuba), or 3 pounds of smoking tobacco; and (3) $100 worth of gifts. These exemptions are offered to travelers who spend at least 72 hours in the United States and who have not claimed them within the preceding 6 months. It is forbidden to bring into the country almost any meat products (including canned, fresh, and dried meat products such as buillion, soup mixes, and so on). Generally, condiments including vinegars, oils, spices, coffee, tea, and some cheeses and baked goods are permitted. Avoid rice products, as rice can often harbor insects. Bringing fruits and vegetables is not advised, though not prohibited. Customs will allow produce depending on where you got it and where you're going after you arrive in the U.S. Foreign tourists may carry in or out up to $10,000 in U.S. or foreign currency with no formalities; larger sums must be declared to U.S. Customs on entering or leaving, which includes filing form CM 4790. For details regarding U.S. Customs and Border Protection, consult your nearest U.S. embassy or consulate, or the **U.S. Customs** website (www.customs.ustreas.gov).

What You Can Take Home from Colorado

Canadian Citizens: For a clear summary of Canadian rules, write for the booklet *I Declare,* issued by the **Canada Border Services Agency** (✆ **800/461-9999** in Canada, or 204/983-3500; www.cbsa-asfc.gc.ca).

U.K. Citizens: For information, contact **HM Customs & Excise** at ✆ **0845/010-9000** (from outside the U.K., 020/8929-0152), or consult their website at **www.hmce.gov.uk**.

Australian Citizens: A helpful brochure available from Australian consulates or Customs offices is *Know Before You Go.* For more information, call the **Australian Customs Service** at ✆ **1300/363-263** or log on to **www.customs.gov.au**.

New Zealand Citizens: Most questions are answered in a free pamphlet available at New Zealand consulates and Customs offices: *New Zealand Customs Guide for Travellers, Notice no. 4.* For more information, contact **New Zealand Customs,** The Customhouse, 17–21 Whitmore St., Box 2218, Wellington (✆ **04/473-6099** or 0800/428-786; www.customs.govt.nz).

3 WHEN TO GO

Colorado has two main tourist seasons: warm and cold. Those who want to see the state's parks and other scenic wonders by hiking, mountain biking, or rafting usually visit from May through October; those who prefer skiing, snowboarding, and snowmobiling will have to wait for winter, usually from late November through March or April, depending on snow levels. Although you can visit most museums year-round, some close in winter.

The best way to avoid crowds at the more popular destinations, such as Rocky Mountain National Park, Garden of the Gods, and Pikes Peak, is to try to visit during the shoulder seasons of March through May and October through mid-December. Generally, those traveling without children will want to avoid visiting during school vacations.

To hear Coloradans tell it, the state has perfect weather all the time. Although they may be exaggerating just a bit, the weather here is usually quite pleasant, with an abundance of sun and relatively mild temperatures in most places—just avoid those winter snowstorms.

Along the Front Range, where Denver and Colorado Springs are located, summer days are hot and dry, and evenings mild. Humidity is low, and temperatures seldom rise above the 90s (30s Celsius). Evenings start to get cooler by mid-September, but even as late as November the days are often warm. Surprisingly, winters here are warmer and less snowy than winters in the Great Lakes or New England.

Most of Colorado is considered semi-arid, and overall the state has an average of 296 sunny days a year—more sunshine than San Diego or Miami Beach. The prairies average about 16 inches of precipitation annually; the Front Range, 14 inches; the western slope, only about 8 inches. Rain, when it falls, is commonly a short afternoon thunderstorm. However, if you want to see snow, simply head to the mountains, where snowfall is measured in feet rather than inches, and mountain peaks may still be white in July. Mountain temperatures can be bitterly cold, especially if it's windy, but even at the higher elevations of some of the nation's top ski resorts, you'll find plenty of sunshine.

Average Monthly High/Low Temperatures & Precipitation

	Jan	Feb	Mar	Apr	May	June	July	Aug	Sept	Oct	Nov	Dec
Denver												
Temp. (°F)	43/16	47/20	52/26	62/35	71/44	82/53	88/59	86/57	77/48	66/37	52/25	45/18
Temp. (°C)	6/–9	8/–6	11/–3	16/1	21/6	27/11	31/15	30/13	25/8	18/2	11/–3	7/–7
Precip. (in.)	0.5	0.6	1.3	1.8	2.5	1.7	1.9	1.5	1.1	1.0	0.9	0.6
elev. 5,280'												
Col. Springs												
Temp. (°F)	41/17	44/20	51/26	60/34	68/42	79/52	85/57	82/56	75/48	63/36	50/25	42/18
Temp. (°C)	5/–8	6/–6	10/–3	15/1	20/5	26/11	29/13	27/13	23/8	17/2	10/–3	5/–7
Precip. (in.)	0.3	0.4	1.2	1.4	2.8	2.5	2.5	3.3	1.1	0.9	0.6	0.5
elev. 6,035'												
Grand Junction												
Temp. (°F)	36/16	44/23	54/31	65/39	76/48	87/57	93/64	90/62	81/53	68/41	51/92	39/19
Temp. (°C)	2/–8	6/–5	12/0	18/3	24/8	30/13	33/17	32/16	27/11	20/5	10/–1	3/–7
Precip. (in.)	0.6	0.5	0.9	0.8	0.8	0.4	0.6	0.9	0.8	0.9	0.7	0.6
Elev. 4,586'												

CALENDAR OF EVENTS

Below are some of the major annual events in Colorado. You'll find additional events on the Internet at **www.colorado.com**, **www.coloradofestival.com**, and **www.denver365.com**, as well as on each city's website. I strongly recommend, however, that if a particular event is especially important to you, confirm the date by telephone before you leave home. For an exhaustive list of events beyond those listed here, check **http://events.frommers.com**, where you'll find a searchable, up-to-the-minute roster of what's happening in cities all over the world.

January

Great Fruitcake Toss, Colorado Springs. This zany event, where contestants compete to see who can throw a fruitcake the farthest, is among the most outlandish and festive spectacles of the year. It takes place in Manitou Springs's Memorial Park, 5 miles west of downtown Colorado Springs. Call ✆ **800/642-2567** or 719/685-5089 for more information. Early January.

Mahlerfest, Boulder. This may be the only festival celebrating the work of composer Gustav Mahler. Attend a full orchestra concert, free chamber concerts, or the free symposium. Call ✆ **303/447-0513** or visit **www.mahlerfest.org** for more information. Early January.

National Western Stock Show and Rodeo, Denver. This is the world's largest livestock show and indoor rodeo, with about two dozen rodeo performances, a trade exposition, Western food and crafts booths, and livestock auctions. Call ✆ **303/297-1166** for details. Second and third week of January.

Ullr Fest, Breckenridge. A week of wacky events dedicated to Ullr, the Norse snow god, culminates in a wackier parade. Call ✆ **970/453-6018** or visit **www.gobreck.com**. Mid-January.

Wintersköl Carnival, Aspen and Snowmass. A 4-day event that includes a parade, fireworks, and a torchlight descent. Call ✆ **970/925-1940** or see **www.aspenchamber.org**. Mid-January.

International Snow Sculpture Championships, Breckenridge. Four-person teams transform 20-ton blocks of snow into works of art. Call ✆ **970/453-6018** or visit **www.gobreck.com**. Late January.

Boulder Bach Festival, Boulder. Music of the master baroque composer. Call ✆ **303/652-9101** or visit **www.boulder bachfest.org** for details. Last weekend in January.

February

Loveland Valentine Remailing Program, Loveland. More than 200,000 valentines are remailed annually from Loveland. Call ✆ **970/667-6311** or see **www.loveland.org** for details. Early February.

Steamboat Springs Winter Carnival, Steamboat Springs. Festivities include races, jumping, broomball, and skijoring—that's horse-powered skiing—street events. Call ✆ **970/879-0695** or visit **www.sswsc.org**. First full week in February.

Leadville Valentine's Day Wine Tasting, Leadville. Wine tasting, good food, workshops, and related activities cosponsored by the National Mining Hall of Fame and Museum. Call ✆ **888/532-3845** or see **www.leadvilleusa.com** for information. Mid-February.

Buffalo Bill's Birthday Celebration, Golden. Ceremonies and live entertainment that commemorate the life of the legendary scout and entertainer take place at the Buffalo Bill Memorial Museum. Call ✆ **303/526-0744** or 303/526-0747, or check **www.buffalo bill.org** for further information. Late February.

March

Colorado Springs Dance Theatre Wine Festival, Colorado Springs. Sample the best wines at this 3-day benefit for the Colorado Springs Dance Theatre. Call ✆ **719/630-7434** for further information. Early March.

Pow Wow, Denver. More than 1,500 American Indians (as well as 60 drum groups), representing some 85 tribes from 32 states, perform traditional music and dances. Arts and crafts are also sold. Call ✆ **303/934-8045** or browse **www.denvermarchpowwow.org** for details. Mid-March.

Saint Patrick's Day, Denver. Among the largest Irish holiday parades in the United States, with floats, marching bands, and thousands of horses. Call ✆ **303/892-1112** for further information. Saturday before March 17.

April

Easter Sunrise Service, Colorado Springs and Denver. Worshipers watch the rising sun illuminate red sandstone formations in the Garden of the Gods in Colorado Springs. For details, call ✆ **719/634-6666.** Denver's Easter Sunrise Service takes place at Red Rocks Amphitheatre, also in the midst of stunning geological formations. Call ✆ **303/295-4444** or visit **www.red rocksonline.com** for further information. Easter Sunday.

Spring Barrel Tasting, Grand Junction. Wine sampling, talks on winemaking, and good food. Call ✆ **970/244-1480** or see **www.visitgrandjunction.com** for information. Late April.

May

Cinco de Mayo, Denver and Colorado Springs. More than 250,000 people from around the Denver area celebrate this annual event centered on north Federal Boulevard with mariachi bands, dancers, Mexican food, and other activities. Call ✆ **303/534-8342** for information. Memorial Park is the site for the Colorado Springs celebration. Call ✆ **719/635-5001** for information. May 5.

Plant and Book Sale, Denver. The largest volunteer-run plant and book sale in the nation, this event at Denver Botanic Gardens offers more than 250,000 plants, thousands of new and used books, and free gardening advice. Call ✆ **720/865-3500** or visit **www.botanicgardens.org** for details. Early May.

Boulder Kinetic Fest, Boulder. A wacky event that's a real crowd pleaser. Most years an average of 70 teams race over land and water at Boulder Reservoir in a variety of imaginative human-powered conveyances. Activities include the kinetic parade, kinetic concerts, the kinetic ball, and a hot-air-balloon launch. Call ✆ **303/444-5600** for details. Early May.

Iron Horse Bicycle Classic, Durango. Mountain bikers race against a steam train from Durango to Silverton. Call ✆ **970/259-4621** or see **www.ironhorsebicycleclassic.com**. Memorial Day weekend.

Taste of Creede, Creede. A festival of fine arts, with live music, artists' demonstrations, food, and an art auction. Call **800/327-2102** or see **www.creede.com** for information. Memorial Day weekend.

Bolder Boulder, Boulder. This footrace attracts some 40,000 entrants each year, plus numerous spectators. Participants walk, jog, or run the 10K course. Call ✆ **303/444-RACE** (444-7223) or visit **www.bolderboulder.com** for details. Memorial Day.

June

FIBArk Whitewater Festival, Salida. North America's longest and oldest downriver kayak race highlights this festival, which includes carnival rides, a parade, a white-water rodeo, and live entertainment. Call ✆ **719/539-6918** or visit **www.fibark.net**. Mid-June.

Strawberry Days, Glenwood Springs. One of Colorado's oldest civic celebrations, with a rodeo, talent show, music, dancing, an arts-and-crafts fair, parade, carnival, and footraces. Call ✆ **970/945-2425** or visit **www.strawberrydaysfestival.com**. Mid-June.

Glenn Miller Dancin' on the Plains, Fort Morgan. A big-band music extravaganza in the hometown of the legendary big band leader. Call ✆ **800/354-8660** or see **www.fortmorganchamber.org** for information. Mid-June.

International Buskerfest, Denver. An international street performers' festival featuring amazing shows by world-class jugglers, sword swallowers, magicians, tightrope artists, mimes, and acrobats. Call ✆ **303/478-7878** for more information. Mid-June.

Wool Market, Estes Park. This huge natural-fiber show boasts contests, demonstrations, a children's tent, and a sale of animals (sheep, llamas), plus products made from their wool. Kids love it. Call ✆ **970/586-5800** or go to **www.estesnet.com**. Mid-June.

Aspen Music Festival, Aspen. Considered one of the finest summer music festivals in the country, featuring world-renowned artists in classical, chamber, and opera performances. Call ✆ **970/925-9042** or see **www.aspenmusicfestival.com**. Mid-June through mid-August.

Strings Music Festival, Steamboat Springs. Top-notch classical, jazz, country, and pop musicians perform. Call ✆ **970/879-5056** or see **www.stringsinthemountains.com**. June through mid-August.

Greeley Stampede, Greeley. One of the West's biggest rodeos, with top national entertainers, plus concerts, kids' events, art exhibits, fireworks, and more. Call ✆ **800/982-2855** or go to **www.**

greeleystampede.org for details. Late June to early July.

Colorado Brewers' Festival, Fort Collins. Samples of more than 40 Colorado beers plus food and music. Call ✆ **800/274-3678** or see **www.downtownfortcollins.com**. Late June.

Telluride Bluegrass Festival, Telluride. This major international music gathering features bluegrass, folk, and country music. Call ✆ **800/624-2422** or see **www.telluridebluegrass.com**. Late June.

Colorado Shakespeare Festival, Boulder. Considered among the top Shakespeare festivals in the country, with most performances in an outdoor theater. Call ✆ **303/492-0554** for details. Late June through late August.

Garden Concerts, Denver. Jazz, blues, and folk concerts take place in the outdoor amphitheater at **Denver Botanic Gardens.** Call ✆ **720/865-3500** or visit **www.botanicgardens.org** for information. June through September.

July

Brush Rodeo, Brush. Billed as Colorado's largest professional rodeo, with hundreds of participants, this event offers traditional rodeo competition, children's activities, an art show, a parade, a free barbecue, a footrace, a dance, and fireworks. Call ✆ **970/842-5001** or see **www.brushcolo.com.** Early July.

Colorado State Mining Championship, Creede. Entrants from six states compete in old-style hand steeling, hand mucking, spike driving, and newer methods of machine drilling and machine mucking. Call ✆ **800/327-2102** or visit **www.creede.com**. July 4th weekend.

Pikes Peak Auto Hill Climb, Colorado Springs. This "race to the clouds," held annually since 1916, takes drivers to the top of 14,110-foot Pikes Peak. Call ✆ **719/685-4400** for additional information. Saturday close to July 4th.

Woodcarvers Rendezvous, Creede. This weeklong event includes woodcarving classes, demonstrations, and an auction. Call ✆ **800/327-2102** or see **www.creedewoodcarvers.com**. Early to mid-July.

Rooftop Rodeo & Parade, Estes Park. Award-winning rodeos Tuesday through Sunday evenings. A grand parade kicks it all off on Tuesday morning. Call ✆ **970/586-5800** or visit **www.estesnet.com** for details. Mid-July.

Crested Butte Wild Flower Festival, Crested Butte. This mountain community shows off its spectacular wildflowers with hikes, photo workshops, classes, and other activities. Call ✆ **800/455-1290** or see **www.crestedbuttewildflowerfestival.com**. Mid-July.

Art Fair, Boulder. Some 150 local and regional artists display their works in downtown Boulder, offering "fine art to fun art" plus live musical performances. Call ✆ **303/449-3774** or visit **www.boulderdowntown.com** for more information. Third weekend in July.

Buffalo Bill Days, Golden. A parade, kids' rides, a burro race, arts and crafts displays, a petting zoo, a car show, and a pancake breakfast mark Golden's largest event. Call ✆ **303/384-0003** or visit **www.buffalobilldays.com** for more information. Late July.

August

Boom Days, Leadville. Events celebrate Leadville's mining and Wild West heritage with a parade, a carnival, gun-slinger reenactments, a mine-drilling competition, and a burro race. Call ✆ **888/532-3845** or see **www.leadvilleboomdays.com.** First weekend in August.

Pikes Peak or Bust Rodeo, Colorado Springs. Colorado's largest outdoor rodeo, and a popular stop on the professional rodeo circuit. Call ✆ **719/635-3547** or visit **www.coloradospringsrodeo.com** for details. Early August.

Sculpture in the Park, Loveland. This outdoor juried exhibit of sculpture includes works by close to 200 sculptors from around the world. Call ✆ **970/663-2940** or see **www.sculptureinthepark.org**. Mid-August.

Colorado State Fair, Pueblo. National professional rodeo, carnival rides, food booths, industrial displays, horse shows, animal exhibits, and entertainment by top-name performers. Call ✆ **800/876-4567** or visit **www.coloradostatefair.com** for additional information. Mid-August through Labor Day.

September

Telluride Film Festival, Telluride. This influential festival has premiered some of the finest independent films in recent years. Call ✆ **510/665-9494** or see **www.telluridefilmfestival.org**. Early September.

Colorado Springs Balloon Classic, Colorado Springs. More than 100 colorful hot-air balloons launch from Memorial Park, making this one of the largest balloon rallies in the country. Call ✆ **719/471-4833** or visit **www.balloonclassic.com** for more information. Labor Day weekend.

A Taste of Colorado, Denver. This is Denver's largest celebration, with an annual attendance of about 400,000. Local restaurants serve house specialties; there are also crafts exhibits and free concerts. Call ✆ **303/295-6330** or visit **www.atasteofcolorado.com** for details. Labor Day weekend.

Vail Oktoberfest, Vail. A traditional village-wide weekend celebration, it features street entertainment, German beer and food, dancing, games, and singalongs. Call ✆ **970/476-6797** or go to **www.vailoktoberfest.com**. Mid-September.

Fall Festival, Boulder. An Oktoberfest celebration, this festival includes polka bands, food, carnival rides, and an art fair. Call ✆ **303/449-3774** or visit **www.boulderdowntown.com** for more information. Late September or early October.

October

Great American Beer Festival, Denver. Hundreds of American beers are available for sampling, and seminars are presented at what is considered the largest and most prestigious beer event in the United States. Call ✆ **303/447-0816** or visit **www.beertown.org/events/gabf** for information. Early October.

Cowboy Gathering, Durango. Cowboy poetry, Western art, motorless parade, a dance, historical lectures, and demonstrations. Call ✆ **970/382-7494** or go to **www.durangocowboygathering.org**. Early October.

Pumpkin Festival, Denver. This family event, sponsored by **Denver Botanic Gardens** and held at Chatfield Nature Preserve southwest of town, includes pumpkin picking, food, crafts, hayrides, and other activities. Call ✆ **720/865-3500** or visit **www.botanicgardens.org** for details. Mid-October.

November

Holiday Gift & Garden Market, Denver. Handmade Christmas ornaments, gifts, dried-flower arrangements, and food items are among the unique merchandise at this annual sale at the Denver Botanic Gardens. Call ✆ **720/865-3500** or visit **www.botanicgardens.org** for information. Mid-November.

Christmas Mountain USA, Salida. More than 3,000 lights outline a huge tree; it also boasts a parade of lights and a visit from Santa Claus. Call ✆ **877/772-5432** or see **www.salidachamber.org**. Day after Thanksgiving.

December

World's Largest Christmas Lighting Display, Denver. Some 40,000 colored floodlights illuminate the Denver City and County Building. All month.

Blossoms of Light, Denver. Over 12,000 sparkling lights cascade through the Botanic Gardens. Grand topiaries, nightly entertainment, "kissing spots," whimsical displays, and warm treats make for an unforgettable winter evening. Call ✆ **303/865-3500** or visit **www.botanicgardens.org** for information. All month.

Parade of Lights, Denver. A holiday parade winds through downtown Denver, with floats, balloons, and marching bands. Call ✆ **303/478-7878** or visit **www.denverparadeoflights.com** for information. Early December.

Festival of Lights Parade, Colorado Springs. A nighttime parade kicks off this month-long celebration of the holidays. Features include decorated live trees and holiday scenes from cultures around the world. Call ✆ **719/634-5581** or visit **www.csfineartscenter.org** for information. Early December.

Country Christmas Jubilee at Old Town, Burlington. Victorian carolers and Christmas music, historic buildings decorated in individual themes, bell ringing, plus other Victorian Christmas activities. Call ✆ **800/288-1334** or check **www.burlingtoncolo.com**. Early December.

Christmas with Cody, Golden. Buffalo Bill Cody playing Santa? He sure did, and a reenactor continues the tradition, with gifts for the kids at the Buffalo Bill Memorial Museum. Call ✆ **303/526-0744** or 303/526-0747, or check **www.buffalobill.org** for further information. First Sunday in December.

Olde Golden Christmas, Golden. Come to Golden for an old-fashioned candlelight walk on the first Friday in December, and stay for weekend festivities in town. Call ✆ **303/279-3113** or visit **www.goldencochamber.org** for information. Begins in early December.

Pikes Peak Summit Fireworks, Colorado Springs. A wondrous fireworks display to ring in the New Year. Call (✆ **800/888-4748** or 719/635-7506, or check out **www.coloradosprings-travel.com**. December 31.

4 GETTING THERE & GETTING AROUND

GETTING TO COLORADO

By Plane

Those flying to Colorado will probably land at Denver International Airport or Colorado Springs Airport. Both airports are on the fringes of their respective city, so it can be a tossup depending on your route. Denver certainly has the best average prices. Both offer car rentals and shuttle services to their city's hotels.

Denver International Airport (DIA) is 23 miles northeast of downtown Denver, about a 35- to 45-minute drive. It is the sixth-busiest airport in the nation, with six runways and 93 gates. An information line (✆ **800/AIR-2-DEN** [247-2336] or 303/342-2000; www.flydenver.com) provides data on flight schedules and connections, parking, ground transportation, current weather conditions, and local accommodations. The local airport information and paging number is ✆ **303/342-2300.** Airlines serving Denver include **Air Canada** (✆ 888/247-2262; www.aircanada.ca), **Alaska Airlines** (✆ 800/252-7524; www.alaskaair.com), **American** (✆ 800/433-7300; www.aa.com), **Continental** (✆ 800/523-3273; www.continental.com), **Delta** (✆ 800/221-1212; www.delta.com), **Frontier** (✆ 800/432-1359; www.frontierairlines.com), **jetBlue Airways** (✆ 800/538-2583; www.jetblue.com), **Mexicana** (✆ 800/531-7921; www.mexicana.com), **Midwest Airlines** (✆ 800/452-2022; www.midwestairlines.com), **Northwest** (✆ 800/225-2525; www.nwa.com), **Southwest**

(© 800/435-9792; www.southwest.com), **United** (© 800/241-6522; www.ual.com), and **US Airways** (© 800/428-4322; www.usair.com).

Colorado Springs Airport (COS), located in the southeast corner of Colorado Springs (© **719/550-1900**), has nearly 100 flights each day, with connections to most major U.S. cities. **Allegiant** (© 702/505-8888; www.allegiantair.com), **American, Continental, ExpressJet** (© 888/958-9538; www.expressjet.com), **Frontier, Northwest, United,** and **US Airways** serve Colorado Springs.

Flights from the United Kingdom

British Airways (© **800/247-9297** or 0845/773-3377 in London; www.british-airways.com) offers one daily nonstop flight between London and Denver. Travelers from the United Kingdom can also take British Airways to other U.S. cities and make connecting flights to Denver or Colorado Springs.

Arriving at the Airport

International visitors arriving by air, no matter what the port of entry, should cultivate patience and resignation before setting foot on U.S. soil. U.S. airports have considerably beefed up security clearances in the years since the terrorist attacks of September 11, 2001, and clearing **Customs and Immigration** can take as long as 2 hours.

Getting into Town from the Airport

Bus, taxi, and limousine services shuttle travelers between the airport and downtown, and most major car-rental companies have outlets at the airport. Many major hotels are some distance from the airport, so travelers should check on the availability and cost of hotel shuttle services when making reservations.

The cost of a **city bus** ride from the airport to downtown Denver is $9; from the airport to Boulder and suburban Park-n-Ride lots, it is about $11. The **SuperShuttle** (© **800/525-3177** or 303/370-1300; www.supershuttle.com) provides transportation to and from a number of hotels downtown and in the Denver Tech Center for $19 each way; door-to-door service is also available. **Taxi** companies are another option, with fares generally in the $30-to-$50 range, and you can often share a cab and split the fare by calling the cab company ahead of time. For instance, **Yellow Cab** (© **303/777-7777**) will take up to five people from DIA to most downtown hotels for a flat rate of $45. **Metro Taxi** (© **303/333-3333**) is the other service in Denver.

Long-Haul Flights: How to Stay Comfortable

- Your choice of airline and airplane will definitely affect your legroom. Find more details about U.S. airlines at **www.seatguru.com**. For international airlines, the research firm Skytrax has posted a list of average seat pitches at **www.airlinequality.com**.
- Emergency exit seats and bulkhead seats typically have the most legroom. Emergency exit seats are usually left unassigned until the day of a flight (to ensure that someone able-bodied fills the seats); it's worth checking in online at home (if the airline offers that option) or getting to the ticket counter early to snag one of these spots for a long flight. Many passengers find that bulkhead seating offers more legroom, but keep in mind that bulkhead seats have no storage space on the floor in front of you.
- To have two seats for yourself in a three-seat row, try for an aisle seat in a center section toward the back of coach. If you're traveling with a companion, book an aisle and a window seat. Middle seats are usually booked last, so chances are good you'll end up with three seats to yourselves. And in the event that a third passenger is assigned the middle seat, he or she will probably be more than happy to trade for a window or an aisle.

- To sleep, avoid the last row of any section or the row in front of an emergency exit, as these seats are the least likely to recline. Avoid seats near highly trafficked toilet areas. Avoid seats in the back of many jets—these can be narrower than those in the rest of coach. Or reserve a window seat so you can rest your head and avoid being bumped in the aisle.
- Get up, walk around, and stretch every 60 to 90 minutes to keep your blood flowing. This helps avoid **deep vein thrombosis,** or "economy-class syndrome."
- Drink water before, during, and after your flight to combat the lack of humidity in airplane cabins. Avoid caffeine and alcohol, which will dehydrate you.
- Jet lag is a pitfall of traveling across time zones. If you're flying north–south and you feel sluggish when you touch down, your symptoms will be the result of dehydration and the general stress of air travel. When you travel east–west or vice versa, your body becomes confused about what time it is, and everything from your digestive system to your brain is knocked for a loop. Traveling east is more difficult on your internal clock than traveling west because most peoples' bodies are more inclined to stay up late than to fall asleep early. To combat jet lag, reset your watch to your destination time before you board the plane, drink lots of water, avoid alcohol, and exercise and sleep well for a few days before your trip.

By Car

An excellent road system, connecting to interstate highways heading in all directions, makes driving a good and economical choice. This is especially true for those planning excursions out of Denver. Although these cities have good public transportation within their boundaries, a car (either your own or a rental) is practically mandatory for those intent on getting out into the country.

Most major car-rental companies have locations in all three cities; metro Denver has the lion's share of them. For listings of the major car rental agencies, please see the "Fast Facts, Toll-Free Numbers & Websites" appendix (p. 448).

Some 1,000 miles of interstate highways form a star on the map of Colorado, with its center at Denver. (See the state map on the inside back cover.) **I-25** crosses the state from south to north, extending from New Mexico to Wyoming; over its 300 miles, it goes through nearly every major city of the Front Range, including Pueblo, Colorado Springs, Denver, and Fort Collins. **I-70** crosses from west to east, extending from Utah to Baltimore, Maryland. It enters Colorado near Grand Junction; passes through Glenwood Springs, Vail, and Denver; and exits just east of Burlington, a distance of about 450 miles. **I-76** is an additional 190-mile spur that begins in Denver and extends northeast to Nebraska, joining I-80 just beyond Julesburg.

Denver is about 1,025 miles from Los Angeles, 780 miles from Dallas, 600 miles from Kansas City, 510 miles from Salt Lake City, 440 miles from Albuquerque, 750 miles from Las Vegas, 820 miles from Phoenix, 1,010 miles from Chicago, and 1,800 miles from New York.

Fun Facts **Take the High Road**

The world's highest automobile tunnel, the Eisenhower Tunnel, crosses the Continental Divide 65 miles west of Denver, at an elevation of 11,000 feet.

By Train

Amtrak (© **800/USA-RAIL** [872-7245]; www.amtrak.com) has two routes through Colorado. The California Zephyr, which links San Francisco and Chicago, passes through Grand Junction, Glenwood Springs, Granby, Winter Park, Denver, and Fort Morgan en route to Omaha, Nebraska. The Southwest Chief, which runs between Los Angeles and Chicago, travels from Albuquerque, New Mexico, via Trinidad, La Junta, and Lamar before crossing the southeastern Colorado border into Kansas.

GETTING AROUND

Since most visitors to Colorado will probably be traveling between cities and also into surrounding areas, you will most likely want to rent a car. However, you can save a bit of cash by doing your downtown city exploring, which can be done quite conveniently using public transportation, at either the beginning or the end of your stay, and only renting a car when you plan to leave town.

Each of the individual city chapters that follows contains information on car rentals and public transportation. A good first stop: Denver's largest map store, **Mapsco Map and Travel Center,** 800 Lincoln St., Denver, CO 80203 (© **800/456-8703** or 303/830-2373; www.mapsco.com), offers USGS and recreation maps, state maps and travel guides, raised relief maps, and globes.

By Car

In Colorado in general, the most cost-effective way to travel is by car, but Denver, Boulder, and Colorado Springs have pedestrian- and bicycle-friendly routes and at least decent public transportation.

If you're visiting from abroad and plan to rent a car in the United States, keep in mind that foreign driver's licenses are usually recognized in the U.S., but you should get an international one if your home license is not in English.

Check out **Breezenet.com**, which offers domestic car-rental discounts with some of the most competitive rates around. Also worth visiting are **Orbitz.com**, **Hotwire.com**, **Travelocity.com,** and **Priceline.com**, all of which offer competitive online car-rental rates. For additional car-rental agencies, see the "Fast Facts, Toll-Free Numbers & Websites" appendix, p. 448.

By Plane

Although you can fly between Denver and Colorado Springs, it's not nearly as economical as driving the 70 miles. Overseas visitors can take advantage of the APEX (Advance Purchase Excursion) reductions offered by all major U.S. and European carriers. In addition, some large airlines offer transatlantic or transpacific passengers special discount tickets under the name **Visit USA,** which allows mostly one-way travel from one U.S. destination to another at very low prices. Unavailable in the U.S., these discount tickets must be purchased abroad in conjunction with your international fare. This system is the easiest, fastest, cheapest way to see the country.

By Train

Although you can catch an Amtrak train from Union Station in Denver, it's not a particularly good method of travel between Denver, Boulder, and Colorado Springs—not until a light-rail build-out takes place in the next decade, at least. In Denver, existing light rail is useful for navigating certain attractions.

International visitors can buy a **USA Rail Pass,** good for 15 or 30 days of unlimited travel on **Amtrak** (© **800/USA-RAIL** [872-7245]; www.amtrak.com). The pass is available online or through many overseas travel agents. See Amtrak's website for the cost of travel within the western, eastern, or northwestern United States. Reservations are generally required and should be made as early as possible. Regional rail passes are also available.

By Bus

Bus travel is often the most economical form of public transit for short hops between U.S. cities, but it's certainly not an option for everyone (particularly when Amtrak, which is far more luxurious, offers similar rates). Between Colorado Springs and Denver, the **Front Range Express** (✆ **719/636-3739;** www.frontrangeexpress.com) offers bus service for $9 one-way. **Greyhound** (✆ **800/231-2222;** www.greyhound.com) is the sole nationwide bus line. International visitors can obtain information about the **Greyhound North American Discovery Pass** from foreign travel agents or through **www.discoverypass.com**; it provides unlimited travel and stopovers in the U.S. and Canada.

5 MONEY & COSTS

Generally, Colorado is not particularly expensive, especially compared to destinations on the East and West coasts. You'll find a wide range of prices for lodging and dining; admission to most museums is less than $10. Hotel rooms in the state are typically $100 to $200, but there are exceptions that are lower and higher—particularly higher when it comes to peak seasons. You'll find main courses for dinner typically running $10 to $20 up and down the Front Range.

Those traveling away from the major cities will discover prices in small towns are usually quite reasonable, but ski resorts such as Vail and Aspen can be rather pricey, especially during winter holidays. Hotel rooms tend to start well over $200 a night in ski season in these resorts, and condos are more.

Traveler's checks and **credit cards** are accepted at almost all hotels, restaurants, shops, and attractions, plus many grocery stores; automated teller machines for all the major national networks are practically everywhere.

The most common bills are the $1 (a "buck"), $5, $10, and $20 denominations. There are also $2 bills (seldom encountered), $50 bills, and $100 bills. (The last two are usually not welcome as payment for small purchases.)

Coins come in seven denominations: 1¢ (1 cent, or a penny); 5¢ (5 cents, or a nickel); 10¢ (10 cents, or a dime); 25¢ (25 cents, or a quarter); 50¢ (50 cents, or a half-dollar); the gold-colored Sacagawea coin, worth $1; and the rare silver dollar.

The easiest and best way to get cash away from home is from an **ATM** (automated teller machine). Look at the back of your bank card to see which network you're on; then call or check online for ATM locations at your destination. Be sure you know your personal identification number (PIN) and daily withdrawal limit before you depart. Also, if you have a five- or six-digit PIN, change it to a four-digit PIN before coming to Colorado.

Remember that many banks impose a fee every time you use a card at another bank's ATM, and that fee can be higher for international transactions (up to $5 or more) than for domestic ones (where they're rarely more than $2). In addition, the bank from which you withdraw cash may charge its own fee.

6 HEALTH

STAYING HEALTHY

Colorado's Front Range has its fair share of regional health concerns to be aware of before your trip, most of them relating to the altitude and the wildlife, but these can easily be avoided in most cases.

General Availability of Health Care

Contact the **International Association for Medical Assistance to Travelers (IAMAT; ✆ 716/754-4883** or, in Canada, 416/652-0137; www.iamat.org) for tips on travel and health concerns in the United States, and for lists of local, English-speaking doctors. The United States **Centers for Disease Control and Prevention** (**✆ 800/311-3435;** www.cdc.gov) provides up-to-date information on health hazards by region or country and offers tips on food safety. The website **www.tripprep.com**, sponsored by a consortium of travel medicine practitioners, may also offer helpful advice on traveling to the U.S. You can find listings of reliable U.S. clinics at the **International Society of Travel Medicine** (www.istm.org).

COMMON AILMENTS

ALTITUDE SICKNESS About two-thirds of Colorado is more than a mile above sea level, which means there is less oxygen and lower humidity than many travelers are accustomed to. This creates a unique set of problems for short-term visitors, such as the possibility of shortness of breath, fatigue, and other physical concerns.

Those not used to higher elevations should get sufficient rest, avoid large meals, and drink plenty of nonalcoholic fluids, especially water. Individuals with heart or respiratory problems should consult their personal physicians before planning a trip to the Colorado mountains. Those in generally good health need not take any special precautions, but it is best to ease the transition to high elevations by changing altitude gradually. For instance, spend a night or two in Denver (elevation 5,280 ft.) or Colorado Springs (elevation 6,035 ft.) before driving or taking the cog railway to the top of Pikes Peak (elevation 14,110 ft.).

Lowlanders can also help their bodies adjust to higher elevations by taking it easy for their first few days in the mountains, cutting down on cigarettes and alcohol, and avoiding sleeping pills and other drugs. Your doctor can provide prescription drugs to help prevent and relieve symptoms of altitude sickness.

Because the sun's rays are more direct in the thinner atmosphere, they cause sunburn more quickly. The potential for skin damage increases when the sun reflects off snow or water. A good sunblock is strongly recommended, as are good-quality ultraviolet-blocking sunglasses. Remember that children need more protection than adults.

HANTAVIRUS State health officials warn outdoor enthusiasts to take precautions against the Hantavirus, a rare but often fatal respiratory disease first recognized in 1993. About half of the country's confirmed cases have been reported in the Four Corners states of Colorado, New Mexico, Arizona, and Utah. The disease is usually spread by the urine and droppings of deer mice and other rodents, and health officials recommend that campers avoid areas with signs of rodent droppings. Symptoms of Hantavirus are similar to flu and lead to breathing difficulties and shock.

WEST NILE VIRUS Colorado has also had its share of cases of the West Nile virus illness. The best prevention is mosquito repellant. The virus can be fatal but typically is not. Symptoms include fever, headache, and body aches.

Fun Facts **High & Mighty**

Colorado boasts 75% of the land in the continental United States above 10,000 feet in elevation.

WHAT TO DO IF YOU GET SICK AWAY FROM HOME

Hospitals and **emergency numbers** are listed in the "Fast Facts" appendix, p. 448.

If you suffer from a chronic illness, consult your doctor before your departure. Pack **prescription medications** in your carry-on luggage, and carry them in their original containers, with pharmacy labels—otherwise, they won't make it through airport security. Visitors from outside the U.S. should carry generic names of prescription drugs. For U.S. travelers, most reliable health-care plans provide coverage if you get sick away from home. Foreign visitors may have to pay all medical costs upfront and be reimbursed later.

7 SAFETY

STAYING SAFE

While there are many reasons to visit Colorado and its major cities, two of the reasons most often cited are its historic sites and its magnificent outdoor activities. However, visiting historic sites and participating in outdoor activities can lead to accidents.

When visiting such historic sites as ghost towns, gold mines, and railroads, keep in mind that they were probably built more than 100 years ago, at a time when safety standards were extremely lax, if they existed at all. Never enter abandoned buildings, mines, or railroad equipment on your own. When you're visiting commercially operated historic tourist attractions, use common sense and don't be afraid to ask questions.

Walkways in mines are often uneven and poorly lit, and are sometimes slippery due to seeping groundwater that can also stain your clothing with its high iron content. When entering old buildings, be prepared for steep, narrow stairways; creaky floors; and low ceilings and doorways. Steam trains are a wonderful experience as long as you remember that steam is very hot, and that oil and grease can ruin your clothing.

When heading to the great outdoors, keep in mind that injuries often occur when people fail to follow instructions. Pay attention when the experts tell you to stay on established ski trails, hike only in designated areas, carry rain gear, and wear a life jacket when rafting. Mountain weather can be fickle, and many of the most beautiful spots are in remote areas. Be prepared for extreme changes in temperature at any time of year, and watch out for sudden summer-afternoon thunderstorms that can leave you drenched and shivering in minutes.

8 SPECIALIZED TRAVEL RESOURCES

TRAVELERS WITH DISABILITIES

Most disabilities shouldn't stop anyone from traveling in the U.S. Thanks to provisions in the Americans with Disabilities Act, most public places are required to comply with disability-friendly regulations. Almost all public establishments (including hotels, restaurants, and museums, but not including certain National Historic Landmarks) and at least some modes of public transportation provide accessible entrances and other facilities for those with disabilities.

The **America the Beautiful—National Park and Federal Recreational Lands Pass—Access Pass** (formerly the **Golden Access Passport**) gives the visually impaired or persons with permanent disabilities (regardless of age) free lifetime entrance to federal recreation sites administered by the National Park Service, including the Fish and Wildlife Service, the Forest Service, the Bureau of Land Management, and the Bureau of Reclamation. This may include national parks, monuments, historic sites, recreation areas, and national wildlife refuges.

For more on organizations that offer resources to travelers with disabilities, go to **Frommers.com**.

GAY & LESBIAN TRAVELERS

In general, gay and lesbian travelers will find they are treated just like any other travelers in Colorado. Even cities such as Colorado Springs, home of Focus on the Family and other conservative groups, have become somewhat more open-minded about alternative lifestyles recently. Those with specific concerns can contact **Gay, Lesbian, Bisexual, and Transgender Community Services Center of Colorado** (✆ **303/733-7743;** www.glbtcolorado.org) in Denver; the organization can also provide information on events and venues of interest to gay and lesbian visitors.

The International Gay and Lesbian Travel Association (IGLTA; ✆ **954/776-2626;** www.iglta.org) is the trade association for the gay and lesbian travel industry, and offers an online directory of gay- and lesbian-friendly travel businesses; go to its website and click on "Members."

For more gay and lesbian travel resources, visit **Frommers.com**.

SENIOR TRAVEL

Many Colorado hotels and motels offer special rates to senior citizens, and an increasing number of restaurants, attractions, and public transportation systems offer discounts as well, some for "oldsters" as young as 55.

Members of **AARP** (formerly known as the American Association of Retired Persons), 601 E St. NW, Washington, DC 20049 (✆ **888/687-2277;** www.aarp.org), get discounts on hotels, airfares, and car rentals. AARP offers members a wide range of benefits, including *AARP The Magazine* and a monthly newsletter. Anyone 50 or older can join.

The U.S. National Park Service offers an **America the Beautiful—National Park and Federal Recreational Lands Pass—Senior Pass** (formerly the **Golden Age Passport**), which gives seniors 62 years or older lifetime entrance to all properties administered by the National Park Service—national parks, monuments, historic sites, recreation areas, and national wildlife refuges—for a one-time processing fee of $10. The pass must be purchased in person at any NPS facility that charges an entrance fee. Besides free entry, the America the Beautiful Senior Pass also offers a 50% discount on some federal-use fees charged for such facilities as camping, swimming, parking, boat launching, and tours. For more information, see p. 59. To purchase, go to **www.nps.gov/fees_passes.htm** or call the United States Geological Survey (USGS), which issues the passes, at ✆ **888/275-8747.**

Frommers.com offers more information and resources on travel for seniors.

FAMILY TRAVEL

Colorado is loaded with family attractions, although many touristy areas tend to focus on more adult pursuits. Nonetheless, such kids' landmarks as Tiny Town, Casa Bonita, and Elitch Gardens continue to thrive, and pony rides and kiddie ski schools are widely available in the high country. To locate accommodations, restaurants, and attractions that are particularly kid friendly, refer to the "Kids" icon throughout this guide.

If your travels are taking you to Rocky Mountain National Park, *Frommer's Family Vacations in the National Parks* is a good resource.

For a list of more family-friendly travel resources, turn to the experts at **Frommers.com**.

STUDENT TRAVEL

A valid student ID will often qualify students for discounts on airfare, accommodations, entry to museums, cultural events, movies, and more throughout Colorado.

Check out the **International Student Travel Confederation** (**ISTC;** www.istc.org) website for comprehensive travel services information and details on how to get an **International Student Identity Card (ISIC),** which qualifies students for substantial savings on rail passes, plane tickets, entrance fees, and more. It also provides students with basic health and life insurance and a 24-hour helpline. The card is valid for a maximum of 18 months. You can apply for the card online or in person at **STA Travel** (✆ **800/781-4040** in North America, 13/27-82 in Australia, or 08712/300-040 in the U.K.; www.statravel.com), the biggest student travel agency in the world; check out the website to locate STA Travel offices worldwide. If you're no longer a student but are still under 26, you can get an **International Youth Travel Card (IYTC)** from the same people, which entitles you to some discounts. **Travel CUTS** (✆ **800/592-2887;** www.travelcuts.com) offers similar services for both Canadians and U.S. residents. Irish students may prefer to turn to **USIT** (✆ **01/602-1904;** www.usit.ie), an Ireland-based specialist in student, youth, and independent travel.

TRAVELING WITH PETS

Many of us wouldn't dream of going on vacation without our pets. Under the right circumstances, it can be a wonderful experience for both you and your animals. Dogs and cats are accepted at many lodgings in Colorado, but not as universally in resorts and at the more expensive hotels. Throughout this book, I've tried to consistently note those lodgings that take pets. Some properties require you to pay a fee or damage deposit in advance, and most insist they be notified at check-in that you have a pet.

Be aware, however, that national parks and monuments and other federal lands administered by the National Park Service are not pet friendly. Dogs are usually prohibited on all hiking trails, must always be leashed, and in some cases cannot be taken more than 100 feet from established roads. On the other hand, U.S. Forest Service and Bureau of Land Management areas and most state parks are pro-pet, allowing dogs on trails and just about everywhere except inside buildings. State parks require that dogs be leashed; regulations in national forests and BLM lands are generally looser.

Aside from regulations, though, you need to be concerned with your pet's well-being. Just as people need extra water in Colorado's dry climate, so do pets. I especially like those clever spill-resistant travel water bowls sold in pet shops. And keep in mind that many trails are rough, and jagged rocks can cut the pads on your dog's feet.

For more resources about traveling with pets, go to **Frommers.com**.

9 SUSTAINABLE TOURISM

Sustainable tourism is conscientious travel. It means being careful with the environments you explore and respecting the communities you visit. Two

Tips It's Easy Being Green

Here are a few simple ways you can help conserve fuel and energy when you travel:

- Each time you take a flight or drive a car, greenhouse gases release into the atmosphere. You can help neutralize this danger to the planet through "carbon offsetting"—paying someone to invest your money in programs that reduce your greenhouse gas emissions by the same amount you've added. Before buying carbon offset credits, just make sure that you're using a reputable company, one with a proven program that invests in renewable energy. Reliable carbon offset companies include **Carbonfund** (www.carbonfund.org), **TerraPass** (www.terrapass.org), and **Carbon Neutral** (www.carbonneutral.org).
- Whenever possible, choose nonstop flights; they generally require less fuel than indirect flights that stop and take off again. Try to fly during the day—some scientists estimate that nighttime flights are twice as harmful to the environment. And pack light—each 15 pounds of luggage on a 5,000-mile flight adds up to 50 pounds of carbon dioxide emitted.
- Where you stay during your travels can have a major environmental impact. To determine the green credentials of a property, ask about trash disposal and recycling, water conservation, and energy use; also question if sustainable materials were used in the construction of the property. The website **www.greenhotels.com** recommends green-rated member hotels around the world that fulfill the company's stringent environmental requirements. Also consult **www.environmentallyfriendlyhotels.com** for more green accommodations ratings.
- At hotels, request that your sheets and towels not be changed daily. (Many hotels already have programs like this in place.) Turn off the lights and air-conditioner (or heater) when you leave your room.
- Use public transport where possible—trains, buses and even taxis are more energy-efficient forms of transport than driving. Even better is to walk or cycle; you'll produce zero emissions and stay fit and healthy on your travels.
- If renting a car is necessary, ask the rental agent for a hybrid, or rent the most fuel-efficient car available. You'll use less gas and save money at the tank.
- Eat at locally owned and operated restaurants that use produce grown in the area. This contributes to the local economy and cuts down on greenhouse gas emissions by supporting restaurants where the food is not flown or trucked in across long distances. Visit **Sustain Lane** (www.sustainlane.org) to find sustainable eating and drinking choices around the U.S.; also check out **www.eatwellguide.org** for tips on eating sustainably in the U.S. and Canada.

Frommers.com: The Complete Travel Resource

Planning a trip or just returned? Head to **Frommers.com**, voted Best Travel Site by *PC Magazine.* We think you'll find our site indispensable before, during, and after your travels—with expert advice and tips; independent reviews of hotels, restaurants, attractions, and preferred shopping and nightlife venues; vacation giveaways; and an online booking tool. We publish the complete contents of over 135 travel guides in our **Destinations** section, covering over 4,000 places worldwide. Each weekday, we publish original articles that report on **Deals and News** via our free **Frommers.com Newsletters.** What's more, **Arthur Frommer** himself blogs five days a week, with cutting opinions about the state of travel in the modern world. We're betting you'll find our **Events** listings an invaluable resource; it's an up-to-the-minute roster of what's happening in cities everywhere—including concerts, festivals, lectures, and more. We've also added weekly **podcasts, interactive maps,** and hundreds of new images across the site. Finally, don't forget to visit our **Message Boards,** where you can join in conversations with thousands of fellow Frommer's travelers and post your trip report once you return.

overlapping components of sustainable travel are **eco-tourism** and **ethical tourism.** The **International Ecotourism Society (TIES)** defines eco-tourism as responsible travel to natural areas that conserves the environment and improves the well-being of local people. TIES suggests that eco-tourists follow these principles:

- Minimize environmental impact
- Build environmental and cultural awareness and respect
- Provide positive experiences for both visitors and hosts
- Provide direct financial benefits for conservation and for local people
- Raise sensitivity to host countries' political, environmental, and social climates
- Support international human rights and labor agreements

You can find some eco-friendly travel tips and statistics, as well as touring companies and associations—listed by destination under "Travel Choice"—at the TIES website, **www.ecotourism.org**. Also check out **Ecotravel.com**, which lets you search for sustainable touring companies in several categories (water based, land based, spiritually oriented, and so on).

While much of the focus of eco-tourism is about reducing impacts on the natural environment, ethical tourism concentrates on ways to preserve and enhance local economies and communities, regardless of location. You can embrace ethical tourism by staying at a locally owned hotel or shopping at a store that employs local workers and sells locally produced goods.

Responsible Travel (www.responsibletravel.com) is a great source of sustainable travel ideas; the site is run by a spokesperson for ethical tourism in the travel industry. **Sustainable Travel International** (www.sustainabletravelinternational.org) promotes ethical tourism practices, and manages an extensive directory of sustainable properties and tour operators around the world.

In the U.K., **Tourism Concern** (www.tourismconcern.org.uk) works to reduce social and environmental problems connected to tourism. The **Association of**

Independent Tour Operators (AITO; www.aito.co.uk) is a group of specialist operators leading the field in making holidays sustainable.

Volunteer travel has become increasingly popular among those who want to venture beyond the standard group-tour experience to learn languages, interact with locals, and make a positive difference while on vacation. Volunteer travel usually doesn't require special skills—just a willingness to work hard—and programs vary in length from a few days to a number of weeks. Some programs provide free housing and food, but many require volunteers to pay for travel expenses, which can add up quickly. For general info on volunteer travel, visit **www.volunteerabroad.org** and **www.idealist.org**.

Before you commit to a volunteer program, it's important to make sure any money you're giving is truly going back to the local community, and that the work you'll be doing will be a good fit for you. **Volunteer International** (www.volunteerinternational.org) has a helpful list of questions to ask to determine the intentions.

10 PACKAGES FOR INDEPENDENT TRAVELERS

Package tours are simply a way to buy the airfare, accommodations, and other elements of your trip (such as car rentals, airport transfers, and even activities) at the same time and often at discounted prices. Many of the hotels in Denver, Boulder, and Colorado Springs offer specific packages, like the Broadmoor and golf or Hotel Teatro and theatre, and many offer packages involving outdoor recreation in the Rockies. Ski packages are available from all the major resorts, and there is often significant savings available if you bundle lift tickets, lodging, and airfare.

For more information on package tours and for tips on booking your trip, see **Frommers.com**.

11 ESCORTED GENERAL-INTEREST TOURS

Escorted tours are structured group tours, with a group leader. The price usually includes everything from airfare to hotels, meals, tours, admission costs, and local transportation. Below are some of the better companies that offer escorted tours in the Denver, Boulder, and Colorado Springs areas.

Gray Line, 5855 E. 56th Ave. (P.O. Box 646), Denver, CO 80217 (✆ **303/289-2841;** www.coloradograyline.com), provides traditional bus and van tours to the U.S. Air Force Academy, Pikes Peak, Rocky Mountain National Park, and historic sites of Denver.

Maupintour, 2688 Rainbow Blvd., Las Vegas, NV 89146 (✆ **800/255-4266;** www.maupintour.com), offers a variety of tours, including well-planned multiday tours of Rocky Mountain National Park and other scenic and historic areas.

See also the "Organized Tours" section in chapter 7 for Denver and chapter 8 for Colorado Springs.

Despite the fact that escorted tours require big deposits and predetermined hotels, restaurants, and itineraries, many people derive security and peace of mind from the structure they offer. Escorted tours let travelers sit back and enjoy the trip without having to worry about details. They take you to the maximum number of sights in the minimum amount of time with the least amount of hassle. They're particularly convenient for people with limited mobility and they can be a great way to make new friends.

On the downside, you'll have little opportunity for serendipitous interactions with locals. The tours can be jam-packed with activities, leaving little room for individual sightseeing or adventure—plus they often focus on the heavily touristed sites, so you miss out on many a lesser-known gem.

12 SPECIAL-INTEREST TRIPS

Hikers, bikers, and other outdoor recreationalists can head into the mountains with a variety of companies. See chapter 5, "The Active Vacation Planner," for details.

13 STAYING CONNECTED

TELEPHONES

The area codes for Denver and Boulder are **303** and **720.** In Colorado Springs, it's **719.** In Denver and Boulder, the full 10-digit phone number is required to make local calls, whereas the area code is not necessary in Colorado Springs. Most convenience stores and supermarkets carry calling cards for national and international calls. Pay phones still exist in the area, but their numbers have been on the decline in recent years. However, they are readily available in the downtowns of all three cities.

CELLPHONES

All major U.S. cellular networks work fine on the Front Range, but things quickly get spotty outside of the urban cores. If you're not from the U.S., you'll be appalled at the poor reach of the **GSM (Global System for Mobile Communications) wireless network,** which is used by much of the rest of the world. Your phone will probably work in most major U.S. cities; it may not work in many rural areas. To see where GSM phones work in the U.S., check out **www.t-mobile.com/coverage**. And you may or may not be able to send SMS (text messaging) home.

VOICE-OVER INTERNET PROTOCOL (VOIP)

If you have Web access while traveling, consider a broadband-based telephone service (in technical terms, **Voice-over Internet Protocol,** or **VoIP**) such as Skype (www.skype.com) or Vonage (www.vonage.com), which allow you to make free international calls from your laptop or in a cybercafe. Neither service requires the people you're calling to also have that service (though there are fees if they do not). Check the websites for details.

INTERNET & E-MAIL

With Your Own Computer

Wi-Fi is readily available at hotels and hundreds of public places in Denver, Boulder, and Colorado Springs, including Denver's 16th Street Mall. For specific spots, check out the website **www.jiwire.com**.

Without Your Own Computer

Most major airports have **Internet kiosks** that provide basic Web access for a per-minute fee that's usually higher than cybercafe prices. Check out copy shops like **Kinko's** (FedEx Office), which offers computer stations with fully loaded software (as well as Wi-Fi).

For help locating cybercafes and other establishments where you can go for Internet access, please see "Internet Access" in the "Fast Facts" appendix (p. 451).

14 TIPS ON ACCOMMODATIONS

Denver, Boulder, and Colorado Springs offer a variety of lodging options, from typical American chains to luxury hotels, cozy bed-and-breakfasts to inexpensive mom-and-pop independent motels, cabins to magnificent grande dame hotels.

The chains here are the same ones you see everywhere else in America: Best Western, Comfort, Days Inn, Embassy Suites, Hampton Inn, Hilton, Holiday Inn, Motel 6, Quality Inn, Sheraton, Super 8, Travelodge, and so on. They look just about the same as those found elsewhere and have the same levels of service. In most cases, their rooms are little more than boring boxes of various sizes, with beds and the appropriate plumbing and heating fixtures, and, if you're lucky, a decent view out the window. These chains, even the high-end ones like Hilton and Sheraton, are fine if you just want a place to sleep and plan to take advantage of their swimming pools, exercise rooms, and other facilities. However, they do very little to enhance your vacation experience or even to let you know you're in Colorado.

To make your lodging an integral part of your Colorado experience, I suggest choosing a historic property. I discuss numerous historic bed-and-breakfast inns in the following pages, and—especially when you take into consideration the wonderful breakfasts most of them serve—the rates are fairly reasonable. Why spend $90 for a boring motel room and then another $10 to $15 for breakfast when for just a bit more you can sleep in a handsome, antiques-decorated Victorian home and enjoy a home-cooked breakfast?

This area of Colorado also has several magnificent but pricey historic hotels, including the absolutely wonderful Brown Palace in Denver and the family-friendly Broadmoor in Colorado Springs. These hotels are as much attractions as lodgings, and what better way to see them than to book a room for the night, just as others have done for the better part of a century?

Tips House-Swapping

House-swapping is becoming a more popular and viable means of travel: You stay in their place, they stay in yours, and you both get an authentic and personal view of the area, the opposite of the escapist retreat that many hotels offer. Try **HomeLink International** (www.homelink.org), the largest and oldest home-swapping organization, founded in 1952, with over 11,000 listings worldwide ($75 for a yearly membership). **HomeExchange.org** ($50 for 6,000 listings) and **InterVac.com** ($69 for over 10,000 listings) are also reliable. Many travelers find great housing swaps on **Craigslist** (www.craigslist.org), too, though the offerings cannot be vetted or vouched for. Swap at your own risk.

Other lodging choices here include cabins and a handful of small independent motels. Both are usually fairly inexpensive, although they often lack the facilities, such as pools, spas, and exercise equipment, that you'll find in most chains. I still prefer the cabins and independents, though, because they're often a very good value and the rooms usually have at least some personality (can anybody actually describe the decor of the last Super 8 or Days Inn he or she stayed at?), and cabins, although sometimes a bit primitive, are often in beautiful settings.

For tips on surfing for hotel deals online, visit **Frommers.com**.

4

Suggested Colorado Itineraries

At the risk of oversimplifying, let me suggest that there are essentially three activities for visitors to Colorado—viewing the scenery, visiting historic and cultural sites, and participating in outdoor sports. While there are some visitors whose only goal is to explore prehistoric American Indian sites or historic mining towns, and perhaps hard-core skiers or hikers who are interested solely in pursuing their preferred form of recreation, the vast majority of Colorado visitors want a smorgasbord of experiences: This might include a scenic drive over a mountain pass, a visit to a small-town museum in a Victorian mansion, and a hike to a picturesque lake.

My suggested itineraries assume that you're looking for a mix of experiences; those interested primarily in outdoor activities should see chapter 5. I'll look at the most efficient routes and the must-see destinations. All of the following start in Denver.

These are all driving tours and, in fact, a motor vehicle is almost mandatory for anyone who wants to explore Colorado. Visitors to Denver don't need a car, and if you're heading to a major resort to ski for a week you can be car-less, but many of the best destinations here require that you drive.

Colorado has a well-maintained network of roadways that will take you to most places you want to visit, although not always directly. Unfortunately, Colorado is a big state, with everything spread out, so you'll end up doing a lot of driving. One consolation is that traffic congestion, even in the cities, is not nearly as bad as in many other states. Services along rural highways are often limited, though, so be careful about checking fuel levels. Also, because of seasonal road closures, the tours that leave the Front Range are for summer use only, although parts of them can be adapted for winter use.

1 THE REGIONS IN BRIEF

THE FRONT RANGE The state's three major cities—**Denver, Boulder,** and **Colorado Springs**—form a line along the eastern slope of the Rocky Mountains known as the Front Range. These cities are a blend of old and new, rustic and sophisticated, urban and rural. Founded in the mid–19th century by both East Coast gold-seekers and European and Asian immigrants in search of a better life, they became home to what we might call the more civilized pioneer—the mine owner instead of the prospector, the merchant rather than the gambler.

Today Denver, Boulder, and Colorado Springs have virtually all the amenities you'd expect to find in major U.S. metropolises: opera, theater, dance, art, excellent restaurants, and sophisticated hotels and convention centers. You'll also find historic Victorian mansions, working steam trains, and old gold mines. You can go horseback riding, hiking, skiing, or shopping; or spend hours exploring museums, galleries, and shops. See chapters 6 through 9.

NORTHEASTERN COLORADO This region is quite different from the major cities and even more of a departure from the rugged mountain towns to the west. Northeastern Colorado contains the sparsely populated plains, a place where buffalo once roamed and pioneer farmers endured drought, dust, snow, and wind to create farms and ranches.

Here is the college town of **Fort Collins,** home of the large Anheuser-Busch brewery; the town of **Loveland,** known primarily for its name and Valentine card remailing; plus smaller communities such as **Fort Morgan,** the boyhood home of big band leader Glenn Miller. This region is dotted with pioneer homes and museums, frontier forts, and preserved downtown districts, plus a surprising number of lakes and seemingly endless fields of wheat and corn. See chapter 10.

THE NORTHERN ROCKIES For many people, the northern Rockies epitomize Colorado. Here you'll find some of the West's most spectacular and inspiring scenery at **Rocky Mountain National Park,** as well as America's top ski resorts, including **Vail** and **Aspen,** playgrounds to many of Hollywood's beautiful people. But tucked away amid the ski slopes, overpriced boutiques, and towering peaks are delightful historic Old West towns such as **Leadville** and **Steamboat Springs,** where you can step back to a simpler, more rugged era. This region is ideal for year-round outdoor activities, from skiing and snowboarding to hiking, mountain biking, fishing, boating, and four-wheeling. See chapter 11.

THE WESTERN SLOPE This region more closely resembles the canyon country of Utah than Colorado's famed Rocky Mountains. The area is defined in large part by its rivers—the Colorado, Gunnison, and Yampa—which over tens of thousands of years have carved ruggedly beautiful canyons. The **Black Canyon of the Gunnison National Park** encompasses an awe-inspiring narrow chasm, and colorful layers of rock define the canyon walls and unusual formations of the **Colorado and Dinosaur national monuments.** The latter also boasts one of the best dinosaur quarries you'll see anywhere. In addition, the western slope offers about a dozen wineries near the region's largest city, **Grand Junction,** and mineral hot springs and eye-opening caves in **Glenwood Springs,** where Old West gunfighter Doc Holliday is buried. See chapter 12.

SOUTHWESTERN COLORADO Those curious about the prehistoric peoples who once populated the West should head to this part of the state, where **Mesa Verde National Park** and a number of other sites preserve ancient cliff dwellings and other archaeological sites that help explain what life was like here 1,000 years ago. Also in this region is the historic community of **Durango,** with its main street (ca. 1880) and narrow-gauge steam railroad. Another Old West town, **Telluride,** retains its historic charm while emerging as a major ski and summer resort. In addition, the **San Juan Mountains** rival the vistas in Colorado's northern Rockies. See chapter 13.

THE SOUTHERN ROCKIES An exciting mix of terrain and experiences awaits visitors to the southern Rockies, which contain 30 peaks soaring over 14,000 feet, as well as white-water rafting near **Salida,** the historic picturesque mining town of **Creede,** and the tallest sand dunes in North America at **Great Sand Dunes National Monument and Preserve.** This area also contains splendid boating and fishing at **Curecanti National Recreation Area,** plus skiing and mountain biking, and a historic narrow-gauge steam train at **Antonito,** south of Alamosa. See chapter 14.

SOUTHEASTERN COLORADO History and a scenic stark beauty are the main draws of this region, which is best known for one of the world's most spectacular canyons—the deep, narrow **Royal Gorge,** which is carved by the Arkansas River as it makes its way down from the Rocky Mountains to the plains. The sector's largest city, **Pueblo,** offers outdoor recreation, several good museums, and a fine zoo. Boating and fishing opportunities abound on two lakes—Pueblo and Trinidad—both operated as state parks; and **Bent's Old Fort** is a national historic site that has re-created one of the West's most important frontier trading posts. The towns of **Trinidad** and **La Junta** also have a number of historic attractions, and you'll find dinosaur tracks in the **Comanche National Grassland.** See chapter 15.

2 THE FRONT RANGE CITIES IN 1 WEEK

Colorado's three major Front Range cities are quite different from each other, offering very different experiences, but they are also close and convenient. They are also near Colorado's famed Rocky Mountains, making it very easy to leave the city lights behind and enjoy the serenity of the great outdoors.

Day 1: Arrive in Denver ★★

Whether you arrive by car or by air, the best place to base yourself is downtown, where you can see all of the attractions on foot and by public transportation. Get acquainted with the lay of the land by walking the **16th Street Mall** (p. 114) and wandering down Wynkoop Street in LoDo. Have dinner at one of the many top dining spots in the area, such as the **Wynkoop Brewing Company** (p. 94) or **Rioja** (p. 92).

Days 2 & 3: Explore Denver

Start the next morning at **Larimer Square,** Denver's birthplace, with a self-guided walking tour of the historic sites (p. 113). Then stroll the 16th Street pedestrian mall and head toward the **state capitol** (p. 100), just across Broadway. En route, take a 1-block detour for an early lunch or a cup of tea at the **Brown Palace Hotel** (p. 79). After seeing the capitol, explore other Civic Center sites, especially the **Denver Art Museum** (p. 100). On your third day, explore more of Denver. The city has numerous historic homes, beautiful parks, attractive shopping centers, and several highly touted museums—for example, the **Denver Museum of Nature and Science** (p. 101), the **Botanic Gardens** (p. 109), and the **Black American West Museum** (p. 106).

Day 4: Boulder ★★

From Denver, rent a car and make the 30-minute trip to Boulder. Split your time between the **Pearl Street Mall** (p. 200) and an attraction or two: I'm particularly fond of the **Celestial Seasonings tour** (p. 201) and the **Boulder Museum of Contemporary Art** (p. 203). Explore a bit of the Boulder Creek Path by foot or bike as well, if time allows, before dinner and a show at one of many venues—Boulder is renowned for its music.

Day 5: Explore Rocky Mountain National Park ★★★

Boulder is about an hour's drive from Estes Park, the eastern gateway to **Rocky Mountain National Park** (p. 254). Stop for lunch in **Lyons** (p. 212) and then explore the park by car, parking to take a hike. Stay in Estes Park for the night. See p. 245.

Day ❻: Rocky Mountain National Park to Golden ★

Drive over **Trail Ridge Road** (p. 257) and south to Berthoud Pass to get back to I-70. This scenic drive gives you the option to hike in the park, or else hightail it back south to Golden for a tour of the **Coors Brewery** (p. 137) or a stroll around the pleasant downtown. Either way, it's an ideal overnight stop that lets you avoid the bulk of the traffic in central Denver. See p. 134.

Day ❼: Colorado Springs ★★

Leave for the 70-mile trip in the morning and you can easily make it to downtown Colorado Springs for lunch. Spend the afternoon in Manitou Springs, or drive or take the train up to the summit of **Pikes Peak** (p. 163). In the evening, if your pocketbook allows, head to **The Broadmoor** (p. 150) for a fitting dinner to cap the trip. From Colorado Springs it's about an hour and a half back to Denver International Airport. See p. 69.

3 THE FRONT RANGE CITIES IN 2 WEEKS

Taking 2 weeks to explore these cities and surrounding areas provides time for a more in-depth examination of their attractions, and to spend more time in the mountains.

Days ❶, ❷, ❸ & ❹: Denver ★★

Follow the Denver itinerary above, but take the extra day in Denver to explore a neighborhood by bike and foot. Get a rental and a map from **Campus Cycles** (p. 127), then hop on one of the in-city trails that converges on **Confluence Park** for lunch in the vicinity. After lunch, get your rental car and head to one of the attractions farther afield, or if the schedule allows, take in a Rockies game at **Coors Field,** or another sporting event in this sports-crazy city.

Days ❺, ❻ & ❼: Boulder ★★★

Explore the Pearl Street Mall and a museum on your first day, but take the second day to hike some of the trails in the area (p. 206), packing a lunch before descending for dinner. On your third day in Boulder, visit the **National Center for Atmospheric Research** (p. 200) or the **Redstone Meadery** (p. 202), and take time to do more hiking, biking, or Pearl Street Mall people-watching.

Days ❽ & ❾: Rocky Mountain National Park ★★★

Use Estes Park as a base on the first night and camp in the park (or else stay in Grand Lake, the park's western gateway) on the second. Spending 2 full days in the area allows for the second day to be centered on a significant day hike, like the **Mills Lake Trail** or the **Bierstadt Lake Trail.** See p. 259.

Day ❿: Rocky Mountain National Park to Golden ★★

Follow the 1-week itinerary, above.

Days ⓫, ⓬, ⓭ & ⓮: Colorado Springs ★★

Take your time to explore the Pikes Peak region over 3 unhurried days. Spend your entire first day and night exploring downtown and its attractions, namely the **Fine Arts Center** (p. 166) and the **Pioneers Museum** (p. 161). On the second day, head to Manitou Springs before ascending **Pikes Peak** (p. 163) by rail or car, then descend for an overnight in Manitou Springs or Old Colorado City. The last full day's foci: **Garden of the Gods** (p. 162) and **The Broadmoor** (p. 150) for a final farewell dinner. From Colorado Springs it's about an hour and a half back to Denver International Airport.

4 THE FRONT RANGE CITIES FOR FAMILIES

Denver, Boulder, and Colorado Springs are all great family vacation destinations, with plenty of museums, kid-friendly restaurants and accommodations, and parks to romp around in—not to mention easy access to the Rocky Mountains.

Day ❶: Arrive in Denver ★★

As with the 1-week itinerary earlier in this chapter, start in Denver and base your time there out of downtown. However, kid-friendly destinations are more far-flung, so rent a car from the get-go.

Days ❷ & ❸: Explore Denver ★★

Start with a stop at **Confluence Park** before boarding the **Platte Valley Trolley** (p. 76); then hit the **Children's Museum** (p. 111) and the **Downtown Aquarium** (p. 110). For dinner, **Casa Bonita** (p. 98) is a beloved birthday place. On the third day, hit the **Colorado State Capitol** (p. 100) and the **U.S. Mint** (p. 101) in the morning, and then head to the southern suburbs to **Wildlife Experience** (p. 108) or to **City Park,** home of the **Denver Zoo** (p. 110) and the **Denver Museum of Nature & Science** (p. 101).

Days ❹ & ❺: Explore Colorado Springs ★★

Take your time leaving Denver on the fourth day, but make time to make it to Old Colorado City for lunch at **Meadow Muffins** (p. 178). In the afternoon, visit **Garden of the Gods** (p. 162) before returning downtown for dinner at **Giuseppe's Old Depot Restaurant** (p. 159). Center your next day around Manitou Springs and a trip up **Pikes Peak** (p. 163) by car or rail.

Days ❻ & ❼: Explore Boulder ★★ and Rocky Mountain National Park ★★★

Return north on the sixth day of your trip. En route to Boulder, stop off U.S. 36 at the **Butterfly Pavilion** (p. 109) in Westminster. Visit **Pearl Street Mall** (p. 200) and **Celestial Seasonings** (p. 201) in the afternoon. On the last day of your trip, make a trip up to Estes Park for a quick taste of the Rockies. See p. 241.

5 COLORADO IN 2 WEEKS

Yes, Colorado is a big state with a lot to offer, and I won't pretend that you can actually see and do everything here in only 2 weeks. But this somewhat rushed driving tour hits many of the highlights—what you might call the best of the best. If nothing else, it will show you why Colorado is one of America's top vacation destinations.

Days ❶ & ❷: Denver and Boulder ★★

Arrive in Denver, preferably in the late morning or early afternoon. Browse **Larimer Square** and the **16th Street Mall** (p. 114). The next morning, visit the **Denver Art Museum** (p. 100), the **Colorado History Museum** (p. 106), and the **state capitol** (p. 100). After lunch, take the short drive to Boulder; browse the **Pearl**

Street Mall (p. 200), where you might see a juggler or mime (or just a sleeping University of Colorado student); and settle in for the night.

Day 3: Estes Park ★

Take Canyon Boulevard (Colo. 119) west to Nederland, then follow the foothills north on Colo. 72 and Colo. 7 to Estes Park, where you can visit the **Enos Mills Homestead Cabin** (p. 244), **Estes Park Museum** (p. 244), and take in some spectacular panoramic views on a ride on the **Estes Park Aerial Tramway** (p. 244).

Day 4: Rocky Mountain National Park ★★★

In the morning, enjoy spectacular **Trail Ridge Road** through Rocky Mountain National Park (p. 257), across the Continental Divide to **Grand Lake** (p. 252). After lunch, proceed south on U.S. 40 to **Winter Park, Berthoud Pass,** and **Georgetown** (p. 278).

Day 5: Leadville ★

I-70 and Colo. 91 will take you up to Leadville, Colorado's 2-mile-high city. See the historic district and **National Mining Hall of Fame and Museum** (p. 314), then continue across Independence Pass to the famed resort town of Aspen (p. 317).

Day 6: Aspen ★★

Give yourself a day in Aspen to shop, sightsee, hike, bike, or just enjoy the clean mountain air.

Day 7: Montrose ★

Drive to Montrose. The route follows the Roaring Fork River west to Carbondale, then south along scenic Colo. 133 over McClure Pass (elevation 8,755 ft.), and through the quaint historic village of Redstone. Try to complete the 140-mile drive by early afternoon, leaving time for a visit to the **Ute Indian Museum** (p. 358) and the wondrous deep, dark gorge at **Black Canyon of the Gunnison National Park** (p. 360).

Day 8: The Million Dollar Highway to Durango ★★★

It's 98 miles via the Million Dollar Highway (p. 383), U.S. 550, to Durango. En route, between the memorable old mining towns of **Ouray** (p. 399) and **Silverton** (p. 381), you'll cross spectacular Red Mountain Pass in the San Juan Mountains. **Durango's historic district** (p. 370) is one of Colorado's largest and best preserved.

Day 9: Mesa Verde National Park ★★

Visit the cliff dwellings of Mesa Verde National Park (p. 386), about 40 miles west of Durango.

Day 10: Great Sand Dunes National Park & Preserve ★★

Get an early start for the 150-mile drive across Wolf Creek Pass on U.S. 160 to Alamosa, and continue northeast to explore **Great Sand Dunes National Park & Preserve** (p. 422) before returning to **Alamosa** (p. 425) for the night.

Day 11: Salida and Cañon City ★

Head north to the rafting capital of Salida, perhaps stopping for a dip in the **hot springs pool** (p. 419), then head east on U.S. 50 to Cañon City. See the **Royal Gorge** (p. 435), the re-created Old West town of **Buckskin Joe** (p. 436), and the **Museum of Colorado Prisons** (p. 436).

Days 12 & 13: Colorado Springs ★★

Spend 2 full days seeing the attractions in Colorado Springs and nearby Manitou Springs. Choose among the **Pikes Peak Cog Railway** (p. 163), the **U.S. Olympic Training Center** (p. 164), the **Garden of the Gods** (p. 162), and the **Cheyenne Mountain Zoo** (p. 170), among other sights.

Day 14: Back to Denver

Stop and visit the **U.S. Air Force Academy** (p. 164) on your way back to Denver, where your flight home awaits.

6 COLORADO IN 3 WEEKS

Taking 3 weeks to explore this great state provides the opportunity to see many of its top attractions and get a feel for its cities, towns, and spectacular scenery. It covers top celebrity-watching centers such as Aspen and Vail, some of Colorado's most picturesque Old West communities, and takes you to four major national parks.

Days ❶ & ❷: Denver ★★

Arrive in Denver, preferably in the late morning or early afternoon. Browse **Larimer Square** and the **16th Street Mall** (p. 114). Explore the **state capitol** (p. 100), the **Denver Art Museum** (p. 100), numerous other museums, and **City Park** (p. 109). If there's time, visit nearby Golden, home of **Coors Brewery** (p. 137) and the historic buildings from Colorado's territorial days.

Day ❸: Boulder ★★

Enjoy a leisurely day in Boulder. Stroll the **Pearl Street Mall** (p. 200) and **University of Colorado campus** (p. 200), or visit the **Celestial Seasonings Tea factory** (p. 201) for a guided tour. (The mint room will knock your socks off!) Another option is to rent a bike and explore the city's many bike paths.

Day ❹: Estes Park ★

Take Canyon Boulevard (Colo. 119) west to Nederland, then follow the foothills north on Colo. 72 and Colo. 7 to Estes Park, where you can visit the **Enos Mills Homestead Cabin** (p. 244) and **Estes Park Museum** (p. 244), and take in some spectacular panoramic views on a ride on the **Estes Park Aerial Tramway** (p. 244).

Day ❺: Rocky Mountain National Park ★★★

Spend the day in **Rocky Mountain National Park** (p. 254)—perhaps taking a hike in the high country—and crossing the Continental Divide on **Trail Ridge Road** (p. 257) before enjoying the sunset on **Grand Lake** (p. 252).

Day ❻: Georgetown ★

Take U.S. 40 south through the Winter Park resort community, over Berthoud Pass, to Georgetown, an old Victorian mining town (p. 141).

Day ❼: Breckenridge and Vail ★

Follow I-70 to Frisco, seat of Summit County, and detour on a 10-mile spur to Breckenridge (p. 284). After lunch and some window shopping, return to I-70 and proceed west to Vail (p. 298), America's most popular ski resort (and a booming summer resort as well).

Day ❽: Leadville ★

Take U.S. 24 south to Leadville, the state's highest city, at over 10,000 feet elevation. See the historic district (p. 313) and the **National Mining Hall of Fame** (p. 314), then continue across Independence Pass to Aspen (p. 317).

Day ❾: Aspen ★★

Shop, hike, bike, or just enjoy Aspen's clean mountain air, and if the timing works, attend a concert at the **Aspen Music Festival** (p. 31).

Day ❿: Black Canyon of the Gunnison National Park

Drive to Montrose via Carbondale, the historic villages of Redstone, Paonia, and Delta. Leave a few afternoon hours to visit **Black Canyon of the Gunnison National Park** (p. 360).

Days ⓫, ⓬ & ⓭: Durango and Mesa Verde National Park ★★

The **Million Dollar Highway** (p. 383), U.S. 550 to Durango, where you'll be based for the next few days, passes through the picturesque historic mining towns of **Ouray** (p. 399) and **Silverton** (p. 381) and across Red Mountain Pass, an alpine locale worthy of Switzerland. **Durango's historic district** (p. 370) is one of Colorado's largest and best preserved. Explore historic downtown Durango and take a ride on the **Durango & Silverton Narrow Gauge Railroad** (p. 368), which traverses a magnificent route to Silverton and back. Day 13 will be one of archaeological discovery. Spend most of it at **Mesa Verde National Park** (p. 386), some 40 miles west of Durango, or at **Ute Mountain Tribal Mountain Park** (p. 389), south of Cortez.

Day ⓮: Great Sand Dunes National Park & Preserve ★★

It's 150 miles on U.S. 160 via Wolf Creek Pass to **Alamosa** (p. 421), your base while exploring the seemingly misplaced **Great Sand Dunes National Park and Preserve** (p. 422).

Day ⓯: La Junta ★★

Continue east again on U.S. 160 over La Veta Pass to Walsenburg, then pick up Colo. 10 to La Junta. Visit the **Koshare Indian Museum** (p. 444; a surprising find with wonderful early-20th-century art) and **Bent's Old Fort National Historic Site** (p. 444), the reconstructed hub of a trading empire in the 1830s and 1840s. Proceed to Pueblo for dinner.

Day ⓰: Pueblo & Cañon City ★

Browse Pueblo in the morning, including the impressive Victorian mansion that contains the **Rosemount Museum** (p. 431), and then take a walk at the **Greenway and Nature Center** (p. 430) or along the **Historic Arkansas Riverwalk of Pueblo** (p. 432). Then take U.S. 50 west to Cañon City to see the **Royal Gorge** (p. 435) and the Western theme village of **Buckskin Joe** (p. 436).

Days ⓱, ⓲ & ⓳: Colorado Springs ★★

Head north on I-25 to Colorado Springs, where there's plenty to do: the **Pikes Peak Cog Railway** (p. 163), the **U.S. Air Force Academy** (p. 164), the **United States Olympic Complex** (p. 164), **Garden of the Gods' rock formations** (p. 162), **Cave of the Winds** (p. 169), and a variety of museums and historic sites.

Days ⓴ & ㉑: Back to Denver

Return to Denver and catch up on some of the sites you may have missed earlier, or stop at the **Tattered Cover Bookstore** (p. 125) for some reading matter for the trip home.

The Active Vacation Planner

The variety and sheer number of active sports and recreational activities Colorado has to offer is staggering. It's a place where you can easily arrange a weeklong, hard-core mountaineering expedition, but it's also a place where you can just as easily take one of the most scenic bike rides of your life right in downtown Boulder. Then there's the superb winter activities, from skiing to snowshoeing to ice climbing. This chapter outlines your choices and offers a few tips for planning everything from a guided, multisport vacation to an afternoon's outing.

1 PREPARING FOR YOUR ACTIVE VACATION

Once you've picked the sport or activities you want to pursue, ask yourself a few questions: How physically fit am I *really?* How much skill in this particular activity do I have? How dangerous is this activity? How much money am I willing to spend? Answering these questions honestly can make the difference between a successful vacation and an unmitigated disaster. Some activities, such as cattle drives, require an outfitter, while others, such as biking, camping, or hiking, you can do on your own. If you're attempting a dangerous sport in which you're inexperienced, such as rock or ice climbing, it's imperative to go with someone who (literally) knows the ropes.

If cost is an issue, prearranged escorted tour packages that include virtually everything can sometimes save you money. On the other hand, you'll be with a group, with limited freedom and flexibility to strike out on your own. Some people enjoy the company of their fellow tour members and the convenience of having everything arranged; others can't stand it. It's your choice.

The best outfitters run well-organized trips and are willing to answer any and all questions promptly and fully. They should have well-maintained equipment, possess appropriate land-use permits, and be fully insured. If you have any doubts, ask for the name and phone number of a satisfied former customer, and call that person and ask about his or her experience.

Several government agencies and other organizations provide maps and information that can be extremely useful for a variety of activities. These include **Colorado State Parks** (for state park, boating, RV, and snowmobile regulations), 1313 Sherman St., Ste. 618, Denver, CO 80203 (© **303/866-3437;** www.parks.state.co.us); the **Colorado Outfitters Association** (for a list of licensed guides and outfitters in the state), P.O. Box 849, Craig, CO 81626 (© **970/824-2468;** www.colorado-outfitters.com); the **U.S. Bureau of Land Management** (for topographical maps and information on activities on the vast amount of BLM land in the state), 2850 Youngfield St., Lakewood, CO 80215 (© **303/239-3600;** www.co.blm.gov); the **U.S. Forest Service,** Rocky Mountain Region (for maps and information about activities and facilities in national forests), 740 Simms St., Golden, CO 80401 (© **303/275-5350;** www.fs.fed.us/r2); and the **National Park**

Service, Intermountain Region (for information on national parks, monuments, historic sites, and recreation areas), 12795 Alameda Pkwy., Denver, CO 80225 (✆ **303/969-2500;** www.nps.gov). Another good online government source for information on outdoor recreation opportunities is **www.recreation.gov**.

Of the hundreds of commercial outdoor recreation sites on the Internet, I like **GORP** (Great Outdoor Recreation Page; www.gorp.com); you can go right to the Colorado section at **www.gorp.com/gorp/location/co/co.htm**, which provides detailed information about hiking trails, fishing, watersports, and other activities on Colorado's public lands. Lately, however, that site has been getting a bit too cluttered and commercial; the very informative and user-friendly **Public Lands Information Center** website, **www.publiclands.org**, is an alternative. The ***Denver Post,*** the state's major daily newspaper, also has an especially good website (www.denverpost.com) with quite a bit of outdoor recreation information.

Those looking to buy or rent equipment will find shops practically everywhere in the state, particularly in resort towns. A convenient statewide resource is **Sports Authority** (formerly Gart Brothers; www.sportsauthority.com), the state's largest sporting-goods chain. For the location of the store nearest you, check the website or visit the chain's flagship store at 1000 Broadway in Denver (✆ **303/863-2260**).

2 VISITING COLORADO'S NATIONAL PARKS

Some of the most beautiful parts of Colorado have been preserved within the federal government's national park and monument system.

Rocky Mountain National Park, easily the most popular of the state's national parks in terms of number of visitors, is also the most spectacular. Because photos of its magnificent snowcapped peaks have graced so many calendars and coffee-table books, people often envision Rocky Mountain National Park when they think of Colorado. **Black Canyon of the Gunnison National Park** also offers fine scenery, but it's entirely different from Rocky. Black Canyon is an extremely narrow, rocky river canyon that's wild and beautiful, but difficult to explore because of its steep canyon walls. And then there's **Mesa Verde National Park;** its reason for being is history, with the best-preserved ancient cliff dwellings in the Southwest.

The state's national monuments may not be as well known as Rocky Mountain National Park, but each has its own charm and is well worth a visit. For instance, **Colorado National Monument** is similar to the national parks of southern Utah—somewhat barren but with marvelous red-rock formations. And **Dinosaur National Monument** is really two parks—arid yet scenic canyons in Colorado and its namesake dinosaur quarry just across the border in Utah.

To get the most from your visit, try to avoid school-vacation periods and the dead of winter, when Rocky's high country and parts of Mesa Verde and Black Canyon of the Gunnison may be inaccessible. Although the parks are beautiful under a frosting of snow, you won't be able to see as much.

If you can, take a hike. Most park visitors tend to stay on the beaten track, stopping at the same scenic vistas before rushing to the next one. If you can spend even an hour or two on the trail, it's often possible to simply walk away from the crowds.

Tips Saving Money with a National Parks Pass

Those who make a habit of vacationing at national parks, national forests, and other federal lands may get some use out of a new annual pass to federal lands (which, unfortunately, costs more than the old passes it's replacing). The **America the Beautiful—National Parks and Federal Recreational Lands—Access Pass,** which went on sale in 2007, costs $80 for the general public. It provides free admission for the pass holder and those in his or her vehicle to recreation sites that charge vehicle entrance fees on lands administered by the National Park Service, U.S. Forest Service, U.S. Fish and Wildlife Service, Bureau of Land Management, and Bureau of Reclamation. At areas that charge per-person fees, the passes are good for the pass holder plus 3 additional adults. Children under 16 are admitted free.

The pass, which is good for 1 year from the date of purchase, replaces the National Parks Pass, which was limited to only properties administered by the National Park Service but cost only $50, and the **Golden Eagle Passport,** which provided free entry to all the federal lands covered by the new pass and cost $65. The new passes are also available for U.S. citizens and permanent residents 62 and older for a lifetime fee of $10 (same as the former Golden Age passports), and are free for U.S. residents and permanent residents with permanent disabilities (also the same as the former Golden Access passports). For information or to purchase the pass, go to **http://store.usgs.gov/pass** or **www.nps.gov/fees_passes.htm**, or call the United States Geological Survey (USGS), which issues the passes, at ✆ **888/275-8747.** They can also be bought at park entrance stations.

If you plan to visit a number of national parks and monuments within the time frame of a year, **America the Beautiful—National Park and Federal Recreational Lands—Access Passes,** which cost you $80 (good for 365 days from the date of purchase), will save you money. The passes are good at all properties under the jurisdiction of the National Park Service, as well as fee areas administered by the Bureau of Land Management, National Forest Service, and other federal agencies. See "Saving Money with a National Parks Pass," above.

3 OUTDOOR ACTIVITIES A TO Z

Throughout this book I recommend outfitters and guides that will help you enjoy the great outdoors in their particular areas. One highly regarded company that offers trips throughout the West, including several areas in Colorado, is the **World Outdoors,** 2840 Wilderness Place, Ste. F, Boulder, CO 80301 (✆ **800/488-8483** or 303/413-0938; www.theworldoutdoors.com), which leads a variety of hiking and multisport adventures. Most trips are 6 days long and include transportation, lodging, and dining.

Fun Facts **Elk, Elk & More Elk**

There are over 400,000 elk in Colorado, more than any other state or Canadian province.

BALLOONING You can take a hot-air balloon ride virtually anywhere in the state, but the most awe-inspiring scenery is in the mountains. Hot-air ballooning is expensive, and it's one sport where you don't want to cut corners. Choose an experienced and well-established balloon company and, if you have any qualms, ask about their safety record. And of course, you'll pay the highest rates at resorts.

BICYCLING Road biking is popular throughout Colorado, but especially in Boulder, which has just as many bikes as it has people; in Fort Collins, public buses have bike racks. My favorite city path is the **Boulder Creek Path,** which meanders through miles of Boulder parklands, with no motor vehicle intrusion of any kind.

BOATING Those who take their powerboats along on their visit to Colorado will find lakes scattered across the state. Most have boat ramps, some have fuel and supplies, and some of the larger lakes offer boat rentals. Popular choices include Bonny Lake near Burlington (known for water-skiing), Lake Pueblo, and Trinidad Lake. Because Colorado has been experiencing drought conditions in recent years, it's a good idea to call ahead to check on water conditions. In several instances, lake levels have dropped well below the boat ramps, leaving boaters literally "high and dry."

CAMPING With so many acres of public land, Colorado offers practically unlimited opportunities for camping, especially in the mountains. There are over 400 public campgrounds in the national forests alone, plus sites in Bureau of Land Management areas, national parks, national monuments, and state parks. In addition, most communities have commercially operated campgrounds with RV hookups. If you plan to drive an RV in Colorado, a word of advice: Have the mechanical systems checked out first, as there are some extremely steep grades in the mountains.

One of the best places to camp in the state is Rocky Mountain National Park, but it can be crowded, especially in summer. Visit in late September or early October, if possible. Backpackers will find numerous camping opportunities along the Colorado Trail and in State Forest State Park west of Fort Collins. Mueller State Park, west of Colorado Springs, is tops for RV camping.

The **Colorado Directory, Inc.,** 5101 Pennsylvania Ave., Boulder, CO 80303-2799 (© **888/222-4641** or 303/499-9343; www.coloradodirectory.com), publishes a free booklet that describes commercial campgrounds, cabin facilities, and resorts throughout the state. For a free copy of ***Colorado State Parks,*** which contains details on the state's 40-plus parks, contact state park offices (see "Preparing for Your Active Vacation," above).

CATTLE DRIVES As elsewhere in the West, opportunities abound for city slickers to play cowboy by riding and roping cattle on actual drives that last from a day to a week or more. Each drive is different, so ask very specific questions about food, sleeping arrangements, and other conditions before plunking down your money. The best places for joining a drive are Steamboat Springs and Durango, with their beautiful mountain scenery and fun towns—perfect for relaxing at the end of the trail.

CROSS-COUNTRY SKIING Practically every major downhill ski area also offers cross-country skiing, and there are thousands of miles of trails throughout Colorado's national forests—often over old mining and logging roads—that are perfect for cross-country skiing. Among top choices are Breckenridge, with trails winding through open meadows and a spruce forest, and the beautiful San Juan Mountains near Durango and Telluride. Information is available from the **Colorado Cross Country Ski Association** (www.colorado-xc.org) and from the **U.S. Forest Service** (see "Preparing for Your Active Vacation," above).

DOG SLEDDING If your fantasy is to be a Canadian Mountie mushing across the frozen Yukon, save the airfare and head to the mountains of Colorado instead. Dog-sled rides are offered at several ski resorts; at Aspen, dog power takes you far from the crowds into the rugged backcountry; some rides end with a fancy dinner.

FISHING Many cold-water species of fish live in the state's mountain lakes and streams, including seven kinds of trout (native cutthroat, rainbow, brown, brook, lake, kokanee, and whitefish), walleye, yellow perch, northern pike, tiger muskie, and bluegill. Warm-water sport fish (especially in eastern Colorado and in large rivers) include catfish, crappie, and bass (largemouth, smallmouth, white, and wiper). The best fishing spots are

Fun Facts A Wimpy State Fish

Mistakenly believed to be extinct in 1937 and listed as an endangered species in the early 1970s, the **greenback cutthroat trout** has made a comeback, and in 1994 was named the official Colorado State Fish by the state legislature. It replaced the rainbow trout, a California transplant that had been listed on maps and other documents as the state fish, although state Division of Wildlife officials couldn't say why.

Part of the greenback's problem is that it fails to live up to its cutthroat name, letting other trout invade its waters and practically jumping on any hook dropped into the water. But rumors of its demise were premature, and two native populations were discovered just outside Rocky Mountain National Park in 1973. Efforts were begun to reintroduce the fish to its native waters, as government agencies and the conservation group Trout Unlimited provided it with places to live that are free from more aggressive newcomers. By 1978, its status had improved from "endangered" to "threatened." State wildlife officials hope that if the greenback continues to prosper, it can eventually be removed from the "threatened" list.

Today the greenback cutthroat can be found in some four dozen bodies of water around the state, including several lakes in Rocky Mountain National Park. A good place in the national park to see the greenback cutthroat close-up is from the boardwalks through the Beaver Ponds on Trail Ridge Road.

Although the greenback's designation as official state fish does not provide any additional protection, Division of Wildlife officials say it strengthens the public's willingness to protect the fish and encourages anglers to throw it back if they catch it, as should be the rule with any threatened species.

the Arkansas River near Salida, the Roaring Fork River near Aspen, and the numerous streams and lakes in the mountains surrounding Steamboat Springs.

The fishing season is year-round, except in certain specified waters, and licenses are required for all anglers 16 and older. A 1-year license costs $56 for a nonresident and $26 for a resident. A 5-day license for nonresidents costs $21, and 1-day license costs $9 for both residents and nonresidents. The **Colorado Division of Wildlife,** 6060 Broadway, Denver, CO 80216 (✆ **303/297-1192;** www.wildlife.state.co.us), can answer your questions; for a recorded statewide-fishing report, call ✆ **303/291-7534.**

FOUR-WHEELING For years, skiers have known that four-wheel-drive vehicles make getting to and from the slopes easier. But SUVs and 4WD trucks are also popular for exploring Colorado's backcountry in summer, especially its miles upon miles of old logging and mining roads. Top locations for four-wheeling include the San Juan Mountains around Ouray and Telluride. You can get information on events and tips on places to go from the **Colorado Off Highway Vehicle Coalition,** P.O. Box 620523, Littleton, CO 80162 (✆ **303/539-5010;** www.cohvco.org).

GOLF Clear blue skies and beautiful scenery are hallmarks of Colorado golf courses, but don't think they're merely pretty faces; these courses can be as challenging as any in the country. Balls travel farther here than at sea level, and golfers tend to tire more quickly, at least until they've adapted to the higher elevation. Be prepared for cool mornings and afternoon thunderstorms even at the height of summer. High-elevation courses, such as those in Steamboat Springs and Vail, are shut down by snow in winter, but those at lower elevations, such as along the western slope, in the southwest corner, and around Denver, are often open year-round.

Good golf resorts can be found in Crested Butte, Winter Park, Pueblo, and Alamosa; for high-altitude putting, try Leadville. For what is probably the best golf resort in the state, go to the Broadmoor in Colorado Springs. For information on the state's major golf courses, check with the **Colorado Golf Association,** 5990 Greenwood Plaza Blvd., Ste. 130, Greenwood Village, CO 80111 (✆ **800/228-4675** or 303/366-4653; www.cogolf.org). Another information resource is ***Colorado Golf*** (www.golfcolorado.com), an annual magazine published jointly by several statewide golf organizations and available free at state welcome centers.

HIKING, BACKPACKING & MOUNTAINEERING Colorado is literally crisscrossed with hiking trails and dotted with mountains begging to be climbed. Rocky Mountain National Park's trails are especially beautiful, but they can be crowded. The highly respected **Colorado Mountain School,** 341 Moraine Ave., Estes Park, CO 80517 (✆ **800/836-4008** or 303/447-2804; www.totalclimbing.com), leads climbs up Longs Peak in the national park and provides advice on mountaineering in other parts of the state.

The 500-mile **Colorado Trail** ★★, which winds from Denver to Durango, crosses seven national forests and six designated wilderness areas, and is open to hikers, bikers, and equestrians. Scenery and terrain are varied, from grassy plains to snowcapped mountains. Although those in excellent physical condition can hike the entire trail in 6 to 8 weeks, most hikers make shorter excursions, and many enjoy day hikes. Most of the trail is above 10,000 feet elevation (the highest point is at 13,334 ft.), and hikes of more than a day or two will inevitably include some steep climbs. However, most of the trail has grades of no more than 10%. You'll find the easiest sections of the trail in the first 90 miles from Denver, but other sections, such as one 20-mile stretch near Salida, are also

Impressions

You can't see anything from your car. You've got to get out of the damn thing and walk!

—Edward Abbey, author

easy to moderate. In the Breckenridge and Winter Park areas, the trail is fairly rugged, and most sections below U.S. 50 are mountainous and at least somewhat strenuous. South of U.S. 50, where the trail winds through the San Juan Mountains, is serenely peaceful, but there are also fewer services, and if you're injured, it could be a long wait for help.

If it's serenity you seek, consider climbing one of the fourteeners—peaks over 14,000 feet—just off the Colorado Trail. Among the easiest is the climb to the summit of 14,420-foot Mount Harvard, the state's third-highest peak. The trail branches off the Colorado Trail about 8 miles north of Buena Vista.

Those planning multiday hikes on the Colorado Trail should carry maps or the official guidebook, which includes maps and details of the entire trail—elevation changes, trail conditions, vehicle access points, closest services, and general descriptions. Contact the **Colorado Trail Foundation,** 710 10th St., #210, Golden, CO 80401 (✆ **303/384-3729;** www.coloradotrail.org).

Although the Colorado Trail may be the state's most famous hike, there are plenty of other opportunities. The hike to **Long Lake** in the **Routt National Forest** outside Steamboat Springs is a moderately difficult 12-mile round-trip hike that leads through a forest and past several waterfalls to a peaceful alpine lake. Another pleasant hike in the Denver area is the easy 9-mile walk around **Barr Lake,** 18 miles northeast of the city, which offers excellent viewing of wildlife and birds. For the best city hike, try the **Boulder Creek Path,** a 16-mile trail leading from downtown Boulder into the nearby mountains, offering wildlife- and bird-watching and good views of the mountains and city. Those in Colorado Springs can hike among the beautiful red sandstone formations in the **Garden of the Gods,** or head west 30 miles to **Mueller State Park,** with 75 miles of trails through magnificent mountain scenery. From Aspen or Crested Butte—or from Aspen *to* Crested Butte—the trails in the **Maroon Bells Wilderness Area** are great for day hikes and week-long backpacking trips alike.

The **Continental Divide Trail Alliance (CDTA),** P.O. Box 628, Pine, CO 80470 (✆ **888/909-2382** or 303/838-3760; www.cdtrail.org), is building a trail—using volunteers—along the mountains of the Great Divide from Canada to Mexico, and that means it shoots right through the middle of Colorado. Each year, the CDTA publishes a schedule for the next summer, complete with volunteer needs, project descriptions, and difficulty ratings. This is an opportunity to experience some incredible backcountry, and to help create something your grandchildren will enjoy as well.

HORSEBACK RIDING It's fun to see the Old West the way 19th-century pioneers did: from a horse's saddle. Plenty of stables and outfitters lead rides lasting from 1 hour to several days, but I recommend those near Estes Park, Steamboat Springs, Grand Junction, Durango, and Telluride. If you'd like to spend your entire vacation on horseback, the **Sylvan Dale Guest Ranch** (✆ **877/667-3999** or 970/667-3915; www.sylvandale.com) just outside of Loveland is among the best.

MOUNTAIN BIKING The town of Crested Butte claims to be the mountain-biking capital of Colorado, but Telluride, Vail, and Durango are also top spots for fat-tire explorations. Those planning to go mountain biking in western Colorado can get current trail information from the **Colorado Plateau Mountain-Bike Trail Association,** P.O. Box 4602, Grand Junction, CO 81502 (© **970/244-8877;** www.copmoba.org).

The **Colorado Trail** (see above) is also open to mountain bikers, but they need to detour around six wilderness areas that are closed to all forms of mechanized travel. Riding the entire 500 miles—it takes at least 4 weeks—is easily the state's top mountain-bike adventure, but you can join or leave the trail at almost any point. One easily accessible stretch runs 24 miles from Copper Mountain Ski Resort to Tennessee Pass, crossing 12,280-foot Elk Ridge and descending into the ghost town of Camp Hale. On the trail, bikers yield to hikers and equestrians, and detour around designated wilderness areas. Contact the **Colorado Trail Foundation** (see "Hiking, Backpacking & Mountaineering," above).

RAFTING & KAYAKING Rivers swollen with melted snow lure rafters and kayakers from spring through midsummer, when rivers are at their fullest. Salida has become a famous rafting center; other popular destinations include Fort Collins, Estes Park, Grand Junction, and Glenwood Springs.

Rivers are classified from Class I to VI, depending on the roughness of their rapids. Class I is an easy float trip, practically calm; Class II has some rapids alternating with calm; Class III has some difficult rapids, with waves and boulders, and can be narrow in spots; Class IV is considered very difficult, with long stretches of rough, raft-flipping rapids; Class V is extremely difficult, with violent rapids and steep drops; and Class VI is considered unrunnable. The Arkansas River near Salida offers a variety of rapids from easy to almost unrunnable, and the Colorado River through Glenwood Canyon is a particularly scenic Class II to III river, wild enough for some thrills but with enough calm stretches to let you catch your breath and enjoy the view.

You'll find a range of trips from numerous reliable outfitters. For a free directory of licensed river outfitters and tips on choosing a rafting company, contact the **Colorado River Outfitters Association,** P.O. Box 1662, Buena Vista, CO 81211 (© **303/229-6075;** www.croa.org).

ROCK CLIMBING Although rock climbing is not as big here as in other parts of the West, Colorado does attract its share of climbers. One of the best spots is the Black Canyon of the Gunnison near Montrose, an extremely narrow chasm that sees little daylight; there are also several good spots near Durango. You can get information from the **Colorado Mountain Club,** American Mountaineering Center, 710 10th St., #200, Golden, CO 80401 (© **303/279-3080;** www.cmc.org).

ROCKHOUNDING & GOLD PANNING The state's mining heritage continues in many areas among rockhounders, who search for semiprecious gemstones, petrified woods, and agatized fossil bones. The Salida area has some of the best rockhounding opportunities in the state, and amateur gold panners should visit Idaho Springs (near Denver), Silverton, and Country Boy Mine in Breckenridge. Contact the **Colorado Geological Survey,** 1313 Sherman St., Rm. 715, Denver, CO 80203 (© **303/866-2611** or 303/866-4762 for publications; www.geosurvey.state.co.us), for information, maps, and a list of locations.

SKIING & SNOWBOARDING The most popular winter sport in Colorado is, of course, downhill skiing. Since the state's first resort (Howelsen Hill in Steamboat Springs) opened in 1915, Colorado has been synonymous with skiing in the western

Tips A Word about Rates

In the write-ups for each ski area in the regional chapters, you'll find the daily lift-ticket rates. Although handy for comparison, few people actually pay these prices. Most skiers buy packages that include lift tickets for a given number of days, and may also include transportation, rental equipment, lessons, lodging, meals, and lift tickets for nearby ski areas. There are also season passes that can be worthwhile for skiers who plan lengthy stays or several trips to the same resort. And for high rollers, Colorado Ski Country USA (see above) sells a coveted Gold Pass good at almost all of the state's resorts any day they're open. The possibilities are almost endless.

Some resorts charge more for lift tickets at busy times, and offer discounts at slow times, so it's impossible to guarantee the accuracy of even the daily lift-ticket prices in this book. Certainly, the most expensive time to ski is between December 20 and January 1, as well as on Martin Luther King, Jr., and Presidents' Day weekends. February through March is next; nonholiday times in January are generally cheaper; and the least expensive time is from Thanksgiving until mid-December and April until ski areas close. I generally prefer the last few weeks of the season—the snow's still great, the weather's nice, and the slopes are less crowded because many skiers are turning their thoughts to golf and tennis.

United States: It attracts more skiers per day than any other Western state, and its resorts continue to win accolades.

The snowboarding craze hit Colorado just as hard as other winter-sports destinations and, after some initial resistance, has been welcomed with open arms. Many resorts have opened snowboarding parks and offer lessons and rentals.

For **current ski conditions** and general information, call **Colorado Ski Country USA,** 1507 Blake St., Denver, CO 80202 (✆ **303/837-0793** or 303/825-7669 for snow conditions; www.coloradoski.com), or check ***Ski* magazine**'s website (www.skimag.com). Colorado's slopes are most crowded over Christmas and New Year's, and on Martin Luther King, Jr., and Presidents' Day weekends, when lodging rates are at their highest. Those who can ski midweek will find more room on the slopes, and the beginning and end of the season are the best times to avoid crowds—assuming snow conditions are good.

Colorado's ski areas range from predominately day-use areas, with little beyond a mountain with trails and a few lifts, to full-fledged resorts, with a variety of accommodations, restaurants, and nightlife all within a half-hour of the slopes. The overview that follows describes the key mountains at these ski areas and resorts.

Arapahoe Basin (Summit County) Arapahoe Basin, called "A-Basin" by its loyal fans, is the highest ski area in the state and one of the oldest. Because of its elevation, it gets a bit more snow than elsewhere, so some prefer to ski it during spring's warmer temperatures.

Aspen Highlands (Aspen) An intense mountain for only the most skilled and athletic of skiers. The views from the top are stupendous.

Tips Ski Packages & Tours

While many skiers enjoy planning their trips, others prefer making one phone call or sending an e-mail, and then letting someone else handle the details. Packages not only save time, but also are sometimes cheaper than doing the planning yourself. The key is to make sure you get all the features you want, without paying for things you don't want. Packages often include air and ground transportation, lodging, and lift tickets, and some include trip-cancellation insurance and meals.

A good first step is to check with a ski club in your hometown. These nonprofit organizations often offer some of the best deals if they happen to be planning a trip to where you want to ski at a time you want to go. Many travel agents can arrange ski vacations, and the central reservations service for a particular resort and the reservations desks of nearby lodgings can give you the scoop on the latest packages. Good bets among the well-established companies that offer ski packages throughout Colorado are **Ski.com** (✆ **800/908-5000** or 970/429-3099; www.ski.com) and **Ski the Rockies** (✆ **800/291-2588;** www.skitherockies.com).

Aspen Mountain (Aspen) With more than 100 restaurants and bars, Aspen is one of Colorado's most sophisticated resorts. Aspen Mountain was designed for advanced skiers and is the second most challenging of Aspen's four slopes.

Beaver Creek (Vail) Beaver Creek is probably the most refined ski community in Colorado. The mountain has a good mix of runs for everyone but the super expert, and lift lines are usually shorter than at Vail Mountain, especially on weekends.

Breckenridge (Summit County) Colorado's second most popular resort, Breckenridge is the crown jewel of Summit County's ski areas. There's something for all levels of skiers, and it makes a great base camp for those who want to ski a different Summit County mountain every day.

Buttermilk (Aspen) The usually uncrowded Buttermilk is a great place for affluent novices to practice their moves. It's located just outside the main village and is known for its great ski school.

Copper Mountain (Summit County) With its four superb high-alpine bowls and variety of trails for all levels, Copper is a fun place to ski, and the village is less expensive than nearby Breckenridge.

Crested Butte (Crested Butte) Dependable snow, good beginner and intermediate trails, and lots of extreme skiing—but very little expert terrain—mark this area.

Durango Mountain (Durango) This small, low-key ski area offers mostly intermediate, narrow, hilly trails meandering through the trees amid the breathtakingly beautiful San Juan Mountains.

Echo Mountain Park (Near Idaho Springs) Targeting snowboarders and beginning skiers, Echo Mountain Park is the closest slope to Denver but sports only one lift.

Eldora (Nederland) Just 21 miles from Boulder, Eldora is one of the state's smaller resorts, but has a good mix of terrain and is the closest ski area to the Denver–Boulder metropolitan area.

Howelsen Hill (Steamboat Springs) The oldest ski area in continuous use in Colorado—it opened in 1915—Howelsen Hill is a fun little downtown ski area as well as a training facility for ski jumpers.

Keystone (Summit County) Of Summit County's ski areas, Keystone is the closest to Denver, about 90 miles west of the airport. Its three separate mountains make it a good place for cruising, and night skiing draws locals from miles around.

Loveland (North of Denver) Less than an hour from Denver by car, Loveland is an old-fashioned local's ski area: There's no village, but enough beginner and advanced trails to satisfy the average skier. If you're staying in Denver in winter, give it a whirl.

Monarch (Salida) This family-oriented resort in southern Colorado has low rates, with good terrain and fewer crowds.

Powderhorn (Grand Junction) This is a good mountain for groups of varying abilities, with half its slopes intermediate and another 30% advanced or expert.

Silverton Mountain (Silverton) This new ski/snowboard area plans to be less expensive than most of Colorado's resorts and is geared to expert/advanced skiers and snowboarders only.

Ski Cooper (Leadville) A small, inexpensive resort at a high elevation, Ski Cooper is known for its all-natural snow and beautiful mountain scenery. There's a good balance of trails for beginners, intermediates, and experts.

Snowmass (Aspen) The highlight of Aspen, with plenty of wide-open spaces and trails for absolutely every level of ability. This is, by far, the largest mountain at Aspen. The base village has plenty of beds, but not much nightlife—most night owls hop the free shuttle bus to Aspen, 20 minutes down the road.

SolVista Basin at Granby Ranch (near Winter Park) Created by the merging of several smaller ski areas, Solvista is an all-season resort comprising two interconnected mountains, with mostly beginner and intermediate runs, and just 20% expert.

Steamboat (Steamboat Springs) One of Colorado's three largest mountains (the other two are Vail and Snowmass), Steamboat offers near-perfect skiing. It's well laid out and has gorgeous valley views, and the base village offers a wide choice of accommodations and restaurants. Another draw is the authentic old ranching town of Steamboat Springs, just a few miles away. Most of the mountain's trails are for intermediates, but there are beginner and expert trails as well.

Sunlight Mountain (Glenwood Springs) Sunlight is family oriented, geared to intermediate skiers, and very affordable.

Telluride (Telluride) Set at the top of a lovely box canyon, Telluride caters mainly to intermediate skiers but also has novice trails some $2^1/_2$ miles long and a number of steep expert trails.

Vail (Vail Valley) Colorado's most popular resort, Vail mountain has a top-notch ski school and trails for everyone. The completely self-contained village at its base was created for skiers and is serviced by free shuttle buses.

Winter Park (Winter Park) Young and athletic in spirit, Winter Park is unique—the focus is on value, with a variety of trails for all levels, plus well-regarded programs for children and skiers with disabilities.

Wolf Creek (near Pagosa Springs) One of the state's oldest ski areas, Wolf Creek is famous for consistently having the most snow in the state—an annual average of 465 inches (almost 39 ft.). There is terrain for skiers of all ability levels, but especially intermediates.

SNOWMOBILING If you've never been snowmobiling, the best places for a guided snowmobile tour are Steamboat Springs and Aspen. If you're an experienced snowmobiler and you plan to bring your rig with you, national forest trails are prime snowmobiling spots. Some of the state's best and most scenic rides are in Roosevelt National Forest, about 50 miles west of Fort Collins (via U.S. 287 and Colo. 14) at Chambers Lake. Because many of these trails are multiuse, snowmobilers should watch out for cross-country skiers and snowshoers, and slow down when passing. Colorado's light, dry snow is usually suitable for snowmobiling all winter long, although warm spring days can result in sticky snow, especially at lower elevations, which can gum up the works and make the going rough.

Information on snowmobiling in the state, including current trail conditions, is available online from **SledCity** (formerly the Colorado Snowmobile Association) at **www.coloradosledcity.com**. For information on snowmobile regulations, contact **Colorado State Parks** (see "Preparing for Your Active Vacation," earlier in this chapter).

WILDLIFE- & BIRD-WATCHING There are numerous locations in Colorado to see animals and birds in the wild, including some that are close to the state's major cities. The South Platte River Greenway near Denver is a good spot to see ducks and other waterfowl, songbirds, deer, and beaver; the Monte Vista and Alamosa national wildlife refuges in the San Luis Valley are some of the best spots in the country to see migratory greater sandhill cranes; and if you head to the prairie in southeastern Colorado, the Comanche National Grasslands is the place to see the rare lesser prairie chicken. Other top spots for wildlife include Durango, Telluride, Winter Park, Vail, Rocky Mountain National Park, and Colorado National Monument.

6

Settling into Denver

It's no accident that Denver is called "the Mile High City": When you climb up to the state capitol, you're precisely 5,280 feet above sea level when you reach the 13th step. Denver's location at this altitude was purely coincidental; Denver is one of the few cities not built on an ocean, a lake, a navigable river, or even (at the time) an existing road or railroad.

In the summer of 1858, eager prospectors discovered a few flecks of gold where Cherry Creek empties into the shallow South Platte River, and a tent camp quickly sprang up on the site. (The first permanent structure was a saloon.) When militia Gen. William H. Larimer arrived in 1859, he claim-jumped the land on the east side of the Platte, laid out a city, and, hoping to gain political favors, named it after James Denver, governor of the Kansas Territory, which included this area. Larimer was not aware that Denver had recently resigned.

Larimer's was one of several settlements on the South Platte. Three others also sought recognition, but Larimer had a solution. For the price of a barrel of whiskey, he bought out the other would-be town fathers, and the name "Denver" caught on.

Although the gold found in Denver was but a teaser for much larger strikes in the nearby mountains, the community grew as a shipping and trade center, in part because it had a milder climate than the mining towns it served. A devastating fire in 1863, a deadly flash flood in 1864, and American Indian hostilities in the late 1860s created many hardships. But the establishment of rail links to the east and the influx of silver from the rich mines to the west kept Denver going. Silver from Leadville and gold from Cripple Creek made Denver a showcase city in the late 19th and early 20th centuries. The U.S. Mint, built in 1906, established Denver as a banking and financial center.

In the years following World War II, Denver mushroomed to become the largest city between the Great Plains and the Pacific Coast, with almost 600,000 residents within the city limits and over 3 million in the metropolitan area. It remains a growing city, with a booming downtown and suburbs. Denver is noted for its tree-lined boulevards, 200 city parks that cover more than 20,000 acres, and architecture ranging from Victorian to postmodern.

1 ORIENTATION

ARRIVING

By Plane

Denver International Airport (DIA) is 23 miles northeast of downtown, usually a 35- to 45-minute drive. Covering 53 square miles (twice the size of Manhattan), DIA has one of the tallest flight-control towers in the world, at 327 feet. The airport, which has 95 gates and six full-service runways, can handle around 50 million passengers annually.

Major national airlines serving Denver include American, Continental, Delta, Frontier, jetBlue, Northwest, Southwest, United, and US Airways. **International airlines** include Air Canada, British Airways, Lufthansa, and Mexicana de Aviación.

Regional and **commuter airlines** connecting Denver with other points in the Rockies and Southwest include Alaska Airlines and Great Lakes Airlines.

For airlines' national reservations phone numbers and websites, see "Getting There," in chapter 3. For other information, call the Denver International Airport **information line** (✆ **800/AIR-2DEN** [247-2336] or 303/342-2000; TDD 800/688-1333; www.flydenver.com). Other important airport phone numbers include **ground transportation,** ✆ 303/342-4059; **lost and found,** ✆ 303/342-4062; **paging,** ✆ 303/342-2300; **parking,** ✆ 303/342-7275; **police,** ✆ 303/342-4211; and **security wait times,** ✆ 303/342-8477.

GETTING TO & FROM THE AIRPORT Bus, taxi, and limousine services shuttle travelers between the airport and downtown, and most major car-rental companies have outlets at the airport. Because many major hotels are some distance from the airport, travelers should check on the availability and cost of hotel shuttle services when making reservations.

The **city bus** fare from the airport to downtown Denver is $9; from the airport to Boulder and suburban Park-n-Ride lots, it is about $11. The **SuperShuttle** (✆ **800/525-3177** or 303/370-1300; www.supershuttledenver.com) provides transportation to and from a number of hotels downtown and in the Denver Tech Center. The SuperShuttle has frequent scheduled service between the airport and downtown hotels for $19 per person each way; door-to-door service is also available. **Taxi** companies (see "Getting Around," below) are another option, with fares generally in the $30-to-$50 range, and you can often share a cab and split the fare by calling the cab company ahead of time. For instance, **Yellow Cab** (✆ **303/777-7777;** www.yellowtrans.com) will take up to five people from DIA to most downtown hotels for a flat rate of $45.

Those who prefer a bit of luxury should call **White Dove Limousine** (✆ **800/910-7433** or 303/399-3683; www.whitedovelimo.com). Rates to different parts of the Denver metro area start around $70 but vary, so call for prices. The company operates sedan, stretch, and Hummer limousines, as well as a minibus. Charter services are also available.

By Car

The principal highway routes into Denver are **I-25** from the north (Fort Collins and Wyoming) and south (Colorado Springs and New Mexico), **I-70** from the east (Burlington and Kansas) and west (Grand Junction and Utah), and **I-76** from the northeast (Nebraska). If you're driving into Denver from Boulder, take **U.S. 36;** from Salida and the southwest, **U.S. 285.**

By Train

Amtrak serves Union Station, 17th and Wynkoop streets (✆ **800/USA-RAIL** [872-7245] or 303/825-2583; www.amtrak.com), in the lower downtown historic district. Denver is a stop for **California Zephyr** (Chicago to Emeryville, Calif.); there are two trains daily in each direction.

By Bus

Greyhound, 1055 19th St. (at Arapahoe St.; ✆ **800/231-2222;** www.greyhound.com), is the major bus service in Colorado, with about 60 daily arrivals and departures to communities in and out of the state.

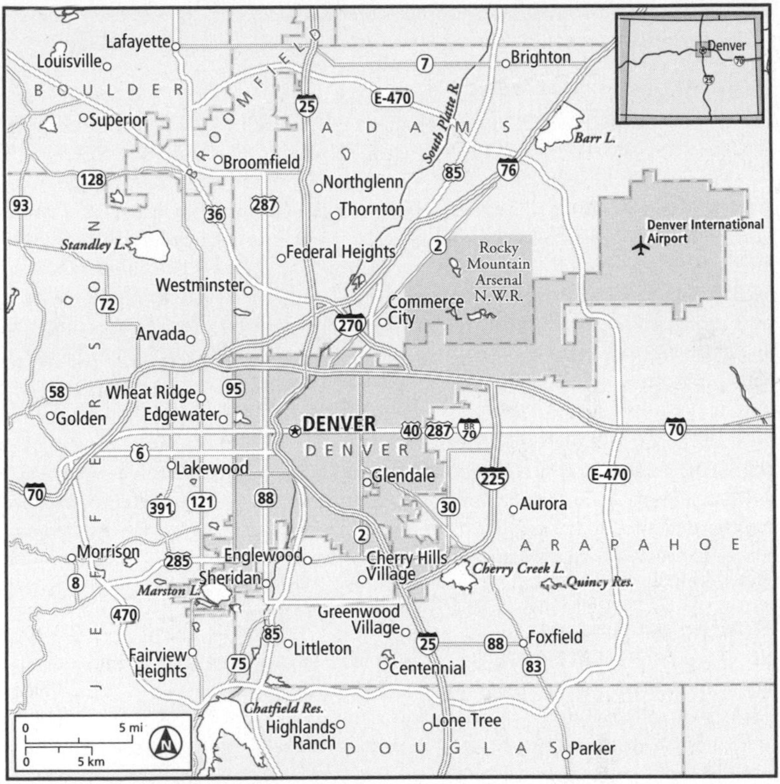

VISITOR INFORMATION

The **Denver Metro Convention and Visitors Bureau** operates a visitor center in the 16th Street Mall at 1600 California St. (✆ **303/892-1505**). It's open Monday through Friday from 9am to 5pm. In summer, it is open until 6pm on weekdays, as well as on Saturday from 9am to 5pm and Sunday from 11am to 3pm. Visitor information is also available at Denver International Airport. Ask for the ***Official Visitors Guide,*** a 150-plus-page full-color booklet with a comprehensive listing of accommodations, restaurants, and other visitor services in Denver and surrounding areas.

For advance information, contact the Denver Metro Convention and Visitors Bureau, 1555 California St., Ste. 300, Denver, CO 80202-4264 (✆ **800/233-6837** or 303/892-1112; www.denver.org).

CITY LAYOUT

It's tough to get lost in Denver—just remember that the mountains, nearly always visible, are to the west. Nonetheless, getting around a city of half a million people can be a challenge. One element of confusion is that Denver has both an older grid system downtown, which is oriented northeast–southwest to parallel the South Platte River, and a newer north–south grid system that surrounds the older one.

The *Official Visitors Guide,* available free of charge from the Denver Metro Convention and Visitors Bureau (see "Visitor Information," above), contains a good map.

Main Arteries & Streets

It's probably easiest to get your bearings from Civic Center Park. From here, Colfax Avenue (U.S. 40) extends east and west as far as the eye can see. The same is true for Broadway, which reaches north and south.

DOWNTOWN DENVER North of Colfax and west of Broadway is the center of downtown, where the streets follow the old grid pattern. A mile-long pedestrian mall, **16th Street,** cuts northwest off Broadway just above this intersection. (The numbered streets parallel 16th to the northeast, extending to 44th; and to the southwest, as far as 5th.) Intersecting the numbered streets at right angles are **Lawrence Street** (which runs one-way northeast) and **Larimer Street** (which runs one-way southwest), 12 and 13 blocks north, respectively, of the Colfax–Broadway intersection.

I-25 skirts downtown Denver to the west, with access from Colfax or **Speer Boulevard,** which winds diagonally along Cherry Creek past Larimer Square.

OUTSIDE DOWNTOWN Outside the downtown sector, the pattern is a little less confusing. But keep in mind that the numbered *avenues* that parallel Colfax to the north and south (Colfax is equivalent to 15th Ave.) have nothing in common with the numbered *streets* of the downtown grid. In fact, any byway labeled an "avenue" runs east–west, never north–south.

Finding an Address

NORTH–SOUTH ARTERIES The thoroughfare that divides avenues into east and west is **Broadway,** which runs one-way south between 19th Street and I-25. Each block east or west adds 100 to the avenue address; thus, if you wanted to find 2115 E. 17th Ave., it would be a little more than 21 blocks east of Broadway, just beyond Vine Street.

Main thoroughfares that parallel Broadway to the east include **Downing Street** (1200 block), **York Street** (2300 block; it becomes **University Blvd.** south of 6th), **Colorado Boulevard** (4000 block), **Monaco Street Parkway** (6500 block), and **Quebec Street** (7300 block). Colorado Boulevard (Colo. 2) is the busiest street in the whole state, intersecting I-25 on the south and I-70 on the north. North–south streets that parallel Broadway to the west include **Santa Fe Drive** (U.S. 85; 1000 block); west of I-25 are **Federal Boulevard** (U.S. 287 N.; 3000 block) and **Sheridan Boulevard** (Colo. 95; 5200 block), the boundary between Denver and Lakewood.

EAST–WEST ARTERIES Denver streets are divided into north and south at **Ellsworth Avenue,** about 2 miles south of Colfax. Ellsworth is a relatively minor street, but it's a convenient dividing point because it's just a block south of **1st Avenue.** With building numbers increasing by 100 each block, that puts an address like 1710 Downing St. at the corner of East 17th Avenue. **First, 6th, Colfax** (1500 block), and **26th** avenues, and **Martin Luther King Jr. Boulevard** (3200 block) are the principal east–west thoroughfares. There are no numbered avenues south of Ellsworth. Major east–west byways south of Ellsworth are **Alameda** (Colo. 26; 300 block), **Mississippi** (1100 block), **Louisiana** (1300 block), **Evans** (2100 block), **Yale** (2700 block), and **Hampden** avenues (U.S. 285; 3500 block).

NEIGHBORHOODS IN BRIEF

Lower Downtown (LoDo) A 25-block area surrounding Union Station, and encompassing **Wynkoop Street** southeast to **Market Street** and **20th Street** southwest to **Speer Boulevard,** this delightful and busy historic district was until recently a somewhat seedy neighborhood of deteriorating Victorian houses and redbrick warehouses. A major restoration effort has brought it back to life. Today it is home to chic shops, art galleries, nightclubs, and restaurants. Listed as both a city and a county historic district, it boasts numerous National Historic Landmarks; skyscrapers are prohibited by law. Coors Field, the 50,000-seat home of the Rockies baseball team, opened here in 1995.

Central Business District This extends along **16th, 17th, and 18th streets between Lawrence Street and Broadway.** The ban on skyscrapers certainly does not apply here. In this area you'll find the Brown Palace Hotel, the Westin Hotel at Tabor Center, and other upscale lodgings; numerous restaurants and bars; plus the popular 16th Street Mall.

Far East Center Denver's Asian community is concentrated along this strip of **Federal Boulevard,** between **West Alameda** and **West Mississippi** avenues. It burgeoned in the aftermath of the Vietnam War to accommodate throngs of Southeast Asian refugees, especially Thai and Vietnamese. Look for authentic restaurants, bakeries, groceries, gift shops, and clothing stores. The Far East Center Building at Federal and Alameda is built in Japanese pagoda style.

Five Points The "five points" actually meet at 23rd Street and Broadway, but the cultural and commercial hub of Denver's black community, from **23rd** to **38th** streets, northeast of downtown, covers a much larger area and incorporates four historic districts. Restaurants offer soul food, barbecued ribs, and Caribbean cuisine, while jazz and blues musicians and contemporary dance troupes perform in theaters and nightclubs. The Black American West Museum and Heritage Center is also in this area.

Highlands Perched northwest of downtown from **32nd** to **38th** avenues between **Federal** and **Zuni** streets, the historic, increasingly chic Highland neighborhood is the most densely populated neighborhood in the city outside of Capitol Hill. Mexican and Italian eateries brush elbows with stylish boutiques and galleries. In the neighboring West Highlands neighborhood, the eclectic retail district centered on 32nd Avenue and Lowell Boulevard is one of the most vibrant in the city.

La Alma Lincoln Park/Auraria Hispanic culture, art, food, and entertainment predominate along this strip of **Santa Fe Drive,** between **West Colfax** and **West 6th** avenues. It's notable for its Southwestern character and architecture. This neighborhood is well worth a visit for its numerous restaurants, art galleries, and crafts shops. Denver's annual Cinco de Mayo celebration takes place here.

Uptown Denver's oldest residential neighborhood, from **Broadway** east to **York Street** (City Park) and **23rd Avenue** south to **Colfax Avenue,** is best known today for two things: It's bisected by 17th Avenue, home to many of the city's finest restaurants, and several of its classic Victorian and Queen Anne–style homes have been converted to captivating bed-and-breakfasts (see "Where to Stay," below).

Denver Neighborhoods

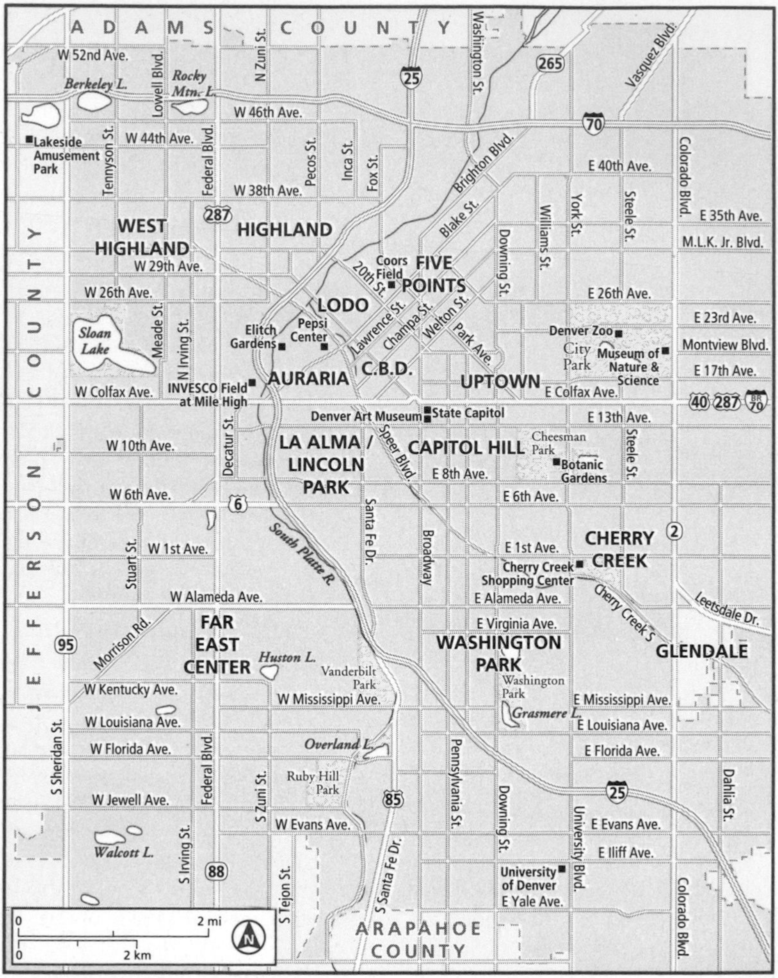

Washington Park A grand Victorian neighborhood centered on the lush park of its namesake, "Wash Park" is one of Denver's trendiest and most popular neighborhoods. Bounded by **Broadway** east to **University Boulevard,** and **Alameda Avenue** south to **Evans Avenue,** it features a good deal of dining and recreational opportunities, but little in the way of lodging. It is a great place, however, for architecture and history buffs to drive or walk past the grand rows of houses.

Capitol Hill One of Denver's most diverse and oldest neighborhoods lies just southeast of downtown. Capitol Hill centers on the gold-domed Capitol Building, encompassing **Broadway** east to **York,** and **Colfax Avenue** south to

6th Avenue. The north edge is improving after years of neglect and criminal activity, and now features such attractions as the Fillmore Auditorium and a lively restaurant and bar scene. There are several commercial and retail districts in the area, nestled amid Victorian houses and modern lofts and apartments. Also here are the Molly Brown House Museum (see chapter 7) and several lodging options, ranging from B&Bs to luxury hotels (see "Where to Stay," below). You'll notice that there are no old wooden buildings here. After a disastrous fire in 1863, the government forbade the construction of wooden structures, a ban that stood until after World War II.

Cherry Creek Home of the Cherry Creek Shopping Center and Denver Country Club, this area extends north from **East 1st Avenue** to **East 8th Avenue,** and from **Downing Street** east to **Steele Street.** You'll find huge, ostentatious stone mansions here, especially around Circle Drive (southwest of 6th and University), where many of Denver's wealthiest families have lived for generations.

Glendale Denver surrounds Glendale, an incorporated city. The center of a lively entertainment district that is home to a slew of topless clubs, Glendale straddles Cherry Creek on **South Colorado Boulevard** south of **East Alameda Avenue.**

Tech Center At the southern end of the metropolitan area is the Denver Tech Center, along **I-25** between **Belleview Avenue** and **Arapahoe Road.** In this district, about a 25-minute drive from downtown, you will find the headquarters of several international and national companies, high-tech businesses, and a handful of upscale hotels heavily oriented toward business travelers.

2 GETTING AROUND

BY PUBLIC TRANSPORTATION

The **Regional Transportation District,** or **RTD** (© **800/366-7433,** 303/299-6000, or TDD 303/299-6089 for route and schedule information; 303/299-6700 for other business; www.rtd-denver.com), calls itself "The Ride." It operates bus routes and a light-rail system, with free transfer tickets available. It provides good service within Denver and its suburbs and outlying communities (including Boulder, Longmont, and Evergreen), as well as free parking at 65 Park-n-Ride locations throughout the Denver–Boulder metropolitan area. The light-rail service is designed to get buses and cars out of congested downtown Denver; many of the bus routes from outlying areas deliver passengers to light-rail stations rather than to downtown.

The local one-way fare is $1.75; seniors and passengers with disabilities pay 85¢, and children age 5 and under travel free. Regional bus fares vary (for example, Denver to Boulder costs $4). Exact change is required for buses, and train tickets can be purchased at vending machines beneath light-rail station awnings.

Depending on the route, the departure time of the last bus or train varies from 9pm to 2am. Maps for all routes are available at any time at the RTD **Civic Center Station,** 16th Street and Broadway; and the **Market Street Station,** Market and 16th streets. RTD also provides special service to Colorado Rockies (baseball) and Denver Broncos (football) games. All RTD buses and trains are completely wheelchair accessible.

Free buses run up and down the 16th Street Mall between the Civic Center and Market Street, daily from 6am to 1am.

The light rail is also useful for exploring downtown and the greater metro area. The **C Line** diverts from the main north–south **D Line** at Colfax Avenue, and it veers west and stops at Invesco Field at Mile High, the Pepsi Center, and Six Flags Elitch Gardens before chugging into Union Station at 17th and Wynkoop streets in lower downtown. The D Line continues along northeast through the east side of downtown before its terminus at 30th Avenue and Downing Street. The **E Line** runs along I-25 from Broadway to Lincoln Avenue in the south suburbs. The **F Line** connects 18th and California streets downtown with Lincoln Avenue. The **G Line** runs from Nine Mile in Aurora at I-225 and Parker Road to Lincoln; the **H Line** connects Nine Mile and 18th and California.

The open-air **Platte Valley Trolley** (**✆ 303/458-6255;** www.denvertrolley.org) operates year-round. From April to October between 12:30 and 4pm Friday through Sunday, there's a 25-minute "Riverfront Ride" ($3 adults, $2 seniors and children), which operates from 15th Street at Confluence Park, south to the Denver Children's Museum along the west bank of the Platte River. From Memorial Day to Labor Day, the ride is also available on Monday. Different routes are offered at other times.

BY TAXI

The main companies are **Yellow Cab** (**✆ 303/777-7777;** www.yellowtrans.com) and **Metro Taxi** (**✆ 303/333-3333;** www.metrotaxidenver.com). Taxis can be hailed on the street, though it's preferable to telephone for a taxi or to wait for one at a taxi stand outside a major hotel. On weekends, hailing a taxi can be difficult when the bars close down for the night.

BY CAR

Because cars are not necessary downtown, visitors can save money by staying downtown while in Denver and then renting a car to leave the area.

The Denver office of the **American Automobile Association (AAA)** is at 4100 E. Arkansas Ave., Denver, CO 80222-3405 (**✆ 800/222-4357** or 303/753-8800; www.aaacolorado.com); there are several other locations in the Denver area.

CAR RENTALS Most major car-rental agencies have outlets in or near downtown Denver, as well as at Denver International Airport. These include **Alamo,** 24530 E. 78th Ave. (**✆ 800/462-5266** or 303/342-7373); **Avis,** 1900 Broadway (**✆ 800/331-1212** or 303/839-1280; 303/342-5500 at DIA); **Dollar,** 10343 N. Federal Blvd., Westminster (**✆ 866/434-2226;** 303/342-9678 at DIA); **Enterprise,** 7720 Calawba Court (**✆ 800/261-7331** or 303/794-3333; 303/342-7350 at DIA); **Hertz,** 2001 Welton St. (**✆ 800/654-3131** or 303/297-9400; 303/342-3800 at DIA); **National,** at Denver International Airport (**✆ 800/227-7368** or 303/342-0717); and **Thrifty,** 8006 E. Arapahoe Ave. (**✆ 800/847-4389** or 303/342-9400; 877/283-0898 at DIA). You can rent campers, travel trailers, motor homes, and motorcycles from **Cruise America** (**✆ 800/671-8042;** www.cruiseamerica.com).

Per-day rentals for midsize cars range from $35 to $70, although AAA and other discounts are often available, and weekend and multiday rates can also save money. Four-wheel-drive vehicles, trucks, and campers cost more.

PARKING Downtown parking-lot rates vary from 75¢ per half-hour to $20 or more per full day. Rates are higher near the 16th Street Mall, in the central business district, and in hotel lots. Keep a handful of quarters available if you plan to use on-street parking meters.

Fast Facts Denver

American Express The American Express travel agency, 555 17th St. (✆ **303/383-5050**), is open Monday through Friday from 8am to 5pm. It offers full member services and currency exchange. To report a lost card, call ✆ **800/528-4800;** to report lost traveler's checks, call ✆ **800/221-7282.**

Area Code Area codes are **303** and **720,** and local calls require 10-digit dialing.

Babysitters Front desks at major hotels can often arrange for babysitters for their guests.

Business Hours Generally, business offices are open weekdays from 9am to 5pm, and government offices are open from 8am until 4:30 or 5pm. Stores are open 6 days a week, with many also open on Sunday; department stores usually stay open until 9pm at least 1 day a week. Discount stores and supermarkets are often open later than other stores, and some supermarkets are open 24 hours a day.

Banks are usually open weekdays from 9am to 5pm, occasionally a bit later on Friday, and sometimes on Saturday. There's 24-hour access to automated teller machines (ATMs) at most banks, plus in many shopping centers and other outlets.

Car Rentals See "Getting Around," above.

Dentists & Doctors Doctor and dentist referrals are available by calling ✆ **800/DOCTORS** (362-8677). **Ask-A-Nurse Centura** (✆ **800/327-6877** or 303/777-6877) provides free physician referrals and answers health questions.

Drugstores Throughout the metropolitan area, you will find Walgreens and other chain pharmacies, as well as Safeway and King Soopers grocery stores (which also have drugstores). The **Walgreens** at 2000 E. Colfax Ave. (✆ **303/331-0917**) is open 24 hours a day. For the locations of other Walgreens, call ✆ **800/925-4733.**

Emergencies Call ✆ **911.** For the **Colorado Poison Center,** call ✆ **303/739-1123.** For the **Rape Crisis and Domestic Violence Hotline,** call ✆ **303/318-9989.**

Eyeglasses One-hour replacements and repairs are available at **Pearle Vision,** 2720 S. Colorado Blvd. at Yale Avenue (✆ **303/758-1292**), and **LensCrafters,** in Cherry Creek Shopping Center (✆ **303/321-8331**).

Hospitals Among Denver-area hospitals are **St. Joseph Hospital,** 1835 Franklin St. (✆ **303/837-7111**), just east of downtown, and **Children's Hospital,** 13123 E. 16th Ave. (✆ **720/777-1234**).

Maps Denver's largest map store, **Mapsco Map and Travel Center,** 800 Lincoln St., Denver, CO 80203 (✆ **800/456-8703** or 303/830-2373; www.mapsco.com), offers USGS and recreation maps, state maps and travel guides, raised relief maps, and globes.

Newspapers & Magazines The *Denver Post* (www.denverpost.com) is Colorado's largest daily newspaper. The *Rocky Mountain News* (www.rockymountainnews.com) also covers the metropolitan area. Under a joint operating agreement, each publishes a separate weekday edition, only the *News* prints on Saturday, and only the *Post* appears on Sunday. A widely read free weekly, *Westword* (www.westword.com), is known as much for its coverage of local politicians and celebrities and its entertainment and dining listings. National newspapers such as *USA Today* and the *Wall Street Journal* can be purchased at newsstands and at major hotels.

Photographic Needs For photographic supplies, equipment, 1-hour processing, and repairs, visit **Wolf Camera** at one of its 18 Denver locations; the downtown branch, at 1545 California St. (✆ **303/623-1155;** www.wolfcamera.com), claims to be the biggest single-floor camera store in the world. Another good source for photo supplies and film processing is **Mike's Camera,** 759 S. Colorado Blvd. (✆ **303/733-2121;** www.mikescamera.com).

Post Office The main downtown post office, 951 20th St., is open Monday through Friday from 7am to 10:30pm, Saturday and Sunday from 8:30am to 10:30pm. For full 24-hour postal service, go to the General Mail Facility, 7500 E. 53rd Place. For other post office locations and hours, check with the U.S. Postal Service (✆ **800/275-8777;** www.usps.com).

Safety Although Denver is a relatively safe city, it is not crime free. Safety is seldom a problem on the 16th Street Mall, but even streetwise Denverites avoid late-night walks along certain sections of Colfax Avenue, just a few blocks away. If you are unsure of the safety of a particular area you wish to visit, ask your hotel concierge or desk clerk.

Taxes State and local sales tax in Denver is about 7.75% (it varies slightly in neighboring counties and suburbs). The hotel tax is 10.75%, bringing the total tax on accommodations to about 18.5%.

Useful Telephone Numbers For a weather report, time, and temperature, call ✆ **303/337-2500.** Statewide road condition reports are available at ✆ **303/639-1111.** For information on possible road construction delays in the Denver area and statewide, see **www.cotrip.org**.

3 WHERE TO STAY

Although most hotels and motels in the Denver area do not have seasonal rates (as you'll find in many other parts of Colorado), hotels that cater to business travelers, such as the **Brown Palace** and the **Warwick** (see below), often offer substantial weekend discounts, sometimes as much as 50% off the regular rates. Rates listed below do not include the 18.5% accommodations tax.

The lodging industry is catching up with the construction of Denver International Airport, and you'll find that many of the major chains and franchises have built or are in the process of constructing facilities near the airport—there's also a proposed hotel at the terminal itself. Among those now open are **Courtyard by Marriott at DIA,** 6901 Tower Rd., Denver, CO 80249 (✆ **800/321-2211** or 303/371-0300), with rates of $219 to $249 for a double; and **Hampton Inn DIA,** 6290 Tower Rd., Denver, CO 80249 (✆ **800/426-7866** or 303/371-0200), with a rate of $139 to $179 for a double.

Reliable (and relatively inexpensive hotels) in the downtown area include **Comfort Inn,** 401 17th St., Denver, CO 80202 (✆ **800/228-5150** or 303/296-0400), with a convenient location and rates of $149 for a double and $189 to $329 for a suite; **La Quinta Inn Downtown,** 3500 Park Ave. W. (at I-25, exit 213), Denver, CO 80216 (✆ **800/531-5900** or 303/458-1222), charging $99 for a double; and **Hotel VQ,** 1975 Mile High Stadium Circle (at I-25, exit 210B), Denver, CO 80204 (✆ **800/388-5381** or 303/433-8331), with rates of $89 to $129 for a double.

These official, or "rack," rates, do not include any discounts, such as those offered to members of AAA or AARP. Be sure to ask if you qualify for a reduced rate. Because a chain hotel's national reservation service may not be able to offer discounts, your best bet may be to call the hotel directly.

DOWNTOWN

Hotels in downtown Denver, "the central business district of the Rocky Mountain West," generally cater to businesspeople, with high-tech amenities and locations convenient to the Convention Center or the financial district. These properties are more than adequate for leisure travelers, and especially enticing on weekends when they lower their rates.

Very Expensive

Brown Palace Hotel ★★ Moments For more than 100 years, the city's finest hotel has been the place to stay for anyone who is anyone. It combines great rooms and amenities with the intangibles: interesting history, romantic atmosphere, regional personality, and impeccable service. A National Historic Landmark, the Brown Palace has operated continuously since it opened in 1892. Designed with an odd triangular shape by the renowned architect Frank Edbrooke, it was built of Colorado red granite and Arizona sandstone. The lobby's walls are paneled with Mexican onyx, and elaborate cast-iron grillwork surrounds six tiers of balconies up to the stained-glass ceiling. Every president since 1905 (except Calvin Coolidge) has visited the hotel, and Dwight Eisenhower made the Brown his home away from the White House. His former room, now known as the Eisenhower Suite, is a vision of stately elegance, with a preserved dent in the fireplace trim that is the alleged result of an errant golf swing. There are also lavish, unique suites named after Teddy Roosevelt, Ronald Reagan, and The Beatles.

Standard rooms are also lush and comfortable, either Victorian or Art Deco in style with reproduction furnishings and fixtures. Each has a desk, a duvet, and individual climate control. The clientele is a mix of leisure travelers and businesspeople with a taste—and a budget—for luxury. The staterooms on the ninth floor are especially enticing, with cordless phones, big-screen TVs, fridges, fax/printers, and safes. The water is great here: The Brown Palace has its own artesian wells!

321 17th St., Denver, CO 80202. ✆ **800/321-2599** or 303/297-3111. Fax 303/312-5900. www.brownpalace.com. 241 units. $210–$385 double; $360–$535 suite. Lower rates Sat–Sun. AE, DC, DISC, MC, V. Valet parking $24 overnight. Pets up to 20 lb. accepted. **Amenities:** 3 restaurants (all American; see "Where to Dine," later in this chapter); 2 lounges; exercise room; concierge; courtesy car; business center; 24-hr. room service; in-room massage (for an extra charge). *In room:* A/C, cable TV w/pay movies, 2-line phone w/dataport, voice mail, free Wi-Fi, hair dryer, iron.

Denver Accommodations

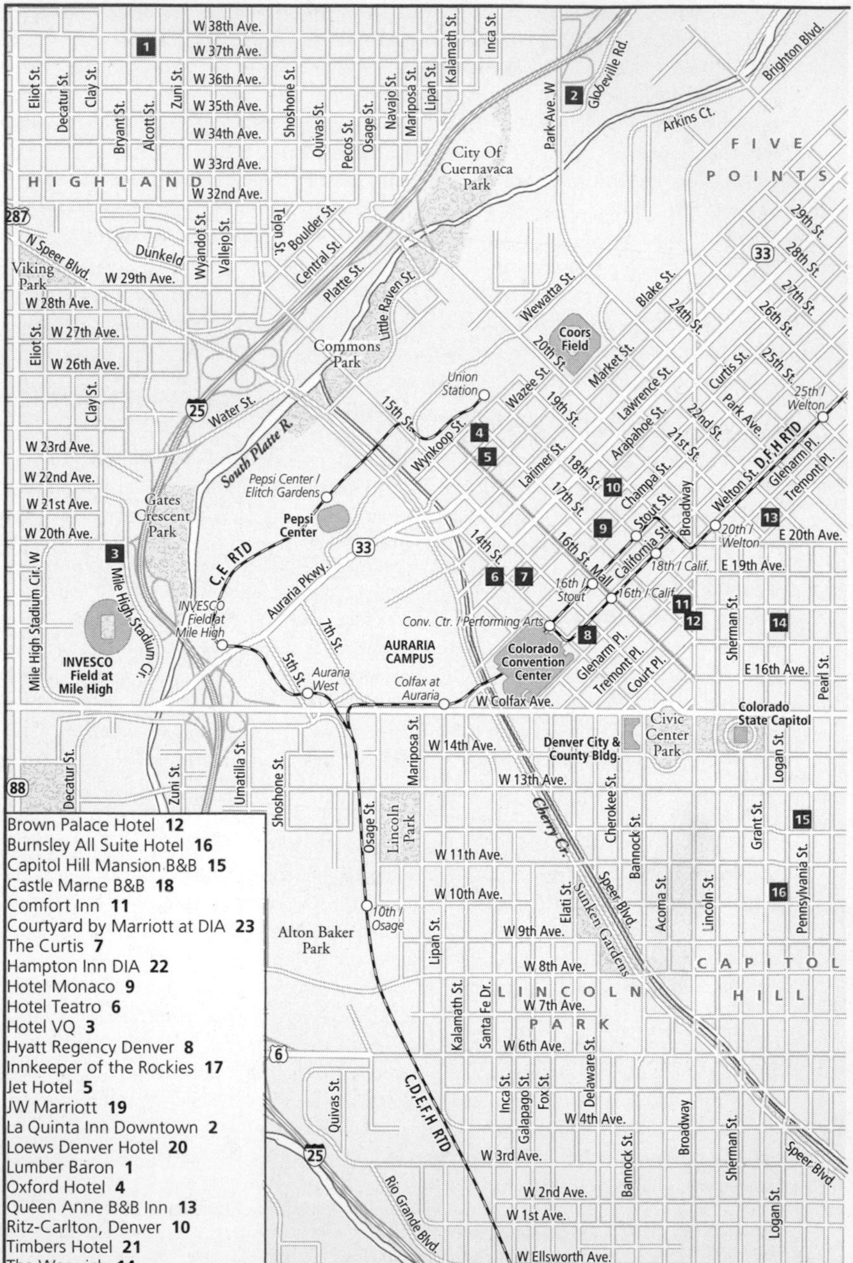
Brown Palace Hotel 12
Burnsley All Suite Hotel 16
Capitol Hill Mansion B&B 15
Castle Marne B&B 18
Comfort Inn 11
Courtyard by Marriott at DIA 23
The Curtis 7
Hampton Inn DIA 22
Hotel Monaco 9
Hotel Teatro 6
Hotel VQ 3
Hyatt Regency Denver 8
Innkeeper of the Rockies 17
Jet Hotel 5
JW Marriott 19
La Quinta Inn Downtown 2
Loews Denver Hotel 20
Lumber Baron 1
Oxford Hotel 4
Queen Anne B&B Inn 13
Ritz-Carlton, Denver 10
Timbers Hotel 21
The Warwick 14
HIGHLAND
FIVE POINTS
City Of Cuernavaca Park
Viking Park
Commons Park
Coors Field
Union Station
Pepsi Center
Gates Crescent Park
INVESCO Field at Mile High
AURARIA CAMPUS
Colorado Convention Center
Civic Center Park
Colorado State Capitol
Denver City & County Bldg.
Lincoln Park
Alton Baker Park
CAPITOL HILL
LINCOLN PARK
South Platte R.
Cherry Cr.
C,E RTD
D,F,H RTD
C,D,E,F,H RTD

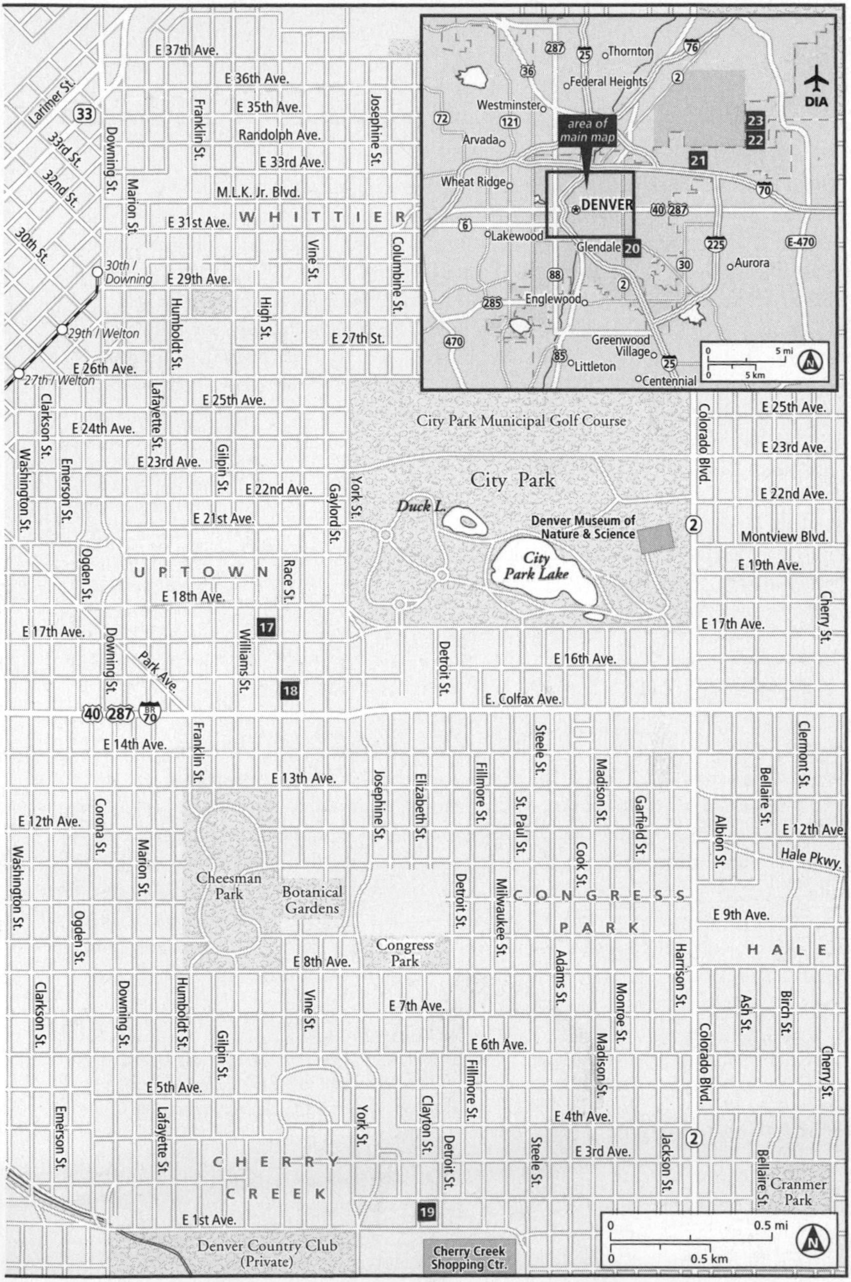

area of main map
DENVER
Thornton
Federal Heights
Westminster
Arvada
Wheat Ridge
Lakewood
Glendale
Aurora
Englewood
Greenwood Village
Littleton
Centennial
DIA
5 mi
5 km
E 37th Ave.
E 36th Ave.
E 35th Ave.
Randolph Ave.
E 33rd Ave.
M.L.K. Jr. Blvd.
E 31st Ave.
E 29th Ave.
E 27th St.
E 26th Ave.
E 25th Ave.
E 24th Ave.
E 23rd Ave.
E 22nd Ave.
E 21st Ave.
E 19th Ave.
E 18th Ave.
E 17th Ave.
E 16th Ave.
E. Colfax Ave.
E 14th Ave.
E 13th Ave.
E 12th Ave.
E 9th Ave.
E 8th Ave.
E 7th Ave.
E 6th Ave.
E 5th Ave.
E 4th Ave.
E 3rd Ave.
E 1st Ave.
Montview Blvd.
Hale Pkwy.
Park Ave.
Larimer St.
33rd St.
32nd St.
30th St.
30th / Downing
29th / Welton
27th / Welton
WHITTIER
UPTOWN
CONGRESS PARK
HALE
CHERRY CREEK
Franklin St.
Josephine St.
Downing St.
Marion St.
Vine St.
Columbine St.
High St.
Humboldt St.
Lafayette St.
Gilpin St.
Gaylord St.
York St.
Race St.
Williams St.
Clarkson St.
Washington St.
Emerson St.
Ogden St.
Corona St.
Elizabeth St.
Detroit St.
Fillmore St.
Steele St.
St. Paul St.
Milwaukee St.
Madison St.
Cook St.
Garfield St.
Adams St.
Monroe St.
Harrison St.
Jackson St.
Clayton St.
Colorado Blvd.
Albion St.
Bellaire St.
Clermont St.
Cherry St.
Ash St.
Birch St.
City Park Municipal Golf Course
City Park
Duck L.
Denver Museum of Nature & Science
City Park Lake
Cheesman Park
Botanical Gardens
Congress Park
Cranmer Park
Denver Country Club (Private)
Cherry Creek Shopping Ctr.
0.5 mi
0.5 km

Fun Facts On the Hoof

If you're in town for the National Western Stock Show, make sure to visit the Brown Palace Hotel for a study in contrasts—the champion steer is traditionally corralled in the lobby during one of the event's final mornings.

Hotel Monaco ★★ Kids Billing itself as "Denver's hippest high-style luxury hotel," the Hotel Monaco is a standout for Kimpton Hotels. With eye-catching interiors inspired equally by Art Deco and French design, the hotel occupies a pair of renovated historic buildings in the heart of the central business district. This is one of the few downtown hotels that is 100% pet friendly—the staff even delivers guests a named goldfish upon request. (The establishment also has a "Director of Pet Relations," a Jack Russell terrier named Lily Sopris.) Rooms have a rich style, equal parts sinful red and snazzy yellow, with perks such as CD stereos, plush animal-print robes, and Starbucks coffee. With jetted tubs, wet bars, and VCRs, the generously sized suites are even more luxurious. You might bump into a celebrity here—the Monaco is a favorite of pro sports teams, rock bands, and Hollywood types, who often stay in the "music suites," named for and decorated after John Lennon, Grace Slick, and Miles Davis. Another perk is the nightly "Altitude Adjustment Hour" in the lobby, where guests enjoy complimentary wine and munchies along with 5-minute massages from the employees of the on-site Aveda Spa.

1717 Champa St. (at 17th St.), Denver, CO 80202. ✆ **800/397-5380** or 303/296-1717. Fax 303/296-1818. www.monaco-denver.com. 189 units. $329–$349 double; from $349 suite. Call for weekend rates. AE, DC, DISC, MC, V. Valet parking $21. Pets accepted. **Amenities:** Restaurant (Panzano; see "Where to Dine," later in this chapter); lounge; exercise room; spa; concierge; 24-hr. room service; in-room massage (for an extra charge); laundry service. *In room:* A/C, cable TV w/pay movies, fax, free Wi-Fi, minibar, fridge, coffeemaker, hair dryer, iron, safe.

Hotel Teatro ★★ Finds Hotel Teatro is one of Denver's most luxurious hotels. It's also the most dramatic: The Denver Center for the Performing Arts (across the street) inspired the decor, which features masks, playbills, and wardrobes from past productions of its resident theater company. The hotel caters to both business and leisure travelers with exquisitely furnished guest rooms that hold Indonesian marble, cherrywood desks and fixtures, and Frette linens and towels. The nine-story building is a historic landmark, constructed as the Denver Tramway Building in 1911. Cutting-edge perks include iPod docking stations and 36-inch plasma-screen TVs in each room. All rooms also feature Aveda amenities and a rainforest shower head. Kevin Taylor, one of Denver's best-known chefs, runs both restaurants and the room service.

1100 14th St. (at Arapahoe St.), Denver, CO 80202. ✆ **303/228-1100.** Fax 303/228-1101. www.hotelteatro.com. 111 units. $269–$399 double; $469–$1,500 suite. AE, DC, DISC, MC, V. Valet parking $24 overnight. Pets accepted. **Amenities:** 2 restaurants (Italian, French); lounge; concierge; courtesy car; 24-hr. room service; massage; laundry service; dry cleaning. *In room:* A/C, cable TV w/pay movies, fax, dataport, free Wi-Fi, minibar, fridge, coffeemaker, hair dryer, iron.

Hyatt Regency Denver ★★ The 37-story Hyatt Regency is the city's crisp new convention center hotel, one of the biggest and best such properties in the Rockies and the first skyscraper to rise in downtown Denver since the early 1980s. With an ideal location—adjacent to the newly expanded Colorado Convention Center and its trademark "Blue Bear" sculpture—and a thorough, modern list of amenities, the Hyatt immediately emerged as the top convention hotel in the Rockies. Showcasing a terrific contemporary art collection with a local bent, the sleek lobby features automated check-in kiosks and the Strata bar. On the 27th floor, another bar, Peaks Lounge, offers the best views downtown. In between, the hotel's guest rooms are contemporary but comfortable, with plush furnishings and an ergonomic workstation. The suites are the biggest downtown, ranging from 500 all the way up to 3,000 square feet.

650 15th St., Denver, CO 80202. ✆ **800/233-1234** or 303/436-1234. Fax 303/436-9102. www.denverregency.hyatt.com. 1,100 units, including 60 suites. $125–$429 double; $550–$5,000 suite. AE, DC, DISC, MC, V. Underground valet parking $24, self-parking $20. **Amenities:** Restaurant (steaks/seafood); 2 lounges; heated indoor pool; health club (weight room, cardiovascular machines); spa; outdoor Jacuzzi; sauna; concierge; car-rental desk; business center; room service (6am–midnight); dry cleaning; executive level. *In room:* A/C, cable TV w/pay movies, free Wi-Fi, fridge, coffeemaker, hair dryer, iron, safe.

Ritz-Carlton, Denver ★★ Opening in early 2008, the Ritz-Carlton is downtown Denver's only household-name luxury hotel (at least until the Four Seasons opens in late 2009). The former Embassy Suites was gutted and rebuilt to Ritz-Carlton's exacting standards and now has a distinctive style and a long list of perks for guests. The plush rooms—at 550 square feet—feature such amenities as steam-free mirrors, iPod-ready clock radios, down comforters, and combination coffee/tea/cappuccino makers. Beyond the rooms, the lavish common areas lead the way to **Elway's,** the downtown sibling to the Denver quarterbacking legend's Cherry Creek steakhouse, a spa, and a fully equipped business center.

1881 Curtis St., Denver, CO 80202. ✆ **303/312-3800.** Fax 303/312-3801. www.ritzcarlton.com. 202 units, including 48 suites. $309–$429 double; $409–$1,200 suite. Weekend rates from $209. AE, DC, DISC, MC, V. Underground valet parking $26, self-parking $15. **Amenities:** Restaurant (steaks); lounge; heated indoor lap pool; health club (weight room, cardiovascular machines, basketball court); spa; concierge; business center; 24-hr. room service; dry cleaning; executive level. *In room:* A/C, cable TV w/pay movies, high-speed Internet access (fee), fridge, coffeemaker, hair dryer, iron, safe.

Expensive

Burnsley All Suite Hotel ★★ Built as an apartment in 1963 but converted into a lodging by an ownership group that included Kirk Douglas and Ella Fitzgerald, this small, elegant hotel offers suites with private balconies and separate living, bedroom, dining, and fully stocked kitchen areas. The units are handsome, featuring marble entrance floors and antiques. The suites are expansive (averaging 700 sq. ft.) and popular with travelers who prefer to be a bit away from the hubbub of downtown. The hotel sits on a relatively quiet one-way street a few blocks southeast of the state capitol. The restaurant serves breakfast, lunch, and dinner on weekdays, and breakfast and dinner on weekends. The lounge is a local favorite, a swank space with live jazz Friday and Saturday. The hotel is conveniently situated near the Cherry Creek shopping areas and is only 5 blocks from downtown.

1000 Grant St. (at E. 10th Ave.), Denver, CO 80203. ✆ **800/231-3915** or 303/830-1000. Fax 303/830-7676. www.burnsley.com. 80 suites. $179–$389 double. Lower weekend rates available. AE, DC, MC, V. Free covered parking. **Amenities:** Restaurant (continental); lounge; seasonal outdoor pool; courtesy car; business center; room service until 10pm; laundry service. *In room:* A/C, cable TV, free Wi-Fi, kitchen, coffeemaker, hair dryer, iron.

The Curtis ★ Finds A convention center lodging reimagined as a pop-culture-themed hotel, the Curtis reopened in 2007, with nostalgic board games in the lobby, floors with various themes (from "The Big Hair Floor" with art of oversized hairdos to "The 13th Floor," the hallway graced by Jack Nicholson's leering mug from *The Shining*), and wakeup calls by Darth Vader and Austin Powers sound-alikes. Featuring a toned-down version of the theme in the hallway, the rooms are modern and outfitted with techie perks like iPod-friendly speaker systems and flatscreen TVs. The staff has a sense of humor and there is a "5 & Dime" store selling toys and candy in the lobby. Corner rooms have fridges and great downtown views.

1405 Curtis St., Denver, CO 80202. ✆ **800/525-6651** or 303/572-3300. Fax 303/825-4301. www.thecurtis.com. 336 units, including 2 suites. $229–$425 double; suites from $450. AE, DC, DISC, MC, V. Valet parking $24, self-parking $15. **Amenities:** Restaurant (seafood); lounge; limited room service; indoor heated pool (large); exercise room; concierge. *In room:* A/C, TV w/DVD player, free Wi-Fi, coffeemaker, hair dryer, iron.

Jet Hotel ★ This contemporary boutique hotel is one of the few lodging options in the lively LoDo neighborhood. Located in a historic redbrick, the property underwent a metamorphosis to the Jet Hotel in the new millennium, newly renovated in 2008. It's sleek and smart, combining the personal service of a B&B with the conveniences of a full-service hotel. The guest rooms are spare studies in efficiency, with perks like CD and DVD players, unique art prints, and large armoires. Some rooms have private balconies and others have jetted tubs; the suite has a copper-topped table and a small kitchen. On weekend nights, the lobby morphs into a popular nightspot. The hotel is entirely non-smoking.

1612 Wazee St., Denver, CO 80202. ✆ **303/572-3300.** Fax 303/623-0773. www.thejethotel.com. 18 units. $169–$199 double; $211–$299 suite. Rates include complimentary continental breakfast. AE, DC, DISC, MC, V. Parking $10. **Amenities:** 2 restaurants (cafe, eclectic); lounge; exercise room; concierge; limited room service. *In room:* A/C, TV w/DVD player, free Wi-Fi, kitchenette, coffeemaker, hair dryer, iron.

Oxford Hotel ★ Finds Designed by the architect Frank Edbrooke and listed on the National Register of Historic Places, this is one of Denver's few hotels to have survived from the 19th century (another being the Brown Palace, described above). The facade is simple red sandstone, but the interior boasts marble walls, stained-glass windows, frescoes, and silver chandeliers, all of which were restored between 1979 and 1983 using Edbrooke's original drawings.

Antique pieces imported from England and France furnish the large rooms, which were created by combining smaller rooms during the restoration. No two units are alike (they're either Art Deco or Western Victorian in style), but all are equipped with one king or queen bed, individual thermostats, dressing tables, and large closets.

An Art Deco gem, the Cruise Room Bar boasts perhaps the swankest cocktail atmosphere in Denver, and the spa is the largest in the area.

1600 17th St. (at Wazee St.), Denver, CO 80202. ✆ **800/228-5838** or 303/628-5400. Fax 303/628-5413. www.theoxfordhotel.com. 80 units. $230–$300 double; $370–$500 suite. AE, DC, DISC, MC, V. Valet parking $21. **Amenities:** Restaurant (McCormick's Fish House & Bar; see "Where to Dine," later in this chapter); 2 lounges; exercise room; spa (w/Jacuzzi and sauna); concierge; courtesy car; salon; 24-hr. room service; massage; laundry service; dry cleaning. *In room:* A/C, TV, free Wi-Fi, minibar, hair dryer, iron.

The Warwick ★★ One of five Warwicks in the United States (the others are in New York, San Francisco, Dallas, and Seattle), this handsome midsize choice boasts an exterior and rooms reminiscent of hotels in Paris, where the corporate office is located. In contrast, the earth-tone lobby stylishly reflects the region, with classic European design, contemporary Western furnishings, and slate and red-stone stonework.

Similarly stylish, every room features a full private balcony with a great city view, and most are equipped with a fridge and wet bar. Each has one king- or two full-size beds, contemporary mahogany furniture, floral prints on the walls, cable TV (with pay-per-view movies), and two incoming phone lines. The standard rooms are very spacious, averaging 450 square feet each, and the 60 suites, which range from two-room parlor suites to grand luxury suites, are even more so.

1776 Grant St. (at E. 18th Ave.), Denver, CO 80203. ✆ **800/525-2888** or 303/861-2000. Fax 303/832-0320. www.warwickdenver.com. 220 units, including 60 suites. $189–$379 double; $269–$1,000 suite. Weekend rates $139–$209 double; from $195 suite. Children 17 and under stay free in parent's room. AE, DC, DISC, MC, V. Valet parking $15 per day, self-parking $12 per day, both underground. **Amenities:** Restaurant (contemporary); lounge; rooftop heated pool; exercise room; concierge; courtesy town car; business center; 24-hr. room service; laundry service. *In room:* A/C, cable TV w/pay movies, dataport, coffeemaker, hair dryer, iron, safe.

Bed & Breakfasts

Those seeking an alternative to a hotel or motel might consider one of Denver's many bed-and-breakfast inns. Often located in historic 19th-century homes, bed-and-breakfasts offer a more personalized lodging experience than you could expect in all but the very best hotels, because you rarely find more than 10 rooms in a B&B, and you are, literally, a guest in someone's home.

Capitol Hill Mansion Bed & Breakfast ★★ Located on Denver's "Mansion Row" just southeast of downtown and the State Capitol, this turreted B&B exemplifies Richardsonian Romanesque design with its ruby sandstone exterior and curving front porch. Built in 1891, the mansion is listed on the National Register of Historic Places and has the original woodwork and stained glass.

The inn is outfitted for the 21st century, with refrigerators, color TVs, and wireless Internet access. Each individually decorated room is named after a Colorado wildflower; some feature two-person Jacuzzi tubs, fireplaces, and private balconies. The elegant Elk Thistle Suite, on the third floor, features a panoramic view of the Rockies, a claw-foot tub, and a kitchen. Honeymooners might enjoy the second-floor Shooting Star Balcony Room, which has a separate whirlpool tub and shower, and a private balcony with a city view.

Breakfasts include such items as crème brûlée French toast and pecan bread pudding. Smoking is not permitted inside the inn.

1207 Pennsylvania St., Denver, CO 80203. ✆ **800/839-9329** outside 303 and 720 area codes, or 303/839-5221. www.capitolhillmansion.com. 8 units. $114–$179 double; $159–$199 suite. Rates include full breakfast and evening wine and refreshments. AE, DC, DISC, MC, V. Free off-street parking. *In room:* A/C, cable TV, free Wi-Fi, fridge, coffeemaker, hair dryer, iron.

Castle Marne Bed & Breakfast ★★ A National Historic Landmark, Castle Marne is an impressive stone fortress designed and built in 1889 by the renowned architect William Lang for a contemporary silver baron. It was so named because a subsequent owner's son fought in the Battle of the Marne during World War I.

The inn is furnished with antiques, fine reproductions, and family heirlooms. Three rooms have private balconies with hot tubs. Three rooms have old-fashioned bathrooms with pedestal sinks and cast-iron claw-foot tubs. A gourmet breakfast (two seatings) is served in the original formal dining room, and a proper afternoon tea is served daily in the parlor. There are also a computer and printer for guest use. Smoking is not permitted, but well-behaved kids over 10 are welcome.

1572 Race St., Denver, CO 80206. ✆ **800/92-MARNE** (800/926-2763) or 303/331-0621 for reservations. Fax 303/331-0623. www.castlemarne.com. 9 units. $95–$235 double; $210–$270 suite. Rates include full breakfast and afternoon tea. AE, DC, DISC, MC, V. Free off-street parking. *In room:* A/C, free Wi-Fi.

Kids Family-Friendly Hotels

Hotel Monaco (p. 82) Kids get a kick out of the colorful decor, the complimentary goldfish, and the house mascot, a Jack Russell terrier named Lily Sopris.

JW Marriott (p. 87) This Cherry Creek hostelry is right in the vicinity of the bike trail, the mall, and other kid-friendly attractions, and has plenty of perks to keep the kids occupied when they're in their rooms.

Loews Denver Hotel (p. 87) Kids get a teddy bear and coloring books when they arrive; the Tuscany Restaurant has a special children's menu.

Lumber Baron ★ Finds After buying this turreted mansion in Denver's Highlands neighborhood on April Fool's Day 1991, Walt Keller began a 4-year, $1.5-million renovation. Built in 1890 by lumber baron John Mouat (hence the name), the 8,500-square-foot house held many surprises: myriad ornate wood fixtures (cherry, poplar, maple, and oak, to name a few) and a once-hidden third-story ballroom under an ornate pyramidal dome. Featuring flatscreen TVs and jetted tubs, the rooms have antique furnishings from around the world and unique themes: The Honeymoon Suite has a neoclassical bent, a four-poster mahogany queen bed, and a gargantuan mirror; and the Mary Ann Keller Suite (named for Walt's mother) has a garden motif with historic photos and intricate Anglo-Japanese wallpapering. For those seeking entertainment, the Lumber Baron hosts 50 "murder mystery parties" annually for $37 (dinner included; two-for-one pricing for guests), comedic events with a handful of actors among the 50 to 100 partygoers.

2555 W. 37th Ave., Denver, CO 80211. ✆ **303/477-8205.** Fax 303/477-0269. www.lumberbaron.com. 5 units. $149 double; $199–$239 suite. Much lower weekday rates. Rates include full breakfast. AE, DISC, MC, V. *In room:* A/C, hair dryer, iron.

Queen Anne Bed & Breakfast Inn ★★ A favorite of both business travelers and couples, the Queen Anne might be considered the perfect bed-and-breakfast in the perfect home. It consists of two Victorian houses: one built by the well-known architect Frank Edbrooke in 1879, and the other built in 1886, now featuring piped-in chamber music, fresh flowers, and wireless Internet access. Each of the 10 double rooms in the 1879 Pierce-Tabor House is decorated with period antiques. Three rooms have original murals: All four walls of the Aspen Room are filled with (what else?) aspen trees, the third-floor Park Room overlooks a park and has a mural depicting the view that visitors would have seen in 1879, and the Rooftop Room has an outdoor hot-tub deck with a superb skyline view. Each of the four two-room suites in the adjacent 1886 Roberts house is dedicated to a famous artist (Norman Rockwell, Frederic Remington, John Audubon, and Alexander Calder). The suites have deep soaking tubs, and the Remington suite has a hot tub. Half of the rooms have cable television. Located in the Clements Historic District, the Queen Anne borders downtown Denver and is within easy walking distance of the major attractions. Smoking is not permitted.

2147–51 Tremont Place, Denver, CO 80205. ✆ **800/432-4667** or 303/296-6666. Fax 303/296-2151. www.queenannebnb.com. 14 units. $135–$185 double; $215 suite. Rates include hot breakfast and Colorado wine each evening. AE, DC, DISC, MC, V. Free off-street parking. *In room:* A/C, free Wi-Fi.

OUTSIDE DOWNTOWN

Very Expensive

JW Marriott ★★ Kids Opened in 2004, the high-end JW Marriott was the first hotel in the Cherry Creek neighborhood, and it was well worth the wait. Sumptuous interiors and bold primary colors make for a distinctive ambience, and the attention to detail is excellent. The little touches are what this hotel is all about: jumbo flatscreen, high-definition TVs with DVD players; spectacular views; big bathrooms with granite aplenty; user-friendly thermostats; and excellent service. For shoppers, it's beyond ideal, a block from the Cherry Creek Mall and surrounded by chic retailers of all stripes. The standout amenities: Second Home Kitchen and Bar, a sleek eatery; a huge exercise room; a 9,300-square-foot day spa; and an upscale shopping arcade. The hotel is also very close to the Cherry Creek bike path.

150 Clayton Lane, Denver, CO 80206. ✆ **866/706-7814** or 303/316-2700. Fax 303/316-4697. www.jwmarriottdenver.com. 196 units. $309–$379 double; $599–$1,200 suite; weekend rates from $199. AE, DC, DISC, MC, V. Pets accepted. **Amenities:** Restaurant (Mirepoix; see "Where to Dine," below); lounge; exercise room; spa; 2 outdoor Jacuzzis; concierge; courtesy car; business center; shopping arcade; salon; 24-hr. room service; massage; coin-op washers and dryers; dry cleaning; executive level. *In room:* A/C, cable TV w/pay movies and DVD player, dataport (w/high-speed Internet access), minibar, coffeemaker, hair dryer, iron, safe.

Expensive

Loews Denver Hotel ★★ Kids Located just east of Colorado Boulevard and south of Cherry Creek, the Loews Denver's sleek, towering exterior is black steel with a reflecting glass tower. Inside, it's bella Italia, with columns finished in imitation marble, and Renaissance-style murals and paintings that look 500 years old. The location, about a 15-minute drive from downtown, is good for those who want access to scattered attractions or the Denver Tech Center. Throughout the hotel, much use has been made of floral patterns, Italian silk wall coverings, and marble-top furnishings. All the spacious rooms have elegant decor, and they include all the business perks any traveler could want: at least three phones, wireless Internet access, and a fax machine. The resident eatery, the Tuscany, is excellent.

4150 E. Mississippi Ave., Denver, CO 80246. ✆ **800/345-9172** or 303/782-9300. Fax 303/758-6542. www.loewshotels.com. 200 units, including 18 suites. $119–$239 double; $239–$389 suite; weekend rates from $99. Children 17 and under stay free in parent's room. AE, DC, DISC, MC, V. Free valet and self-parking. Pets accepted. **Amenities:** Restaurant (Mediterranean); lounge; exercise room; access to nearby health club; concierge; courtesy van; business center; secretarial services; 24-hr. room service; massage; laundry service; dry cleaning; business traveler rooms. *In room:* A/C, cable TV w/pay movies, free Wi-Fi, minibar, coffeemaker, hair dryer, iron, safe.

Moderate

The Timbers Hotel ★ Value About midway between the Colorado State Capitol and Denver International Airport, the Timbers is my pick for a slick place to hang your hat east of downtown. That means the rates are lower than in central Denver, but the style is just as high: The place exudes contemporary Western ambience, hitting the right notes between colorful and comfortable. Each room is dubbed a suite, but only the one-bedroom suites actually have separate bedrooms and living areas. Done up in earth tones and plenty of hardwood, the executive studio suites have kitchens, but they are smaller one-room units without a separate bedroom; the studio suites are one-room units with one king or two queens and a fridge and a microwave. Most rooms have private patios or balconies.

4411 Peoria St., Denver, CO 80239. ✆ **800/844-9404** or 303/373-1444. Fax 303/373-1975. www.timbersdenver.com. 127 units. $119–$209 studio suite; $159–$259 1-bedroom suite. Lower weekend and off-season rates. Rates include complimentary continental breakfast. AE, DISC, MC, V. Free self-parking. **Amenities:** Restaurant (American); lounge; indoor and outdoor pools; exercise room; 2 Jacuzzis; sauna; courtesy airport shuttle; business center; 24-hr. room service; complimentary washers and dryers; dry cleaning. *In room:* A/C, cable TV w/pay movies, free Wi-Fi, kitchen, minibar, coffeemaker, hair dryer, iron.

Inexpensive

Innkeeper of the Rockies *Value* This centrally located hostel moved to spiffy new digs in 2005, about 2 miles east of downtown. Now housed in a converted 1905 apartment building—along with private rooms at a nearby house—the hostel is a clean and convenient choice. Facilities include a community kitchen, laundry machines, Internet access, and barbecue grills. There are two men's rooms, two women's rooms, and two co-ed rooms, each with six bunks.

1717 Race St., Denver, CO 80206. ✆ **303/861-7777.** Fax 720/225-9321. www.innkeeperrockies.com. 36 beds, 4 private units. $20 per person; $43 private double. AE, DISC, MC, V. Free street parking. **Amenities:** Complimentary Internet access; coin-op laundry. *In room:* No phone.

CAMPING

Chatfield State Park ★ On the south side of Denver, 1 mile south of the intersection of Colo. 121 (Wadsworth) and Colo. 470, Chatfield has a 1,550-acre reservoir with ample opportunities for boating, water-skiing, fishing, and swimming, plus around 20 miles of trails for horseback riding, mountain biking, and hiking. Facilities include hot showers, picnic areas, a dump station, boat ramps and rentals, and full hookups.

11500 N. Roxborough Park Rd., Littleton, CO 80125. ✆ **303/791-7275,** or 800/678-2267 for state park reservation service (outside Denver) or 303/4170-1144. www.parks.state.co.us. 197 sites. $18–$22, plus $8 for reservations fee and $7 day-use fee. MC, V only for advance reservations.

Chief Hosa Campground Those seeking the amenities and easy accessibility of a commercial campground close to Denver will find a nice (but often quite busy) campground at this long-standing establishment 20 miles west of Denver. There are tent and RV sites, and most of the latter have electric and water hookups. When it opened in 1913, the south campground here was dubbed "America's First Motor-Camping Area." The campground is open year-round. The amenities include showers, grills, and a volleyball court.

27661 Genessee Dr., Golden, CO 80401. ✆ **303/526-1324.** www.chiefhosa.org. 61 sites. $22–$26. AE, DC, DISC, MC, V. Just off I-70, exit 253, 20 miles west of Denver.

4 WHERE TO DINE

Denver abounds with Mexican hole-in-the-walls, chain eateries, steak joints, and even a few bison joints, and the restaurants in LoDo and Cherry Creek become more like those in Los Angeles and Manhattan every year. Below, I've primarily listed independent restaurants, unique to this area and a cut above others in their price ranges.

DOWNTOWN

Very Expensive

Buckhorn Exchange ★★ ROCKY MOUNTAIN In the same rickety premises where it was established in 1893, this landmark restaurant displays its Colorado Liquor

License No. 1 above the 140-year-old bar in the upstairs saloon. On the first level, the densely decorated dining room, dominated by a daunting menagerie of taxidermy, will alarm vegetarians, but meat lovers will not be disappointed. The Buckhorn's game dishes (slow-roasted buffalo prime rib, lean and served medium rare; elk; and quail) are the best in the city. The beefsteaks, ranging from 8-ounce tenderloins to 64-ounce table steaks for five, are also quite good. With fried alligator tail, Rocky Mountain oysters, and smoked buffalo sausage among the options, the appetizers will surely broaden one's palate. My recommendation: rattlesnake, served in cream cheese–chipotle dip with tricolor tortilla chips. For dessert, try a slab of hot Dutch apple pie—if you have room. Lunch is lighter and more affordable, with an assortment of charbroiled meat entrees, sandwiches, and hearty homemade soups. A mile southwest of the State Capitol, the Buckhorn has its own light-rail stop, making it a fun and easy trip from downtown.

1000 Osage St. (at W. 10th Ave.). ✆ **303/534-9505.** www.buckhorn.com. Reservations recommended. Main courses $8–$16 lunch, $18–$44 dinner. AE, DC, DISC, MC, V. Mon–Fri 11am–2pm; Mon–Thurs 5:30–9pm; Fri–Sat 5–10pm; Sun 5–9pm. Bar all day. Light rail: Osage.

Palace Arms ★★ CONTINENTAL/REGIONAL Despite its dramatic Napoleonic decor—antiques dating from 1700s include a dispatch case and a pair of dueling pistols that may have belonged to Napoleon—the Palace Arms' cuisine is a combination of traditional American, contemporary regional, Mediterranean, and Japanese influences. To begin, the Caesar salad is superb, prepared tableside for two. For an excellent main course, try the Wagyu Master premium Japanese beef ($20 an oz.), lobster with ravioli and vegetables, or truffled Colorado bison. The wine list has received *Wine Spectator*'s "Best Of" award.

In the Brown Palace Hotel (p. 79), 321 17th St. ✆ **303/297-3111.** www.brownpalace.com. Reservations recommended. Main courses $40–$100 dinner. AE, DC, DISC, MC, V. Daily 6–10pm.

Expensive

Bistro Vendome ★★ FRENCH BISTRO Across the street from sister eatery Rioja (see below), Bistro Vendome serves up splendid interpretations of Gallic standbys (dubbed "French soul food") in an intimate space on Larimer Square. The house interpretations of lamb, poultry, and veal dishes mix tradition and invention, and there is always a vegetarian plate on the menu. The pomme frites (aka french fries) are also beloved by locals, and the side dishes and desserts don't disappoint. Brunch brings crepes, quiches, and eggs Benedict. The patio is one of the best in Denver.

1424-H Larimer Sq. ✆ **303/825-3232.** www.bistrovendome.com. Reservations accepted. Main courses $7–$13 brunch, $16–$23 dinner. AE, DC, DISC, MC, V. Mon–Thurs 5–10pm; Fri–Sat 5–11pm; Sun 5–9pm; brunch Sat–Sun 10am–2pm.

Denver ChopHouse & Brewery ★ STEAKS A LoDo mainstay since it opened alongside Coors Field in 1995, this is one of the Mile High City's best places for carnivores. Set in the steeped brick-and-wood atmosphere of a restored early-19th-century train depot, the ChopHouse does classic meat and potatoes (not to mention microbrews) as well as anybody in town. My picks are always the juicy steaks, from filet mignon to New York strip, and the other hearty classics, such as huge, cheese-stuffed pork chops and herb-crusted racks of lamb; white cheddar mashers are my side of choice. The restaurant also serves a nice selection of fresh seafood and some less expensive sandwiches and pizzas, and even a few vegetarian items.

1735 19th St. ✆ **303/296-0800.** www.chophouse.com. Reservations recommended for dinner. Main courses $11–$36. AE, DC, MC, V. Mon–Thurs 11am–11pm; Fri–Sat 11am–midnight; Sun 11am–10pm.

Denver Dining

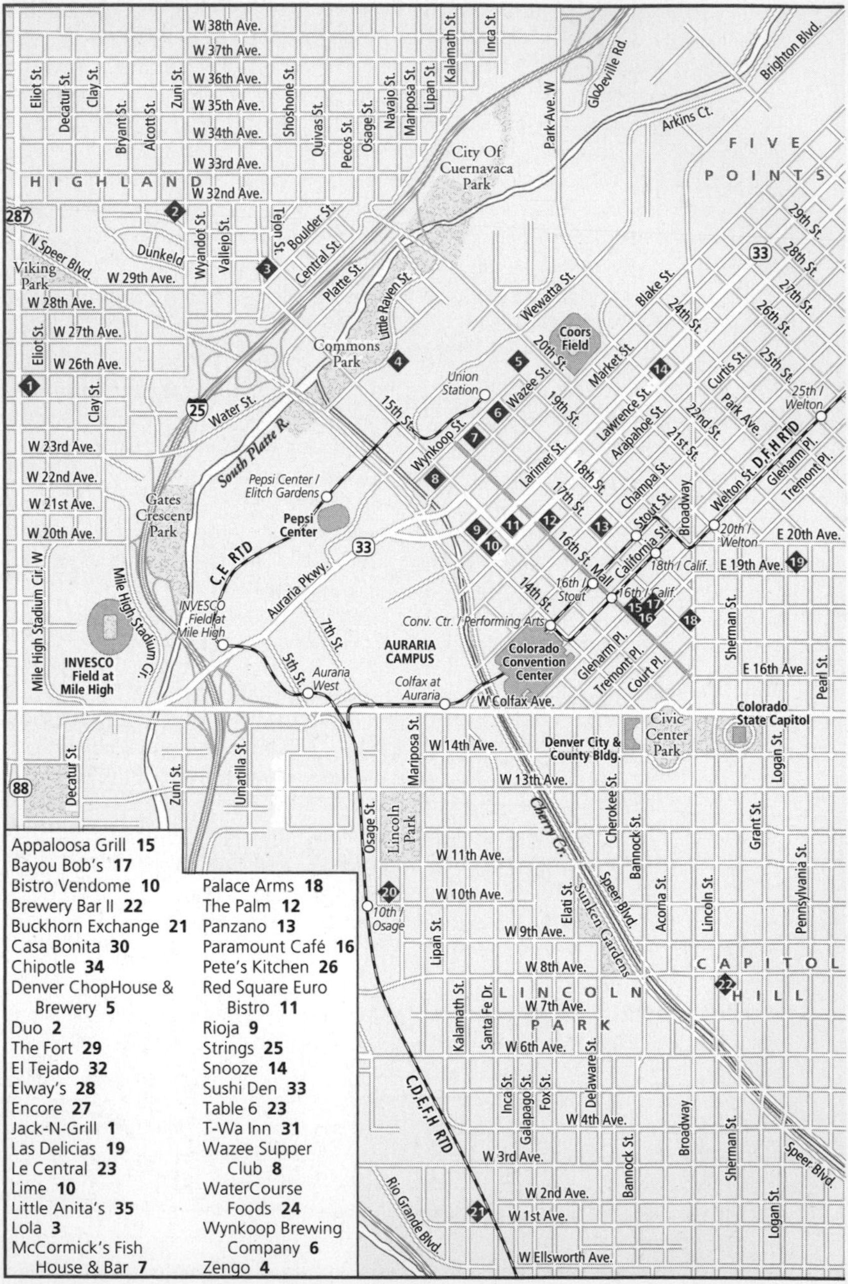

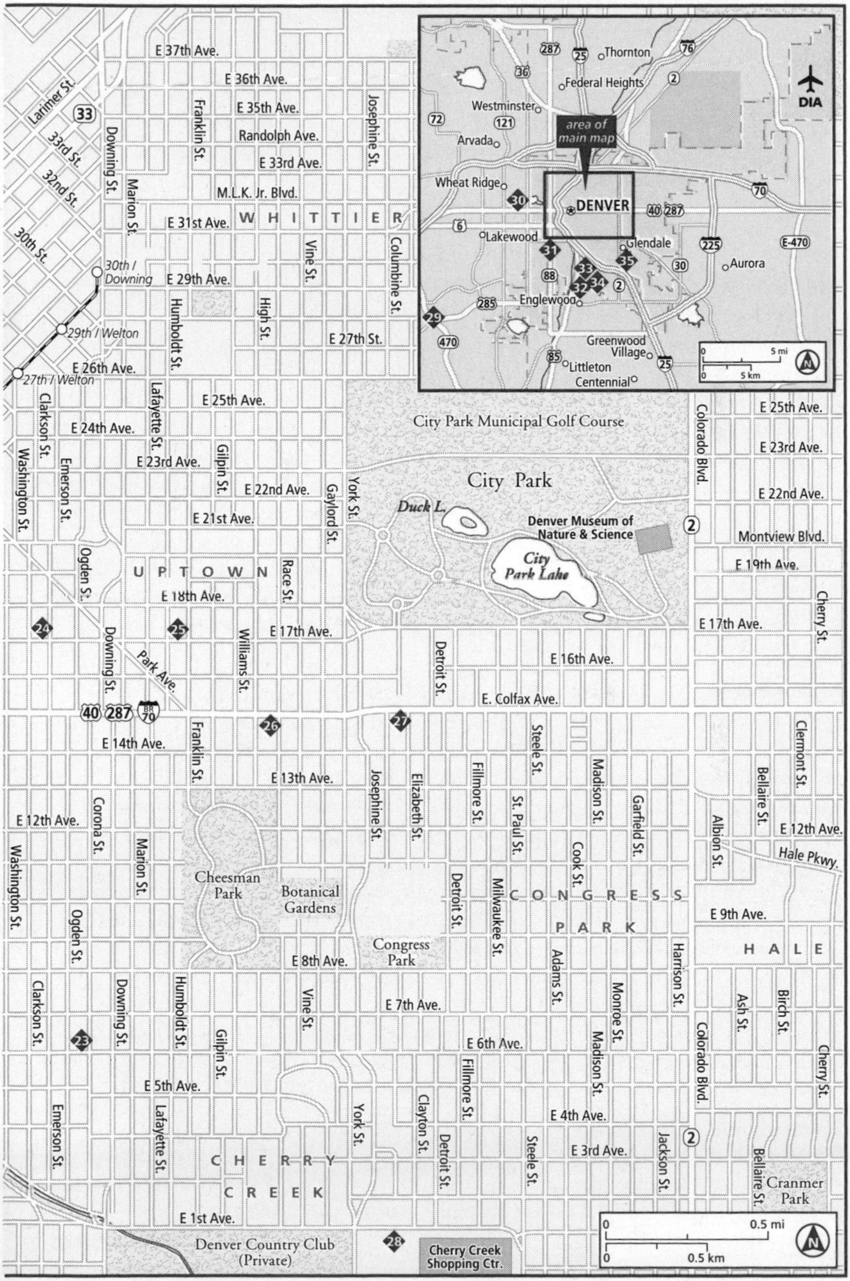

E 37th Ave.
E 36th Ave.
E 35th Ave.
Randolph Ave.
E 33rd Ave.
M.L.K. Jr. Blvd.
E 31st Ave.
WHITTIER
E 29th Ave.
E 27th St.
E 26th Ave.
E 25th Ave.
E 24th Ave.
E 23rd Ave.
E 22nd Ave.
E 21st Ave.
UPTOWN
E 18th Ave.
E 17th Ave.
E 16th Ave.
E. Colfax Ave.
E 14th Ave.
E 13th Ave.
E 12th Ave.
E 9th Ave.
E 8th Ave.
E 7th Ave.
E 6th Ave.
E 5th Ave.
E 4th Ave.
E 3rd Ave.
E 1st Ave.
Larimer St.
33rd St.
32nd St.
30th St.
30th / Downing
29th / Welton
27th / Welton
Downing St.
Marion St.
Franklin St.
Josephine St.
Vine St.
Columbine St.
Humboldt St.
High St.
Lafayette St.
Clarkson St.
Washington St.
Emerson St.
Gilpin St.
Gaylord St.
York St.
Ogden St.
Race St.
Williams St.
Park Ave.
Detroit St.
Elizabeth St.
Fillmore St.
Steele St.
St. Paul St.
Madison St.
Garfield St.
Cook St.
Milwaukee St.
Adams St.
Monroe St.
Harrison St.
Colorado Blvd.
Albion St.
Bellaire St.
Clermont St.
Cherry St.
Ash St.
Birch St.
Corona St.
Clayton St.
Jackson St.
City Park Municipal Golf Course
City Park
Duck L.
City Park Lake
Denver Museum of Nature & Science
E 25th Ave.
E 23rd Ave.
E 22nd Ave.
Montview Blvd.
E 19th Ave.
E 17th Ave.
E 12th Ave.
Hale Pkwy.
HALE
Cheesman Park
Botanical Gardens
Congress Park
CONGRESS PARK
CHERRY CREEK
Cranmer Park
Denver Country Club (Private)
Cherry Creek Shopping Ctr.
0 0.5 mi
0 0.5 km
Thornton
Federal Heights
Westminster
Arvada
Wheat Ridge
DENVER
Lakewood
Glendale
Aurora
Englewood
Greenwood Village
Littleton
Centennial
DIA
area of main map
0 5 mi
0 5 km

Kids Family-Friendly Restaurants

Casa Bonita (p. 98) If the kids aren't concentrating on the tacos, the puppet shows, high divers, fun house, and video arcade will enthrall them.

Wynkoop Brewing Company (p. 94) With a dining area separate from the bar, this pub and restaurant has a loud, bustling atmosphere and plenty of kid-friendly menu options.

The Palm ★ ITALIAN/STEAK/SEAFOOD Pio Bozzi and John Ganzi opened the first Palm restaurant in New York City in 1926. It originally specialized in cuisine from their hometown of Parma, Italy, but whenever a customer requested steak, Ganzi ran to a nearby butcher shop, bought a steak, and cooked it to order. This eventually led to the Palm's having its own meat wholesale company to ensure the quality of its steaks. The current third-generation owners introduced seafood to the menu and expanded the business by opening a dozen more restaurants across the country. Most famous for its prime cuts of beef and live Nova Scotia lobsters, the Palm celebrates tradition, with some of Ganzi's original Italian dishes still popular (and cheaper) items on the menu. The dining room is plastered with caricatures of local celebrities; customers are seated at either booths or tables.

In the Westin at Tabor Center, 1672 Lawrence St. ✆ **303/825-7256.** www.thepalm.com. Reservations recommended. Main courses $9–$22 lunch, $20–$55 dinner. AE, DC, DISC, MC, V. Mon–Fri 11am–11pm; Sat 5–11pm; Sun 5–10pm.

Panzano ★★ CONTEMPORARY ITALIAN The Hotel Monaco's resident eatery is one of the best Italian restaurants in town. Served in a densely decorated dining room with a busy open kitchen, chef Elise Wiggins's menu changes regularly but employs both traditional preparations and inventive variations of Italian plates. You'll likely find the signature *buridda,* a Genovese seafood stew with mussels, calamari, and shrimp in a savory lobster broth; *capesante,* scallops with citrus-fennel-cheese ravioli; and an array of pastas prepared fresh in-house daily. There are also innovative variations on steak, poultry, soups, and salads, which change according to available ingredients: In the summer, for example, a sweet-corn soup appears on the menu. For dessert, don't pass on the tiramisu, which manages to be heavenly and sinful at once. With lighter, similar fare (including killer salads), lunch attracts power meetings. Happy hours are good for getting small portions of the dinner specialties.

In Hotel Monaco (p. 82), 909 17th St. ✆ **303/296-3525.** www.panzano-denver.com. Reservations recommended. Main courses $6–$20 breakfast and brunch, $9–$23 lunch, $17–$30 dinner. AE, DC, DISC, MC, V. Mon–Fri 7–10am and 11am–2:30pm; Mon–Thurs 5–10pm; Fri–Sat 5–11pm; Sat–Sun 8am–2:30pm; Sun 4:30–9:30pm. Closed Thanksgiving and Christmas.

Rioja ★★★ CONTEMPORARY MEDITERRANEAN Chef-owner Jennifer Jasinski emerged as Denver's most creatively inspired restaurateur since opening Rioja in 2004. In the time since, the slick Larimer Square eatery has become a national standout, a critical darling, and my pick for dinner in downtown Denver. With a copper-topped bar and an atmosphere that's formal without being stuffy, Rioja is the perfect vehicle for

Jasinski's menu of contrasting flavors and textures. Offerings range from fresh bacon and cardamom-spiced pork belly to curried cauliflower soup served with fresh apple salad to grilled Colorado lamb. Jasinski keeps the menu fresh, but you'll always get a selection of her delectable handmade pastas for dinner—the artichoke tortellini is my pick—and truly transcendent beignets for dessert.

1431 Larimer Sq. ✆ **303/820-2282.** www.riojadenver.com. Reservations recommended. Main courses $10–$20 brunch and lunch, $16–$30 dinner. AE, DISC, MC, V. Wed–Fri 11:30am–2:30pm; Sat–Sun 10am–2:30pm; Sun–Thurs 5–10pm; Fri–Sat Sat 5–11pm.

Strings ★★ CONTEMPORARY Open for 20 years in Denver's Uptown neighborhood, Strings attracts a hip crowd of loyal locals, as well as visiting celebrities who contribute to a wall of autographed photos. Popular and typically crowded, the restaurant welcomes guests in T-shirts as well as tuxedos; it's especially busy during the before- and after-theater hours. The menu focuses on "New American" cuisine, creative noodle dishes, and fresh seafood—such as cashew-crusted sea bass with saffron couscous and vanilla bean butter. Lunch and dinner specials change weekly to match the season and the mood of the chef. Strings has an outdoor patio for summer dining.

1700 Humboldt St. (at E. 17th Ave.). ✆ **303/831-7310.** www.stringsrestaurant.com. Reservations recommended. Main courses $9–$25 lunch, $14–$35 dinner. AE, DISC, MC, V. Mon–Fri 11am–10pm; Sat 5–10:30pm; Sun 5–9pm.

Zengo ★ LATIN/ASIAN With a menu that runs the gamut from dim sum and sushi to empanadas and ceviche, Zengo—Japanese for "give and take"—is the standout eatery in the booming Riverfront area just west of LoDo. Under the guidance of chef Richard Sandoval (who also owns restaurants in New York, San Francisco, Las Vegas, and elsewhere, as well as Tamayo in Denver), the restaurant is a favorite of the young and hip, and just the place to see and be seen. The colorful contemporary decor matches the lively social scene and the vibrant dishes. Entrees are often Latin-Asian fusions, such as miso-chipotle soup, achiote barbecue salmon, and Szechuan-grilled pork loin with sweet corn salsa. Lunch includes dim sum, sushi, ensaladas, and tortas. There are also numerous vegetarian options.

1610 Little Raven St. ✆ **720/904-0965.** www.modernmexican.com. Reservations recommended. Main courses $16–$28. AE, DISC, MC, V. Sun–Thurs 5–10pm; Fri–Sat 5–11pm; Sat–Sun 11am–3pm. Bar later.

Moderate

Appaloosa Grill CONTEMPORARY/ECLECTIC The employee-owned Appaloosa features an eclectic menu, merging Asian, Southwestern, and bar grub. The ribs are a good bet, as are the tamales, and the all-natural Highland Heritage steaks, originating in the Rockies. The lunch menu includes salads, sandwiches, and assorted lighter entrees. With a casual, semi-intimate atmosphere and a handsome antique bar, this is a good place for dinner to morph into a night on the town. The bar menu is available until 1am and there is live musical entertainment nightly.

535 16th St. Mall (at Welton St.). ✆ **720/932-1700.** www.appaloosagrill.com. Main courses $9–$12 lunch, $9–$32 dinner. AE, DISC, MC, V. Daily 11am–1am. Bar open later.

Le Central ★ (Value) FRENCH Seven blocks south of the Colorado State Capitol, Le Central is a romantic restaurant that since 1980 has prided itself on creating French dishes that are both top quality and affordable. Housed in an aged urban structure with a distinctive European vibe, the restaurant changes its menus daily, but you can always expect to find a selection of fresh chicken, pork, beef, lamb, and seafood. They're available grilled, sautéed, or roasted and finished with some of the tastiest sauces this side of Provence. Bouillabaisse and paella are usually available, and every menu features a vegetarian dish. Shellfish fanatics, take note: Le Central's mussel menu is legendary, and served with all the french fries you can eat.

112 E. 8th Ave. (at Lincoln St.). ✆ **303/863-8094.** www.lecentral.com. Reservations recommended. Main courses $7–$14 lunch, $14–$22 dinner. AE, DC, DISC, MC, V. Mon–Fri 11:30am–2:15pm; Sat–Sun 11am–2pm; Mon–Thurs 5:30–10pm; Fri–Sat 5–10pm; Sun 5–9pm.

McCormick's Fish House & Bar ★ SEAFOOD In lower downtown's historic Oxford Hotel, McCormick's maintains a late-19th-century feel with stained-glass windows, oak booths, and a fine polished-wood bar. Come here for the best seafood in town—it's flown in daily and might include Alaskan salmon and halibut, mussels from Florida, lobsters from Maine, Hawaiian mahimahi, red rockfish from Oregon, and trout from Idaho. The menu also offers pasta, chicken, and a full line of prime beef. Across the hall, the Corner Bar's happy hour (served 3–6pm every day and 10pm–midnight on Fri and Sat) is legendary, featuring $1.95-to-$4.95 crab cakes, cheeseburgers, and steamed mussels. There is breakfast service from the same kitchen at the adjacent bar from 7am until 10:30am daily.

In the Oxford Hotel (p. 84), 1659 Wazee St. ✆ **303/825-1107.** www.msmg.com. Reservations recommended. Lunch and light dishes $7–$17; dinner $17–$35. AE, DC, DISC, MC, V. Mon–Fri 11am–2pm; Sun–Thurs 5–10pm; Fri–Sat 5–11pm.

Red Square Euro Bistro ★★ RUSSIAN/CONTEMPORARY After the Little Russian Café closed in 2003, its all-Russian staff reunited under owner Steve Ryan and opened Red Square. They did their old place one better, with a rich red interior, tucked-away patio, contemporary Russian art, and a vodka bar stocked with infusions made in-house (ranging from raspberry to garlic) and about 100 brands from 17 countries, including Russia, Holland, Poland, Sweden, and even Mexico. The excellent entrees are not purely Russian: The steak stroganoff has a salmon counterpart, the menu has Asian and French influences, and the appetizers include pâté and Dungeness crab ravioli. But there is borscht (cold in summer, hot in winter), a roasted Russian wild boar chop, and, of course, the vodka—lots and lots of vodka.

1512 Larimer St. at Writer Sq. ✆ **303/595-8600.** www.redsquarebistro.com. Main courses $16–$23. AE, DC, DISC, MC, V. Daily 5–10pm. Bar open later.

Wynkoop Brewing Company ★ Kids REGIONAL AMERICAN/PUB Denver's biggest and best brewpub took on an even more esteemed significance in 2003 when founder John Hickenlooper took office as the mayor of Denver. ("Hick" sold his restaurants to an employee group after taking office.) Occupying a renovated warehouse across from Union Station and close to Coors Field, the Wynkoop is one of the country's model microbreweries and even served as a catalyst for the rebirth of surrounding LoDo. The menu offers pub fare, sandwiches, soups, and salads, plus dinners of steak, chicken burritos, bangers and mash, and buffalo meatloaf—not to mention a nice variety of beers on tap, including a spicy standout in Patty's Chile Beer. See also "Denver After Dark," in chapter 7.

1634 18th St. (at Wynkoop St.). ✆ **303/297-2700.** www.wynkoop.com. Reservations recommended for large parties. Main courses $9–$22. AE, DC, DISC, MC, V. Mon–Thurs 11am–11pm; Fri–Sat 11am–midnight; Sun 11am–10pm. Bar open later.

Tips A Good City for Green Chile Fiends

Green chile (green *chil*-ee) *n.* A fiery-sweet stew made of chile peppers and other ingredients, often but not always including chunks of pork, tomato, and onion. Denver's eateries serve bowl after bowl of good green chile, stuff that ranges from merely spicy to flat-out nuclear. If you have a serious weakness for a bowl of green (as I do), here are six hot spots in the Mile High City, in no particular order:

1. **Las Delicias,** 439 E. 19th Ave. (✆ **303/839-5675**): A Denver tradition, Las Delicias serves up some of the city's best green chile from its downtown location among its four metro-area eateries.
2. **Brewery Bar II,** 150 Kalamath St. (✆ **303/893-0971**): Inconspicuously nestled in a warehouse district, the Brewery Bar serves up some of the hottest green chile in Denver. It also happens to be some of the tastiest.
3. **Jack-N-Grill,** 2524 N. Federal Blvd. (✆ **303/964-9544**): Sweet and typically served in a bowl with beans, Jack Martinez's green chile is excellent, as is his red.
4. **Little Anita's,** 1550 S. Colorado Blvd. (✆ **303/691-3337**): Relatively new in Denver, this longtime Albuquerque eatery cooks up wicked green chile from a strip mall in southeast Denver.
5. **Lime,** 1414 Larimer St. (✆ **303/893-5463**): Almost too hip for its own good, Larimer Square's Lime eschews pork for chicken and dresses up the bowl with tortilla strips. Defying tradition tastes pretty good.
6. **El Tejado,** 2651 S. Broadway. (✆ **303/722-3987**): This local's favorite in the southern reaches of the city serves a unique thick green chile plate, as well as some of the best authentic Mexican dishes in the Rockies.

Inexpensive

In addition to the options listed below, there are a number of great breakfast spots in the downtown area. **Snooze,** 2262 Larimer St. (✆ **303/297-0700**), is a great new breakfast and lunch spot in the Ballpark neighborhood, serving delicacies like pineapple upside-down pancakes and bison meatball subs. Established in 1942, **Pete's Kitchen,** 1962 E. Colfax Ave. (✆ **303/321-3139**), is a prototypical urban diner, with checkerboard floors, a breakfast bar, booths, plenty of local color, and killer breakfast burritos. Pete's is open 24 hours on weekends, making it a favorite of the barhopping crowd. For burrito aficionados, the world's first **Chipotle** is located near the University of Denver, at 1644 E. Evans Ave. (✆ **303/777-4121**).

Bayou Bob's Finds CAJUN Fishnets, street signs, and Southern-tinged bric-a-brac cover the walls of Bayou Bob's, which serves Denverites reasonably priced Cajun food in its bar and dining room. Gumbo, red beans and rice, fresh crawfish étouffée, and jambalaya are all favorites, as are the huge Mardi Gras–style Hurricanes. The spicy fried alligator is a great starter, and the many combination plates are a good bet for almost any taste. Catfish, po' boys, and hamburgers are also available.

1635 Glenarm St. (in the Paramount Theatre Bldg.). ✆ **303/573-6828.** Main courses $6–$14. AE, DC, DISC, MC, V. Mon 11am–9pm; Tues–Sat 11am–10pm.

Paramount Cafe AMERICAN Housed in the restored lobby of Denver's historic Paramount Theatre on the 16th Street Mall, this bar and grill is popular, lively, and a bit noisy. A plethora of televisions, a poolroom with five tables plus satellite trivia games, and a year-round patio on the mall make this a good choice for people-watching. The menu features exotic subs, excellent burgers, large salads, and some Tex-Mex fare.

519 16th St. (at Glenarm St.). ✆ **303/893-2000.** Main courses $6–$10. AE, DC, DISC, MC, V. Daily 11am–1am. Bar open until 2am.

Wazee Supper Club ★ Finds PIZZA/SANDWICHES A former plumbing-supply store in lower downtown, the Wazee is a Depression-era relic with a black-and-white tile floor and a bleached mahogany burl bar—a magnificent example of 1930s Art Deco. It's been popular for more than 30 years with artists, architects, theatergoers, entertainers, businesspeople, and just about everybody else. Pizza lovers throng to the place (some believe the pizza here is the best in town, if not the world), but you'll also find an array of overstuffed sandwiches, from New York Reubens to Philly cheese steaks, plus buffalo burgers, and more than 20 draft beers. Don't miss the dumbwaiter used to shuttle food and drinks to the mezzanine floor—it's a converted 1937 garage-door opener.

1600 15th St. (at Wazee St.). ✆ **303/623-9518.** Most menu items $7.50–$10; pizzas $8.50–$21. AE, MC, V. Mon–Sat 11am–midnight; Sun noon–11pm. Bar open until 2am.

OUTSIDE DOWNTOWN

Very Expensive

Elway's ★★ STEAKS/SEAFOOD Owned by retired Denver Broncos quarterback John Elway, this popular Cherry Creek eatery—unlike many celebrity restaurants—is no flash in the pan. Dim but lively, the restaurant is a model of "New West" design, with a menu that melds swank and comfortable. On the swank side: crab cakes, hand-cut USDA Prime steaks, Alaskan halibut, and veggies served a la carte. And the comfy: burgers, enchiladas, and mac and cheese. But it's the little details, such as buttonholes in the napkins, milk bottles full of water, and delectable desserts, that won me over in the end. Service is smooth and business is brisk, in both the cavernous dining room and the bustling bar. If you're lucky, you might bump into Elway himself here—he's not just the owner, but a regular, too. There is also an **Elway's Downtown** in the Ritz-Carlton Denver, 1881 Curtis St. (✆ **303/312-3107**), that opened in 2007.

2500 E. 1st Ave. (immediately west of the Cherry Creek Shopping Center). ✆ **303/399-5353.** www.elways.com. Reservations recommended. Main courses $10–$33 lunch and brunch, $16–$50 dinner. AE, DC, DISC, MC, V. Mon–Thurs 11am–10pm; Fri–Sat 11am–11pm; Sun 11am–9pm.

The Fort ★★★ Moments ROCKY MOUNTAIN There are several reasons to drive 18 miles southwest (and 800 ft. up) from downtown to the Fort in Denver's foothills. First: the atmosphere. The building was hand-constructed of adobe bricks in 1962 as a full-scale reproduction of Bent's Fort, Colorado's first fur-trading post. The equally authentic interior boasts striking views of Denver's city lights. Second: the Fort's impeccable, gracious service, which might just be the finest in town. The third and best reason to go is the food. The Fort built its reputation on high-quality, low-cholesterol buffalo, of which it claims to serve the largest variety and greatest quantity of any restaurant in the world. There's steak, roast marrow, tongue, and even "bison eggs"—hard-boiled quail eggs wrapped in buffalo sausage. My pick is the game plate, with elk chop, teriyaki-style quail, and buffalo filet, served with a salad (and extraordinary homemade dressings), rice, and vegetables. Other house specialtics include Rocky Mountain Oysters and elk medallions with wild-huckleberry sauce. Die-hards can get good ol' beefsteak.

19192 Colo. 8 (just north of the intersection of Colo. 8 and W. Hampden Ave./U.S. 285), Morrison. ✆ **303/697-4771.** www.thefort.com. Reservations recommended. Main courses $22–$52. AE, DC, DISC, MC, V. Mon–Fri 5:30–9:30pm; Sat 5–9:30pm; Sun 5–9pm. Call for special holiday hours.

Moderate to Expensive

Duo ★★ Finds CONTEMPORARY AMERICAN Nestled in the back of a very homey and warm room with brick, worn wood, and a wall of suspended old window frames, Duo's open kitchen plates up a variety of dishes that start with tradition but exude creativity in terms of both presentation and flavor. The menu changes seasonally, but you might find expertly grilled pork chops, buttery buttermilk-fried chicken, or an artful tower of vegetarian gratin. Appetizers are similarly remarkable, my favorite being the leek tart, topped with the transcendental contrast of creamy goat cheese and salty pancetta. For dessert, the house-made ice cream will leave you wanting more.

2413 W. 32nd Ave. ✆ **303/477-4141.** www.duodenver.com. Reservations recommended. Main courses $8–$12 brunch; $17–$25 dinner. AE, DISC, MC, V. Mon–Sat 5–10pm; Sun 5–9pm; Sat–Sun 10am–2pm.

Encore ★ CONTEMPORARY MEDITERRANEAN This smart and hip eatery adjoins the Tattered Cover Book Store and an art cinema, and is a good pick for lunch or dinner east of downtown. With black-and-white tiled floors, great happy-hour deals, and excellent service, Encore is a nice fit for a variety of options, from vegetarian (falafel burgers) to carnivorous (black pepper–crusted rib-eye). In between are great appetizers, wood-fired pizzas, mussels, pastas, and big salads. To finish, the house carrot cake is a delectable dessert in a pumpkin pie–like guise.

2250 E. Colfax Ave. ✆ **303/355-1112.** www.encoreoncolfax.com. Reservations accepted. Main courses $9–$27. AE, DISC, MC, V. Daily 11am–10pm. Bar open until later.

Lola ★★ COASTAL MEXICAN Moving from south Denver to the hip Highlands neighborhood in 2006 quadrupled this popular eatery's floor space, and it still fills to the rafters. It's easy to see why: Lola has oodles of pizzazz, in terms of both its art and airy design—complete with a killer patio with an indoor/outdoor bar and great city views—and the savory dishes on its menu. Start off with some guacamole, prepared fresh tableside, before moving on to a bowl of shellfish of some kind or perhaps an inventively prepared grouper. Most entrees use creative Mexican preparations on fresh seafood with terrific results. Served Saturday and Sunday from 10am to 2pm, the brunch favorite is steak and eggs served with sweet potato hash and chorizo gravy. Lola's margaritas and caipirinhas, sweet Brazilian cocktails with entire quartered limes, are also hard to beat. Below the restaurant is a hip, aptly named lounge, Belola.

1575 Boulder St. ✆ **720/570-8686.** www.loladenver.com. Main courses $18–$26. AE, DC, MC, V. Mon–Thurs 4–10pm; Fri 4–11pm; Sat 10am–11pm; Sun 10am–9pm.

Sushi Den ★★ SUSHI/JAPANESE The long-standing Sushi Den is not only the best sushi restaurant in Denver; it's on the short list of the top sushi restaurants in the country. Owned by three Kizaki brothers—one of whom is based in Japan and sends a daily shipment of ingredients—the Sushi Den's landlocked location is incidental: This is some of the freshest fish you'll find anywhere. The formidable sushi menu, running the gamut from squid and salmon to smoked trout, is complemented by lunch and dinner menus with a wide variety of Japanese fare and sushi and sashimi combination plates. Located in south Denver in the charming Old South Pearl Street retail district, the Sushi Den is one of two locations worldwide—its sister restaurant is in Fukuoka, Japan.

1487 S. Pearl St. ✆ **303/777-0826.** www.sushiden.net. Main courses $8–$18 lunch, $9–$28 dinner; sushi rolls $4.50–$14. AE, DC, MC, V. Mon–Fri 11am–2:30pm; Mon–Thurs 4:45–10:30pm; Fri–Sat 4:30pm–midnight; Sun 5–10:30pm.

Table 6 ★★ Finds CONTEMPORARY MEDITERRANEAN A bistro with a bit of Southern comfort, Table 6 balances a hip but unpretentious sensibility, great food, and one of the best wine lists in town, offered on a tableside stand in an antique photo album. Directed by chef Scott Parker, the open kitchen plates up such tantalizing dishes as mushroom risotto, crisp duck confit, and spaghetti and meatballs in citrus marinara. The atmosphere is lived-in and homey, with rough hardwood floors, brick walls, and ceiling fans, with a blackboard showcasing the day's specials. The desserts are hard to turn down, especially the Nutella beignets and margarita nachos.

609 Corona St. ✆ **303/831-8800.** www.table6denver.com. Reservations recommended. Main courses $16–$26. AE, MC, V. Daily 5–10pm.

Inexpensive

Casa Bonita Kids MEXICAN/AMERICAN A west Denver landmark, Casa Bonita is more of a theme park than a restaurant. A pink Spanish cathedral–type bell tower greets visitors, who discover nonstop action inside: divers plummeting into a pool below a 30-foot waterfall, puppet shows, a video arcade, "Black Bart's Cave," and strolling mariachi bands. The 52,000-square-foot restaurant is said to be the largest restaurant in the Western Hemisphere. There's standard Mexican fare—enchiladas, tacos, and fajitas—along with country-fried steak and fried chicken dinners. Although the food is average, at best, many plates are all-you-can-eat, and patrons need only raise a miniature flag to get another round of tacos. Meals include hot sopaipillas (deep-fried sweet dough) served with honey.

In the JCRS Shopping Center, 6715 W. Colfax Ave., Lakewood. ✆ **303/232-5115.** www.casabonitadenver.com. Reservations not accepted. All-you-can-eat dinners $10–$20; children's meals around $4. DISC, MC, V. Mon–Thurs 11am–9:30pm; Fri–Sat 11am–10pm.

Jack-N-Grill ★ Finds NEW MEXICAN WE ARE NOT FAST FOOD, reads a sign at Jack-N-Grill, and it's spot on: This is clearly a restaurant that takes its time, and its food is worth the wait. Named for Jack Martinez and his ever-present grill, the food reflects Jack's father's motto: *"Comida sin chile, no es comida,"* or "A meal without chile is not a meal." Not surprisingly, just about everything at Jack-N-Grill has chiles in it, roasted on-site by the Martinez family. Both the green and the red chile are top notch, as are the Mexican dishes and the fresh homemade salsa. Also popular: Frito pies and calabasitas, bowls with squash, zucchini, corn, green chiles, and onions. Don't expect Jack to add any chile-free dishes to the menu. "What's the use?" he says.

2524 N. Federal Blvd. ✆ **303/964-9544.** www.jackngrill.com. Plates $6–$14; a la carte dishes $2–$6. AE, MC, V. Sun–Thurs 7am–9pm; Fri–Sat 7am–10pm.

T-Wa Inn Finds VIETNAMESE Denver's oldest Vietnamese restaurant is still the best. With simple, pleasant decor and relics from the Far East on display, it looks the part, but the food is what makes it work. Everything is excellent, but I especially like the succulent shrimp, the spicy pork tenderloin, and the attention to authentic Vietnamese flavors. T-Wa also serves several spicy Thai dishes, as well as Asian beers and a whole rainbow of neon-colored specialty drinks.

555 S. Federal Blvd. (2 blocks south of Alameda Ave.). ✆ **303/922-2378.** www.twainn.com. Most main courses $6–$13. AE, DISC, MC, V. Sun–Thurs 11am–9pm; Fri–Sat 11am–10pm.

WaterCourse Foods ★ Finds VEGETARIAN Beloved by local vegetarians and vegans, WaterCourse is a bustling restaurant that recently relocated to the Uptown neighborhood after outgrowing its old Capitol Hill digs. Breakfast is served all day—the menu includes scrambles (cage-free eggs or tofu with tomatoes, chiles, cheese, and other ingredients), meatless tamales, and banana-bread French toast—and there is also a selection of sandwiches, pasta dishes, salads, and other uniformly tasty vegetarian and vegan specialties for lunch and dinner. Beer and wine are available.

837 E. 17th Ave. ✆ **303/832-7313.** www.watercoursefoods.com. Main courses $5–$9 breakfast, $7–$10 lunch and dinner. AE, DISC, MC, V. Mon–Fri 7am–10pm; Mon–Sat 8am–10pm.

7

What to See & Do in Denver

Denver, an intriguing combination of modern American city and overgrown Old West town, offers a wide variety of attractions, activities, and events. Thanks to its geographic isolation, it's a true cultural hub for a significant chunk of the country: You'll discover art, history, sports, recreation, shopping, and plenty of nightlife. It is quite easy to spend an entire week of vacation in the city, but Denver also makes a convenient base for trips to Boulder, Colorado Springs, or the mountains.

1 THE TOP ATTRACTIONS

Colorado State Capitol ★★ Built to last 1,000 years, the capitol was constructed in 1886 of granite from a Colorado quarry. The dome, which rises 272 feet above the ground, was first sheathed in copper and then replaced with gold leaf after a public outcry: Copper was not a Colorado product.

Murals depicting the history of water in the state adorn the walls of the first-floor rotunda, which offers a splendid view upward to the underside of the dome. The rotunda resembles the layout of the U.S. Capitol in Washington, D.C. South of the rotunda is the governor's office, paneled in walnut and lit by a massive chandelier.

On the first floor, the west lobby hosts revolving temporary exhibits. To the right of the main lobby is the governor's reception room. The second floor has main entrances to the House, Senate, and old Supreme Court chambers. On the third floor are entrances to the public and visitor galleries for the House and Senate (open to the public during legislative session from Jan to early May).

Lincoln St. and Colfax Ave. ✆ **303/866-2604.** Free admission. 45-min. tours offered year-round (more frequently in summer), Memorial Day to Labor Day Mon–Fri 9am–3:30pm; rest of year Mon–Fri 9:15am–2:30pm. Bus: 0, 2, 7, 12, 15, or 50.

Denver Art Museum ★★ Founded in 1893, this seven-story museum has two distinct buildings. The main 1972 building, designed by Gio Ponti, is wrapped by a thin 28-sided wall faced with one million sparkling tiles. The second, a jagged, avant-garde addition, designed by renowned architect Daniel Libeskind, opened in fall 2006, doubling the size of the museum and giving Denver a unique architectural highlight in the process.

The museum's collection of Western and regional works is its cornerstone. Included are Frederic Remington's bronze *The Cheyenne,* Charles Russell's painting *In the Enemy's Country,* plus 19th-century photography, historical pieces, and works by Georgia O'Keeffe. In 2001, Dorothy and William Harmsen, longtime Colorado residents and founders of the Jolly Rancher Candy Company, donated their prestigious Western art collection to the museum. Assembled over 40 years, the collection immediately made the museum's inventory of Western art one of the most impressive in the nation. The American Indian collection is also excellent, consisting of more than 18,000 pieces from

Impressions

. . . Cash! Why, they create it here.

—Walt Whitman, on Denver, in *Specimen Days,* 1881

150 tribes of North America, and spanning nearly 2,000 years. The collection is growing through the acquisition of historic pieces as well as the commissioning of works by contemporary artists. Other collections include architecture and design; graphics; and Asian, African, Oceanic, European, and American painting and sculpture; modern and contemporary, pre-Columbian, Spanish Colonial, and textile art.

Overview tours are available Tuesday through Sunday at 1:30pm, as well as at 11am on Saturday; an in-depth tour of a different area of the museum is offered each Wednesday and Friday at noon and 1pm; and a variety of child-oriented and family programs are scheduled regularly. There are gift shops in both buildings. Allow 2 to 3 hours.

100 W. 14th Ave. Pkwy. (at Civic Center Park). ✆ **720/865-5000.** www.denverartmuseum.org. Admission $13 adults, $10 college students and seniors 65 and over, $5 children 6–18, free for children 5 and under; free for Colorado residents the first Sat of each month. Tues–Thurs and Sat 10am–5pm; Fri 10am–10pm; Sun noon–5pm. Bus: 0, 2, 7, 12, 15, or 50.

Denver Museum of Nature & Science ★★ Kids The largest museum of its kind in the Rocky Mountain region, the Denver Museum of Nature & Science features scores of world-renowned dioramas, an extensive gems and minerals display, a pair of Egyptian mummies, a terrific fossil collection, and several other award-winning exhibitions. The museum focuses on six areas of science: anthropology, health science, geology, paleontology, space science, and zoology.

At "Space Odyssey," visitors experience a carefully crafted mix of exhibits, live programming, digital multimedia, and interactive modules that engage them in contemporary stories of space exploration. The state-of-the-art Gates Planetarium has an advanced computer graphics and video system, unlike any other in the world. "Prehistoric Journey" traces the history of life on Earth through 3.5 billion years with dinosaur skeletons, fossils, interactive exhibits, and dioramas of ancient ecologies. New in 2009, "Expedition Health" is a state-of-the-art exhibit that allows visitors an eye-opening look at the workings of their own bodies, gathering information on themselves as they move through the exhibits and getting a printout about their own physical condition at the end.

An **IMAX theater** (✆ **303/322-7009**) presents science-, nature-, or technology-oriented films with surround sound on a screen that measures four and a half stories tall. Allow 2 to 4 hours.

City Park, 2001 Colorado Blvd. ✆ **800/925-2250** outside Metro Denver, or 303/322-7009; 303/370-8257 for those with hearing impairment. www.dmns.org. Admission to museum $11 adults, $6 children 3–18 and seniors 65 and older, free for children 2 and under; IMAX $8 adults, $6 children and seniors; planetarium $5 subsequent adults, $4 subsequent children and seniors. Daily 9am–5pm. Closed Christmas. Bus: 32 or 40.

U.S. Mint ★★ Whether we worship it or simply consider money a necessary commodity, we all have to admit a certain fascination with the coins and bills that seem to make the world turn. There are four mints in the United States, but the Denver Mint is one of only two (the other is the Philadelphia Mint) where you can actually see the process of turning lumps of metal into shiny coins.

Denver Attractions

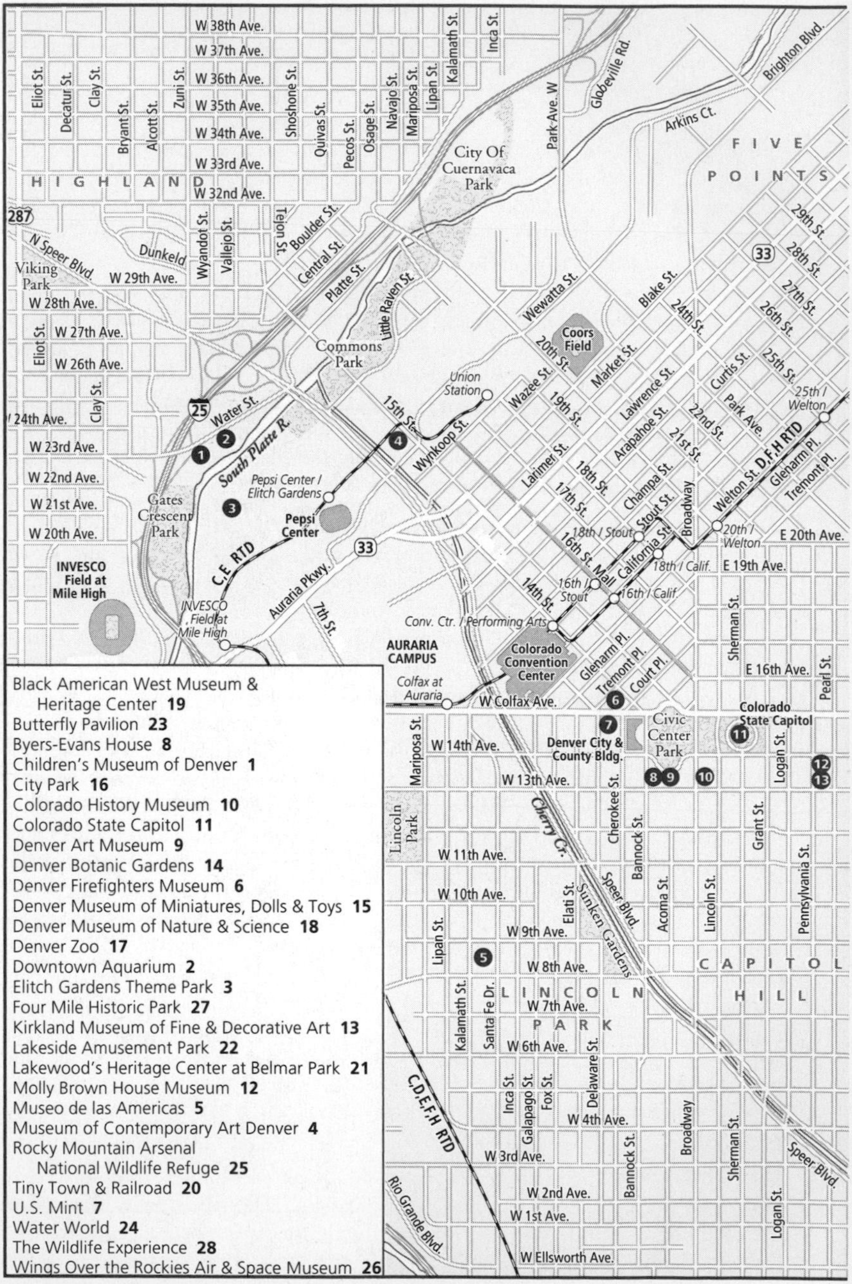

Black American West Museum & Heritage Center **19**
Butterfly Pavilion **23**
Byers-Evans House **8**
Children's Museum of Denver **1**
City Park **16**
Colorado History Museum **10**
Colorado State Capitol **11**
Denver Art Museum **9**
Denver Botanic Gardens **14**
Denver Firefighters Museum **6**
Denver Museum of Miniatures, Dolls & Toys **15**
Denver Museum of Nature & Science **18**
Denver Zoo **17**
Downtown Aquarium **2**
Elitch Gardens Theme Park **3**
Four Mile Historic Park **27**
Kirkland Museum of Fine & Decorative Art **13**
Lakeside Amusement Park **22**
Lakewood's Heritage Center at Belmar Park **21**
Molly Brown House Museum **12**
Museo de las Americas **5**
Museum of Contemporary Art Denver **4**
Rocky Mountain Arsenal National Wildlife Refuge **25**
Tiny Town & Railroad **20**
U.S. Mint **7**
Water World **24**
The Wildlife Experience **28**
Wings Over the Rockies Air & Space Museum **26**

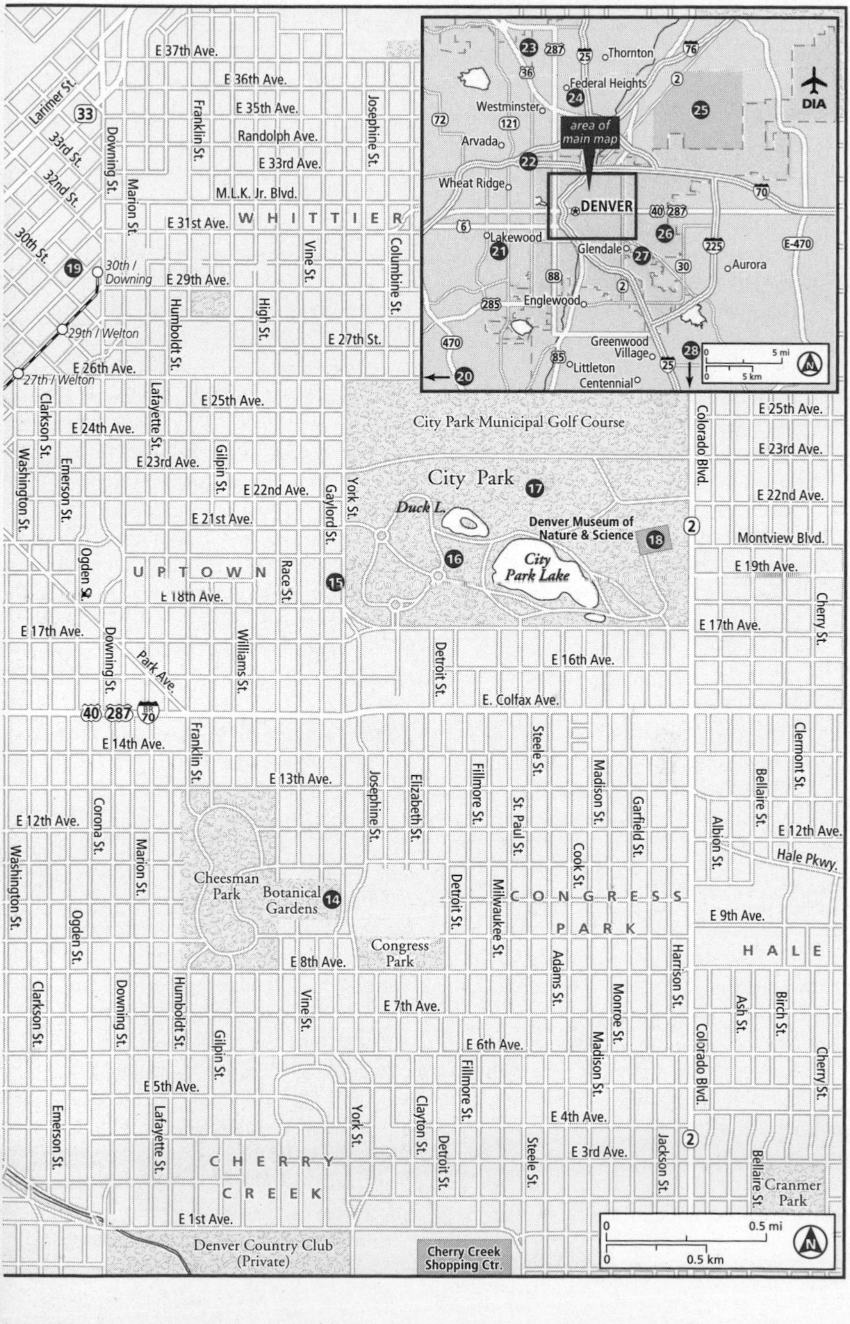
E 37th Ave.
E 36th Ave.
E 35th Ave.
Randolph Ave.
E 33rd Ave.
M.L.K. Jr. Blvd.
E 31st Ave.
W H I T T I E R
E 29th Ave.
E 27th St.
E 26th Ave.
E 25th Ave.
E 24th Ave.
E 23rd Ave.
E 22nd Ave.
E 21st Ave.
U P T O W N
E 18th Ave.
E 17th Ave.
E 16th Ave.
E. Colfax Ave.
E 14th Ave.
E 13th Ave.
E 12th Ave.
E 9th Ave.
E 8th Ave.
E 7th Ave.
E 6th Ave.
E 5th Ave.
E 4th Ave.
E 3rd Ave.
E 1st Ave.
Larimer St.
33rd St.
32nd St.
30th St.
30th / Downing
29th / Welton
27th / Welton
Downing St.
Marion St.
Franklin St.
Josephine St.
Columbine St.
Vine St.
High St.
Humboldt St.
Lafayette St.
Gilpin St.
Gaylord St.
York St.
Clarkson St.
Emerson St.
Washington St.
Ogden St.
Race St.
Williams St.
Park Ave.
Detroit St.
Elizabeth St.
Fillmore St.
St. Paul St.
Steele St.
Madison St.
Cook St.
Garfield St.
Milwaukee St.
Adams St.
Monroe St.
Harrison St.
Colorado Blvd.
Albion St.
Bellaire St.
Clermont St.
Cherry St.
Ash St.
Birch St.
Clayton St.
Jackson St.
Corona St.
E 25th Ave.
E 23rd Ave.
E 22nd Ave.
Montview Blvd.
E 19th Ave.
E 17th Ave.
E 12th Ave.
Hale Pkwy.
City Park Municipal Golf Course
City Park
Duck L.
Denver Museum of Nature & Science
City Park Lake
Cheesman Park
Botanical Gardens
Congress Park
C O N G R E S S
P A R K
H A L E
C H E R R Y
C R E E K
Cranmer Park
Denver Country Club (Private)
Cherry Creek Shopping Ctr.
0 0.5 mi
0 0.5 km
Thornton
Federal Heights
Westminster
Arvada
Wheat Ridge
area of main map
DENVER
Lakewood
Glendale
Aurora
Englewood
Greenwood Village
Littleton
Centennial
DIA
0 5 mi
0 5 km

Fun Facts Robbery at the Mint

A daring armed robbery took place at the Denver Mint in 1922, just 1 week before Christmas, and although police were certain they knew who the culprits were, no one ever served a day in jail for the crime. The most secure building in Denver, the Mint seemed an unlikely target for a robbery. In fact, the thieves did not rob the Mint itself—they simply waited for guards to carry the money out the front door.

A Federal Reserve Bank truck was parked outside the Mint on West Colfax Avenue at about 10:30am on December 18. It was being loaded with $200,000 worth of brand-new $5 bills, which were to be taken to a bank about 12 blocks away, when a black Buick touring car pulled up. Two men jumped out and began firing sawed-off shotguns, killing one guard and spraying the Mint and nearby buildings, while a third robber grabbed the bags of money. Guards inside the Mint quickly pulled their guns and returned fire, but within a minute and a half the robbers were gone—$200,000 richer.

Mint guards were certain they had hit one of the thieves, and 4 weeks later the Buick turned up in a dusty Denver garage. Lying in the front seat was the frozen, bloody body of Nick Trainor, a convicted criminal who had recently been released on parole from the Nebraska State Penitentiary. Trainor had been shot several times.

Secret Service agents recovered $80,000 of the missing loot the following year in St. Paul, Minnesota, but no arrests were made, and little more was mentioned until 1934, when Denver police announced that they knew the identities of the other men involved. Still, no charges were filed. Two of the suspects were already serving life sentences for other crimes.

At the time, police said a Midwest gang had pulled off the robbery and immediately fled to the Minneapolis–St. Paul area. The robbers gave the money to a prominent Minneapolis attorney, who also was never charged.

Opened in 1863, the Mint originally melted gold dust and nuggets into bars. In 1904 the office moved to this site, and 2 years later began making gold and silver coins. Copper pennies were added a few years later. The last silver dollars (containing 90% silver) were coined in 1935. In 1970, all silver was eliminated from dollars and half-dollars (today they're made of a copper-nickel alloy). The Denver Mint stamps billions of coins each year, and each has a small D on it.

Although visitors today don't get as close as they once did, a self-guided tour along the visitors' gallery provides a good look at the process, with a bird's-eye view from the mezzanine of the actual coin-minting process. A variety of displays help explain the minting process, and an adjacent **gift shop** on Cherokee Street (© **303/572-9500**) offers a variety of souvenirs. Allow 1 hour.

320 W. Colfax Ave. (btw. Cherokee and Delaware sts.). © **303/405-4757** or 303/405-4761; 303/572-9500 for gift shop. www.usmint.gov. Free admission. Tours Mon–Fri 8am–2pm. Gift shop 8am–3:30pm. Reservations recommended; online reservations available. Closed 1–2 weeks in summer for audit; call for exact dates. Bus: 7.

2 MORE ATTRACTIONS

HISTORIC BUILDINGS

Denver encompasses 17 recognized historic districts, including Capitol Hill, the Clements District (around 21st St. and Tremont St., just east of downtown), and 9th Street Park in Auraria (off 9th St. and West Colfax Ave.). **Historic Denver** (✆ **303/534-5288;** www.historicdenver.org) offers publications covering many of these areas and organizes several annual events. For additional information on some of Denver's historic areas, see the "Neighborhoods in Brief" section in chapter 6.

Byers-Evans House This elaborate Victorian home, built by *Rocky Mountain News* founding editor William Byers in 1883, has been restored to its appearance of 1912–24, when it was owned by William Gray Evans, son of Colorado's second territorial governor. (The Evans family continued to reside here until 1981.) Guided tours describe the architecture and explain the fascinating lives of these prominent Denver families. There is a gift shop. Allow 45 minutes.

1310 Bannock St. (in front of the Denver Art Museum). ✆ **303/620-4933.** Admission $5 adults, $4 seniors, $3 children 6–16, free for children 5 and under. Tues–Sun 11am–3pm. Closed state holidays. Bus: 7.

Larimer Square ★ This is where Denver began. Larimer Street between 14th and 15th streets was the entire community of Denver City in 1858, with false-fronted stores, hotels, and saloons to serve gold-seekers and other pioneers. In the mid-1870s it was the main street of the city and the site of Denver's first post office, bank, theater, and streetcar line. By the 1930s, however, this part of Larimer Street had deteriorated so much that it had become a skid row of pawnshops, gin mills, and flophouses. Plans had been made to tear these structures down, when a group of investors purchased the entire block in 1965.

The Larimer Square project became Denver's first major historic preservation effort. All 16 of the block's commercial buildings, constructed in the 1870s and 1880s, were renovated, providing space for street-level retail shops, restaurants, and nightclubs, as well as upper-story offices. A series of courtyards and open spaces was created, and in 1973 it was added to the National Register of Historic Places. Allow at least a half-hour—but this is a great spot for a meal if you have more time. In June, Larimer Square hosts La Piazza dell'Arte, featuring hundreds of artists creating pastel masterpieces on the street.

1400 block of Larimer St. ✆ **303/534-2367** or 303/685-8143 (events line). www.larimersquare.com. Bus: 2, 12, 15, 28, 31, 32, 38, or 44.

Molly Brown House Museum ★★ Built in 1889 of Colorado rhyolite with sandstone trim, this was the residence of J.J. and Margaret (Molly) Brown from 1894 to 1932. The "unsinkable" Molly Brown became a national heroine in 1912 when the *Titanic* sank. She took charge of a group of immigrant women in a lifeboat and later raised money for their benefit.

Restored to its 1910 appearance, the Molly Brown House has a large collection of early-20th-century furnishings and art objects, many of which belonged to the Brown family. There are also temporary exhibits (recent ones detailed the lives of servants in Brown's day and trends in Victorian undergarments), and a carriage house with a museum store at the rear is open to visitors. The house can be seen on guided tours. Allow 1 hour.

1340 Pennsylvania St. ✆ **303/832-4092.** www.mollybrown.org. Guided tour $6.50 adults, $5 seniors over 65, $3 children 6–12, free for children 5 and under. June–Aug Mon–Sat 10am–4pm, Sun noon–4pm; Sept–May Tues–Sat 10am–4pm, Sun noon–4pm. Guided tours every 30 min.; last tour of the day begins at 3:30pm. Closed major holidays. Bus: 2 on Logan St. to E. 13th, and then 1 block east to Pennsylvania.

MUSEUMS & GALLERIES

Black American West Museum & Heritage Center ★ Nearly one-third of the cowboys in the Old West were black, and this museum chronicles their little-known history, along with that of black doctors, teachers, miners, farmers, newspaper reporters, and state legislators. The extensive collection occupies the Victorian home of Dr. Justina Ford, the first black woman licensed to practice medicine in Denver. Known locally as the "Lady Doctor," Ford (1871–1951) delivered more than 7,000 babies—most of them at home because she was denied hospital privileges—and consistently served the disadvantaged and underprivileged of Denver.

The museum's founder and curator emeritus, Paul Stewart, loved to play cowboys and Indians as a boy, but his playmates always chose him to be an Indian because "There was no such thing as a black cowboy." He began researching the history of blacks in the West after meeting a black cowboy who had led cattle drives in the early 20th century. Stewart explored almost every corner of the American West, gathering artifacts, memorabilia, photographs, oral histories—anything to document the existence of black cowboys—and his collection served as the nucleus for this museum when it opened in 1971. Allow 1 hour.

3091 California St. (at 31st St.). ✆ **303/482-2242.** www.blackamericanwestmuseum.com. Admission $8 adults, $7 seniors, $6 children 12 and under. June–Aug Tues–Sat 10am–5pm; Sept–May Tues–Sat 10am–2pm. Light rail: 30th and Downing.

Colorado History Museum ★ The Colorado Historical Society's permanent exhibits include "The Colorado Chronicle," an 1800-to-1949 timeline that uses biographical plaques and a remarkable collection of photographs, news clippings, and paraphernalia to illustrate Colorado's past. Dozens of dioramas portray episodes in state history, including an intricate re-creation of 19th-century Denver. Among the other standouts, "Ancient Voices" and "Confluence of Cultures" are slickly produced multimedia exhibits dedicated to the history of Colorado's native tribes and the state's Pioneer era, respectively. The museum offers a series of lectures and statewide historical and archaeological tours. Allow 1 hour.

1300 Broadway. ✆ **303/866-3682.** www.coloradohistory.org. Admission $7 adults, $6 seniors and students, $5 children 6–12, free for children 5 and under. Mon–Sat 10am–5pm; Sun noon–5pm. Bus: 0, 2, 7, 12, 15, or 50.

Denver Firefighters Museum Kids The history of the Denver Fire Department is preserved and displayed here, in historic Fire Station No. 1. Built in 1909 for Engine Company No. 1, it was one of the largest firehouses in Denver, occupying 11,000 square feet on two floors. In its early years, it lodged men, fire engines, and horses. Motorized equipment replaced horse-drawn engines by 1923, and in 1932 the firehouse was "modernized." Concrete replaced the wooden floor, the stables and hayloft were removed, and the plumbing was improved. Visitors today see firefighting equipment dating to 1866, as well as historic photos and newspaper clippings. Allow 45 minutes.

1326 Tremont Place. ✆ **303/892-1436.** www.denverfirefightersmuseum.org. Admission $6 adults, $5 students and seniors, $4 children 12 and under. Mon–Sat 10am–4pm. Closed major holidays. Located 2 blocks west of Civic Center Park on the north side of Colfax.

Denver Museum of Miniatures, Dolls & Toys *Finds* This late-19th-century property is home to an intriguing collection of antique and collectible dolls, from rag and wood to exquisite German and French bisque. Also on display are dollhouses, from a Santa Fe adobe with hand-carved furniture, to a replica of a 16-room home in Newport, Rhode Island. The museum also displays wonderful old toys, from teddy bears to model cars, and temporary exhibits that change every 3 months. The gift shop is equally delightful. Allow 45 to 60 minutes.

1880 Gaylord St. (just west of City Park). ✆ **303/322-1053.** www.dmmdt.org. Admission $6 adults, $5 seniors, $4 children 5–16, free for children 4 and under. Wed–Sat 10am–4pm; Sun 1–4pm.

Four Mile Historic Park ★ Four miles southeast of downtown Denver—thus the name—the city's oldest extant log home (1859) serves as the centerpiece for this 12-acre open-air museum. Everything is authentic to the period from 1859 to 1883, including the house (a former stagecoach stop), its furnishings, outbuildings, and farm equipment. There are draft horses and chickens in the barn, and crops in the garden. Weekend visitors can enjoy horse-drawn carriage rides ($2), weather permitting. Seasonal "Heritage Events" feature pioneer-era musicians and actors, as well as many food and craft demonstrations. Big events include July 4th and an outdoor theater series. Allow 1 hour.

715 S. Forest St. (at Exposition Ave.). ✆ **303/399-1859.** www.fourmilepark.org. Free admission; museum tours $3.50 adults, $2 seniors and children 6–15, free for children 5 and under. Apr–Sept Wed–Fri noon–4pm, Sat–Sun 10am–4pm; Oct–Mar Sat–Sun noon–4pm.

Kirkland Museum of Fine & Decorative Art ★★ *Finds* This terrific museum covers Colorado's most illustrious artist, Vance Kirkland (1904–81), in grand fashion, while also presenting a world-class collection of decorative arts. Kirkland was a watercolor painter focused on Western landscapes when he started experimenting, combining oils and watercolors on one canvas. The Denver arts establishment discounted his modern ideas, but Kirkland later won accolades for creating his own artistic universe in his stunning paintings, about 60 of which are on display here. First built in 1911, his preserved brick studio has an unusual harness he used for painting on flat canvases facedown (dating from his "dot" period). The museum's decorative-arts collection, located here and in a separate gallery across the street, includes more than 3,300 pieces ranging from teacups to armchairs, and there are also more than 700 works by notable Colorado artists other than Kirkland.

1311 Pearl St. ✆ **303/832-8576.** www.kirklandmuseum.org. Admission $6 adults; $5 students, teachers, and seniors. No one 12 or under permitted due to the fragile nature of the collection. Children 13–17 must be accompanied by an adult. Tues–Sun 1–5pm. Guided tour Wed–Sat at 1:30pm. Closed major holidays.

Lakewood's Heritage Center at Belmar Park In Denver's early days, many wealthy residents maintained summer estates in the rural Lakewood area, and this historic village tells their story, as well as that of others who lived and worked here. For an introduction to the museum, your first stop should be the visitor center; you can begin a personalized guided or self-guided tour here. The village includes an 1870s farmhouse, a 1920s one-room school, a 1950s variety store, and the Barn Gallery. There's an exhibit on "Lakewood People and Places," antique and vintage farm machinery, self-guided history walks through the surrounding 127-acre park, changing art exhibits, and a picnic area. Also on-site are an amphitheater and festival area, which hosts a summer concert series and a slate of seasonal fairs and celebrations. Allow 1 to 2 hours.

Another worthwhile attraction in the area is the **Lab at Belmar,** 404 S. Upham St., Lakewood (✆ **303/934-1777;** www.belmarlab.org), an art museum/public forum that opened in 2006; it features weekly lectures and seminars, as well as a regularly rotating gallery.

801 S. Yarrow Blvd. (near Wadsworth and Ohio), Lakewood. ✆ **303/987-7850.** Free admission; guided tours $5 adults, $4 seniors, $3 children 4–18, free for children 3 and under. Tues–Sat 10am–4pm; guided tours on the hour until 3pm. Closed Sun and Mon.

Museo de las Americas ★ Finds Billed as the only museum in the Rocky Mountains focusing exclusively on the art, culture, and history of Latinos, the Museo is worth a stop, as is a stroll through the colorful surrounding gallery- and *taquería*-laden neighborhood. The exhibits here change regularly, and a semipermanent exhibit tells the story of pre-Columbian Latin America, with a replica of an ornate sunstone and exhibits on Tenochtitlán, the Aztec metropolis (on the site of present-day Mexico City) destroyed by invading Spaniards in the 16th century. Allow 1 to 2 hours.

861 Santa Fe Dr. ✆ **303/571-4401.** www.museo.org. Admission $4 adults, $3 seniors and students, free for children 12 and under. Tues–Fri 10am–5pm; Sat–Sun noon–5pm.

Museum of Contemporary Art Denver ★ Having moved in 2007 into a translucent new LEED-certified structure in LoDo (actually three buildings wrapped in glass), this is a stark canvas for the artists who are on center stage here. Five galleries are dedicated to five different disciplines (photography, paper works, large works, new media, and projects), and only one artist at a time occupies a given gallery; most works were created for their exhibition or are a year or two old. An interesting library showcases influences of the artists currently on display. There is also a small gift shop full of books and oddball knickknacks. Allow 1 hour.

1485 Delgany St. ✆ **303/298-7554.** www.mcadenver.org. Admission $10 adults, $5 seniors and students, free for children 5 and under. $1 discount for those who come by public transportation, foot, or bike. Tues–Sun 10am–6pm; Sun noon–5:30pm.

The Wildlife Experience ★ Kids Located near the Denver Technological Center, this impressive museum has three focuses: natural history, nature films, and wildlife art, with nine galleries of paintings, sculptures, and photography. The museum's aim is to educate visitors about conservation and the delicate balance between people and the environment, and to do it in an aesthetically pleasing fashion. It accomplishes the task with such highlights as a National Geographic Channel screening room and an interactive Children's Gallery. Also here are a 315-seat Iwerks Extreme Screen Theater, a restaurant, and a gift shop. Allow 1 hour.

10035 S. Peoria St. ✆ **720/488-3300.** www.thewildlifeexperience.org. Admission or theater tickets $7.95 adults, $6.95 seniors, $4.95 children; combination museum/theater tickets $12 adults, $11 seniors, $6.95 children. Tues–Sun 9am–5pm. Closed major holidays and nonholiday Mon. Located 1 mile east of I-25 via Lincoln Ave. (exit 193).

Wings Over the Rockies Air & Space Museum ★ Kids More than 40 planes and spacecraft occupy cavernous Hangar No. 1, which became a museum when Lowry Air Force Base closed in 1995; now it's a burgeoning residential area about 6 miles southeast of downtown. On display are antique biplanes, a search-and-rescue helicopter, an F-14 Tomcat, a massive B-1A bomber—one of only two in existence—and most of the F-100 fighter series. You can also see a World War II uniform collection, a Norden bombsight, a U3A Blue Canoe, and the Freedom space module, plus seasonal exhibits. On each month's second Saturday, the museum hosts "Demo Cockpit Day," when visitors get to climb into the planes' cockpits from 10am to 2pm. Sci-fi fans, take note: A full-size X-Wing prop used in the filming of *Star Wars* is on permanent display. The store is filled with aviation- and space-oriented souvenirs. Allow 1½ hours.

7711 E. Academy Blvd., Hangar No. 1. ✆ **303/360-5360.** www.wingsmuseum.org. Admission $9 adults, $8 seniors, $6 children 4–12, free for children 3 and under. Mon–Sat 10am–5pm; Sun noon–5pm. Bus: 65.

PARKS, GARDENS & ZOOS

Butterfly Pavilion ★★ Kids A walk through the butterfly conservatory introduces the visitor to a world of grace and beauty. The constant mist creates a hazy habitat to support the lush green plants that are both food and home to the 1,200 butterfly inhabitants representing 50 species at any given time. If you stand still for a few minutes, a butterfly might land on you, but don't try to pick up the butterflies—the oils on your hands contaminate their senses, interfering with their ability to find food. One display describes the differences among butterflies, moths, and skippers, and color charts help with identification.

In the "Crawl-A-See-Um," meet arthropods (the scientific name for insects) that are native to Colorado, and see exotic species from around the world. A fascinating "touch cart" allows you to get up close to a cockroach or tarantula, assuming that you really want to. "Shrunk!" features giant animatronic insects (it can be scary for little ones) and nifty interactive exhibits about the biomechanics of bugs. Also on the premises are a large gift shop and a snack bar. Outside, a .5-mile nature trail meanders amid cactuses and other desert-friendly plants. Allow 2 to 3 hours.

6252 W. 104th Ave., Westminster. ✆ **303/469-5441.** www.butterflies.org. Admission $7.95 adults, $5.95 seniors, $4.95 children 3–12, free for children 2 and under. Daily 9am–5pm. Take the Denver–Boulder Tpk. (U.S. 36) to W. 104th Ave. and go east for about a block. The pavilion is on your right.

City Park Denver's largest urban park covers 330 acres on the east side of uptown. Established in 1881, it retains Victorian touches. The park encompasses two lakes (with boat rentals and fishing), athletic fields, jogging and walking trails, a free children's water feature, playgrounds, tennis courts, picnic areas, and an 18-hole municipal golf course. In summer, there are concerts. The park is also the site of the Denver Zoo (see below) and the Denver Museum of Nature and Science (p. 101), including its IMAX Theater.

E. 17th to E. 26th aves., between York St. and Colorado Blvd. Free admission to park. Separate admission to zoo, museum, golf course, and other sites. Bus: 24 or 32.

Denver Botanic Gardens ★★ Twenty-three acres of outstanding outdoor and indoor gardens display plants native to the desert, plains, mountain foothills, and alpine zones. There's also a traditional Japanese garden, an herb garden, a water garden, a fragrance garden, and a garden inspired by the art of Monet. Even in the cold of winter, the dome-shaped, concrete-and-Plexiglas Tropical Conservatory houses thousands of species of tropical and subtropical plants. Huge, colorful orchids and bromeliads share space with a collection of plants used for food, fibers, dyes, building materials, and medicines. The Botanic Gardens also have a gift shop, a library, and an auditorium. Special events, scheduled throughout the year, range from garden concerts in summer to a spring plant sale, to a cornfield maze southwest of Denver in the fall. Allow 1 to 2 hours.

1005 York St. ✆ **720/865-3500.** www.botanicgardens.org. Admission $11 adults, $7.50 seniors, $6 children 4–15 and students with ID, free for children 3 and under. May to mid-Sept Sat–Tues 9am–8pm, Wed–Fri 9am–5pm; mid-Sept to Apr daily 9am–5pm. Bus: 2 or 10.

Denver Mountain Parks ★★ Formally established in August 1913, the city's Mountain Parks system immediately began acquiring land in the mountains near Denver to be set aside for recreational use. Today it includes more than 14,000 acres, with 31 developed mountain parks and 16 unnamed wilderness areas that are wonderful places for hiking, picnicking, bird-watching, golfing, or lazing in the grass and sun.

The first and largest, **Genesee Park,** is 20 miles west of Denver off I-70, exit 254; its 2,341 acres contain the Chief Hosa Lodge and Campground (the only overnight camping available in the system), picnic areas with fireplaces, a softball field, a scenic overlook, and an elk-and-buffalo enclosure.

Among the system's other parks is **Echo Lake,** about 45 minutes from downtown Denver on Colo. 103. At 10,600 feet elevation on Mount Evans, the park has good fishing, hiking, and picnicking, plus a restaurant and curio shop. Other parks include 1,000-acre **Daniels Park** (23 miles south of Denver; take I-25 to Castle Pines Pkwy., and then go west to the park), which offers picnic areas, a bison enclosure, and a scenic overlook; **Red Rocks Park,** just southwest of Denver in Morrison, featuring the famed amphitheater, a trading post, a museum that covers both natural history and rock 'n' roll, and hiking trails amid the red sandstone formations (see www.redrocksonline.com); and **Dedisse Park** (2 miles west of Evergreen on Colo. 74), which provides picnic facilities, a golf course, a restaurant, a clubhouse, and opportunities for ice-skating, fishing, and volleyball.

Dept. of Parks and Recreation. ✆ **303/697-4545.** www.denvergov.org. Free admission.

Denver Zoo ★★ Kids More than 700 species of animals (nearly 4,000 individuals) live in this spacious zoological park, home to the rare deerlike okapi as well as to Siberian tigers, Komodo dragons, and western lowland gorillas. The newest (and most ambitious) habitat here is Predator Ridge, a re-created African savanna with lions, hyenas, and other African predators. The exhibit is modeled after a Kenyan preserve, complete with artificial termite mounds that dispense insects for the banded mongoose that live here. The zoo has long been an innovator in re-creating realistic habitats: Bear Mountain, built in 1918, was the first animal exhibit in the United States constructed of simulated concrete rockwork.

The zoo is home to the nation's first natural gas–powered train ($2). The electric Safari Shuttle ($2.50 adults, $1.50 children) tours all zoo paths spring through fall. An especially kid-friendly attraction is the Conversation Carousel ($2), featuring wood-carved renditions of such endangered species as okapi, polar bears, Komodo dragons, and hippos. The Hungry Elephant, a cafeteria with an outdoor eating area, serves full meals, and picnicking is popular, too. Feeding times are posted near the zoo entrance so you can time your visit to see the animals when they are most active. Allow from 2 hours to a whole day.

City Park, 2300 Steele St. (main entrance btw. Colorado Blvd. and York St. on 23rd Ave.). ✆ **303/376-4800.** www.denverzoo.org. Admission $12 adults summer, $9 adults winter; $9 seniors 62 and over summer, $7 seniors winter; $7 children 3–12 (accompanied by an adult) summer, $5 children winter; free for children 2 and under. Apr–Sept daily 9am–5pm; Oct–Mar daily 10am–4pm. Bus: 24 or 32.

Downtown Aquarium Denver's state-of-the-art aquarium—the largest between Chicago and Monterey, California—opened in 1999 as a nonprofit, went belly-up, and in 2003 was sold to the for-profit Landry's seafood restaurant chain. The sale brought the aquarium stability, not to mention new exhibits and a theme restaurant and lounge on-site. Residents include greenback cutthroat trout (the Colorado state fish), river otters, tigers, nurse sharks, sea turtles, and moray eels. Among the other exhibits: a flash-flood simulation, a gold-panning and mining display, "Stingray Reef" (visitors can pet and feed the slippery denizens), and a lifelike animatronic orangutan. On Saturdays, licensed divers and novice snorkelers can swim in the big tanks for a fee (about $175 for divers, $75 for snorkelers). Allow 2 hours.

700 Water St., just east of I-25 via 23rd Ave. (exit 211). ✆ **303/561-4444.** www.aquariumrestaurants.com. Admission before 6pm $14 adults, $13 seniors, $8.25 children 3–11, free for children 2 and under. Discounts available after 6pm or with receipt from restaurant. Sun–Thurs 10am–9pm; Fri–Sat 10am–9:30pm. Closed Christmas. Bus: 28.

Rocky Mountain Arsenal National Wildlife Refuge Once a site where the U.S. Army manufactured chemical weapons such as mustard gas and GB nerve agent, and later leased to a private enterprise to produce pesticides, the Rocky Mountain Arsenal has become an environmental success story. The 27-square-mile Superfund cleanup site, an area of open grasslands and wetlands just west of Denver International Airport, is home to more than 330 species, including deer, coyotes, prairie dogs, and birds of prey. This is one of the country's largest eagle-roosting locales during the winter.

The Rocky Mountain Arsenal Wildlife Society Bookstore is at the visitor center, and there are about 15 miles of hiking trails, as well as catch-and-release fishing. Allow at least an hour.

56th Ave. at Quebec St. ✆ **303/289-0930.** www.fws.gov/rockymountainarsenal. Free admission. Tues–Sun 6am–6pm. Bus: 88.

3 PLACES ESPECIALLY FOR KIDS

Denver abounds in child-oriented activities, and the listings below will probably appeal to young travelers of any age. In addition, some sights listed in the previous sections may appeal to families. They include the Butterfly Pavilion and Insect Center; Colorado History Museum; Downtown Aquarium; Denver Art Museum; Denver Museum of Miniatures, Dolls & Toys; Denver Museum of Nature and Science; Denver Zoo; Four Mile Historic Park; and U.S. Mint.

Children's Museum of Denver ★ Kids Denver's best hands-on experience for children, this intriguing museum is both educational and just plain fun. Focusing on children 8 years old and younger, the museum uses educational "playscapes" to entertain and activate young minds. These exhibits include "CMD Fire Station No. 1," which teaches fire safety, and "My Market," a faux supermarket that allows kids to role-play as shoppers and clerks. There are several other playscapes with themes ranging from biology to engineering. There's also a resource center that provides parenting information to adults, and a cafe that serves sandwiches, snacks, and beverages. Allow at least 2 hours.

2121 Children's Museum Dr. ✆ **303/433-7444.** www.mychildsmuseum.org. Admission $7 ages 1–59, $5 seniors 60 and over, free for children under 1. Mon–Fri 9am–4pm; Sat–Sun 10am–5pm. Take exit 211 (23rd Ave.) east off I-25; turn right on 7th St., and again on Children's Museum Dr. Bus: 28.

Elitch Gardens Theme Park ★ Kids A Denver tradition established in 1889, this amusement park moved to its present downtown site in 1995. The 45-plus rides include Twister II, an unbelievable 10-story roller coaster with a 90-foot drop and dark tunnel; the Flying Coaster, a one-of-a-kind "hang gliding" experience in which passengers lie facedown; the Halfpipe, a snowboarding-themed thrill ride that involves 16 passengers

Fun Facts The Big Blue Bear

Denver has a new face to the world, and it's peering into the second floor of the Colorado Convention Center. Known popularly as "The Big Blue Bear," the 40-foot blue ursine immediately became Denver's most photogenic piece of public art when it was installed in 2005. Sculptor Lawrence Argent designed the big fella—officially named *I See What You Mean*—and then a California-based fabricator shaped him out of 5 tons of steel, fiberglass, and cement; transported him to Colorado in sections; and bolted him into place.

The sculpture is located right by the convention center's 14th Street entrance and can be photographed from inside or out. For a Denver souvenir, it's hard to beat the little blue bear replicas available at the Denver Art Museum, inside the Colorado Convention Center, and at the visitor information center at 16th and California streets.

on a 39-foot board; the 220-foot, free-fall Tower of Doom; and a fully restored 1925 carousel with 67 hand-carved horses and chariots. Patrons of all ages can enjoy the Island Kingdom Water Park while the little ones have fun on pint-sized rides in StarToon Studios. There are also musical revues and stunt shows, games and arcades, food, shopping, and beautiful flower gardens. Allow 3 hours.

Speer Blvd., at I-25, exit 212A. ✆ **303/595-4386.** www.elitchgardens.com. Gate admission with unlimited rides $35 for those taller than 4 ft., $20 for those 4 ft. and under, free for children 3 and under and seniors over 69. Online ticket specials available. Parking $10. Memorial Day to Labor Day daily 10am–9pm; Apr to late May and early Sept to Oct weekends (call for hours). Light rail: C Line, Pepsi Center/Elitch Gardens.

Lakeside Amusement Park (Kids) Among the largest and most historic amusement parks in the Rocky Mountains, Lakeside has about 40 rides, including a Cyclone roller coaster, a midway with carnival and arcade games, and a rare steam-powered miniature train from the early 20th century that circles the lake. There are also food stands and picnic facilities, plus a separate Kiddie's Playland with 15 rides. Allow 3 hours.

4601 Sheridan Blvd. (just south of I-70, exit 271). ✆ **303/477-1621.** www.lakesideamusementpark.com. Admission $2.50. Ride coupons 50¢ (rides require 1–4 coupons each); unlimited rides $14 Mon–Fri, $20 Sat–Sun and holidays. May Sat–Sun and holidays noon–10pm; June to Labor Day Mon–Fri 6–10pm, Sat–Sun and holidays noon–10pm. Kiddie's Playland Mon–Fri 1–10pm, Sat–Sun and holidays noon–10pm. Closed from the day after Labor Day to Apr.

Tiny Town and Railroad (Kids) (Finds) Originally built in 1915 at the site of a Denver–Leadville stagecoach stop, Tiny Town is exactly what its name implies—a one-sixth-scale Western village. Nestled in a scenic mountain canyon about 20 miles southeast of downtown Denver, Tiny Town is made up of 100 colorful buildings and a steam-powered locomotive that visitors can ride for an additional $1. Allow 1 hour.

6249 S. Turkey Creek Rd., Tiny Town. ✆ **303/697-6829.** www.tinytownrailroad.com. Admission $5 adults, $3 children 2–12, free for children 1 and under. Memorial Day to Labor Day daily 10am–5pm; May and Sept Sat–Sun 10am–5pm. Closed Oct–Apr. Located 20 miles southeast of downtown via U.S. 285 (Hampden Ave.).

Water World ★ (Kids) This 64-acre complex, billed as America's largest family water park, has two oceanlike wave pools, river rapids for inner tubing, twisting water slides, several kids' play areas, a gondola to the country's first water-based funhouse, plus other attractions—more than 40 in all—as well as food service and other amenities. Allow at least 4 hours.

88th Ave. and Pecos St., Federal Heights. ✆ **303/427-SURF** [427-7873]. www.waterworldcolorado.com. Admission $34 for those 48 in. and taller, $29 for those 40–48 in., free for seniors and children under 40 in. Memorial Day to Labor Day daily 10am–6pm. Closed rest of year and some school days in Aug. Take the Thornton exit (exit 219, 84th Ave.) off I-25 north.

WALKING TOUR DOWNTOWN DENVER

START: Denver Information Center, Civic Center Park.
FINISH: State Capitol, Civic Center Park.
TIME: 2 to 8 hours, depending on how much time you spend shopping, eating, and sightseeing.
BEST TIMES: Any Tuesday through Friday in late spring.
WORST TIMES: Monday and holidays, when the museums are closed.

Start your tour of the downtown area at Civic Center Park, on West Colfax Avenue at 14th Street.

1 Civic Center Park

This 2-square-block oasis features a Greek amphitheater, fountains, statues, flower gardens, and 30 different species of trees, 2 of which (it is said) were originally planted by Abraham Lincoln at his Illinois home.

Overlooking the park on its east side is the State Capitol. On its south side is the:

2 Colorado History Museum

The staircaselike building houses exhibits that make the state's colorful history come to life.

Also on the south side of the park are the Denver Public Library and the:

3 Denver Art Museum

With buildings designed by Gio Ponti of Italy and Daniel Libeskind of Germany, the art museum is an architectural wonder. Inside are more than 35,000 works of art, including renowned Western and American Indian collections.

On the west side of Civic Center Park is the:

4 City and County Building

During the Christmas season, a rainbow of colored lights decorates it in spectacular fashion.

A block farther west is the:

5 U.S. Mint

Modeled in Italian Renaissance style, the building resembles the Palazzo Riccardi in Florence. More than 60,000 cubic feet of granite and 1,000 tons of steel went into its construction in 1904.

Cross over Colfax and go diagonally northwest up Court Place. Two blocks ahead is the:

6 Denver Pavilions

The city's newest retail hot spot sits at the south end of the 16th Street Mall, featuring a Hard Rock Cafe, a 15-screen movie theater, and a Barnes & Noble Superstore.

Three blocks up the 16th Street Mall, head southwest 2 blocks on California Street past the Colorado Convention Center and turn right on 14th Street. Walk 2 blocks to the:

7 Denver Performing Arts Complex

The complex covers 4 square blocks between 14th Street and Cherry Creek, Champa Street and Arapahoe Street. The entrance is under a block-long, 80-foot-high glass archway. The center includes seven theaters, a symphony hall in the round, a voice research laboratory, and a smoking solar fountain. Free tours are offered.

Two more blocks up 14th Street, past the arts center, is:

8 Larimer Square

This is Denver's oldest commercial district. Restored late-19th-century Victorian buildings accommodate more than 30 shops and a dozen restaurants and clubs. Colorful awnings, hanging flower baskets, and quiet open courtyards accent the square, once home to such notables as Buffalo Bill Cody and Bat Masterson. Horse-drawn carriage rides originate here for trips up the 16th Street Mall or through lower downtown.

> **TAKE A BREAK**
> Stop at **Rioja,** 1431 Larimer St., between 14th and 15th sts. (✆ **303/820-2282**), or one of the patios on Larimer Square for a drink and people-watching. (See review on p. 92.)

A walkway at the east corner of Larimer and 15th leads through:

9 Writer Square

Quaint gas lamps, brick walkways, and outdoor cafes dot this shopping-and-dining complex.

At 16th Street, cross to the:

10 Tabor Center

The glass-enclosed shopping and entertainment complex spreads over three levels, in effect a 2-block-long greenhouse.

To the east, the Tabor Center is anchored by the:

11 D&F Tower

The city landmark was patterned after the campanile of St. Mark's Basilica in Venice, Italy, in 1910. In the basement is a performing arts venue, Lannie's Clocktower Cabaret.

Head northwest along 16th Street, then turn right on Wynkoop Street and go 4 blocks to LoDo's centerpiece:

12 Coors Field

The anchor of the vital LoDo ("Lower Downtown") neighborhood and the home of baseball's Colorado Rockies, the stadium is right at home amid the Victorian redbricks. There are plenty of eateries and bars in the area, as well as transportation hubs in Union Station and Market Street Station, plus a few shops.

Here, head southeast to 16th Street to begin a leisurely stroll down the:

13 16th Street Mall

The $76-million pedestrian path affords the finest people-watching spot in the city. You'll see everyone from street entertainers to lunching office workers to travelers like yourself. Built of red and gray granite, it is lined with 200 red oak trees, a dozen fountains, and a lighting system straight out of *Star Wars.* You'll also see outdoor cafes, restored Victorian buildings, modern skyscrapers, and hundreds of shops—with an emphasis on sports—plus restaurants and department stores. If you are done with walking, sleek European-built shuttle buses run through, offering free transportation up and down the mall as often as every 90 seconds.

You'll walk 7 blocks down 16th Street from the Tabor Center before reaching Tremont Place. Turn left, go 1 block farther, and across the street, on your right, you'll see the:

14 Brown Palace Hotel

One of the most beautiful grande dame hotels in the United States, it was built in 1892 and features a nine-story atrium lobby topped by a Tiffany stained-glass ceiling. Step into the lobby for a look.

Continue across Broadway on East 17th Avenue. Go 2 blocks to Sherman Street, turn right, and proceed 2 blocks south on Sherman to East Colfax Avenue. You're back overlooking Civic Center Park, but this time you're at the:

15 State Capitol

If you stand on the 13th step on the west side of the building, you're exactly 5,280 feet (1 mile) above sea level. Architects modeled the Colorado capitol after the U.S. Capitol in Washington, D.C., and used the world's entire known supply of rare rose onyx in its interior wainscoting.

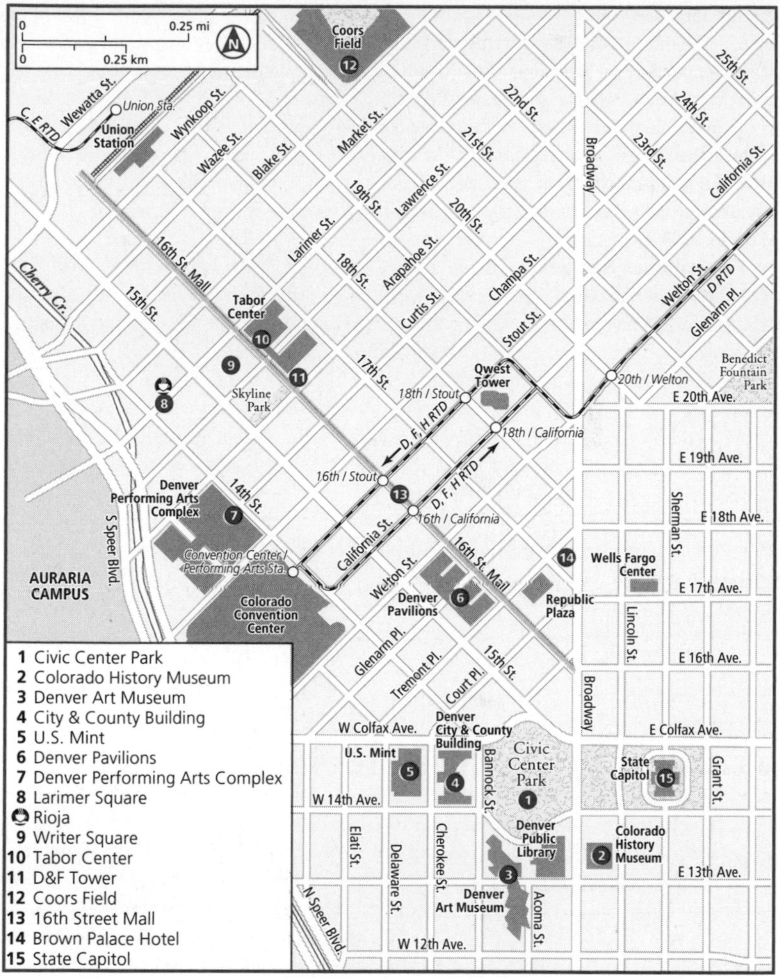

4 ORGANIZED TOURS

Visitors who want to be personally guided to the attractions of Denver and the surrounding areas by those in the know have a variety of choices. In addition to the following, see "Escorted General-Interest Tours" and "Special-Interest Trips," in chapter 3.

Half- and full-day bus tours of Denver and the nearby Rockies are offered by the ubiquitous **Gray Line,** P.O. Box 17646, Denver, CO 80217 (✆ **800/348-6877** for information only; 303/289-2841 for reservations and information; www.coloradograyline.com). Fares for children under 13 are half the adult prices listed below. Prices include entry fees but usually no food. Tours depart from the Cherry Creek Shopping Center at 1st Avenue and Milwaukee Street, as well as from local hotels and hostels on a reservation basis.

A 4-hour tour (no. 27), leaving at 1:30pm, takes in Denver's mountain parks: Red Rocks Park, Bergen Park, and Buffalo Bill's grave atop Lookout Mountain. It costs $40 for adults. The Denver city tour (no. 28), which departs daily at 8:30am and takes about 3$^1/_2$ hours, gives you a taste of both old Denver—through Larimer Square and other historic buildings—and the modern-day city. It's $35 for adults. The city tour combined with the mountain-parks tour costs $70. Gray Line also offers tours of Rocky Mountain National Park, Golden and Morrison, and the Colorado Springs area; call or check the website for information.

The Colorado Sightseer, 6780 W. 84th Circle, Ste. 60, Arvada, CO 80003 (✆ **303/423-8200;** www.coloradosightseer.com), offers guided tours of Denver and environs. The Historic Denver tour includes a visit to LoDo and some of the city's earliest buildings, the State Capitol, the Molly Brown House, and Four Mile Historic Park. It lasts about 4 hours and costs $45 for adults, $35 for children 5 to 12, and it's free for children under 5. A Rocky Mountain National Park tour, lasting about 9$^1/_2$ hours, costs $85 for adults and $65 for children 5 to 12, including a box lunch. The 4$^1/_2$-hour Foothills Tour includes stops at Coors Brewery, the Buffalo Bill memorial, and scenic Red Rocks Park. The costs are $45 for adults, $35 for children 5 to 12, and free for children under 5.

The **LoDo District** (✆ **303/628-5428;** www.lodo.org) leads guided walking tours of the storied area June to October. Tours depart from Union Station (17th and Wynkoop sts.) on Tuesday at 10am and Saturday at 1pm; the cost is $10 adults, $5 students, and free for those under 13. They also offer different walking tours on Thursday and Saturday afternoons. Take advantage of your cellphone with **Rocky Mountain Audio Guides** (✆ **303/898-7073;** www.rmaguides.com), which delivers 40- and 80-minute walking tours of downtown Denver. Call 24 hours before your tour to purchase; then you simply dial a number and walk around town, guided via satellite.

BICYCLING & MULTISPORT TOURS

The World Outdoors (✆ **800/488-8483** or 303/413-0938; www.theworldoutdoors.com) offers a 6-day, 5-night multisport hut-to-hut tour that begins and ends in Vail (100 miles west of Denver). The huts, described by *Mountain Bike Magazine* as "luxurious backcountry accommodations," serve as recreational headquarters for guests, who have plenty of hiking, rafting, and sightseeing opportunities between mountain-biking treks. The trips aren't cheap, costing around $1,500 per person, but this might be the best way for the outdoors enthusiast to enjoy the Rockies west of Denver. Available in June and August, tours include meals but not biking and camping gear.

Colorado Mountain Expeditions (✆ **888/CME-HIKE** [263-4453]; www.coloradotrailhiking.com) offers supported weeklong treks on the Colorado Trail (which runs 483 miles from Denver to Durango) for $925 per person, all meals included. The beauty of these trips: You only carry a day pack. A support crew sets up your camp and makes your meals while you focus on the trail, not the campsite.

Another company that offers weeklong tours in the area is **Bicycle Tour of Colorado** (✆ **303/985-1180;** www.bicycletourcolorado.com). For $300 to $400, a biker can join a tour involving more than 1,000 riders and 70 volunteers—including medical and bike-tech support as well as guiding services—on a 400-mile journey that hits six different cities each year, crossing the Continental Divide several times in the process. Although accommodations can be prearranged at hotels, most riders elect to stay at facilities provided by the city (for example, the local high school). All meals are provided for the one fee for the week.

A good resource for bicyclists is the **Denver Bicycle Touring Club** (www.dbtc.org), which organizes local rides and publishes a monthly newsletter. See also "Bicycling & Skateboarding," below.

5 OUTDOOR ACTIVITIES

Denver's proximity to the Rocky Mountains makes it possible to spend a day skiing, snowmobiling, horseback riding, hiking, river running, sailing, fishing, hunting, mountain climbing, or rockhounding, and return to the city by nightfall. Within the city limits and nearby, visitors will find more than 200 miles of jogging and bicycle paths, more than 100 free tennis courts, and several dozen public golf courses.

The city has an excellent system of **Mountain Parks** (✆ **303/697-4545**), covering more than 14,000 acres, which are discussed earlier in this chapter in the "Parks, Gardens & Zoos" section.

Campsites are easy to reach from Denver, as are suitable sites for hang gliding and hot-air ballooning. Sailing is popular within the city at Sloan's Lake and in Washington Park (both Denver City Parks), and the Platte River is clear for many miles of river running in rafts, kayaks, and canoes.

The Skinny on Denver

According to the statisticians, Denver has the highest proportion of thin people of any city in the country. A 2008 study showed Colorado to be the state with the lowest percentage of the population to be overweight.

The Denver Metro Convention and Visitors Bureau (see "Visitor Information," in chapter 6) can supply detailed information about activities in the city. Information on nearby outdoor activities is available from **Colorado State Parks,** 1313 Sherman St., Ste. 618, Denver, CO 80203 (✆ **303/866-3437;** www.parks.state.co.us); the **U.S. Forest Service,** Rocky Mountain Region, 740 Simms St., Golden, CO 80401 (✆ **303/275-5350;** www.fs.fed.us/r2); the **U.S. Bureau of Land Management,** 2850 Youngfield St., Lakewood, CO 80215 (✆ **303/239-3600;** www.co.blm.gov); and the **National Park Service**'s Intermountain Region headquarters, 12795 W. Alameda Pkwy., Lakewood, CO 80228 (✆ **303/969-2000;** www.nps.gov).

Visitors who don't bring the necessary equipment should hit the **REI** flagship store, 1416 Platte St. (✆ **303/756-3100**); its rental department is stocked with tents, backpacks, stoves, mountaineering equipment, kayaks, and other gear.

BALLOONING You can't beat a hot-air balloon ride for viewing the magnificent Rocky Mountain scenery. **Life Cycle Balloon Adventures, Ltd.** (✆ **800/980-9272** or 303/216-1990; www.lifecycleballoons.com), and **Colorado Rocky Ballooning** (✆ **888/468-9280** or 970/468-9280; www.coloradoballoonrides.com) both offer sunrise flights daily. The cost at both companies is usually $195 to $250 per person.

BICYCLING & SKATEBOARDING The paved bicycle paths that crisscross Denver include a 12-mile scenic stretch along the bank of the South Platte River and along

Cherry Creek beside Speer Boulevard. All told, the city has more than 85 miles of off-road trails for bikers and runners. Bike paths link the city's 205 parks, and many streets have bike lanes. In all, the city has more than 130 miles of designated bike paths and lanes. Mountain bikers will take delight in the foothills; one option is **Waterton Canyon,** where singletrack connects metro Denver and Deckers. For more information, contact **Bike Denver** (www.bikedenver.org) or **Bicycle Colorado** (© **303/417-1544;** www.bicyclecolo.org). Bike tours are available from several companies and clubs (see "Organized Tours," above). The **Cherry Creek Bike Rack,** 171 Detroit St. (© **303/388-1630;** www.cherrycreekbikerack.com), offers rentals, service, and free parking for bikes.

Denver also has the largest free skateboarding park (3 acres) in the country, the **Denver Skatepark,** 19th and Little Raven sts. (© **720/913-1311;** www.denverskatepark.com). It is quite popular and open between the hours of 5am and 11pm.

BOATING A quiet way to view some of downtown Denver is from a punt on scenic Cherry Creek. **Venice on the Creek** (© **303/893-0750;** www.veniceonthecreek.com) operates from June to August Thursday to Sunday from 5 to 10pm. On weekdays it accommodates only groups of 12 or more; smaller groups are taken on weekends. Guides describe the history of the city while pointing out landmarks. Tickets are available at the kiosk at Creekfront Plaza, at the intersection of Speer Boulevard and Larimer Street. A 1-hour trip costs $25 to $30 per bench (each accommodates two) or $75 for a private boat. Also downtown, you can rent a kayak ($50 a day) and take kayaking classes ($49 per session) at **Confluence Kayaks,** 1615 Platte St. (© **303/433-3676**).

In the outlying areas, you'll find powerboat marinas at **Cherry Creek State Park,** 4201 S. Parker Rd., Aurora (© **303/699-3860**), 11 miles from downtown off I-225; and **Chatfield State Park,** 11500 N. Roxborough Park Rd., Littleton (© **303/791-7275**), 16 miles south of downtown Denver. Jet-skiing and sailboarding are also permitted at both parks. Sailboarding, canoeing, and other wakeless boating are popular at **Barr Lake State Park,** 13401 Picadilly Rd., Brighton (© **303/659-6005**), 21 miles northeast of downtown on I-76.

For a different watersports experience, try riverboarding with **RipBoard** (© **866/311-2627** or 303/904-8367; www.ripboard.com), which entails going down Clear Creek face-first with flippers on your feet and a helmet on your head. It's exciting and exhausting, but can be a lot of fun in the right water. Lessons (including equipment) are $75 for 4 hours; rentals and sales are also available.

For information on other boating opportunities, contact Colorado State Parks, the National Park Service, or the U.S. Forest Service (see above).

FISHING A couple of good bets in the metropolitan area are Chatfield State Park, with trout, bass, and panfish, and Cherry Creek State Park, which boasts trout, walleye pike, bass, and crappie (see "Boating," above). In all, there are more than 7,100 miles of streams and 2,000 reservoirs and lakes in Colorado. For information, contact Colorado State Parks, the Colorado Division of Wildlife (© **303/297-1192**), or the U.S. Fish and Wildlife Service (© **303/236-7917**). Within Denver city limits, the **Denver Department of Parks and Recreation** (© **720/913-1311**) stocks a number of lakes with fish.

A number of sporting-goods stores can provide more detailed information. The skilled and experienced staff at **Anglers All,** 5211 S. Santa Fe Dr. (© **303/794-1104;** www.anglersall.com), can help with equipment choices and recommendations for where to go. Anglers All also offers lessons, seminars, clinics, and guided wade and float trips (about $400 a day for two people).

GOLF Throughout the Front Range, it's often said that you can play golf at least 320 days a year, because the sun always seems to be shining, and even when it snows, the little snow that sticks melts quickly. There are more than 50 courses in the Denver area, including seven municipal golf courses, with nonresident greens fees up to $24 for 18 holes. City courses are **City Park Golf Course,** East 25th Avenue and York Street (✆ 303/295-2096); **Evergreen Golf Course,** 29614 Upper Bear Creek Rd., Evergreen (✆ 303/674-4128); the par-3 **Harvard Gulch Golf Course,** East Iliff Avenue and South Clarkson Street (✆ 303/698-4078); **Kennedy Golf Course,** 10500 E. Hampden Ave. (✆ 303/751-0311); **Overland Park Golf Course,** South Santa Fe Drive and West Jewell Avenue (✆ 303/698-4975); **Wellshire Golf Course,** 3333 S. Colorado Blvd. (✆ 303/692-5636); and **Willis Case Golf Course,** 4999 Vrain St. near West 50th Avenue (✆ 303/458-4877). Wellshire is the best overall course, but I prefer Willis Case for its spectacular mountain views.

You can make same-day reservations by calling the course; otherwise, nonresident golfers must purchase a $10 card at City Park, Wellshire, or Willis Case, and then make reservations through the **automated phone system** (✆ **303/784-4000**). The one exception to this policy is Evergreen Golf Course, where you can call the starter for reservations 3 days in advance. For information on any course, you can also call the **Department of Parks and Recreation** (✆ **720/913-1311**).

An 18-hole Frisbee golf course is located at Lakewood Gulch, near Federal Boulevard and 12th Street. Call the **Department of Parks and Recreation** (✆ **720/913-1311**) for more information.

HIKING & BACKPACKING The **Colorado Trail** ★★ is a hiking, horse, and mountain-biking route stretching 500 miles from Denver to Durango. The trail is also open to cross-country skiing, snowshoeing, and llama-pack hiking. Opened in 1988, the trail is still being fine-tuned. It took 15 years to establish, using volunteer labor, and crosses eight mountain ranges and five river systems, winding from rugged terrain to pristine meadows. For information, contact the **Colorado Trail Foundation,** 710 10th St., Rm. 210, Golden, CO 80401-1022 (✆ **303/384-3729;** www.coloradotrail.org). Beyond being a source of information, the foundation maintains and improves the trail, publishes relevant guidebooks, and offers supported treks (see "Bicycling & Multisport Tours," above) and accredited courses.

For hikes in the Denver area, contact the city **Department of Parks and Recreation** (✆ **720/913-1311**) for information on Denver's park system. Or contact any of the following agencies: Colorado State Parks, Colorado Division of Wildlife, National Park Service, U.S. Bureau of Land Management, or U.S. Forest Service (see the introduction to this section and "Fishing," above). A good source for the many published area maps and hiking guides is **Mapsco Map and Travel Center,** 800 Lincoln St., Denver (✆ **303/830-2373**).

Above Red Rocks Park, **Mount Falcon Park** ★ (✆ **303/271-5925**) offers excellent trails that are easy to moderate in difficulty, making this a good place for families with children. There are also picnic areas, shelters, and ruins of an old castlelike home. From Denver, go west on U.S. 285, north on Parmalee Gulch Road, and follow the signs; the park is open daily from dawn to dusk, and admission is free. Mountain bikes and horseback riding are permitted, as are leashed dogs.

Other relatively easy trails near Denver are in **Roxborough State Park** (✆ **303/973-3959**), 10 miles south of Littleton—the 1-mile **Willow Creek Trail** and the 2.3-mile **Fountain Valley Trail** ★. There are several more strenuous trails at Roxborough, which

Tips Denver's Dog Parks

In 2004, Denver began to allow canines to roam free at five parks within city limits, and there are dozens of off-leash parks in the metropolitan area as a whole. Contact the Department of Parks and Recreation (✆ **720/913-1311**) for more information or visit **www.denvergov.org**.

are worth the effort if you enjoy beautiful red rocks and the chance to see wildlife. To get to Roxborough Park, exit Colo. 470 south onto U.S. 85, turn west onto Titan Road, and then go south again at Roxborough Park Road to the main entrance. Admission is $6 per passenger vehicle. The park is open daily from 8am to 8pm in summer, with shorter hours the rest of the year. Dogs, bikes, and horseback riding are not permitted.

HORSEBACK RIDING Equestrians can find a mount year-round at **Stockton's Plum Creek Stables,** 7479 W. Titan Rd., Littleton (✆ **303/791-1966;** www.stocktonsplumcreek.com), near Chatfield State Park, 15 miles south of downtown. Stockton's offers hayrides and barbecue picnics, as well as lessons. **Paint Horse Stables,** 4201 S. Parker Rd., Aurora (✆ **303/690-8235;** www.painthorsestables.net), at Cherry Creek State Park, also rents horses, boards horses, and provides riding lessons, trail rides, hayrides, and pony rides for kids.

RECREATION CENTERS The **Denver Department of Parks and Recreation** (✆ **720/913-1311**) operates about 30 recreation centers around the city, several of which have facilities oriented to seniors. Daily guest passes for all facilities, including swimming pools, cost $5 for adults, $2 for children under 18. Facilities vary but may include basketball courts, indoor or outdoor pools, gyms, and weight rooms. The centers offer fitness classes and other recreation programs, including programs for those with special needs. Call ✆ **720/913-0693** for current program information.

Among the city's recreation centers are the following: **Scheitler Recreation Center,** 5031 W. 46th Ave. (✆ **303/458-4898**), which has an indoor pool and a weight room; **Martin Luther King, Jr., Recreation Center,** 3880 Newport St. (✆ **303/331-4034**), which is the nearest full-service center to Denver International Airport and has an indoor pool, a large gym, and a racquetball court; **20th Street Recreation Center,** downtown at 1011 20th St., between Arapahoe and Curtis streets (✆ **303/295-4430**), with an indoor pool and a weight room; and **Washington Park Recreation Center,** 701 S. Franklin St. (✆ **303/698-4962**), with an indoor pool, an advanced weight room, a large gym, and walking and jogging trails.

SKIING Several ski resorts close to the Front Range target primarily locals. They include **Eldora Mountain Resort,** 45 miles west (✆ **303/440-8700;** www.eldora.com), which covers almost 700 acres and has 53 trails, with skiing rated 20% beginner, 50% intermediate, and 30% advanced. **Loveland Basin and Valley,** 56 miles west on I-70, exit 216 (✆ **800/736-3754** or 303/569-3203; www.skiloveland.com), covers 1,365 acres and has 70 trails, rated 13% beginner, 41% intermediate, and 46% advanced. **Winter Park Resort ★**, 67 miles west of Denver on I-70 and U.S. 40 (✆ **970/726-5514** or 303/316-1564; www.winterparkresort.com), boasts 2,762 skiable acres with 134 trails, rated 8% beginner, 17% intermediate, and 75% advanced. Winter Park is accessible by car and via the **Ski Train** (✆ **303/294-4754;** www.skitrain.com) from Union

Station in downtown Denver. Fares are about $50 to $75 per person round-trip; packages including lift tickets are also available. Eldora and Winter Park offer Nordic as well as alpine terrain.

Full information on statewide skiing is available from **Colorado Ski Country USA** (✆ **303/837-0793;** www.coloradoski.com) and the **Colorado Cross Country Ski Association** (www.colorado-xc.org).

Some useful Denver telephone numbers for skiers include **ski-area information and snow report** (✆ 303/825-7669), **weather report** (✆ 303/337-2500), and **road conditions** (✆ 303/639-1111).

SWIMMING The Denver Department of Parks and Recreation (✆ **720/913-1311**) operates 16 outdoor swimming pools (open daily mid-June to mid-Aug) and 12 indoor pools (open Mon–Sat year-round). Nonresident fees are $3 for adults and $2 for children. See "Recreation Centers," above.

TENNIS The Denver Department of Parks and Recreation (✆ **720/913-1311**) manages or owns close to 150 tennis courts, more than one-third of them lit for night play. Among the most popular courts are those in City Park (York St. and E. 17th Ave.), Berkeley Park (Tennyson St. and W. 17th Ave.), Green Valley East Ranch Park (Jebel St. and E. 45th Ave.), Washington Park (S. Downing St. and E. Louisiana Ave.), and Sloan's Lake Park (Sheridan Blvd. and W. 17th Ave.). The public courts are free. For more information, contact the **Colorado Tennis Association** (✆ **303/695-4116;** www.coloradotennis.com).

GREAT NEARBY STATE PARKS

Colorado has a number of excellent state parks offering a wide range of activities and scenery. Information on the state's parks is available at **www.parks.state.co.us**.

BARR LAKE STATE PARK About 25 miles northeast of Denver on I-76 in Brighton, this wildlife sanctuary of almost 2,800 acres comprises a prairie reservoir and surrounding wetlands and uplands. Boats with motors exceeding 10 horsepower are not allowed, but you can sail, paddle, row, and fish. A 9-mile hiking and biking trail circles the lake. A boardwalk from the nature center at the south parking lot leads to a good view of a heron rookery, and bird blinds along this trail allow wildlife observation and photography. Three picnic areas provide tables and grills; there's a commercial campground opposite the park on the west side. The entrance is at 13401 Picadilly Rd. Admission costs $6 per vehicle. Call ✆ **303/659-6005** for more information.

CASTLEWOOD CANYON STATE PARK ★ Steep canyons, a meandering stream, a waterfall, lush vegetation, and considerable wildlife distinguish this 2,000-acre park. You can see the remains of Castlewood Canyon Dam, which was built for irrigation in 1890; it collapsed in 1933, killing two people and flooding the streets of Denver. The park, 30 miles south of Denver on Colo. 83, east of Castle Rock in Franktown, provides picnic facilities and hiking trails. The entrance is at 2989 S. State Hwy. 83; admission is $6 per vehicle. Call ✆ **303/688-5242** for more information.

CHATFIELD STATE PARK ★ Sixteen miles south of downtown Denver on U.S. 85 in Littleton, this park occupies 5,600 acres of prairie against a backdrop of the steeply rising Rocky Mountains. Chatfield Reservoir, with a 26-mile shoreline, invites swimming, boating, fishing, and other watersports. The area also has 18 miles of paved bicycle trails, plus hiking and horseback-riding paths. In winter, there's ice fishing and cross-country skiing. The park also has a hot-air-balloon launch pad, a radio-controlled model aircraft field, and a 21-acre man-made wetlands area.

Facilities include 197 pull-through campsites, showers, laundry, and a dump station. Admission is $7 per vehicle; the camping fee is $18 to $22 daily. The entrance is 1 mile south of C-470 on Wadsworth Boulevard (✆ **303/791-7275**).

CHERRY CREEK STATE PARK The 880-acre Cherry Creek Reservoir, created for flood control by the construction of a dam in 1950, is the central attraction of this popular park, which draws 1.5 million visitors each year. Located at the southeast Denver city limits (off Parker Rd. and I-225) about 12 miles from downtown, the park encompasses 4,200 acres in all.

Watersports include swimming, water-skiing, boating, and fishing. There's a nature trail, dog-training area, model-airplane field with paved runways, jet-ski rental facility, rifle range, pistol range, and trap-shooting area. Twelve miles of paved bicycle paths and 12 miles of bridle trails circle the reservoir (horse rentals are available). Rangers offer guided walks by appointment, as well as evening campfire programs in an amphitheater. In winter, there are skating, ice fishing, and ice boating.

Each of the park's 102 campsites has access to showers, laundry, and a dump station. Most sites have full hookups with water and electric. Many lakeshore day-use sites have picnic tables and grills.

Admission is $7 to $8 per vehicle; campsites are $14 to $22 daily. Campgrounds are open year-round. The entrance is at 4201 S. Parker Rd. in Aurora. Call ✆ **303/690-1166** for general information or ✆ 800/678-2267 for camping reservations.

GOLDEN GATE STATE PARK ★ About 30 miles west of Denver, this 12,000-acre park ranges in elevation from 7,400 to 10,400 feet and offers camping, picnicking, hiking, biking, fishing, hunting, and horseback-riding opportunities. A daily vehicle pass costs $6, and camping fees range from $14 to $18 in developed campgrounds, $8 for backcountry camping. There are around 160 developed campsites, with a limited number of electrical hookups. Reverend's Ridge, the park's largest campground, has coin-operated showers and laundry facilities.

To get to Golden Gate, take Colo. 93 north from Golden 1 mile to Golden Gate Canyon Road. Turn left and continue 13 miles to the park. For more information, call ✆ **303/582-3707.**

6 SPECTATOR SPORTS

Tickets to many sporting events can be obtained from **Ticketmaster** (✆ **303/830-TIXS** [830-8497]; www.ticketmaster.com), which has several outlets in the Denver area.

AUTO RACING For drag racing and other motorsports, head to **Bandimere Speedway,** 3051 S. Rooney Rd., Morrison (✆ **303/697-6001,** or 303/697-4870 for a 24-hr. recording; www.bandimere.com), with races scheduled April through October. There are motorcycles, pickup trucks, street cars, and sports cars, plus car shows, swap meets, and other special events.

BASEBALL The **Colorado Rockies** (✆ **800/388-7625** or 303/762-5437; www.coloradorockies.com) of Major League Baseball's National League West initially enjoyed record-breaking fan support, but attendance has fallen recently, a 2007 run to the World Series notwithstanding. The team plays at the attractive Coors Field, located at 20th and Blake streets in historic Lower Downtown. The 50,000-seat stadium, with a redbrick exterior and on-site microbrewery, was designed in the style of baseball stadiums of old. Tickets are easy to come by, from either the box office or the scalpers on the street.

BASKETBALL The **Denver Nuggets** (**© 303/405-1111** for ticket information; www.nuggets.com) of the National Basketball Association have gained fans thanks to young superstar Carmelo Anthony. The Nuggets play their home games at the handsome Pepsi Center (downtown at Speer Blvd. and Auraria Pkwy.). There are 41 home games a year between November and April, with playoffs continuing into June.

The **University of Denver** (**© 303/871-2336** for ticket office or 303/830-2497; www.denverpioneers.com) plays a competitive college basketball schedule from late November to March.

FOOTBALL The **Denver Broncos** (**© 720/258-3333** for tickets; www.denverbroncos.com) of the National Football League make their home at Invesco Field at Mile High. Home games are sold out months in advance, so call early; there are also a few tickets sold on game day. Your best bet may be to find someone hawking tickets outside the stadium entrance on game day. Pricing tickets above face value is technically illegal, but the law is rarely enforced.

You might have better luck getting into a college game. The **University of Colorado Buffaloes** (**© 303/492-8337;** www.cubuffs.com), of the Big 12 Conference, play in Boulder. Other top college football teams in the area are Colorado State University in Fort Collins and the Air Force Academy in Colorado Springs.

HOCKEY Denver's National Hockey League team, the **Colorado Avalanche** (**© 303/405-1111** for ticket information; www.coloradoavalanche.com), plays in front of sellout crowds at the Pepsi Center (Speer Blvd. and Auraria Pkwy.). The season runs from October to April.

For a cheaper ticket (and a fun atmosphere), the **University of Denver** men's hockey team (**© 303/871-2336** for ticket office or 303/830-2497; www.denverpioneers.com) is consistently top tier and plays a competitive schedule between October and mid-March at the Ritchie Center.

HORSE RACING **Arapahoe Park,** 26000 E. Quincy Ave., Aurora (**© 303/690-2400;** www.milehiracing.com), offers horse racing May to August, with simulcast wagering the rest of the year. Admission varies.

RODEO The **National Western Stock Show, Rodeo, and Horse Show** (**© 303/297-1166;** www.nationalwestern.com) is held the second and third weeks of January. While a move to the plains near Denver International Airport is on the drawing board, the rodeo takes place at the Denver Coliseum, and other activities are at the National Western Complex and the Event Center. With more than $500,000 available in prize money and 700,000 people in attendance, this is one of the world's richest and largest rodeos.

SOCCER The **Colorado Rapids** (**© 303/405-1100;** www.coloradorapids.com), of Major League Soccer, play home games at Dick's Sporting Goods Park, a new, soccer-only stadium at Quebec Street and 60th Avenue in Commerce City.

7 SHOPPING

If you're in Denver on foot, you'll find that most visitors do their shopping along the **16th Street Mall** (the mile-long pedestrian walkway between Market St. and Tremont

Place) and adjacent areas, including **Larimer Square, The Shops at Tabor Center, Writer Square,** and the newest retail development downtown, **Denver Pavilions.**

Outside the downtown area there are more options, primarily the huge **Cherry Creek Shopping Center**—a shopper's dream—south of downtown. There are also numerous funky urban retail areas within the city limits, as well as suburban shopping malls.

Business hours vary from store to store and from mall to mall. Generally, stores are open 6 days a week, with many open on Sunday, too; department stores usually stay open until 9pm at least 1 evening a week. Discount stores and supermarkets are often open later than other stores, and some supermarkets are open 24 hours a day.

SHOPPING A TO Z

Antiques

Denver's main antiques area is **Antique Row** (www.antique-row.com) along **South Broadway,** between Mississippi and Iowa streets, with hundreds of dealers selling all sorts of fine antiques, collectibles, and junk. Wandering through the wide variety of stores, where each dealer has his or her own unique bent, is great fun. Just remember that prices are often negotiable; unless you're quite knowledgeable about antiques, it wouldn't hurt to do some comparison shopping before making a major purchase.

Art & Fine Crafts

The preeminent arts destination in Denver is the **ArtDistrict on Santa Fe.** In recent years, Santa Fe Drive has emerged as home to about 40 galleries and studios between 5th and 11th avenues. Most of the galleries are contemporary or Latin American and there is a popular First Friday Art Walk here from 6 to 9pm the first Friday of every month. For additional information, visit **www.artdistrictonsantafe.com**.

Also, the renaissance of Denver's lower downtown (LoDo) has resulted in the creation of the **Lower Downtown Arts District,** where you can explore a number of galleries. The district runs from Larimer to Wynkoop streets between 14th and 20th streets. Call ✆ **303/628-5428** or browse **www.lodo.org** for additional information.

A mile to the southeast, the Golden Triangle neighborhood, bordered by Lincoln Street, Speer Boulevard, and Colfax Avenue, has more than 25 galleries and a number of museums. The **Golden Triangle Museum District** (✆ **303/534-0771;** www.gtmd.org) puts together an open gallery event the first Friday night of every month, complete with a free shuttle.

Andenken Open weekends, this hip gallery shows the work of contemporary young artists working in every medium under the sun, usually outside the boundaries of tradition. 2990 Larimer St. ✆ **303/941-2458.**

Camera Obscura (Finds) This highly respected gallery exhibits vintage and contemporary photographs, including works by internationally renowned photographers. Closed Monday. 1309 Bannock St. ✆ **303/623-4059.**

Dori Quilts & Lodge Furniture This 10,000-square-foot gallery, which calls itself the largest quilt gallery in America, has some 3,000 to 5,000 handmade quilts on display at any given time. It also sells handmade red cedar log and dried cactus furniture and accessories. Colorado Mills Mall, 14500 W. Colfax Ave., Lakewood. ✆ **303/590-1490.**

Native American Trading Company Older weavings, pottery, baskets, jewelry, and other American Indian works from the Rocky Mountain region are the focus at this fine gallery. It's located in a 1906 Mission Revival building across the street from the Denver Art Museum. Closed Monday. 213 W. 13th Ave. ✆ **303/534-0771.**

Pirate Denver's oldest arts co-op, Pirate has showcased the work of cutting-edge contemporary artists of all kinds for more than 20 years. It's in a funky north Denver neighborhood with several eateries and a theater. 3655 Navajo St. ✆ **303/458-6058.**

Pismo Contemporary Art Glass Nationally renowned glass artists, as well as emerging stars, are represented in this gallery, located in Cherry Creek North. 2770 E. 2nd Ave. ✆ **303/333-2879.**

Sandy Carson Gallery Established regional artists are represented at this respected gallery in the arts district on Santa Fe Drive, which is known for showing contemporary works in traditional media. Closed Sunday and Monday. 760 Santa Fe Dr. ✆ **303/573-8585.**

Books

Barnes & Noble This two-story location is in the Denver Pavilions retail area on the south side of downtown Denver. There's a particularly good travel section, where you'll find local and regional maps. 500 16th St. (in the Denver Pavilions). ✆ **303/825-9166.**

Mile High Comics Megastore Kids One of five Mile High Comics locations in the Denver area, this is the largest comic-book store in the nation. Its 11,000 square feet are packed with comics of all descriptions, plus games, toys, posters, and other books. 9201 N. Washington St., Thornton (10 miles north of downtown Denver). ✆ **303/457-2612.**

Tattered Cover ★★ One of the country's largest bookstores, the locally beloved Tattered Cover moved to new digs on East Colfax Avenue in 2006 after more than 30 years in Cherry Creek. Taking over the old Lowenstein Theater, the store remains a bibliophile's paradise, with comprehensive selections on every subject and a design that incorporates elements of the old theater. Also in the development: Twist & Shout, Denver's top independent record store; an art-house movie theater with its own cocktail lounge; a restaurant, Encore; and a coffee shop. 2526 E. Colfax Ave. (opposite East High School). ✆ **303/322-7727.** www.tatteredcover.com. There are also locations at Denver's LoDo at 16th and Wynkoop sts. (✆ **303/436-1070**) and in the Town Center development in Highlands Ranch (✆ **303/470-7050**).

Fashion

Eddie Bauer This is the place to come for good deals on the famous Eddie Bauer line of upscale outdoor clothing. This extralarge store features a wide variety of men's and women's fashions alongside outdoor-oriented gadgetry. 3000 E. Cherry Creek Ave. (in the Cherry Creek Mall). ✆ **303/377-2100.**

Lawrence Covell This renowned upscale shop, established in 1967 by Lawrence and Cathy Covell, offers the finest men's and women's fashions, including designer clothing by Kiton, John Lobb, Etro, and Paul Smith. 225 Steele St. (in Cherry Creek N.). ✆ **303/320-1023.**

Rockmount Ranch Wear ★★ Founded in 1946 by Jack A. Weil—who passed away in 2008 at the age of 107—Rockmount is one of the last real Western landmarks in town. The three-generation family business—which was the first company to put a snap on a shirt!—recently turned its landmark warehouse into a retail store, and it's even got a small museum of Western wear and memorabilia. The place sells hats, shirts, scarves, and everything else anyone might need to dud up like a cowboy or cowgirl. Rock bands and movie stars love the brand, and even stop by the store on a regular basis. 1626 Wazee St. ✆ **303/629-7777.** www.rockmount.com.

Food & Drink

King Soopers, Safeway, and **Albertson's** are the main grocery-store chains.

Applejack Wine & Spirits Value This huge store, which covers some 40,000 square feet and is one of America's largest beer, wine, and liquor supermarkets, offers some of the best prices in the area. It also delivers. The store has a wide choice of single-malt scotches; an extensive wine section, which includes a number of Colorado wines; and a good selection of cigars. 3320 Youngfield St. (in the Applewood Shopping Center), Wheat Ridge (I-70, exit 264). ✆ **303/233-3331.**

Corks/Wine Complements Side by side near Confluence Park, these two stores offer oenophiles a nice selection of reasonably priced bottles (Corks) and every wine gadget and edible wine accompaniment imaginable (Wine Complements). 1620 Platte St. ✆ **303/477-5799** or 303/480-9463.

The Market at Larimer Square A combination deli/gourmet market/coffee shop right downtown, the Market is something of a community hub for all of downtown Denver. Its location on Larimer Square is ideal for people-watching and convenience. 1445 Larimer Sq. ✆ **303/534-5140.**

Whole Foods This enormous store helps perpetuate Coloradans' healthy lifestyles. No food sold here contains artificial flavoring or preservatives, nor was any grown using pesticides, chemicals, or other additives. There's sushi, a salad bar, and many to-go lunch and dinner offerings as well. This Cherry Creek–area store, part of the national chain, is one of several locations scattered throughout the metropolitan area. 2375 E. 1st Ave. (at University Blvd.). ✆ **720/941-4100.**

Gifts & Souvenirs

Colorado History Museum Store This museum shop carries unique made-in-Colorado gifts and souvenirs, including American Indian jewelry and sand paintings, plus an excellent selection of books on Colorado. 1300 Broadway. ✆ **303/866-4993.**

Where the Buffalo Roam Here you'll find the gamut of traditional Denver and Colorado souvenirs, from T-shirts to buttons to hats to mugs. 535 16th St. ✆ **303/260-7347.**

Jewelry

Jeweler's Center at the University Building Here you'll find about a dozen retail and wholesale outlets in what is billed as Denver's largest concentration of jewelers. 910 16th St. ✆ **303/534-6270.**

John Atencio A highly regarded Colorado artist, John Atencio has received several awards for his unique jewelry designs. Located on historic Larimer Square, his store offers 14- and 18-karat gold jewelry accented with high-quality stones, plus special collections such as "Elements," which features unusual combinations of gold, sterling silver, and stones. 1440 Larimer St. (on Larimer Sq.). ✆ **303/534-4277.**

Malls & Shopping Centers

Cherry Creek Shopping Center Saks Fifth Avenue, Neiman Marcus, and Nordstrom anchor this deluxe million-square-foot mall, with more than 160 shops, restaurants, and services, including an eight-screen movie theater. Across the street is Cherry Creek North, an upscale retail neighborhood. The mall is open Monday through Friday from 10am to 9pm, Saturday from 10am to 8pm, and Sunday from 11am to 6pm. 3000 E. 1st Ave. (btw. University Blvd. and Steele St.). ✆ **303/388-3900.**

Colorado Mills This relatively new mall, on the western fringe of metro Denver, has over 200 stores and outlet centers, as well as theaters, restaurants, and a skatepark. Stores include Super Target, Eddie Bauer Outlet, and Sports Authority. I-70 and W. Colfax Ave., Lakewood. ✆ **303/384-3000.**

Denver Pavilions Located on the southern end of the 16th Street Mall, this three-level complex jammed with entertainment and dining options features Denver's Hard Rock Cafe, a movie-plex, Niketown, a bowling alley, Virgin Records, and Barnes & Noble megastores (see "Books," above). Store hours are Monday to Saturday from 10am to 9pm and Sunday from 11am to 6pm; the restaurants and movie theaters are open later. 500 16th St. (btw. Welton and Tremont sts.). ✆ **303/260-6000.**

Larimer Square This restored quarter of old Denver (see "More Attractions," earlier in this chapter) includes numerous art galleries, boutiques, restaurants, and nightclubs. Most shops are open Monday through Thursday from 10am to 7pm, Friday and Saturday from 10am to 6pm, and Sunday from noon to 5pm. Restaurant and nightclub hours vary, and hours are slightly shorter during the winter. 1400 block of Larimer St. ✆ **303/534-2367.**

Mile High Flea Market Just 10 minutes northeast of downtown Denver, this huge market attracts more than 1.5 million shoppers a year to 2,000 vendors on more than 80 paved acres. Besides closeouts, garage sales, and seasonal merchandise, it has more than a dozen places to eat and snack, plus family rides. It's open year-round on Friday, Saturday, and Sunday from 7am to 5pm. Admission is $2 Friday, $3 Saturday and Sunday, and always free for children under 12. 7007 E. 88th Ave. (at I-76), Henderson. ✆ **303/289-4656.**

The Outlets at Castle Rock This outlet mall between Denver and Colorado Springs, about 30 minutes south of Denver, has about 100 stores, including Levi's/Dockers, Van Heusen, Eddie Bauer, Bass, Nike, Big Dog, Gap, Borders, and Coleman, plus a food court. Open Monday through Saturday from 10am to 8pm and Sunday from 11am to 6pm. I-25, exit 184. ✆ **303/688-4494.**

Park Meadows Retail Resort Located at the C-470/I-25 interchange south of Denver, this is the largest shopping center in Colorado, and now the heart of a mind-boggling retail area. Very posh and upscale—the interior is reminiscent of a luxurious mountain lodge—Park Meadows features Nordstrom, Dillard's, Macy's, and 160 specialty shops and restaurants. Stores are open Monday through Saturday from 10am to 9pm, Sunday from 11am to 6pm. 8401 Park Meadows Center Dr. (south of C-470 on Yosemite St.), Littleton. ✆ **303/792-2533.**

Sporting Goods

Those in need of a bike should talk to the experts at **Campus Cycles,** 2102 S. Washington St. (✆ **303/698-2811**), which carries the Gary Fisher, Trek, and Giant brands. Sports fans looking for that Rockies cap or Broncos shirt will have no trouble finding it at the appropriately named **Sportsfan,** 1962 Blake St., across from Coors Field (✆ **303/295-3460**). There are several other locations in the Denver area, and mail orders are accepted.

For information on where to rent sporting-goods equipment, see the "Outdoor Activities" section, earlier in this chapter.

REI ★★ Although the Seattle-based co-op has several stores in the metro area, its flagship store, a beautifully restored redbrick just west of downtown, is one of the country's best and biggest outdoor-oriented retailers. (It is one of only three flagship stores; the others are in Seattle and the Minneapolis area.) This is the place to go before heading for an excursion in the Rockies. The gargantuan store features a 45-foot climbing wall, an outdoor bike-testing area, a kayaking area on adjacent Cherry Creek, and a "cold room" to try out outerwear and sleeping bags. 1416 Platte St. ✆ **303/756-3100.**

Sports Authority Sportscastle Active travelers will be pleased to discover that Denver has sporting-goods stores that match the scale of the outdoor opportunities in Colorado—namely, this five-story monster. With everything from footballs to golf clubs to tents, the selection is comprehensive. Extras include a driving cage for golfers, ball courts on the roof, and the annual Sniagrab (that's *bargains* spelled backward), featuring rock-bottom prices on ski equipment every Labor Day weekend. 1000 Broadway. ✆ **303/863-2260.**

Toys & Hobbies

Caboose Hobbies Model-train buffs should plan to spend at least half a day here. Billed as the world's largest train store, it stocks electric trains, accessories, books, and so much train-related stuff (over 100,000 items on nearly 20,000 sq. ft. of floor space) that it's hard to know where to start. The knowledgeable employees seem just as happy to talk about trains as to sell them. Naturally, there are model trains of every scale winding through the store, as well as test tracks so that you can check out a locomotive before purchasing it. There are also mugs, patches, and decals from just about every railroad line that ever existed in North America. 500 S. Broadway. ✆ **303/777-6766.** www.caboosehobbies.com.

Wizard's Chest Kids This store's magical design—a castle with drawbridge and moat—and legendary wizard out front are worth the trip alone, but be sure to go inside. The Wizard's Chest is paradise for kids of all ages, specializing in games, toys, and puzzles. The costume department is fully stocked with attire, wigs, masks, and professional makeup. 230 Fillmore St. in Cherry Creek N. ✆ **303/321-4304.** www.wizardschest.com.

8 DENVER AFTER DARK

The anchor of Denver's performing arts scene, an important part of this increasingly sophisticated city, is the 4-square-block **Denver Performing Arts Complex,** located downtown just a few blocks from major hotels. The complex houses nine theaters, a concert hall, and what may be the nation's first symphony hall in the round. It is home to the Colorado Symphony, Colorado Ballet, Opera Colorado, and Denver Center for the Performing Arts (an umbrella organization for resident and touring theater companies). In all, Denver has some 30 theaters, more than 100 cinemas, and dozens of concert halls, nightclubs, discos, and bars. Clubs offer country-and-western music, jazz, rock, and comedy.

Current entertainment listings appear in special Friday-morning sections of the two daily newspapers, the *Denver Post* and *Rocky Mountain News. Westword,* a weekly newspaper distributed free throughout the city every Wednesday evening, has perhaps the best listings: It focuses on the arts, entertainment, and local politics.

You can get tickets for nearly all major entertainment and sporting events from **Ticketmaster** (✆ **303/830-TIXS** [830-8497]), which has several outlets in the Denver area.

Rock, Jazz & Blues

Bluebird Theater This historic theater, built in 1913 to show silent movies, has been restored and now offers a diverse selection of rock, alternative, and other live music, as well as films. The performers generally target teens and 20-somethings. Tickets usually run $7 to $20. 3317 E. Colfax Ave. (at Adams St.). ✆ **303/377-1666.** www.bluebirdtheater.net.

The Church Located just a few blocks southeast of downtown, this cavernous and historic former church features three dance floors and several bars, including wine and sushi bars. One of Denver's most popular dance clubs, it attracts celebrity DJs and a throng of beautiful people on a regular basis. The semireligious decor and diverse crowd, in conjunction with the loud music, make for near sensory overload. 1160 Lincoln St. ✆ **303/832-3528.** www.the-church.com.

El Chapultepec Denver's oldest jazz club, the "Pec" offers live jazz nightly in a noisy, friendly atmosphere. You'll often find standing room only, not to mention a hearty helping of local color—young and old, poor and rich, in equal measure. A small burrito kitchen and poolroom adjoin the club. There is never a cover. 1962 Market St. ✆ **303/295-9126.**

Gothic Theatre One of metro Denver's best-looking (and best-sounding) midsize venues, the Gothic is light-years beyond the heavy-metal dive it was in the 1980s. Both local and national acts play the stage here. Tickets usually cost $7 to $30. 3263 S. Broadway, Englewood. ✆ **303/788-0984.** www.gothictheatre.com.

hi-dive A standout for indie rock and experimental music, the hi-dive is popular with young and in-the-know hipsters and features an adjoining no-cover bar, **Sputnik,** with a kitchen in the back. 7 S. Broadway. ✆ **303/570-4500.** www.hi-dive.com.

Larimer Lounge This bar on old Larimer Street has been serving drinks since 1892 and serving loud punk rock and alternative music since 2003. The place is out of the hustle and bustle of LoDo, in an old neighborhood east of Broadway, and has seen such national acts as the Arcade Fire and Mudhoney take the stage. The average patron is young, tattooed, and a bit rough around the edges. 2721 Larimer St. ✆ **303/291-1007.** www.larimerlounge.com.

Mercury Cafe It's hard to classify the Mercury as specializing in any genre of music, but there's always something exciting happening, even on poetry night. It attracts a casual, eclectic clientele. Offerings usually range from tango lessons to avant-garde jazz to classical violin to tarot readings to progressive rock. A health-oriented restaurant is also here. 2199 California St. (at 22nd St.). ✆ **303/294-9258.** www.mercurycafe.com.

3 Kings Tavern A relatively new venue in the Baker neighborhood, 3 Kings offers a hip vibe and interesting decor (Elvis paraphernalia, pop culture bric-a-brac, comic-book wallpapering, and a big "Sanatorium" sign above the bar) to go with the touring and local rockabilly, punk, metal, and country acts that grace the stage. 60 S. Broadway. ✆ **303/777-7352.** www.3kingstavern.com.

Country Music

Grizzly Rose Known to locals as "the Griz" or "the Rose," its 5,000-square-foot dance floor beneath a 1-acre roof has drawn such national acts as Garth Brooks, Willie Nelson, LeAnn Rimes, and Johnny Paycheck. There's live music Tuesday through Saturday; Sunday is family night. Dance lessons are available Wednesday night. 5450 N. Valley Hwy., at I-25, exit 215. ✆ **303/295-1330.**

Stampede This colossal nightclub offers free country-and-western dance lessons on Friday and Saturday, a huge solid-oak dance floor, pool tables, a restaurant, and seven bars. Its Wednesday ladies' nights are notoriously rowdy. Closed Sunday through Tuesday. 2430 S. Havana St. (at Parker Rd.), Aurora. ✆ **303/696-7686.** www.stampedeclub.net.

The Bar Scene

The first permanent structure on the site of modern Denver was supposedly a saloon, and the city has built on that tradition ever since. Today there are sports bars, dance bars, lots of brewpubs, outdoor cafe bars, English pubs, Old West saloons, city-overlook bars, Art Deco bars, gay bars, and a few bars I don't want to discuss here.

> **Bottoms Up!**
>
> More beer is brewed in metropolitan Denver than in any other city in the United States.

Appropriately, the newest Denver "in" spot for barhopping is also the oldest part of the city—LoDo—which has been renovated and upgraded, and now attracts all the young partiers and upwardly mobile professionals. Its trendy nightspots are often noisy and crowded, but if you're looking for action, this is where you'll find it.

Other popular "strips" are along Broadway (centered on 10th and Ellsworth aves., respectively), and along East Colfax Avenue from about Ogden to Monroe streets. For those who prefer caffeine to alcohol, there are also a number of good coffee bars throughout downtown Denver, as well as in the Capitol Hill and Uptown neighborhoods.

The following are among the popular bars and pubs, but there are plenty more, so be sure to check out the publications mentioned at the beginning of this section.

Bull & Bush Pub & Brewery A neighborhood hangout in Cherry Creek, this re-creation of a famous London pub always has about 10 of its own award-winning beers on tap. On Sunday evening, there's traditional jazz by regional groups. A full brew-house menu is available. 4700 Cherry Creek Dr. S., Glendale. ✆ **303/759-0333.** www.bullandbush.com.

Charlie Brown's Just south of downtown, Charlie Brown's is a piano bar, some version of which has been in existence since 1927. The atmosphere is casual, with a baby grand piano and a diverse crowd. The grill serves three meals a day, inside and outside on a great patio. 980 Grant St. (at 10th Ave.). ✆ **303/860-1655.**

Churchill Bar You'll find an excellent selection of fine cigars, single-malt Scotches, and after-dinner drinks at this refined lounge, which caters to older, well-to-do professional types. In the Brown Palace Hotel, 321 17th St. ✆ **303/297-3111.**

Cruise Room Bar Modeled after a 1930s-era bar aboard the *Queen Mary,* the Cruise Room opened in 1933 on the day Prohibition ended. Restored to its Art Deco best, the very red room features decorative panels depicting toasts around the world and mixes one of the best martinis in town. In the Oxford Hotel, 1600 17th St. (at Wazee St.). ✆ **303/825-1107.**

Falling Rock Tap House Comfy, woody, and just down the street from Coors Field, this LoDo pub has 69 beers on tap—the best selection of good beer in Denver. You'll also find darts and pool, happy hours, and occasional live music. 1919 Blake St. ✆ **303/293-8338.** www.fallingrocktaphouse.com.

JR's A cavernous gay bar with a little bit of country, JR's is centered on a horseshoe-shaped bar and known for its drink specials and busy dance floor. 777 E. 17th Ave. ✆ **303/831-0459.** www.myjrs.com.

Finds Brewery Tours

Whether or not you drink beer, it can be fun to look behind the scenes and see how beer is made. Denver's first modern microbrewery, the **Wynkoop Brewing Co.,** 1634 18th St., at Wynkoop Street (✆ **303/297-2700;** www.wynkoop.com), offers tours every Saturday between 1 and 5pm. Housed in the renovated 1898 J. S. Brown Mercantile Building across from Union Station, the Wynkoop is also a popular restaurant (see "Where to Dine," in chapter 6). At least 10 beers are always on tap, including a few exotic recipes—the spicy chile beer is my favorite. If you can't decide which one to try, the "taster set" provides a nice sampling: nine 4-ounce glasses of different brews. For non–beer drinkers, the Wynkoop offers some of the best root beer in town. On the second floor is a top-notch pool hall with billiards, snooker, and darts.

Also downtown, **Great Divide Brewing Co.,** 2201 Arapahoe St. (✆ **303/296-9460,** ext. 26; www.greatdivide.com), has a terrific taproom and free samples. Tours are offered Monday through Friday at 3pm and on the hour on Saturday from 2 to 7pm. Great Divide is known for being a beer lover's brewery, crafting such favorites as the rice-based Samurai and the aptly named Yeti Imperial Stout.

Since it opened in 1991, **Rock Bottom Brewery,** 1001 16th St. (✆ **303/534-7616;** www.rockbottom.com), has been one of the leading brewpubs in the area. Tours, which are given upon request, offer great views of the brewing process, plus a sampling of the product.

A mile south of downtown, **Breckenridge Brewery,** 471 Kalamath St. (✆ **303/623-BREW** [623-2739]; www.breckenridgebrewery.com), also lets you see the brewing process. Free brewery tours are given by appointment. In addition to its award-winning ales, the brewery serves traditional pub fare.

East of downtown in the Uptown neighborhood, the same folks behind Mountain Sun in Boulder opened **Vine Street Pub & Brewery** in 2008; it's at 1700 Vine St. (✆ **303/388-2337**) and has a fun and funky neighborhood vibe with a healthful bent to its menu. In Cherry Creek, **Bull & Bush Pub & Brewery,** 4700 Cherry Creek Dr. S. (✆ **303/759-0333;** www.bullandbush.com), produces about 10 handcrafted ales and will give tours of its facilities upon request.

For a look at the other side of the coin, take a trip to nearby Golden for a look at **Coors,** one of the world's largest breweries (see "A Side Trip to Colorado's Gold Circle Towns," below).

Meadowlark This dim, hip subterranean bar oozes style, featuring plenty of industrial chic, great margaritas and other mixed drinks, and an eclectic music calendar both live and prerecorded. 2721 Larimer St. ✆ **303/293-0251.**

My Brother's Bar A Platte Valley fixture since the Beat Generation (this was one of Jack Kerouac's favorite Denver hangouts), this is the locals' choice for big, juicy burgers, wrapped in wax paper and served with an array of condiments and a side helping of friendly, unpretentious vibes. 2376 15th St. ✆ **303/455-9991.**

Old Curtis Street Bar A classic family-owned bar, complete with vinyl booths and a Mexican menu, Old Curtis Street is my pick for a low-key evening downtown. There is an eclectic entertainment calendar featuring punk bands, DJs, and stand-up comedy nights. 2100 Curtis St. ✆ **303/292-2083.** www.oldcurtis.com.

Samba Room The atmosphere at the Samba Room—Cuban murals, booming Latin music, a fashionable young clientele—is right up there with Denver's flashiest nightclubs. The menu of Latin-Caribbean fusion, albeit a bit pricey and uneven, adds to the theme. 1460 Larimer St. ✆ **720/956-1701.**

Sing Sing A noisy, eclectic crowd dominates the scene at this LoDo hot spot, located beneath the Denver ChopHouse & Brewery (see "Where to Dine," in chapter 6). You'll often find low-priced beer specials, which encourage the hard-partying college types to sing along (loudly and badly) with the dueling pianos. A fun place, but hang on tight. Closed Sunday. 1735 19th St. ✆ **303/291-0880.** www.singsing.com.

Wynkoop Brewing Company Owned by Denver Mayor John Hickenlooper, Denver's first modern brewpub is still the city's best. Among its most interesting offerings are India pale ale, chile beer, and Scotch ale, but you really can't go wrong with any of the selections. Added attractions: a large upstairs pool hall, which generally draws a more party-hearty crowd than the restaurant and bar, and an improv and comedy theater in the basement. 1634 18th St. (at Wynkoop St.). ✆ **303/297-2700.** www.wynkoop.com.

THE PERFORMING ARTS

Classical Music & Opera

Colorado Symphony Orchestra This international-caliber orchestra performs more than 100 classical, pops, and family concerts each year at locations throughout the metropolitan area, mostly at the Denver Center for the Performing Arts. Most tickets run $20 to $80. 1000 14th St., #15. ✆ **303/623-7876.** www.coloradosymphony.org.

Opera Colorado Every season, the company stages three operas (four performances each), with English supertitles, at the stunning Ellie Caulkins Opera House at the Denver Performing Arts Complex. Internationally renowned singers and local favorites sing the lead roles. The typical schedule is three evening performances and one matinee each week from February to May. Tickets usually cost $30 to $125. 695 S. Colorado Blvd., #20. ✆ **303/357-2787** for tickets or 303/778-1500. www.operacolorado.org.

Theater & Comedy

Buntport Theater Injecting a fresh dose of creativity and zaniness into the Denver theater scene, the Buntport plays host to a number of original productions and adaptations (including "live sit-coms") as well as improv and open mics at its black box–style theater south of downtown. 717 Lipan St. ✆ **720/946-1388.** www.buntport.com.

Comedy Works Considered one of the region's top comedy clubs for more than 20 years, this is your best bet for seeing America's hot comics at work—Bob Saget and *Last Comic Standing* winner (and Denver local) Josh Blue recently took the stage. Admission is $7 to $10 on weekdays, more on weekends and for marquee performers. A second Comedy Works opened at Belleview and I-25 in the Denver Tech Center. 1226 15th St. ✆ **303/595-3637.** www.comedyworks.com.

Denver Center for the Performing Arts An umbrella organization for resident and touring theater, youth outreach, and conservatory training, the DCPA includes the **Denver Center Theatre Company,** the largest professional resident theater company in the Rockies. With 40 artists on its payroll, the troupe performs about 10 plays in repertory from October to June, including classical and contemporary dramas, musicals, and premieres of new plays. Tickets cost roughly $30 to $60. **Denver Center Attractions** brings in more than 10 touring Broadway productions annually. Tickets run $25 to $80. For both companies, many shows sell out well in advance. 14th and Curtis sts. ✆ **800/641-1222** or 303/893-4100. www.denvercenter.org.

Denver Civic Theatre A restored 1921 gem, the Denver Civic Theatre is a new outlet for touring productions, typically a bit edgy. Tickets usually cost $30 to $50. 721 Santa Fe Dr. ✆ **303/309-3773.** www.denvercivic.com.

El Centro Su Teatro A Hispanic theater and cultural center, El Centro presents bilingual productions on a regular basis. Tickets cost $10 to $20. 4725 High St. ✆ **303/296-0219.** www.suteatro.org.

Lannie's Clocktower Cabaret In the basement of the landmark D&F Tower on the 16th Street Mall, Lannie's is a funky bordello-inspired theater that sees a wide variety of entertainers on its stage, including hostess/singer Lannie Garrett (known for her portrayal of "Patsy DeCline"), as well as burlesque, comedy, and music. In the D&F Tower, 1601 Arapahoe St. ✆ **303/293-0075.** www.lannies.com.

Dance

Cleo Parker Robinson Dance A highly acclaimed multicultural modern-dance ensemble and school, the Cleo Parker Robinson group performs a varied selection of programs each year, both on tour around the world and at several Denver locations. Tickets usually run $20 to $35. 119 Park Ave. W. ✆ **303/295-1759.** www.cleoparkerdance.org.

Colorado Ballet The state's premier professional resident ballet company performs at the Ellie Caulkins Opera House and other venues. The company presents five productions during its fall-through-spring season—a balance of classical and contemporary works that always includes *The Nutcracker* at Christmastime. Tickets range from $25 to $150. 1278 Lincoln St. ✆ **303/837-8888.** www.coloradoballet.org.

MAJOR CONCERT HALLS & AUDITORIUMS

Arvada Center for the Arts & Humanities This multidisciplinary arts center is in use almost every day of the year for performances by internationally known artists and its own theater companies, its historical museum and art gallery exhibitions, and its hands-on education programs for all ages. In addition, the children's theater program performs in front of an annual audience of 60,000. A new, fully accessible playground features a 343-foot sea creature by the name of Squiggles. 6901 Wadsworth Blvd., Arvada (2½ miles north of I-70). ✆ **720/898-7200.** www.arvadacenter.org.

Denver Performing Arts Complex Covering 4 square downtown blocks, from Speer Boulevard to 14th Street and Champa to Arapahoe streets, the Center for the Performing Arts (called the "Plex" by locals) is impressive even to those not attending a performance. Its numerous theaters seat from 157 to 2,800, and there's also a restaurant. 14th and Curtis sts. ✆ **800/641-1222** or 303/893-4100. www.denvercenter.org.

Fiddler's Green Amphitheatre The alfresco summer concerts here feature national and international stars of rock, jazz, classical, and country music. The amphitheater has about 6,500 reserved seats and room for 10,000 more on its spacious lawn. Located in the southwestern section of the metropolitan area, just west of I-25 between Arapahoe and Orchard roads, it's open from May to September. The surrounding streets are a gallery for the Museum of Outdoor Arts featuring numerous characters from *Alice in Wonderland.* 6350 Greenwood Plaza Blvd., Englewood. ✆ **303/220-7000.**

Fillmore Auditorium The 3,600-seat Fillmore is the former Mammoth Gardens, which was renovated by proprietors of the legendary Fillmore in San Francisco. The slickly remodeled venue is now one of Denver's best, loaded with bars and countless vintage rock photos. It attracts national rock acts from Ween to Bob Dylan. Tickets generally cost $20 to $100. 1510 Clarkson St. ✆ **303/837-0360.** www.fillmoreauditorium.com.

Paramount Theatre A performing arts center since 1929, this restored 2,000-seat downtown theater is a wonderful place to enjoy jazz, pop, and folk performances, as well as comedy, lectures, and theater. Recent bookings have included Foreigner and Chelsea Handler. 1621 Glenarm Place. ✆ **303/623-0106.** www.paramountdenver.com.

Red Rocks Amphitheatre ★★★ Quite possibly the country's best and most beautiful venue for top-name outdoor summer concerts, Red Rocks is in the foothills of the Rocky Mountains, 15 miles southwest of the city. Four-hundred-foot-high red sandstone rocks flank the 9,000-seat amphitheater, a product of the Civilian Conservation Corps. At night, with the lights of Denver spread across the horizon, the atmosphere is magical. The Beatles performed here, as have Jimi Hendrix, Paul Simon, the Grateful Dead, Sting, Bonnie Raitt, Lyle Lovett, Willie Nelson, and top symphony orchestras from around the world. The venue has a sparkling new **visitor center** at the amphitheater's apex, which affords amazing views and displays detailing the varied performances that have taken place here since it opened in 1941. There are also a restaurant, a network of hiking trails, and the **trading post,** carrying a good selection of American Indian jewelry and pottery, plus a variety of other curios and souvenirs. I-70, exit 259 S., 16351 C.R. 93, Morrison. ✆ **720/865-2494.** www.redrocksonline.com.

9 A SIDE TRIP TO COLORADO'S GOLD CIRCLE

Golden, Idaho Springs, and **Georgetown** make up most of the fabled Gold Circle—those towns that boomed with the first strikes of the gold rush in 1859. Central City, once the richest of the four towns but now the least attractive, completes the circle. Central City is trying to relive its glory days with a return to gambling, largely supported by locals from Denver, and although the exteriors of its historic buildings remain appealing, the rows of electronic slot machines and other gambling devices inside are a turnoff. Visitors to the area might like to make a brief stop and then move on to Idaho Springs.

GOLDEN ★★

Golden, 15 miles west of downtown Denver by way of U.S. 6 or Colo. 58 off I-70, is better known for the Coors Brewery (founded in 1873) and the Colorado School of Mines (established in 1874) than for its years as territorial capital. For tourist information, contact the **Greater Golden Area Chamber of Commerce,** 1010 Washington Ave., Golden, CO 80402 (✆ **303/279-3113;** www.goldencochamber.org).

What to See & Do

Historic downtown Golden centers on the **Territorial Capitol** in the **Loveland Building,** 12th Street and Washington Avenue. Built in 1861, it housed the first state legislature from 1862 to 1867, when the capital was moved to Denver. Today it contains offices

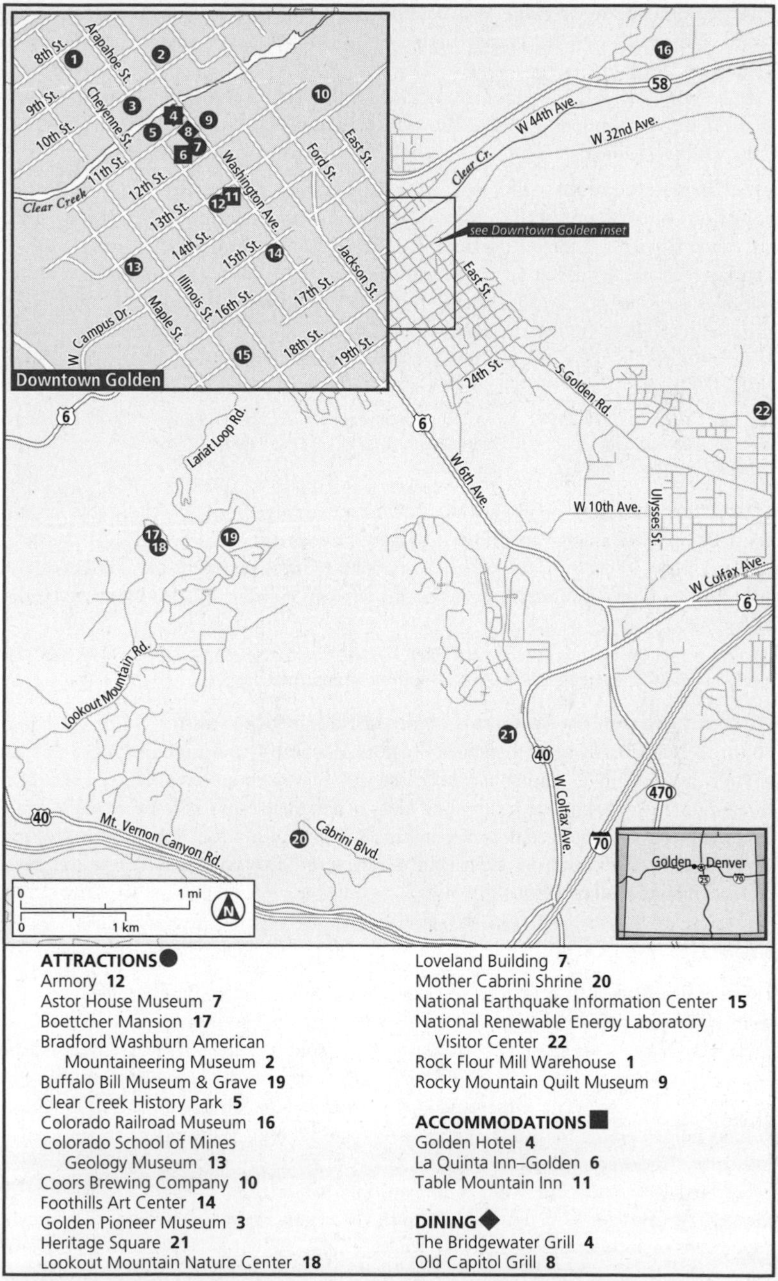

ATTRACTIONS ●
Armory **12**
Astor House Museum **7**
Boettcher Mansion **17**
Bradford Washburn American Mountaineering Museum **2**
Buffalo Bill Museum & Grave **19**
Clear Creek History Park **5**
Colorado Railroad Museum **16**
Colorado School of Mines Geology Museum **13**
Coors Brewing Company **10**
Foothills Art Center **14**
Golden Pioneer Museum **3**
Heritage Square **21**
Lookout Mountain Nature Center **18**
Loveland Building **7**
Mother Cabrini Shrine **20**
National Earthquake Information Center **15**
National Renewable Energy Laboratory Visitor Center **22**
Rock Flour Mill Warehouse **1**
Rocky Mountain Quilt Museum **9**

ACCOMMODATIONS ■
Golden Hotel **4**
La Quinta Inn–Golden **6**
Table Mountain Inn **11**

DINING ◆
The Bridgewater Grill **4**
Old Capitol Grill **8**

and a restaurant. The **Armory,** 13th and Arapahoe streets, is probably the largest cobblestone structure in the United States; 3,300 wagonloads of stone and quartz went into its construction. **The Rock Flour Mill Warehouse,** 8th and Cheyenne streets, dates from 1863; it was built with red granite from nearby Golden Gate Canyon and still has its original cedar beams and wooden floors.

In addition to the attractions listed below, see the section on Golden Gate State Park, in the Denver "Outdoor Activities" section, and RipBoard, in the "Boating" section, earlier in this chapter.

Astor House Museum This handsome native stone structure, believed to be the first stone hotel built west of the Mississippi River, was constructed in 1867 to house legislators when Golden was the territorial capital. Scheduled for demolition to make space for a parking lot, the Astor House was instead restored in the 1970s and is now listed on the National Register of Historic Places. Today the Western-style Victorian hotel offers glimpses into life in Golden during the town's heyday in the late 19th century. Allow 30 to 60 minutes. While there, you can obtain a walking-tour guide for the 12th Street Historic District or visit the Victorian Gift Shop, whose proceeds benefit the museum.

822 12th St. ✆ **303/278-3557.** www.astorhousemuseum.org. Admission $3 adults ($4.50 for combo ticket that also includes Clear Creek History Park), $2 children 12 and under ($3 combo ticket). Tues–Sat 10am–4:30pm; June–Aug also Sun 11am–3pm.

Boettcher Mansion This historic Jefferson County estate was built by Charles Boettcher in 1917 as a summer home and hunting lodge. It contains displays of furnishings and other items from the American Arts and Crafts period of the late 1800s and early 1900s. Other exhibits explore the history of Golden and the Boettcher family. Allow 1 hour.

900 Colorow Rd. (on Lookout Mountain). ✆ **720/497-7630.** http://jeffco.us/boettcher/index.htm. Free admission, donations accepted. Mon–Fri 8am–4pm, or by appointment.

Bradford Washburn American Mountaineering Museum Named for pioneering mountaineer and cartographer Bradford Washburn, this museum, which opened in 2008, takes on the daunting task of telling the story of conquering the world's toughest mountains in an indoor facility and does a remarkable job keeping the epic scale. Exhibits cover mountain and rock-climbing history, technique, and technology, and showcase the contributions of the legends of the sport. The scale model of Mount Everest is a highlight. Allow 1 hour.

710 10th St. ✆ **303/996-2755.** www.bwamm.org. Admission $6.50 adults, $4.50 children. Tues–Sat 10am–6pm (Thurs until 7pm).

Buffalo Bill Museum & Grave ★ Kids William Frederick "Buffalo Bill" Cody, the famous Western scout, is buried atop Lookout Mountain, south of Golden. (Some folks claim that friends stole Cody's body after his sister sold it to the City of Denver and the *Denver Post,* hightailed it north, and buried it in Wyoming, but I was assured that this was the real McCoy.) The museum contains memorabilia from the life and legend of Buffalo Bill, who rode for the Pony Express, organized buffalo hunts for foreign royalty, and toured the world with his Wild West Show. There are also displays of American Indian artifacts, guns, and Western art; an observation deck provides a great view of Denver. The museum is in 66-acre **Lookout Mountain Park,** a Denver municipal park popular for picnicking. Allow 1 to 1½ hours.

987 1/2 Lookout Mountain Rd. ✆ **303/526-0747.** www.buffalobill.org. Admission $3 adults, $2 seniors, $1 children 6–15, free for children 5 and under. May–Oct daily 9am–5pm; Nov–Apr Tues–Sun 9am–4pm. Closed Christmas. I-70, exit 256.

Clear Creek History Park This 3-acre creekside park illustrates the history of the area's ranching, with two log cabins, several animal barns, a blacksmith's shop, and a one-room schoolhouse from the 1870s. The buildings were moved to this site to save them from development in nearby Golden Gate Canyon, their original location. Allow about an hour.

11th and Arapahoe sts. in downtown Golden. ✆ **303/278-3557.** www.clearcreekhistorypark.org. Admission $3 adults ($4.50 for combo ticket that also includes the Astor House Museum), $2 children 12 and under ($3 combo ticket). June–Aug Tues–Sat 10am–4:30pm, Sun 1–4pm; May and Sept Sat 10am–4:30pm. Closed Oct–Apr.

Colorado Railroad Museum ★ Housed in a replica of an 1880 railroad depot, this museum 2 miles east of Golden is a must-see for railroad buffs. On display are more than 100 narrow- and standard-gauge locomotives, cabooses, and cars, plus other historic equipment, artifacts, photos, documents, and model trains. The exhibits cover 12 acres, including the two-story depot and a working roundhouse. You can climb into many of the old locomotives and wander through the parlor cars. The excellent gift-and-souvenir shop sells hundreds of railroad-related items, from coffee mugs to posters to T-shirts. Allow 1 to 2 hours.

17155 W. 44th Ave. ✆ **800/365-6263** or 303/279-4591. www.coloradorailroadmuseum.org. Admission $8 adults, $7 seniors over 60, $5 children 2-15, free for children 1 and under, $18 families. Daily 9am–5pm. Closed Thanksgiving, Christmas, and New Year's Day. Follow signs from I-70, exit 265, westbound; exit 266, eastbound.

Colorado School of Mines Geology Museum ★ Exhibits here help explain the history of mining in Colorado with a replica of a uranium mine and other displays. On exhibit are some 50,000 minerals, gems, fossils, and artifacts from around the world, plus displays on geology, Earth history, and paleontology. The Colorado School of Mines, founded in 1874, has an enrollment of about 3,000. Allow 1 hour.

13th and Maple sts. ✆ **303/273-3815** or 303/273-3823. Free admission. School year Mon–Sat 9am–4pm, Sun 1–4pm; summer Mon–Sat 9am–4pm. Closed Colorado School of Mines holidays.

Coors Brewing Company Reputedly the world's largest single-site brewery, this facility produces 1.5 million gallons of beer each day. Coors conducts free public tours, followed by free samples of the various beers produced. The entire presentation lasts about 1 1/2 hours. Tours leave a central parking lot at 13th and Ford streets, where visitors board a bus for a short drive through historic Golden before arriving at the brewery. There, a 30-minute prerecorded walking tour covers the history of the Coors family and company, the barley malting process, the 13,640-gallon gleaming copper kettles, and the entire production process all the way to packaging. Children are welcome, and arrangements can be made for visitors with disabilities. There's also a gift shop and an interactive timeline in the reception area. Allow about 2 hours—unless you take the "short tour," which actually skips the tour altogether and heads straight to the hospitality lounge. ***Note:*** Visitors under 18 must be accompanied by an adult.

13th and Ford sts. ✆ **866/812-2337** or 303/277-2337. www.coors.com. Free admission. Tours Thurs–Sat and Mon 10am–4pm; Sun noon–4pm. Closed Tues, Wed, and holidays. Visitors 17 and under must be accompanied by an adult.

Foothills Art Center Housed in an 1872 Gothic-style Presbyterian church (which is on the National Register of Historic Places), this exhibition center evolved from the annual Golden Sidewalk Art Show and features changing national and regional exhibits. A gift shop sells crafts by local artisans. Allow 30 minutes.

809 15th St. ✆ **303/279-3922.** www.foothillsartcenter.org. Admission $5 adults, $3 seniors, free for children and students. Mon–Sat 10am–5pm; Sun 1–5pm.

Golden Pioneer Museum This museum exhibits an impressive collection of furniture, household articles, photographs, and other items, including a re-created 19th-century parlor and boudoir. Especially impressive is its collection of 200 American Indian dolls, representing 39 different groups from all around North America. There are also a genealogical and historic research library and a gift shop. Allow 1 hour.

923 10th St. ✆ **303/278-7151.** www.goldenpioneermuseum.com. Admission $3 adults, $2 seniors and children 6–18, free for children 5 and under, $10 families. Mon–Sat 10am–4:30pm. Closed major holidays.

Heritage Square Kids A family-oriented shopping, dining, and entertainment village with a Wild West theme, Heritage Square features some Victorian specialty shops, a Ferris wheel, a stocked fishing pond, and a dinner theater. Warm-weather activities include go-carts, bumper boats, and a 2,350-foot alpine slide with bobsled-style carts. Heritage Square Music Hall offers shows for adults and children, and there's a nostalgic ice-cream parlor. Allow 1 to 2 hours.

18301 Colfax Ave. (U.S. 40). ✆ **303/279-2789.** www.heritagesquare.info. Free admission; separate charges for individual activities. Memorial Day to Labor Day Mon–Sat 10am–8pm, Sun noon–8pm; rest of year Mon–Sat 10am–6pm, Sun noon–6pm. I-70, exit 259.

Lookout Mountain Nature Center Kids A 1.5-mile self-guided nature trail winds through this 110-acre preserve among ponderosa pines and pretty mountain meadows. A free trail guide is available at the Nature Center when it's open, and a map is on display at a kiosk for those walking the trail at other times. The nonprofit Nature Center has displays on the pine beetle, pollination, and Colorado wildlife, plus an interactive exhibit on the ponderosa pine forest. The building is also worth a look—it's constructed of used and recycled materials such as ground-up plastic soda containers and the pulp of aspen trees. The center schedules free naturalist-guided environmental education activities year-round. Topics vary but could include the flowers, butterflies, or wildlife of the area, or a look at the night sky. Advance registration is required for most programs, and age restrictions may apply. Call for details. Allow at least 1 hour.

910 Colorow Rd. (on Lookout Mountain). ✆ **720/497-7600.** Free admission. Trail daily 8am–dusk; Nature Center Tues–Sun 10am–4pm; also Sat–Sun 9am–5pm in winter.

Mother Cabrini Shrine A 22-foot statue of Jesus stands at the top of a 373-step stairway adorned by carvings representing the stations of the cross and mysteries of the rosary. Terra-cotta benches provide rest stops along the way. The shrine is dedicated to the country's first citizen saint, St. Frances Xavier Cabrini, who founded the Order of the Missionary Sisters of the Sacred Heart. The order has a convent here with a gift shop that's open from 9am to 5pm daily. Allow 45 to 90 minutes.

20189 Cabrini Blvd. (I-70, exit 259), Lookout Mountain. ✆ **303/526-0758.** www.den-cabrini-shrine.org. Free admission, donations welcome. Summer daily 7am–7pm; winter daily 7am–5:30pm; masses daily 7:30am, Sun also 11am.

National Earthquake Information Center The U.S. Geological Survey operates this facility to collect rapid earthquake information, transmit warnings over the Earthquake

Early Alerting Service, and publish and disseminate earthquake data. Tours of 30 to 45 minutes can be scheduled by appointment when a guide is available. They include information about the NEIC, the Earthquake Early Alerting Service, and earthquakes in general.

1711 Illinois St. ✆ **303/273-8500** or 303/273-8420. http://neic.usgs.gov. Free admission. Tues–Thurs 9–11am and 1–3pm, by appointment only.

National Renewable Energy Laboratory Visitor Center This federal lab's public face features interactive exhibits covering all things renewable, from solar to biomass. The structure is a model for efficient design, with state-of-the-art heating, lighting, cooling, and insulation. Allow 1 hour.

15013 Denver West Pkwy. ✆ **303/384-6565.** www.nrel.gov/visitors_center. Free admission. Mon–Fri 9am–5pm.

Rocky Mountain Quilt Museum This museum presents changing exhibits, including works from its permanent collection of more than 350 quilts. Consigned works are for sale in the gift shop. Allow 30 minutes.

1111 Washington Ave. ✆ **303/277-0377.** www.rmqm.org. Admission $6 adults, $4 seniors, $3 children 6–12, free for children 5 and under. Mon–Sat 10am–4pm; mid-May to Aug also Sun noon–4pm.

Where to Stay & Dine

La Quinta Inn–Golden, just off I-70, exit 264, at 3301 Youngfield Service Rd. (✆ **800/531-5900** or 303/279-5565), is a dependable choice, with 129 units and rates of $79 to $99 for a double room. **Table Mountain Inn,** 1310 Washington Ave. (✆ **800/762-9898** or 303/277-9898; www.tablemountaininn.com), is a smaller, slightly more expensive alternative. Rates are $149 to $189 double, $189 to $234 suite. Completely renovated in 2004, the **Golden Hotel,** 800 11th St. (✆ **800/233-7214** or 303/279-0100; www.thegoldenhotel.com), offers the best of the West, old and new, in its attractive guest rooms. Doubles run $159 to $179, suites $259 to $299.

For a good meal in a historic setting, try the **Old Capitol Grill** in downtown Golden, 1122 Washington Ave. at 12th Street (✆ **303/279-6390**), which offers steak and burgers plus a good selection of sandwiches. Located in the Territorial Capitol Building constructed in 1862, the restaurant is open daily for lunch and dinner, with dinner prices in the $10-to-$20 range. A more upscale dinner choice is **The Bridgewater Grill,** in the Golden Hotel, 800 11th St. (✆ **303/279-2010**). It serves creative regional fare in the $15-to-$25 range.

IDAHO SPRINGS ★

For visitor information, contact the **Idaho Springs Chamber of Commerce,** P.O. Box 97, Idaho Springs, CO 80452 (✆ **303/567-4382;** www.idahospringschamber.org). Information on Idaho Springs and the nearby towns of Empire, Georgetown, and Silver Plume is available from the **Clear Creek County Tourism Bureau,** P.O. Box 100, Idaho Springs, CO 80452 (✆ **866/674-9237** or 303/567-4660; www.clearcreekcounty.org).

What to See & Do

The scenic "Oh My God" dirt road, a steep, winding thoroughfare, runs from Central City through Virginia Canyon to Idaho Springs, although most visitors prefer to take I-70 directly to this community 35 miles west of Denver. Site of a major gold strike in 1859, Idaho Springs today beckons visitors to try their luck at panning for any gold that may remain. The quaint Victorian downtown is worth a look; don't miss the Bridal Veil Falls tumbling through the largest waterwheel in Colorado across from City Hall.

The **Argo Gold Mine, Mill, and Museum,** 2350 Riverside Dr. (✆ **303/567-2421;** www.historicargotours.com), is listed on the National Register of Historic Places and offers tours daily from mid-April to October from 9am to 6pm. Visitors can see the Double Eagle Gold Mine, relatively unchanged since the early miners first worked it more than 100 years ago, and the mill, where ore was processed into gold. Everyone is welcome to take part in gold- and gemstone-panning. Admission is $15 for adults, $7.50 for children 7 to 12, and free for kids under 7. Allow at least 45 minutes.

At the **Phoenix Gold Mine** ★, on Trail Creek Road (✆ **303/567-0422;** www.phoenixgoldmine.com), you can don a hard hat and follow a working miner through narrow tunnels to see what mining 100 years ago was all about. You can also pan for gold on the property and relax in the picnic area. Weather permitting, the mine is open daily from 10am to 5pm in the summer (until 4pm in the winter); the tours are informal and entertaining. Cost is $10 for adults, $8 for seniors, $5 for children 6 to 11, and free for children under 6. Panning only is $5. Allow about 1 hour.

Just outside Idaho Springs is **Indian Springs Resort,** 302 Soda Creek Rd. (✆ **303/989-6666;** www.indianspringsresort.com), a fine spot for a relaxing soak in the hot springs after a long day of skiing or hiking. The resort has a covered swimming pool, indoor and outdoor private baths, and a vapor cave with soaking pools. Rates are $18 to $24 per person for an hour in the private baths or all-day use of the vapor cave, $14 to $16 for all-day use of the pool, and $10 for a mud bath in "Club Mud." Lodging is in rooms and cabins ($63–$119 for two) or a campground ($24 nightly); meals and weekend entertainment are also offered. The resort is open daily from 7:30am to 10:30pm year-round.

Idaho Springs is the starting point for a 28-mile drive to the summit of 14,260-foot **Mount Evans** ★★. From I-70, exit 240, follow Colo. 103—also called Mt. Evans Highway—as it winds along Chicago Creek through Arapahoe National Forest to **Echo Lake Park,** another Denver mountain park with fireplaces, hiking trails, and fishing. From here, Colo. 5—the highest paved auto road in North America—climbs to the Mount Evans summit. Views along this highway are of spectacular snowcapped peaks even in June, and you're likely to see mountain goats, bighorn sheep, marmots, eagles, and other wildlife. The road is generally open from Memorial Day to Labor Day. Allow at least 4 hours.

Another way to see this area's great scenery is by horseback. **A&A Historical Trails Stables,** 5 miles up Virginia Canyon from Idaho Springs (✆ **303/567-4808;** www.aastables.com), offers a variety of trail rides, including breakfast and moonlight rides. Rides are usually offered May through November, weather permitting. A 1-hour ride costs $30 per person, and a 2-hour ride costs $70.

Where to Stay & Dine

H&H Motor Lodge, 2445 Colorado Blvd. (P.O. Box 1359), Idaho Springs, CO 80452 (✆ **800/445-2893** or 303/567-2838), is a mom-and-pop motel on the east side of town. It offers bright and cheery rooms, TVs with HBO, a hot tub, and a sauna. The 34 rooms and suites include several larger family units. Rates are $59 for a standard double, kitchenettes $69 to $109 extra; two-bedroom suites start at $69.

Beau Jo's Colorado Style Pizza, 1517 Miner St. (✆ **303/567-4376;** www.beaujos.com), offers a wide variety of so-called mountain pizzas, including standard pepperoni; "Skier Mike's," with Canadian bacon, green peppers, and chicken breast; and a roasted-garlic and veggie combo. Sandwiches are also available, plus a salad bar set up in a pair of old claw-foot bathtubs. The bill usually comes out to $10 to $20 per person.

GEORGETOWN ★

A pretty village of Victorian-era houses and stores, Georgetown, 45 miles west of Denver on I-70, at an elevation of 8,500 feet, is named for an 1860 gold camp. Among the best preserved of the foothill mining towns, Georgetown is one of the few that didn't suffer a major fire during its formative years. Perhaps to acknowledge their blessings, townspeople built eye-catching steeples on top of their firehouses, not their churches.

For information on attractions and travel services, drop by or contact the **Georgetown Visitors Center,** 613 6th St. (P.O. Box 444), Georgetown, CO 80444 (✆ **800/472-8230** or 303/569-2888), which runs a visitor information center at 6th and Argentine streets across from the Georgetown post office; or **Historic Georgetown, Inc.,** 15th and Argentine streets, P.O. Box 667, Georgetown, CO 80444 (✆ **303/569-2840;** www.historicgeorgetown.org).

What to See & Do

The Georgetown–Silver Plume Mining Area was declared a National Historic Landmark District in 1966, and more than 200 of its buildings have been restored.

A convenient place to begin a **walking tour** is the Old County Courthouse, at 6th and Argentine streets. Now the community center and tourist information office, it was built in 1867. Across Argentine Street is the Old Stone Jail (1868); 3 blocks south, at 3rd and Argentine, is the Hamill House (see below).

Sixth Street is Georgetown's main commercial strip. Walk east from the Old Courthouse. On your left are the Masonic Hall (1891), the Fish Block (1886), the Monti and Guanella Building (1868), and the Cushman Block (1874); on your right, the Hamill Block (1881) and the Kneisel & Anderson Building (1893). The Hotel de Paris (see below) is at the corner of 6th and Taos. Nearly opposite, at 6th and Griffith, is the Star Hook and Ladder Building (1886), along with the town hall and marshal's office.

If you turn south on Taos Street, you'll find Grace Episcopal Church (1869) at 5th Street, and the Maxwell House (1890) a couple of steps east on 4th. Glance west on 5th to see Alpine Hose Company No. 2 (1874) and the Courier Building (1875). North on Taos Street from the Hotel de Paris are the Old Georgetown School (1874), at 8th Street; First Presbyterian Church (1874), at 9th Street; Our Lady of Lourdes Catholic Church (1918), at 9th Street; and the Old Missouri Firehouse (1870), at 10th Street and Taos.

If you turn west on 9th at the Catholic church, you'll find two more historic structures: the Bowman-White House (1892), at Rose and 9th; and the Tucker-Rutherford House (ca. 1860), a miner's log cabin with four small rooms and a trapper's cabin in back, on 9th Street at Clear Creek.

Georgetown Energy Museum This small museum is dedicated to educating people about the history of hydropower in Georgetown and Colorado. Located at Georgetown's power plant—built in 1900 and still operating—the museum allows visitors an up-close look at a pair of hydroelectric-generating units in action. The museum also features photographic and text displays detailing the history of similar plants in the region, as well as a collection of antiques: washing machines, stoves, and generator meters. Allow 30 minutes.

600 Griffith St. ✆ **303/569-3557.** www.georgetownenergymuseum.org. Free admission, donations accepted. June to mid-Oct Mon–Sat 10am–4pm, Sun noon–4pm; Mid-Oct to May weekdays by appointment only.

Hamill House Built in Country Gothic Revival style, this house dates from 1867, when silver speculator William Hamill owned it. When Historic Georgetown, Inc., acquired it in 1971, the house had its original woodwork, fireplaces, and wallpaper. A delicately carved outhouse had two sections: one with walnut seats for the family, the other with pine seats for servants. Allow 30 to 60 minutes.

305 Argentine St. ✆ **303/569-2840.** Admission $4 adults, $3 seniors 60 and older and students, free for children 9 and under. Memorial Day to Sept daily 10am–4pm; Oct–Dec Sat–Sun noon–4pm. Closed Jan to late May except for prearranged tours.

Hotel de Paris ★ The builder of the hotel, Louis Dupuy, once explained his desire to build a French inn so far away from his homeland: "I love these mountains and I love America, but you will pardon me if I bring into this community a remembrance of my youth and my country." The hotel opened in 1875 and soon became famous for its French Provincial luxury.

Today it's a historic museum run by the National Society of Colonial Dames of America, embellished with many of its original furnishings, including Haviland china, a big pendulum clock, paintings and etchings, photographs by William Henry Jackson, and carved walnut furniture. The kitchen contains an antique stove and other cooking equipment, and the wine cellar houses early wine barrels, with their labels still in place. Allow 45 to 60 minutes.

409 6th St. (at Taos St.). ✆ **303/569-2311.** www.hoteldeparismuseum.org. Admission $4 adults, $3 seniors 60 and older, $2 children 6–16, free for children 5 and under. Memorial Day to Labor Day daily 10am–4:30pm; early Sept to Dec and May Sat–Sun noon–4pm, weather permitting. Closed Jan–Apr and major holidays.

Where to Stay & Dine

Colorado's oldest continuously operating hotel, about 5 minutes from Georgetown, is the **Peck House Hotel and Restaurant,** 83 Sunny Ave. (P.O. Box 428), on U.S. 40 off I-70, exit 232, Empire, CO 80438 (✆ **303/569-9870;** www.thepeckhouse.com). Established in 1862 as a stagecoach stop for travelers and immigrants from the East Coast, the hotel has an antiques-filled parlor lined with photos of the Peck family and their late-19th- and early-20th-century guests, and a panoramic view of the Empire Valley afforded by the wide veranda. The rooms are comfortable and quaint (claw-foot tubs grace many bathrooms). There are 11 rooms (9 with private bathroom), and rates for two are in the $65-to-$140 range. The hotel's excellent **restaurant** serves fish and steak entrees and seriously delicious hot-fudge cake and raspberries Romanoff. The restaurant serves dinner daily year-round; prices for entrees are $13 to $30.

Back in Georgetown, **The Happy Cooker,** 412 6th St. (✆ **303/569-3166**), serves unusual soups, sandwiches on homemade breads, crepes, quiches, and more substantial fare such as frittatas and eggs Benedict, in a converted home in Georgetown's historic business district. It's open Monday through Friday from 7am to 4pm, Saturday and Sunday from 7am to 5pm. Prices are in the $4-to-$8 range, and breakfast is served all day. For a beer, a burger, and a dose of local color, head to the **Red Ram Restaurant & Saloon,** 606 6th St. (✆ **303/569-2300**). The menu also has Mexican plates and slow-cooked baby back ribs; prices run $7 to $17 for a main course, and the Red Ram has two family suites for rent to overnight guests.

Colorado Springs

Magnificent scenic beauty, a favorable climate, and dreams of gold have lured visitors to Colorado Springs and neighboring Pikes Peak Country for well over 100 years.

In 1806, army Lieut. Zebulon Pike led a company of soldiers on a trek around the base of an enormous mountain. He called it "Grand Peak," declared it unconquerable, and moved on. Today the 14,110-foot mountain we know as Pikes Peak has been conquered so often that an auto highway and a cog railway take visitors to the top.

Unlike many Colorado towns, neither mineral wealth nor ranching was the cornerstone of Colorado Springs's economy during the 19th century—tourism was. In fact, Colorado Springs, founded in 1871, was the first genuine resort community west of Chicago. Gen. William J. Palmer, builder of the Denver & Rio Grande Railroad, established the resort on his rail line, at an elevation of 6,035 feet. The state's growing reputation as a health center, with its high mountains and mineral springs, convinced him to build at the foot of Pikes Peak. In an attempt to lure affluent Easterners, he named the resort Colorado Springs, because most fashionable Eastern resorts were called "springs." The mineral waters at Manitou Springs were only 5 miles away, and soon Palmer exploited them by installing a resident physician, Dr. Samuel Solly, who exuberantly trumpeted the benefits of Manitou's springs both in print and in person.

The 1890s gold strikes at Cripple Creek, on the southwestern slope of Pikes Peak, added a new dimension to life in Colorado Springs. Among those who cashed in on the boom was Spencer Penrose, a middle-aged Philadelphian and Harvard graduate who arrived in 1892, made some astute investments, and became quite rich. Penrose, who believed that the automobile would revolutionize life in the United States, promoted the creation of new highways. To show the effectiveness of motorcars in the mountains, he built the Pikes Peak Highway (1913–15), using more than $250,000 of his own money. Then, during World War I, at a cost of more than $2 million, he built the luxurious Broadmoor hotel at the foot of Cheyenne Mountain. World War II brought the military and defense industry to this area, and in 1958 the $200-million U.S. Air Force Academy opened.

Modern Colorado Springs is a growing city of about 400,000, with more than 600,000 in the metropolitan area. The majority of its residents are conservative, and the city is also home to some of the country's largest nondenominational churches and conservative groups.

To many visitors, the city retains the feel and mood of a small Western town. Most tourists come to see the Air Force Academy, marvel at the scenery at Garden of the Gods and Pikes Peak, and explore the history of America's West. I'm pleased to report that Colorado Springs also has some of the best lodging and dining in the state.

1 ORIENTATION

ARRIVING

By Plane

Major airlines offer nearly 100 flights a day to **Colorado Springs Airport,** located north of Drennan Road and east of Powers Boulevard in the southeastern part of the city (✆ **719/550-1972;** www.flycos.com).

Airlines serving Colorado Springs include **Allegiant** (✆ 702/505-8888; www.allegiant air.com), **American** (✆ 800/433-7300; www.aa.com), **Continental** (✆ 800/525-0280; www.flycontinental.com), **Delta** (✆ 800/221-1212; www.delta.com), **ExpressJet** (✆ 888/958-9538; www.expressjet.com), **Frontier** (✆ 800/432-1359; www.frontierair lines.com), **Northwest** (✆ 800/225-2525; www.nwa.com), **United** (✆ 800/864-8331; www.united.com), and **US Airways** (✆ 800/428-4322; www.usairways.com).

GETTING TO & FROM THE AIRPORT Several companies provide airport shuttle services; call ✆ **719/550-1930** for information.

By Car

The principal artery to and from the north and south, I-25, bisects Colorado Springs. Denver is 70 miles north; Pueblo, 42 miles south. U.S. 24 is the principal east–west route through the city.

Visitors arriving on I-70 from the east can take exit 359 at Limon and follow U.S. 24 into the Springs. Arriving on I-70 from the west, the most direct route is exit 201 at Frisco, then Colo. 9 through Breckenridge 53 miles to U.S. 24 (at Hartsel), and finally east 66 miles to the Springs. This route is mountainous, so check road conditions before setting out in winter.

VISITOR INFORMATION

The **Experience Colorado Springs at Pikes Peak Convention and Visitors Bureau** is at 515 S. Cascade Ave., Colorado Springs, CO 80903 (✆ **800/888-4748** or 719/635-7506; fax 719/635-4968; www.experiencecoloradosprings.com). Ask for the free *Official Visitor Guide to Colorado Springs and the Pikes Peak Region,* a colorful booklet with a comprehensive listing of accommodations, restaurants, and other area visitor services, as well as a basic but efficient map. Inquire at the Visitor Information Center or local bookstores for more detailed maps. An excellent one is the Pierson Graphics Corporation's *Colorado Springs and Monument Valley Street Map.* The **Visitor Information Center,** at the southeast corner of Cascade Avenue and Cimarron Street, is open from 8:30am to 5pm daily in summer, Monday through Friday in winter. From I-25, take the Cimarron Street exit (exit 141) and head east about 4 blocks.

> **Heads Up**
>
> At an elevation of 6,035 feet, Colorado Springs has two-thirds the oxygen found at sea level; Pikes Peak, at 14,110 feet, has only one-half the oxygen.

Visitors to Manitou Springs—and every Colorado Springs visitor should also get to Manitou Springs—can get information from the **Manitou Springs Chamber of Commerce & Visitors Bureau,** 354 Manitou Ave., Manitou Springs, CO 80829 (✆ **800/642-2567** or 719/685-5089; www.manitousprings.org). You can also contact the **Pikes**

Peak Country Attractions Association at the same address (© **800/525-2250;** www.pikes-peak.com).

CITY LAYOUT

It's easy to get around central Colorado Springs, which is laid out on a classic grid pattern.

If you focus on the intersection of I-25 and U.S. 24, downtown Colorado Springs lies in the northeast quadrant, bounded on the west by I-25 and on the south by U.S. 24 (Cimarron St.). Boulder Street to the north and Wahsatch Avenue to the east complete the downtown frame. Nevada Avenue (Bus. 25 and Colo. 115) parallels the freeway for 15 miles through the city, intersecting it twice; Tejon Street and Cascade Avenue also run north–south through downtown between Nevada Avenue and the freeway. **Colorado Avenue** and **Platte Avenue** are the busiest east–west downtown cross streets.

West of downtown, Colorado Avenue extends through the historic Old Colorado City district and the quaint foothill community of **Manitou Springs,** rejoining U.S. 24—a busy but less interesting artery—as it enters Pike National Forest.

South of downtown, **Nevada Avenue** intersects **Lake Avenue,** the principal boulevard into the Broadmoor hotel (see below), and proceeds south as Colo. 115 past Fort Carson to Cañon City.

North and east of downtown, **Academy Boulevard** (Colo. 83) is a good street name to remember. From the south gate of the Air Force Academy north of the Springs, it winds through residential hills, crosses Austin Bluff Parkway, and then runs without a curve 8 miles due south, finally bending west to intersect I-25 and Colo. 115 at Fort Carson. U.S. 24, which exits downtown east as Platte Avenue, and Fountain Boulevard, which leads to the airport, are among its cross streets. Austin Bluffs Parkway extends west of I-25 as **Garden of the Gods Road,** leading to that natural wonder.

City street addresses are divided by Pikes Peak Avenue into north and south, by Nevada Avenue into east and west.

2 GETTING AROUND

Although Colorado Springs has public transportation, most visitors prefer to drive. Parking and roads are good, and some of the best attractions, such as the Garden of the Gods (p. 162), are accessible only by car (or foot or bike for the truly ambitious).

BY CAR

For regulations and advice on driving in Colorado, see "Getting There & Getting Around," in chapter 3. The **American Automobile Association (AAA)** maintains an office in Colorado Springs at 3525 N. Carefree Circle (© **800/283-5222** or 719/591-2222; www.aaa.com), open Monday through Friday from 8:30am to 5:30pm and Saturday from 9am to 1pm.

CAR RENTALS Car-rental agencies in Colorado Springs, some of which have offices in or near downtown as well as at the airport, include **Avis** (© **800/331-1212** or 719/596-2751), **Budget** (© **800/527-7000** or 719/473-6535), **Enterprise** (© **800/736-8222** or 719/636-3900), **Hertz** (© **800/654-3131** or 719/596-1863), and **National/Alamo** (© **800/227-7368** or 719/574-8579). You can rent campers, travel trailers, motor homes, and motorcycles from **Cruise America** (© **800/671-8042;** www.cruiseamerica.com).

PARKING Most downtown streets have parking meters; the rate is 25¢ for a half-hour. Look for city-run parking lots, which charge 25¢ per half-hour and also offer day rates. Outside downtown, free parking is generally available on side streets.

BY BUS

Mountain Metropolitan Transit (✆ **719/385-7433;** www.springsgov.com) provides city bus service. Buses operate Monday through Friday from 5:10am to 10:45pm, Saturday from 5:30am to 10:45pm, and Sunday from 7:30am to 5:35pm, except major holidays. Fares on in-city routes are $1.50 for adults; 75¢ students, children 6 to 11, seniors, and passengers with disabilities; and free for children under 6. There is also a free downtown shuttle and free seasonal trolley service in Manitou Springs. Bus schedules can be obtained at terminals, city libraries, and the Colorado Springs Convention and Visitors Bureau.

BY TAXI

Call **Yellow Cab** (✆ **719/634-5000**) for taxi service.

ON FOOT

Each of the main sections of town can easily be explored without a vehicle. It's fun, for instance, to wander the winding streets of Manitou Springs or explore the Old Colorado City "strip." Between neighborhoods, however, distances are considerable. Unless you're particularly fit, it's wise to drive or take a bus or taxi.

Fast Facts Colorado Springs

American Express To report a lost card, call ✆ **800/528-4800;** to report lost traveler's checks, call ✆ **800/221-7282.**

Area Code The telephone area code is **719.**

Babysitters Front desks at major hotels often can make arrangements.

Business Hours Most banks are open Monday through Friday from 9am to 5pm, and some have Saturday hours. Major stores are open Monday through Saturday from 9 or 10am until 5 or 6pm (sometimes until 9pm Fri), and often Sunday from noon until 5pm. Stores that cater to tourists are usually open longer in the summer, with shorter hours in winter.

Car Rentals See "Getting Around," above.

Dentists For referrals for dentists who accept emergency patients, contact the **Colorado Springs Dental Society** (✆ **719/598-5161**).

Doctors For referrals and other health information, call **HealthLink** (✆ **719/444-2273**).

Drugstores **Walgreens,** 920 N. Circle Dr. (✆ **719/473-9090**), has a 24-hour prescription service.

Emergencies For police, fire, or medical emergencies, dial ✆ **911.** To reach **Poison Control,** call ✆ **800/332-3073.**

Eyeglasses You can get 1-hour replacement of lost or broken glasses at **Pearle Vision** in the Citadel Mall (✆ **719/597-0757**) and at **LensCrafters** in Erindale Centre on North Academy Boulevard (✆ **719/548-8650**).

Hospitals **Memorial Hospital,** 1400 E. Boulder St. (✆ **719/365-5000**), offers full medical services, including 24-hour emergency treatment, as does **Penrose-St. Francis Hospital,** 2215 N. Cascade Ave. (✆ **719/776-5000**).

Newspapers & Magazines The *Gazette* (www.gazette.com), published daily in Colorado Springs, is the city's most widely read newspaper. The *Denver Post* is also available at newsstands throughout the city. The glossy *Colorado Springs Style* magazine and the politically oriented *Independent* are other local periodicals. *USA Today* and the *Wall Street Journal* can be purchased on the street and at major hotels.

Photographic Needs There are dozens of photofinishing outlets throughout the city, including **Walgreens** and **Shewmaker's Camera Shop,** in the Woodmen Valley Shopping Center, 6902 N. Academy Blvd. (✆ **719/598-6412;** www.shewmakers.com). For camera and video supplies and repairs as well as photofinishing, go to the downtown location of **Shewmaker's,** 30 N. Tejon St. (✆ **719/636-1696**).

Post Office The main post office is downtown at 201 E. Pikes Peak Ave. Contact the U.S. Postal Service (✆ **800/275-8777;** www.usps.com) for hours and locations of other post offices.

Safety Although Colorado Springs is generally a safe city, it is not crime free. Try to be aware of your surroundings at all times, and ask at your hotel or the visitor center about the safety of neighborhoods you plan to explore, especially after dark.

Taxes Total taxes on retail sales in Colorado Springs amount to about 7.4%; room taxes total about 9.4%. Rates in Manitou Springs are a bit higher.

Useful Telephone Numbers For **weather and road conditions,** including road construction, throughout the state, call ✆ **303/639-1111** or visit www.cotrip.org.

3 WHERE TO STAY

You'll find a wide range of lodging possibilities here, from Colorado's ritziest resort—the Broadmoor—to basic budget motels. There are also several particularly nice bed-and-breakfasts; the **Colorado Bed and Breakfasts of the Pikes Peak Area** is a good resource (✆ **888/835-8900** or 719/685-1120; www.pikespeakareabnbs.com). The rates listed here are the officially quoted prices ("rack rates") and don't take into account individual or group discounts. Generally, rates are highest from Memorial Day to Labor Day, and lowest in the spring. During graduation and other special events at the Air Force Academy, rates can increase markedly, and you may have trouble finding a room at any price. Rates listed below do not include the lodging tax (about 9% in Colorado Springs, 10% in Manitou Springs). Parking is free unless otherwise specified.

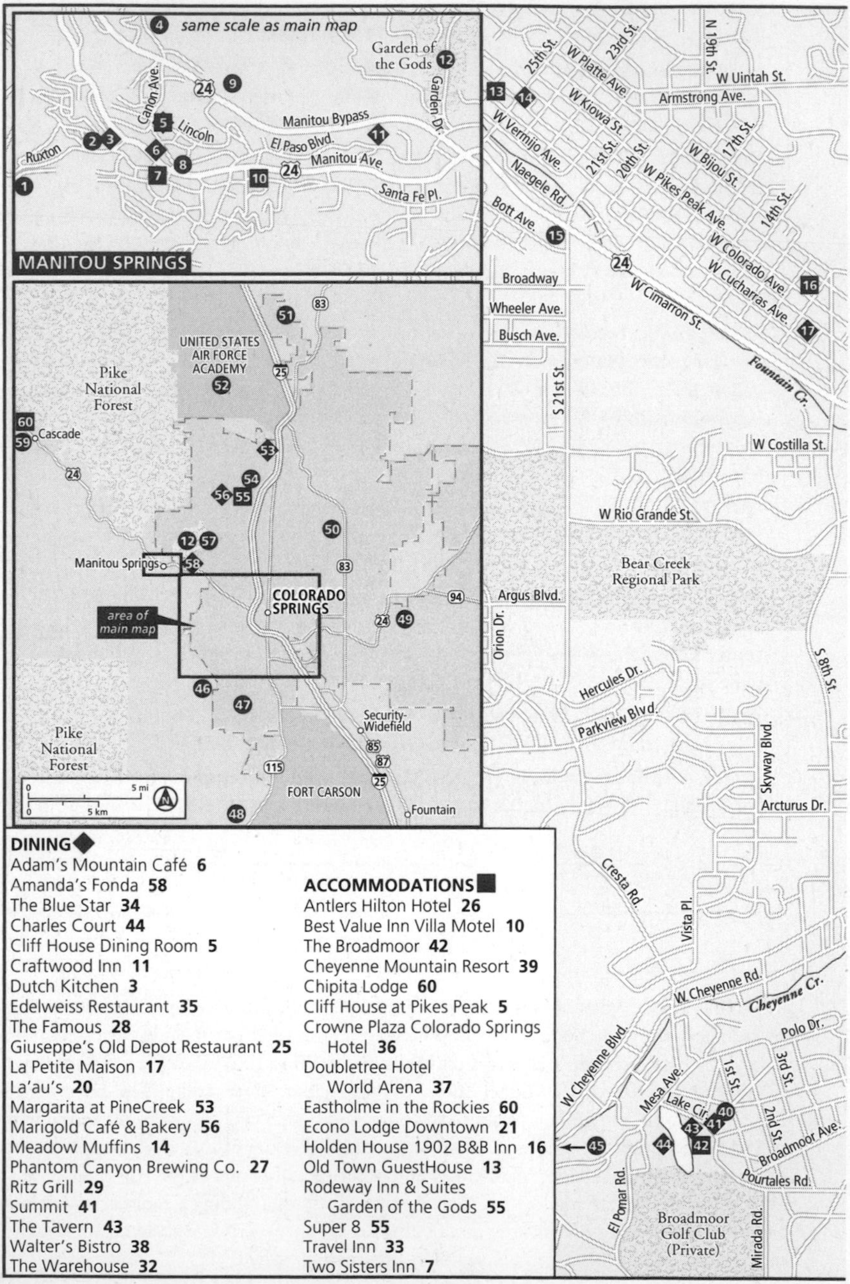

DINING◆

Adam's Mountain Café **6**
Amanda's Fonda **58**
The Blue Star **34**
Charles Court **44**
Cliff House Dining Room **5**
Craftwood Inn **11**
Dutch Kitchen **3**
Edelweiss Restaurant **35**
The Famous **28**
Giuseppe's Old Depot Restaurant **25**
La Petite Maison **17**
La'au's **20**
Margarita at PineCreek **53**
Marigold Café & Bakery **56**
Meadow Muffins **14**
Phantom Canyon Brewing Co. **27**
Ritz Grill **29**
Summit **41**
The Tavern **43**
Walter's Bistro **38**
The Warehouse **32**

ACCOMMODATIONS■

Antlers Hilton Hotel **26**
Best Value Inn Villa Motel **10**
The Broadmoor **42**
Cheyenne Mountain Resort **39**
Chipita Lodge **60**
Cliff House at Pikes Peak **5**
Crowne Plaza Colorado Springs Hotel **36**
Doubletree Hotel World Arena **37**
Eastholme in the Rockies **60**
Econo Lodge Downtown **21**
Holden House 1902 B&B Inn **16**
Old Town GuestHouse **13**
Rodeway Inn & Suites Garden of the Gods **55**
Super 8 **55**
Travel Inn **33**
Two Sisters Inn **7**

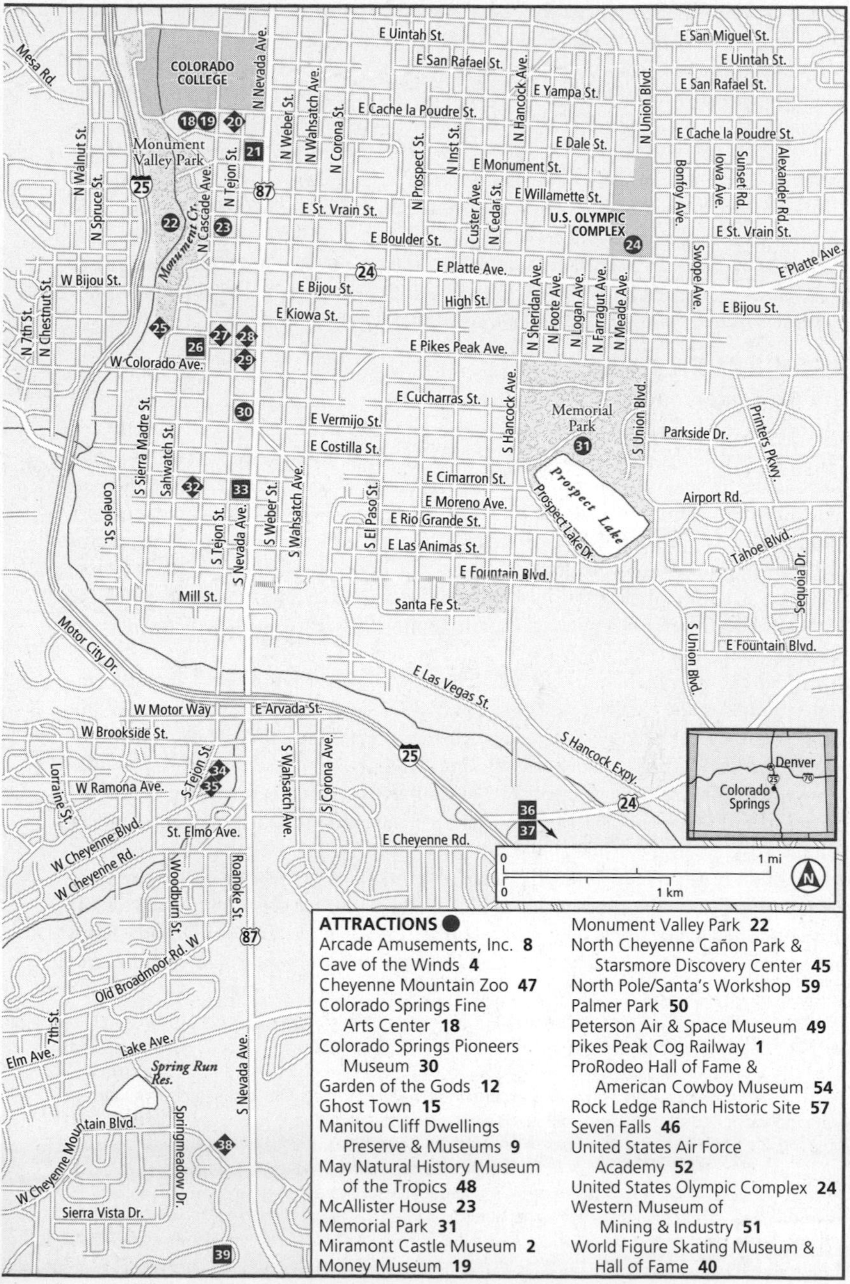

ATTRACTIONS ●

Arcade Amusements, Inc. **8**
Cave of the Winds **4**
Cheyenne Mountain Zoo **47**
Colorado Springs Fine Arts Center **18**
Colorado Springs Pioneers Museum **30**
Garden of the Gods **12**
Ghost Town **15**
Manitou Cliff Dwellings Preserve & Museums **9**
May Natural History Museum of the Tropics **48**
McAllister House **23**
Memorial Park **31**
Miramont Castle Museum **2**
Money Museum **19**
Monument Valley Park **22**
North Cheyenne Cañon Park & Starsmore Discovery Center **45**
North Pole/Santa's Workshop **59**
Palmer Park **50**
Peterson Air & Space Museum **49**
Pikes Peak Cog Railway **1**
ProRodeo Hall of Fame & American Cowboy Museum **54**
Rock Ledge Ranch Historic Site **57**
Seven Falls **46**
United States Air Force Academy **52**
United States Olympic Complex **24**
Western Museum of Mining & Industry **51**
World Figure Skating Museum & Hall of Fame **40**

In addition to the accommodations described below, a number of moderately priced chain and franchise motels offer reliable lodging. These include the economical **Econo Lodge Downtown,** 714 N. Nevada Ave., Colorado Springs, CO 80903 (✆ **800/553-2666** or 719/636-3385), with doubles from $39 to $89; the attractive and well-maintained **Rodeway Inn & Suites Garden of the Gods,** 555 W. Garden of the Gods Rd., Colorado Springs, CO 80907 (✆ **800/828-4347** or 719/593-9119), with rates for two of $69 to $119; and **Super 8,** near Garden of the Gods at 4604 Rusina Rd., Colorado Springs, CO 80907 (✆ **800/800-8000** or 719/594-0964), which charges $42 to $57 for a double. Those looking for a more upscale chain won't go wrong with the **Doubletree Hotel World Arena,** 1775 E. Cheyenne Mountain Blvd. (I-25, exit 138), Colorado Springs, CO 80906 (✆ **800/222-TREE** [222-8733] or 719/576-8900), with double rates from $115 to $145 and suites from $300; or the **Crowne Plaza Colorado Springs Hotel,** 2886 S. Circle Dr. (I-25, exit 138), Colorado Springs, CO 80906 (✆ **800/981-4012** or 719/576-5900), with doubles from $89 to $199.

VERY EXPENSIVE

The Broadmoor ★★★ Kids This storied resort keeps itself on the forefront of luxury, where it's been since Spencer Penrose originally opened it in 1918. (The first names entered on the guest register were those of John D. Rockefeller, Jr., and his party.) Today the Broadmoor is an enormous resort complex of historic pink Mediterranean-style buildings with modern additions, set at the foot of Cheyenne Mountain on magnificently landscaped 3,000-acre grounds about 3½ miles southwest of downtown Colorado Springs. The original Italian Renaissance–style main building features marble staircase, chandeliers, Italian tile, hand-painted beams and ceilings, and a carved-marble fountain, not to mention a priceless art collection with original work by Toulouse-Lautrec and Ming dynasty ceramicists.

Behind the main building is lovely Cheyenne Lake; a swimming pool almost seamlessly attached to the west end looks like a part of the lake. This swimming complex will make you think you're at an oceanside beach resort, with water slides, two outdoor hot tubs, 13 cabanas, and an outdoor cafe. The guest rooms occupy a series of separate buildings centered on the lake and pool area. The spacious, luxurious rooms are beautifully decorated in European style, with chandeliers, Italian fabrics, rich wood, and limited-edition works of art. Most units hold two double beds or one king-size bed, desks and tables, plush seating, and two-line portable phones. Many rooms contain large soaking tubs and separate marble showers; some in the South Tower have high-tech touch screens that control the lights, the drapes, and even the "Privacy" and "Do Not Disturb" lights in the hall. The service is impeccable: The hotel averages two employees for every guest.

Lake Circle, at Lake Ave. (P.O. Box 1439), Colorado Springs, CO 80901. ✆ **800/634-7711** or 719/634-7711. Fax 719/577-5700. www.broadmoor.com. 700 units. May–Oct $420–$565 double, $625–$1,000 standard suite; Nov–Apr $300–$420 double, $425–$850 standard suite; year-round up to $3,400 large suite. AE, DC, DISC, MC, V. Self-parking $14; valet $16. **Amenities:** 12 restaurants (all Continental, American, or Contemporary); 4 lounges; outdoor pool cafe; 3 swimming pools (indoor, outdoor w/water slide, outdoor lap pool); 2 outdoor hot tubs; 3 18-hole golf courses; 9 all-weather tennis courts (1 clay court); state-of-the-art fitness center and full-service spa w/aerobics classes, saunas, and whirlpool tubs; paddle boats; bicycle rentals; children's programs (summer); riding concierge; car-rental agency; shopping arcade; 24-hr. room service; in-room massage; valet laundry; stables; fly-fishing school; movie theater; shuttle bus btw. buildings; service station. *In room:* A/C, cable TV, dataport, free Wi-Fi, minibar, coffeemaker, hair dryer, iron, safe.

EXPENSIVE

Antlers Hilton Hotel ★ The Antlers has been a Colorado Springs landmark for more than a century. Although it is in many ways geared to business travelers, for vacationers it offers the best accommodations within a short walking distance of many of downtown Colorado Springs's major attractions and restaurants. There have been three different Antlers on this site. The first, a turreted Victorian showcase built in 1883, was named for Gen. William Palmer's collection of deer and elk trophies. After it was destroyed by fire in 1898, Palmer built an extravagant Italian Renaissance–style building that survived until 1964, when it was leveled to make room for the more contemporary hotel, which Hilton renovated to the tune of $15 million in recent years. Antique black-walnut nightstands from the previous incarnation provide a touch of historic continuity to the spacious guest rooms, which are handsomely decorated in earth tones with rich wood furnishings. The corner rooms are larger, and I prefer the west-side rooms: They are more expensive but worth every penny because of their unparalleled Pikes Peak views.

4 S. Cascade Ave., Colorado Springs, CO 80903. ✆ **877/754-9940** or 719/473-5600. Fax 719/389-0259. www.antlers.com. 292 units. Summer $139–$189 double; $250–$695 suite. AE, DC, DISC, MC, V. Self-parking $8; valet $12. **Amenities:** 2 restaurants (American); indoor pool; fitness center; whirlpool; salon; room service (6:30am–11pm); laundry. *In room:* A/C, cable TV, free Wi-Fi, coffeemaker, hair dryer, iron.

Cheyenne Mountain Resort ★★ Set at the foot of Cheyenne Mountain, this resort was built at a preexisting country club with a Pete Dye–designed golf course in 1985, and is something of a less expensive alternative to the swank Broadmoor (above), just a few miles uphill. With a stunning view of the mountain from the lobby, the Cheyenne Mountain Resort features top-notch recreational facilities and attracts numerous conferences and meetings, but is an outstanding choice for tourists as well. The rooms—which are in a series of buildings set off from the main lodge—are rich and masculine, and have either one king or two queens (or both in some suites). The bathrooms are a cut above, with granite counters and tub/shower combos, as well as jetted soakers in the executive suites. All rooms have a private balcony, and most have great views.

3225 Broadmoor Valley Rd., Colorado Springs, CO 80906. ✆ **800/428-8886** or 719/538-4000. Fax 719/540-5779. www.cheyennemountain.com. 316 units, including 5 suites. Summer $169–$209 double; $485–$650 suite. Lower rates fall through spring. AE, DC, DISC, MC, V. **Amenities:** 2 restaurants (American); 2 lounges; indoor pool; 18-hole golf course; 18 indoor tennis courts; health club; Jacuzzi; sauna; bike rental; children's programs; concierge; business center; room service (7am–11pm); massage; dry cleaning. *In room:* A/C, cable TV w/pay movies, free Wi-Fi, coffeemaker, hair dryer, iron.

Cliff House at Pikes Peak ★★ **Finds** Striving to compete with the best that Colorado has to offer (and doing a pretty good job), the Cliff House is an old yet new facility. Built in 1874, it was designated a National Historic Landmark in 1980 and has hosted such eminent guests as Theodore Roosevelt, Clark Gable, and Thomas Edison. A major fire forced the Cliff House to close in 1982, and it remained closed until a massive reconstruction in 1997. The project incorporated several pieces of the hotel's original decor, including ornate woodwork and a tile fireplace, and what the fire destroyed was replicated with an emphasis on attention to detail. Once again a grand and luxurious hotel, the Cliff House reopened in 1999.

Today the lovely, uniquely decorated accommodations vary in size and personality, although the overall decor is Queen Anne–Victorian. Units range from average-size, relatively simple studios to large, luxurious celebrity suites named for former guests.

Some units have gas fireplaces, two-person spas, steam showers, and terrific views of the mountains. All have live flowering plants, robes, heated toilet seats, and working desks. I wouldn't turn down any room at the Cliff House, but my favorite is definitely the Clark Gable Suite ($475 double in summer), which is decorated in subdued Hollywood style—if you can call leopard-print wallpaper subdued—and contains a shower for two, a jetted tub, a wet bar and refrigerator, two TVs, a gas fireplace, and photos of Clark, who stayed at the hotel in the early 1940s.

There's a fine-dining restaurant (see "Where to Dine," below), and the entire property is nonsmoking.

306 Cañon Ave., Manitou Springs, CO 80829. ✆ **888/212-7000** or 719/685-3000. Fax 719/685-3913. www.thecliffhouse.com. 55 units. $145–$200 double; $189–$475 suite. Children 12 and under stay free in parent's room. Rates include breakfast buffet. AE, DC, MC, V. **Amenities:** 2 restaurants (American/bar and grill); bar; fitness center; concierge; activities desk; airport pickup; room service 7am–11pm; on-call massage; valet laundry service. *In room:* A/C, cable TV w/DVD players, CD player, free Wi-Fi, coffeemaker, hair dryer, iron, safe.

Old Town GuestHouse ★★ Just a half-block south of the main street of Colorado Springs's historic Old Colorado City stands this three-story redbrick inn. It may appear to be from the 1890s, but it actually dates from the 1990s. As a result, it features all the modern amenities, not to mention great service from innkeepers Don and Shirley Wick, who've owned the inn since 2005.

All eight of the individually decorated rooms are named for flowers: for example, Colorado Columbine, with a mountain mural above the king bed; Moroccan Jasmine, with a Sahara Desert theme; Oriental Poppy, decorated with collectibles from the Orient; and romantic Victorian Rose. Each room has individual climate control, robes, and a queen or king bed. Several have gas-log fireplaces, seven have a private porch or balcony, and some have steam showers for two or private outdoor hot tubs. There's an elevator, and one room is ADA compliant.

The attractive library has a fireplace, music, and overstuffed chairs. Downstairs is a game room with pool table and exercise equipment, plus wireless Internet access throughout the inn.

115 S. 26th St., Colorado Springs, CO 80904. ✆ **888/375-4210** or 719/632-9194. Fax 719/632-9026. www.oldtown-guesthouse.com. 8 units. $99–$210 double. AE, DISC, MC, V. Free off-street parking. Children 11 and under not accepted. *In room:* A/C, cable TV w/VCR/DVD player, free Wi-Fi, fridge, coffeemaker, hair dryer, iron.

MODERATE

Chipita Lodge ★★ (Finds) In dinky Chipita Park, below the looming majesty of Pikes Peak—and above a peaceful lake—is the Chipita Lodge. The historic 1927 structure began as a hotel but served as both the local post office and a real-estate office before becoming an inn again in 1997. The common area has shelves of games, a TV, and a huge fireplace; there is also an outdoor hot tub. The rooms feature interesting furnishings—a vanity made from old P.O boxes, for one, and a rocker made from muleshoes; antiques and private baths help give the accommodations a woodsy elegance. The Chipita also rents nearby **cabins** for $135 to $165 a night, with a 3-night minimum.

9090 Chipita Park Rd., Chipita Park, CO 80809. ✆ **877/CHIPITA** [244-7482] or 719/684-8454. www.chipitalodge.com. 8 units (6 with bathroom), including 2 cottages. $100–$135 double. Rates include full breakfast. AE, MC, V. 10 miles west of I-25, then 1.5 miles east on Chipita Park Rd. **Amenities:** Outdoor hot tub. *In room:* Free Wi-Fi.

(Kids) Family-Friendly Hotels

Best Value Inn Villa Motel (p. 154) A swimming pool and easy access to parks and the attractions in Manitou Springs keep most kids occupied.

The Broadmoor (p. 150) A lake and pool area with a terrific water slide, plus tennis, golf, riding stables, and a great summer kids' program that includes a visit to the Cheyenne Mountain Zoo all add up to a wonderful family experience.

Eastholme in the Rockies ★ Nestled in the quaint Pikes Peak mountain village of Cascade, 10 miles west of downtown Colorado Springs, this Victorian B&B gives guests an opportunity to see the city and get away from it all in the same day. Originally built in 1885 as a resort hotel, this property has a storied history that includes a stint as a boarding house before becoming a guest inn in 1988. Today it's a favorite of vacationers who want to be within striking distance of city attractions but whose main interests lie in the Rockies. The parlor holds a bay window, a fireplace, and antiques. Most of the inn's large rooms feature 10-foot ceilings, and all provide plush quilts and remarkable views. The Marriott and Eisenhower suites feature original furnishings and a plethora of antiques, and the cottages offer DVD players, fireplaces, and spacious bathrooms with whirlpool tubs.

4445 Hagerman Ave. (P.O. Box 98), Cascade, CO 80809. ✆ **800/672-9901** or 719/684-9901. www.eastholme.com. 8 units (6 with bathroom), including 2 cottages. $95–$135 double; $135 suite; $150 cottage. Rates include full breakfast. DISC, MC, V. 10 miles west of I-25, about 1 mile off U.S. 24. **Amenities:** Outdoor hot tub. *In room:* Cable TV w/VCR, free Wi-Fi, fridge, coffeemaker, hair dryer.

Holden House 1902 Bed & Breakfast Inn ★★ Innkeepers Sallie and Welling Clark restored this storybook 1902 Colonial Revival–style Victorian house, the adjacent carriage house, and the 1898 house next door, filling the rooms with antiques and family heirlooms. Located near Old Colorado City, the inn has a living room with a tile fireplace, a front parlor with a bay window, verandas, and a lovely garden out back. Guests enjoy 24-hour coffee-and-tea service with a bottomless cookie jar, an afternoon wine social, and a gourmet breakfast in the formal dining room. Two suites are in the main house, two are in the adjacent carriage house, and one is in the second home. Each guest room bears the name of a Colorado mining area and contains memorabilia of that district. All have sitting areas, queen-size beds, fireplaces, CD/DVD players, and tubs for two. The Cripple Creek Suite features Victorian fretwork in the sitting area, a mahogany fireplace, and a magnificent Roman marble tub. The Independence Suite, in the adjacent building, is accessible to guests with disabilities. Smoking is not allowed and pets are not permitted—except the two resident cats, Mingtoy and Mei-Lin.

1102 W. Pikes Peak Ave., Colorado Springs, CO 80904. ✆ **888/565-3980** or 719/471-3980. Fax 719/471-4740. www.holdenhouse.com. 5 suites. $140–$160 double. Rates include full breakfast. AE, DC, DISC, MC, V. Children not accepted. *In room:* A/C, TV w/DVD player, free Wi-Fi, fridge, hair dryer, iron.

Two Sisters Inn ★★ Built by two sisters in 1919 as a boarding house, this splendid bed-and-breakfast has been owned and operated by two women—sisters in spirit if not in blood—since 1990. Wendy Goldstein and Sharon Smith have furnished the four bedrooms and separate honeymoon cottage with family heirlooms and photographs, in a style best described as informal elegance. The rooms in the main house feature Victorian frills and furnishings, such as quilts and claw-foot bathtubs. The two rooms that share a bathroom are only rented together ($79 for the second bedroom, plus $15 for an additional person), which is a great choice for two couples. Across a splendid garden area, the small cottage, with a separate bedroom and living room, has a feather bed, gas-log fireplace, refrigerator, and shower with skylight. Fresh flowers adorn each room, and homemade chocolates and baked goods are served upon arrival.

The rooms are great, but I especially like the breakfasts, which the proprietors describe as "healthy decadence." They often cook with herbs and vegetables from their garden, and they do some marvelous things with fruit. In the summer, Wendy and Sharon's lemonade, made fresh with naturally sparkling Manitou Springs water, is the perfect refreshment. Smoking is not permitted.

10 Otoe Place, Manitou Springs, CO 80829. ✆ **800/2SISINN** [274-7466] or 719/685-9684. www.twosisinn.com. 5 units. $94–$188 double; $155 cottage. Rates include full breakfast. DISC, MC, V. Children 9 and under not accepted. Located 1 block south of the town clock on Manitou Ave.

INEXPENSIVE

Best Value Inn Villa Motel (Kids) A solid option right off the main drag in Manitou Springs, the Villa offers well-kept rooms and reasonable rates within walking distance of all of Manitou's restaurants and shops, as well as some older cottages that are the least expensive rooms on-site. The cottages have two double beds, the newer motel rooms have two queens or a king, and deluxe rooms have a jetted tub and a kitchenette, to boot. For the kids, there's a small pool and easy access to the family-friendly attractions downtown.

481 Manitou Ave., Manitou Springs, CO 80829. ✆ **888/315-2378** or 719/685-5492. www.villamotel.com. 47 units. Summer $82–$120 double; fall–spring $59–$109. AE, DC, DISC, MC, V. **Amenities:** Large outdoor pool. *In room:* A/C, cable TV, free Wi-Fi, fridge, coffeemaker, hair dryer, iron, microwave.

Travel Inn (Value) Popular with both business travelers and vacationers on a budget, the Travel Inn offers a comfortable place to sleep at very reasonable rates. The two-story motel with bright turquoise trim is conveniently located near downtown Colorado Springs, with easy access to all the area attractions on I-25 and U.S. 24. The remodeled rooms are simple and comfortable, with white stucco walls and dark-wood furnishings. There is one apartment with a kitchenette that is designed for longer stays.

512 S. Nevada Ave., Colorado Springs, CO 80903. ✆ **719/636-3986.** Fax 719/636-3980. 36 units (most with shower only). Summer $49–$89 double; fall–spring $40–$60 double. Rates include continental breakfast. AE, DC, DISC, MC, V. **Amenities:** Outdoor heated pool (seasonal); coin-op washers and dryers. *In room:* A/C, cable TV, free Wi-Fi, kitchenette.

CAMPING

Also see the section on **Mueller State Park,** under "Parks & Zoos," later in this chapter.

Garden of the Gods Campground Located near Garden of the Gods (see "Attractions," p. 161), this large, tree-shaded campground offers 250 full RV hookups (30- and 50-amp service, some with modems and phones) and additional tent sites. Facilities include tables, barbecue grills, bathhouses, grocery store, wireless Internet access, laundry, heated swimming pool, whirlpool tub, playground, and clubhouse with pool tables and game room. The 12 camping cabins, which share the campground's bathhouse, rent for $45 to $50 for a double. There are also motel-style rooms for $60 to $110 for a double. The bunkhouse and the cabins are available in summer only.

3704 W. Colorado Ave., Colorado Springs, CO 80904. © **800/248-9451** or 719/475-9450. www.coloradocampground.com. Summer $36–$49; fall–spring $22–$32. Extra person $3. DISC, MC, V. Take I-25, exit 141, head west on U.S. 24, then north (right) on 31st St., then left on Colorado Ave. for 6 blocks (keep right), and turn right to gate.

4 WHERE TO DINE

Colorado Springs has an excellent variety of above-average restaurants, with a good sampling of continental cuisine, Mexican restaurants, and steak joints. See also the section on dinner theaters in "Colorado Springs After Dark," later in this chapter. A good online resource for information on area restaurants and nightlife is www.sceneinthesprings.com.

VERY EXPENSIVE

Charles Court ★★ PROGRESSIVE AMERICAN The English country-manor atmosphere of this outstanding restaurant at the Broadmoor resort (p. 150), with picture windows looking across Cheyenne Lake to the renowned hotel, lends itself to a fine-dining experience. The creative American menu, which changes seasonally, has a decidedly Rocky Mountain emphasis. You'll usually find such delicacies as a Colorado lamb rib-eye, beef tenderloin, wild King salmon, Rocky Mountain trout, and a wild-game selection such as buffalo or venison. The wine list includes more than 600 selections, service is superlative, and the desserts are extraordinary. A seasonal outdoor patio provides splendid views of the mountains across the lake. A comparable experience can be had on the top of the tower on the other side of the lake at the **Penrose Room,** an equally refined eatery with a Continental bent and even more formality (jackets required).

Broadmoor W., in the Broadmoor, Lake Circle. © **719/577-5733.** www.broadmoor.com. Reservations recommended. Breakfast $8–$18; dinner main courses $23–$42. AE, DC, DISC, MC, V. Daily 7–11am and 6–10pm.

Cliff House Dining Room ★★ AMERICAN The Cliff House Dining Room is an excellent choice for a romantic occasion. The Villeroy & Boch china, damask linen, crystal glassware, and 19th-century tiled fireplace evoke the charm of the Victorian era. The main event is dinners: old favorites expertly prepared in new ways. While the menu changes regularly, I recommend the filet mignon, charbroiled with roasted garlic pepper, and the seafood (trout to scallops and prawns) when they're available, but everything is quite good. As would be expected, service is impeccable. The breakfast menu offers traditional American selections, plus a nifty wild-mushroom Florentine with smoked bacon, and lunches are upscale sandwiches and entrees like quiche du jour and blackened ruby-red trout. The excellent wine list includes some 600 selections.

Cliff House Inn, 306 Cañon Ave., Manitou Springs. © **719/785-2415.** Reservations recommended. Lunch main courses $7–$24; dinner main courses $19–$32. AE, DC, DISC, MC, V. Daily 6:30–10:30am, 11:30am–2:30pm, and 5:30–9:30pm.

Craftwood Inn ★★★ *Finds* COLORADO CUISINE Ensconced in an English Tudor building with beamed ceilings, stained-glass windows, and a copper-hooded fireplace, the casually elegant Craftwood Inn, built in 1912, was originally a coppersmith's shop. Today this excellent restaurant specializes in regional game and also offers steak, seafood, and vegetarian dishes. The extensive selection of game—elk, venison, pheasant, quail, caribou, antelope, wild boar, ostrich, and buffalo—attracts the most acclaim. I especially recommend grilled Rocky Mountain elk steak (when available), marinated in herb and smoke–infused oil, and served with a cabernet sauvignon hunter's sauce. The adventurous might opt for the wild grill: elk, antelope, and venison, each accompanied by a distinctive sauce. Be sure to save room for one of the superb—and somewhat unusual—desserts, such as jalapeño white chocolate mousse with raspberry sauce, or prickly pear sorbet. The outdoor patio provides wonderful views of Pikes Peak.

404 El Paso Blvd., Manitou Springs. ✆ **719/685-9000.** www.craftwood.com. Reservations recommended. Main courses $24–$38. AE, DC, DISC, MC, V. Daily 5:30–8:30pm. Turn north off Manitou Ave. onto Mayfair Ave., go uphill 1 block, and turn left onto El Paso Blvd.; the Craftwood is on your right.

The Famous ★★ STEAK A swank urban steakhouse, the Famous is a magnet for beefeaters, serving up choice cuts of U.S. Prime. It's hard to go wrong here, but bring an appetite: Except for two filets, no steak is less than a pound. I like the Kansas City bone-in strip, but everything is top shelf here, even the nonbeef fare, like fresh seafood (flown in daily), Colorado lamb, and chicken Oscar. The lunch menu is similarly carnivorous, with a few salads for good measure. There are shiny booths and jet-black tables, as well as a full bar and live piano every night.

31 N. Tejon St. ✆ **719/227-7333.** Reservations recommended. Lunch main courses $10–$15, dinner main courses $28–$50. AE, DISC, MC, V. Mon–Fri 11am–3pm; Sun–Thurs 5–10pm; Fri–Sat 5–11pm.

Summit ★★★ CONTEMPORARY AMERICAN Flashy, modern, and new in 2006, Summit is a departure from the Broadmoor's typical eatery formula—Continental has long ruled the roost here—but it quickly rose to the top of the local culinary stratosphere. Designed by acclaimed architect Adam Tihany, the strikingly contemporary room is at once slick and romantic, with cloth chandeliers, contemporary metalwork on the windows and walls, and a glassed-in, rotating turret holding 432 bottles of wine behind the bar. The visual spectacle is aesthetically matched by the innovative and adventurous fare—the seasonal menu might have a terrific roasted beet salad or monkfish *osso buco,* but it depends on what's currently domestically available. The service is impeccable, and the sommelier is skilled at wine pairings, with a focus on biodynamic and organic wines, and wines from small wineries.

In the Broadmoor, 19 Lake Circle. ✆ **719/577-5896.** www.summitatbroadmoor.com. Reservations recommended. Main courses $18–$32. AE, DC, DISC, MC, V. Daily 5:30–9pm.

Walter's Bistro ★★ CONTINENTAL Slick but not stuffy, Walter's manages to be classy, casual, and classic, all at once. Proprietor Walter Iser, a native of Salzburg, Austria, has long worked the front of the house in various upscale properties in the Springs and environs, but he's truly hit his stride with Walter's, which opened in 1999 and relocated to a handsome new location in 2004. Watching over four dining areas—including a richly decorated "red room" and a chef's table beneath windows into the kitchen—Iser has a gracious style and steady direction that inform an expertly prepared menu of Continental staples, which manage to simultaneously taste traditional but original. The menu changes regularly, but my visit included a terrific rack of lamb, herb roasted and served with a creamy English pea risotto, pan-roasted Chilean sea bass, and a truly phenomenal bone-in filet mignon with an equally superlative bread pudding with wild mushrooms and andouille sausage. Desserts are decadent, including a chocolate "bag" filled with tiramisu, and the wine list is long and varied.

136 E. Cheyenne Mountain Blvd. ✆ **719/630-0201.** Reservations recommended. Lunch main courses $7–$24; dinner main courses $24–$32. AE, DC, DISC, MC, V. Mon–Fri 11am–2pm; Mon–Sat 5:30–9pm.

EXPENSIVE

The Blue Star ★★ INTERNATIONAL FUSION In a quiet area just south of downtown, the Blue Star is one of the most popular eateries in Colorado Springs, and deservedly so. The menu changes monthly, but it always includes filet mignon, fresh fish (flown in daily), pork, and chicken, prepared with a nose for invention. The culinary inspiration comes from Mediterranean and Pacific Rim cultures, but it is ultimately unclassifiable and in a local class of its own. The restaurant might serve Thai chili beef tips with avocado sorbet one week and beef bourguignon the next. Social and colorful, the bar features sleek wood and metal decor, and walls are adorned with well-lit artwork, whereas the dining room's atmosphere is milder with an open kitchen. Each room serves its own menu: The bar menu is "eating" (lunch and dinner in a social atmosphere), while the main room is serious "dining," dinner only in a more refined space. Blue Star has won *Wine Spectator*'s "Best of" Award of Excellence with its 8,500-bottle cellar since 2003.

1645 S. Tejon St. ✆ **719/632-1086.** www.thebluestar.net. Reservations recommended. Main courses $6–$14 lunch, $9–$25 dinner. AE, MC, V. Dining room Sun–Thurs 5:30–9pm; Fri–Sat 5:30–10pm. Bar during restaurant hours; bar food service Mon–Wed 11:30am–10:30pm, Thurs–Fri 11:30am–midnight, Sat 3pm–midnight, Sun 3–10:30pm.

La Petite Maison ★★ CONTEMPORARY FRENCH This delightful 1894 Victorian cottage houses a gem of a restaurant, chef-owned by Henri Chaperont. Since 1978, it has served a blend of classic French and eclectic modern cuisine in a friendly, intimate setting with jazz playing in the background. The food is innovative, interesting, and well presented; service is impeccable. The menus change monthly; if they're available, I suggest Colorado rack of lamb Provençale or the baked monkfish with three-grain mustard. Chaperont's skills are on full display with his three-course tasting menus, available for $30 Tuesday through Friday and Sunday; a typical meal could include traditional French onion soup, roasted pork tenderloin, and chocolate pâté with lavender crème anglaise for dessert.

1015 W. Colorado Ave. ✆ **719/632-4887.** Reservations recommended. Main courses $19–$30. AE, DC, DISC, MC, V. Tues–Sun 5–10pm.

Margarita at PineCreek ★★ ECLECTIC A delightful spot to sit and watch the sun set over Pikes Peak, the Margarita is tucked away above two creeks on the north side of the city. The decor is attractively simple, with tile floors and stucco walls; a tree-shaded outdoor patio is open in summer and even features outdoor movies on occasion. Saturday evenings bring live harpsichord music to the dining room, and Friday nights often feature live acoustic music—from bluegrass to Celtic. Although the style of cooking may vary, depending on the chef's whim, the emphasis is on fresh ingredients, and everything is prepared from scratch, including breads and stocks. Lunches feature a choice of two homemade soups, salad, and fresh bread; there are also Southwestern and weekly specials. Six-course dinners offer three entree choices, usually fresh fish, veal, steak, pasta, lamb, or duckling.

7350 Pine Creek Rd. ✆ **719/598-8667.** Reservations recommended. Fixed-price lunch $10–$11; fixed-price dinner $30–$38; brunch $10–$15. AE, DISC, MC, V. Tues–Fri 11:30am–2pm; Tues–Sat 5:30–9pm; Sun 10:30am–2pm.

Kids Family-Friendly Restaurants

Edelweiss Restaurant (see below) Kids will enjoy the strolling musicians who play German folk music on weekends, and they'll love the apple and cherry strudels.

Giuseppe's Old Depot Restaurant (p. 159) An original locomotive stands outside this old Denver & Rio Grande Railroad station. Most kids will adore the spaghetti and pizza.

Meadow Muffins (p. 161) The junk-store appearance and kid-friendly food (like a burger with peanut butter) make this place a hit with the younger set.

The Tavern ★★ STEAK/SEAFOOD Authentic Toulouse-Lautrec lithographs on the walls and knotty pine furniture and paneling mark the Tavern, open since 1939, as a restaurant with unusual ambience. In the front dining room, nightly piano music is followed by a four-piece ensemble—guests are welcome to take a turn around the dance floor between courses. The quieter garden room, with luxuriant tropical foliage, gives the feeling of outdoor dining without being outdoors. Service in both rooms is impeccable.

Many selections are prepared in the restaurant's stone grill, and the emphasis is on fresh ingredients and classic cuisine. The lunch menu changes seasonally but typically includes steaks, gourmet burgers, crab cakes, and a variety of sandwiches and salads. Dinners are more elaborate: Choose from slow-roasted prime rib, filet mignon, Rocky Mountain trout, or roast chicken. All entrees come with a selection of homemade breads.

Broadmoor Main, at the Broadmoor, Lake Circle. ✆ **719/577-5733.** www.broadmoor.com. Reservations recommended. Main courses $10–$29 lunch, $16–$58 dinner. AE, DC, DISC, MC, V. Daily 11am–11pm.

The Warehouse ★★ CONTEMPORARY/FUSION This stalwart locals' joint, which opened in 1997, emanates the style that helped launch a revitalization of the south side of downtown Colorado Springs. The Warehouse is located in, yes, a converted century-old warehouse, a mixed-use building that's one of the most stylish addresses in the city. One side of the restaurant is the main dining area, with an array of tables centered on a copper-topped bar; across the hall is a gallery with couches where many people enjoy libations or wait for a table. The attractive industrial chic atmosphere is a nice match for the diverse menu, which is known for a filet "Oskar," seared beef tenderloin with lemon-pepper asparagus, blue crab, and Béarnaise sauce; and venison with a tart cherry sauce and mountain mushroom risotto. Lunch is lighter, mainly unique sandwiches and salads, and the wine and beer lists—focused on Colorado producers—are excellent.

25 W. Cimarron St. ✆ **719475-8880.** www.thewarehouserestaurant.com. Reservations recommended. Main courses $8–$15 lunch, $15–29 dinner. AE, DISC, MC, V. Mon–Fri 11:30am–9pm; Sat 5–10pm.

MODERATE

Edelweiss Restaurant ★ Kids GERMAN The Edelweiss occupies an impressive stone building with a trio of fireplaces and an outdoor biergarten. It underscores its

Bavarian atmosphere with strolling folk musicians on weekends, which gives it a party feel that makes this a fun place for kids. It offers a hearty menu of Jägerschnitzel, Wiener schnitzel, sauerbraten, bratwurst, and other old-country specials, as well as New York strip steak, fresh fish, and chicken. The fruit strudels are excellent, and there are some great beers, many of them German imports.

34 E. Ramona Ave. (southwest of I-25, 1 block west of Nevada Ave.). ✆ **719/633-2220.** www.edelweissrest.com. Reservations recommended. Main courses $7–$9 lunch, $12–$25 dinner. AE, DC, DISC, MC, V. Daily 11:30am–9pm.

Giuseppe's Old Depot Restaurant ★ Kids ITALIAN/AMERICAN Located in a restored Denver & Rio Grande train station with glass ticket windows lining the walls, Giuseppe's is a fun place with a lot of historic ambience. You can see freight trains going by just outside the windows. The same extensive menu is served all day. Spaghetti, lasagna (vegetarian spinach or spicy sausage and ground beef), and stone-baked pizza are house specialties. American dishes include my favorite—baby back pork ribs, smothered in Giuseppe's secret sauce—plus prime rib, grilled salmon filet, and fried chicken.

10 S. Sierra Madre St. ✆ **719/635-3111.** www.giuseppes-depot.com. Menu items $8–$31; pizzas $11–$21. AE, DC, DISC, MC, V. Sun–Thurs 11am–9pm; Fri–Sat 11am–10pm.

Marigold Café and Bakery ★ Finds INTERNATIONAL This bustling restaurant and bakery is known for its fresh ingredients and homemade breads and pastries. A low wall separates the bakery counter from the cafelike dining area. Breakfast and lunch are casual, featuring traditional menus and gourmet-savvy items such as Greek pizzas and innovative sandwiches served on fresh breads. The restaurant takes on a more refined atmosphere at dinner, when the menu reflects a wide range of international influences. Favorites include flat iron steak, served with a balsamic and red-wine reduction, salmon with sautéed spinach and goat cheese and dried tomato pesto, jambalaya, and fresh pasta dishes. The bakery counter bustles through the early afternoon, offering splendid breads, pastries, and sandwiches. Box lunches, coffee, lattes, and cappuccinos are also available.

4605 Centennial Blvd. (at Garden of the Gods Rd.). ✆ **719/599-4776.** Main courses $5–$8.50 breakfast, $7–$10 lunch, $11–$32 dinner. AE, DC, DISC, MC, V. Restaurant Mon–Sat 7–10:30am, 11am–2:30pm, and 5–9pm. Coffee bar and bakery Mon–Fri 6am–9pm; Sat 7am–9pm. Closed Sun.

Phantom Canyon Brewing Co. ★ CONTEMPORARY AMERICAN This popular, busy brewpub is in the Cheyenne Building, home to the Chicago Rock Island & Pacific Railroad in the early 1900s. On any given day, 8 to 10 of Phantom Canyon's specialty beers are on tap, including homemade root beer. The signature beer is the Phantom, a traditional India pale ale; others include the Cascade Amber and a light ale called Queen's Blonde.

The dining room is large and wide open, with ceiling fans, hardwood floors, and large brewing vats, visible in the corner. Lunch is typical but well-prepared brewpub fare: hearty salads, half-pound burgers, fish and chips, and the like. The dinner menu is varied and more innovative, with choices such as roasted chicken and hot bacon salad, Queen's Blonde Ale soup, steak, and trout. The menus change periodically. On the second floor is a billiards hall with TVs and foosball. See also "Colorado Springs After Dark," later in this chapter.

2 E. Pikes Peak Ave. ✆ **719/635-2800.** Main courses $8–$13 lunch, $9–$25 dinner. AE, DC, DISC, MC, V. Mon–Thurs 11am–10pm; Fri–Sat 11am–midnight; Sun 10am–10pm. Bar open later.

Ritz Grill ★ NEW AMERICAN This lively restaurant-lounge with a large central bar is where it's at for many of the city's young professionals. The decor is Art Deco, the service fast and friendly. The varied, trendy menu offers such specialties as Garden Ritz veggie pizza, with fresh spinach, sun-dried tomatoes, bell peppers, onions, mushrooms, fresh pesto, and three cheeses; and Siamese tuna salad—served rare with wild greens, mango salsa, radish sprouts, pickled ginger chestnuts, and wasabi peas. I would recommend the Cajun chicken and shrimp, sautéed with bell peppers in a spicy alfredo sauce, or the peppered Ahi, spiced with pastrami and served with gingered white rice and sautéed spinach. See also "Colorado Springs After Dark," later in this chapter.

15 S. Tejon St. ✆ **719/635-8484.** www.ritzgrill.com. Main courses $7–$15 brunch and lunch, $12–$26 dinner. AE, MC, V. Mon–Thurs 11am–10pm; Fri–Sat 11am–10:30pm; Sun 9:30am–10pm. Bar open later with a limited menu.

INEXPENSIVE

Adam's Mountain Cafe ★★ Finds AMERICAN/VEGETARIAN Not strictly vegetarian, Adam's Mountain Cafe is one of the best restaurants in the area for those seeking vegetarian or healthy, largely organic—but not entirely meatless—fare. While Adam's relocated from its longtime Cañon Avenue address to the ground floor of the restored Spa Building in 2007, the country-meets-French-Victorian vibe is still there. The menu includes grilled items, fresh fish, and many Mediterranean-style entrees. Breakfast specialties include orange-almond French toast, my top choice, and the P. W. Busboy Special, consisting of two whole-grain pancakes, two scrambled eggs, and slices of fresh fruit. Lunch offerings include sandwiches, soups, salads, fresh pasta, and Southwestern plates. Come dinner, I recommend the harvest crepes, packed with roasted butternut squash and finished with a vegetarian red chile, and the Caribbean jerked chicken.

934 Manitou Ave. (in the Spa Building)., Manitou Springs. ✆ **719/685-1430.** www.adamsmountain.com. Main courses $4.50–$9 breakfast and lunch, $8–$19 dinner. AE, DISC, MC, V. Daily 8am–3pm; Tues–Sat 5–9pm. Closed Mon Oct–Apr.

Amanda's Fonda ★ Finds AMERICAN My pick for Mexican food in Colorado Springs, Amanda's Fonda is the handiwork of a family that has owned Mexican restaurants for six generations. Clearly they've honed the art of making remarkable chile in that time: Both the chile Colorado and the green chile are excellent; the former is red with big hunks of steak, the latter spicier with pork. The burritos, spinach-and-mushroom enchiladas, and seafood are also quite tasty, and on weekends the menu includes both *menudo* (tripe soup) and pozole (pork and hominy stew). The interior of the place is a funky maze, one part log cabin, one part family restaurant, and one part Mexican bar and grill. The shady creekside patio is a great place for a summertime meal.

3625 W. Colorado Ave. ✆ **719/227-1975.** Main courses $6–$14. AE, DISC, MC, V. Mon–Sat 11:30am–9pm; Sun noon–9pm.

Dutch Kitchen ★ Value AMERICAN Good homemade food served in a casual, friendly atmosphere is the draw at this relatively small restaurant, which the Flynn family has owned and operated since 1959. I especially like the corned beef, pastrami, and ham sandwiches, and if you're there in summer, be sure to try the fresh rhubarb pie. Other house specialties include the pies (the buttermilk, pecan chocolate, and candied apple are award-winners) and homemade soups.

1025 Manitou Ave., Manitou Springs. ✆ **719/685-9962.** Main courses $4–$8 lunch, $7–$13 dinner. No credit cards. Sat–Thurs 11:30am–3:30pm and 4:30–8pm. Closed Thurs in spring and fall. Closed Dec–Feb.

La'au's (Finds HAWAIIAN TACOS An unexpected hybrid that works quite well, La'au's is a Colorado College student favorite that takes Mexican tradition and filters it through a Pacific Rim lens—it's one of the few taco joints on the mainland offering its customers chopsticks and sriracha sauce. With counter service and indoor and outdoor seating, Lau'au's tacos are topped with papaya or cabbage and often filled with Hawaiian staples like huli chicken or mahimahi. Besides tacos, borrachas (make-your-own taco plates), salads, and bowls (tacos minus the tortillas) are available, as are bottles of beer and premade margaritas.

830 N. Tejon St., Ste. 110. © **719/578-5228.** www.laaustacoshop.com. Plates $5.50–$9. No credit cards. Mon–Sat 11am–10pm; Sun noon–8pm.

Meadow Muffins ★ (Value (Kids AMERICAN A fun spot for a good, inexpensive meal in a lively atmosphere, Meadow Muffins is a boisterous bar packed with movie memorabilia and assorted oddities. The decorations range from two buckboard wagons (hung from the ceiling near the front door), which were supposedly used in *Gone with the Wind,* to a 5-ton cannon used in a number of war movies. The menu includes chicken wings, onion rings, sandwiches, salads, and the like. The burgers are especially good—just ask anyone in the Springs—but I have to admit that I couldn't bring myself to try the Jiffy Burger: a large ground-beef burger topped with bacon, provolone cheese, and—believe it or not—peanut butter. On most days, there are great food and drink specials. See also "Colorado Springs After Dark," later in this chapter.

2432 W. Colorado Ave., in Old Colorado City. © **719/633-0583.** www.meadowmuffins.com. Most menu items $4.50–$9. AE, DISC, MC, V. Daily 11am–10pm. Bar open later, with a limited menu.

5 ATTRACTIONS

Most of the attractions of the Pikes Peak region fit in two general categories: natural, such as Pikes Peak, Garden of the Gods, and Cave of the Winds; and historic/educational, including the Air Force Academy, Olympic Complex training center, museums, historic homes, and art galleries. There are also gambling houses in Cripple Creek.

If you visit Colorado from a sea-level area, you might want to schedule mountain excursions, such as the cog railway to the top of Pikes Peak, at the end of your stay. This will give your body time to adapt to the lower oxygen level at these higher elevations. See also "Health," in chapter 3.

THE TOP ATTRACTIONS

Colorado Springs Pioneers Museum ★★ (Value Housed in the former El Paso County Courthouse (1903), which is on the National Register of Historic Places, this museum is an excellent place to begin your visit to Colorado Springs. Exhibits depict the community's rich history, including its beginning as a fashionable resort, the railroad and mining eras, and its growth and development in the 20th century. Also here is the Victorian home of writer Helen Hunt Jackson.

You can ride an Otis birdcage elevator, which dates to the early 1900s, to the restored original courtroom, where several *Perry Mason* episodes were filmed. A recent renovation uncovered intriguing gold and silver images of goddesses, painted on the courtroom walls in part to represent the two key resources of the state's economy at the time. However, it's believed that they were also painted as a subtle protest when the country was changing

Fun Facts Fit for the Gods

In 1859 large numbers of pioneers were arriving in Colorado hoping to find gold (their motto: "Pikes Peak or Bust"). Many of them established communities along what is now called the Front Range, including Colorado City, which was later incorporated within Colorado Springs.

Legend has it that certain pioneers who explored the remarkable sandstone formations in the area wanted to establish a beer garden there. However, one Rufus Cable objected: "Beer Garden! Why this is a fit place for a Garden of the Gods!"

Fortunately for posterity, Charles Elliott Perkins (head of the Burlington Railroad) bought the area some 20 years later and kept it in its natural state. Upon Perkins's death in 1907, his heirs gave the remarkable area to Colorado Springs on the condition that it be preserved as a park and open to the public. The park was dedicated in 1909 and is now a Registered National Landmark.

from a gold and silver standard to a gold-only monetary standard. Another series of murals depicts over 400 years of Pikes Peak region history.

Changing exhibit areas house traveling shows such as quilts, historic photographs, aviation, American Indian culture, and art pottery. The museum has hosted a wide range of events, including lectures on the American cowboy, antique auto shows, jazz concerts, and Hispanic celebrations. The historic reference library and archives are available by appointment. Allow 1 to 3 hours.

215 S. Tejon St. ✆ **719/385-5990.** www.cspm.org. Free admission, donations accepted. Year-round Tues–Sat 10am–5pm. Take I-25, exit 141, east to Tejon St.; turn right and go 4 blocks.

Garden of the Gods ★★★ Value One of the West's unique geological sites, the 1,300-acre Garden of the Gods is a giant rock garden composed of spectacular red sandstone formations sculpted by rain and wind over millions of years. Located where several life zones and ecosystems converge, the beautiful city-run park harbors a variety of plant and animal communities. The oldest survivors are the ancient, twisted junipers, some 1,000 years old. The strangest animals arc the honey ants, which gorge themselves on honey in the summer and fall, becoming living honey pots to feed their colonies during winter hibernation.

The park has a number of hiking trails—mostly easy to moderate—that offer great scenery and an opportunity to get away from the crowds. Leashed dogs are permitted on trails (owners should clean up after their pets). Many trails are also open to horseback riding and mountain biking. You can get trail maps for the park at the **visitor center,** which also offers exhibits on the history, geology, plants, and wildlife of the area; a cafeteria; and other conveniences.

A 12-minute multimedia theater presentation, *How Did Those Red Rocks Get There?* ($5 adults, $2 children 5–12, free for children under 5), newly remade by local filmmaker John Bourbonais in 2008 in high definition with a unique BluRay projection system, is an excellent introduction to the geologic history of the area. In summer, park naturalists lead free 45-minute walks through the park and conduct free afternoon interpretive programs. You can also take a 20-minute bus tour of the park ($5 adults, $2.50

children 5–12, free for children under 5). You may spot technical rock climbers on some of the park spires; they are required to register at the visitor center.

Also in the park is the **Rock Ledge Ranch Historic Site** (see "More Attractions," below).

1805 N. 30th St. ✆ **719/634-6666.** www.gardenofgods.com. Free admission. Park May–Oct daily 5am–11pm; Nov–Apr daily 5am–9pm. Visitor Center Memorial Day to Labor Day daily 8am–8pm; Labor Day to Memorial Day 9am–5pm. Take Garden of the Gods Rd. west from I-25, exit 146, and turn south on 30th St.

Pikes Peak Cog Railway ★★ For those who enjoy rail travel, spectacular scenery, and the thrill of mountain climbing without all the work, this is the trip to take. The first passenger train climbed Pikes Peak on June 30, 1891, and diesel slowly replaced steam power between 1939 and 1955. Four custom-built Swiss twin-unit rail cars, each seating 216 passengers, went into service in 1989. The 9-mile route, with grades up to 25%, takes 75 minutes to reach the top of 14,110-foot Pikes Peak; the round-trip requires 3 hours and 10 minutes (including a 40-min. stopover at the top). Runs depart between 8am and 5pm in midsummer, with shorter hours at other times.

> **Fun Facts — Top of the Charts**
>
> Teacher Katharine Lee Bates (1859–1929) wrote the patriotic song "America the Beautiful" after an 1895 wagon trip to the top of Pikes Peak.

The journey is exciting from the start, but passengers really begin to ooh and aah when the track leaves the forest, creeping above timberline at about 11,500 feet. The view from the summit takes in Denver, 75 miles north; New Mexico's Sangre de Cristo range, 100 miles south; the Cripple Creek mining district, on the mountain's western flank; wave after wave of Rocky Mountain subranges to the west; and the seemingly endless sea of Great Plains to the east. This is also where you'll want to watch for Rocky Mountain bighorn sheep and yellow-bellied marmots. The Summit House at the top of Pikes Peak has a restaurant (sandwiches, snacks, beverages, and box lunches), a gift shop, and even a flavored oxygen bar.

Take a jacket or sweater—it can be cold and windy on top, even on warm summer days. This trip is not recommended if you have cardiac or respiratory problems. Even those in good health may feel faint or light-headed.

515 Ruxton Ave., Manitou Springs. ✆ **800/745-3773** or 719/685-5401. www.cograilway.com. $31–$33 adults, $17–$18 children 3–11, free for children 2 and under held on an adult's lap. Mid-Apr to mid-Nov, with 2 to 8 departures daily; call or check schedules online. Closed mid-Nov to mid-Apr, except for special events. Reservations required (available online). Take I-25, exit 141, west on U.S. 24 for 4 miles, turn onto Manitou Ave. west and go 1½ miles to Ruxton Ave., turn left and go about ½ mile.

Pikes Peak Highway ★ Perhaps no view in Colorado equals the 360-degree panorama from the 14,110-foot summit of Pikes Peak. Whether you go by cog railway (see above) or private vehicle, the ascent is a spectacular, exciting experience—although not for those with heart or breathing problems or a fear of heights. The 19-mile toll highway (paved for 10 miles, all-weather gravel thereafter) starts at 7,400 feet, some 4 miles west of Manitou Springs. There are numerous photo-op stops as you head up the mountain, and deer, mountain sheep, marmots, and other animals often appear on the slopes, especially above the timberline (around 11,500 ft.). This 156-curve road is the site of the annual Pikes Peak International Hill Climb (see "Spectator Sports," later in this chapter). Allow 3 hours minimum.

 Off U.S. 24 at Cascade Ave. ✆ **800/318-9505** or 719/385-7325. www.pikespeakcolorado.com. Admission $10 adults, $5 children 6–15, free for children 5 and under, $35 maximum per car. Fri before Memorial Day to Labor Day daily 7am–7pm; Labor Day to late Sept daily 7am–5pm; Oct to Memorial Day daily 9am–3pm, weather permitting. Take I-25, exit 141, west on U.S. 24 about 10 miles.

United States Air Force Academy ★★ Colorado Springs's pride and joy got its start in 1954 when Congress authorized the establishment of a U.S. Air Force Academy and chose this 18,000-acre site from among 400 prospective locations. The first class of cadets enrolled in 1959, and each year since, about 4,000 cadets have enrolled for the 4 years of rigorous training required to become Air Force officers.

The Academy is 12 miles north of downtown; enter at the North Gate, off I-25, exit 156B. Soon after entering the grounds, at the intersection of North Gate Boulevard and Stadium Boulevard, you'll see an impressive outdoor B-52 bomber display. Where North Gate Boulevard becomes Academy Drive (in another mile or so), look to your left to see the Cadet Field House, where the basketball and ice-hockey teams play (see "Spectator Sports," later in this chapter), and the Parade Ground, where you can sometimes spot cadets marching.

Academy Drive soon curves to the left. Six miles from the North Gate, signs mark the turnoff to the Barry Goldwater Air Force Academy Visitor Center. Open daily, it offers a variety of exhibits and films on the academy's history and cadet life, extensive literature and self-guided tour maps, and the latest information and schedules on academy activities. There are also a large gift shop and coffee shop.

A short trail from the visitor center leads to the unmistakable Cadet Chapel. Its 17 gleaming aluminum spires soar 150 feet, and within the building are separate chapels for the major Western faiths as well as an "all faiths" room. The public can visit Monday through Saturday from 9am to 5pm; Sunday services at 10am are open to the public. The chapel is closed for 5 days around graduation and during special events.

Also within easy walking distance of the visitor center is Arnold Hall, the social center that houses historical exhibits, a cafeteria, and a theater featuring a variety of public shows and lectures.

Off I-25, exit 156B. ✆ **719/333-2025.** www.usafa.af.mil. Free admission. Visitor center daily 9am–5pm; grounds 8am–6pm; additional hours for special events.

United States Olympic Complex So you think your local fitness center is state-of-the-art? Check out the 37-acre United States Olympic Complex, a sophisticated center where thousands of athletes train each year in a variety of Olympic sports. Free guided tours, available daily, take about an hour and include a film depicting the U.S. Olympic effort. Visitors may also see athletes in training. The visitor center includes the U.S. Olympic Hall of Fame, interactive kiosks on Olympics subjects, various other displays, and a gift shop that sells Olympic-logo merchandise.

The complex includes the **Olympic Sports Center I,** with five gymnasiums and a weight-training room; **Sports Center II,** which accommodates 14 sports; the **Indoor Shooting Center,** the largest facility of its kind in the Western Hemisphere, with areas for rifle and pistol shooting, rapid-fire and women's sport pistol bays, running-target rifle ranges, and air-rifle and pistol-fire points; and the **Aquatics Center,** which contains a 50m-by-25m pool with two movable bulkheads, 10 50m and 20 25m lanes, and more than 800,000 gallons of water. The U.S. Olympic Committee also operates the **7-Eleven Velodrome,** with a banked track for bicycle and roller speed skating, about 1 mile south of the Olympic Complex, in Memorial Park (see "Parks & Zoos," later in this chapter) off Union Boulevard. Olympic figure skaters train at the **World Arena,** southwest of downtown. Allow 1 to 2 hours.

1 Olympic Plaza, corner of Boulder St. (entrance) and Union Blvd. ✆ **888/659-8687** or 719/866-4618. www.usolympicteam.com. Free admission. Complex daily 9am–6pm. Guided tours begin every half-hour 9am–4pm (hourly Aug–May); reservations required for groups of 10 or more (✆ 719/866-4656). From I-25, take exit 143.

MORE ATTRACTIONS

Architectural Highlights

The Broadmoor This famous Italian Renaissance–style resort hotel has been a Colorado Springs landmark since Spencer Penrose built it in 1918. (See "Where to Stay," earlier in this chapter.) Stroll around the lake, have a drink at one of the watering holes, and look at the "Walk of Fame" near Charles Court, a hallway of photographs of celebrities at the resort, everyone from Jackie Gleason to the Shah of Iran to Aerosmith.

Lake Circle, at Lake Ave. ✆ **719/634-7711.** www.broadmoor.com. Free admission. Daily year-round.

Miramont Castle Museum Architecture buffs will love this place. Built into a hillside by a wealthy French priest as a private home in 1895 and converted by the Sisters of Mercy into a sanatorium in 1907, this unique Victorian mansion has always aroused curiosity. The structure incorporates at least nine identifiable architectural styles in its four stories, 46 rooms, 14,000 square feet of floor space, and 2-foot-thick stone walls. If you like tiny stuff, don't miss the room housing the miniatures museum. In summer, lunches, desserts, and tea are served Tuesday through Saturday from 11am to 4pm in the Queen's Parlour. The museum lies on the route from Manitou Avenue to the Pikes Peak Cog Railway. Allow at least 1 hour.

9 Capitol Hill Ave., Manitou Springs. ✆ **888/685-1011** or 719/685-1011. www.miramontcastle.org. Admission $6 adults, $5.50 seniors 60 and over, $2 children 6–15, free for children 5 and under. Memorial Day to Labor Day daily 9am–5pm; rest of year Tues–Sun 10am–4pm. Located 1 block west of the intersection of Manitou and Ruxton aves.

Historic Buildings

McAllister House This Gothic cottage, listed on the National Register of Historic Places, is a good place for a quick look at the Colorado of the late 19th century. It was built in 1873, and the builder, an army major named Henry McAllister, decided to construct the house with brick when he learned that the local wind was so strong it had blown a train off the tracks nearby. The house has many original furnishings, including three marble fireplaces. It is now owned by the Colonial Dames of America, whose knowledgeable volunteers lead guided tours. Allow about 1 hour.

423 N. Cascade Ave. (at St. Vrain St.). ✆ **719/635-7925.** Admission $5 adults, $4 seniors 62 and older, $3 children 6–12, free for children 5 and under. Summer Wed–Sat 10am–4pm, Sun noon–4pm; winter Thurs–Sat 10am–4pm. Take I-25, exit 141, east to Cascade Ave.; go left and continue for about 6 blocks.

Rock Ledge Ranch Historic Site Visitors can explore the history of three pioneer eras at this living-history farm, at the east entrance to Garden of the Gods Park. Listed on the National Register of Historic Places, the ranch presents the rigors of the homestead era at the 1860s Galloway Homestead, the agricultural difficulties of the working-ranch era at the 1880s Chambers Farm and Blacksmith Shop, and the more sophisticated estate period at the 1907 Orchard House. Special events, which take place frequently, include an old-fashioned Fourth of July celebration, an 1860s vintage baseball game in late summer, a Victorian Halloween party, and holiday celebrations Thanksgiving through Christmas. The General Store stocks a wide selection of historic reproductions, books, and gift items, and the proceeds help with preservation and restoration of the ranch. Allow 1 to 2 hours.

N. 30th St. and Gateway Rd., Garden of the Gods. ✆ **719/578-6777.** www.rockledgeranch.com. Admission $6 adults, $4 seniors 55 and older and students 13–18, $2 children 6–12, free for children 5 and under. June to Labor Day Wed–Sun 10am–5pm. Closed Labor Day to May. Take I-25, exit 146, and then follow signs west to Garden of the Gods.

Historic Neighborhoods

Manitou Springs, which centers on Manitou Avenue off U.S. 24 West, is a separate town with its own government. It is one of the country's largest National Historic Districts. Legend has it that Utes named the springs Manitou, their word for "Great Spirit," because they believed that the Great Spirit had breathed into the waters to create the natural effervescence of the springs. Pikes Peak soars above the town nestled at its base.

Today the community offers visitors a chance to step back to a slower and quieter time. It boasts numerous elegant Victorian buildings, many of which house delightful shops, galleries, restaurants, and lodgings. Manitou Springs is also home to many fine artists and artisans, whom you might spot painting or sketching about town. A small group of sculptors began the Manitou Art Project in 1992; it installed more than 20 sculptures in various locations downtown and in the parks, creating a large sculpture garden for all to enjoy. The works, which stay on display for a year, are for sale, with 25% of the proceeds used to purchase permanent sculpture for the city.

Visitors are encouraged to take the self-guided tour of the nine restored mineral springs of Manitou. Pick up the *Manitou Springs Visitor's Guide,* which contains a map and descriptions to help you find each spring. It's available at the Manitou Springs Chamber of Commerce & Visitors Bureau, 354 Manitou Ave. (✆ **800/642-2567** or 719/685-5089; www.manitousprings.org), which is open daily.

Old Colorado City, Colorado Avenue between 21st and 31st streets, was founded in 1859, 12 years before Colorado Springs. The town boomed in the 1880s after General Palmer's railroad came through. Tunnels led from the respectable side of town to this saloon and red-light district so that the city fathers could carouse without being seen coming or going—or so the legend goes. Today this historic district has an interesting assortment of shops, galleries, and restaurants.

Museums & Galleries

Colorado Springs Fine Arts Center ★ The center's permanent American collection includes works by legends like Georgia O'Keeffe, John James Audubon, John Singer Sargent, Charles Russell, Dale Chihuly, and other famed painters and sculptors, as well as a world-class collection of Native American and Latin American works. Opened in 1936 and fabulously expanded in 2007, the center also houses a 450-seat performing-arts theater, a 32,000-volume art-research library, the Bemis School of Art, a tactile gallery for those who are visually impaired, and a delightful sculpture garden. The expansion doubled the gallery space and won raves from architectural critics. Changing exhibits showcase local collections as well as touring international exhibits. Designed by renowned Santa Fe architect John Gaw Meem (whose work is nicely complemented by Denver-based David Tryba's colorful expansion), the Art Deco–style building reflects Southwestern mission and Pueblo influences. There is **Cafe 36** for lunch and the **Deco Lounge** for coffee and cocktails on weekend nights. Allow 1 to 3 hours.

30 W. Dale St. (west of N. Cascade Ave.). ✆ **719/634-5581.** www.csfineartscenter.org. Admission to galleries and museum $7.50 adults, $6.75 seniors and students 5–17, $3 for children 3–12, free for children 4 and under. Separate admission for performing-arts events. Galleries and museum Tues–Fri and Sun 10am–5pm; Sat 10–8pm. The 1st Thurs of every month until 9pm for a wine tasting. Closed federal holidays. Take I-25, exit 143, east to Cascade St., turn right to Dale St., and then turn right again.

Ghost Town Kids A fun place to take the family, Ghost Town is part historic attraction, part theme park. Made up of authentic 19th-century buildings relocated from other parts of Colorado, this "town" is sheltered from the elements in Old Colorado City. There's a sheriff's office, jail, saloon, general store, livery stable, blacksmith shop, rooming house, and assay office. Animated frontier characters tell stories of the Old West, while a shooting gallery, antique arcade machines, and nickelodeons provide additional entertainment. During the summer you can even pan for real gold. Allow about 2 hours.

400 S. 21st St. (on U.S. 24). ✆ **719/634-0696.** www.ghosttownmuseum.com. Admission $6.50 adults, $3.50 children 6–16, free for children 5 and under. June–Aug Mon–Sat 9am–6pm, Sun 11am–6pm; Sept–May Mon–Sat 10am–5pm, Sun 11am–5pm. Take I-25, exit 141; town is just west of exit.

Manitou Cliff Dwellings Preserve & Museums ★ Kids The cliff-dwelling ruins here are real, although originally they were located elsewhere. This put me off at first—they would be more authentic if they were in their original location—but the move here may have saved them. In the early 1900s, archaeologists, who saw such dwellings being plundered by treasure hunters, dismantled some of the ancient buildings, gathered artifacts found there, and hauled them away. Some of these ruins, constructed from A.D. 1200 to 1300, can be seen here in a village reconstructed by archaeologists. There are also two museums with exhibits on prehistoric American Indian life, and several gift shops that sell Indian-made jewelry, pottery, and other crafts, plus Colorado souvenirs. American Indian dancers perform during the summer. Allow 2 hours.

U.S. 24, Manitou Springs. ✆ **800/354-9971** or 719/685-5242. www.cliffdwellingsmuseum.com. Admission $9.50 adults, $8.50 seniors 60 and over, $7.50 children 7–11, free for children 6 and under. May–Sept daily 9am–6pm; Oct–Nov and Mar–Apr daily 9am–5pm; Dec–Feb daily 10am–4pm. Closed Thanksgiving and Christmas. Take I-25, exit 141, and go west on U.S. 24 about 5 miles.

May Natural History Museum of the Tropics Kids Here you'll find one of the world's best public collections of giant insects and other tropical invertebrates, not to mention a statue out front touted to be the world's largest Hercules beetle. James F. W. May (1884–1956) spent more than half a century exploring the world's jungles while compiling his illustrious collection, which has grown to more than 100,000 invertebrates, about 8,000 of which are on display at any given time. The specimens are irreplaceable, because many came from areas that are now so politically unstable that no one is willing or able to explore the backcountry to collect them again. Exhibits change periodically.

Also on the grounds is the **Museum of Space Exploration,** where you can take a pictorial trip through the history of space exploration, beginning with man's first attempts to fly and continuing through the most recent photos from NASA. Also on display are numerous models of early aircraft, World War II planes, and spacecraft. Take time to view one or more of the NASA space films, which include the first moon landing. Allow 2 to 3 hours for both museums. There's also a 500-site campground ($24–$26 for campsites) with hiking trails, fishing, and a playground area.

710 Rock Creek Canyon Rd. ✆ **719/576-0450.** www.maymuseum-camp-rvpark.com. Admission (includes Museum of Space Exploration) $6 adults, $5 seniors 60 and older, $3 children 6–12, free for children 5 and under. May–Sept daily 9am–6pm. Closed Oct–Apr except for groups of 10 or more. Take Colo. 115 and drive southwest out of Colorado Springs for 9 miles; watch for signs and the Hercules Beetle of the West Indies that mark the turnoff to the museum.

Money Museum ★ Finds Operated by the American Numismatic Association, this museum is the largest collection of its kind west of the Smithsonian Institution, consisting of four galleries of coins, tokens, medals, and paper money from around the world. Of special note is the earliest *reale* (Spanish coin) struck in the New World (Mexico), dating from 1536. There's also an 1804 dollar, a 1913 "V" nickel, and a nice collectors' library. Allow 1 hour.

818 N. Cascade Ave., on the campus of Colorado College. ✆ **719/632-2646.** www.money.org. Free admission, donations welcome. Tues–Fri 9am–5pm; Sat 10am–5pm; Sun noon–5pm. Take I-25, exit 143, east to Cascade Ave.; then turn right and go about 6 blocks.

Peterson Air & Space Museum Through its exhibits, this museum traces the history of Peterson Air Force Base, NORAD, the Air Defense Command, and Air Force Space Command. Of special interest are 16 historic aircraft, including P-47 Thunderbolt and P-40 Warhawk fighters from World War II, plus a number of missiles and jets from the Korean War to the present. To mark the 50th anniversary of the U.S. Air Force, a memorial grove of 58 conifer trees honoring the USAF Medal of Honor recipients was planted. There's also a small gift shop. Allow 1 to 2 hours. ***Note:*** Visitors must have a military ID or give administration at least 24 hours' advance notice to get on the base (72 hr. for Sat visits).

Peterson Air Force Base main gate, off U.S. 24 7 miles east of downtown. ✆ **719/556-4915.** www.petemuseum.org. Free admission. Tues–Sat 9am–4:30pm. Closed holidays and occasionally during military exercises; call ahead. Take I-25, exit 141, and then follow U.S. 24 east about 7½ miles.

ProRodeo Hall of Fame & American Cowboy Museum ★★ Kids No rhinestone cowboys here. This is the real thing, with exhibits on the development of rodeo, from its origins in early ranch work to major professional sport. You'll learn about historic and modern cowboys, including those brave (or crazy) enough to climb onto bucking broncos and wild bulls, in Heritage Hall. The Hall of Champions displays photos, gear, personal memorabilia, and trophies honoring rodeo greats. There are two multimedia presentations, and the museum features changing exhibits of Western art. Outside you'll find a replica rodeo arena, live rodeo animals, and a sculpture garden. Allow 2 hours.

101 ProRodeo Dr. (off Rockrimmon Blvd.). ✆ **719/528-4764.** www.prorodeohalloffame.com. Admission $6 adults, $5 seniors 55 and older, $3 children 6–12, free for children 5 and under. Memorial Day to Aug daily 9am–5pm; Sept to day before Memorial Day Wed–Sun 9am–5pm. Closed Easter, Thanksgiving, Christmas, and New Year's Day. Take I-25 to exit 147.

Western Museum of Mining & Industry ★★ Machines are fun, and the bigger the better. Historic hard-rock mining machinery and other equipment from Cripple Creek and other late-19th-century Colorado gold camps form the basis of this museum's 4,000-plus-item collection. Visitors can see an operating Corliss steam engine with an enormous 17-ton flywheel, a life-size underground mine reconstruction, and an exhibit on mining-town life showing how early Western miners and their families lived. You can also pan for gold—there's a wheelchair-accessible trough—and view a 23-minute video presentation on life in the early mining camps. Various hands-on family activities focus

Impressions

The air is so refined that you can live without much lungs.

—Shane Leslie, *American Wonderland,* 1936

on themes such as life in a mining town, minerals in everyday products, and recycled art. Free guided tours are available; call for information and times. Allow at least 2 hours.

1025 North Gate Rd., at I-25, exit 156A (off Gleneagle Dr. just east of the north gate of the U.S. Air Force Academy). ✆ **800/752-6558** or 719/488-0880. www.wmmi.org. Admission $8 adults, $6 seniors 60 and older and students 13–17, $4 children 3–12, free for children 2 and under. Mon–Sat 9am–4pm. Guided tours begin at 10am and 1pm. Located just east of I-25 via Gleneagle Dr.

World Figure Skating Museum & Hall of Fame This is the only museum of its kind in the world, exhibiting 1,200 years of ice skates—from early versions of carved bone to highly decorated cast-iron examples and finally the steel blades of today. There are also skating costumes, medals, and other memorabilia; changing exhibits; films; a library; and a gift shop. A gallery displays skating-related paintings, including works by the 17th-century Dutch artist Pieter Brueghel and Americans Winslow Homer and Andy Warhol. The museum is recognized by the International Skating Union, the sport's international governing body, as the repository for the history and official records of figure skating and the sport's official hall of fame. Here also are the U.S. national, regional, sectional, and international trophies. Allow 1 to 2 hours.

20 1st St. ✆ **719/635-5200.** www.worldskatingmuseum.org. Admission $3 adults, $2 seniors 60 and over and children 6–12, free for children 5 and under. Summer Mon–Sat 10am–4pm; closed Sat rest of yr. Closed major holidays. Take I-25, exit 138, west on Lake Ave.; just before the Broadmoor, turn right onto 1st St.

Natural Attractions

Cave of the Winds ★ Kids Discovered by two boys on a church outing in the 1880s, this impressive underground cavern has offered public tours for well over a century. It provides a good opportunity to see the beauty of the underworld. The 45-minute Discovery Tour takes visitors along a well-lit 3/4-mile passageway through 20 subterranean chambers, complete with classic stalagmites, stalactites, crystal flowers, and limestone canopies. In the Adventure Room, modern lighting techniques return visitors to an era when spelunking was done by candle and lantern. The 1 1/2-hour Lantern Tour follows unpaved and unlighted passageways and corridors. This tour is rather strenuous, with some stooping required in areas with low ceilings; it might muddy your shoes, but not your clothes.

Kids especially like the outdoor laser shows (with stereophonic sound) presented nightly during the summer at 9pm ($10 adults, $5 children 6–15, free for children under 6).

U.S. 24, Manitou Springs. ✆ **719/685-5444.** www.caveofthewinds.com. Discovery Tour $18 adults, $9 children 6–15, free for children 5 and under. Tours depart every 15–30 min. Memorial Day to Labor Day daily 9am–8pm; early Sept to late May daily 10am–4:30pm. Lantern Tours (3 times daily in summer and on weekends; other times by reservation) $22 adults, $12 children 6–15, children 5 and under are not permitted. Visitors with heart conditions, visual impairment, or other physical limitations are advised not to take Lantern Tour. Take I-25, exit 141, and go 6 miles west on U.S. 24.

Seven Falls This is a good choice for those who have not yet gotten their fill of Colorado's spectacular mountain scenery. A picturesque 1-mile drive through a box canyon takes you between the Pillars of Hercules, where the canyon narrows to just 42 feet, ending at these cascading falls. Seven separate waterfalls dance down a granite cliff, cascading some 181 feet. A free elevator takes visitors to the Eagle Nest viewing platform. A mile-long trail atop the plateau passes the grave of 19th-century novelist Helen Hunt Jackson, the author of *Ramona,* and ends at a panoramic view of Colorado Springs. Watch for birds and other wildlife along the way. Allow 2 hours.

At the end of S. Cheyenne Canyon Rd. © **719/632-0765.** www.sevenfalls.com. Day admission $9 adults, $8 seniors, $5.50 children 6–15, free for children 5 and under; night admission $11 adults, $9.50 seniors, $6.50 children 6–15, free for children 5 and under; lower rates in winter. Mid-May to Memorial Day daily 8:30am–9:30pm; June to mid-Aug daily 8:30am–10:30pm; rest of year daily 9am–4:15pm (to 5:15pm during daylight saving time). Christmas lighting daily mid- to late Dec 5–9:30pm. Closed major holidays. Take I-25, exit 141; head west on U.S. 24, turn south on 21st St. for about 3 miles, turn west on Cheyenne Blvd., and then left onto S. Cheyenne Canyon Rd.

Parks & Zoos

Cheyenne Mountain Zoo ★ Kids On the lower slopes of Cheyenne Mountain, at 6,800 feet above sea level, this medium-size zoological park is my top choice for a family outing. The zoo's 800-plus animals, many in "natural" environments, include wolves, lions, leopards, red pandas, elephants, hippos, monkeys, giraffes, reptiles, snakes, and lots of birds. Rocky cliffs have been created for the mountain goats; there's a pebbled beach for penguins and a new animal-contact area for children. The zoo is home to more than 30 endangered species, including the Siberian tiger, Amur leopard, and black-footed ferret. The zoo's giraffe herd is the largest and most prolific captive herd in the world; there have been about 200 live births since the 1950s. Visitors can actually feed the long-necked beasts ($1 for three crackers).

There's also a colorful antique carousel, built in 1926, the year the zoo was founded. New in 2008, the $8.2-million **Rocky Mountain Wild** lets visitors get up close and personal with mountain lions, grizzly bears, moose, and other local denizens. A stroller- and wheelchair-accessible tram makes a full loop of the zoo in about 15 minutes; it operates from Memorial Day to Labor Day. Admission to the zoo includes road access to the nearby **Will Rogers Shrine of the Sun,** a granite tower built in 1937, with photos and information on the American humorist. The tower also affords great views of the city and surrounding countryside. Strollers, double strollers, wheelchairs, and wagons are available for rent at Thundergod Gift and Snack Shop. Allow 2 to 4 hours for the zoo and an extra 45 minutes for the shrine.

4250 Cheyenne Mountain Zoo Rd. © **719/633-9925.** www.cmzoo.org. Admission $14 adults, $12 seniors 65 and over, $7.25 children 3–11, free for children 2 and under. Summer daily 9am–6pm; off season daily 9am–5pm. Take I-25, exit 138; drive west to the Broadmoor hotel and follow signs.

Memorial Park One of the largest parks in the city, Memorial is home to the Mark "Pa" Sertich Ice Center and the Aquatics and Fitness Center, as well as to the famed 7-Eleven Velodrome, which is used for world-class bicycling events. Other facilities include baseball and softball fields, volleyball courts, tennis courts, a bicycle criterium, and jogging trails. The park also stages a terrific fireworks display on Independence Day. See the sections on ice-skating, swimming, and tennis under "Outdoor Activities," below.

1605 E. Pikes Peak Ave. (btw. Hancock Ave. and Union Blvd.). © **719/385-5940.** www.springsgov.com (follow links). Free admission. Daily year-round. Located 1 mile east of downtown.

Monument Valley Park This long, slender park follows Monument Creek through downtown Colorado Springs. At its south end are formal zinnia, begonia, and rose gardens, and in the middle are demonstration gardens of the Horticultural Art Society. Facilities include softball and baseball fields, a swimming pool (open daily in summer; $5.50 adults, $4 children), volleyball and tennis courts, children's playgrounds, and picnic shelters. Also in the park are the 4.3-mile Monument Creek Trail for walkers, runners, and cyclists, and the 1-mile Monument Valley Fitness Trail at the north end, beside Bodington Field.

170 W. Cache La Poudre Blvd. ✆ **719/385-5940.** www.springsgov.com (follow links). Free admission. Daily year-round.

Mueller State Park ★★★ Finds Somewhat like a junior version of Rocky Mountain National Park, Mueller contains over 5,000 acres of prime scenic beauty along the west slope of Pikes Peak. The 55 miles of trails, designated for hikers, horseback riders, and mountain bikers, provide opportunities to observe elk, bighorn sheep, black bear, and the park's other wildlife. The best times to spot wildlife are spring and fall, just after sunrise and just before sunset. In the summer, rangers lead hikes and offer campfire programs in a 100-seat amphitheater. The park has 132 campsites (✆ **800/678-2267** for reservations), with fees ranging from $14 for walk-in sites to $18 for drive-in sites with electricity; coin-operated pay showers are available from mid-May to mid-October. Also available are two- to four-bedroom cabins for $120 to $240 a night.

P.O. Box 39, Divide, CO 80814. ✆ **719/687-2366.** www.parks.state.co.us. Admission $6 per vehicle. Take U.S. 24 west from Colorado Springs to Divide (25 miles), and then go 3½ miles south on Colo. 67.

North Cheyenne Cañon Park and Starsmore Discovery Center ★★ A delightful escape on a hot summer day, this 1,600-acre park includes North Cheyenne Creek, which drops 1,800 feet over the course of 5 miles in a series of cascades and waterfalls. The heavily wooded park contains picnic areas and about 15 miles of hiking/biking/horseback riding trails. The small visitor center at the foot of scenic Helen Hunt Falls has exhibits on history, geology, flora, and fauna. The **Starsmore Discovery Center** (✆ **719/385-6086**), at the entrance to the park, holds maps, information, and interactive exhibits for both kids and adults, including audiovisual programs and a climbing wall where you can learn about rock climbing. Call for current climbing-wall hours. During the summer, the center schedules a series of free programs on subjects such as rock climbing, butterflies, and hummingbirds, and guided walks and hikes (call for the current schedule). The park also has excellent rock-climbing areas for experienced climbers; pick up information at the Starsmore Discovery Center or Helen Hunt Falls Visitor Center.

2120 S. Cheyenne Cañon Rd. (west of 21st St.). ✆ **719/578-6146.** www.springsgov.com (follow links). Free admission. Park daily year-round. Starsmore Discovery Center summer daily 9am–5pm; call for hours at other times. Helen Hunt Falls Visitor Center Memorial Day to Labor Day daily 9am–5pm; closed rest of year. Located just west of the Broadmoor Golf Club via Cheyenne Blvd.

Palmer Park Deeded to the city in 1899 by Colorado Springs founder Gen. William Jackson Palmer, this 737-acre preserve offers hiking, biking, and horseback riding across a mesa overlooking the city. It contains a variety of minerals (including quartz, topaz, jasper, and tourmaline), rich vegetation (including a yucca preservation area), and considerable wildlife. The Edna Mae Bennet Nature Trail is a self-guided excursion, and there are numerous other trails. Other facilities include 12 separate picnic areas, softball and baseball fields, and volleyball courts.

3650 Maizeland Rd. off Academy Blvd. ✆ **719/385-5940.** www.springsgov.com (follow links). Free admission. Daily year-round. Located 3 miles east of I-25 via Austin Bluffs Pkwy. (exit 146).

ESPECIALLY FOR KIDS

In addition to the listings below, children will probably enjoy the **Cheyenne Mountain Zoo** (p. 170), **May Natural History Museum**, (p. 167), and **Ghost Town** (p. 167).

Arcade Amusements, Inc. ★ (Kids) Among the West's oldest and largest amusement arcades, this game complex just might be considered a hands-on arcade museum as well as a fun place for kids of all ages. Some 250 machines range from original working penny pinball machines to modern video games, skee-ball, and 12-player horse racing.

900 Block Manitou Ave., Manitou Springs. ✆ **719/685-9815.** Free admission; arcade games from 1¢. Early May to Labor Day daily 10am–10pm. Call for winter hours. Located in downtown Manitou Springs.

North Pole/Santa's Workshop (Kids) A Christmas-themed amusement park, Santa's Workshop is busy from mid-May until December 24. Not only can kids visit shops where elves have some early Christmas gifts for sale, but they can also see Santa and whisper their requests in his ear. This 26-acre village features numerous rides, including a miniature train, a 60-foot Ferris wheel, and a space-shuttle replica that swings to and fro, as well as magic shows and musical entertainment, snack shops, and an ice-cream parlor.

At the foot of Pikes Peak Hwy. off U.S. 24, 5 miles west of Manitou Springs. ✆ **719/684-9432.** www.santas-colo.com. Admission (includes all rides, shows, and attractions) $17 ages 2–59, free for seniors 60 and over and children under 2. Mid-May to late June daily 10am–5pm; late June to mid-Aug daily 10am–5:30pm; mid-Aug to Dec 23 (weather permitting) Fri–Tues 10am–5pm; Dec 24 10am–4pm. Closed Christmas to mid-May. Take I-25, exit 141, and go west on U.S. 24 about 10 miles.

ORGANIZED TOURS

Half- and full-day bus tours of Colorado Springs, Pikes Peak, the Air Force Academy, and other nearby attractions are offered by **Gray Line of Colorado Springs,** 3704 W. Colorado Ave. (✆ **800/345-8197** or 719/633-1181; www.coloradograyline.com). Prices range from $35 to $50 per person.

A free downtown **walking tour** brochure, with a map and descriptions of more than 30 historic buildings, is available at the Colorado Springs Convention and Visitors Bureau, as well as at local businesses.

Another free brochure, ***Old Colorado City,*** shows the location of more than a dozen historic buildings and lists shops, galleries, and other businesses.

The **Manitou Springs Chamber of Commerce & Visitors Bureau** (see "Visitor Information," earlier in this chapter) distributes the free *Manitou Springs Visitor's Guide,* which includes a self-guided walking-tour map of Mineral Springs, as well as information on where to find a variety of outdoor sculptures. See "Historic Neighborhoods," earlier in this chapter.

6 OUTDOOR ACTIVITIES

For information on the city's parks and programs, contact the **Colorado Springs Parks and Recreation Department** (✆ **719/385-5940;** www.springsgov.com). Most of the state and federal agencies concerned with outdoor recreation are headquartered in Denver. There are branch offices in Colorado Springs for **Colorado State Parks,** 2128 N. Weber St. (✆ **719/471-0900;** www.parks.state.co.us); the **Colorado Division of Wildlife,** 4255 Sinton Rd. (✆ **719/227-5200;** www.wildlife.state.co.us); and the **U.S.**

Impressions

Could one live in constant view of these grand mountains without being elevated by them into a lofty plane of thought and purpose?

—Gen. William J. Palmer, founder of Colorado Springs,1871

Forest Service, Pikes Peak Ranger District of the Pike National Forest, 601 S. Weber St. (✆ **719/636-1602;** www.fs.fed.us/r2/psicc/pp).

You can get hunting and fishing licenses at many sporting-goods stores, as well as at the Colorado Division of Wildlife office listed above.

AERIAL SPORTS The **Black Forest Soaring Society,** 24566 David C. Johnson Loop, Elbert, CO 80106 (✆ **303/648-3623;** www.soarbfss.org), some 50 miles northeast of Colorado Springs, offers glider rides, rentals, and instruction. Rides start at about $100 for a 15-minute ride; rentals (to those with gliding licenses) and instruction are also available. Advance reservations are required.

The area's commercial ballooning companies include **High but Dry Balloons,** 4164 Austin Bluffs Pkwy., #146, Colorado Springs, CO 80918 (✆ **719/260-0011;** www.highbutdryballoons.com), for tours, champagne flights, and weddings. Sunrise flights are scheduled daily year-round, weather permitting. Cost depends on the number of passengers, locations, and type of flight, but start at about $195 per person. Generally, flights last 2 or 3 hours, with a minimum of 1 hour. On Labor Day weekends since 1977, the **Colorado Springs Balloon Classic ★★** (✆ **719/471-4833;** www.balloonclassic.com) sees over 100 hot-air balloons launched from the city's Memorial Park. Admission is free.

BICYCLING Aside from the 4.3-mile loop trail around Monument Valley Park (see "Parks & Zoos," under "Attractions," above), there are numerous other urban trails for bikers. You can get information at the city's Visitor Information Center (see "Visitor Information," earlier in this chapter). For rentals ($30 per day), contact **Colorado Springs West Bikes,** 2403 W. Colorado Ave. (✆ **719/633-5565**).

FISHING Most serious Colorado Springs anglers drive south 40 miles to the Arkansas River or west to the Rocky Mountain streams and lakes, such as those found in Eleven Mile State Park and Spinney Mountain State Park on the South Platte River west of Florissant. Bass, catfish, walleye pike, and panfish are found in the streams of eastern Colorado; trout is the preferred sport fish of the mountain regions.

Angler's Covey, 295 S. 21st St. (✆ **800/75-FISHN** [753-4746] or 719/471-2984; www.anglerscovey.com), is a specialty fly-fishing shop and a good source of general fishing information for southern Colorado. It offers guided half- and full-day trips ($245–$395 for one to three persons), as well as state fishing licenses, rentals, flies, tackle, and clinics.

GOLF Public courses include the **Patty Jewett Golf Course,** 900 E. Española St. (✆ **719/385-6950**), and **Valley Hi Golf Course,** 610 S. Chelton Rd. (✆ **719/385-6917**). Nonresident greens fees range from $26 to $28 for 18 holes (not including a cart). **Pine Creek Golf Club,** 9850 Divot Trail (✆ **719/594-9999**), is another public course, with greens fees of $42 to $52.

The finest golf courses in the Colorado Springs area are private. Guests of the Broadmoor hotel (p. 150) can play the 54-hole **Broadmoor Golf Club** (✆ **719/577-5790**).

HIKING Opportunities abound in municipal parks (see "Parks & Zoos," under "Attractions," above) and Pike National Forest, which borders Colorado Springs to the west. The U.S. Forest Service district office can provide maps and general information (see address and phone number in the introduction to this section).

Especially popular are the 7.5-mile **Waldo Canyon Trail,** with its trail head just east of Cascade Avenue off U.S. 24; the 6-mile **Mount Manitou Trail,** starting in Ruxton Canyon above the hydroelectric plant; and the 12-mile **Barr Trail** to the summit of Pikes Peak. **Mueller State Park** (✆ **719/687-2366**), 3½ miles south of Divide en route to Cripple Creek, has 50 miles of trails. See "Parks & Zoos" under "Attractions," above.

HORSEBACK RIDING You'll find good opportunities at city parks, including Garden of the Gods, North Cheyenne Cañon Park, and Palmer Park, plus Mueller State Park (see "Attractions," earlier in this chapter). The **Academy Riding Stables,** 4 El Paso Blvd., near the Garden of the Gods (✆ **888/700-0410** or 719/633-5667; www.academyriding stables.com), offers guided trail rides for children and adults by reservation ($38 for 1 hr., $55 for 2).

ICE-SKATING The **Mark "Pa" Sertich Ice Center** at Memorial Park (✆ **719/385-5983**) is open daily and offers prearranged instruction and rentals. (Admission is $1.50 to $5; skate rentals are $2.) The U.S. Olympic Complex operates the **Colorado Springs World Arena Ice Hall,** 3185 Venetucci Blvd. (✆ **719/477-2150;** www.worldarena.com), with public sessions daily. Admission is $1 to $4; skate rentals are $2. If you have hockey equipment, you can join a pickup game ($7); call for times. To get there, take I-25, exit 138, go west on Circle Drive to Venetucci Boulevard, and go south to the arena.

MOUNTAIN BIKING There are abundant mountain-biking opportunities in the Colorado Springs area; contact the U.S. Forest Service for details (see address and phone number in the introduction to the section). From May to early October, **Challenge Unlimited,** 204 S. 24th St. (✆ **800/798-5954** or 719/633-6399; www.bikithikit.com), hosts fully equipped, guided rides for every level of experience. Your guide on the 19-mile ride down the Pikes Peak Highway, from the summit at 14,110 feet to the tollgate at 7,000 feet, presents an interpretation of the nature, history, and beauty of the mountain. Participants must be at least 10 years old; advance reservations are recommended. Rates are $45 to $110 per person. For rentals ($30 per day), contact **Colorado Springs West Bikes,** 2403 W. Colorado Ave. (✆ **719/633-5565**).

RIVER RAFTING Colorado Springs is 40 miles from the Arkansas River near Cañon City. Several licensed white-water outfitters tackle the Royal Gorge. **Echo Canyon River Expeditions,** 45000 U.S. 50 West, Cañon City, CO 81212 (✆ **800/755-3246** or 719/275-3154; www.raftecho.com), offers half-day to 3-day trips on "mild to wild" stretches of river. The company uses state-of-the-art equipment, including self-bailing rafts. Costs range from $49 (half-day, adult) to $645 (for a 4-day expedition). **Arkansas River Tours,** P.O. Box 337, Cotopaxi, CO 81223 (✆ **800/321-4352** or 719/942-4362; www.arkansasrivertours.com), offers white-water trips of lengths from a quarter of a day to a full day for $32 to $110, and 2-day trips for $259 to $289.

SWIMMING & TENNIS Many city parks have pool or lake swimming, for which they charge a small fee, and free tennis courts. Contact the Colorado Springs Parks and Recreation Department (✆ **719/385-5940**) for locations and hours.

7 SPECTATOR SPORTS

The **Air Force Academy Falcons** football team dominates the sports scene, and there are also competitive baseball, basketball, ice hockey, and soccer teams. Call for schedules and ticket information (✆ **800/666-USAF** [8723] or 719/472-1895; www.goairforce falcons.com).

AUTO RACING The **Pikes Peak International Hill Climb** (✆ **866/464-2626** for tickets or 719/685-4400; www.ppihc.com), known as the "Race to the Clouds," takes place annually in late June or early July. An international field of drivers negotiates the hairpin turns of the final 12¹/₃ miles of the Pikes Peak Highway to the top of the 14,110-foot mountain. On the way up, there are 156 turns, 2,000-foot cliffs, and no guardrails.

BASEBALL The **Colorado Springs Sky Sox,** of the Pacific Coast League, the AAA farm team for the Colorado Rockies of Denver, play a full 144-game season, with 72 home games at Security Service Field, 4385 Tutt Blvd., off Barnes Road east of Powers Boulevard (✆ **719/591-7699** for tickets or 719/597-1449; www.skysox.com). The season runs from April to Labor Day. Tickets cost $6 to $11.

HOCKEY In addition to Air Force Academy hockey (see above), the **World Arena,** 3185 Venetucci Blvd. (✆ **719/477-2100;** www.worldarena.com), is home to the perennial power Colorado College Tigers (✆ **719/389-6324;** www.cctigers.com). Tickets are $13 to $18.

RODEO Held annually since 1941, the **Pikes Peak or Bust Rodeo** (✆ **719/576-2626** for tickets or 719/635-3547; www.coloradospringsrodeo.com), which takes place in mid-July, is a major stop on the Professional Rodeo Cowboys Association circuit. Its purse of more than $150,000 makes it the second-largest rodeo in Colorado, after Denver's National Western Stock Show. It takes place at the **Norris-Penrose Events Center,** 945 W. Rio Grande St., and tickets run $5 to $30. Various events around the city, including a parade and a street breakfast, mark the rodeo.

8 SHOPPING

Five principal areas attract shoppers in Colorado Springs. The Manitou Springs and Old Colorado City neighborhoods are fun places to browse for art, jewelry, arts and crafts, books, antiques, and other specialty items. The Chapel Hills and Citadel malls combine major department stores with a variety of national chain outlets. Downtown Colorado Springs also has numerous shops.

SHOPPING A TO Z

Antiques

Antique Emporium at Manitou Springs The shop's 4,000-square-foot floor space provides ample room for displaying its collection of antique furniture, china, glassware, books, collectibles, and primitives. 719 Manitou Ave., Manitou Springs. ✆ **719/685-9195.**

Colorado Country Antique Mall This well-established multidealer mall, covering some 10,000 square feet, is filled with a wide variety of antiques and collectibles, including a good selection of lower-priced items. 2109 Broadway St. ✆ **719/520-5680.**

Art Galleries

Business of Art Center Primarily an educational facility to help artists learn the business end of their profession, the center also has workshops, classes, and lectures, plus numerous artists' studios (open for viewing), six exhibition galleries, and a gift shop. Featured are renowned Colorado artists and juried exhibits of regional art. The shop offers a varied selection of regional artwork, including prints, photographs, jewelry, sculpture, ceramics, wearable art, hand-blown glass, and carved-wood objects. Theater, music, and dance performances are occasionally staged. 513 Manitou Ave., Manitou Springs. ✆ **719/685-1861.** www.thebac.org.

Commonwheel Artists Co-op Original art and fine crafts by area artists fill this excellent gallery, where you'll find a good selection of paintings, photography, sculpture, jewelry, textiles, and other items. 102 Cañon Ave., Manitou Springs. ✆ **719/685-1008.** www.commonwheel.com.

Flute Player Gallery This gallery offers contemporary and traditional American Indian silver and turquoise jewelry, Pueblo pottery, Navajo weavings, and Hopi kachina dolls. 2511 W. Colorado Ave., Old Colorado City. ✆ **719/632-7702.** www.fluteplayergallery.com.

Michael Garman's Gallery (Kids) A showcase for Garman's sculptures and casts depicting urban and Western life, this gallery also holds "Magic Town," a large model of an old-time inner city, with sculptures and holographic actors. Admission to Magic Town is $5 for adults, $3.50 for seniors, $1.50 for children 7 to 12, and free for children 6 and under. 2418 W. Colorado Ave., Old Colorado City. ✆ **800/731-3908** or 719/471-9391. www.michaelgarman.com.

Books

There are numerous chain bookstores around the city, including **Barnes & Noble,** 795 Citadel Dr. E., just east of the Citadel Mall (✆ **719/637-8282**).

Book Sleuth (Finds) For all your mystery needs, visit this bookstore. In addition to a wide selection of mystery novels (including a good stock of out-of-print books), the shop offers numerous puzzles and games. 2501 W. Colorado Ave., #105, Old Colorado City. ✆ **719/632-2727.**

Crafts

Van Briggle Art Pottery Founded in 1899 by Artus Van Briggle, who applied Chinese matte glaze to Rocky Mountain clays molded into imaginative Art Nouveau shapes, this is one of the oldest active art potteries in the United States. Artisans demonstrate their craft, from throwing on the wheel to glazing and firing. Free tours are available, and finished works are sold in the showroom. 600 S. 21st St., Old Colorado City. ✆ **800/847-6341** or 719/633-7729. www.vanbriggle.com.

Jewelry

Manitou Jack's Jewelry & Gifts Black Hills gold, 10- and 14-karat, is the specialty here. There's also an extensive collection of American Indian jewelry, pottery, sand paintings, and other art. The shop will create custom jewelry and make repairs. 814 Manitou Ave., Manitou Springs. ✆ **719/685-5004.**

Velez Galeria This well-established downtown Colorado Springs store sells the work of indigenous jewelers from the Southwest and Mexico, as well as artworks in many media. 220 N. Tejon St. ✆ **719/630-3710.**

Malls & Shopping Centers

Chapel Hills Mall Macy's, JCPenney, and Dillard's are among the 150 stores at this mall, which also houses a glow-in-the-dark minigolf course, a children's play area, a 15-screen movie theater, and about two dozen food outlets. 1710 Briargate Blvd. (N. Academy Blvd., at I-25, exit 150A). ✆ **719/594-0110.** www.chapelhillsmall.com.

The Citadel This is southern Colorado's largest regional shopping mall, with Dillard's, Macy's, JCPenney, and more than 170 specialty shops and restaurants. 750 Citadel Dr. E. (N. Academy Blvd. at E. Platte Ave.). ✆ **719/591-5516.** www.shopthecitadel.com.

The Promenade Shops at Briargate Among the shops and restaurants at this chic outdoor shopping center on the city's northern suburban fringe are Pottery Barn, Ann Taylor, P.F. Chang's China Bistro, and Ted's Montana Grill. 1885 Briargate Pkwy. ✆ **719/265-6264.** www.thepromenadeshopsatbriargate.com.

Sporting Goods

In business since 1968, the independent **Mountain Chalet,** 226 N. Tejon St. (✆ **719/633-0732;** www.mtnchalet.com), sells camping gear, outdoor clothing, hiking and climbing gear, and winter sports equipment. Another good source for all sorts of outdoor clothing and equipment is **Sports Authority,** with stores at 7730 N. Academy Blvd. (✆ **719/532-1020**) and 1409 N. Academy Blvd. (✆ **719/574-1400**).

Western Wear

Lorig's Western Wear ★ This Colorado Springs institution is where real cowboys get their hats, boots, jeans, and those fancy belts with the big buckles. 15 N. Union Blvd. ✆ **719/633-4695.**

Wine & Liquor

Cheers Liquor Mart This 35,000-square-foot liquor supermarket has a huge selection of beer and wine, including Colorado wines, at good prices. 1105 N. Circle Dr. ✆ **719/574-2244.**

The Wines of Colorado This tasting room and sales outlet offers the greatest number of Colorado wines available for tasting under one roof. There are also gift items, and the restaurant offers a grill menu. 8045 W. U.S. 24, Cascade (about 10 miles west of Colorado Springs). ✆ **719/684-0900.**

9 COLORADO SPRINGS AFTER DARK

The Colorado Springs entertainment scene spreads throughout the metropolitan area. Pikes Peak Center, the Colorado Springs Fine Arts Center, City Auditorium, Colorado College, and various facilities at the U.S. Air Force Academy are all outstanding venues for the performing arts. The city also supports dozens of cinemas, nightclubs, bars, and other after-dark attractions. Downtown is the major nightlife hub, but Old Colorado City and Manitou Springs also have their fair share of interesting establishments.

Weekly entertainment schedules appear in the Friday *Gazette.* Also look at the listings in the *Independent,* a free entertainment tabloid. A good online resource for information on events and nightlife, as well as for restaurants, is www.sceneinthesprings.com.

Tickets for many major entertainment and sporting events can be obtained from **Ticketmaster** (✆ **719/520-9090;** www.ticketmaster.com).

THE CLUB & MUSIC SCENE

Black Sheep A good bet for punk and indie rock, the Black Sheep features graffiti art on the walls and an edgy vibe throughout. 2106 E. Platte Ave. ✆ **719/227-7625.**

Cowboys Two-steppers and country-and-western music lovers flock to this east-side club, which boasts the largest dance floor in the area. It's open Wednesday to Sunday, and dance lessons are available. 25 N. Tejon St. ✆ **719/596-1212.**

Poor Richard's Restaurant An eclectic variety of performers appear at this bohemian landmark 1 or 2 nights a week, presenting everything from acoustic folk to Celtic melodies to jazz to bluegrass. The menu includes pizza, sandwiches, and the Springs's best nachos (blue corn chips and mozzarella), as well as beer and wine. Adjacent are Poor Richard's Bookstore and Little Richard's Toy Store, all owned by local politico Richard Skorman. 324½ N. Tejon St. ✆ **719/632-7721.**

Rum Bay Located in the renovated Woolworth Building downtown, the lively Rum Bay is a massive nightclub sporting a wall full of rum bottles and a tropical theme. Disc jockeys spin records for two dance floors; there's also a piano bar featuring dueling players. The entire block contains a number of additional bars under the same management, ranging from Cowboys (see above) to "the world's smallest bar," to Rum Bay–like clubs focusing on tequila and bourbon. 20 N. Tejon St. ✆ **719/634-3522.**

The Underground This popular hangout attracts a diverse crowd, from college students and other young people to baby boomers and retirees. Patrons come to dance or just listen to the equally eclectic music (live or recorded), which ranges from rock to jazz to reggae, with some occasional folk. 110 N. Nevada Ave. ✆ **719/578-7771.**

THE BAR SCENE

Bijou Bar and Grill Southern Colorado's longest-standing gay and lesbian bar, the Bijou Bar has a Mexican menu, regular drink specials, Wednesday karaoke nights, and DJs spinning dance music on Friday and Saturday. 2510 E. Bijou Ave. ✆ **719/473-5718.**

15C An unmarked speak-easy-style joint with an alley entrance, 15C is a slick martini-and-cigar bar with an upscale ambience accented by dim lighting and leather couches. Located just off Bijou St. in the alley between Cascade Ave. and Tejon St. ✆ **719/635-8303.**

Golden Bee (Moments) An opulent 19th-century English pub was disassembled, shipped from Great Britain, and reassembled piece by piece to create this delightful drinking establishment. You can have imported English ale by the yard or half-yard while enjoying steak-and-potato pie, Devonshire cheddar-cheese soup, sandwiches, or other British specialties. Evenings bring a ragtime pianist to enliven the atmosphere; interested guests are given songbooks for singalongs. Lower-level entrance of the Broadmoor International Center, Lake Circle. ✆ **719/634-7711.**

Meadow Muffins A boisterous barroom packed to the gills with movie memorabilia and assorted knickknacks, Meadow Muffins certainly doesn't lack personality. It features DJs or live music several nights a week. The food is standard bar fare, but the burgers are great. On most days, there are several specials, with happy hour from 4 to 7pm daily (until closing on Fri). There are pool tables, a pair of big-screen TVs, and arcade games. See also the restaurant listing on p. 161. 2432 W. Colorado Ave., in Old Colorado City. ✆ **719/633-0583.**

Oscar's Featuring aquariums above the bar, this downtown hangout shucks more oysters than anyplace in the Springs, including the Broadmoor's eateries. The menu here

is Cajun, the crowd eclectic, the music tending toward jazz and blues. 333 S. Tejon St.
✆ **719/471-8070.**

Phantom Canyon Brewing Co. This popular brewpub generally offers 8 to 10 of its specialty beers, including homemade root beer. The beers are unfiltered and unpasteurized, served at the traditional temperature for the style. I recommend Railyard Ale, a light amber ale with a smooth, malty taste; Hefeweizen, a traditional German wheat beer; and a very hoppy India pale ale. A billiards hall is on the second floor. See also the restaurant listing on p. 159. 2 E. Pikes Peak Ave. ✆ **719/635-2800.**

Ritz Grill Especially popular with young professionals after work and the chic clique later in the evening, this noisy restaurant/lounge, known for its martinis and large central bar, brings an Art Deco feel to downtown Colorado Springs. There's live music (usually rock) starting at 9pm Thursday through Saturday. See also the restaurant listing on p. 159. 15 S. Tejon St. ✆ **719/635-8484.**

Tony's Laden with plenty of brick and Green Bay Packers memorabilia, this neighborhood bar just north of Acacia Park has a laid-back vibe, Wisconsin roots, and the best fried cheese curds in the state. 311 N. Tejon St. ✆ **719/228-6566.**

THE PERFORMING ARTS

Among the major venues for performing arts is the 8,000-seat **Colorado Springs World Arena,** 3185 Venetucci Blvd., at I-25, exit 138 (✆ **719/477-2100;** www.worldarena.com). The area's newest entertainment center, it presents big-name country and rock concerts and a wide variety of sporting events. Other major facilities include the handsome **Pikes Peak Center,** 190 S. Cascade Ave. (✆ **719/520-7469** for the ticket office or 719/477-2100; www.pikespeakcenter.org), a 2,000-seat concert hall in the heart of downtown that has been acclaimed for its outstanding acoustics. The city's symphony orchestra and dance theater call the Pikes Peak Center home, and top-flight touring entertainers, Broadway musicals, and symphony orchestras appear here as well. The **Colorado Springs Fine Arts Center,** 30 W. Dale St. (✆ **719/634-5581** for general information, or 719/634-5583 for the box office; www.csfineartscenter.org), is a historic facility (see "Museums & Galleries" under "Attractions," earlier in this chapter) that includes a children's theater program, a repertory theater company, dance programs and concerts, and classic films. Recent productions have included *Annie* and *Oklahoma.* At the historic **City Auditorium,** 221 E. Kiowa St. (✆ **719/385-5969;** www.springsgov.com, follow links), you can often attend a trade show or big-name concert—Willie Nelson has performed here—or drop in at the Lon Chaney Theatre for a dramatic production.

Theater & Dance

BlueBards The Air Force Academy's cadet theater group performs Broadway and other productions; it recently staged *Kiss Me Kate.* Arnold Hall Theater, U.S. Air Force Academy. ✆ **719/333-4497.**

Colorado Springs Dance Theatre This nonprofit organization presents international dance companies from September to May at Pikes Peak Center, Colorado College's Armstrong Hall, and other venues. Notable productions have included Mikhail Baryshnikov, Alvin Ailey Repertory Ensemble, Ballet Folklorico of Mexico, and other traditional, modern, ethnic, and jazz dance programs. Each year, three to five performances are scheduled, and master classes, lectures, and other programs often coincide with the performances. Tickets typically run $20 to $40. 7 E. Bijou St., Ste. 209. ✆ **719/630-7434.** www.csdance.org.

Star Bar Players Each year, this resident theater company presents several full-length plays, ranging from Greek comedies to modern murder mysteries. Recent productions have included *The Heidi Chronicles* and *The Rabbit Hole.* Tickets are typically $10 to $15. Osborne Studio Theatre, Theatreworks, 3955 Cragwood Dr. ✆ **719/573-7411.** www.starbarplayers.org.

Dinner Theaters

Flying W Ranch ★ This working cattle and horse ranch, just north of the Garden of the Gods, encompasses a Western village of more than a dozen restored buildings and a mine train. There are also demonstrations of Navajo weaving and horse-shoeing. A Western stage show features bunkhouse comedy, cowboy balladry, and foot-stompin' fiddle, mandolin, and guitar music. From mid-May to September the town opens each afternoon at 5pm (Thurs–Sun in Sept); a chuck-wagon dinner (barbecued beef or chicken, potatoes, beans, biscuits, and cake) is served ranch style at 7pm, and the show begins at 8pm. The winter steakhouse is open October to December and March to May on Friday and Saturday, with seatings at 5 and 8pm and a Western stage show at each seating.

3330 Chuckwagon Rd. ✆ **800/232-FLYW** (232-3599) or 719/598-4000. www.flyingw.com. Reservations recommended. Chuck-wagon dinners $20 adults, $10 children 6–12; winter steakhouse $24–$26 adults, $12–$15 children 8 and under.

Iron Springs Chateau Melodrama ★ Located near the foot of the Pikes Peak Cog Railway, this popular comedy and drama dinner theater urges patrons to boo the villain and cheer the hero. Past productions have included *Farther North to Laughter or Buck of the Yukon, Part Two,* and *When the Halibut Start Running or Don't Slam the Door on Davy Jones' Locker.* A family-style dinner, with free seconds, includes oven-baked chicken and barbecued beef brisket, mashed potatoes, green beans almandine, pineapple coleslaw, and buttermilk biscuits. A singalong and a vaudeville-style olio show follow the performance. Iron Springs Chateau is open from April to mid-October and in December. Dinner is served on Tuesday, Wednesday, Friday, and Saturday between 6 and 6:45pm; the show follows at 8pm.

444 Ruxton Ave., Manitou Springs. ✆ **719/685-5104** or 719/685-5572. Reservations required. Dinner and show $29 adults, $27 seniors, $16 children; show only $16 adults, $15 seniors, $9.50 children.

10 SIDE TRIPS FROM COLORADO SPRINGS

FLORISSANT FOSSIL BEDS NATIONAL MONUMENT ★★

Approximately 35 miles west of Colorado Springs on U.S. 24 is the small village of Florissant, which means "flowering" in French. It couldn't be more aptly named—every spring its hillsides virtually blaze with wildflowers. Just 2 miles south is one of the most spectacular, yet relatively unknown, fossil deposits in the world, Florissant Fossil Beds National Monument. From Florissant, follow the signs along Teller County Road 1.

The fossils in this 6,000-acre National Park Service property are preserved in the rocks of ancient Lake Florissant, which existed 34 million years ago. Volcanic eruptions spanning half a million years trapped plants and animals under layers of ash and dust; the creatures were fossilized as the sediment settled and became shale.

The detailed impressions, first discovered in 1873, offer the most extensive record of its kind in the world. Scientists have removed thousands of specimens, including 1,100 separate species of insects. Dragonflies, beetles, and ants; more fossil butterflies than anywhere else in the world; plus spiders, fish, some mammals, and birds are all perfectly preserved from 34 million to 35 million years ago. Leaves from willows, maples, and hickories; extinct relatives of birches, elms, and beeches; and needles of pines and sequoias are also plentiful. These fossil plants, markedly different from those living in the area today, show how the climate has changed over the centuries.

Mudflows also buried forests during this long period, petrifying the trees where they stood. Nature trails pass petrified tree stumps; one sequoia stump is 10 feet in diameter and 11 feet high. There's a display of carbonized fossils at the visitor center, which also offers interpretive programs. An added attraction within the monument is the homestead of Adeline Hornbek, who pioneered the area with her children in 1878. The national monument also has over 14 miles of hiking trails.

Nearby, about 1/2 mile north of the monument, there's superb fishing for German browns and cutthroats at Spinney Mountain Reservoir.

Admission to the monument is $3 per adult and free for children under 15, making a visit here an incredibly affordable outing. It's open from 8am to 6pm daily in summer and 9am to 5pm daily the rest of the year (closed Thanksgiving, Christmas, and New Year's Day). Contact Florissant Fossil Beds National Monument, P.O. Box 185, Florissant, CO 80816-0185 (✆ **719/748-3253;** www.nps.gov/flfo).

CRIPPLE CREEK

This old mining town on the southwestern flank of Pikes Peak was known as the world's greatest gold camp after the precious metal was first discovered here in 1890. During its heyday at the beginning of the 20th century, Cripple Creek (elevation 9,494 ft.) had a stock exchange, two opera houses, five daily newspapers, 16 churches, 19 schools, and 73 saloons, plus an elaborate streetcar system and a railroad depot that saw 18 arrivals and departures a day. By the time mining ceased in 1961, more than $800 million worth of ore had been taken from the surrounding hills.

Today Cripple Creek has several dozen limited-stakes gambling casinos, most lining Bennett Avenue. They cash in not only on the lure of gambling, but also on the nostalgia for the gambling houses that were once prominent throughout the Old West. Although gamblers must be at least 21 years old, some casinos offer special children's areas, along with other family activities. Among the more interesting of the many casinos in town is the **Imperial Casino Hotel,** 123 N. 3rd St. at Bennett Avenue (P.O. Box 869), Cripple Creek, CO 80813 (✆ **800/235-2922** or 719/689-7777; www.imperialcasinohotel.com). Built in 1896 following a disastrous fire that razed most of the city, the fully renovated Imperial offers Victorian accommodations in a handsome historic building, a casino, and several restaurants and bars.

One of the town's unique attractions is a herd of wild donkeys, descendants of the miners' runaways, that roam freely through the hills and into the streets. The year's biggest celebration, **Donkey Derby Days** in late June, culminates with a donkey race.

Although gambling takes place year-round, many of the historic attractions are open in summer only or have limited winter hours. Among those you'll want to check out is the 1891 **Mollie Kathleen Gold Mine,** 1 mile north of Cripple Creek on Colo. 67 (✆ **719/689-2466;** www.goldminetours.com). It offers visitors a rare chance to join hard-rock miners on a 1,050-foot underground descent into a genuine gold mine and take home a gold-ore specimen as a souvenir. Tours last about 40 minutes; temperatures in the mine are 45° to 50°F (7°–10°C), and jackets are provided. Admission is $15 for adults, $10 for children 3 through 12, and free for children under 3. The mine is open from early April to mid-September daily from 9am to 5pm, with shorter hours the rest of the year (call ahead).

The **Cripple Creek District Museum,** at the east end of Bennett Avenue (✆ **719/689-2634;** www.cripple-creek.org), includes three historic buildings packed with late-19th-century relics, including mining and railroad memorabilia. There's a gold-ore exhibit, Victorian fashions and furniture, exhibits on local wildlife, historic photos, a fully restored Victorian-era flat, and an assay office where fire-testing of local ores took place. The museum is open daily from 10am to 5pm Memorial Day through September, and Friday to Sunday from 10am to 4pm the rest of the year. Admission is $5 adults, $3 seniors and children. There is another museum, the Old Homestead Museum, covering the world's oldest profession in a family-friendly tour for $4 adults and $3 kids and seniors.

The **Cripple Creek & Victor Narrow Gauge Railroad Co. ★★**, at the Midland Terminal Depot, east end of Bennett Avenue at 5th Street (✆ **719/689-2640;** www.cripplecreekrailroad.com), takes visitors on a 4-mile narrated tour. The route runs past abandoned mines and over a reconstructed trestle to the ghost town of Anaconda, powered by a 15-ton "iron horse" steam locomotive. The train operates daily from mid-May to mid-October. The first train leaves the station at 10am and subsequent trains leave about every 40 minutes, until 5pm. Tickets are $13 for adults, $11 for seniors, $7.75 for children 3 to 12, and free for kids under 3.

Cripple Creek is 45 miles west of Colorado Springs; take U.S. 24 west and Colo. 67 south. For additional information, contact the **Cripple Creek Chamber of Commerce,** P.O. Box 430, Cripple Creek, CO 80813 (✆ **877/858-4653** or 719/689-3461; www.cripple-creek.co.us).

Nearby Scenic Drives

When you leave Cripple Creek, two drives of particular beauty offer alternatives to Colo. 67. Neither is paved and both are narrow and winding, but both are usually acceptable for everyday vehicles under dry conditions. Each is roughly 30 miles long but requires about 90 minutes to negotiate. First, take Colo. 67 south out of Cripple Creek for 6 miles to the historic mining town of **Victor,** a delightful, picturesque destination.

The **Gold Camp Road** leads east from Victor to Colorado Springs via the North Cheyenne Cañon. Teddy Roosevelt said that this trip up the old Short Line Railroad bed had "scenery that bankrupts the English language." The **Phantom Canyon Road** leads south from Victor to Florence, following another old narrow-gauge railroad bed known as the Gold Belt Line. A number of ghost towns and fossil areas mark this route.

Boulder

Although Boulder is known primarily as a college town (the University of Colorado is here), it would be inaccurate to begin and end the description there. Sophisticated and artsy, Boulder is home to numerous high-tech companies and research concerns; it also attracts countless outdoor sports enthusiasts with its delightful climate, vast open spaces, and proximity to Rocky Mountain National Park.

Set at the foot of the Flatirons of the Rocky Mountains, just 30 miles northwest of downtown Denver and only 74 feet higher than the Mile High City, Boulder was settled by hopeful miners in 1858 and named for the large rocks in the area. Welcomed by Chief Niwot and the resident southern Arapaho, the miners struck gold in the nearby hills the following year. By the 1870s, Boulder had become a regional rail and trade center for mining and farming. The university, founded in 1877, became the economic mainstay of the community after mining collapsed around the beginning of the 20th century.

In the 1950s, Boulder emerged as a national hub for scientific and environmental research. The National Center for Atmospheric Research and the National Institute of Standards and Technology are located here, as are dozens of high-tech and aerospace companies. Alongside the ongoing high-tech boom, the university and attendant vibrant culture have attracted a diverse mix of intellectuals, individualists, and eccentrics. Writers William S. Burroughs, Jr.; Stephen King; and Allen Ginsberg, co-founder of the city's Naropa Institute, all called Boulder home at one time or another.

Today's residents are a mix of students attending the University of Colorado (called CU by locals); employees of the many computer, biotech, and research firms; and others attracted by the casual, bohemian, environmentally aware, and otherwise hip lifestyles that prevail here. Whatever differences exist among the residents, they are united by a common love of the outdoors. Boulder has 43,000 acres of open space within its city limits, 56 parks, and 200 miles of trails. On any given day, seemingly three-quarters of the population is outside making great use of this land, generally from the vantage point of a bicycle seat, the preferred mode of transport—there are about 100,000 bicycles in Boulder, one for each of the city's 100,000 residents.

1 ORIENTATION

ARRIVING

By Plane

Boulder doesn't have a commercial airport. Air travelers must fly into Denver International Airport and then make ground connections to Boulder, a trip of about an hour.

GETTING TO & FROM THE AIRPORT The **SuperShuttle Boulder** (© **303/227-0000;** www.supershuttle.com) leaves Denver International Airport hourly from 5:10am to 12:10am, and Boulder hourly between 3:30am and 9:30pm, with fewer departures on holidays. Scheduled pickups in Boulder are at the University of Colorado campus and area hotels; pickups from other locations are made on call. The one-way fare from a scheduled pickup point to the airport is $25 per person, or $28 for residential pickup service from other points; round-trips run $46.

Boulder Yellow Cab (✆ **303/777-7777;** www.yellowtrans.com) charges $70 one-way to the airport for up to five passengers.

Buses operated by the **Regional Transportation District,** known locally as **RTD** (✆ **800/366-7433** or 303/299-6000; www.rtd-denver.com), charge $11 for a one-way trip to the airport (exact change required); those under 16 ride free. Buses leave from and return to the main terminal at 14th and Walnut streets daily every hour from before 4am to after midnight.

Boulder Limousine Service (✆ **303/449-5466**) charges $108 and up (plus any highway tolls) to take up to three people from DIA to Boulder (or vice versa) in a limousine.

By Car

The Boulder Turnpike (U.S. 36) branches off I-25 north of Denver and passes through the suburbs of Westminster, Broomfield, and Louisville before reaching Boulder. The trip takes about 30 minutes. If you are coming from Denver International Airport, take E-470 west, which becomes the Northwest Parkway (both are toll roads; $6 for two axles) to U.S. 36. If you're arriving from the north, take the Longmont exit from I-25 and follow Colo. 119 all the way. Longmont is 7 miles due west of the freeway; Boulder is another 15 miles southwest on the Longmont Diagonal Highway.

VISITOR INFORMATION

The **Boulder Convention and Visitors Bureau,** 2440 Pearl St. (at Folsom St.), Boulder, CO 80302 (✆ **800/444-0447** or 303/442-2911; www.bouldercoloradousa.com), is open Monday through Friday from 8:30am to 5pm and can provide excellent maps, brochures, and general information on the city. There are also visitor information kiosks on **Pearl Street Mall** and at the **Davidson Mesa overlook,** several miles southeast of Boulder on U.S. 36. Brochures are available at both sites year-round.

CITY LAYOUT

The north–south streets increase in number going from west to east, beginning with 3rd Street. (The eastern city limit is at 61st St., although the numbers continue to the Boulder County line at 124th St. in Broomfield.) Where U.S. 36 enters Boulder (and does a 45-degree turn to the north), it becomes 28th Street, a major commercial artery. The Longmont Diagonal Highway (Colo. 119) enters Boulder from the northeast and intersects 28th Street at the north end of the city.

To reach downtown Boulder from U.S. 36, turn west on Canyon Boulevard (Colo. 119 west) and north on Broadway, which would be 12th Street if it had a number. It's 2 blocks to the Pearl Street Mall, a 4-block, east–west pedestrian-only strip from 11th to 15th streets that constitutes the historic downtown district. Boulder's few one-way streets circle the mall: 13th and 15th streets are one-way north, 11th and 14th one-way south, Walnut Street (a block south of the mall) one-way east, and Spruce Street (a block north) one-way west.

Broadway continues across the mall, eventually joining U.S. 36 north of the city. South of Arapahoe Avenue, Broadway turns southeast, skirting the University of Colorado campus and becoming Colo. 93 (the Foothills Hwy. to Golden) after crossing Baseline Road. Baseline follows a straight line from east Boulder, across U.S. 36 and Broadway, past Chautauqua Park and up the mountain slopes. To the south, Table Mesa Drive takes a similar course.

The Foothills Parkway (not to be confused with the Foothills Hwy.) is the principal north–south route on the east side of Boulder, extending from U.S. 36 at Table Mesa Drive to the Longmont Diagonal; Arapahoe Avenue, a block south of Canyon Boulevard, continues east across 28th Street as Arapahoe Road.

2 GETTING AROUND

BY PUBLIC TRANSPORTATION

The **Regional Transportation District,** known as the **RTD** (✆ **800/366-7433** or 303/299-6000; www.rtd-denver.com), provides bus service throughout Boulder as well as the Denver greater metropolitan area. The Boulder Transit Center, 14th and Walnut streets, is open Monday through Friday from 5am to midnight and Saturday and Sunday from 6am to midnight. Fares within the city are $1.75 for adults and children (85¢ for seniors and passengers with disabilities; children under 6 ride free). Schedules are available at the Transit Center, the Chamber of Commerce, and other locations. Buses are wheelchair accessible.

The city of Boulder runs a shuttle bus service called the **HOP** (✆ **303/447-8282**), connecting downtown, University Hill, the University of Colorado, and 30th and Pearl. The HOP operates Monday through Thursday from 7am to 10pm, Friday and Saturday from 9am to 11:30pm, and Sunday from 10am to 6pm. While the University of Colorado is in session, the night HOP runs Friday and Saturday from 10pm to 3am. Buses run about every 8 to 15 minutes during the day, every 15 to 20 minutes at night; the fare is $1.75 (85¢ for seniors; children under 6 ride free).

The RTD runs a complementary local shuttle, the **SKIP,** Monday through Friday from 5:08am to 12:30am, Saturday from 7am to 12:30am, and Sunday from 7am to 11pm. Buses run north and south along Broadway, with a loop through the west Table Mesa neighborhood, every 6 to 10 minutes during peak weekday times and less frequently in the evenings and on weekends.

BY CAR

The **American Automobile Association (AAA)** has an office at 1933 28th St., #200 (✆ **303/753-8800**). It's open Monday through Friday from 8:30am to 5:30pm, Saturday from 9am to 1pm.

CAR RENTALS Most people who fly to Colorado land at Denver International Airport and rent a car there. To rent a car in Boulder, contact **Avis** (✆ 800/331-1212), **Dollar** (✆ 800/800-4000), **Enterprise** (✆ 800/736-8222), **Hertz** (✆ 800/654-3131), or **National** (✆ 888/227-7368).

PARKING Most downtown streets have parking meters, with rates of about 25¢ per 20 minutes. Downtown parking lots cost $1 to $3 for 3 hours. Parking can be hard to find around the Pearl Street Mall, but new lots have eased the pain. Outside downtown, free parking is generally available on side streets.

BY BICYCLE

Boulder is a wonderful place for bicycling; there are bike paths throughout the city and an extensive trail system leading for miles beyond Boulder's borders (see "Bicycling" under "Sports & Outdoor Activities," later in this chapter).

You can rent and repair mountain bikes and buy trail and city maps at **University Bicycles,** 839 Pearl St., about 2 blocks west of the Pearl Street Mall (✆ **303/444-4196;** www.ubikes.com), and **Full Cycle,** 1211 13th St., near the campus (✆ **303/440-7771;** www.fullcyclebikes.com). Bike rentals cost $20 to $40 (or $85 for a luxury model) daily. Maps and other information are also available at the **Boulder Convention and Visitors Bureau,** 2440 Pearl St. (✆ **303/442-2911**).

BY TAXI

Boulder Yellow Cab (✆ **303/777-7777**) operates 24 hours, but you need to call for service—there are no taxi stands, and taxis won't stop for you on the street. Another company that serves Boulder is **Metro Taxi** (✆ **303/333-3333**).

ON FOOT

You can walk to most of what's worth seeing in downtown Boulder, especially around the Pearl Street Mall and University of Colorado campus. **Historic Boulder, Inc.,** 4735 Walnut St. (✆ **303/444-5192;** www.historicboulder.org), can provide advice about exploring the city's historic neighborhoods on foot. Books and brochures covering historic walking tours are available at the Convention and Visitors Bureau, 2440 Pearl St.

Fast Facts Boulder

Area Code Area codes are **303** and **720,** and local calls require 10-digit dialing.

Babysitters The front desk at a major hotel often can make arrangements on your behalf. Boulder's **Child Care Referral Service** (✆ **303/441-3180**) can also help if you call in advance.

Business Hours Most banks are open Monday through Friday from 9am to 5pm, and some have Saturday hours, too. Major stores are open Monday through Saturday from 9 or 10am until 5 or 6pm, and often Sunday from noon to 5pm. Department and discount stores often have later closing times.

Car Rentals See "Getting Around," above.

Drugstores Reliable prescription services are available at the Medical Center Pharmacy in the **Boulder Medical Center,** 2750 N. Broadway (✆ **303/440-3111**). The pharmacy at **King Soopers Supermarket,** 1650 30th St., in Sunrise Plaza (✆ **303/444-0164**), is open from 8am to 9pm weekdays, 9am to 6pm Saturday, and 10am to 6pm Sunday.

Emergencies For police, fire, or medical emergencies, call ✆ **911.** For the **Poison Control Center,** call ✆ **303/739-1123.** For the **Rape Crisis Hotline,** call ✆ **303/443-7300.**

Eyeglasses You can get fast repair or replacement of your glasses at **Visions Optical,** 1933 28th St. (✆ **303/442-4521**).

Hospitals Full medical services, including 24-hour emergency treatment, are available at **Boulder Community Hospital,** 1100 Balsam Ave., at North Broadway (✆ **303/440-2273**).

Newspapers & Magazines Newspaper options include the *Daily Camera* and the *Boulder Weekly.* Many Boulderites also read the campus paper, the *Colorado Daily,* available all over town. Both Denver dailies—the *Denver Post* and *Rocky Mountain News*—are available at newsstands throughout the city. You can also find the *New York Times* and *Wall Street Journal.*

Photographic Needs For standard processing requirements (including 2-hr. slide processing), as well as custom lab work, contact **Photo Craft,** 3550 Arapahoe Ave. (✆ **303/442-6410**). For equipment, supplies, and repairs, visit **Mike's Camera,** 2500 Pearl St. (✆ **303/443-1715;** www.mikescamera.com).

Post Office The main downtown post office is at 15th and Walnut streets. Contact the U.S. Postal Service (✆ **800/275-8777;** www.usps.com) for hours and other locations.

Safety Although Boulder is generally a safe city, it is not crime free. Be aware of your surroundings, especially if walking alone at night.

Taxes State and city sales taxes total about 7%; room taxes are 10.25%, although there is the possibility of an increase for 2009.

Useful Telephone Numbers Call ✆ **303/639-1111** for **road conditions,** ✆ **303/825-7669** for **ski reports,** and ✆ **303/494-4221** for **weather reports.**

3 WHERE TO STAY

You'll find a good selection of comfortable lodgings in Boulder, with a wide range of rates to suit almost every budget. Be aware, though, that the town literally fills up during the popular summer season, making advance reservations essential. It's also almost impossible to find a place to sleep during any major event at the University of Colorado, particularly graduation. Those who do find themselves in Boulder without lodging can check with the Boulder Convention and Visitors Bureau (see "Visitor Information," under "Orientation," above), which keeps track of availability. You can usually find a room in Denver, a half-hour or so away. Rates listed below do not include the 10.25% accommodations tax. Parking is free unless otherwise specified.

Major chains and franchises that provide reasonably priced lodging in Boulder include **Best Western Boulder Inn,** 770 28th St., Boulder, CO 80303 (✆ **800/780-7234** or 303/449-3800), with rates of $89 to $149 double; **Boulder Creek Quality Inn and Suites,** 2020 Arapahoe Ave., Boulder, CO 80302 (✆ **800228-5151** or 303/449-7550; www.qualityinnboulder.com), with rates of $79 to $149 double; and **Days Inn,** 5397 S. Boulder Rd., Boulder, CO 80303 (✆ **800/329-7466** or 303/499-4422), with rates of $89 to $129 double. Among the nonchains, **Boulder University Inn,** just south of downtown at 1632 Broadway (✆ **303/417-1700;** www.boulderuniversityinn.com), is a solid option, with reasonable double rates of $69 to $119.

Boulder

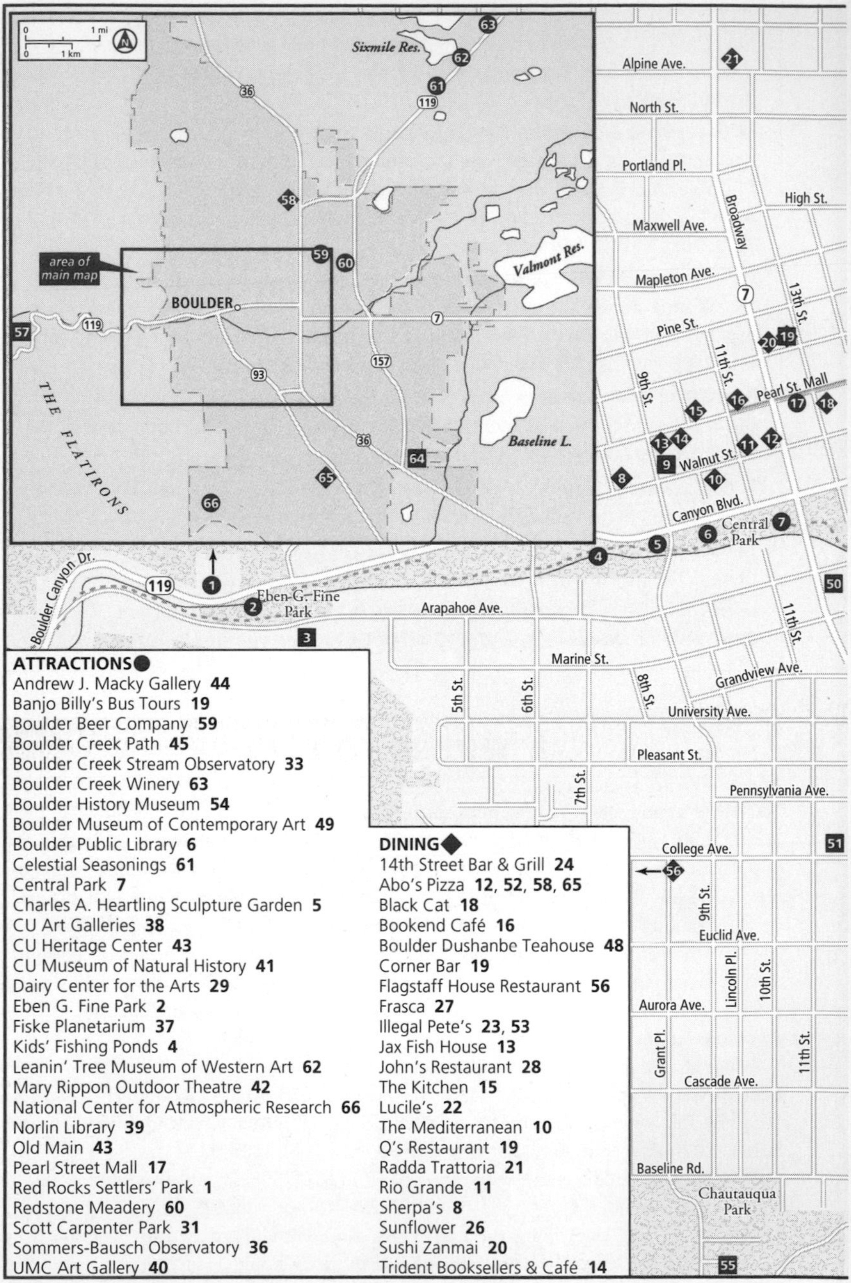

ATTRACTIONS ●

Andrew J. Macky Gallery **44**
Banjo Billy's Bus Tours **19**
Boulder Beer Company **59**
Boulder Creek Path **45**
Boulder Creek Stream Observatory **33**
Boulder Creek Winery **63**
Boulder History Museum **54**
Boulder Museum of Contemporary Art **49**
Boulder Public Library **6**
Celestial Seasonings **61**
Central Park **7**
Charles A. Heartling Sculpture Garden **5**
CU Art Galleries **38**
CU Heritage Center **43**
CU Museum of Natural History **41**
Dairy Center for the Arts **29**
Eben G. Fine Park **2**
Fiske Planetarium **37**
Kids' Fishing Ponds **4**
Leanin' Tree Museum of Western Art **62**
Mary Rippon Outdoor Theatre **42**
National Center for Atmospheric Research **66**
Norlin Library **39**
Old Main **43**
Pearl Street Mall **17**
Red Rocks Settlers' Park **1**
Redstone Meadery **60**
Scott Carpenter Park **31**
Sommers-Bausch Observatory **36**
UMC Art Gallery **40**

DINING ◆

14th Street Bar & Grill **24**
Abo's Pizza **12**, **52**, **58**, **65**
Black Cat **18**
Bookend Café **16**
Boulder Dushanbe Teahouse **48**
Corner Bar **19**
Flagstaff House Restaurant **56**
Frasca **27**
Illegal Pete's **23**, **53**
Jax Fish House **13**
John's Restaurant **28**
The Kitchen **15**
Lucile's **22**
The Mediterranean **10**
Q's Restaurant **19**
Radda Trattoria **21**
Rio Grande **11**
Sherpa's **8**
Sunflower **26**
Sushi Zanmai **20**
Trident Booksellers & Café **14**

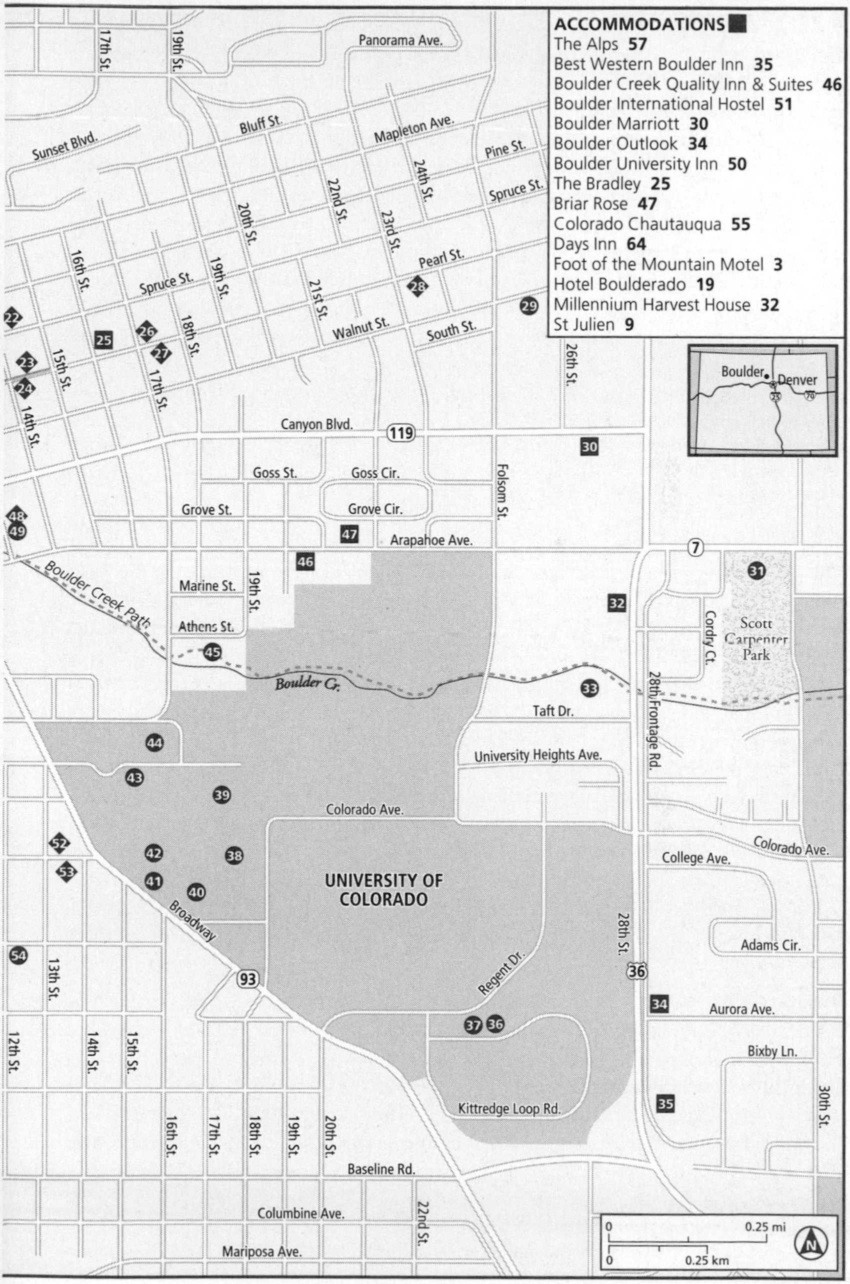
ACCOMMODATIONS
The Alps 57
Best Western Boulder Inn 35
Boulder Creek Quality Inn & Suites 46
Boulder International Hostel 51
Boulder Marriott 30
Boulder Outlook 34
Boulder University Inn 50
The Bradley 25
Briar Rose 47
Colorado Chautauqua 55
Days Inn 64
Foot of the Mountain Motel 3
Hotel Boulderado 19
Millennium Harvest House 32
St Julien 9
Boulder
Denver
Panorama Ave.
Sunset Blvd.
Bluff St.
Mapleton Ave.
Pine St.
Spruce St.
Pearl St.
Walnut St.
South St.
Canyon Blvd.
Goss St.
Goss Cir.
Grove St.
Grove Cir.
Arapahoe Ave.
Boulder Creek Path
Marine St.
Athens St.
Boulder Cr.
Folsom St.
Taft Dr.
University Heights Ave.
Colorado Ave.
College Ave.
Adams Cir.
Aurora Ave.
Bixby Ln.
Cordry Ct.
28th/Frontage Rd.
28th St.
30th St.
Scott Carpenter Park
UNIVERSITY OF COLORADO
Broadway
Regent Dr.
Kittredge Loop Rd.
Baseline Rd.
Columbine Ave.
Mariposa Ave.
12th St.
13th St.
14th St.
15th St.
16th St.
17th St.
18th St.
19th St.
20th St.
21st St.
22nd St.
23rd St.
24th St.
26th St.
0 0.25 mi
0 0.25 km

VERY EXPENSIVE

St Julien ★★★ The first new hotel in downtown Boulder since the Boulderado debuted in 1909, the swank St Julien instantly raised the bar for lodging in Boulder when it opened in 2005. The flagstone and Norman brick exterior, accented by patina copper and red roof tiles, sheaths a sumptuous lobby and exquisite guest rooms, averaging a healthy 400 square feet each. Everything from the walnut floors to the luxurious linens to the premium bath amenities to the artistic Boulder photographs on the wall is first rate. Honeyed tones and French doors accent the guest rooms, which feature either one California king or two queens. The bathrooms are the best in town; there are separate tubs and showers in every granite-laden one. Perks include live music Tuesday through Saturday in the lobby or picture-perfect back terrace, a two-lane lap pool, complimentary yoga classes on summer weekend mornings, and a spa that offers "indigenous therapies" using local minerals and plants. Expect to be wowed.

900 Walnut St., Boulder, CO 80302. ✆ **877/303-0900** or 720/406-9696. Fax 720/406-9697. www.stjulien.com. 201 units, including 15 suites. $239–$329 double; $399–$489 suite. AE, DC, DISC, MC, V. Valet parking $15 per night. **Amenities:** Restaurant (American); lounge; indoor heated pool; indoor Jacuzzi; fitness center; spa; salon; complimentary bikes; concierge; business center; dry cleaning. *In room:* A/C, cable TV w/pay movies, dataport, free Wi-Fi, coffeemaker, hair dryer, iron, safe.

EXPENSIVE

The Alps ★ Finds A stage stop in the late 1800s, this historic log lodge sits on a mountainside about a 7-minute drive (3 miles) west of downtown Boulder. Converted into a beautiful bed-and-breakfast decorated with Arts and Crafts and Mission furnishings by owners Jeannine and John Vanderhart, the Alps is ideal for travelers planning to split time between Boulder and its outlying wilderness and scenery. Each room here is different and named after a Colorado mining town, including Magnolia, Salina, and Wall Street. All have functional fireplaces with Victorian mantels, king or queen beds with down comforters, and individual thermostats. Most are spacious, with a claw-foot or double whirlpool tub plus a double shower, and many have private porches. Shared spaces include a beautiful lounge with a huge rock fireplace, plus delightful gardens and patio areas. The entrance is the original log cabin built in the 1870s. Smoking is not permitted.

38619 Boulder Canyon Dr., Boulder, CO 80302. ✆ **800/414-2577** or 303/444-5445. Fax 303/444-5522. www.alpsinn.com. 12 units. $149–$269 double. Rates include full breakfast. AE, DC, DISC, MC, V. **Amenities:** Jacuzzi; concierge; activities desk; in-room massage. *In room:* A/C, cable TV, dataport, hair dryer, iron.

Boulder Marriott ★ Until the St Julien came along (see above), the Marriott was the newest full-service hotel in the city. It is conveniently located just a block off 28th Street (U.S. 36), providing great access to everything in town. Furnished with Southwestern touches, the rooms are geared to the business traveler, with multiline phones, large work desks, and ergonomic chairs. Local and toll-free calls cost $1. The concierge level has a private lounge, and rates include continental breakfast, happy hour, and hors d'oeuvres. Three-quarters of the rooms feature mountain views.

2660 Canyon Blvd., Boulder, CO 80302 (1 block west of Canyon and 28th St.). ✆ **303/440-8877.** Fax 303/440-3377. www.marriott.com/denbo. 157 units. $159–$239 double; $279–$299 suite. AE, DC, DISC, MC, V. Free valet and self-parking. **Amenities:** Restaurant (steakhouse); lounge; indoor heated pool; exercise room; spa; Jacuzzi; 24-hr. business center; shopping arcade; limited room service; massage; laundry service; dry cleaning; executive level. *In room:* A/C, cable TV w/pay movies, dataport, free Wi-Fi, coffeemaker, hair dryer, iron, safe.

The Bradley ★★ Built as an upscale inn in the 1990s, the Bradley nicely blends into the surrounding historic neighborhood, just northeast of the Pearl Street Mall. The striking Great Room and uniquely decorated guest rooms are all adorned with bold contemporary art from local galleries, and it's all for sale. Some of the rooms have hot tubs and balconies; all have standout Bob Timberlake furnishings from North Carolina, rainforest shower heads, and tiny sleeping cat sculptures at the foot of the bed. The eclectic inn has a very homey feel, and the breakfasts—featuring huge fresh fruit salads and bread that is baked on-site—and the nightly wine and cheese are big events.

2040 16th St., Boulder, CO 80302. ✆ **800/858-5811** or 303/545-5200. Fax 303/440-6740. www.thebradleyboulder.com. 12 units. $175–$245 double. Rates include full breakfast. AE, DC, DISC, MC, V. **Amenities:** Complimentary access to a nearby health club; concierge; business center; dry cleaning. *In room:* A/C, cable TV w/DVD player, free Wi-Fi, hair dryer, iron.

Briar Rose ★ A country-style brick home built in the 1890s, this midcity bed-and-breakfast might remind you of Grandma's place. Every room is furnished with antiques, from the bedrooms to the parlor to the sunny back porch, and the lovely gardens offer a quiet escape. Two of the six units in the main house have fireplaces; two in a separate carriage house come with either a patio or a balcony. All are furnished with feather comforters. The full organic breakfast is gourmet quality: homemade granola, fresh nut breads, yogurt with fruit, and much more. Refreshments are available in the lobby from 8am to 9pm. There are two guest computers off of the sitting room. Smoking is permitted only in the outside garden areas.

2151 Arapahoe Ave., Boulder, CO 80302. ✆ **303/442-3007.** Fax 303/786-8440. www.briarrosebb.com. 10 units (6 with shower only). $149–$189 double. Rates include full breakfast. AE, MC, V. *In room:* A/C, cable TV, free Wi-Fi, hair dryer.

Hotel Boulderado ★★ Opened on January 1, 1909, this elegant and historic hotel still has the same Otis elevator that wowed visiting dignitaries that day. The colorful stained-glass ceiling and cantilevered cherrywood staircase are other reminders of days past, along with the rich woodwork of the balusters around the mezzanine and the handsome armchairs and settees in the main-floor lobby. The hotel's Christmas tree, a 28-footer with more than 1,000 white lights, is a Boulder tradition and the setting for afternoon tea on the mezzanine in December.

Five stories tall and just a block off the Pearl Street Mall, this contemporary of Denver's Brown Palace has 42 original guest rooms, all bright and cozy, individually decorated with panache. Although the rooms are continuously renovated and refurbished, they retain a Victorian flavor, with lush floral wallpapering, custom bedspreads, and furnishings alternately stately and plush. The construction of a spacious North Wing in 1989 almost quadrupled the number of rooms; although these are larger and more typical of a modern hotel, they also embody the early-20th-century theme. All have a few high-tech touches: electronic locks and two-line phones with voice mail; most rooms have refrigerators, and a few have jetted tubs.

2115 13th St. (at Spruce St.), Boulder, CO 80302. ✆ **800/433-4344** or 303/442-4344. Fax 303/442-4378. www.boulderado.com. 160 units. $174–$304 double; $274–$394 suite. AE, DC, DISC, MC, V. **Amenities:** 2 restaurants (contemporary American; see "Where to Dine," below); 3 lounges; access to nearby health club; business center; laundry service. *In room:* A/C, cable TV w/pay movies, dataport, free Wi-Fi, coffeemaker, hair dryer, iron.

Millennium Harvest House (Kids) The Harvest House is a full-service hotel with spacious and lovely grounds. Located on 16 acres just west of U.S. 36 in south Boulder,

Kids Family-Friendly Hotels

Millennium Harvest House (p. 191) A good place to stay with the kids, especially in the summer. The Harvest House has a nice swimming pool and lots of nearby green space; it's also next to the Boulder Creek Path and within walking distance of 29th Street.

Foot of the Mountain Motel (p. 193) There's lots of space here where the kids can expend their energy. Across the street is a lovely park with a playground, as well as the Boulder Creek Path.

Boulder Outlook (see below) At this eco-friendly motel, kids can use the pool and play inside even when the weather is bad, and the diversions are many (bouldering rocks, game room, dog park).

the former Regal Harvest House looks like almost any other four-story hotel from the front—but its backyard melts into a park that surrounds the east end of the 10-mile Boulder Creek Path (see "Attractions," later in this chapter), where bike rentals are available. All rooms hold one king-size or two double beds, a lounge chair and ottoman, remote-control cable TV, and direct-dial phone. My favorite rooms here are those that look out on the Boulder Creek Path.

1345 28th St., Boulder, CO 80302. ✆ **800/545-6285** or 303/443-3850. Fax 303/443-1480. www.millenniumhotels.com/boulder. 269 units. $129–$299 double; $229–$499 suite. AE, DC, DISC, MC, V. **Amenities:** Restaurant (American); 2 lounges (sports bar/cigar bar); indoor lap pool; outdoor heated swimming pool; 15 tennis courts (5 indoor); fitness center; 2 Jacuzzis (indoor and outdoor); bike rental; courtesy shuttle (local); Internet-access kiosks (fee); 24-hr. room service; on-call masseur; valet and self-service laundry. *In room:* A/C, cable TV w/pay movies, coffeemaker, hair dryer, iron.

MODERATE

Boulder Outlook ★★ Value Kids The proprietors of this former Holidome have outdone every chain motel in town. The Outlook is fun, fresh, and definitively Boulder, with such unique perks as two bouldering rocks (one is 11 ft. high, the other 4 ft.), a fenced 4,000-square-foot dog run, and an ecologically conscious approach and comprehensive recycling program. The brightly painted motel has 40 rooms that have an outdoor entrance; the rest are accessed indoors. Overall, the rooms are contemporary and larger than average; the baths are nicely tiled. In-room recycling containers and all-natural bath amenities are two more distinctly Boulder touches. The indoor pool is superb, complete with a waterfall and a mural of a cloud-speckled sky, and the bar and grill here features live music Thursday, Saturday, and Sunday nights, as well as Wednesdays during the school year.

800 28th St., Boulder, CO 80303. ✆ **800/542-0304** or 303/443-3322. Fax 303/449-5130. www.boulderoutlook.com. 162 units. $109–$159 double. Rates include continental breakfast. AE, DC, DISC, MC, V. Pets accepted, $10 per night. **Amenities:** Restaurant (American); lounge; indoor heated pool; exercise room; Jacuzzi; men's and women's saunas; game room; activities desk; 24-hr. business center; limited room service; massage; coin-op washers and dryers; dry cleaning; executive level. *In room:* A/C, cable TV, dataport, coffeemaker, hair dryer, iron, safe.

Colorado Chautauqua ★★ (Finds During the late 19th and early 20th centuries, more than 400 Chautauquas—adult education and cultural entertainment centers—sprang up around the United States. This 26-acre park, a peaceful world apart at the foot of the Flatiron Mountains, is one of the few remaining and a National Historic Landmark. In summer, it hosts a wide-ranging arts program, including the Colorado Music Festival (see "Boulder After Dark," p. 210).

Lodging is in attractive cottages and in rooms and apartments in two historic lodges. All units were outfitted with new furnishings in recent years and come with linens and towels. They have balconies or porches, and either private or shared kitchens. The trim and tidy cottages range from efficiencies to three-bedroom, two-bathroom units. Larger groups might take the newly restored Mission House, which has eight bedrooms, a kitchen, and a screened-in porch and rents for $1,143 a night. From September to May, many cottages and apartments are rented by the month or longer, but nightly accommodations are generally available.

Guests have access to the park's playgrounds, picnic grounds, and hiking trail heads. The historic Chautauqua Dining Hall, which opened on July 4, 1898, serves three moderately priced meals a day year-round.

900 Baseline Rd. (at 9th St.), Boulder, CO 80302. ✆ **303/952-1611** for lodging, 303/440-3776 for restaurant. Fax 303/449-0790. www.chautauqua.com. 87 units. $71–$118 lodge room; $104–$147 efficiency cottage; $126–$162 1-bedroom cottage; $152–$275 2- or 3-bedroom cottage. AE, MC, V. Bus: 203. Pets accepted in cottages, $10 per night. Pets not accepted in lodges. **Amenities:** Restaurant (creative American); 4 tennis courts; children's programs during summer; self-service laundry. *In room:* Kitchen, coffeemaker, no phone.

Foot of the Mountain Motel (Value (Kids This nicely preserved motel, a series of connected, cabin-style units with bright red trim near the east gate of Boulder Canyon, dates from the 1930s but has kept up with the times. The location is inspiring, on the west edge of town where city meets mountains, and right across the street is the top end of the Boulder Creek Path and the trail head that leads to the summit of Flagstaff Mountain. The pleasant pine-walled cabins are furnished with queen or double beds and individual water heaters; two suites are big enough for families and outfitted with full kitchens and a shared hot tub.

200 Arapahoe Ave., Boulder, CO 80302. ✆ **866/773-5489** or 303/442-5688. www.footofthemountainmotel.com. 20 units (2 with shower only), including 2 suites. $90 double; $115–$185 suite. Rates include complimentary continental breakfast. AE, DISC, MC, V. Pets accepted for $5 nightly fee and a $50 refundable deposit. *In room:* Cable TV, free Wi-Fi, kitchen, fridge.

INEXPENSIVE

Boulder International Hostel ★ (Value Established in 1961, this hostel, spread over 12 buildings with a maximum occupancy of 400, has a little something for everybody: communal dorm rooms, private rooms, and even extended-stay apartments. Wonderfully international, the hostel has a social and intellectual vibe you won't find at the hotels. The toilets, showers, kitchen, laundry, and TV room are communal. Just 2 blocks from the University of Colorado campus, the hostel is open for registration daily from 8am to 11pm. To stay in a bunk, you must present identification proving you are not a resident of Colorado.

1107 12th St., Boulder, CO 80302-7029. ✆ **888/442-0522** or 303/442-0522. Fax 303/442-0523. www.boulderhostel.com. 250 units. $27 dorm bed; $49–$55 private unit. AE, DISC, MC, V. **Amenities:** Coin-op washers and dryers; free Wi-Fi. *In room:* No phone.

4 WHERE TO DINE

Partly because Boulder is a young, hip community, it has attracted a variety of small, with-it restaurants. At these chef-owned-and-operated establishments, innovative and often-changing cuisine is the rule. You'll find a lot of California influences here, as well as a number of top-notch chefs doing their own thing.

A Boulder city ordinance prohibits smoking inside restaurants.

VERY EXPENSIVE

Flagstaff House Restaurant ★★ Moments NEW AMERICAN/REGIONAL Named for its perch on Flagstaff Mountain, this restaurant attracts patrons from across the state and nation with excellent cuisine and service, and the spectacular nighttime view of the lights of Boulder spread out 1,000 feet below. The Monette family has owned and operated this restaurant, a local institution, since 1951 and kept ahead of the curve by sticking with tradition in an elegant, candlelit dining room with glass walls that maximize the view. The prices aren't for the budget-minded, but those seeking a romantic setting and superlative food can't miss with the Flagstaff House.

The menu, which changes daily, offers an excellent selection of fresh fish, flown in from the source, and Rocky Mountain game, all prepared with a creative flair. Typical appetizers include pancetta-wrapped rabbit loin or pheasant breast, calamari, black trumpet mushrooms, and caviar. Entrees, many of which are seasonal, might include Colorado rack of lamb, Maine lobster, veal cheeks, and mahimahi. The restaurant also has dessert soufflés, a world-renowned wine cellar (at, 20,000 bottles, perhaps the best in Colorado), and an impressive selection of after-dinner drinks.

1138 Flagstaff Rd. (west up Baseline Rd.). ✆ **303/442-4640.** www.flagstaffhouse.com. Reservations recommended. Main courses $32–$56. AE, DC, MC, V. Sun–Fri 6–10pm; Sat 5–10pm.

EXPENSIVE

Black Cat ★★ Finds CONTEMPORARY/ECLECTIC One of the smallest restaurants in Boulder, the Black Cat is also one of the best. In the intimate space with contrasting walls of cloth, metal, and glass, owner-chef Eric Skokan changes the menu nightly, using herbs and vegetables he harvests from his own half-acre garden in Boulder. Skokan's zero-inventory approach makes for some of the freshest food on the Front Range, but it's his creativity that shines through. The menu might include starters like warm mozzarella with rosemary coulis, inventively prepared seafood, garlic-polenta gratin, and anything else that is in season or strikes the kitchen staff's fancy. One of the few places where the menu might have a "Study of Rabbit" or "Juxtaposition of Duck," the Black Cat is a restaurant where the proprietor's passion is visible on every plate. For a special evening, the Black Cat offers a tasting menu for $62 for five courses, $99 with wine pairings.

1964 13th St. ✆ **303/444-5500.** www.blackcatboulder.com. Reservations recommended. Main courses $15–$30. AE, DISC, MC, V. Daily 5:30–11pm.

Frasca ★★★ ITALIAN Winning raves since its 2004 opening, Frasca is the critical darling in Boulder for its upscale atmosphere, impeccable service, and peerless cuisine, drawn exclusively from the culinary traditions of Friuli-Venezia Giulia, a subalpine region in northeastern Italy. Using fresh ingredients, with a special emphasis on terrific seafood, cheese, and wine, the masterful kitchen delivers some of the best fare in the West. The menu changes daily but always includes a vast selection of small plates leading up to pasta, seafood, pork loin, and other specialties of the region. Every year the staff takes a trip to Italy for a refresher course in Italian culinary appreciation, and it shows.

1738 Pearl St. ✆ **303/442-6966.** www.frascafoodandwine.com. Reservations recommended. Main courses $20–$30, $60–$70 for 4-course dinner. AE, DISC, MC, V. Mon–Thurs 5:30–9pm; Fri–Sat 5:30–10pm. Closed Sun and 2 weeks in early June.

John's Restaurant ★★ Finds CONTINENTAL/MEDITERRANEAN This funky but elegant converted house has set the pace for the Boulder dining scene for nearly 30 years. The emphasis here is squarely on the food. Sibling chef-owners Corey Buck and Ashley Maxwell (who bought the place from founder John Bizzarro in 2003) start with the classic cuisine of southern Europe, but add their own creative signature spin to each dish; compared to Bizzarro, Buck prepares bigger plates and is more fond of game dishes. For starters, apple Stilton pecan salad and ricotta-and-spinach gnocchi verde set the stage for the continually changing main-course offerings. Menu mainstays include filet mignon with Stilton ale sauce, surrounded by grilled Bermuda onions; phyllo-wrapped pork tenderloin with garlic whipped potatoes; and a variety of fresh seafood dishes. The menu also includes a few vegetarian items and near-transcendent homemade desserts.

2328 Pearl St. ✆ **303/444-5232.** www.johnsrestaurantboulder.com. Reservations recommended. Main courses $20–$40. AE, DISC, MC, V. Tues–Sat from 5:30pm.

The Kitchen ★★ ECLECTIC Since it opened in 2004, the Kitchen has emerged as a standout in a competitive dining market. Locals flock here for the fresh, often organic food; the expert service; and the casual atmosphere that melds metropolitan flair with Boulder funkiness. The lunch menu changes seasonally, often depending on what ingredients are locally available, but the buttery, melt-in-your mouth slow-roasted pork sandwich, topped with a mellow salsa verde, and lamb burger are always available. The daily-evolving dinner slate might include chargrilled pork chops, gnocchi, Maine oysters, and a vegetarian selection or two, once again with an emphasis on local and organic ingredients. On Monday "Community Nights," food is presented family style for $35; reservations are necessary. Upstairs is the aptly named [Upstairs], a swank wine bar that serves a light menu and libations from the 4,500-bottle cellar, staying open into the wee hours.

1039 Pearl St. ✆ **303/544-5973.** www.thekitchencafe.com. Reservations recommended. Main courses $4–$14 breakfast, $9–$16 lunch, $20–$36 dinner. AE, MC, V. Mon–Fri 8am–2pm; Sat–Sun 9am–2pm; Mon–Wed 5:30–9:30pm; Thurs–Sat 5:30–10pm; Sun 5:30–9pm. Bar open later.

Q's Restaurant ★★ CONTEMPORARY AMERICAN The historic ambience that makes the Hotel Boulderado such a delightful place to stay also makes its way into Q's, the hotel's main restaurant. The dining room combines the old—rich polished wood and stained glass—with the comfortable, casually elegant feel of today. Of course, the important thing is the food, and chef-owner John Platt does an excellent job, using locally grown organic vegetables whenever possible.

Platt, who claims seafood as his specialty after years on Cape Cod, always includes several fresh fish selections on the menu, such as seared Hawaiian ono with fresh hearts of palm and artichoke purée. Other meat dishes often include Nebraskan buffalo rib-eye, served with posole and seared greens, shoestring onions, and chile jus. Other specialties: seared scallops, gnocchi in Parmesan broth, and Caesar salad.

In the Hotel Boulderado, 2115 13th St. (at Spruce St.). ✆ **303/442-4880.** www.qsboulder.com. Reservations recommended. Main courses $6–$11 breakfast, $8–$16 lunch, $16–$28 dinner. AE, DC, DISC, MC, V. Mon–Fri 6:30–11am and 11:30am–2pm; Sat–Sun 6:30am–2pm; daily 5–10pm.

Sushi Zanmai ★★ (Kids) SUSHI/JAPANESE Boulder is a hot spot for great sushi: Zanmai is a go-to stalwart but faces stiff competition from a number of like-minded upstarts. I still prefer the place for its festive atmosphere, impeccable service, and traditional sushi. Prepared while you watch—at the sushi bar or tableside—the options include everything from tuna and trout to sea urchin and octopus, with such exotic rolls as Colorado (raw filet mignon), Z-No. 9 (shrimp tempura, avocado, salmon, and eel sauce), and Two Dragon (shrimp tempura and eel). There are lunch specials as well as sushi happy-hour specials during lunch and dinner. Karaoke singalong takes place every Saturday from 10pm to midnight. Under the same ownership next door is **Amu** (✆ **303/440-0807**), a traditional sake bar with its own menu of artfully prepared sashimi and other Japanese staples. Amu, which translates approximately as "to have nothingness," requires patrons to leave their shoes at the door.

1221 Spruce St. (at Broadway). ✆ **303/440-0733.** www.sushizanmai.com. Reservations recommended for groups of 4 or more. Main courses $7.50–$13 lunch, $15–$26 dinner; sushi rolls $2–$12. AE, DC, MC, V. Mon–Fri 11:30am–2pm; Sun–Fri 5–10pm; Sat 5pm–midnight.

MODERATE

Boulder Dushanbe Teahouse ★ (Finds) ETHNIC WORLD CUISINE In 1990, 200 crates were shipped to Colorado as a gift from Dushanbe, Tajikistan, Boulder's sister city. From the ornately hand-carved and -painted pieces of a Persian teahouse in the crates, the building was assembled at its present site with help from four Tajik artisans. It's the only teahouse of its kind in the Western Hemisphere. Lavishly and authentically decorated, the teahouse holds 14 pillars carved from Siberian cedar, and a grand central fountain. The cuisine includes traditional ethnic dishes from the Middle East, Asia, and elsewhere, including several noodle and vegetarian options. There are even a few Tajik specialties, often a lamb dish, and cuisine prepared with specialty tea. Pastries, coffees, and more than 70 teas are also available. There is a full bar on-site as well.

1770 13th St. ✆ **303/442-4993.** www.boulderteahouse.com. Main courses $5–$9 breakfast, $9–$16 lunch, $11–$19 dinner. AE, DISC, MC, V. Mon–Fri 8–10:30am and 11am–3pm; Sat–Sun 8am–3pm; daily 5–10pm. Tea and coffee bar daily 8am–10pm.

14th Street Bar & Grill ★ CONTEMPORARY AMERICAN An open restaurant with large windows facing the street, this is a great spot for people-watching as well as dining. The open wood grill and pizza oven; the long, crowded full-service bar; and a changing display of abstract art let you know that this is a fun place. The menu centers on what chef-owner Kathy Andrade calls "American grill" cuisine, which includes grilled sandwiches, Southwestern chicken salads, and unusual homemade pizzas, such as a pie topped with prosciutto, poached egg, charred green chiles, and radish sprouts. A seafood

(Kids) Family-Friendly Restaurants

Sushi Zanmai (p. 196) Flashing knives and tableside cooking keep kids fully entertained.

Rio Grande (p. 198) The busy atmosphere is a great match for kids' energy level and potential mood swings.

stew is also offered, plus fantastic food and drink specials during the daily social hour (3–6pm).

1400 Pearl St. (at 14th St.). ✆ **303/444-5854.** www.14thstreetboulder.com. Main courses $10–$26. AE, MC, V. Daily 11:30am–10pm.

Jax Fish House ★ SEAFOOD Fresh seafood is flown in daily from the East and West coasts to supply this restaurant, a lively space with colored chalk graffiti and oceanic art on its brick walls, social patrons, and a great happy hour. At patio, bar, and table seating, you can order one of the house specialties—the Mississippi catfish skillet is a good bet—or simply slurp down raw oysters and martinis to your heart's content. Entrees usually include scallops, New Zealand bluenose, wild King salmon, and halibut, along with soft-shell crab when in season. Or try a seafood po' boy, with slaw or fresh mussels or clams in mango–lemon grass broth or white wine and garlic. Those who prefer beef can choose from a filet and all-natural burgers.

928 Pearl St. (1 block west of the mall). ✆ **303/444-1811.** www.jaxfishhouseboulder.com. Main courses $10–$35. AE, MC, V. Mon–Thurs 4–10pm; Fri–Sat 4–11pm; Sun 4–9pm.

The Mediterranean ★ MEDITERRANEAN/TAPAS Known as "The Med," this local favorite is designed in homage to the casual eateries of Spain and Italy. With a multihued tile interior and an enjoyable breezy patio, the Med draws a bustling after-work drinking crowd for its weekday tapas hour (3–6:30pm), which includes such reasonably priced delicacies as fried artichoke hearts, Moroccan spiced BBQ pork, and hummus. For a full dinner, the selection is extensive, ranging from pasta to poultry, steaks to gourmet wood-fired pizzas, with several vegetarian dishes to please the health-conscious Boulder crowd. The lunch menu is similar, with a nice selection of panini sandwiches (including lamb, salmon, and vegetarian). There are also several daily specials.

1002 Walnut St. ✆ **303/444-5335.** www.themedboulder.com. Main courses $9–$26; most tapas $3–$5. AE, DC, DISC, MC, V. Sun–Wed 11am–10pm; Thurs–Sat 11am–11pm.

Radda Trattoria ★★ Finds ITALIAN A popular neighborhood eatery north of downtown, Radda Trattoria has a social atmosphere and a terrific sense of invention in the kitchen. In a room that belies its shopping-center location next to a supermarket—centered on a large rectangular bar—the well-oiled operation serves plates of Northern Italian cuisine, such as gnocchi, *cinghiale* (wild boar), and pizzas, as well as fantastic soups and salads. The vibe is casual and smart, with more young professionals and CU faculty than the student hangouts downtown. Radda's older and more formal sister restaurant is **Mateo,** 1837 Pearl St. (✆ **303/443-7766**).

1265 Alpine Ave. ✆ **303/442-6200.** www.raddatrattoria.com. Reservations not accepted. Main courses $9–$16. AE, DISC, MC, V. Mon–Fri 7am–10pm; Sat–Sun 9am–10pm.

Sunflower ★ Finds CONTEMPORARY/ORGANIC This pleasant contemporary eatery, eclectically decorated with murals, rotating local art, and a flagstone floor, touts its menu as healthy and environmentally friendly. The ingredients include certified organic produce, fresh seafood, and free-range, hormone-free poultry and game. The kitchen takes a multicultural approach: Sunflower features a diverse selection of dinner entrees, including sesame-crusted ahi tuna served with coconut-scallion basmati; buffalo sirloin tenderloin with gorgonzola crust; and tempeh korma with spinach, potatoes, raisins, and cashews. Lunch includes fresh variations on sandwiches—such as a blackened salmon burger—as well as specialties like pad Thai and vegetarian Malay fried rice. An all-you-can-eat organic salad buffet is served daily until 4pm, organic juices and wines are available, and there's a popular weekend brunch.

1701 Pearl St. (2 blocks east of the mall). ✆ **303/440-0220.** www.sunflowerrestaurant.net. Main courses $9–$19 lunch and brunch, $19–$31 dinner. AE, DISC, MC, V. Tues–Fri 11am–2:30pm; Tues–Sat 5–10pm; Sat–Sun brunch 10am–3pm; Sun 5–9pm.

INEXPENSIVE

In addition to the choices below, try a slice of Boulder's best New York–style pie at any **Abo's Pizza** location: 1110 13th St. (✆ **303/443-3199**), 1911 Broadway (✆ **303/443-9113**), 2761 Iris Ave. (✆ **303/443-1921**), and 637 S. Broadway (✆ **303/494-1274**). **Lucile's,** 2124 14th St. (✆ **303/442-4743**), is a Boulder breakfast mainstay, serving beignets, buttermilk biscuits, and other morning delicacies that take inspiration from the Big Easy.

Corner Bar ★ CONTEMPORARY AMERICAN With the same kitchen as the highly rated Q's Restaurant (see above), the Hotel Boulderado's Corner Bar is far above your average sandwich shop, although sandwiches and burgers are on the menu, too. Here you can savor a grilled-salmon sandwich, served with red-onion marmalade, spinach, and horseradish aioli. Or you might try a roast turkey BLT with herbed mayo, a grilled Angus sirloin, or pan-roasted halibut with sweet corn–shiitake chowder and zucchini-scallion confit. Those not in search of a full meal can opt for an appetizer, such as fried oysters or chipotle-tomato soup.

In the Hotel Boulderado, 2115 13th St. (at Spruce St.). ✆ **303/442-4560.** Main courses $9–$17. AE, DC, DISC, MC, V. Daily 11:30am–11:45pm.

Illegal Pete's (Value) MEXICAN Located at the far east end of the Pearl Street Mall, Illegal Pete's is renowned locally for its creative, healthy burritos packed with chicken, steak, veggies, or fish. The menu also includes a similar range of tacos, as well as salads, quesadillas, and chile. There's a full bar you can belly up to in the back, and a patio out front. Another Illegal Pete's is on the Hill at 1320 College Ave. (✆ **303/444-3055**).

1447 Pearl St. ✆ **303/440-3955.** www.illegalpetes.com. Menu items $5–$7. AE, DISC, MC, V. Sun–Thurs 11am–10pm; Fri–Sat 11am–2:30am.

Rio Grande MEXICAN This popular neighborhood restaurant and bar, just south of the Pearl Street Mall, is probably best known for its huge, award-winning margaritas—so potent that the staff enforces a strict limit of three. Frequented by college students and Boulder's under-30 crowd, the Rio is bustling for reasons beyond its alcoholic concoctions—the loud, social atmosphere and the food, a good variety of oversize Mexican entrees and combos. My favorites are the hearty fajitas (steak or veggie, with handmade tortillas), zesty Yucatan shrimp, and creative chiles rellenos.

1101 Walnut St. ✆ **303/444-3690.** www.riograndemexican.com. Meals $7–$15. AE, MC, V. Mon–Thurs 11am–2pm; Mon–Wed 5–10pm; Thurs 5–10:30pm; Fri–Sun 11am–10:30pm.

Sherpa's ★ (Finds) TIBETAN/NEPALI Owned by Pemba Sherpa—a native of Nepal who, in fact, is a Sherpa, or Himalayan mountain guide—Sherpa's is located in a converted Victorian house just southwest of the Pearl Street Mall. Decorated with Himalayan relics and photography of the peaks of Nepal and Tibet, the restaurant serves up food to match: Tibetan dishes like *thupka* (noodle bowls) and sherpa stew, as well as spicier Nepali and Indian cuisine, including *saag* (creamed spinach with garlic, cumin, ginger, and your choice of veggie or meat) and curry dishes. There are lunch specials daily, as well as a comfortable bar with a library full of climbing tomes.

825 Walnut St. ✆ **303/440-7151.** Reservations accepted. Main courses $5–$10 lunch, $9–$15 dinner. AE, DISC, MC, V. Daily 11am–3pm; Sun–Thurs 5–9:30pm; Fri–Sat 5–10pm.

ESPRESSO BARS, COFFEEHOUSES & RELATED ESTABLISHMENTS

Espresso fans will have no problem finding a decent espresso, cappuccino, or latte: Boulder has a number of **Starbucks** establishments, as well as many more-interesting independent coffeehouses. Many of the independents, located near the Pearl Street Mall, provide outdoor seating in nice weather. Attached to the Boulder Book Store, the **Bookend Cafe,** 1115 Pearl St. (✆ **303/440-6699**), offers a variety of coffee drinks and a delightful array of baked goods, soups, and pies. **Trident Booksellers & Café,** 940 Pearl St. (✆ **303/443-3133**), features indoor and outdoor seating as well as a comprehensive selection of used books. The **Boulder Dushanbe Teahouse,** 1770 13th St. (✆ **303/442-4993;** p. 196), offers an authentic Persian setting for quaffing more than 70 varieties of tea and a good selection of coffees from 8am to 10pm daily. Homemade baked goods are also available.

5 ATTRACTIONS

THE TOP ATTRACTIONS

Boulder Creek Path ★★ Kids Following Boulder Creek, this nature corridor provides about a 16-mile-long oasis and recreation area through the city and west into the mountains. With no street crossings (there are bridges and underpasses instead), the path is popular with Boulder residents, especially on weekends, when you'll see numerous walkers, runners, bicyclists, and in-line skaters. (Walkers should stay to the right; the left lane is for faster traffic.) The path links the CU campus, several city parks, and office buildings. Near the east end, watch for deer, prairie-dog colonies, and wetlands, where some 150 species of birds have been spotted. You might see Canada geese, mallard ducks, spotted sandpipers, owls, and woodpeckers.

At 30th Street, south of Arapahoe Road, the path cuts through **Scott Carpenter Park** (named for the astronaut and Colorado native), where you can enjoy swimming in summer and sledding in winter. Just west of Scott Carpenter Park, you'll find **Boulder Creek Stream Observatory,** which is adjacent to the Millennium Harvest House. In addition to observing trout and other aquatic wildlife, you're invited to feed the fish with trout food purchased from a vending machine (25¢). **Central Park,** at Broadway and Canyon Boulevard, preserves some of Boulder's history with a restored steam locomotive. The **Boulder Public Library** is also in this area.

Traveling west, watch for the **Charles A. Heartling Sculpture Garden** (with the stone image of local Indian chief Niwot) and the **Kids' Fishing Ponds;** the Boulder Fish and Game Club stocks the ponds, which are open only to children under 12, who can fish for free and keep what they catch. Near 3rd Street and Canyon Boulevard, you'll find the **Xeriscape Garden,** where drought-tolerant plants are tested for reduced water intake.

The **Eben G. Fine Park** is named for the Boulder pharmacist who discovered Arapaho Glacier on nearby Arapaho Peak. To the west, **Red Rocks Settlers' Park** marks the

Impressions

If heaven has a college town, it's probably as beautiful as Boulder.

—*Sunset Magazine*

beginning of the **Boulder Canyon Pioneer Trail,** which leads to a continuation of Boulder Creek Path. The park is named for Missouri gold-seekers who camped at this spot in 1858 and later found gold about 12 miles farther west. Watch for explanatory signs along the 1.3-mile path. The **Whitewater Kayak Course** has 20 slalom gates for kayakers and canoeists to use free; to the west, **Elephant Buttresses** is one of Boulder's more popular rock-climbing areas. The path ends at **Four Mile Canyon,** the old town site of Orodell.

55th St. and Pearl Pkwy., to the mouth of Boulder Canyon. ✆ **303/413-7200.** Free admission. Daily 24 hr. Bus: HOP.

National Center for Atmospheric Research ★ Finds Inspired by the cliff dwellings at Mesa Verde National Park, I. M. Pei designed this striking pink-sandstone building, which overlooks Boulder from high atop Table Mesa in the southwestern foothills. (You might recognize the center from Woody Allen's *Sleeper;* scenes were shot here.) Scientists study such phenomena as the greenhouse effect, wind shear, and ozone depletion to gain a better understanding of Earth's atmosphere. Among the technological tools on display are satellites, weather balloons, interactive computer monitors, robots, and supercomputers that can simulate the world's climate. There are also hands-on, weather-oriented exhibits and a theater. The **Walter Orr Roberts Weather Trail** outside the building's west doors takes visitors on a .4-mile, wheelchair-accessible loop along a path with interpretive signs describing various aspects of weather and climate plus the plants and animals of the area. The center also houses a changing art exhibit and a science-oriented gift shop. Allow 1 to 2 hours.

1850 Table Mesa Dr. ✆ **303/497-1174.** www.ncar.ucar.edu. Free admission. Self-guided tours Mon–Fri 8am–5pm; Sat–Sun and holidays 9am–4pm. 1-hr. guided tours daily at noon; there is also a self-guided audio tour. Take Broadway heading southwest out of town to Table Mesa Dr., and follow it west to the center.

Pearl Street Mall ★★ Kids This 4-block-long tree-lined pedestrian mall marks Boulder's downtown core and its center for dining, shopping, strolling, and people-watching. Musicians, mimes, jugglers, and other street entertainers hold court on the landscaped mall day and night, year-round. Buy your lunch from one of the many vendors and sprawl on the grass in front of the courthouse to relax and eat. Locally owned businesses and galleries share the mall with trendy boutiques, sidewalk cafes, and major chains including Peppercorn, Banana Republic, and Abercrombie & Fitch. There's a wonderful play area for youngsters, with climbable boulders set in gravel. Don't miss the bronze bust of Chief Niwot (of the southern Arapaho) in front of the Boulder County Courthouse between 13th and 14th streets. Niwot, who welcomed the first Boulder settlers, was killed in southeastern Colorado during the Sand Creek Massacre of 1864.

Pearl St. from 11th to 15th sts. Bus: HOP.

University of Colorado ★ The largest university in the state, with nearly 29,000 students (including about 4,600 graduate students), "CU" dominates the city. Its student population, cultural and sports events, and intellectual atmosphere have helped shape Boulder into the city it is today. The school boasts 16 alumni astronauts who have flown in space and three Nobel laureates on the faculty.

Old Main, on the Norlin Quadrangle, was the first building erected after the university was established in 1876; at that time, it housed the entire school. Later, pink-sandstone Italian Renaissance–style buildings came to dominate the campus. Visitors may want to take in the university's **Heritage Center,** on the third floor of Old Main; the **University of Colorado Museum** (see "More Attractions," below), a natural-history museum in the Henderson Building on Broadway; the **Mary Rippon Outdoor Theatre,** behind the Henderson Building, site of the annual Colorado Shakespeare Festival; **Fiske Planetarium,** between Kittredge Loop Drive and Regent Drive on the south side of campus; and the **Norlin Library,** on the Norlin Quadrangle, the largest research library in the state, with extensive holdings of American and English literature. Other attractions include the CU Art Museum, University Memorial Center (the student center), and the Integrated Teaching and Learning Laboratory in the College of Engineering. Prospective students and their parents can arrange campus tours by contacting the admissions office (✆ **303/492-6301**).

The **Sommers-Bausch Observatory** (✆ **303/492-6732** during the day, 303/492-2020 at night) offers tours and Friday-evening open houses. Among the telescopes there are 16-, 18-, and 24-inch Cassegrain reflectors and a 10-inch-aperture heliostat.

East side of Broadway, btw. Arapahoe Ave. and Baseline Rd. ✆ **303/492-1411.** www.colorado.edu. Bus: HOP, SKIP, STAMPEDE, and Denver buses.

MORE ATTRACTIONS

Beyond the attractions listed below, the **Boulder Creek Winery,** 6440 Odell Place (✆ **303/516-9031;** www.bouldercreekwine.com), offers a complimentary tasting Thursday through Sunday from 1 to 5:30pm in summer and 1 to 5pm Friday to Sunday fall through spring.

Banjo Billy's Bus Tours A rollicking journey through Boulder and its storied history, Banjo Billy's Bus Tours utilize one of the funkiest vehicles you've ever seen. Featuring armchairs for guests inside, the exterior looks like the offspring of a log cabin and a school bus—and features 13 disco balls, five saddles, and a rubber chicken! The 90-minute tours delve into ghost stories and lurid tales of crime, but the tone is tongue-in-cheek and entertaining.

Tours depart from the Hotel Boulderado (p. 191). ✆ **720/771-0087.** www.banjobilly.com. Tickets $16 adults, $14 seniors, $10 children 5–12, free for children 4 and under. Tours depart Tues–Sun 2pm and 4pm in the summer, less frequently at other times of year.

Celestial Seasonings ★ Value The nation's leading producer of herbal teas, housed in a modern building in northeastern Boulder, offers tours that are an experience for the senses. The company began in a Boulder garage in 1969 and now produces more than 90 varieties of tea from more than 75 different herbs and spices imported from 35 countries. You'll understand why the company invites you to "see, taste, and smell the world of Celestial Seasonings" as you move from a consumer taste test in the lobby to their famed tea-box art, and finally into the production plant where nine million tea bags roll off the line daily. The exhilaratingly aromatic "Mint Room" is a highlight. The tour lasts 45 minutes, and there are a cafe and gift shop on-site.

4600 Sleepytime Dr. © **303/581-1202** or 303/530-5300. www.celestialseasonings.com. Free admission. Mon–Fri 10am–4pm; Sat 10am–3pm; Sun 11am–3pm; tours on the hour. Reservations required for groups of 8 or more. Exit Colo. 119, Longmont Diagonal; at Jay Rd. go east to Spine, and then north to Sleepytime. Bus: J.

Redstone Meadery ★ Finds Drunk by Beowulf and Shakespeare, mead is the original fermented beverage. There are about 60 active meaderies in the United States, including this standout in Boulder. Founded by David Myers in 2000, the meadery crafts several beverages (ranging from sparkling to portlike) that quickly demonstrate why this amateur mead maker turned pro. The meadery offers free 30-minute tours and tasting, and sells its wares ($17–$25 a bottle) and other regional foods and gifts.

4700 Old Pearl St., #2A. © **720/406-1215.** www.redstonemeadery.com. Free admission. Tours Mon–Fri 1 and 3pm, Sat 12:30pm; tasting room Mon–Fri noon–6:30pm, Sat noon–5pm. Located 1 block northeast of the Pearl St. exit off Foothills Pkwy.

Boulder Beer Company From the grinding of the grain to the bottling of the beer, the 25-minute tour of Colorado's original microbrewery ends as all brewery tours should: in the pub. Tours pass by glistening copper vats that turn out hundreds of kegs of Boulder Beer a day. The pub overlooks the bottling area, so even if you visit without taking a tour, you still get a good view of the brewing process. The menu includes burgers, burritos, salads, and appetizers; most entrees run $6 to $9.

2880 Wilderness Place. © **303/444-8448.** www.boulderbeer.com. Free admission. Tours Mon–Fri 2pm (or by appt.); pub Mon–Fri 11am–9pm. Take U.S. 36 north to Valmont Rd.; then head east to Wilderness Place.

Museums & Galleries

There are three art galleries on the University of Colorado campus, all with free admission. The **CU Art Museum** (© **303/492-8300**) displays the work of CU students and faculty, as well as pieces from the Colorado Collection, about 5,000 works by international artists, including Warhol, Dürer, Rembrandt, Tiepolo, Hogarth, Hiroshige, Matisse, and Picasso. There are also rotating exhibits. ***Note:*** The museum is closed until fall 2009 and will reopen at that time in the new Visual Arts Complex.

At the University Memorial Center, the **UMC Art Gallery** (© **303/492-7465**) organizes and hosts a variety of exhibitions featuring regional and national artists. In the music-listening rooms, visitors can peruse current periodicals while listening to modern and classical music. The gallery is on the second floor of the center, just left of the information desk; it's open Monday to Friday from 9am to 6pm (bus: HOP, SKIP, STAMPEDE).

The **Andrew J. Macky Gallery** (© **303/492-8423**), at the main entrance of Macky Auditorium, shows touring exhibits and works by local artists. It's open Wednesday from 9am to 4pm (bus: HOP, SKIP, STAMPEDE).

There are also studios and a gallery at the **Dairy Center for the Arts,** 2590 Walnut St. (© **303/440-7826;** www.thedairy.org), which also houses two theaters, classrooms, and several dance, theater, and arts organizations. See "Theater & Dance," later in this chapter.

Boulder History Museum ★ Ensconced on University Hill in the 1899–1900 Harbeck-Bergheim House, a Victorian mansion with a Dutch-style front door and Italian tile fireplaces, the museum houses one of the most comprehensive local-history collections in the region. There are more than 35,000 artifacts (from snake oil to sidesaddles), plus hundreds of thousands of photographs and historical documents from Colorado's early days to the present.

Permanent exhibits include "Storymakers: A Boulder History," featuring a rich collection of oral histories and late-19th-to-early-20th-century photographs. There are also rotating exhibits that stay up for 6 to 10 months. The museum also hosts numerous lectures, programs, tours, and community events. Allow 1 to 2 hours.

1206 Euclid Ave. ✆ **303/449-3464.** www.boulderhistorymuseum.org. Admission $5 adults, $3 seniors, $2 children and students, free for children 4 and under. Tues–Fri 10am–5pm; Sat–Sun noon–4pm. Guided tours by appt. Closed Mon and major holidays. Bus: HOP.

Boulder Museum of Contemporary Art This multidisciplinary art museum, created in 1972 to exhibit the work of contemporary artists, has evolved into an exciting venue where one can expect to see almost anything art related, from the lighthearted to the elegant, political to religious, by regional and international contemporary artists. There are special programs for young children and a variety of other events throughout the year. Performing arts—from poetry and dance to music and drama—are occasionally presented in the museum's "black box" performance venue. There are free tours during Farmer's Market (summer Sat) at 11am and kid's programs. Allow 30 to 45 minutes.

In addition, a separate organization puts on Saturday evening movie screenings in the adjacent parking lot in summer; classic movies such as *Citizen Kane* and cult classics are shown outside ($5 suggested donation per person; see **www.boulderoutdoorcinema.com** for information). Take a lawn chair or blanket.

1750 13th St. ✆ **303/443-2122.** www.bmoca.org. Admission $5 adults, $4 students and seniors, free for children 11 and under. Tues–Sat 11am–5pm (Sat 9am–4pm and until 8pm Wed in summer); Sun noon–3pm. Hours change seasonally; call ahead for current information. Closed Sun–Mon and major holidays. Bus: HOP, SKIP.

CU Heritage Center Located in the oldest building on campus, this museum reflects the history of the university. Its seven galleries hold exhibits on early student life (together with a complete set of yearbooks), CU's contributions to space exploration, campus architecture, distinguished alumni, and an overview of the university's history. Allow 30 minutes—or a lot more if you're an alum.

3rd floor of Old Main, University of Colorado. ✆ **303/492-6329.** Free admission. Mon–Fri 10am–4pm. Bus: HOP, SKIP, STAMPEDE.

CU Museum of Natural History ★ Kids The natural history and anthropology of the Rocky Mountains and Southwest are the focus of this campus museum, founded in 1902 and one of the best of its kind. Featured exhibits include Ancestral Puebloan pottery and collections pertaining to dinosaurs, geology, paleontology, botany, entomology, and zoology. A children's area has interactive exhibits, and one gallery is devoted to special displays that change throughout the year. Allow 1 to 3 hours.

University of Colorado, Henderson Bldg., just east of Broadway btw. 15th and 16th sts. ✆ **303/492-6892.** http://cumuseum.colorado.edu. Admission $3 adults, $1 seniors and children 6–18, free for children 5 and under. Mon–Fri 9am–5pm; Sat 9am–4pm; Sun 10am–4pm. Bus: HOP.

Leanin' Tree Museum of Western Art You may know Leanin' Tree as the world's largest publisher of Western-art greeting cards. What's not so well known is that the company's headquarters houses an outstanding 400-plus-piece collection of original paintings and bronze sculptures by contemporary artists. All depict scenes from the Old or New West, including a collection of humorous cowboy art. There is also an outdoor sculpture garden of likenesses of human and animal Western icons. Free guided tours are available. Allow 1 hour.

6055 Longbow Dr. (exit Jay Rd. and Longmont Diagonal). ✆ **800/777-8716** or 303/530-1442, ext. 4299. www.leanintreemuseum.com. Free admission; donations suggested. Mon–Fri 8am–5pm; Sat–Sun 10am–5pm. Closed major holidays. Bus: 205.

Especially for Kids

City parks (see "Sports & Outdoor Activities," below) offer the best diversions for children.

On the **Boulder Creek Path** (see "The Top Attractions," earlier in this chapter), the underwater fish observatory behind the Millennium Harvest House fascinates youngsters. They can feed the huge trout swimming behind a glass barrier on the creek (machines cough up handfuls of fish food for 25¢). Farther up the path, on the south bank around 6th Street, Kids' Fishing Ponds, stocked by the Boulder Fish and Game Club, are open to children under 12. There's no charge for either activity.

The **Fiske Planetarium** (✆ **303/492-5001;** http://fiske.colorado.edu) offers visitors a walk through the solar system. Dedicated to the memory of CU alumnus Ellison Onizuka and the six other astronauts who died in the space shuttle *Challenger* explosion, the outdoor scale model begins at the entrance to the planetarium with the sun and inner planets, and continues across Regent Drive to the outer planets, located along the walkway to the Engineering Center. Admission is free; allow at least a half-hour. The planetarium offers kids' after-school and summer discovery programs, star shows, and other programs in which you get a chance to look at the sky through the planetarium's telescopes. Admission for these events is usually around $5; call for the latest schedule (bus: HOP).

6 SPORTS & OUTDOOR ACTIVITIES

Boulder is one of the leading spots for outdoor sports in North America. The city manages more than 38,000 acres of parklands, including more than 200 miles of hiking trails and bicycle paths. Several canyons lead down from the Rockies directly into Boulder, attracting mountaineers and rock climbers. Families enjoy picnicking and camping in the beautiful surroundings. It seems that everywhere you look, people of all ages are running, walking, biking, skiing, or engaged in other active sports.

The **Boulder Parks and Recreation Department** (✆ **303/413-7200;** www.ci.boulder.co.us/parks-recreation) manages many of the outdoor facilities and schedules a variety of year-round activities for children as well as adults. Seasonal booklets on activities and city parks are available free from the Chamber of Commerce office and through the parks and recreation department's website (see above). Although many of the programs last for several weeks or months, some are half- or full-day activities that visiting children can join, usually at a slightly higher price than that for city residents. The department sponsors hikes, fitness programs, ski trips, watersports, special holiday events, and performances in local parks, and even operates a skate park and a pottery lab. (TV trivia buffs, take note: Mork, of *Mork and Mindy,* first touched down on Planet Earth in Chautauqua Park, on the city's south side, and the house used as their residence's exterior is at 1619 Pine St.)

One destination where you can enjoy several kinds of outdoor activities is **Eldorado Canyon State Park ★**. This mountain park, just 5 miles southwest of Boulder in

Impressions

This is Mork from Ork signing off from Boulder, Colorado. Nanu, Nanu!

—Mork from Ork (Robin Williams), on TV's *Mork & Mindy,* 1978–82

Eldorado Springs, is a favorite of technical rock climbers, but the 850-foot-high canyon's beauty makes it just as popular with hikers, picnickers, and others who want to get away from it all. The 1,448-acre park features 9 miles of hiking and horseback-riding trails, plus 7.5 miles of trails suitable for mountain bikes; fishing is permitted, but camping is not. An exhibit at the brand-new visitor center describes the history of the park; there's also a bookstore and rotating displays covering topics from wildflowers to climbing. Admission is $6 to $7 per vehicle and $3 per pedestrian; the park is open daily from dawn to dusk. For further information, contact Eldorado Canyon State Park, Box B, Eldorado Springs, CO 80025 (✆ **303/494-3943;** parks.state.co.us).

BALLOONING Float above the majestic Rocky Mountains in a hot-air balloon, watching as the early-morning light gradually brightens to full day. Flights often include champagne and an elaborate continental breakfast or brunch. **Fair Winds Hot Air Balloon Flights** (✆ **303/939-9323;** www.fairwindsinc.com) flies 7 days a week year-round, weather permitting. Prices are $195 to $275 per person and include a certificate, T-shirt, and photograph.

BICYCLING On some days, you see more bikes than cars in Boulder. Paths run along many of the city's major arteries, and local racing and touring events are scheduled year-round. Bicyclists riding at night are required to have lights; perhaps because of the large number of bicyclists in Boulder, the local police actively enforce traffic regulations that apply to them. Generally, bicyclists must obey the same laws that apply to operators of motor vehicles.

For current information on biking events, maps of the city's trails, tips on the best places to ride, and equipment sales and repairs, check with **University Bicycles,** 839 Pearl St., about 2 blocks west of the Pearl Street Mall (✆ **303/444-4196;** www.ubikes.com), and **Full Cycle,** 1211 13th St., near the campus (✆ **303/440-7771;** www.fullcyclebikes.com). Daily bike rentals cost $20 to $40 (or $85 for a luxury model). See also "By Bicycle," under "Getting Around," earlier in this chapter.

CLIMBING & BOULDERING If you want to tackle the nearby mountains and cliffs with ropes and pitons, contact **Boulder Mountaineering,** 1335-B Broadway (✆ **303/442-8355;** www.bouldermountaineering.com), which sells clothing and technical equipment, and can also provide maps and advice on climbing and trail running. Other good information sources are **Colorado Athletic Training School,** 2800 30th St. (✆ **303/939-9699;** www.catsgym.com), and **Total Climbing,** 2829 Mapleton Ave. (✆ **800/447-4008;** www.totalclimbing.com). The latter is home to the Boulder Rock Club, featuring 10,000 square feet of indoor climbing surfaces and offers guiding services.

Boulderers (those who climb without ropes) flock to **The Spot,** billed as the country's largest bouldering gym, at 3240 Prairie Ave. (✆ **303/379-8806;** www.thespotgym.com). Lessons and guide service are available, and there are a cafe and a yoga studio on-site.

The Flatiron Range (easily visible from downtown Boulder) and nearby Eldorado Canyon are two favorite destinations for expert rock scalers. The Third Flatiron is 1,400 feet high, taller than the Empire State Building, and has been climbed by people without using their hands, on roller skates, naked, and in a record 8 minutes (by separate climbers). For bouldering, Carter Lake (30 miles north on U.S. 36) and Boulder Canyon (west of the city on Canyon Blvd.) are two of the top spots.

FISHING Favored fishing areas near Boulder include **Boulder Reservoir,** North 51st Street, northeast of the city off the Longmont Diagonal, where you can try your luck at walleye, catfish, largemouth bass, bluegill, crappie, and carp. The Boulder Parks and Recreation Department (✆ **303/441-3461**) manages the reservoir. Other favorite fishing holes include **Lagerman Reservoir,** west of North 73rd Street off Pike Road, about 15 miles northeast of the city, where only nonmotorized boats can be used; **Barker Reservoir,** just east of Nederland on the Boulder Canyon Drive (Colo. 119), for bank fishing; and **Walden Ponds Wildlife Habitat,** about 6 miles east of downtown on North 75th Street. Fly-fishing is also popular in the area; guide service is available through **Kinsley Outfitters,** 2070 Broadway (✆ **800/442-7420** or 303/442-6204; www.kinsleyoutfitters.com), for $250 for one person for a full day or $350 for two. Kinsley's fly shop offers a good selection of supplies.

GLIDER FLYING & SOARING The atmospheric conditions generated by the peaks of the Front Range are ideal for year-round soaring and gliding. **Mile High Gliding,** 5534 Independence Rd. (✆ **303/527-1122;** www.milehighgliding.com), offers rides and lessons on the north side of Boulder Municipal Airport, 2 miles northeast of downtown. Rides for one person range from $79 to $259 and last from 15 minutes to an hour or more; a 40-minute ride for two costs $219.

GOLF Local courses include the 18-hole **Flatirons Golf Course** (run by Boulder Parks and Recreation), 5706 E. Arapahoe Ave. (✆ **303/442-7851;** www.flatironsgolf.com), and the 9-hole **Haystack Mountain Golf Course,** 5877 Niwot Rd. in Niwot., 5 miles north of Boulder (✆ **303/530-1400;** www.golfhaystack.com). Nonresident greens fees range from $13 to $32.

HIKING & BACKPACKING There are plenty of opportunities in the Boulder area—the Boulder Mountain Parks system includes 4,625 acres bordering the city limits, including the Flatirons and Flagstaff Mountain. You can obtain a map with descriptions of more than 60 trails from the **Boulder Convention and Visitors Bureau,** 2440 Pearl St. (✆ **303/442-2911**).

Numerous Roosevelt National Forest trail heads leave the Peak-to-Peak Scenic Byway (Colo. 72) west of Boulder. Check with the **U.S. Forest Service,** Boulder Ranger District, 2140 Yarmouth Ave. (✆ **303/541-2500**), for hiking and backpacking information. During dry weather, check on possible fire and smoking restrictions before heading into the forest. The trail heads leading to Long, Mitchell, and Brainard lakes are among the most popular, as is the 2-mile hike to Isabel Glacier.

About 70 miles west of Boulder, on the Continental Divide, is the **Indian Peaks Wilderness Area** (✆ **303/541-2500**). More than half of the area is fragile alpine tundra; a $5 permit is required for camping from June 1 to September 15. North of Boulder, via Estes Park, is **Rocky Mountain National Park** (✆ **970/586-1206**), one of the state's prime destinations for hikers and those seeking beautiful mountain scenery. The 2.5-mile **Mills Lake Trail ★**, one of my favorites, is here; see "A Side Trip to Rocky Mountain National Park," later in this chapter. Another good hike is the 6-mile Mesa Trail, which departs from the Bluebell Shelter in Chautauqua Park.

RUNNING The Boulder Creek Path (see "The Top Attractions," earlier in this chapter) is one of the most popular routes for runners in Boulder. A good resource for the traveling runner is **Boulder Road Runners** (www.boulderroadrunners.org). They organize group runs in the area and can provide information. The **Bolder Boulder** (✆ **303/444-RACE** [444-7223]; www.bolderboulder.com), held every Memorial Day, attracts about 50,000 runners who circle its 6.3-mile course. The **Boulder Running Company,** 2775 Pearl St. (✆ **303/786-9255;** www.boulderrunningcompany.com), sells a wide variety of running shoes and gear, going as far as analyzing customers' strides on a treadmill to find the perfect shoe.

SKIING Friendly **Eldora Mountain Resort,** P.O. Box 1697, Nederland, CO 80466 (✆ **888/235-3672** or 303/440-8700; fax 303/440-8797; www.eldora.com), is just 21 miles west of downtown Boulder. It's about a 40-minute drive on Colo. 119 through Nederland. RTD buses leave Boulder for Eldora four times daily during ski season. For downhill skiers and snowboarders, Eldora has 53 trails, rated 30% novice, 50% intermediate, and 20% expert terrain on 680 acres. It has snowmaking on 320 acres and a terrain park with a 600-foot superpipe. The area has two quad lifts, two triple and four double chairlifts, four surface lifts, and a vertical rise of 1,500 feet. Lift tickets (2007–08 rates) were $59 for adults, $37 for seniors 65 to 74 or children 6 to 15, and just $7 for those under 6 and over 74. There are also discount packages that include lessons and rental equipment for both skiers and snowboarders. Snowshoeing is also gaining popularity in the area. The season runs from mid-November to mid-April, snow permitting.

For cross-country skiers, Eldora has 25 miles of groomed and backcountry trails, and an overnight hut available by reservation. About 15% of the trails are rated easy, 50% intermediate, and 35% difficult. The trail fee is $18, $10 for children 6 to 15 and seniors 65 to 74, and $2 for those under 6 and over 74.

You can rent all your ski, snowboard, and snowshoeing equipment at the ski-rental center, and Nordic equipment at the Eldora Nordic Center. A free base-area shuttle runs throughout the day from the lodge to the Little Hawk area and the Nordic Center.

In Boulder, you can rent or buy telemark and alpine touring equipment from **Eldora Mountain Sports,** 2775 Canyon Blvd. (✆ **303/447-2017**).

SWIMMING Five public pools are located within the city. Indoor pools, all open daily year-round, are at the newly renovated **North Boulder Recreation Center,** 3170 N. Broadway (✆ **303/413-7260**); the **East Boulder Community Center,** 5660 Sioux Dr. (✆ **303/441-4400**); and the **South Boulder Recreation Center,** 1360 Gillaspie Dr. (✆ **303/441-3448**). The two outdoor pools (both open daily from Memorial Day to Labor Day) are **Scott Carpenter Pool,** 30th Street and Arapahoe Avenue (✆ **303/441-3427**), and **Spruce Pool,** 2102 Spruce St. (✆ **303/441-3426**). Swimming fees for all municipal pools are $6 adults, $4 seniors, $3.50 teens, $3 children 3 to 12, and free for children 2 and under.

TENNIS There are more than 30 public courts in the city. The North and South Boulder Recreation centers (see "Swimming," above) each have four lighted courts and accept reservations ($8 per hr.). The North Boulder Recreation Center also has two platform tennis courts. Play is free if you arrive and there's no one using the courts, or with a reservation. For locations of other public tennis courts, contact the Boulder Parks and Recreation Department (✆ **303/413-7200**).

WATERSPORTS For both motorboating and human-powered boating, sailboard instruction, or swimming at a sandy beach, head for the square-mile **Boulder Reservoir** (✆ **303/441-3461**), on North 51st Street off the Longmont Diagonal northeast of the city. Human-powered boats and canoes (no personal watercraft) can be rented at the

boathouse (✆ **303/441-3468**). Rates start at $8 per hour, with sailboards at $20 per hour. There are also a boat ramp and other facilities.

SPECTATOR SPORTS

The major attractions are **University of Colorado football, women's volleyball,** and **men's and women's basketball.** For tickets, contact the Ticket Office, Campus Box 372, Boulder, CO 80309 (✆ **303/49-BUFFS** [492-8337]; www.cubuffs.com). Football tickets sometimes sell out early, particularly for homecoming and games against Nebraska and Oklahoma.

7 SHOPPING

For the best shopping in Boulder, head to the **Pearl Street Mall** (see "The Top Attractions," earlier in this chapter), where you'll find not only shops and galleries galore, but also street entertainers.

Twenty Ninth Street, centered on the former site of the Crossroads Mall at the intersection of Canyon Boulevard and 29th Street (✆ **303/449-1189;** www.twentyninthstreet.com), is a major new multiuse development featuring an outdoor shopping center. Open since 2006, tenants include Eddie Bauer, Ruby's Diner, MontBell, Borders Books & Music, Apple, and Century Theatres. Hours are 10am to 9pm Monday through Saturday and 11am to 6pm on Sunday.

The indoor-outdoor, 1.5-million-square-foot **FlatIron Crossing** (✆ **720/887-7467;** www.flatironcrossing.com), an upscale mall featuring Nordstrom, Dillard's, and Brookstone among its 200 shops, is a more comprehensive option for the devout shopper. It's 9 miles southeast of Boulder off U.S. 36 in Broomfield. Hours are 10am to 9pm Monday through Saturday and 11am to 6pm on Sunday.

SHOPPING A TO Z

Arts & Crafts

Art Source International Natural-history prints, maps, and other items relevant to Western Americana, mainly from the 18th and 19th centuries, are the specialty here, along with collections of 100-year-old Colorado photographs, maps, and prints. The store also features a great selection of new globes, as well as a few reproductions. 1237 Pearl St. ✆ **303/444-4079.** www.rare-maps.com.

Boulder Arts & Crafts Cooperative This is a good place to find a unique gift or souvenir. The shop, owned and operated by its artist members since 1971, features a wide variety of original handcrafted works. Pieces range from watercolors, serigraphs, and other fine art to top-quality crafts, including blown glass, stained glass, handmade jewelry, and functional pottery. Many of the items are made in Colorado or the Rocky Mountain region. 1421 Pearl St. ✆ **303/443-3683.** www.boulderartsandcrafts.com.

Niwot Antiques *Finds* With dozens of dealers (including New England antiques specialist Elysian Fields), this antiques mall, in business since the 1950s, is the area's best, and a good excuse to make a trip to Niwot, 5 miles north of Boulder on the Longmont Diagonal. 136 2nd Ave., Niwot. ✆ **303/652-2587.** www.niwotantiques.com.

Books

Being a college town, Boulder is one of the best cities in the world for a browsing bookworm. It reportedly has more used-book stores per capita than any other U.S. city. Chain outlets include **Barnes & Noble,** 2915 Pearl St. (© **303/442-1665**). The independents run the gamut from the Kerouac and Burroughs specialists at **Beat Bookshop,** 1717 Pearl St. (© **303/444-7111**), to the lesbian/feminist/gay selection at **Word Is Out,** 2015 10th St. (© **303/449-1415**). **Trident Booksellers,** 940 Pearl St. (© **303/443-3133**), is a good used-book shop with a coffeehouse attached.

Boulder Book Store This meandering, four-story, 20,000-square-foot bookstore has been locally owned and operated since the 1970s. It attracts students, bohemians, and businesspeople alike with its homey vibe, and features great selections of Buddhism tomes and travel guides. Attached is the Bookend Cafe, a coffeehouse with patio seating on the Pearl Street Mall (see "Espresso Bars, Coffeehouses & Related Establishments," earlier in this chapter). 1107 Pearl St. © **303/447-2074.** www.boulderbookstore.com.

Fashion

Alpaca Connection Come here for natural-fiber clothing from around the world, including alpaca-and-wool sweaters from South America. 1326 Pearl St. © **303/447-2047.**

Rocky Mountain Kids (Kids) Offering clothing for newborns to 12-year-olds, this bright store specializes in quality brands and is known for its kid-friendliness: complimentary animal crackers and plenty of toys in the box. 2525 Arapahoe Ave. © **303/447-2267.**

Weekends The selection of men's and women's fashions is somewhat pricey but chosen for comfort and style—and it shows. 1200 Pearl St. © **303/444-4231.** www.weekendsboulder.com.

Food & Drink

Boulder Wine Merchant This store has a solid selection of wines from around the world, plus knowledgeable salespeople (and more than one master sommelier) who can help you make the right choice. 2690 Broadway. © **303/443-6761.**

Liquor Mart Here you'll find a huge choice of discounted wine and liquor, with more than 5,000 wines and 900 beers, including a wide selection of imported and microbrewed beers. 1750 15th St. (at Canyon Blvd.). © **303/449-3374.**

Whole Foods The latest and greatest of Boulder's organic supermarkets, this huge store—part of the national chain—has a wide-ranging, fresh inventory and is a favorite lunch spot of locals. Offerings include a deli, soup and salad bar, sushi, and more free samples than you could possibly eat. 2905 Pearl St. © **303/545-6611.**

Gifts & Souvenirs

The best stops for T-shirts, University of Colorado paraphernalia, and other Boulder souvenirs are **Jackalope and Company,** 1126 Pearl St. (© **303/939-8434**); **Where the Buffalo Roam,** 1320 Pearl St. (© **303/938-1424**); and the **CU Bookstore,** 1111 Broadway (© **303/442-5051**). Long a hub for Eastern religion, Boulder also has a plethora of Tibetan gift shops—**Old Tibet,** 948 Pearl St. (© **303/440-0323**) is the longest standing.

Hardware

McGuckin Hardware McGuckin claims to have the world's largest hardware selection, with more than 200,000 items in stock. In addition to the nuts, bolts, brackets, paints, tools, and assorted whatchamacallits that most hardware stores carry, you'll also find sporting goods, kitchen gizmos, automotive supplies, stationery, some clothing, electronics, outdoor furniture, fresh flowers, and a whole lot of other stuff. 2525 Arapahoe Ave. © **303/443-1822** or 86-MCGUCKIN (866-2482). www.mcguckin.com.

Jewelry

Angie Star Jewelry A gallery for some of the area's top jewelry designers, Angie Star's store is a showcase for one-of-a-kind pieces. 1807 Pearl St. ✆ **720/565-0288.**

El Loro Distinctively Boulder, this bohemian jewelry shop has been a Pearl Street Mall resident for more than 25 years. Aside from a nice selection of sterling silver items with semiprecious stones, El Loro also sells clogs and incense. 1416 Pearl St. ✆ **303/449-3162.**

Kitchenware

Peppercorn From cookbooks to pasta makers, you can find anything and everything for the kitchen here at "the Smithsonian of cookstores." In business since 1977, this vast store (12,000 sq. ft.!) has hundreds of kitchen gadgets and appliances—everything you might need to prepare, serve, and consume the simplest or most exotic meal. 1235 Pearl St. ✆ **800/447-6905** or 303/449-5847. www.peppercorn.com.

Sporting Goods

Sports Authority, 3320 N. 28th St. (✆ **303/449-9021**), is a good all-purpose source, while the following are more specialized—and interesting—retail outlets.

Boulder Army Store Just east of the Pearl Street Mall, this shop has the best inventory of camping gear in the city, along with a limited amount of fishing equipment. There is also a good supply of outdoor clothing and military surplus items such as fatigues, helmets, and that disarmed hand grenade you've always wanted. 1545 Pearl St. ✆ **303/442-7616.**

Boulder Mountaineering This shop specializes in equipment, clothing, and accessories for backpacking, camping, rock and ice climbing, mountaineering, backcountry skiing, and snowshoeing. Equipment rentals include sleeping bags, tents, backpacks, and snowshoes; backcountry and telemark ski packages are available. Eldora Mountain Sports (see above) also sells maps and guidebooks, and the knowledgeable staff—which includes several trained guides—can help you plan your trip. 1335 Broadway. ✆ **303/442-8355.**

8 BOULDER AFTER DARK

As a cultured and well-educated community (59% of adult residents have at least one college degree), Boulder is especially noted for its summer music, dance, and Shakespeare festivals. Major entertainment events take place year-round, both downtown and on the University of Colorado campus. There's also a wide choice of nightclubs and bars, but it hasn't always been so: Boulder was dry for 60 years, from 1907 (13 years before national Prohibition) to 1967. The first new bar in the city opened in 1969, in the Hotel Boulderado. The notoriously healthy city banned smoking in 1995, 11 years before the state did the same thing.

Entertainment schedules can be found in the *Daily Camera*'s weekly *Friday Magazine;* in either of the Denver dailies, the *Denver Post* or the *Rocky Mountain News;* in *Westword,* the Denver weekly; or in the free *Boulder Weekly.*

THE CLUB & MUSIC SCENE

Boulder Theater (Finds) Rock, folk, bluegrass, jazz, hip-hop, comedy, and who knows what else—performed by notables such as Lou Reed, Bill Maher, Herbie Hancock, and Norah Jones—take the stage here. During the week, you'll also find independent and otherwise alternative films; there are also annual film festivals here. 2032 14th St. ✆ **303/786-7030.** www.bouldertheater.com.

The Catacombs This popular bar books live blues and jazz by local and regional performers. The loud, somewhat raucous atmosphere (and smoking room) draws a crowd of CU students and an eclectic mix of locals and traveling businesspeople. A limited pub menu is served. In the basement of the Hotel Boulderado, 13th and Spruce sts. ✆ **303/443-0486.**

Fox Theatre and Cafe *Finds* A variety of live music (including, but not limited to, bluegrass, funk, blues, hip-hop, reggae, and punk) is presented here 5 or 6 nights a week, featuring a mix of local, regional, and national talent. You'll find three bars at this converted movie theater, which is revered for its great acoustics. 1135 13th St. ✆ **303/443-3399** or 303/447-0095. www.foxtheatre.com.

'Round Midnight A hip basement joint on the Pearl Street Mall, 'Round Midnight specializes in malt scotch, good beer, and dancing. An eclectic array of performers (hip-hop, techno, jazz, rock) takes the stage here on weekends and there are DJs during the week. 1005 Pearl St. ✆ **303/442-2176.** www.roundmidnight.tv.

THE BAR SCENE

Conor O'Neill's *Finds* Everything in this pub—from the bar to the art to the timber floors—was designed and built in Ireland. The atmosphere is rich, with a "shop pub" up front and two back rooms centered on a pair of fireplaces that were constructed by visiting Irish stonemasons. There are more than a dozen beers on tap, primarily from (where else?) Ireland, and the pub menu features fish and chips, burgers, and a mean shepherd's pie. There is regular live music (surf to Celtic), and an Irish jam session Sunday afternoons. 1922 13th St. ✆ **303/449-1922.** www.conoroneills.com.

Lazy Dog With a great rooftop deck and a plethora of TVs tuned into games of all kinds, the Lazy Dog has emerged as the best sports bar in Boulder, especially after its recent relocation to the Pearl Street Mall. 1346 Pearl St. ✆ **303/440-3355.** www.thelazydog.com.

Mountain Sun Pub & Brewery An English-style neighborhood pub and microbrewery, Mountain Sun produces dozens of barrels of beer each week and provides tours on request during the day. The mostly made-from-scratch menu features soups, salads, burgers, sandwiches, and a few Mexican dishes. There's live folk, acoustic, and bluegrass music on Sunday night. There is also the **Southern Sun** in south Boulder at 627 S. Broadway (✆ 303/543-0886). 1535 Pearl St. (east of the mall). ✆ **303/546-0886.** www.mountainsunpub.com.

The Sink *Finds* This off-campus establishment opened in 1923 (CU dropout Robert Redford was once the janitor) but has been updated with new spacy wall murals that help make it one of Boulder's funniest—and most fun—nightspots. There's a full bar with more than a dozen regional microbrews, live music, and fare such as Sinkburgers and "ugly crust" pizza. 1165 13th St. ✆ **303/444-SINK** [444-7465]. www.thesink.com.

Sundown Saloon This raucous dive is a CU institution. In a spacious basement on the west end of the Pearl Street Mall, pool is the pastime of choice and the drinks are reasonably priced. 1136 Pearl St. **303/449-4987.** www.thesundownsaloon.com.

Walnut Brewery In a historic brick warehouse a block from the Pearl Street Mall, this large restaurant/bar/microbrewery is popular with the after-work crowd, both young and old. 1123 Walnut St. (near Broadway). ✆ **303/447-1345.** www.walnutbrewery.com.

Tips Lyons: On the Beaten Path

Most tourists driving U.S. 36 to Rocky Mountain National Park from Boulder or Denver blaze through the dinky town of Lyons without even bothering to slow down. They're missing some top-drawer diversions in the process. For beer and music aficionados, **Oskar Blues Grill & Brew,** 303 Main St. (✆ **303/823-6685;** www.oskarblues.com), is a fun and—to say the least—eclectically decorated place for lunch and a beer, or a blues, rock, or rockabilly show come nighttime. Oskar Blues was the first craft brewery in the country to can its beer (Dale's Pale Ale, Old Chub, Gordon, and Ten-Fidy). The canning now happens in nearby Longmont, but the restaurant is still open daily from 11am to 10pm; the bar is open until midnight Sunday through Thursday and until 2am on Friday and Saturday. Also worth a look is the **Lyons Pinball Arcade,** 339-A Main St. (✆ **303/823-6100;** www.lyonspinball.com), with 30 pinball machines dating from the 1970s and more recent decades, including Kiss, Black Knight, and Addams Family. For silverball fiends, it's a trip down memory lane.

Downtown Lyons is a historic district marked by 16 Victorian sandstones, and just outside of town, the fishing and hiking are excellent. For additional information, contact the **Lyons Chamber of Commerce,** 350 Broadway (P.O. Box 426), Lyons, CO 80540 (✆ **877/LYONS-CO** [596-6726] or 303/823-5215; www.lyons-colorado.com).

West End Tavern A 2004 makeover of this popular neighborhood bar left the brick walls and the classic bar intact, but gave the rest of the joint a contemporary shot in the arm and a slick look. Beyond the 48 bourbons stocked by the bar, fare includes a different specialty burger every day, barbecue, and more upscale items. The tavern's roof garden is an ideal spot to unwind and enjoy some of the best views in town and outdoor cinema on certain summer nights. 926 Pearl St. ✆ **303/444-3535.** www.thewestendtavern.com.

THE PERFORMING ARTS

Music, dance, and theater are important aspects of life for Boulder residents. Many of these activities take place at **Macky Auditorium** at the University of Colorado (✆ **303/492-8008;** www.colorado.edu/music) and other campus venues, as well as the **Chautauqua Auditorium,** 900 Baseline Rd. (✆ **303/442-3282;** www.chautauqua.com), and the **Dairy Center for the Arts,** 2590 Walnut St. (✆ **303/440-7826;** www.thedairy.org).

Classical Music & Opera

Boulder Bach Festival First presented in 1981, this celebration of the music of Johann Sebastian Bach includes not only a late-January festival, but also concerts and other events year-round. Tickets run about $15 to $30. Series tickets are also available. P.O. Box 1896, Boulder, CO 80306. ✆ **303/776-9666.** www.boulderbachfest.org.

Boulder Philharmonic Orchestra This acclaimed community orchestra performs an annual fall-to-spring season, primarily at Macky Auditorium, with world-class artists who have included singer Marilyn Horne, guitarist Carlos Montoya, cellist Yo-Yo Ma, and violinist Itzhak Perlman. Tickets cost $10 to $70, more for concerts that feature premier performers. 2995 Wilderness Place, Ste. 100, Boulder, CO 80301. ✆ **303/449-1343.** www.boulderphil.org.

Colorado MahlerFest Begun in 1988, this international festival is the only one of its kind in the world. For a week each January it celebrates the work of Gustav Mahler with a performance of one of his symphonies, as well as chamber concerts, films, discussions, seminars, and other musical programs. Most events are free; admission to symphony concerts ranges from $10 to $40. P.O. Box 1314, Boulder, CO 80306. ✆ **303/447-0513.** www.mahlerfest.org.

Colorado Music Festival *Finds* Begun in 1976, this series is the single biggest annual arts event in Boulder, with visiting musicians from around the world performing in the acoustically revered Chautauqua Auditorium. The festival presents works by composers of the classical through modern eras, such as Bach, Beethoven, Mozart, Dvorak, and Gershwin, plus living composers. It usually runs from mid-June to mid-August, with symphony orchestra performances Thursday and Friday, chamber-orchestra concerts Sunday, and a chamber-music series Tuesday; all shows start at 7:30pm. There's also a children's concert in late June and a free Independence Day concert at CU's Folsom Field. Adult ticket prices range from $12 to $47. 900 Baseline Rd., Cottage 100, Boulder, CO 80302. ✆ **303/449-1397** for general information, 303/440-7666, or visit website for tickets. www.coloradomusicfest.org.

CU Concerts The university's College of Music presents the Artist Series, Music, Theatre, University of Colorado Summer Opera, Takács String Quartet Series, and Holiday Festival at Macky Auditorium and Grusin Music Hall. The Artist Series features an outstanding lineup of classical soloists, jazz artists, dance companies, and multidisciplinary events. Call early for tickets for performances of the renowned Takács String Quartet. The annual Holiday Festival includes the University Symphony Orchestra, university choirs, several smaller ensembles, and soloists from the College of Music's student body and faculty. General admission tickets usually cost between $10 and $40. University of Colorado. ✆ **303/492-8008.** www.cuconcerts.org.

Theater

Colorado Shakespeare Festival *Moments* Considered one of the top three Shakespearean festivals in the United States, this 2-month annual event attracts more than 40,000 theatergoers between late June and late August. Held since 1958 in the University of Colorado's Mary Rippon Outdoor Theatre, and indoors at the University Theatre Main Stage, it offers more than a dozen performances of each of four plays. Actors, directors, designers, and everyone associated with the productions are fully schooled Shakespearean professionals. Tickets run from $7 to $54 for single performances, with series packages also available. Campus Box 277, University of Colorado, Boulder, CO 80309. ✆ **303/492-0554** for information and the box office. www.coloradoshakes.org.

Upstart Crow Theatre Company Specializing in Shakespeare and more contemporary classics, the Upstart Crow is the resident theater company at the Dairy Center for the Arts. They perform on two stages: a 99-seat theater (where no seat is more than three rows from the stage) and an 86-seat proscenium theater. Tickets are $16 to $19; there are also "name-your-price nights." Dairy Center for the Arts, 2590 Walnut St. ✆ **303/442-1415.** www.theupstartcrow.org.

10 Northeastern Colorado

Spacious skies, stretching without interruption hundreds of miles eastward from the foot of the Rocky Mountains. Golden, rolling, irrigated fields of wheat and corn, spreading along the valleys of the South Platte and Republican rivers and their tributaries. A different Colorado exists on the sparsely populated plains of northeastern Colorado, one that inspired James Michener's novel *Centennial.*

Stories of the prehistoric buffalo hunters who first inhabited the region; trailblazers and railroad crews who opened up the area to Anglo settlement; hardy pioneer farmers who endured drought and economic ruin; and ranchers such as John W. Iliff, who carved a feudal empire built on longhorn cattle come alive here. And they're kept alive by the pioneer museums, frontier forts, old battlefields, and preserved downtown districts. This vivid history and the vast open stretches here—wetlands swollen with migrating waterfowl, the starkly beautiful Pawnee National Grassland—are a reminder that Colorado is not just the Rocky Mountains.

1 FORT COLLINS

65 miles N of Denver, 34 miles S of Cheyenne, Wyoming

A bustling college town, Fort Collins was founded in 1864 as a military post on the Cache la Poudre (pronounced *Poo*-der) River, named for a powder cache left by French fur traders. The fort, named for Lieut. Col. William O. Collins, was abandoned in 1867, but the settlement prospered, first as a center for quarrying and farming, then for sugar-beet processing after 1910.

Today Fort Collins is among the fastest-growing cities in the United States, with an average annual growth rate of about 3%. Population leaped from 43,000 in 1970 to 65,000 in 1980 to roughly 140,000 today, not including the many Colorado State University students. CSU was established in 1870; today it is nationally known for its veterinary medicine and forestry schools, as well as its research advances in space engineering and bone cancer.

Fort Collins, just below 5,000 feet in elevation, makes a good base for fishing, boating, rafting, or exploring Rocky Mountain National Park (see chapter 11). It also has several historic sites and offers a treat for beer lovers, with tours of breweries ranging from micro to the huge facilities operated by Anheuser-Busch.

ESSENTIALS

GETTING THERE **By Car** Coming from south or north, take I-25 to exit 269 (Mulberry St., for downtown Fort Collins), exit 268 (Prospect Rd., for Colorado State University), or exit 265 (Harmony Rd., for south Fort Collins). From Rocky Mountain National Park's Estes Park entrances, follow U.S. 34 to Loveland, then turn north on U.S. 287. The drive takes about 1¼ hours from Denver or Estes Park and about 40 minutes from Cheyenne, Wyoming.

Fort Collins

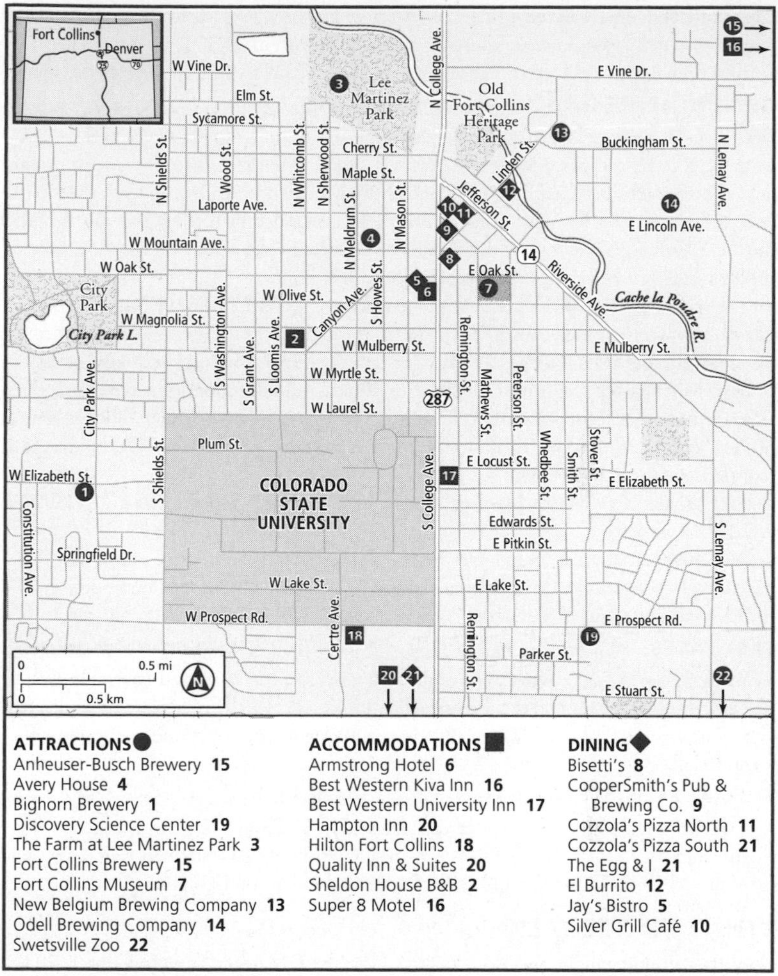

By Plane Many visitors to Fort Collins fly into **Denver International Airport** (see chapter 6). The **Fort Collins–Loveland Municipal Airport** (✆ **970/962-2852;** www.fcgov.com/airport), off I-25 exit 259, 7 miles northeast of downtown Loveland, has charter service.

Shamrock Airport Express (✆ **970/482-0505;** www.rideshamrock.com) provides daily shuttle services between Denver and Fort Collins (one-way rates: $32 adults, $10 children under 13, free for children who sit on a parent's lap). Car rentals in Fort Collins are provided by **Advantage** (✆ **970/224-2211**) and **Enterprise** (✆ **970/224-2592**).

VISITOR INFORMATION The **Fort Collins Convention and Visitors Bureau** operates a visitor information center at 19 Old Town Sq., Ste. 137, Fort Collins, CO 80524 (✆ **800/274-3678** or 970/232-3840; http://visit.ftcollins.com). The state operates a

Colorado Welcome Center, just east of I-25 at Prospect Road (exit 268); the angular, two-story building's unique architecture makes it hard to miss. Both are open daily from 8am to 6pm Memorial Day to Labor Day, and from 8am to 5pm the rest of the year.

GETTING AROUND Fort Collins is located on the Cache la Poudre River, 4 miles west of I-25. College Avenue (U.S. 287) is the main north–south artery and the city's primary commercial strip; Mulberry Street (Colo. 14) is the main east–west thoroughfare. Downtown Fort Collins extends north of Mulberry Street on College Avenue to Jefferson Street; Old Town is a triangle east of and bounded by College Avenue, 4 blocks north of Mulberry. The main Colorado State University campus covers a square mile on the west side of College Avenue 2 blocks south of Mulberry.

The city bus system, known as **Transfort** (✆ **970/221-6620;** www.fcgov.com/transfort), operates more than a dozen routes throughout Fort Collins Monday through Saturday, except major holidays. Its sister system, **Fox Trot,** connects with Loveland's bus system. Most routes run from 6:30am to 6:30pm, and additional runs are made when CSU is in session. All buses have bike racks. Fares are $1.25 for adults, 60¢ for seniors 60 and older and those with disabilities; youths under 18 ride free. Exact change is required. A 10-ride ticket costs $9.

Taxi service is provided 24 hours a day by **Shamrock Yellow Cab** (✆ **970/224-2222**).

Bicycling is a popular and viable means of transportation in Fort Collins. Just about the only place you can't ride is College Avenue. See "Sports & Outdoor Activities," below, for information about bike rentals.

FAST FACTS The **Poudre Valley Hospital** is at 1024 S. Lemay Ave. (✆ **800/252-5784** or 970/495-7000; www.pvhs.org), between Prospect Road and Riverside Avenue just east of downtown. The main **post office** is located at 301 S. Howes St. Contact the U.S. Postal Service (✆ **800/275-8777;** www.usps.com) for hours and other post office locations.

SPECIAL EVENTS Gem & Mineral Show, late March; Cinco de Mayo in Old Town, first weekend in May; Colorado Brewers' Festival in Old Town Square, last full weekend in June; Fabric of Legacies Quilt Show, mid-August; NewWestFest in Old Town and Library Park, mid-August; and Oktoberfest in Old Town, mid-October.

WHAT TO SEE & DO

Families with kids might also want to stop in at the **Discovery Science Center,** 703 E. Prospect Rd. (✆ **970/472-3990;** www.dcsm.org), with interactive exhibits covering everything from dinosaurs to local ecology to electricity.

Anheuser-Busch Brewery ★★ One of Fort Collins's leading employers—and its top tourist attraction—this Anheuser-Busch brewery produces some six million barrels of beer each year, distributed to 10 Western states. The 1¼-hour tours leave from the visitor center and gift shop, and include exhibits on the history of the Anheuser-Busch company, nostalgic displays of ads from the 1950s and other periods, and a complete look at the brewing process, from the huge brew kettles to the high-speed packaging plant that fills 2,000 cans per minute. The tours end at the tasting room with a free sample. You can also visit the barn and see the giant Clydesdale draft horses used to promote Budweiser and other Anheuser-Busch beers since 1933; the first Saturday of each month (year-round) from 1 to 3pm is Clydesdale Camera Day, when the horses are brought out to pose with visitors.

Finds The Great Stupa of Dharmakaya & the Shambhala Mountain Center

Founded by Chögyam Trungpa Rinpoche, a Tibetan Buddhist teacher who was a major figure in bringing his religion to the U.S., the **Shambhala Mountain Center** is about an hour's drive northwest of Fort Collins and a world apart. Located in a rocky, forested mountain valley, the center offers a curriculum ranging from meditation and yoga to gardening and storytelling.

Beyond the educational component, the center is also home to a unique structure: The **Great Stupa of Dharmakaya,** dedicated to Shambhala founder Rinpoche, is the largest and most ornate *stupa* (a spire built in honor of a deceased Buddhist teacher) in the Western Hemisphere. Nuclear-plant engineers were called in to design a structure out of reinforced concrete that would stand for 1,000 years, and artisans hand-painted every last detail. The stupa is open from 9am to 6pm daily; guided tours are offered at 2pm Saturday and Sunday ($10 donation suggested); lunch ($10) is available from 12:30 to 1:30pm.

Lodging ranges from tent-cabins with a communal bathhouse ($69–$79 nightly) to lodge rooms ($80–$139 for a room with a shared bathroom, $159–$199 nightly for one with a private bath), and there is a cafeteria on-site. Many weekend renewal programs are offered, and many programs are open to Bud dhists and non-Buddhists alike. There are also 6 miles of hiking paths on the property.

For further information, contact the Shambhala Mountain Center, 4921 C.R. 68C, Red Feather Lakes, CO 80545 (✆ **888/788-7221** or 970/881-2184; www.shambhalamountain.org).

2351 Busch Dr. (I-25 exit 271). ✆ **970/490-4691.** www.budweisertours.com. Free admission. June–Aug daily 9:30am–4:30pm; Sept daily 10am–4pm; Oct–May Thurs–Mon 10am–4pm. Closed some major holidays.

Avery House Custom-built in 1879 for banker-surveyor Franklin Avery and his wife, Sara, this Victorian home at the corner of Mountain Avenue and Meldrum Street was constructed of red-and-buff sandstone from the quarries west of Fort Collins. The Poudre Landmarks Foundation and the city of Fort Collins purchased the house in 1974, restoring it to its original Victorian splendor—from furniture to wallpaper to wallpapered ceilings. The grounds, with a gazebo, carriage house, and fountain, are popular for weddings and receptions. Allow 30 minutes to 1 hour.

328 W. Mountain Ave. ✆ **970/221-0533.** www.poudrelandmarks.com. Free admission, donations welcome. Wed and Sun 1–3pm except Easter, Christmas, and New Year's Day.

Colorado State University Fort Collins revolves around this university, with its 25,000 students from every state and close to 100 foreign countries. Founded in 1870 as Colorado Agricultural College, it was renamed Colorado A&M in 1935 and became Colorado State University in 1957. The A constructed on the hillside behind Hughes Stadium by students and faculty in 1923 stands for "Aggies" and remains a cherished tradition, even though the school's athletic teams have been called the Rams for decades.

Those wanting to see the campus should stop first at the **visitor center,** at the southwest corner of College Avenue and Pitkin Street (✆ **970/491-4636**), for information, maps, and parking passes. It's open Monday through Friday from 7:45am to 4:45pm when school is in session and 7:30pm to 4:30pm when it is not. Among suggested stops are the **Administration Building,** on the Oval where the school began, and the **Lory Student Center,** at University and Center avenues, which houses a food court, bookstore, art gallery, floral shop, activities center, ballroom, and other facilities. Allow about an hour for a stroll around campus. Guided tours are available daily.

Appointments can be made to visit the renowned **Veterinary Teaching Hospital** and the **Equine Teaching Center.** The **Art Department** has five different galleries with revolving exhibits, and the **University Theatre** in Johnson Hall, on East Drive (✆ **970/491-5562** or 970/491-4849 for tickets), presents student productions year-round. The university's **Environmental Learning Center** covers some 200 acres and has 2.5 miles of trails, with opportunities to see wildlife such as golden eagles, muskrats, and white-tail deer, and a variety of plants. Dogs, horses, and bikes are not permitted on the trails.

Fun Facts Horsing Around

Firecracker, the world's first test-tube horse, was born July 2, 1996, at Colorado State University's Animal Reproduction and Biotechnology Laboratory.

CSU has the full gamut of sports teams. For information on who's playing during your visit, check with the **Athletic Department** (✆ **800/491-7267** or 970/491-5300; www.csurams.com).

University and College aves. ✆ **970/491-1101.** www.colostate.edu.

The Farm at Lee Martinez Park Kids Early-20th-century farm machinery is on display, crafts are sold in the Silo Store, and oats are available to feed the animals. The Farm Museum has exhibits depicting farming techniques from the late 19th and early 20th centuries. Special programs are scheduled year-round, and kids can take advantage of the weekend pony rides ($5) from mid-March through October; group hayrides and tours can be booked in advance. A gift shop is open from mid-March through October. Allow 1 to 2 hours.

600 N. Sherwood St. ✆ **970/221-6665.** $2 admission, free for children under 2. June to mid-Aug Tues–Sat 10am–5pm, Sun noon–5pm; mid-Aug to May Wed–Sat 10am–5pm, Sun noon–5pm.

Fort Collins Municipal Railway One of the few remaining original trolley systems in the nation, this restored 1919 Birney streetcar runs on its original route, along Mountain Avenue for 1½ miles from City Park to Howes Street. It's certainly more for fun than practical urban transport. Allow 30 minutes.

Oak and Roosevelt, at City Park. ✆ **970/482-8246.** www.fortnet.org/trolley. Admission $1 adults, 75¢ seniors, 50¢ children 12 and under. May–Sept Sat–Sun and holidays only, noon–5pm.

Fort Collins Museum Located in the 1903 Carnegie Library Building just a block south of Old Town, this museum boasts the largest collection of Folsom points of any Western museum, plus historical artifacts from Fort Collins as well as pioneer and Victorian objects. You can see an 1850s cabin that is among the oldest surviving pioneer

Brewery Tours

There's no denying that Fort Collins is a beer town. Not only is it home to the giant **Anheuser-Busch Brewery,** with its famous Clydesdale horses (see above), but the city also boasts several excellent microbreweries.

CooperSmith's Pub & Brewing Co. (see "Where to Dine," later in this chapter) provides patrons a view of the brewing process from inside the restaurant and offers tours by appointment. Using English malted barley and hops from the Pacific Northwest, CooperSmith's brews from 6 to 10 ales. For those averse to beer, the brewery also makes its own root beer, ginger ale, and cream soda.

Just northeast of Old Town, across the railroad tracks, **New Belgium Brewing Company ★★**, 500 Linden St. (✆ **888/622-4044** or 970/221-0524; www.newbelgium.com), is a "macro" microbrewery—it ranks in the country's top 15 brewers by volume, second to only Coors of Colorado—producing top-quality Belgian-style ales including the very popular Fat Tire. The always-lively brewery's "Liquid Center" is open Tuesday through Saturday from 10am to 6pm, offering four 3-ounce samples to visitors. Hour-long tours are offered every half-hour Tuesday through Friday from 1 to 3:30pm, and Saturday on the half-hour from 11am to 4pm, with self-guided tours anytime. Beer can be purchased, along with glasses, caps, T-shirts, and other souvenirs.

You'll find **Odell Brewing Company,** Fort Collins's oldest craft brewery, at 800 E. Lincoln Ave. (✆ **970/498-9070;** www.odellbrewing.com). Specializing in English-style ales, Odell produces draft and bottled beers, which are available in restaurants and bars throughout the Rocky Mountains and the Southwest. Tours are given Monday through Saturday at 1, 2, and 3pm, and the tasting room is open Monday through Saturday from 11am to 6pm. Beer, which you can sample before making your choice (or get a taster of each for $4), plus beer glasses, shirts, and other souvenirs are all available.

Also brewing beer in Fort Collins are **Fort Collins Brewery,** 1900 E. Lincoln Ave., #B (✆ **970/472-1499;** www.fortcollinsbrewery.com), which specializes in lagers and has a comfortable tasting room that's open from noon to 6pm Monday through Saturday; and **Bighorn Brewery & Clubhouse,** 1427 W. Elizabeth St. (✆ **970/221-5954**), a bar and grill which brews a variety of beer styles. Contact these breweries for additional information.

buildings in Colorado, an 1864 log officers' mess hall known locally as "Auntie Stone's cabin," and a log one-room schoolhouse built in 1905. Allow 2 hours.

200 Mathews St. ✆ **970/221-6738.** www.fcgov.com/museum. Free admission, $2 suggested donation. Tues–Sat 10am–5pm; Sun noon–5pm.

Old Town A redbrick pedestrian walkway flanked by street lamps and surrounding a bubbling fountain is the focus of this restored historic district, which offers a look at the earliest roots of the city and has plenty of good shopping opportunities. The main plaza, which covers several square blocks, extends diagonally to the northeast from the intersection of College and Mountain avenues; on either side are shops and galleries, restaurants, and nightspots. Outdoor concerts and a string of special events keep the plaza lively, especially from midspring to midfall. Self-guided walking-tour maps are available from the Convention and Visitors Bureau, individual merchants, and city offices. Allow about an hour, more if you want to do a lot of shopping.

Btw. College and Mountain aves. and Jefferson St.

Swetsville Zoo ★ Kids Don't come to Bill Swets's zoo expecting to find animals—not live ones, that is. The sculpture park is a constantly growing menagerie of more than 150 dinosaurs and other real and imaginary animals, flowers, and windmills—all constructed from car parts, farm machinery, and other scrap metal. The whimsical nature of the sculptures is a delight for kids as well as adults. Several galleries offer works by other local artists, ranging from pottery to paintings to sculptures. Allow at least 1 hour.

4801 E. Harmony Rd. ✆ **970/484-9509.** Free admission, donations appreciated. Daily, dawn to dusk. The zoo is 1/4 mile east of I-25, exit 265.

SPORTS & OUTDOOR ACTIVITIES

With its prime location, nestled in the foothills of the Rockies, Fort Collins is ideally situated for those who want to get out under Colorado's clear blue sky and experience the delights of nature. There are several convenient multiuse trails. The **Poudre River Trail** (www.poudretrail.org) is a 10.6-mile paved trail that follows the Poudre River from North Taft Hill Road to East Drake Road and the CSU Environmental Learning Center, passing Lee Martinez Park along the way. Plans call for it eventually to connect with Greeley. The paved **Spring Creek Trail** runs 6.6 miles along Spring Creek, passing through several city parks, from West Drake Road to East Prospect Road at the Poudre River, where you can pick up the Poudre River Trail. Both trails are popular with hikers, cyclers, and skaters during warm weather, and cross-country skiers when the snow flies. Contact the Fort Collins Convention and Visitors Bureau (see "Visitor Information," above) for additional information.

There is a vast amount of public land under the jurisdiction of the U.S. Forest Service within easy access of Fort Collins, offering opportunities for hiking, mountain biking, horseback riding, fishing, camping, snowshoeing, and cross-country skiing. For details, check with the information center of the **Arapaho & Roosevelt National Forests and Pawnee Grasslands,** 2150 Centre Ave., Bldg. E, Fort Collins, CO 80526 (✆ **970/295-6700;** www.fs.fed.us/r2/arnf).

Major Fort Collins city parks include: **City Park,** 1500 W. Mulberry St., with a lake, picnic shelters, playgrounds, playing fields, tennis courts, a fitness course, a pottery studio, miniature train rides, a 9-hole golf course, and an outdoor swimming pool; **Edora Park,** 1420 E. Stuart St., with the excellent Edora Pool Ice Center (a combination of indoor swimming pools and two ice rinks), plus playgrounds, ball fields, tennis courts, a disc golf course, a fitness course, and horseshoe pits; **Rolland Moore Park,** which features an outdoor complex for racquetball and handball players, plus tennis courts, picnic grounds, softball fields, and basketball courts; and **Fossil Creek Park,** with playgrounds, a dog park, a skate park, and a wetlands interpretation site. For information on these and other city recreation facilities, contact the Fort Collins Parks Department (✆ **970/221-6600;** www.fcgov.com/parks).

Among the most popular areas for outdoor recreation is **Horsetooth Reservoir** (✆ **970/679-4554;** www.larimer.org/parks/horsetooth.htm), about 15 minutes west of downtown, just over the first ridge of the Rocky Mountain foothills. The $6^1/_2$-mile-long, man-made lake is named for a distinctive tooth-shaped rock that has long been an area landmark. It's reached via C.R. 44E or 42C, both off Overland Trail, or C.R. 38E off Taft Hill Road. At the reservoir and nearby **Horsetooth Mountain Park,** located several miles west via C.R. 38E (same phone as above), you'll find a wide array of outdoor activities, from fly-fishing to rock climbing to swimming and water-skiing. The entrance fee for the reservoir is $7 per vehicle and $7 per boat; other areas have a day-use fee of $6 per vehicle. Campsites run $10 to $20 a night and basic cabins $30 to $60.

Lory State Park, just west of Fort Collins along the northwest edge of Horsetooth Reservoir (✆ **970/493-1623;** www.parks.state.co.us), is known for its scenic beauty and 20-mile trail system. To get to the park, take U.S. 287 north out of Fort Collins, leaving it to take 54G Road through Laporte, then head west on C.R. 52E for 1 mile, turn left (south) onto C.R. 23N for about $1^1/_2$ miles to C.R. 25G, where you turn right and drive about $1^1/_2$ miles to the entrance. **State Forest State Park,** about 75 miles west of Fort Collins via Colo. 14 (✆ **970/723-8366;** www.parks.state.co.us), covers more than 70,000 acres with spectacular mountain scenery, alpine lakes, and an abundance of wildlife, camping, and trails. See below for details on activities at these areas, and check out **www.parks.state.co.us** on the Web. Day-use fees are $6 per vehicle at both parks; camping runs $8 to $18. At State Forest, a number of cabins and yurts are available for $60 to $110 a night.

BICYCLING There are more than 75 miles of designated bikeways in Fort Collins, including the Spring Creek and Poudre River trails, both paved (see above). There's also a dirt trail, the 5.8-mile Foothills Trail, parallel to Horsetooth Reservoir from Dixon Reservoir north to Campeau Open Space and Michaud Lane. For rentals of road and mountain bikes (about $25 per day), check with **Recycled Cycles,** 4031 S. Mason St. (✆ **970/223-1969;** www.recycled-cycles.com); and if you need repairs for your own bike, visit **Lee's Cyclery,** 202 W. Laurel St. (✆ **970/482-6006;** www.leescyclery.com), or its second location at 931 E. Harmony Rd. (✆ **970/226-6006**). Also see "Mountain Biking," below.

FLY-FISHING Guided fly-fishing trips and clinics are available from **Rocky Mountain Adventures,** 1117 N. U.S. 287 (P.O. Box 1989), Fort Collins, CO 80522 (✆ **800/858-6808** or 970/493-4005; www.shoprma.com). They access the Big Thompson, Cache la Poudre, and North Platte rivers, plus waters on two private ranches and in Rocky Mountain National Park. Half-day guided walk and wade trips cost $135 for one person or $200 for two people, and full-day trips cost $225 and $290, respectively. Those who'd like to strike out on their own might try nearby **Roosevelt National Forest.** For further information, contact the information center of the Arapaho & Roosevelt National Forests and Pawnee Grasslands (see above) and the Colorado Division of Wildlife, 317 W. Prospect Rd. (✆ **970/472-4300;** http://wildlife.state.co.us). Anglers heading out to State Forest State Park have a good chance of catching a variety of trout species; only artificial flies and lures are permitted in some lakes there.

GOLF Fort Collins has three municipal courses: **Collindale Golf Course,** 1441 E. Horsetooth Rd. (✆ **970/221-6651**); **City Park Nine,** 411 S. Bryan Ave. (✆ **970/221-6650**); and **SouthRidge Golf Club,** 5750 S. Lemay Ave. (✆ **970/226-2828**). Tee times should be reserved 3 days in advance. Two privately owned courses open to the public are **Link-N-Greens Golf Course,** 777 E. Lincoln Ave. (✆ **970/221-4818**), and

 Mountain Vista Greens Golf Course, 2808 NE Frontage Rd. (✆ **970/482-4847**). Courses are open year-round, weather permitting, and greens fees are in the $20 to $25 range for 18 holes.

HIKING The **Comanche Peak Wilderness area,** 67,500 acres of pine and spruce-fir forests below expanses of alpine tundra, offers scenic hiking trails along the north and east sides of Rocky Mountain National Park. Contact the information center of the **Arapaho & Roosevelt National Forests and Pawnee Grasslands** (see above).

State Forest State Park has miles of hiking trails and even gives overnight visitors the opportunity to stay in a yurt (see "Skiing & Other Winter Sports," below). There are 26 miles of trails at **Horsetooth Mountain Park** that are shared by hikers, mountain bikers, and horseback riders. Finally, **Lory State Park** has about 20 miles of hiking trails, where the top of Arthur's Rock—a hike of 2 miles—offers a marvelous view across Fort Collins and the northeastern Colorado plains. For more information on these parks, see the introduction to the "Sports & Outdoor Activities" section, above.

HORSEBACK RIDING For the most part, riding is permitted anywhere in the Estes-Poudre District of the Roosevelt National Forest without special permit or license. Horsetooth Mountain Park, State Forest State Park, and Lory State Park have horse trails as well. **Tip Top Guest Ranch,** 22 miles west of Fort Collins in Bellevue (✆ **970/484-1215;** www.tiptopranch.com), offers a variety of guided rides, including 2-hour rides ($40 per person) and pony rides ($8).

KAYAKING **Rocky Mountain Adventures** (see "Fly-Fishing," above) offers kayaking classes covering the Eskimo roll, paddling techniques, and white-water skills. Tuition prices are $60 for the roll, $40 for paddling, and $210 for a 2-day "Fast Track" class. Private instruction is also available.

Classes for all levels are also available from **Poudre River Kayaks, Inc.,** a part of the Mountain Shop, 632 S. Mason St., Fort Collins, CO 80524 (✆ **800/403-5720** or 970/493-5720; www.poudreriverkayaks.com), which also offers kayak rentals ($25 for 2 days, including needed gear).

LLAMA PACKING Using llamas as pack animals is relatively new in the United States, but they are rapidly becoming the pack animal of choice in the Rocky Mountains. Guided llama trips, overnight pack trips, and llama leasing are the specialty of **Buckhorn Llama Co.** (✆ **970/667-7411;** www.llamapack.com). Guided pack trips for one to three people cost $350 per person per day.

MOUNTAIN BIKING A good choice for mountain bikers is the **Foothills Trail,** which runs along the east side of Horsetooth Reservoir from Dixon Dam north almost 7 miles to Michaud Lane. Horsetooth Mountain Park, Lory State Park, and State Forest State Park have excellent trails appropriate for mountain biking as well. In addition, there are yurts for overnighting at State Forest State Park (see "Skiing & Other Winter Sports," below). Also see "Bicycling," above.

RIVER RAFTING River-rafting enthusiasts have ample opportunities for boating the Cache la Poudre, a nationally designated wild-and-scenic river. **Rocky Mountain Adventures** (see "Fly-Fishing," above) offers half-day and full-day trips on the Cache la Poudre and four other regional rivers. Costs range from $44 to $62 for a half-day and $92 for a full day. **A Wanderlust Adventure** (✆ **800/745-7238** or 970/484-1219; www.awanderlustadventure.com) and **A1 Wildwater** (✆ **800/369-4165** or 970/224-3379; www.a1wildwater.com) offer half-day trips on the Cache la Poudre River for similar prices.

SKIING & OTHER WINTER SPORTS Cross-country skiers will find plenty of trails and rolling hills at Lory State Park, surrounding national forests, and in State Forest State Park, where they can stay overnight in a backcountry yurt system owned by **Never Summer Nordic** (✆ **970/723-4070;** www.neversummernordic.com). The eight yurts, which are circular, tentlike canvas-and-wood structures on a high wood deck, have wood-burning stoves, padded bunks, and complete, albeit nonelectrified, kitchens. Most sleep up to 6, and one sleeps at least 10. Winter rates for the entire yurt are $95 to $120. In summer, rates are $65 to $80. State Forest State Park also has an extensive system of snowmobile trails, either groomed or packed, that is separate from its cross-country ski trail system. The park also has several yurts for $60 to $110 a night.

There's year-round **ice skating** at Edora Pool Ice Center (see "Swimming," below); it costs $4.50 for adults to age 59, $3.50 for youths 2 to 17, $4 for seniors 60 to 84, and free for infants under 2 and seniors 85 and older. Call for current hours.

SWIMMING **Edora Pool Ice Center (EPIC),** at 1801 Riverside Dr. in Edora Park (✆ **970/221-6683**), offers swimming, water exercise programs, and diving. The indoor **Mulberry Pool,** 424 W. Mulberry St. (✆ **970/221-6657**), has lap lanes, a diving area, and "Elrog the Frog," a poolside slide. Both have recreational swimming and lap swimming; call for the current schedule or check out **www.fcgov.com/recreation**. The **City Park Outdoor Pool,** 1599 City Park Ave. (✆ **970/416-2489**), is open afternoons during warm weather (closed in inclement weather). Admission at each of the three above pools costs $4 for adults to age 59, $3.25 for youths 2 to 17 and for seniors 60 to 84, and is free for infants under 2 and seniors 85 and older.

WILDLIFE WATCHING Although you'll see some wildlife and water birds at Lory State Park and Horsetooth Reservoir, go to State Forest State Park to try to catch a glimpse of the state's largest moose population, along with elk, mule deer, mountain lions, bighorn sheep, and black bears. State Forest State Park's Moose Visitor Center has wonderful displays and wildlife-viewing information.

SHOPPING

Visitors enjoy shopping in **Old Town Square,** at Mountain and College avenues, with numerous shops, galleries, and restaurants. Old Town is also the site of various events; contact the **Downtown Business Association** (✆ **970/484-6500;** www.downtownfortcollins.com). Northern Colorado's largest enclosed shopping mall is the **Foothills Mall,** just north of the intersection of South College Avenue and Horsetooth Road (✆ **970/226-5555;** www.shopfoothills.com). Anchored by Macy's and Sears, it has more than 100 specialty stores and a food court, and is open Monday through Saturday from 10am to 9pm and on Sunday from 11am to 6pm. There is also a small **antiques district** along South College Avenue between Harmony and Trilby roads.

WHERE TO STAY

Lodging rates in Fort Collins are usually higher in summer, and rooms can be especially expensive and hard to find during college graduation and other major college events. The city has numerous chain motels, including the **Best Western Kiva Inn,** 1638 E. Mulberry St., Fort Collins, CO 80524 (✆ **888/299-5482** or 970/484-2444), with rates of $79 to $119 double; **Best Western University Inn,** 914 S. College Ave., Fort Collins, CO 80524 (✆ **800/937-8376** or 970/484-1984), with rates of $74 to $139 double; **Hampton Inn,** 1620 Oakridge Dr., Fort Collins, CO 80525 (✆ **800/426-7866** or 970/229-5927), with rates of $99 to $139 double; **Quality Inn & Suites,** 4001 S.

Mason St., Fort Collins, CO 80525 (✆ **800/424-6423** or 970/282-9047), with rates of $99 to $199 double; and **Super 8 Motel,** 409 Centro Way, Fort Collins, CO 80524 (✆ **800/800-8000** or 970/493-7701), with rates of $59 to $119 double. Rates may be higher during special events, like college graduation. Room taxes add 9.7% to hotel bills.

Armstrong Hotel ★ Finds The only downtown lodging in Fort Collins, the boutique Armstrong Hotel is a nice balance of new and old. The historic property opened in 1923 but had gone downhill prior to its renovation and reopening under new ownership in 2004. Now it's a model for a downtown hotel turnaround. Some rooms are furnished with antiques, others with contemporary decor, but all have original art on the walls, hardwood floors, and a sleek, spare style that's quite relaxing. The hotel's website offers real-time reservations so you can see exactly which rooms are available, complete with pictures. Interestingly, every room has a different sink, ranging from vintage to modern, and guests enjoy the use of complimentary cruiser bicycles.

259 S. College Ave., Fort Collins, CO 80524. ✆ **866/384-3883** or 970/484-3883. Fax 970/224-5653. www.thearmstronghotel.com. 43 units, including 14 suites. $89–$139 double; $115–$165 suite. AE, DISC, MC, V. **Amenities:** Health club access. *In room:* A/C, cable TV w/pay movies, wireless Internet access (free), kitchen.

Hilton Fort Collins ★ Formerly the Holiday Inn, this newly renovated hotel is the official "Home of the CSU Rams," and boasts a location next to campus and the most complete list of facilities and amenities in town. Guest rooms have contemporary decor and queens or two doubles; the 50 rooms on the hotel's west side are bigger, with king beds and great mountain views, but they're also more expensive. The nine-story hotel, centered on an open lobby, also has a restaurant and lounge, indoor pool, and fitness center.

425 W. Prospect Rd., Fort Collins, CO 80526. ✆ **800/445-8667** or 970/482-2626. Fax 970/224-9209. www.hiltonfortcollins.com. 256 units. $109–$229 double. AE, DISC, MC, V. **Amenities:** Restaurant (American); lounge; indoor pool; fitness center; indoor hot tub; courtesy shuttle. *In room:* A/C, cable TV w/pay movies, wireless Internet access (fee), coffeemaker, hair dryer, iron.

Sheldon House Bed & Breakfast ★★ Step back into the early 20th century at this foursquare Victorian home, with golden oak floors and woodwork, leaded windows, and all the ornate furnishings you would expect from a prominent Fort Collins banker, who had the home built in 1905. The attractive three-story inn has spacious rooms and an abundance of historic charm. It's an ideal choice for couples intent on exploring downtown Fort Collins or visiting the university (just 2 blocks away). Each room is unique—some have four-poster beds—but all have down comforters and attractively appointed private bathrooms with bathrobes. The smallest and least expensive room—Bob's Hideaway—is decorated in Old West style and has one twin bed. Other rooms have queen-size beds, and Miss Olive's Room has a queen and an additional single bed, plus a delightful outdoor balcony. Newly available is the Loft, the former innkeeper's suite, with a microwave, fridge, and washer-dryer.

616 W. Mulberry St., Fort Collins, CO 80521. ✆ **877/221-1918** or 970/221-1917. Fax 970/495-6954. www.thesheldonhouse.com. 5 units. $115–$155 double. Rates include full breakfast. MC, V. Children 10 and older welcome. *In room:* A/C, wireless Internet access (free), no phone.

Camping

There are several full-service campgrounds in the Fort Collins area. The **Fort Collins Poudre Canyon Kampground of America (KOA)** is about 10 miles northwest of downtown at U.S. 287 and Colo. 14 (✆ **800/562-2648** for reservations, or 970/493-9758; www.koa.com), open May through September, with rates of $27 to $30 for tents and $30 to $40 for RVs. A second **KOA,** open year-round, is just off I-25 exit 281, north of Fort Collins at Wellington (✆ **800/562-8142** for reservations, or 970/568-7486; www.fortcollinsnorthkoa.com), with rates of $32 to $37 for RV sites and $27 to $30 for tents per site. Campers looking for a lakeside RV resort might consider the third KOA, **Fort Collins Lakeside KOA,** northwest of Fort Collins at 1910 N. Taft Rd. (✆ **877/254-4063** or 970/484-9880; www.fclakesidecg.com), which is open year-round and has rates of $40 to $72 for RV sites and $32 to $24 for tent sites. Cabins and lodge rooms run about $60 to $130.

Nearby Arapaho and Roosevelt national forests have a number of established campgrounds, many with restrooms, water, and picnic tables. For rates and other information, contact the **Arapaho & Roosevelt National Forests and Pawnee Grasslands** office (see "Sports & Outdoor Activities," above).

WHERE TO DINE

Expensive

Jay's Bistro ★★ CONTEMPORARY/GAME Owned and operated by Jay and Jacki Witlen, longtime local favorite Jay's is an intimate eatery with a creative menu centered on innovative game dishes. Served at the inviting bar or one of several small dining areas decorated in earth tones and blond woods, the menu is interesting to read, from appetizers to dessert, and even better to taste. Try the smoked buffalo carpaccio or a half-dozen fresh oysters to start, before moving on to one of the expertly prepared and presented entrees. The seafood and game, especially the Colorado-raised ostrich filet, deer loin, and lobster ravioli (served in a savory tomato-cognac sauce), are the best choices, but the diverse menu includes pasta and vegetarian dishes, poultry, and beef. There is live jazz Wednesday to Saturday, and the crowd is more mature than most restaurants in town. Lunch is served weekdays until 2pm, and an abbreviated menu is served for 2 more hours.

135 W. Oak St. ✆ **970/482-1876.** www.jaysbistro.net. Reservations recommended. Main courses $16–$33. AE, DC, DISC, MC, V. Mon–Thurs 11am–9pm; Fri 11am–10pm; Sat 5–10pm; Sun 5–8pm.

Moderate

Bisetti's ★★ ITALIAN A delightful atmosphere and good food make Bisetti's one of my favorite dining stops in northeast Colorado. The dining rooms glow with a Tuscan atmosphere and the mahogany bar offers great happy-hour specials. The menu features a variety of homemade pastas, from spaghetti and lasagna to fettuccine and manicotti. (Have the basil fettuccine with chicken.) If it's a romantic dinner you're looking for, ask about the private cubby for two, and split the mouthwatering tiramisu for dessert.

120 S. College Ave. ✆ **970/493-0086.** www.bisettis.com. Reservations accepted for parties of 5 or more only. Main courses $9–$20. AE, DISC, MC, V. Sun–Thurs 11am–9pm; Fri–Sat 11am–10pm.

CooperSmith's Pub & Brewing Co. BREWPUB One of the oldest brewpubs in Colorado, CooperSmith's has been pleasing its customers since 1989. Located in historic Old Town Square, this American brewpub isn't just a place for knocking back a few, but a good place for a feast as well. Within its brick walls is an open kitchen that prepares such traditional pub specialties as fish and chips, as well as less typical bangers and mash and Highland cottage pie, plus fresh fish and steak. You can also get a hamburger or a vegan burger, sandwiches, salads, and soups, plus pizzas baked in a wood-fired oven.

Portions are generous, and the two outdoor patios are popular in good weather. There's also a short children's menu and a great little pool hall with a half-dozen tables, especially popular with university students.

5 Old Town Sq. © **970/498-0483.** www.coopersmithspub.com. Main courses $8–$20. AE, MC, V. Daily 11am–midnight.

Inexpensive

Beyond the restaurants below, **The Egg & I,** 2809 S. College Ave. (© **970/223-5271**), is a good choice for its scrambles and other breakfast favorites; and **El Burrito,** 404 Linden St. (© **970/484-1102**), a family-owned Mexican eatery, specializes in its namesake.

Cozzola's Pizza North ★ PIZZA This is the place to come for the best pizza in Fort Collins. And you don't need to take my word for it: That's been the consensus of the Coloradoan Readers Poll for more than a decade. In addition to offering the traditional chewy white pizza crust, the restaurant offers a whole-wheat poppy-seed or herb crust and several sauce options: sweet basil, fresh garlic, *salsa del drago* (sauce of the dragon), pesto, or spinach ricotta. The long list of available toppings includes artichoke hearts, feta cheese, sun-dried tomatoes, pineapple, and almonds. If you're not in the mood for pizza, you might try the spinach calzone or stromboli.

Cozzola's Pizza South (takeout and delivery only) is located at 1112 Oakridge Dr. (© **970/229-5771**).

241 Linden St. © **970/482-3557.** Pizza $7–$18; lunch main courses $5–$7. AE, MC, V. Tues–Fri 11am–9pm; Sat 11:30am–9pm; Sun 4–8pm.

Silver Grill Cafe ★★ Finds AMERICAN In operation since 1933, this workingman's cafe attracts blue- and white-collar types, as well as seniors, students, and families for tasty, home-style food at very reasonable prices. When there's a line outside, as there often is on weekends, coffee is served to those waiting. You can't go wrong with one of the giant cinnamon rolls, but the rest of the menu is good, too. It's standard American fare: eggs, pancakes, and biscuits 'n' gravy for breakfast (served all day); burgers, sandwiches, and excellent homemade soups for lunch; and "noontime dinners" such as chicken-fried steak and beef pot roast.

218 Walnut St., Old Town. © **970/484-4656.** www.silvergrill.com. Main courses $5–$10. DISC, MC, V. Daily 6:30am–2pm.

PERFORMING ARTS & NIGHTLIFE

The college crowd does much of its drinking and partying at **Washington's,** a large, bustling, multilevel dance and drink emporium at 132 Laporte Ave. (© **970/484-3989**), with a variety of recorded music and drink specials. You might try the somewhat bohemian **Avogadro's Number,** 605 S. Mason St. (© **970/493-5555**), which attracts a mixed crowd for live bluegrass and acoustic music. **Hodi's Half Note,** 167 N. College Ave. (© **970/472-2034**), is a small rock-oriented club. Country-and-western fans head to the big dance floor at the **Sundance Steak House and Country Club,** 2716 E. Mulberry St. (© **970/484-1600**), for live country music and free dance lessons. Sports freaks like the **SportsCaster Bar & Grill,** 165 E. Boardwalk (© **970/223-3553**), which has 50 TV screens and 20 beers on tap. When you just want to quaff a cool beer at the end of the day, **CooperSmith's Pub & Brewing Co.,** 5 Old Town Sq. (© **970/498-0483**), may be the best place in town. Many Fort Collins folk drive 14 miles up the Poudre River to the **Mishawaka Amphitheatre & Restaurant,** 13714 Poudre Canyon (© **970/482-4420;** www.mishawakaconcerts.com), where top regional bands—and occasional national acts—perform during the summer in an outdoor amphitheater on the banks of the Poudre River.

The principal venue for the performing arts in Fort Collins is **Lincoln Center,** 417 W. Magnolia St., at Meldrum Street (✆ **970/221-6730** box office, or 970/221-6735 administration; www.fcgov.com/lctix). Built in 1978, the center includes the 1,180-seat Performance Hall and the 220-seat Mini Theatre, as well as three art galleries and an outdoor sculpture and performance garden. It's home to the Fort Collins Symphony, Opera Fort Collins, Canyon Concert Ballet, Larimer Chorale, OpenStage Theatre, and the Children's Theater. Concert, dance, children's, and travel film series are presented annually. Ticket prices vary considerably, but children's programs are often free or less than $10 and big-name acts and Broadway shows are $30 to $50.

The **Fort Collins Symphony** (✆ **970/482-4823;** www.fcsymphony.org), established in 1948, performs both classical and pops music plus special events with guest performers. There are numerous concerts annually, with July 4 and the December holiday season being two of the big ones.

The **OpenStage Theatre Company,** 400 N. College Ave. (✆ **970/484-5237;** www.openstage.com), is the area's leading professional stage group. It offers six productions annually, as well as various popular, classical, and operatic performances. Recent productions have included *Little Shop of Horrors,* Sam Shepard's *True West,* and Shakespeare's *As You Like It.*

Those who enjoy an intimate theater experience should head to the **Bas Bleu Theatre Company,** 401 Pine St. (✆ **970/498-8949;** www.basbleu.org), which presents a variety of plays, concerts, poetry readings, and other events.

Broadway musicals are presented year-round at **Carousel Dinner Theatre,** 3509 S. Mason St. (✆ **970/225-2555;** www.adinnertheatre.com), Thursday through Saturday at 6pm and Sunday at noon. A choice of three entrees is offered, and prices are $34 to $38, which includes dinner, the show, and tax, but not beverages or dessert. Recent productions have included *The Producers, The Full Monty,* Irving Berlin's *White Christmas,* and *Buddy: The Buddy Holly Story.*

The **Colorado State University School of the Arts** (✆ **970/491-5529;** http://sota.colostate.edu) presents a variety of dramas and musicals, plus concerts by music faculty ranging from jazz to classical during the school year. Many of these events are free or very inexpensive.

2 LOVELAND

13 miles S of Fort Collins, 52 miles N of Denver

Named for Colorado Central Railroad president W. A. H. Loveland in the 1870s, this town now calls itself the "Sweetheart City," because every February, hundreds of thousands of Valentine's Day cards are remailed from here with a Loveland postmark. Established as a trading post in the late 1850s, the community at the foot of the Rockies grew around a flour mill in the late 1860s, before being platted on a wheat field near the railroad tracks in 1877. Today it's a shipping and agriculture center with a population of just over 60,000. It also has a growing arts community and several foundries. Like Fort Collins, its proximity to Rocky Mountain National Park and other outdoor recreation opportunities make this small city a good home base for those exploring the region. Elevation is just under 5,000 feet.

Tips Valentines from Loveland

To get your Valentine's Day cards remailed with a four-line Valentine cachet from Loveland, address and stamp each one, making sure to leave room in the lower left-hand corner of the envelopes for the special Loveland stamp, and mail them in a large envelope to the Postmaster, Attn.: Valentines, Loveland, CO 80538-9998. To ensure delivery by February 14, mail for the United States must be received in Loveland by February 9, and foreign mail should be received by February 3. For additional information, visit the website, **www.withlovefromloveland.com**.

ESSENTIALS

GETTING THERE **By Car** Downtown Loveland is near the junction of U.S. 287 and U.S. 34. Coming from south or north, take I-25 exit 257B. From the west (Rocky Mountain National Park) or east (Greeley), follow U.S. 34 directly to Loveland. The drive takes about 1 hour from Denver.

By Plane Many visitors to Loveland fly into **Denver International Airport** (see chapter 6). The **Fort Collins/Loveland Airport** (✆ **970/962-2852;** www.fcgov.com/airport), off I-25 exit 259, 7 miles northeast of downtown Loveland, offers charter service.

Shamrock Airport Express (✆ **970/482-0505;** www.rideshamrock.com) provides daily shuttle services between Denver and Fort Collins (one-way rates: $32 adults, $10 children under 13, free for children who sit on a parent's lap).

VISITOR INFORMATION The **Loveland Chamber of Commerce** operates a visitor center at 5400 Stone Creek Circle, Loveland CO 80538, just northwest of the junction of I-25 and U.S. 34 (✆ **800/258-1278** or 970/667-5728; www.loveland.org).

GETTING AROUND U.S. 34, Eisenhower Boulevard, is the main east–west thoroughfare and does a slight jog around Lake Loveland, just west of city center. Lincoln Avenue (one-way northbound) and Cleveland Avenue (one-way southbound) make up U.S. 287 through the city. The downtown district is along Lincoln and Cleveland south of Seventh Street, 7 blocks south of Eisenhower.

For a taxi, call **Shamrock Yellow Cab** (✆ **970/224-2222**).

FAST FACTS The hospital, with a 24-hour emergency room, is **McKee Medical Center,** 2000 N. Boise Ave. (✆ **970/669-4640**), in the northeastern part of the city. The **post office** is at 446 E. 29th St., just off Lincoln Avenue. Contact the U.S. Postal Service (✆ **800/275-8777;** www.usps.com) for hours and locations of other nearby post offices.

SPECIAL EVENTS Larimer County Fair and Rodeo, early August; Loveland Invitational Sculpture Show and Sale and Sculpture in the Park, early August; Old-Fashioned Corn Roast Festival, mid- to late August.

SPORTS & OUTDOOR ACTIVITIES

Loveland has more than two dozen city parks, a mountain park, three golf courses, and hiking trails, some of which are discussed below. Information on the city-run recreation sites is available from **Loveland Parks and Recreation Department,** 500 E. Third St. (✆ **970/962-2727;** www.ci.loveland.co.us/parksrec/prmain.htm).

Boyd Lake State Park (✆ **970/669-1739;** www.parks.state.co.us) is located a mile east of downtown Loveland via Madison Avenue and C.R. 24E. One of the largest lakes in the northern Front Range, with 1,700 surface acres when full, Boyd Lake is geared to watersports, including water-skiing (on the south end of the lake only), sailing, and windsurfing. There are sandy beaches for swimming, 148 campsites ($9–$18), including some with electric hookups, plus showers, a dump station, picnic areas, a children's playground, a paved walking/biking trail that connects to the city's path system, two paved boat ramps, and excellent fishing (especially for walleyes). Visitors often see foxes, beavers, coyotes, great horned owls, hawks, eagles, and other wildlife. The daily park entrance fee is $6 to $7. A commercially run **marina** (✆ **970/663-2662**) is open in summer, with boat slips and moorings, a full-service gas dock, boat rentals, bait, groceries, and other supplies.

BICYCLING & JOGGING A combination biking/jogging/walking path that nearly encircles the city joins with a 3-mile path at Boyd Lake State Park. For a map showing completed sections, stop at the Loveland Chamber of Commerce (see above).

GOLF Golfers can enjoy two 18-hole municipal golf courses: **Olde Course at Loveland,** 2115 W. 29th St., which charges $30 for 18 holes; and **Marianna Butte,** 701 Clubhouse Dr., with greens fees of $40 for 18 holes. The 9-hole **Cattail Creek Golf Course,** 2116 W. 29th St. (across the street from Olde Course), charges $8 to $10 for 9 holes. For tee times and other information for all three courses, contact the city (✆ **970/962-2496** or 970/669-5800 for automated reservations; www.ci.loveland.co.us/golf/golfmain.htm).

HIKING The city-run **Viestenz-Smith Mountain Park,** in Big Thompson Canyon 12 miles west of Loveland along U.S. 34, is one of your best bets for hiking, with two trails. The **Summit Adventure Trail,** a moderately difficult 4.8-mile (one-way) hike, climbs 2,700 feet to offer scenic views of the mountains to the west and plains to the east. Those not interested in that much exercise will enjoy the easy 1-mile (one-way) **Foothills Nature Trail.** The park also has picnic tables, a playground, and a fishing stream, and is open year-round.

SWIMMING The city-run **Loveland Swim Beach,** at 29th Street and Taft Avenue, has a free swimming beach, fishing, tennis and racquetball courts, a playground, and a miniature narrow-gauge train. There's also swimming at Boyd Lake State Park (see above).

IN-TOWN ATTRACTIONS

Benson Sculpture Garden ★ More than 100 sculptures—gorillas, giraffes, big pigs, and sledding kids among them—are permanently displayed among the trees, plants, and ponds at this city park, and a few more are added each year. This is also the site of **Sculpture in the Park,** the largest juried outdoor sculpture show in the United States, which takes place each year over the second weekend in August. The show, with all submissions available for purchase, features over 1,000 works by about 200 different sculptors from across the United States and Canada. Show aside, this park is worth a stroll any time of year. Allow 1 hour.

29th St. btw. Aspen and Beech sts. ✆ **970/663-2940.** www.sculptureinthepark.org. Free admission.

Loveland Museum/Gallery Changing exhibits of local historical subjects and the work of regional, national, and international artists fill this fine small museum. The permanent "Life on Main Street" exhibit area depicts Loveland at the turn of the 20th century, and there's an exhibit on the city's Great Western Sugar Factory. The museum also sponsors changing programs on art and history, workshops, concerts, and poetry readings. Allow an hour.

503 N. Lincoln Ave. ✆ **970/962-2410.** www.ci.loveland.co.us. Free admission. Tues–Wed and Fri 10am–5pm; Thurs 10am–9pm; Sat 10am–4pm; Sun noon–4pm.

A FOUNDRY TOUR

For a behind-the-scenes look at an art foundry, make an appointment to tour **Art Castings of Colorado,** 511 Eighth St. SE (✆ **970/667-1114;** www.artcastings.com), which gives foundry tours by appointment.

WHERE TO STAY & DINE

Affordable chain motels in Loveland include the **Best Western Crossroads Inn,** 5542 E. U.S. 34 (at I-25 exit 257B), Loveland, CO 80537 (✆ **888/818-6223** or 970/667-7810), with rates of $85 to $135 double; and **Comfort Inn,** 1500 N. Cheyenne Ave., Loveland, CO 80538 (✆ **800/228-5150** or 970/593-0100), with rates of $89 to $149 double. State and county taxes add about 8% to hotel bills.

For an inexpensive breakfast and lunch, **The Egg & I,** 2525 N. Lincoln Ave. (U.S. 287; ✆ **970/635-0050**), offers numerous egg dishes, plus sandwiches, salads, and Mexican dishes. For dinner, try **Henry's Pub,** 234 E. 4th St. (✆ **970/613-1896;** www.henrys-pub.com), a swank bar and grill behind a historic storefront downtown. Anytime, veer off I-25 at exit 254 for a bite at truck stop extraordinaire **Johnson's Corner,** 2842 S.E. Frontage Rd. (✆ **970/667-2069;** www.johnsonscorner.com), a Colorado classic that hasn't closed its doors since it first opened in 1952.

Sylvan Dale Guest Ranch ★ Kids The Jessup family, owners of this 3,200-acre working cattle and horse ranch on the banks of the Big Thompson River, invites guests to join in with daily ranch chores, horseback riding, and cattle drives, or just kick back, relax, and enjoy the many other available activities. Accommodations here are delightful, quiet, and comfortable; the homey rooms and cabins have a touch of Western charm and are carpeted and furnished with antiques. Some cabins have fireplaces. A lodge, the Heritage, provides a gathering room with a large stone fireplace, library, gift shop, and exhibits on the history of the ranch, which dates to 1946. Horseback-riding lessons, overnight pack trips, breakfast rides, and adventure rides are included in the summer adult riding package. Other activities offered are fly-fishing, hayrides, and white-water rafting. There's also a full slate of entertainment, mostly Western in nature. Summer guests must schedule 6-night full-board stays; the rest of the year, overnight guests are welcome for "bunk and breakfast."

2939 N. C.R. 31D, Loveland, CO 80538. ✆ **877/667-3999** or 970/667-3915. www.sylvandale.com. 26 units, including 11 cabins. Mid-June to late Aug, 6-night packages only, $2,200 per adult, $1,765 nonriding adult package, $1,475 per youth (ages 6–12), $955 per child (ages 3–5); packages include all meals. Year-round nightly rates of $83–$114 room, $96–$155 cabin, $194–$648 guesthouse; includes full breakfast. AE, MC, V. 7 miles west of Loveland via U.S. 34. **Amenities:** Restaurant; outdoor heated pool; 2 tennis courts; children's program (summer); game room. *In room:* No phone.

3 GREELEY

30 miles SE of Fort Collins, 54 miles N of Denver

Greeley is a good spot to see the "other Colorado," the flatlands to the east of the state's famed mountains, as well as to delve into the area's history at several museums. One of the few cities in the world that owes its existence to a newspaper, Greeley was founded in 1870 as a sort of prairie utopia by Nathan C. Meeker, a farm columnist for the *New York Tribune.* Meeker named the settlement—first known as Union Colony—in honor of his patron, *Tribune* publisher Horace Greeley. Through his widely read column,

Meeker recruited more than 100 pioneers from all walks of life and purchased a tract on the Cache la Poudre from the Denver Pacific Railroad. Within a year, the colony's population was 1,000, and it has grown steadily ever since, to nearly 90,000 today.

Greeley's economy is supported in large part by agriculture, with about 75% of Weld County's 1.9 million acres devoted to farming or the raising of livestock. A combination of irrigated and dry-land farms produce grains, including oats, corn, and wheat, and root vegetables such as sugar beets, onions, potatoes, and carrots. The University of Northern Colorado (UNC), with about 11,000 students, offers undergraduate and graduate degree programs. Elevation is 4,658 feet.

ESSENTIALS

GETTING THERE **By Car** Greeley is located at the crossroads of U.S. 34 (east–west) and U.S. 85 (north–south), midway between Denver and Cheyenne, Wyoming—both of which are more directly reached by U.S. 85 than by I-25. U.S. 34 heads west 17 miles to I-25, beyond which are Loveland and Rocky Mountain National Park. To the east, U.S. 34 connects Greeley to Fort Morgan via I-76, 37 miles away.

By Airport Shuttle Visitors who fly into Denver International Airport can travel on to Greeley with the **Rocky Mountain Shuttle Company** (© **888/444-3580** or 970/356-3366; www.rockymountainshuttlecompany.com), with one-way rates of $31 per person.

VISITOR INFORMATION Contact the **Greeley Convention & Visitors Bureau,** 902 7th Ave., Greeley, CO 80631 (© **800/449-3866** or 970/352-3567; www.greeleycvb.com).

GETTING AROUND Greeley is laid out on a standard grid and is an easy city to navigate—provided you don't get confused by the numbered streets (which run east–west) and numbered avenues (which run north–south). It helps to know which is which when you're standing at the corner of 10th Street and 10th Avenue. Eighth Avenue (U.S. 85) is the main north–south street through downtown. Ninth Street is U.S. 34 Business, jogging into 10th Street west of 23rd Avenue. The U.S. 34 Bypass joins U.S. 85 in a cloverleaf just south of town.

The city bus system, called simply **The Bus** (© **970/350-9287;** www.greeleygov.com), provides in-town transportation. For a taxi, call **Shamrock Yellow Cab** (© **970/686-5555**).

FAST FACTS The hospital, **North Colorado Medical Center,** is at 1801 16th St. (© **970/352-4121**), just west of downtown. The **post office** is at 925 11th Ave. Contact the U.S. Postal Service (© **800/275-8777;** www.usps.com) for hours and locations of other area post offices.

SPECIAL EVENTS Colorado Farm Show, late January; the UNC Jazz Festival, April; Semana Latina and Cinco de Mayo, late April and early May; Greeley Stampede, late June and early July (see "Rodeo," later in this chapter); Weld County Fair, early August; Potato Day celebrates Greeley's heritage, early September; Festival of Trees, early December.

SPORTS & OUTDOOR ACTIVITIES

Beginning about 25 miles northeast of Greeley and extending 60 miles east, the 200,000-acre **Pawnee National Grassland** is a popular destination for hiking, mountain biking, birding, wildlife viewing, and horseback riding. Nomadic tribes lived in this desertlike area until the late 19th century, and farmers subsequently had little success in cultivating the grasslands. Although primarily grassland, the dramatic **Pawnee Buttes,** located in the eastern section, are a pair of sandstone formations that rise some 250 feet. A dirt road leads to an overlook that offers good views of the buttes, and from the overlook, a 1.5-mile trail leads to the base of the west butte. The most popular springtime activity is bird-watching, when you're apt to see white-crowned sparrows, lark buntings, meadowlarks, thrushes, orioles, and burrowing owls among the 300-plus species known to frequent the area. Pronghorn, coyotes, mule deer, fox, badger, prairie dogs, and short-horned lizards are among the prolific wildlife.

There are many routes to the grassland; one is to follow U.S. 85 north 11 miles to Ault, then east on Colo. 14 toward Briggsdale, 23 miles away. As much of the grassland is interspersed with private land, those planning to explore the area are advised to stop at the U.S. Forest Service office, 660 O St., Greeley (✆ **970/346-5000;** www.fs.fed.us/r2/arnf).

In Greeley, the 20-mile **Poudre River Trail** is popular with in-line skaters, bikers, walkers, and runners. For more information, call ✆ **970/336-4044** or visit www.poudretrail.org.

SPECTATOR SPORTS

RODEO **Greeley's Stampede ★★** comes to town for 2 weeks, starting in late June, and boasts the world's largest Fourth of July Rodeo. Hundreds of professional cowboys and cowgirls compete for over $400,000 in prize money at Greeley's Island Grove Regional Park, with bareback bronc riding, calf roping, saddle bronc riding, team roping, steer racing, barrel racing, and bull riding. Festivities include country and classic rock concerts, art shows, a carnival, a children's rodeo, fun-runs, a demolition derby, barbecues, and a parade and fireworks display. For information, call ✆ **800/982-2855** or 970/356-2855, or see www.greeleystampede.com.

ATTRACTIONS

Cold war history buffs might also want to schedule a tour of the decommissioned Atlas E silo at **Missile Site Park,** 10611 Spur 257 (✆ **970/381-7451**), which also has basic campsites and a playground.

Centennial Village Museum ★ A fun step back to times long gone, this collection of more than 30 structures—more are added each year—on 5½ acres depicts life on the High Plains of Colorado from the 1860s to the 1940s. Visit the blacksmith shop, print shop, and fire station of the commercial district, and stroll through Hanna Square, surrounded by elegant Victorian homes, a school, depot, and church. Watch for the exhibit on Rattlesnake Kate's dress, a flapper dress made of rattlesnake skins. Frequent living-history demonstrations and special events bring the past alive. In addition, the gardens here are beautiful, with the most colorful displays from July through September. Allow 2 to 3 hours.

1475 A St. at N. 14th Ave., adjacent to Island Grove Regional Park. ✆ **970/350-9220.** www.greeleymuseums.com. Admission $7 adults, $5 seniors 60 and older, $3 children 6–11, free for children 5 and under. Tues–Sat 10am–4pm. Closed mid-Oct to mid-Apr.

Greeley History Museum ★ Opened in 2005, this facility tells the intriguing story of Greeley through its permanent "Utopia: Adaptation of the Great American Desert" exhibit, and it also features several rotating exhibits each year. Housed in the historic former offices of the *Greeley Tribune,* the museum features excellent interpretation of its impressive collection, as well as an interactive children's area. Allow 1 hour.

714 Eighth St. ✆ **970/350-9220.** www.greeleymuseums.com. Free admission. Tues–Fri 8:30am–4:30pm; Sat 10am–4pm. Closed Sun and Mon.

Meeker Home Museum A good place to step back into the 19th century, this impressive two-story adobe home was built in 1870 for Greeley founder Nathan Cook Meeker. Now on the National Register of Historic Places, it is furnished with original family belongings and period antiques, including a 10-foot-tall diamond-dust mirror. Interpretive panels discuss the history of Greeley and vicinity, with an emphasis on the family's struggle for survival after Nathan's death in the 1879 Meeker Massacre. Allow 30 minutes to 1 hour.

1324 Ninth Ave. ✆ **970/350-9220.** www.greeleymuseums.com. Free admission. May–Sept first Sat of the month 10am–4pm. Closed Oct–Apr.

WHERE TO STAY

A building boom of chain motels in the past few years has greatly increased lodging choices. Highest rates are during the summer. Options include the **Country Inn & Suites,** 2501 W. 29th St., Greeley, CO 80631 (✆ **800/456-4000** or 970/330-3404), with rates of $80 to $105 double; and **Comfort Inn,** 2467 W. 29th St., Greeley, CO 80631 (✆ **800/228-5150** or 970/330-6380), which charges $79 to $129 double. Lodging taxes add about 9% to hotel bills.

Greeley Guest House ★ A modern inn—it was built from the ground up and opened in 1996—the Greeley Guest House balances country charm with modern convenience. Centered on a shady courtyard, the brick-and-stucco, ranch-style structure houses two levels of spacious, distinctively furnished rooms, all with gas fireplaces, microwaves, and high-speed wireless Internet access. VCRs and videos are available. The beds are king and queen size, and the wooden furnishings and country-style decor are subtly pleasant.

5401 W. Ninth St., Greeley, CO 80634. ✆ **800/314-3684** or 970/353-9373. Fax 970/353-9297. www.greeleyguesthouse.com. 19 units. $114 double; $134–$164 double for units with whirlpool tubs. Rates include full breakfast. AE, MC, V. Located 1 block north of 10th St. (U.S. 34) in west Greeley. **Amenities:** Access to nearby fitness center; business center; laundry service; dry cleaning. *In room:* A/C, cable TV, wireless Internet access (free), kitchen, fridge, microwave, hair dryer, iron.

Sod Buster Inn Bed & Breakfast ★★ This is a great choice for those who love the ambiance of historic lodging but aren't ready to give up modern conveniences. This attractive three-story inn, which immediately stands out for its octagonal shape and wraparound veranda, is located in a historic district and is surrounded by 100-year-old structures. But the Sod Buster was actually built in 1997, designed to blend in with its older neighbors. The inn offers what may be the best of both worlds—an exceedingly comfortable and attractive modern inn with the look and feel of a historic property, but without the steep staircases, noisy pipes, creaks, groans, and other "charms" you often find in old buildings. Each guest room is individually decorated with a blend of antiques and country-style furnishings, and all include a king or queen bed, desk, good reading lamps, CD players, and comfy seating.

1221 Ninth Ave., Greeley, CO 80631. ✆ **866/501-8667** or 970/392-1221. www.thesodbusterinn.com. 10 units. $119–$149 double. Rates include full breakfast. AE, DISC, MC, V. Well-behaved children accepted with advance notification. *In room:* A/C, cable TV, wireless Internet access (free), hair dryer.

WHERE TO DINE

The Armadillo (Finds (Kids MEXICAN There's a fiesta atmosphere at this downtown Mexican restaurant, which is part of a small regional chain started in 1970 by the Lucio family. The Armadillo serves a variety of Mexican food standards, and many of the recipes come from the Lucio family. Especially recommended are the Mexican Turnover (a deep-fried meat pie) and the Burrito Supreme. Fajitas are also popular.

819 Ninth St. © **970/304-9024.** Main courses $5–$12. AE, DISC, MC, V. Mon–Thurs 11am–9:30pm; Fri–Sat 11am–10pm; Sun 10am–9:30pm.

Fat Albert's Food & Drink AMERICAN A casual and homey family restaurant, this establishment has been in business since 1982. Diners can sit at the bar, tables, or booths bedecked in brick and stained glass, and choose from a lunch menu that includes a good variety of salads, burgers, and sandwiches—ranging from a veggie melt to the perennially popular Monte Cristo. At 5pm, the menu expands to include trout, steak, and several chicken dishes. The award-winning homemade pies and cakes are extra special and include traditional favorites such as apple pie and carrot cake, as well as more exotic recipes such as chocolate zucchini cake and peanut butter pie. For Guinness lovers, Fat Albert's celebrates St. Patrick's Day on the 17th of every month.

1717 23rd Ave., in Cottonwood Square shopping center. © **970/356-1999.** www.fat-alberts.com. Lunch $6–$9; dinner $9–$16. AE, DISC, MC, V. Sun–Thurs 10:30am–9:30pm; Fri–Sat 10:30am–10:30pm.

4 FORT MORGAN

51 miles E of Greeley, 81 miles NE of Denver

A pleasant, laid-back city of just over 11,000 people, Fort Morgan may be best known as the childhood home of famed big-band leader Glenn Miller, who graduated from Fort Morgan High School in 1921 and formed his first band, the Mick-Miller Five, in the city. Established as a military outpost in 1864, the original Fort Morgan housed about 200 troops who protected stagecoaches and pioneers traveling the Overland Trail from marauding Cheyenne and Arapaho warriors. The threat had passed by 1870, and the fort was dismantled, but the name stuck when the city was founded in 1884. Nothing of the fort remains, but a monument on Riverview Avenue marks the fort's site.

The town grew in the 20th century with the establishment of the Great Western Sugar Company for sugar-beet processing, and with a pair of oil discoveries in the 1920s and 1950s. Cattle and sheep ranching remain important today, as well as dairy farming. In addition to sugar beets, the area grows alfalfa, onions, beans, corn, potatoes, sorghum, and wheat. Visitors enjoy the community's historic district and the fine Fort Morgan Museum, and use the town as home base while boating and fishing at Jackson Lake State Park.

About 10 miles east of Fort Morgan is the community of **Brush,** with a population of about 5,000. Also a farming and ranching center, Brush offers food and lodging, easy access to a popular pheasant-hunting area, and a variety of special events. Elevation in the Fort Morgan–Brush area is about 4,300 feet.

ESSENTIALS

GETTING THERE **By Car** Fort Morgan is located on U.S. 34 at I-76, the main east–west route between Denver and Omaha, Nebraska. U.S. 34 proceeds west to Greeley and Estes Park, and east to Wray and southern Nebraska. Colo. 52 is the principal north–south route through Fort Morgan.

By Plane **Denver International Airport** is less than 90 minutes away (p. 69).

By Train **Amtrak** (© **800/872-7245;** www.amtrak.com) trains make daily stops on the Denver-to-Chicago route.

VISITOR INFORMATION Contact the **Fort Morgan Area Chamber of Commerce,** 300 Main St. (P.O. Box 971), Fort Morgan, CO 80701 (✆ **800/354-8660** or 970/867-6702; www.fortmorganchamber.org). For information on events and activities in the nearby community of Brush, contact the **Brush Chamber of Commerce,** 1215 Edison St., Brush, CO 80723 (✆ **800/354-8659** or 970/842-2666; www.brushchamber.org).

GETTING AROUND Platte Avenue (U.S. 34) is Fort Morgan's principal east–west thoroughfare. The north–south artery, Main Street, divides it and other streets into east and west designations. I-76 exits onto Main Street north of downtown.

FAST FACTS The **Colorado Plains Medical Center,** with a 24-hour emergency room, is located at 1000 Lincoln St. in Fort Morgan (✆ **970/867-3391**). The **Fort Morgan Post Office** is at 300 State St. Contact the U.S. Postal Service (✆ **800/275-8777;** www.usps.com) for hours and the addresses of other post offices.

SPECIAL EVENTS Glenn Miller Dancin' on the Plains in Fort Morgan, fourth weekend in June; Brush Rodeo, early July.

WHAT TO SEE & DO

Fort Morgan Museum ★★ Finds Among the most interesting small-town museums in Colorado, the Fort Morgan Museum has an impressive collection of northeastern Colorado American Indian artifacts, beginning with a 13,000-year-old tool. Other permanent exhibits cover the history of farming, ranching, the military, and the railroad in Morgan County. My favorites: a display on the life of native son Glenn Miller and a fully restored 1920s soda fountain. The museum also hosts traveling exhibits and stages temporary shows from its collection, and is a good source for genealogical information in the area. There's a gift shop, and you'll find picnic areas and a playground in the surrounding City Park. Allow about 2 hours.

City Park, 414 Main St. ✆ **970/524-4010.** www.ftmorganmus.org. Free admission. Mon and Fri 10am–5pm; Tues–Thurs 10am–8pm; Sat 11am–5pm.

Rainbow Bridge Also called the James Marsh Arch Bridge, this 11-arch concrete bridge was built over the South Platte River in 1923, at a construction cost of $69,290. Listed on the National Register of Historic Landmarks and the National Register of Engineering Landmarks, the 1,110-foot bridge is the only rainbow-arch design in Colorado. For information, contact the Fort Morgan Museum (see above), and allow 15 to 30 minutes.

At the NW corner of Riverside Park (I-76 and Colo. 52).

Sherman Street National Historic District The Fort Morgan Museum (see above) publishes a walking-tour brochure both for Sherman Street and for the 9-block downtown district, the latter noting 44 buildings that made up the early town. These are available at the chamber of commerce (see "Visitor Information," above) and the museum. Four Victorian mansions in the Sherman Street District are of special interest. Located around the intersection of Sherman Street and East Platte Avenue, they include the Warner House, an 1886 Queen Anne home; the Curry House, an 1898 Queen Anne with decorative spindle work porches, a barn, a carriage house, and a water tower; the Graham House, a 1914 American foursquare home; and the Bloedorn House, a 1926 brick Georgian revival–style building. Each is associated with a prominent city pioneer. They are private homes, not open to the public, but it's worth the walk to see the architecture from the sidewalk. For additional information contact the Fort Morgan Museum (see above). Allow at least 2 hours.

400 block of Sherman St.

SPORTS & OUTDOOR ACTIVITIES

The main recreation spot in this area is **Jackson Lake State Park,** located about 25 miles northwest of Fort Morgan (✆ **970/645-2551;** www.parks.state.co.us). The park offers swimming, boating, fishing, and picnicking in summer; and ice fishing, ice skating, and cross-country skiing in winter ($6 day-use fee).

Water-skiing, sailboarding, and boating are the most popular activities on the park's 2,700-acre reservoir, which has sandy beaches and boat ramps. The **Shoreline Marina** (✆ **970/645-2628;** www.shorelinemarina.biz) has fuel, fishing gear, boating supplies, and a snack bar May through September on weekends (depending on lake water levels).

Anglers try for walleye, bass, and catfish, except when fishing is prohibited during the migratory waterfowl season. There's also a .5-mile nature trail, plus 260 campsites (some with electric hookups), showers, and a dump station ($14–$18). To get to Jackson Lake, follow Colo. 144 northwest for 22 miles; the park is about 2½ miles north of the community of Goodrich via paved C.R. 3.

One of the nicest city parks in the region is **Riverside Park** ★ (✆ **970/867-3808;** www.cityoffortmorgan.com), located off Main Street between I-76 and the South Platte River. Admission is free, and it has a large children's playground, more than 4 miles of nature trails along the river, tennis and basketball courts, horseshoe pits, an in-line hockey rink, a picnic area, a duck pond where kids can fish, and a swimming pool open in summer. The park offers free tent camping and free overnight RV camping with electrical hookups.

SPECTATOR SPORTS

RODEO The **Brush Rodeo,** billed as the world's largest open rodeo (both amateurs and professionals compete), is held in Brush July 2 to 4, with all the usual rodeo events (including the popular wild-cow milking contest), plus a parade, kids' games, a dance, and fireworks. Contact the Brush Chamber of Commerce (see above) or check the Web at **www.brushcolo.com**.

STOCK-CAR RACING Fans head to Fort Morgan's I-76 Speedway (✆ **970/867-2101;** www.i-76speedway.com), where they can see late-model, street stocks, ministocks, midgets, minisprints, microsprints, dwarf cars, and IMCA modifieds race on a quarter-mile, high-banked dirt oval track from late March through October.

WHERE TO STAY & DINE

Lodging possibilities in Fort Morgan include the well-maintained **Best Western Park Terrace Inn,** 725 Main St. (✆ **888/593-5793** or 970/867-8256), which charges $70 to $95 double and has a good restaurant on-site (see below); and the **Super 8,** 1220 N. Main St. (✆ **800/800-8000** or 970/867-9443), charging $60 to $70 double. State and county taxes add 8.5% to hotel bills.

Restaurants in Fort Morgan include **Memories,** at the Best Western Park Terrace Inn (✆ **970/867-8205;** www.memoriesrestaurant.com), which offers a good selection of well-prepared American standards and Mexican plates daily from 6am to 9pm, with prices for lunch $7 to $10, and for dinner $9 to $23.

Another good dining choice in Fort Morgan is **Country Steak Out,** 19592 E. Eighth Ave. (✆ **970/867-7887**), which serves steak and seafood (and has a big salad bar), with prices from $10 to $30 at dinner. It's open Tuesday through Saturday from 6 to 9pm and Sunday for brunch from 10am to 2pm.

5 BURLINGTON

163 miles E of Denver, 385 miles W of Topeka, Kansas

As the first major Colorado community to greet motorists traveling I-70 from the east, Burlington is a good place to overnight at the beginning or end of a Colorado vacation. It's the largest town in east-central Colorado, with a population of about 3,500, and sits at an elevation of 4,165 feet. Those passing through might want to see how the community has preserved its turn-of-the-20th-century heritage with an impressive Old Town and famous carousel. Dry-land farmers established Burlington and other "outback" communities along the Kansas City–Denver rail line in the 1880s, and while wheat is very much the dominant crop today, you'll also find corn, dry beans, and sunflowers.

ESSENTIALS

GETTING THERE **By Car** Burlington is located on east–west I-70, 13 miles from the Kansas border. U.S. 385, which runs the length of Colorado's eastern frontier, makes a north-to-south pass through the town.

VISITOR INFORMATION The **Colorado Welcome Center** is along I-70 beside Burlington Old Town (✆ **800/288-1334** or 719/346-5554), and is open daily from 8am to 6pm in summer and 8am to 5pm in winter. For information specifically on Burlington, contact the **Burlington Chamber of Commerce** (✆ **719/346-8070;** www.burlington colo.com).

GETTING AROUND The town lies on the north side of I-70. Rose Avenue (U.S. 24) runs east–west through the center of Burlington. Main north–south streets are Eighth Street (U.S. 385 N.) on the east side of town, 14th Street (which locals call Main St.), and Lincoln Street (U.S. 385 S.) on the west side of town.

FAST FACTS The **Kit Carson County Memorial Hospital** is at 286 16th St. (✆ **719/346-5311**). The **post office** is at 259 14th St. Contact the U.S. Postal Service (✆ **800/275-8777;** www.usps.com) for hours and other information. During inclement weather (but not at other times), you can get a **road condition report** by calling ✆ **719/ 346-8778.**

SPECIAL EVENTS Kit Carson County Fair, August; Old Town Ghost Town, last Saturday in October; Country Christmas Jubilee at Old Town, first Sunday in December; and Storybook Christmas and Parade of Lights, December.

WHAT TO SEE & DO

Kit Carson County Carousel ★★★ Kids This is the town's pride and joy, the only National Historic Landmark in eastern Colorado, and a must-see for everyone who stops in Burlington. Carved in 1905 by the Philadelphia Toboggan Company for Denver's Elitch Gardens, and one of the few wooden carousels left in America that still wears its original coat of paint, it's fully restored and operational. The 46 stationary animals—mostly horses, but also giraffes, zebras, camels, a hippocampus (sea horse), a lion, a tiger, and others—march counterclockwise around three tiers of oil paintings, representing the lifestyles and interests of the American Victorian middle class. A Wurlitzer Monster Military Band Organ, one of only two of its size and vintage in operation today, provides the music, and a terrific new museum opened in 2007 to provide fascinating historic context. Allow 1 hour.

County Fairgrounds, 15th St. at Colorado Ave. ✆ **719/348-5562.** www.kitcarsoncountycarousel.com. Admission 25¢ per ride. Memorial Day to Labor Day daily 11am–6pm. Private tours given at other times with 2 weeks' advance notice.

Old Town ★ Kids For a look at the real Old West, take a trip to Old Town. Close to 20 turn-of-the-20th-century-style Old West buildings make up this living-history museum, where you're likely to see a gunfight or, in the summer months, a cancan show in the Longhorn Saloon. Nine of the buildings are original historic structures, moved to Old Town, and the rest are reproductions, all furnished with genuine Old West artifacts to show what it was like here 100 years ago. Visit the blacksmith shop, bank, law office, newspaper office and operating print shop, general store, schoolhouse, and barn. The railroad depot, built in 1889 in Bethune, Colorado, is the oldest structure in Old Town. There's the saloon, where you're likely to find the piano player tinkling the ivories, or stop at the church, built in 1921 and still used for weddings. The dollhouse is home to a number of unique dolls, and in the wood shop you'll see tools more than 100 years old. The original Burlington town jail cells are also here, and the two-story, six-bedroom Manor house, built in the early 1900s, is magnificent, furnished with splendid antiques of the period. There's also a sizable gift shop. On summer weekends, the horse-drawn "Old Town Express" gives rides to the Kit Carson County Carousel (see above). Allow 1 to 3 hours.

420 S. 14th St. ✆ **800/288-1334** or 719/346-7382. Admission $6 adults 19–59, $5 seniors 60 and older, $4 youths 12–18, $2 children 3–11. Mon–Sat 9am–5pm, Sun noon–5pm. Last admission at 4pm.

SPORTS & OUTDOOR ACTIVITIES

As soon as the winter snows are gone, the folks in Burlington and other eastern Colorado communities head to the beach, and that means **Bonny Lake State Park,** 23 miles north of Burlington on U.S. 385, then east on county roads 2 or 3 for about 1½ miles (✆ **970/354-7306;** www.parks.state.co.us). Built as a flood control project in 1951, the reservoir contains 1,900 surface acres of relatively warm water, perfect for swimming, water-skiing, windsurfing, and fishing. The 5,000-acre park provides opportunities to see wildlife, with some 250 species of birds, mule and whitetail deer, coyotes, badgers, muskrats, bobcats, beavers, and rabbits. The daily entrance fee is $6 per vehicle.

Finds Plains Kitsch

There are two noteworthy specimens of roadside Americana on the eastern plains. You can supposedly see six states from the **Wonder View Tower,** just off I-70 in Genoa (✆ **719/763-2309**), after you climb the ramshackle staircases to the observation deck, which has been standing for the better part of a century. Below, a former dancehall has morphed into a junk shop over the years, full of bizarre objects in its nooks and crannies, including taxidermy of several two-headed animals. The tower is open 9am to 5pm daily (but it's best to call to make sure if you can) and admission is $1. Just to the east of Genoa in the dinky town of Arriba, **Grandpa Jerry's Clown Museum,** 22 Lincoln Ave. (✆ **719/768-3257**), showcases some 3,000 clowns, from music boxes to paint-by-numbers masterworks to dolls. Admission is free and the museum is open by appointment.

The lake has four campgrounds, with a total of 190 campsites ($14–$18). Some sites have electric hookups, and several are handicapped accessible. Facilities include boat-launching ramps, restrooms, pay showers, picnic areas, a short nature trail (not handicap accessible), and a fish-cleaning station. Fishing for walleye, northern pike, and a variety of bass is good here. While not maintained, the gravel roads around the lake make a 17-mile loop that's perfect for hiking and biking.

A family stop in Burlington is **Outback Territory Park Playground,** which covers a full block between 15th and 16th streets and Railroad and Martin avenues. It's got a marvelous playground (designed by Burlington Elementary School children) and delightful picnic areas with lots of shade. Admission is free. For additional information, contact the Colorado Welcome Center in Burlington or the Burlington Chamber of Commerce (see "Visitor Information," above).

If you're traveling this way in winter, stop by for an afternoon of cross-country skiing, ice skating, or ice fishing, but don't forget your long underwear—winter winds are bone chilling out here on the plains. During winter, electric and water are available in the campgrounds, and there are vault toilets, but the showers and flush toilets are shut down.

WHERE TO STAY

Because Burlington is simply an overnight stop for many travelers along the interstate highway, you won't have any trouble finding a room here, with all the motels easily accessible from I-70 exits 437 and 438. In addition to the motels discussed below, there's a **Comfort Inn,** 282 S. Lincoln St. (✆ **800/228-5150** or 719/346-7676), with double rates of $70 to $120; and an **America's Best Value Inn,** 2100 Fay St. (✆ **719/346-5627**), charging double rates of $50 to $70. Tax adds about 8% to lodging bills.

Chaparral Motor Inn ★ Value This conveniently located modern motel is an excellent choice for those seeking an exceptionally clean and well-maintained place to spend the night at a reasonable price. The rooms are set back a bit from the road, so they're fairly quiet. Rooms and bathrooms are of average size, simply but attractively decorated in a contemporary Southwestern style. All rooms have a small working desk and a table with two chairs; refrigerators and hair dryers are available on request. An adjacent restaurant serves three meals daily.

405 S. Lincoln St., Burlington, CO 80807. ✆ **800/456-6206** or 719/346-5361. Fax 719/346-8502. 39 units. $45–$60 double; rates include continental breakfast. AE, DISC, MC, V. Small pets accepted ($7 per dog per night; $10 per cat per night). **Amenities:** Outdoor heated pool (seasonal); exercise room. *In room:* A/C, cable TV, wireless Internet access (free), coffeemaker.

Claremont Inn ★★ One of the few bed-and-breakfasts on Colorado's eastern plains, the striking Claremont Inn is a good choice for those who want more than a clean place to sleep for the night. The three-story inn blends an intimate atmosphere with modern conveniences, and features uniquely decorated rooms such as the flower- and birdhouse-bedecked Waverly Room and the romantic Secret Garden Room, with its own whirlpool for two. The public rooms, which include the domed-ceiling Hearth Room and a movie theater, are similarly impressive. Breakfasts might include bananas Foster or French toast; the inn also serves eclectic dinners (add about $90 per couple), and it regularly hosts cooking weekends, often with French and Italian themes. Smoking is not permitted.

800 Claremont Dr., Stratton, CO 80836. ✆ **888/291-8910** or 719/348-5125. www.claremontinn.com. 10 units. $149–$219 double; rates include full breakfast. AE, DC, DISC, MC, V. Located 18 miles west of Burlington, off I-70, exit 419. *In room:* A/C, cable TV/VCR, wireless Internet access (free), fridge, coffeemaker, hair dryer, iron.

The Route Steakhouse AMERICAN This family restaurant boasts an especially good salad bar and a large selection of well-prepared American staples. The dining room is what you might call contemporary Western, with solid wood tables and booth seating. There are various half-pound burgers and sandwiches for lunch—try the Trail Boss sandwich, piled high with brisket, turkey, and ham, and topped with melted Swiss and cheddar. From the dinner menu, the 14-ounce rib-eye and the house specialty, chicken-fried steak, are excellent choices. Salads here are also very good, especially the Cobb.

218 S. Lincoln St. ✆ **719/346-8790.** Lunch items $5–$10; dinner entrees $6–$22. AE, DISC, MC, V. Mon–Thurs 5–9pm; Fri–Sat 11am–10pm. Closed Sun.

11

The Northern Rockies

Literally and figuratively, this is the mother lode. It's where scrappy silver and gold miners struck it rich time and time again in the late 19th century, yet it's also where Colorado's rugged beauty is shown off to fullest effect.

The northern Rockies begin just outside of Denver and extend on either side of the meandering Continental Divide down sawtooth ridgelines, through precipitous river canyons, and across broad alpine plains. Here snowfall is measured in feet, not inches; it's where you'll find Colorado's hottest ski resorts—Aspen, Vail, and Steamboat—as well as a few smaller areas that are making headlines, such as Winter Park. And then there's Summit County, with possibly more major ski areas within a half-hour's drive than anywhere else in the country. If you're easily bored, rent a condo or take a room in Breckenridge and spend your days skiing a different mountain every day. With Copper, Keystone, Arapahoe Basin, and even tiny Loveland all within a few miles' drive, you've got plenty of choices.

When spring's sun finally melts away the walls of white, a whole new world opens up amid the brilliantly colored alpine wildflowers. You can head to any of the area's ski resorts to shop their stores and hike or cycle their trails. Perhaps best of all, though, is a trip to the West's premier mountain vacation spot, and my favorite mountain destination in Colorado—Rocky Mountain National Park. Here you can enjoy some of the most spectacular scenery in America, as well as a broad range of outdoor activities, from hiking to wildlife viewing to cross-country skiing.

1 ESTES PARK & GRAND LAKE

71 miles NW of Denver, 42 miles SW of Fort Collins, 34 miles NW of Boulder

Estes Park is the eastern gateway to Rocky Mountain National Park, and Grand Lake is the closest town to the park's western entrance. Of the two, Estes Park is more developed. It has more lodging and dining choices, as well as a few noteworthy sights that are worth a visit. If you're driving to Rocky Mountain National Park via Boulder or Denver, you'll want to make Estes Park your base camp.

Grand Lake is a more rustic spot, with plenty of places to camp, a number of motels, and a few guest ranches. If you're coming from Steamboat Springs or Glenwood Springs, Grand Lake is a more convenient base. At any time of year, you can get there via U.S. 34. In summer, you can also get to Grand Lake by taking the Trail Ridge Road through Rocky Mountain National Park from Estes Park. Both routes are scenic, although the national park route (closed in winter) is definitely prettier.

ESTES PARK

Unlike most Colorado mountain communities where mining was the economic bedrock before tourism emerged, Estes Park (elevation 7,522 ft.) has always been a resort town. Long known by Utes and Arapahos, it was "discovered" in 1859 by rancher Joel Estes. He soon sold his homestead to Griff Evans, who built it into a dude ranch. One of

Evans's guests, the Welsh Earl of Dunraven, was so taken by the region that he purchased most of the valley and operated it as his private game reserve, until thwarted by such settlers as W. E. James, who built Elkhorn Lodge as a "fish ranch" to supply Denver restaurants.

The growth of Estes Park, however, is inextricably linked with two individuals: Freelan Stanley and Enos Mills. Stanley invented the kerosene-powered Stanley Steamer automobile in 1899 together with his brother Francis, then settled in Estes Park in 1907, launched a Stanley Steamer shuttle service from Denver, and in 1909 built the landmark Stanley Hotel. Mills was one of the prime advocates for the establishment of Rocky Mountain National Park. Although less well known than John Muir, Mills is an equally important figure in the history of the U.S. conservation movement. His efforts increased sentiment nationwide for preserving wild lands and resulted in President Woodrow Wilson signing a bill to set aside 400 square miles for Rocky Mountain National Park in 1915. Today the park attracts some three million visitors annually. Estes Park, meanwhile, has a year-round population of about 6,000.

Essentials

GETTING THERE **By Car** The most direct route is U.S. 36 from Denver and Boulder. At Estes Park, U.S. 36 joins U.S. 34, which runs up the Big Thompson Canyon from I-25 and Loveland, and continues through Rocky Mountain National Park to Grand Lake and Granby. An alternative scenic route to Estes Park is Colo. 7, the "Peak-to-Peak Scenic Byway" that traverses Central City (Colo. 119), Nederland (Colo. 72), and Allenspark (Colo. 7) under different designations.

By Plane The closest airport is Denver International Airport, 80 miles away. The **Estes Park Shuttle** (✆ **970/586-5151;** www.estesparkshuttle.com) connects DIA with Estes Park. Rates are $45 one-way and $85 round-trip.

VISITOR INFORMATION The **Estes Park Convention & Visitors Bureau,** 500 Big Thompson Ave., Estes Park, CO 80517 (✆ **800/443-7837** or 970/577-9900; www.estesparkcvb.com), has a visitor center on U.S. 34, just east of its junction with U.S. 36. In summer, it's open Monday through Saturday from 8am to 9pm and Sunday from 9am to 5pm; winter hours are Monday through Saturday from 9am to 5pm and Sunday from 10am to 4pm.

GETTING AROUND Shuttle buses began operating in 2006 throughout the business district of Estes Park and from Estes Park into Rocky Mountain National Park. The buses run daily from July through Labor Day; schedules are available at the Estes Park Visitor Center (see "Visitor Information," above).

Local taxi service is provided by **Stanley Brothers Taxi Company** (✆ **970/577-7433**).

FAST FACTS The hospital, **Estes Park Medical Center,** with a 24-hour emergency room, is at 555 Prospect Ave. (✆ **970/586-2317**). The **post office** is at 215 W. Riverside Dr. Call the U.S. Postal Service (✆ **800/275-8777;** www.usps.com) for hours and locations of other post offices. For statewide **road conditions,** call ✆ **303/639-1111** or check www.cotrip.org. For a **current weather report,** call ✆ **970/586-5555.**

SPECIAL EVENTS Jazz Fest and Art Walk, mid-May; the Wool Market, mid-June; the Scandinavian Mid-Summer Festival, on a weekend near summer solstice; the Rooftop Rodeo, mid-July; Longs Peak Scottish Irish Festival, the weekend after Labor Day; Autumn Gold—A Festival of Brats and Bands, late September; Elk Fest, early October.

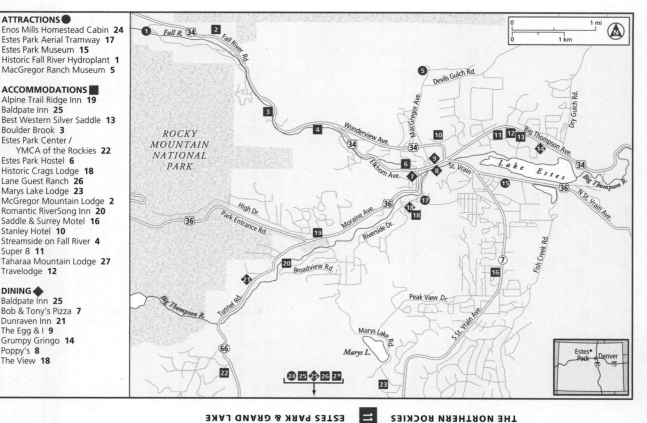

ATTRACTIONS ●
Enos Mills Homestead Cabin **24**
Estes Park Aerial Tramway **17**
Estes Park Museum **15**
Historic Fall River Hydroplant **1**
MacGregor Ranch Museum **5**

ACCOMMODATIONS ■
Alpine Trail Ridge Inn **19**
Baldpate Inn **25**
Best Western Silver Saddle **13**
Boulder Brook **3**
Estes Park Center /
YMCA of the Rockies **22**
Estes Park Hostel **6**
Historic Crags Lodge **18**
Lane Guest Ranch **26**
Marys Lake Lodge **23**
McGregor Mountain Lodge **2**
Romantic RiverSong Inn **20**
Saddle & Surrey Motel **16**
Stanley Hotel **10**
Streamside on Fall River **4**
Super 8 **11**
Taharaa Mountain Lodge **27**
Travelodge **12**

DINING ◆
Baldpate Inn **25**
Bob & Tony's Pizza **7**
Dunraven Inn **21**
The Egg & I **9**
Grumpy Gringo **14**
Poppy's **8**
The View **18**

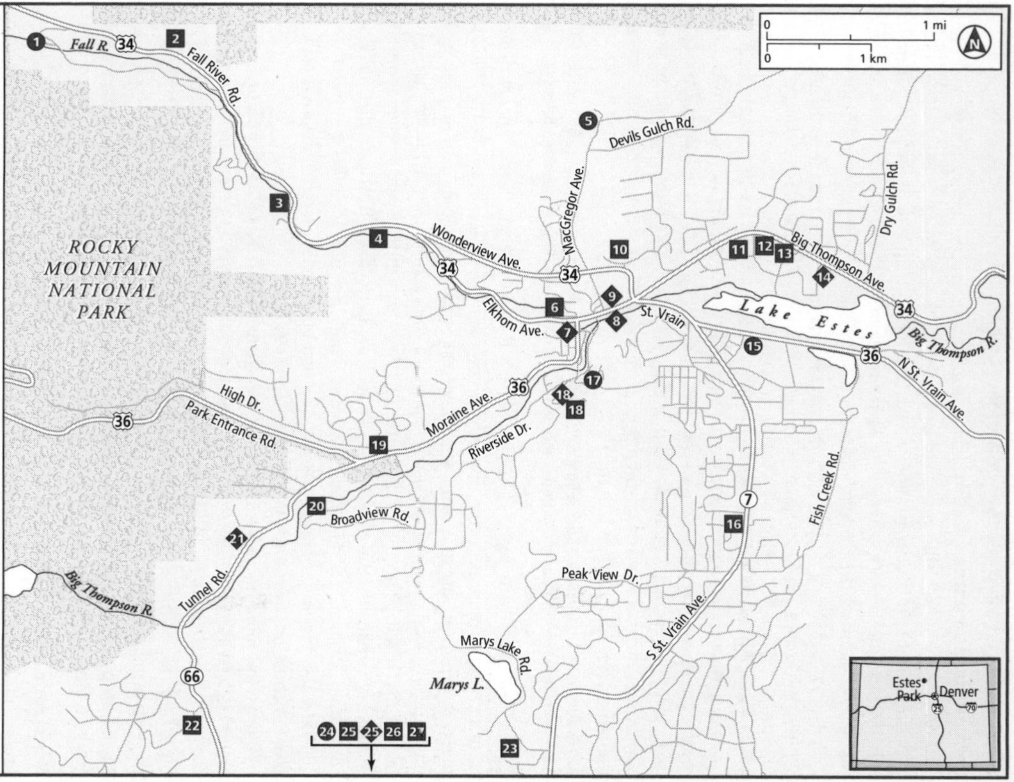

What to See & Do

In addition to the attractions discussed here, be sure to check out the art galleries and other visual arts venues discussed under "Shopping," below.

Enos Mills Homestead Cabin This 1885 cabin and homestead belonged to the late-19th- and early-20th-century conservationist Enos A. Mills, a major force behind the establishment of Rocky Mountain National Park. A short walk down a nature trail brings you to the cabin, still owned by his descendants, with displays of his life and work. Also on the premises are a bookshop and a gallery. Allow 30 minutes to 1 hour.

6760 Colo. 7 (opposite Longs Peak Inn). ✆ **970/586-4706.** $5 adults, $2.50 children 6–12. Memorial Day to Labor Day usually Mon–Tues 11am–4pm, but call to confirm. By appt. Wed–Sun and rest of the year.

Estes Park Aerial Tramway ★ This tram, which climbs 1,100 vertical feet in less than 5 minutes, offers a great ride up the side of Prospect Mountain and provides spectacular panoramic views of Longs Peak, the Continental Divide, and Estes Park village itself. Its lower terminal is a block south of the post office. You'll find a gift shop, a snack bar, and an observation deck at the upper terminal, and numerous trails converge atop the mountain. Allow at least 1 hour.

420 E. Riverside Dr. ✆ **970/586-3675.** www.estestram.com. Admission $9 adults, $8 seniors 60 and older, $4 children 6–11, free for children 5 and under. Late May to mid-Sept daily 9am–6:30pm.

Estes Park Museum ★★ The lives of early homesteaders in Estes Park are depicted in this excellent museum, which includes a completely furnished turn-of-the-20th-century log cabin, an original Stanley Steamer car, and a changing exhibit gallery. The museum also features a permanent "Tracks in Time" exhibit that helps visitors see the impact that ordinary people, from the region's American Indians and women pioneers to today's area residents and travelers, have had on Estes Park. You can also see Rocky Mountain National Park's original headquarters building, which has been moved here. In addition, the museum sponsors a variety of programs and distributes a historical walking-tour brochure on downtown Estes Park. Allow 1½ hours.

Under the museum's administration, the **Historic Fall River Hydroplant,** at 1754 Fish Hatchery Rd., chronicles the 1909 construction and 1982 destruction of the town's one-time power supply, washed away when a dam inside Rocky Mountain National Park built by F. O. Stanley gave way. It's open Memorial Day through Labor Day, Tuesday through Sunday from 1 to 4pm.

200 Fourth St. at U.S. 36. ✆ **970/586-6256.** www.estesnet.com/museum. Free admission; donations accepted. May–Oct Mon–Sat 10am–5pm, Sun 1–5pm; Nov–Apr Fri–Sat 10am–5pm, Sun 1–5pm.

MacGregor Ranch Museum Listed on the National Register of Historic Places, the museum is located on the one-time domain of the MacGregor family, a big name in local ranching lore. Originally founded in 1873, the museum today is a lens into life on a cattle farm in that era. Volunteer-led tours of the restored main house focus on the MacGregors themselves, but the grounds are full of other historic structures, not to mention a working cattle ranch—beef is for sale at the ranch office. Allow 1 hour.

180 MacGregor Lane. ✆ **970/586-3749.** www.macgregorranch.org. Admission $3 adults, free for those 17 and under. June–Aug Tues–Fri 10am–4pm. Closed rest of year.

Shopping

Elkhorn Avenue is the main shopping area in Estes Park, and this is also where you'll find public restrooms and free parking lots. Among the notable galleries and gift shops are those in the **Old Church Shops,** 157 W. Elkhorn Ave. (✆ **970/586-5860;** www.churchshops.com). Also worth looking for are **The Glassworks,** 323 W. Elkhorn Ave. (✆ **970/586-8619**), a gallery and studio with fascinating glass-blowing demonstrations; **Serendipity Trading Company,** 117 E. Elkhorn Ave. (✆ **800/832-8980** or 970/586-8410; www.serendipitytrading.com), traders in American Indian arts and crafts; and **Trendz,** 100 E. Elkhorn Ave. (✆ **970/577-0831;** www.trendzestespark.com), a contemporary home decor shop that gave downtown Estes Park's retail scene a much-needed shot of the upscale.

The **Cultural Arts Council of Estes Park,** 304 E. Elkhorn Ave. (P.O. Box 4135), Estes Park, CO 80517 (✆ **970/586-9203;** www.estesarts.com), has a fine art gallery featuring changing exhibits of works by nationally recognized artists, as well as exhibits on loan from private collections and museums. The council sponsors an Art in Public Places series (call for details) and a film festival, and hosts Art Walks—self-guided tours of galleries, artists' studios, special exhibits, and events throughout the area. The Art Walks take place in mid-May, June through Labor Day, late September, and early December; maps are available. The council also sponsors an outdoor performance series, Thursday Night Live, not too surprisingly held Thursday nights at 7pm from June through August at Estes Park's Performance Park (on the west side of downtown). Events, which are free or have a nominal admission fee, start at 7pm and offer classical, jazz, folk, or contemporary music, plus theater and dance.

Established in 1917, **Eagle Plume's,** 9853 S. Colo. 7, Allenspark (✆ **303/747-2861;** www.eagleplume.com), is a one-of-a-kind museum/gallery that hocks a few souvenirs but mainly focuses on fine art. Plenty of contemporary Native American arts, crafts, and jewelry are on display, many of them part of the collection of the store's namesake, the late Charles Eagle Plume.

The **Art Center of Estes Park** in the Stanley Village Shopping Center, 517 Big Thompson Ave. (✆ **970/586-5882;** www.artcenterofestes.com), is a community visual arts center that features changing exhibits of a wide variety of local and regional art, including paintings, sculpture, photography, textiles, glass work, and wood carvings. Works are for sale, and the center also presents workshops and classes on subjects such as oil painting, sketching, stained glass, and jewelry-making. Cost is usually in the $50-to-$100 range, including materials. The Art Center is a bit hard to find; once you get to the shopping center below the Stanley Hotel, go up the stairs behind the fountain.

Where to Stay

The highest rates here, sometimes dramatically higher, are in summer. For help in finding accommodations, call the **Estes Park Convention and Visitors Bureau** (✆ **800/443-7837;** www.estesparkcvb.com). National chains here include **Best Western Silver Saddle,** 1260 Big Thompson Ave. (U.S. 34), Estes Park, CO 80517 (✆ **800/WESTERN** [937-8376] or 970/586-4476), with rates of $79 to $259 double from June to mid-September, $79 to $199 double during the rest of the year; **Super 8,** 1040 Big Thompson Ave., Estes Park, CO 80517 (✆ **800/800-8000** or 970/586-5338), charging $99 to $119 double in summer, $59 to $89 double during the rest of the year; and **Travelodge,** 1220 Big Thompson Ave., Estes Park, CO 80517 (✆ **800/578-7878** or 970/586-4421), charging $129 to $220 double in summer, $85 to $109 double during the rest of the year.

Although many lodging facilities in the Estes Park area do not have air-conditioning, it is seldom needed at this elevation. Unless otherwise noted, pets are not permitted. Taxes add 7.7% to hotel bills.

Expensive

Boulder Brook ★★ It would be hard to find a more beautiful setting for lodging than this. Surrounded by tall pines and cradled in a ruggedly majestic valley 2 miles from the park entrance, all suites face the Fall River, and all have private riverfront decks and full or partial kitchens. The spa suites are equipped with two-person spas, fireplaces, sitting areas with cathedral ceilings, and king-size beds. One-bedroom suites hold king-size beds, window seats, two TVs, and bathrooms with whirlpool tub/shower combinations. The grounds, a serene jumble of forest, rock, and running water, include an outdoor hot tub and barbecue area. Smoking is not allowed.

1900 Fall River Rd., Estes Park, CO 80517. ✆ **800/238-0910** or 970/586-0910. Fax 970/586-8067. www.boulderbrook.com. 19 units. $109–$225 double. DISC, MC, V. **Amenities:** Year-round outdoor hot tub; large free video and DVD library. *In room:* Cable TV w/DVD/VCR, wireless Internet access (free), kitchen, fridge, coffeemaker, hair dryer, iron.

Historic Crags Lodge ★★ Perched above town on the north shoulder of Prospect Mountain, Crags Lodge has a friendly, comfy warmth to it that's removed from the bustle of downtown Estes Park—but only by a few hundred feet. On the National Register of Historic Places, the lodge opened in 1914 as an alternative to the Stanley Hotel, and it is one of the area's standout lodgings today. While the lobby and public areas retain a woodsy elegance, the guest studios and suites are more modern than historic. The decor keeps the Western trappings to a minimum, aside from a few historic photos, instead opting for an upscale condominium feel. All of the rooms have kitchenettes, queen beds, and sitting areas with a hide-a-bed; a few have balconies. The activities list is long and varied, and self-guided tour pamphlets are provided to guests free of charge. The resident restaurant, **The View** (see "Where to Dine," later in this chapter), is excellent.

300 Riverside Dr., Estes Park, CO 80517. ✆ **970/586-6066.** Fax 970/586-6806. www.ilxresorts.com. 33 units. May–Oct $135–$215 double; Nov–Apr $85–$165 double. AE, DISC, MC, V. **Amenities:** Restaurant; bar; outdoor heated pool (seasonal); outdoor hot tub; activities desk; children's program; concierge. *In room:* A/C, cable TV, wireless Internet access (free), kitchenette, coffeemaker, hair dryer, iron.

Marys Lake Lodge ★★ Open from 1913 and shuttered in 1978, Marys Lake Lodge reopened for the 21st century in grand fashion, renovating its old lodge and building over 50 condominium units on the property, to boot. The old lodge rooms are funky but nice, with terrific views and some original fixtures and claw-foot tubs. The condo units sleep 2 to 10 people and feature full kitchens, flatscreen TVs, DVD players, and other modern perks. There are two restaurants: **The Tavern,** woodsy and casual, serving top-notch bar fare, beef, and pasta; and the upscale **Chalet Room,** with a menu heavy on Mediterranean influences and fresh seafood.

2625 Mary's Lake Rd., Estes Park, CO 80517. ✆ **877/443-6279** or 970/586-5958. Fax 970/586-5308. www.maryslakelodge.com. 16 lodge rooms, 52 condominium units. June–Sept $129–$219 lodge room, $219–$429 condominium; Oct–May $109–$179 lodge room, $179–$389 condominium. AE, DISC, MC, V. **Amenities:** 2 restaurants; lounge; outdoor heated pool (seasonal); outdoor hot tub; spa. *In room:* A/C, cable TV, wireless Internet access (free), kitchen.

Romantic RiverSong Inn ★ A picture-perfect 1920 Craftsman mansion on the Big Thompson River, this elegant bed-and-breakfast has nearly 30 forested acres with hiking trails and a trout pond, as well as prolific wildlife and beautiful wildflowers. Very quiet, the inn is at the end of a country lane, the first right off Mary's Lake Road after it branches off U.S. 36 south. The comfortable bedrooms are decorated with a blend of antique and modern country furniture. All have large tubs, separate showers, and fireplaces; seven units offer jetted or soaking tubs for two, others have claw-foots. Smoking is not permitted. Gourmet candlelight dinners are available by advance arrangement ($124 per couple), but you must supply your own alcoholic beverages.

1765 Lower Broadview Rd. (P.O. Box 1910), Estes Park, CO 80517. ✆ **970/586-4666.** Fax 970/577-1336. www.romanticriversong.com. 10 units. $165–$350 double. Rates include full breakfast. DISC, MC, V. Not suitable for small children. *In room:* Wireless Internet access (free), fridge (in some units).

Stanley Hotel ★★ F. O. Stanley, inventor of the Stanley Steamer, built this elegant hotel in 1909, and a flurry of recent projects have added a spa and a series of lavish condos. The equal of European resorts the day it opened, the Stanley was constructed in solid rock at an elevation of 7,800 feet on the eastern slope of the Colorado Rockies. Today the hotel and its grounds are listed on the National Register of Historic Places as the Stanley Historic District. Each room differs in size and shape, offering a variety of views of Longs Peak, Lake Estes, and surrounding hillsides. I prefer the deluxe rooms in the front of the building, which provide views of Rocky Mountain National Park.

333 Wonderview Ave. (P.O. Box 1767), Estes Park, CO 80517. ✆ **800/976-1377** or 970/586-3371. Fax 970/586-4964. www.stanleyhotel.com. 140 units. $153–$240 double; $300–$400 suite; $400–$600 condominium; from $1,200 presidential cottage. AE, DISC, MC, V. **Amenities:** Restaurant (American); pool (heated outdoor); tennis court (outdoor, unlit); exercise room; spa. *In room:* Cable TV w/pay movies, dataport.

Streamside on Fall River ★ These cabin suites, on 17 acres along the Fall River, about a mile west of Estes Park on U.S. 34, are surrounded by woods and meadows of wildflowers. Deer, elk, and bighorn sheep are such regular visitors that many have been given names. Everything is top drawer inside these cabins: All have king- or queen-size beds, fireplaces, and decks or patios with gas grills. Many have beamed cathedral ceilings, skylights, full kitchens, and whirlpool tubs. Guests can wander the nature trails on the property. A variety of special-occasion packages are offered.

1260 Fall River Rd. (P.O. Box 2930), Estes Park, CO 80517. ✆ **800/321-3303** or 970/586-6464. Fax 970/586-6272. www.sttreamsudeonfallriver.com. 21 units. June–Sept $155–$295 double; Oct–May $99–$195 double. AE, DISC, MC, V. **Amenities:** Indoor hot tub; 2 outdoor hot tubs. *In room:* Cable TV/DVD player, wireless Internet access (free), kitchen.

Taharaa Mountain Lodge ★★★ A luxurious mountain lodge, Taharaa is named for the French Polynesian word for "beautiful view," and it's a fitting moniker: There are jaw-dropping views of the Mummy Range from just about every room in the house. Built in 1997 and expanded in 2005 by Diane and Ken Harlan, Taharaa melds upscale hotel amenities and service with the intimacy of a B&B. With a contemporary, "New West" feel, the sumptuous interiors are a good match with the sublime panoramas, with individually decorated rooms like the Big Thompson, outfitted with trout art of all kinds, and the two-room Cattle Baron Suite, with an imposing antique headboard and a wet bar. All rooms have gas fireplaces and private balconies. The property has a guest library with Internet access and a phenomenal Great Room, with a 30-foot ceiling and fireplace, a wrought-iron chandelier, and picture windows framing the stunning view.

3110 Colo. 7 (P.O. Box 2586), Longs Peak Route, Estes Park, CO 80517. ✆ **800/597-0098** or 970/577-0098. Fax 970/577-0819. www.taharaa.com. 18 units, including 2 suites. May to mid-Oct $185–$255 double, $305–$345 suite; mid-Oct to Apr $155–$225 double, $245–$285 suite. Rates include full breakfast and happy hour. AE, DISC, MC, V. **Amenities:** Indoor hot tub; outdoor hot tub; sauna; exercise room; massage. *In room:* A/C, cable TV/DVD player, wireless Internet access (free).

Moderate & Inexpensive

In addition to the properties discussed here, the **Saddle & Surrey Motel,** 1341 S. St. Vrain Ave. (✆ **800/204-6226** or 970/586-3326; www.saddleandsurrey.com), with queen rooms for $89 and with kitchenettes for $145 in summer, is a good choice. In an attractive stucco building downtown, the **Estes Park Hostel,** 211 Cleave St. (✆ **877/213-0549** or 970/586-3149; www.estesparkhostel.com), rents dormitory bunks for $26 and private rooms for $30 (single) or $52 (double), as well as an apartment that sleeps five people and has its own kitchen for $85 a night. There are also cabins and cottages available at the **Elk Meadow Campground,** listed under "Camping," below.

Allenspark Lodge Bed & Breakfast ★★ Finds This historic property has just the right ambience for a visit to Rocky Mountain National Park. The three-story lodge was built in 1933 of hand-hewn ponderosa pine logs and includes a large native stone fireplace. Located in a tiny village at the southeast corner of the national park, all lodge rooms offer mountain views and original handmade 1930s pine furniture. At the top end is the Hideaway Room, with a queen-size brass bed, bear-claw-foot tub, fine linens, and a gas-log stove. Guests share the large sunroom, the stone fireplace in the Great Room, videos in the recreation room, and books in the library. A hot family-style breakfast, and afternoon and evening coffee, tea, and cookies are complimentary. There is also a hot tub, espresso coffee shop, and wine and beer bar; horseback riding is available across the street in the summer.

184 Main St., Colo. 7 Business Loop (P.O. Box 247), Allenspark, CO 80510. ✆ **303/747-2552.** www.allensparklodge.com. 13 units (7 with bathroom). $95–$150 double. Rates include full breakfast. AE, DISC, MC, V. Children 13 and under not accepted. **Amenities:** Bar; indoor hot tub. *In room:* No phone.

Alpine Trail Ridge Inn ★ Value This top-notch independent motel, right next to the entrance to Rocky Mountain National Park, offers nicely maintained rooms, many with private balconies, with basic Western decor and plenty of functionality. There are rooms with kings and queens, or two doubles, as well as a few two-room family units. Proprietors Jay and Fran Grooters are also great sources for hiking advice—Fran's **Trail Tracks** (www.trailtracks.com) publishes excellent 3-D hiking maps of Rocky Mountain National Park and other hiking meccas.

927 Moraine Ave., Estes Park, CO 80517. ✆ **800/233-5023** or 970/586-4585. Fax 970/586-6249. www.alpinetrailridgeinn.com. 48 units. Summer $80–$139 double, $140–$202 family unit. Closed mid-Oct to Apr. AE, DISC, DC, MC, V. **Amenities:** Restaurant (American); outdoor heated pool; business center. *In room:* A/C, cable TV, wireless Internet access (free), fridge, coffeemaker, hair dryer, iron.

Baldpate Inn ★ Finds Located 7 miles south of Estes Park, the Baldpate was built in 1917 and named for the novel *Seven Keys to Baldpate,* a murder mystery in which seven visitors believe each possesses the only key to the hotel. Guests today can watch several movie versions of the story, read the book, and contribute to the hotel's collection of more than 30,000 keys. Guests can also enjoy complimentary refreshments by the handsome stone fireplace in the lobby, relax on the large sun deck, or view free videos on the library VCR. But it might be difficult to stay inside once you experience the spectacular views from the inn's spacious porch and see the nature trails beckoning. Each of the early-20th-century-style rooms is unique, with handmade quilts on the beds. Several of the rooms are a bit small, and although most of the lodge rooms share bathrooms (five bathrooms for nine units), each room does have its own sink. Among my favorites are the Mae West Room (yes, she was a guest here), with a red claw-foot tub and wonderful views of the valley; and the Pinetop Cabin, which has a whirlpool tub, canopy bed, and gas fireplace. In summer, an excellent soup-and-salad buffet is served for lunch and dinner daily.

4900 S. Colo. 7 (P.O. Box 700), Estes Park, CO 80517. ✆ **866/577-5397** or 970/586-6151. www.baldpateinn.com. 12 units (5 with private bathroom), 4 cabins. $110 double with shared bathroom; $135 double with private bathroom; $200 cabin per double ($15 per additional person). Rates include full breakfast. DISC, MC, V. Closed Nov–Apr. **Amenities:** Restaurant (seasonal). *In room:* Wireless Internet access (free), no phone.

Estes Park Center/YMCA of the Rockies ★ Value This extremely popular family resort is an ideal place to get away from it all, and serves as a great home base while exploring the Estes Park area. Lodge units are simply decorated and perfectly adequate, but I prefer the spacious mountain cabins. These have two to four bedrooms (accommodating up to 10), complete kitchens, and some have fireplaces. The center, which occupies 860 wooded acres, offers hiking, horseback riding, miniature golf, fishing, a skate park, and winter activities.

2515 Tunnel Rd., Estes Park, CO 80511-2550. ✆ **970/586-3341** or 303/448-1616. Fax 970/586-6088. www.ymcarockies.org. 510 lodge rooms (450 with bathroom), 205 cabins. Lodge rooms summer $94–$139, winter $74–$99; cabins year-round $104–$349. YMCA membership required (available at a nominal charge). MC, V. Pets are permitted in the cabins but not the lodge rooms ($5 per pet per night). **Amenities:** Indoor heated pool; tennis courts (3 outdoor); bike rentals. *In room:* Wireless Internet access (free), kitchen (in the cabins).

Lane Guest Ranch Kids Lloyd Lane opened his guest ranch south of Estes Park in 1953 and built it into a great family resort with a focus on the great outdoors. For this, its location on 30 acres abutting Roosevelt National Forest and Rocky Mountain National Park is ideal. The calendar is pretty packed here, with activities ranging from guided hiking to silversmithing classes, and entertainment ranging from bingo to magic. The horseback rides run the gamut from standard trail rides to wine and cheese rides, overnight rides, and even a shopping-oriented ride! All meals are included, with nightly specials and a standard menu. The cabins here accommodate families up to six, complete with bunk beds, stocked fridges, and knotty pine furnishings. There is also the Doctor's House, a large house that accommodates up to 14.

P.O. Box 1766, Estes Park, CO 80517. ✆ **303/747-2493.** Fax 303/747-2306. www.laneguestranch.com. 25 cabins. June–Aug $260 per adult per night, $135–$210 per child per night, children 2 and under free without childcare (childcare packages available for kids). Rates include all meals and activities. 3-night minimum. Pets accepted. MC, V. Closed Sept–May. **Amenities:** Restaurant (American); lounge; outdoor pool; outdoor hot tub; sauna; fitness center; children's program; activities desk; wireless Internet access (free; lodge and pool only). *In room:* TV w/DVD/VCR player, kitchen, hair dryer, no phone.

McGregor Mountain Lodge ★ Kids This smallish, spread-out midpriced pick on the east side of Rocky Mountain National Park is a stone's throw from the park boundary at the foot of McGregor Mountain, a favorite hangout for bighorn sheep. With efficiencies, cottages, and one- and two-bedroom suites, the 19 rooms here are diverse and uniformly well maintained, and the place has a homey, faraway feel, despite its location off one of the area's main thoroughfares. Many of the rooms have hot tubs and balconies—all of them are great spots to unwind. The property is totally nonsmoking.

2815 Fall River Rd., Estes Park, CO 80517. ✆ **800/835-8439** or 970/586-3457. Fax 970/586-4040. www.mcgregormountainlodge.com. 19 units, including 15 cottages and suites. Early June to mid-Aug $119–$135 double, $149–$349 cottage or suite; rest of year $65–$89 double, $75–$229 cottage or suite. DISC, MC, V. Pets accepted ($20 one-time fee). **Amenities:** Indoor hot tub; playground. *In room:* Cable TV/VCR, wireless Internet access (free), kitchen, no phone.

Camping

Elk Meadows Lodge & RV Park Located close to the national park's Beaver Meadows entrance, this campground boasts 30 open and wooded acres, grand views in all directions, and sites that can handle "big rigs." There are several historic cabins on the property, plus a swimming pool, convenience store, laundry facilities, playgrounds, a dump station, and a recreation room. There are also a number of teepees for rent.

 1665 Colo. 66, Estes Park, CO 80517. ✆ **800/582-5342** or 970/586-5342. www.elkmeadowrv.com. 288 sites. Rates for 2 adults $43–$48 RV, $25–$28 tent; $34 teepee; $90–$250 cabin. DISC, MC, V. Open early Early Apr to mid-Oct.

Estes Park Campground ★★ Finds Located at the end of the road, 1 mile past the YMCA of the Rockies, and with the national park on two sides, this attractive campground offers glorious views and lots of quiet. Most campsites are nestled among pine trees and are perfect for tenters and pickup campers; only 21 have water and electric (30 amp) hookups. There are modern restrooms with showers, a small playground, a dump station, and a store that stocks supplies including firewood and ice.

3420 Tunnel Rd. (P.O. Box 3517), Estes Park, CO 80517. ✆ **888/815-2029** or 970/586-4188. www.estesparkcampground.com. 68 sites. Rates for 2 adults $26–$29 site with no hookups, $30–$40 site with hookups. AE, DISC, MC, V. Open mid-May to late Sept.

Mary's Lake Campground Here you'll find mostly open campsites that can accommodate everything from tents to 45-foot RVs, with full hookups that include cable TV. Facilities include bathhouses, a laundry, a dump station, a playground, a basketball court, a small store, a Wi-Fi network, a heated swimming pool, horseshoe pits, and a game room. Fishing licenses, bait, and tackle for shore fishing at the lake and stream fishing in the national park are available. Pets are welcome.

2120 Mary's Lake Rd. (P.O. Box 2514), Estes Park, CO 80517. ✆ **800/445-6279** or 970/586-4411. Fax 970/586-4493. www.maryslakecampground.com. 150 sites. Rates for 2 people $25–$27 site with no hookups; $36–$41 site with hookups. Extra person (over age 5) $3. Extra fee for A/C or electric heater use. DISC, MC, V. Open May–Sept.

Where to Dine

In addition to the restaurants described here, I also like **Bob & Tony's Pizza,** 124 W. Elkhorn Ave. (✆ **970/586-2044**), a busy pizza joint with redbrick walls covered with chalk signatures.

Expensive

Dunraven Inn ★★ ITALIAN This is a great spot to celebrate a special occasion in an intimate setting, but not so fancy that you wouldn't want to take the (well-behaved) kids. The decor is eclectic, to say the least: Images of the *Mona Lisa* are scattered about, ranging from a mustachioed lady to opera posters, and autographed dollar bills are posted in the lounge area. House specialties include shrimp scampi, lasagna, and my favorite, the Dunraven Italiano (a 10-oz. charbroiled sirloin steak in a sauce of peppers, onions, and tomatoes). There's a wide choice of pastas, fresh seafood, vegetarian plates, and desserts, plus a children's menu. The full bar is well stocked, and the wine list reasonably priced.

2470 Colo. 66. ✆ **970/586-6409.** www.dunraveninn.com. Reservations recommended. Main courses $10–$38. AE, DISC, MC, V. Daily 5–10pm; closes slightly earlier in winter.

The View ★★ Finds STEAKS/SEAFOOD Although the restaurant is named for the picture-perfect panorama of the town and surrounding mountainscape, the food is also terrific. Chef Russell Stephens shows an inventive eye for detail with such dishes as the walnut-crusted rainbow trout, served with garlic mashed potatoes and a grapefruit beurre blanc sauce; or a pan-seared rib-eye with garlic–blue cheese crust and merlot sauce. The atmosphere is woodsy but refined, with hardwood floors and red-and-white-checkered tablecloths, and there is often jazz or a Celtic guitarist.

At Historic Crags Lodge (see "Where to Stay," earlier in this chapter), 300 Riverside Dr. ✆ **970/586-6066.** Reservations recommended. Main courses $13–$29 dinner. AE, DISC, MC, V. Daily 5–9pm. Closed mid-Oct to mid-May.

Moderate

Baldpate Inn ★ Finds SOUP/SALAD Don't be misled by the simple cuisine—the buffet is deliciously filling and plentiful. Everything is freshly prepared on the premises, with the cooks barely staying one muffin ahead of the guests. Terrific soups—a choice of two is offered each day—include hearty stews, chile, chicken rice, garden vegetable, and classic French onion. The salad bar provides fresh greens and an array of toppings, chunks of cheese, and fruit and vegetable salads. Honey-wheat bread is a staple, plus wonderful rolls, muffins, and corn bread. Topping off the meal are fresh homemade pies and cappuccino.

4900 S. Colo. 7. ✆ **970/586-6151.** www.baldpateinn.com. Reservations recommended. Buffet $13 adults, $4.95 children 9 and under. DISC, MC, V. Memorial Day to Aug Mon–Sat 11:30am–8pm, Sun 11:30am–7pm. Shorter hours Sept to mid-Oct; call for current schedule.

Grumpy Gringo ★ Kids MEXICAN Dine in style at this classy Mexican restaurant without breaking the bank. The private booths, whitewashed plaster walls, green plants, bright poppies, and a few choice sculptures provide a posh atmosphere. And although the food is excellent and portions are large, the prices are surprisingly low. My choice here is a burrito, but which one to choose? I would also recommend the huge enchilada olé. It's actually three enchiladas: one each of cheese, beef, and chicken. The fajitas—either chicken or beef—are delicious. There are six sauces from which to choose, each homemade, and rated mild, semihot, or hot. Burgers and sandwiches are also offered. The house specialty drink is the Gringo Margarita, made with Sauza Gold tequila from an original (and secret) recipe, and the signature dessert is deep-fried ice cream.

1560 Big Thompson Ave. (U.S. 34). ✆ **970/586-7705.** www.grumpygringo.com. Main courses $8–$14. AE, DISC, MC, V. Daily 11am–9pm summer; 11am–8pm fall through spring. On U.S. 34, 1 mile east of the junction of U.S. Hwy. 34 and Hwy. 36.

Poppy's Kids ITALIAN/AMERICAN This bright, pleasant, and casual eatery right on the Big Thompson River serves up a menu of gourmet pizzas, sandwiches, and entree salads, and also has a good soup and salad bar. I'm partial to some of the Mexican-accented dishes, like the enchilada pizza or the green-chile cheeseburger, not to mention the "Adult Italian Sodas," sweet and fizzy drinks that pack a mild punch. You can dine in the family-friendly room or the great riverfront patio.

342 E. Elkhorn Ave. (on the Riverwalk in Barlow Plaza). ✆ **970/586-8282.** www.poppyspizzaandgrill.com. Main courses $7–$22. AE, DISC, MC, V. Summer daily 11am–9pm; rest of year daily 11am–8pm.

Inexpensive

The Egg & I AMERICAN A bright and cheery place to start your day, the Egg & I is decorated in warm earth tones, with magnificent views of the pristine Rocky Mountains. Breakfast is available at any time, ranging from the simplest fried egg to several variations of eggs Benedict, omelets, frittatas, crepes, and skillet meals—and I do mean meals—plus pancakes and French toast. Those not opting for breakfast can choose among a variety of sandwiches, such as the California Croissant: thinly sliced turkey breast, Swiss cheese, alfalfa sprouts, tomato, and avocado on a fresh tender croissant. Soups and a number of salads are also available, and there is takeout.

393 E. Elkhorn at the corner of U.S. Hwy. 34 and 36. ✆ **970/586-1173.** Main courses $4–$10. AE, DISC, MC, V. Summer Mon–Sat 6am–2pm, Sun 7am–2pm; winter daily 7am–2pm.

Arts & Entertainment

It's impossible to get bored in Estes Park, where you'll find a wide variety of performing arts events—many of them free—presented year-round. You'll hear classical music, from small ensembles to symphony orchestras, plus jazz, country, and Christian; and you'll see dance and theater. The community boasts a nice outdoor entertainment venue, Estes Park Performance Park, on West Elkhorn Avenue on the west side of town. For details on what's going on when you plan to be in town, contact the **Cultural Arts Council of Estes Park,** 304 E. Elkhorn Ave. (P.O. Box 4135), Estes Park, CO 80517 (✆ **970/586-9203;** www.estesarts.com), which represents a number of arts groups and individual artists, and helps coordinate many of the community's arts events. These include a free outdoor concert series, Thursday Night Live, logically held Thursdays at 7pm June through August at the Estes Park Performance Park; a dance festival in November; and Imagine This, a family-oriented festival of performing and visual arts, each February.

Among individual organizations presenting live productions are the **Fine Arts Guild of the Rockies** (www.fineartsguild.org), which sponsors musicals and plays; the **Estes Park Music Festival,** P.O. Box 4290, Estes Park, CO 80517 (✆ **970/586-9519;** www.estespark musicfestival.org), which presents a series of classical music concerts each summer and winter, as well as special events; and the **Chamber Music Society of Estes Park** (✆ **970/586-9467;** www.estesparkchambermusic.org), offering several concerts each year.

Of local watering holes, the **Wheel Bar,** 132 E. Elkhorn Ave. (✆ **970/586-9381;** www.thewheelbar.com), which has been open for a century and owned by the Nagl family since 1945, is one of the best. It's open every day except Christmas, serving as a community hub in more ways than one. The bar is a bit funky, with an excellent steakhouse, **Orlando's,** upstairs, and plenty of wheel decor, including a slowly rotating specimen behind the bar.

Among other bars, the **Rock Inn,** 1675 Colo. 66 (✆ **970/586-4116;** www.rockinn estes.com), plates up an eclectic array of steak, seafood, and salads, and hosts live rock and country music. For live rock music and dancing on weekends, check out **Lonigan's Bar & Grill,** 110 W. Elkhorn Ave. (✆ **970/586-4346;** www.lonigans.com).

GRAND LAKE

The western entrance to Rocky Mountain National Park is at the picturesque little town of Grand Lake, in the shade of Shadow Mountain at the park's southwestern corner.

Here, in the crisp mountain air at 8,370 feet above sea level, you can stroll down an old-fashioned boardwalk as one of the locals rides by on horseback. In fact, take away the automobiles and electric lights, and this town looks and feels like the late 1800s. Located in the Arapaho National Recreation Area, Grand Lake is surrounded by three lakes—Grand Lake itself, Shadow Mountain Reservoir, and Lake Granby—each with a marina that offers boating (with rentals), fishing, and other watersports. In the recreation area, you'll find miles of trails for hiking, horseback riding, four-wheeling, and mountain biking that become cross-country skiing and snowmobiling trails in winter.

The **Grand Lake Yacht Club** (✆ **970/627-3377;** www.grandlakeyachtclub.com) hosts the **Grand Lake Regatta** in July or August. The club was organized in 1902, and the regatta began 10 years later. Sailboats from around the world compete to win the prestigious Lipton Cup, given to the club by Thomas Lipton in 1912. Other summer events include an enormous **Fourth of July fireworks display** over Grand Lake, and **Western Weekend,** with a buffalo barbecue, 5K run, and a pancake breakfast, in mid-July. The **Rocky Mountain Repertory Theatre** (✆ **970/627-3421** or 970/627-5087; www.rockymountainrep.com) offers a summer program of Broadway shows and other theater, plus programs for children and teens.

Usually open daily from 11am to 5pm in summer, the **Kauffman House,** 407 Pitkin Ave., at Lake Ave. (✆ **970/627-9644;** www.kauffmanhouse.org), is a log structure that was built as a hotel in 1892. It has been restored and now serves as the museum of the Grand Lake Historical Society, with many of its original furnishings and exhibits on what life was like here back when everyone arrived on horseback or by stagecoach. Admission is free, although donations are welcome.

Golfers may want to test their skills at the 18-hole championship **Grand Lake Golf Course** (✆ **970/627-8008;** www.grandlakegolf.com), altitude 8,420 feet. Greens fees peak at $83 for 18 holes, although much lower twilight, off-season, and walking rates are available.

For further information on what to do in this area, stop at the **Visitor Information Center** on U.S. 34 at the turnoff into town (open daily 9am–5pm in summer, with shorter hours the rest of the year), or contact the **Grand Lake Area Chamber of Commerce,** P.O. Box 429, Grand Lake, CO 80447 (✆ **800/531-1019** or 970/627-3402; www.grandlakechamber.com). Information is also available from the Forest Service's **Sulphur Ranger District office,** 9 Ten Mile Dr. (P.O. Box 10, Granby, CO 80446), off U.S. 40 about a half-mile south of Granby (✆ **970/887-4100;** www.fs.fed.us/r2), open in summer Monday through Friday from 8am to 6pm, Saturday and Sunday 9am to 5pm, with shorter hours in winter.

Where to Stay

There are plenty of lodging possibilities in Grand Lake. A good source for information is the **Grand Lake Area Chamber of Commerce** (see above). In addition to the properties below, I like the **Grand Lake Terrace Inn,** 813 Grand Ave. (P.O. Box 1791), Grand Lake, CO 80447 (✆ **888/627-3001** or 970/627-3000; www.grandlaketerraceinn.com), a quaint mountain inn with three attractively decorated rooms plus a spacious suite, with rates of $60 to $150 double for the rooms and $125 to $275 for the suite. The inn also has a restaurant serving three meals a day.

Black Bear Lodge Located 3 miles south of town across from Shadow Mountain Lake, this comfortable and well-maintained establishment is a great bet if you're looking for an affordable motel with Rocky Mountain ambiance. Some units have two rooms and some have kitchenettes. Of the 17 units, bathrooms in eight have showers only; the rest have bathrooms with shower/tub combos. All units are nonsmoking.

12255 U.S. 34 (P.O. Box 609), Grand Lake, CO 80447. ✆ **800/766-1123** or 970/627-3654. www.blackbeargrandlake.com. 17 units. $76–$135 double. MC, V. **Amenities:** Outdoor pool; 2 whirlpools (1 indoor, 1 outdoor); sauna. *In room:* Cable TV.

Daven Haven Lodge ★★ Set among pine trees across the street from the lake, this group of cabins is a good choice for those seeking peace and quiet in a secluded mountain resort–type setting. There's a welcoming stone fireplace in the lobby plus old Coke machines and several antique jukeboxes—they actually play 78-rpm records! The cabins vary in size, sleeping from two to eight people; each has its own picnic table and six have stone fireplaces. The decor and furnishings are contemporary Western. You'll also find a lovely patio, a volleyball court, horseshoes, and a bonfire pit. The Backstreet Steakhouse (see "Where to Dine," below) serves dinner nightly in summer and 4 nights a week in winter. All cabins are nonsmoking.

604 Marina Dr. (P.O. Box 1528), Grand Lake, CO 80447. ✆ **970/627-8144.** Fax 970/627-5098. www.davenhavenlodge.com. 16 cabins. $94–$154 for units for 2–4; $164–$236 for units for 5–8. DISC, MC, V. 3-night minimum required on reservations during holidays. **Amenities:** Restaurant (steakhouse). *In room:* TV, wireless Internet access (free), kitchen (no microwaves).

 The Inn at Grand Lake ★ For modern lodging with an Old West feel, stay at this handsome restored historic building, originally constructed in 1881 as Grand Lake's courthouse and jail. Rooms have a variety of bed combinations, and several sleep up to six. They're equipped with Western-style furniture, ceiling fans, white stucco walls, and Indian-motif draperies and bedspreads. Many of the units have refrigerators and microwaves. About half of the units have tub/shower combinations, and the rest have showers only. The best views are on the street side of the building. The inn is located in the center of town, about a half-block from the lake. The Sagebrush BBQ & Grill (see "Where to Dine," below) serves three meals daily. All units are nonsmoking.

1103 Grand Ave. (P.O. Box 2087), Grand Lake, CO 80447. ✆ **800/722-2585** or 970/627-9234. www.innatgrandlake.com. 18 units. $100–$150 double, $120–$180 suite. AE, DISC, MC, V. *In room:* TV, coffeemaker, hair dryer.

Where to Dine

Backstreet Steakhouse ★ STEAK This cozy, country inn–style restaurant in the Daven Haven lodge (see above) offers fine dining in a down-home atmosphere. Steaks—from the 8-ounce filet mignon to the 12-ounce New York strip—are all USDA choice beef, cooked to perfection. The house specialty, Jack Daniel's pork chops (breaded, baked, and served with a creamy Jack Daniel's mushroom sauce), has been featured in *Bon Appétit* magazine. Also on the menu are pasta, chicken, and fish dishes, plus slow-roasted prime rib and children's items. Sandwiches and light entrees, such as the smoked salmon and wild game sausage platter, are served in the lounge.

In the Daven Haven Lodge, 604 Marina Dr. ✆ **970/627-8144.** www.davenhavenlodge.com. Reservations recommended in summer and on winter weekends. Main courses dining room $16–$36, lounge $7–$16. DISC, MC, V. Summer and Christmas holidays daily 5pm–close; winter Thurs–Sun 5pm–close.

Sagebrush BBQ & Grill AMERICAN Come here to enjoy excellent barbecue plus steaks, sandwiches, and seafood in a historic building that also houses the Inn at Grand Lake (see above). The atmosphere here is definitely Wild West, complete with Grand Lake's original jail doors, and so casual that you're encouraged to munch on peanuts and throw the shells on the floor. The specialty here is barbecue—try the super-tender fall-off-the-bone pork ribs—but that doesn't mean the New York strip steak, the pan-fried rainbow trout, and the elk medallions served with roasted raspberry chipotle sauce are anything to pass up. Another good choice is the burrito—pork, chicken, or vegetarian—served with refried beans, green chile, cheese, tomato, and lettuce.

1101 Grand Ave. ✆ **970/627-1404.** www.sagebrushbbq.com. Main courses lunch and dinner $6–$24. MC, V. Sun–Thurs 7am–9pm; Fri–Sat 7am–10pm.

2 ROCKY MOUNTAIN NATIONAL PARK ★★★

Snow-covered peaks—17 mountains above 13,000 feet—stand over the lush valleys and shimmering alpine lakes that cover the 415 square miles (265,727 acres) of Rocky Mountain National Park. The highest, at 14,259 feet, is Longs Peak. But what really sets the park apart (after all, this sort of eye-popping beauty is not unusual in the Rockies) is its variety of distinct ecological zones. As you rise and descend in altitude, the landscape of the park changes dramatically. In relatively low areas, from about 7,500 to 9,000 feet, a lush forest of ponderosa pine and juniper cloaks the sunny southern slopes, with Douglas fir on the cooler northern slopes. Thirstier blue spruce and lodgepole pine cling to streamsides, with occasional groves of aspen. Elk and mule deer thrive. On higher slopes, a subalpine ecosystem exists, dominated by forests of Engelmann spruce and subalpine fir, but it's interspersed with wide meadows covered with wildflowers during spring and summer. The park is also home to bighorn sheep, which have become its unofficial mascots. Above 11,500 feet, the trees become increasingly gnarled and stunted, until they disappear altogether and alpine tundra predominates. Fully one-third of the park is at this altitude, and in this bleak, rocky world, many of the plants are identical to those found in the Arctic.

Trail Ridge Road★, the park's primary east–west roadway, is one of America's great alpine highways. It cuts west through the middle of the park from Estes Park, then south down its western boundary to Grand Lake. Climbing to 12,183 feet near Fall River Pass, it's the highest continuous paved highway in the United States. The road is usually open from Memorial Day into October, depending on snowfall. The 48-mile scenic drive from Estes Park to Grand Lake takes about 3 hours, allowing for stops at numerous scenic outlooks.

Fall River Road, the original park road, leads to Fall River Pass from Estes Park via Horseshoe Park. West of the Endovalley picnic area, the road is one-way uphill and is closed to trailers and motor homes. As you negotiate its gravelly switchbacks, you get a clear idea of what early auto travel was like in the West. It, too, is closed in winter.

One of the few paved roads in the Rockies that leads into a high mountain basin is **Bear Lake Road;** it is kept open year-round, with occasional half-day closings to clear snow. Numerous trails converge at Bear Lake, southwest of the Park Headquarters/Visitor Center, via Moraine Park.

JUST THE FACTS

ENTRY POINTS Entry into the park is from either the east (through the town of Estes Park) or the west (through the town of Grand Lake). The east and west sides of the park are connected by Trail Ridge Road, open during summer and early fall, but closed to all motor vehicle traffic by snow the rest of the year. Most visitors enter the park from the Estes Park side. The **Beaver Meadows Entrance,** west of Estes Park via U.S. 36, leads to the Beaver Meadows Visitor Center and park headquarters, and is the most direct route to Trail Ridge Road. U.S. 34 west from Estes Park takes you to the Fall River Visitor Center, just outside the park, and into the park via the **Fall River Entrance,** which is north of the Beaver Meadows Entrance. From there you can access Old Fall River Road or Trail Ridge Road. Those entering the park from the west side should take U.S. 40 to Granby and then follow U.S. 34 north to the **Grand Lake Entrance.** See the inside front cover of this book for a map.

GETTING AROUND In summer, a free national park **shuttle bus** runs from Moraine Park Campground, Moraine Park Museum, and the Glacier Basin parking area to Bear Lake, with departures every 10 to 20 minutes. Shuttle buses also began operating in 2006 throughout the business district of Estes Park and from Estes Park into Rocky Mountain National Park. The buses run daily from July through Labor Day; schedules are available at the Estes Park Visitor Center (see "Visitor Centers & Information," below).

FEES & REGULATIONS Park admission for up to a week costs $20 per vehicle or $10 per person for motorcyclists, bicyclists, and pedestrians.

As is true for most of the national parks, wilderness permits are required for all overnight backpacking trips, and camping is allowed only in specified campsites. Pets must be leashed, aren't permitted on trails or into the backcountry, and may not be left unattended anywhere, including vehicles and campsites. Both motor vehicles and bicycles must remain on roads or in parking areas. Do not feed or touch any park animals, and do not pick any wildflowers.

VISITOR CENTERS & INFORMATION Entering the park on U.S. 36 from Estes Park, the **Beaver Meadows Visitor Center** (✆ **970/586-1206**) has knowledgeable people to answer questions and give advice, a wide choice of books and maps for sale, and interpretive exhibits, including a relief model of the park and an audiovisual program. It's open daily from 8am to 9pm in summer and from 8am to 5pm the rest of the year.

Just outside the park, on U.S. 34 and just east of the Fall River entrance, is the **Fall River Visitor Center** (✆ **970/586-1206**). Located in a beautiful mountain lodge–style building, it is staffed by park rangers and volunteers from the Rocky Mountain Nature Association. It contains exhibits on park wildlife, including some spectacular full-size bronzes of elk and other animals, plus information and a bookstore. Next door is a large (but somewhat pricey) souvenir and clothing shop plus a cafeteria-style restaurant with snacks and sandwiches. Hours are from 9am to 6pm in summer and 9am to 5pm in spring and fall.

Near the park's west side entrance is the **Kawuneeche Visitor Center** (✆ **970/586-1513**), open daily from 8am to 6pm in summer, from 8am to 5pm in late spring, and 8am to 4:30pm in fall and winter. Located high in the mountains (11,796 ft. above sea level) is the **Alpine Visitor Center** (✆ **970/586-1206**), at Fall River Pass, open from late June to early October daily from 10:30am to 4:30pm, with shorter hours toward the end of the season; exhibits here explain life on the alpine tundra. Visitor facilities are also available at the **Moraine Park Museum** (✆ **970/586-1206**) on Bear Lake Road on the east side of the park, open from mid-April to mid-October daily from 9am to 4:30pm.

For more specifics on planning a trip, contact **Rocky Mountain National Park,** 1000 U.S. 36, Estes Park, CO 80517-8397 (✆ **970/586-1206** or 970/586-1333 for recorded information; www.nps.gov/romo). You can also get detailed information from the **Rocky Mountain Nature Association,** P.O. Box 3100, Estes Park, CO 80517 (✆ **970/586-0108;** www.rmna.org), which sells a variety of maps, guides, books, and videos.

SEASONS Even though the park is technically open daily year-round, Trail Ridge Road, the main east–west thoroughfare through the park, is almost always closed in winter. The road is usually open by late May (after the snow has been cleared) and closes between mid- and late October. However, it is not uncommon for snowstorms to close the road for several hours or even a full day at any time, especially in early June and October. The high country is open during the summer and as snow conditions permit in winter.

AVOIDING THE CROWDS Because large portions of the park are closed in winter, most people visit the park from late spring through early fall. The busiest period, though, is from mid-June to mid-August. In order to avoid the largest crowds, try to visit just before or just after that period. For those who don't mind chilly evenings, late September and early October are less crowded and can be beautiful, although there's always the chance of an early winter storm. Regardless of when you visit, the absolute best way to avoid crowds is by putting on a backpack or climbing onto a horse. Rocky Mountain has some 350 miles of trails leading into all corners of the park (see "Sports & Outdoor Activities," below).

RANGER PROGRAMS Evening programs take place at campground amphitheaters, and additional talks and programs are offered at visitor centers between June and September. Consult the park's free newspaper for scheduled activities, which vary from photo walks to fly-fishing and orienteering.

SEEING THE HIGHLIGHTS

Although Rocky Mountain National Park is generally considered the domain of hikers and climbers, it's surprisingly easy to thoroughly enjoy this park without working up a sweat. For that we can thank **Trail Ridge Road.** Built in 1932 and undoubtedly one of America's most scenic highways, it provides expansive and sometimes dizzying views in all directions. The drive from Estes Park to Grand Lake covers some 48 miles through the park, rising above 12,000 feet in elevation and crossing the Continental Divide. It offers spectacular vistas of snow-capped peaks, deep forests, and meadows of wildflowers, where bighorn sheep, elk, and deer graze. Allow at least 3 hours for the drive, and more if you'd like to take a short hike from one of the many vista points.

To get a close look at the tundra, pull off Trail Ridge Road into the **Rock Cut** parking area (elevation 12,110 ft.), about halfway along the scenic drive. The views of glacially carved peaks along the Continental Divide are spectacular, and signs on the half-mile Tundra Nature Trail identify the hardy plants and animals that inhabit the region and explain how they have adapted to the harsh environment.

TRAIL RIDGE ROAD ★

Along Trail Ridge Road are numbered signs, from 1 to 12, starting on the east side of the park and heading west. These stops are described below, and the route is also discussed in a brochure available at park visitor centers (50¢). Motorists starting from the west side of the park will begin at number 12 and count down.

Stop No. 1: Deer Ridge Junction. This spot offers views of the Mummy Mountain Range to the north. It is the official beginning of Trail Ridge Road, the highest continuous paved road in the United States, reaching an elevation of 12,183 feet. Here you're at a mere 8,940 feet.

Stop No. 2: Hidden Valley. Formerly the site of a downhill ski area, this scenic subalpine valley boasts forests of Engelmann spruce and fir. The elevation is 9,240 feet.

Stop No. 3: Many Parks Curve. This delightfully scenic stop, with one of the best roadside views in the park, is also a good location for birders, who are likely to spot the noisy Steller's jay and Clark's nutcracker. The term "park" is used in the sense of a level valley between mountain ranges (often an open, grassy area), which in this case was carved by glaciers some 10,000 years ago. The elevation is 9,620 feet.

Stop No. 4: Rainbow Curve. Just past a sign announcing your position 2 miles above sea level is Rainbow Curve, an area known for colorful rainbows that are often seen after thunderstorms. It's also famous for ferocious winds and brutal winters. Take a look at the trees that have branches only on their downwind side, where their trunks protect them from the elements. The excellent view from the overlook here extends past Longs Peak and into Hidden Valley and Horseshoe Park, where you can see rock, gravel, and other rubble left by a flood that struck in 1982 after a dam broke. The elevation is 10,829 feet.

Stop No. 5: Forest Canyon Overlook. From this stop's parking area, a short paved walkway leads to an observation platform offering a beautiful but dizzying view into vast Forest Canyon, where the erosion work of glaciers is clearly evident. The peaks of the Continental Divide appear beyond. Near the overlook, watch for pikas (relatives of rabbits), marmots, and other small mammals. The elevation is 11,716 feet.

Stop No. 6: Rock Cut. Practically the highest point along Trail Ridge Road, this is alpine tundra at its harshest. Winds can reach 150 mph, winter blizzards are frequent, and temperatures in midsummer frequently drop below freezing. You'll have splendid views of the glacially carved peaks along the Continental Divide, and on the .5-mile **Tundra World Nature Trail,** you'll find signs identifying the hardy plants and animals that inhabit this cold and barren region. The elevation is 12,110 feet.

Stop No. 7: Lava Cliffs. Here you'll see a dark cliff, created by the carving action of glacial ice through a thick layer of tuff (volcanic ash and debris) that was deposited about 28 million years ago during volcanic eruptions in the Never Summer Range, located about 8 miles west. If you look just below the cliff, you'll see a pretty meadow that is a popular grazing spot for elk. The elevation is 12,080 feet.

Stop No. 8: Fall River Pass. At this spot you'll get a good view of a huge amphitheater, and you can take a break at the Alpine Visitor Center. A viewing platform at the rear of the visitor center offers vistas of a wide, glacially carved valley of grasses, wildflowers, shrubs, and small trees where you're practically guaranteed to see elk grazing. This is also the junction of Trail Ridge Road and Old Fall River Road. The elevation is 11,796 feet.

Stop No. 9: Medicine Bow Curve. Views of a vast subalpine forest of spruce and fir and the distant Cache la Poudre River give way to the Medicine Bow Mountains, which extend into Wyoming. The elevation is 11,640 feet.

Stop No. 10: Milner Pass. This is the Continental Divide, the backbone of North America. From this point, water flows west to the Pacific or east toward the Atlantic. The divide also affects the park's weather—the west side is usually colder, is less windy, and receives much more precipitation than the east side. The elevation is 10,758 feet.

Stop No. 11: Farview Curve. This aptly named overlook provides a look at the beginnings of the Colorado River as it carves its way through the Kawuneeche Valley 1,000 feet below the overlook, before flowing some 1,400 miles to the Gulf of California. There are also panoramic views of the Never Summer Mountains. Looking west from this point, you can see the Grand Ditch, which carries water across the Continental Divide to Colorado's thirsty eastern plains. Engelmann spruce and lodgepole pine grow here, and you'll see ground squirrels and chipmunks scurrying among the rocks. The elevation is 10,120 feet.

Stop No. 12: Holzwarth Trout Lodge Historic Site. Just past the Timber Creek Campground, this stop provides access to a short trail to **Holzwarth Trout Lodge Historic Site,** an early-20th-century homestead that started out as a working cattle ranch and soon evolved into a dude ranch. Rangers give talks and guided walks here during the summer. The elevation is 8,884 feet.

SPORTS & OUTDOOR ACTIVITIES

Rocky Mountain National Park is a fantastic area for a variety of outdoor activities, and many activities also take place just outside the park in the 1,240-square-mile Roosevelt National Forest. In Estes Park, a **Forest Service Information Center** is located at 161 Second St. (✆ **970/586-3440**); it's usually open daily from 9am to 5pm in summer. For year-round information, contact the **Forest Service Information Center,** 2150 Centre Ave., Bldg. E, Fort Collins, CO 80526 (✆ **970/295-6700**; www.fs.fed.us/r2).

BICYCLING Bicyclists share the park roadways with motor vehicles along narrow roads with 5% to 7% grades, and, like most national parks, bikes are not permitted off established roads. However, bicyclists still enjoy the challenge and scenery. One popular 16-mile ride is the **Horseshoe Park/Estes Park Loop,** which goes from Estes Park west on U.S. 34 past Aspenglen Campground and the park's Fall River entrance and visitor center, circles around Horseshoe Park, and then heads east again at the Deer Ridge Junction, following U.S. 36 out through the Beaver Meadows park entrance. There are plenty of beautiful mountain views; allow from 1 to 3 hours. A free park brochure provides information on safety, regulations, and other suggested routes. Tours, rentals, and repairs are available at **Colorado Bicycling Adventures,** 184 E. Elkhorn Ave., Estes Park (✆ **970/586-4241;** www.coloradobicycling.com). Bike rentals range from $17 to $50 for a half-day and $25 to $91 for a full day, depending on the type of bike, which ranges from very basic to absolutely fantastic. The company offers guided downhill tours in the park for about $75 per person, and also leads a variety of free group bike rides in the Estes Park area from May to September (call or check the website for the current schedule).

CLIMBING & MOUNTAINEERING **Colorado Mountain School,** 341 Moraine Ave., Estes Park, CO 80517 (✆ **800/836-4008;** www.totalclimbing.com), is an AMGA (American Mountain Guides Association) accredited year-round guide service and the sole concessionaire for technical climbing and instruction in Rocky Mountain National Park. The school offers a wide range of programs. Among those I especially recommend are the 2-day mountaineering class for $425 and the guided group hike up Longs Peak for $200. The school also offers lodging in a hostel-type setting, at about $35 per night per person in summer with lower rates the rest of the year. (See also "Hiking & Backpacking," below.) Be sure to stop at the ranger station at the Longs Peak trail head for current trail and weather information before attempting to ascend Longs Peak.

EDUCATIONAL PROGRAMS The **Rocky Mountain Nature Association** (see contact information under "Visitor Centers & Information," above) offers a wide variety of seminars and workshops, ranging from 1 full day to several days. Subjects vary but might include songbirds, flower identification, edible and medicinal herbs, painting, wildlife photography, tracking park animals, and edible mushrooms. Rates are $85 to $100 for full-day programs and $170 and up for multiday programs.

FISHING Four species of trout are fished in national park and national forest streams and lakes: brown, rainbow, brook, and cutthroat. A state fishing license is required (nonresidents: $9 for 1 day or $21 for 5 days, plus a $5 habitat stamp), and only artificial lures or flies are permitted in the park. A number of lakes and streams in the national park are closed to fishing, including Bear Lake; free park brochures listing open and closed bodies of water plus regulations and other information are available at visitor centers.

HIKING & BACKPACKING The park visitor centers offer topographic maps and hiking guides for sale, and rangers can direct you to lesser-used trails.

One particularly easy park hike is the **Alberta Falls Trail** from the Glacier Gorge Parking Area (a half-mile one-way), which rises in elevation only 160 feet as it follows Glacier Creek to pretty Alberta Falls. A slightly more difficult option is the **Bierstadt Lake Trail,** accessible from the north side of Bear Lake Road about 6 miles from Beaver Meadows. This 1.5-mile (one-way) trail climbs 566 feet through an aspen forest to Bierstadt Lake, where you'll find excellent views of Longs Peak.

Starting at Bear Lake, the trail up to **Emerald Lake** ★ offers spectacular scenery en route, past Nymph and Dream lakes. The half-mile hike to Nymph Lake is easy, climbing 225 feet; from there the trail is rated as moderate to Dream Lake (another half-mile) and then on to Emerald Lake (another .8 mile), which is 605 feet higher than the starting point at Bear Lake. Another moderate hike is the relatively uncrowded **Ouzel Falls Trail,** which leaves from Wild Basin Ranger Station and climbs about 950 feet to a picture-perfect waterfall. The distance one-way is 2.8 miles.

Among my favorite moderate hikes here is the **Mills Lake Trail ★★**, a 2.5-mile (one-way) hike, with a rise in elevation of about 700 feet. Starting from Glacier Gorge Junction, the trail goes to a mountain lake nestled in a valley among towering mountain peaks. This lake is an excellent spot for photographing dramatic Longs Peak, especially in late afternoon or early evening, and it's the perfect place for a picnic.

If you prefer a more strenuous adventure, you'll work hard but be amply rewarded with views of timberline lakes and alpine tundra on the **Timber Lake Trail,** in the western part of the park. It's 4.8 miles one-way, with an elevation gain of 2,060 feet. Another strenuous trail, only for experienced mountain hikers and climbers in top physical condition, is the 8-mile (one-way) **East Longs Peak Trail,** which climbs some 4,855 feet along steep ledges and through narrows to the top of Longs Peak.

Backcountry permits (required for all overnight hikes) can be obtained ($20 May–Oct, free Nov–Apr) at park headquarters and ranger stations (in summer); for information, call ✆ **970/586-1242.** There is a 7-night backcountry camping limit from June to September, with no more than 3 nights at any one spot.

HORSEBACK RIDING Many of the national park's trails are open to horseback riders. Several outfitters provide guided rides inside and outside the park, including a 1-hour ride (about $35) and the very popular 2-hour rides (about $50). There are also all-day rides ($120–$130, bring your own lunch), plus breakfast and dinner rides and multiday pack trips. Recommended companies include **SK Horses** (www.cowpokecornercorral.com), which operates **National Park Gateway Stables,** at the Fall River entrance of the national park on U.S. 34 (✆ **970/586-5269**), and the **Cowpoke Corner Corral,** at Glacier Lodge, 3 miles west of town, 2166 Colo. 66 (✆ **970/586-5890**). **Sombrero Ranches** (✆ **970/586-4577;** www.sombrero.com) operates two stables inside park boundaries, **Moraine Park Stables** (✆ **970/586-2327**) and **Glacier Creek Stables** (✆ **970/586-3244**), as well as stables in Estes Park, Grand Lake, and Allenspark.

SKIING & SNOWSHOEING During the winter, when deep snow covers roads and trails, much of the park is closed to vehicular travel (including snowmobiles). But this produces ideal conditions for those with cross-country skis or snowshoes to experience the park without the crowds. Snow conditions are usually best January through March. A popular spot for cross-country skiing and snowshoeing in the park is Bear Lake, south of the Beaver Meadows entrance. A lesser-known area of the park is **Wild Basin ★★**, south of the park's east entrances off Colo. 7, about a mile north of the community of Allenspark. A 2-mile road, closed to motor vehicles for the last mile in winter, winds through a subalpine forest to the Wild Basin Trail, from which you follow a picturesque creek to a waterfall, a rustic bridge, and eventually another waterfall. Total distance to the second falls is 2.8 miles. Along the trail, your chances are good for spotting birds such as Clark's nutcrackers, Steller's jays, and the American dipper. On winter weekends, the Colorado Mountain Club often opens a warming hut at the Wild Basin Ranger Station. Before you set forth, stop by park headquarters for maps, information on where the snow is best, and a permit if you plan to stay out overnight. Rangers often lead guided snowshoe walks on winter weekends. Among shops that rent snowshoes is **Estes Park Mountain Shop,** 2050 Big Thompson Ave. (✆ **866/303-6548** or 970/586-6548; www.estesparkmountainshop.com). Daily rental costs $5 per pair of snowshoes or $8 for skis.

WILDLIFE VIEWING & BIRD-WATCHING Rocky Mountain National Park is a premier wildlife-viewing area. Fall, winter, and spring are the best times (although you can see plenty of elk and squirrels, plus a few deer, marmot, and coyote during the summer months if you're lucky). Large herds of elk and bighorn sheep can often be seen in the meadows and on mountainsides. In addition, you may spot mule deer, beavers, coyotes, and river otters. Watch for moose among the willows on the west side of the park. In the forests are lots of songbirds and small mammals; particularly plentiful are gray and Steller's jays, Clark's nutcrackers, chipmunks, and golden-mantled ground squirrels. There's a good chance of seeing bighorn sheep, marmots, pikas, and ptarmigan along Trail Ridge Road. For current wildlife-viewing information, stop by one of the park's visitor centers and check on the many interpretive programs, including bird walks. Rangers stress that it is both illegal and foolish to feed any wildlife. Not only do you risk personal injury and disease, but you also harm the animals by giving them food that is not good for them and making them dependent on humans.

CAMPING

The best place to camp for those visiting the national park is in the park itself. Although you won't have the modern conveniences of commercial campgrounds (see "Camping," in the "Estes Park & Grand Lake: Gateways to Rocky Mountain National Park" section, earlier in this chapter), you will have plenty of trees, an abundance of wildlife scurrying by your tent or RV, and a true national park experience. The park has five campgrounds, with a total of almost 600 sites. Nearly half are at **Moraine Park;** another 150 are at **Glacier Basin.** Moraine Park, **Timber Creek** (98 sites), and **Longs Peak** (26 tent sites) are open year-round; Glacier Basin and **Aspenglen** (54 sites) are seasonal. Camping in summer is limited to 3 days at Longs Peak and 7 days at other campgrounds; the limit is 14 days at all the park's campgrounds in winter. Arrive early in summer if you hope to snare one of these first-come, first-served campsites. Reservations for Moraine Park and Glacier Basin are accepted from Memorial Day through early September and are usually completely booked well in advance. However, any sites not reserved—as well as sites at Timber Creek, Longs Peak, and Aspenglen—are available on a first-come, first-served basis. Make reservations with the **National Park Reservation Service** (© **800/365-2267;** www.recreation.gov). Campsites cost $20 per night during the summer, $14 in the off-season when water is turned off. No showers or RV hookups are available.

3 STEAMBOAT SPRINGS ★★

158 miles NW of Denver, 194 miles E of Grand Junction, 335 miles E of Salt Lake City, Utah

One of my favorite Colorado resort towns, in part because it's a real town in addition to being a resort, Steamboat Springs fuses two very different worlds—a state-of-the-art ski village with a genuine Western ranching center. This historic town, with a population of just under 10,000, is a pleasant laid-back community where ranchers still go about their business in cowboy boots and Stetsons, seemingly unaware of the fashion statement they are making to city-slicker visitors.

At an elevation of 6,695 feet, Steamboat Springs's numerous mineral springs and abundant wild game made this a summer retreat for Utes centuries before the arrival of white settlers. The bubbling mineral springs also caused many a mid-19th-century trapper to swear he heard the chugging sound of "a steamboat comin' round the bend"—hence the name. But prospectors never thrived here as they did elsewhere in the Rockies, though coal mining has proven profitable. Ranching and farming were the economic mainstays until tourism arrived, and agriculture remains of key importance today.

This area is perhaps best known as the birthplace of organized skiing in Colorado. Although miners, ranchers, and mail carriers used primitive skis for transportation as early as the 1880s, it wasn't until Norwegian ski-jumping and cross-country champion Carl Howelsen built Howelsen Hill ski jump here in 1914 that skiing began to be considered a recreational sport in Colorado. In 1963, Storm Mountain was developed for skiing, and Steamboat's future as a modern ski resort was ensured. The mountain was renamed Mount Werner after the 1964 avalanche death in Europe of Olympic skier Buddy Werner, a Steamboat Springs native. Today the mountain is managed by the Steamboat Ski & Resort Corporation and, more often than not, is simply called Steamboat. Howelsen Hill, owned by the city of Steamboat Springs, continues to operate as a facility for ski jumpers, as well as a fun little downtown ski area.

ESSENTIALS

GETTING THERE **By Car** The most direct route to Steamboat Springs from Denver is via I-70 west 68 miles to Silverthorne, Colo. 9 north 38 miles to Kremmling, and U.S. 40 west 52 miles to Steamboat. (***Note:*** Rabbit Ears Pass, 25 miles east of Steamboat, can be treacherous in winter.) If you're traveling east on I-70, exit at Rifle, proceed 88 miles north on Colo. 13 to Craig, then take U.S. 40 east 42 miles to Steamboat. For statewide **road condition reports,** call ✆ **303/639-1111** or visit **www.cotrip.org**.

By Plane The **Yampa Valley Regional Airport,** 22 miles west of Steamboat Springs near Hayden (✆ **970/276-5001;** www.co.routt.co.us), is served by **United Airlines** (✆ **800/241-6522**) with year-round commuter service from Denver and **Continental Airlines** (✆ **800/525-0280**), with summer service to Houston. During the winter, direct flights to major U.S. cities are available from **United** and **Continental** (see above), plus **American Airlines** (✆ **800/433-7300**), **Delta Airlines** (✆ **800/221-1212**), and **Northwest Airlines** (✆ **800/225-2525**). Delta also offers service in the summer and fall.

Ground transportation from Yampa Valley Regional Airport is provided by **Alpine Taxi** (✆ **800/343-7433** or 970/879-2800; www.alpinetaxi.com); the cost is about $50 per adult and $25 per child round-trip. The company also offers shuttle service between Steamboat and Denver International Airport. **Avis** (✆ **970/276-4377**) maintains a location at the airport.

VISITOR INFORMATION The **Steamboat Springs Chamber Resort Association,** 1255 S. Lincoln Ave. (P.O. Box 774408), Steamboat Springs, CO 80477 (✆ **970/879-0880;** www.steamboat-chamber.com and www.steamboatsummer.com), operates a visitor center, open in summer from 8am to 6pm Monday through Saturday and from 10am to 4pm Sunday, with shorter hours the rest of the year.

GETTING AROUND There are really two Steamboats. The ski resort, known as Steamboat Village, is about 2 miles southeast of the historic Steamboat Springs. If you're coming from Denver, U.S. 40 approaches Steamboat from the south and parallels the Yampa River through town. Mount Werner Road, which turns east off U.S. 40, leads directly to the ski resort, centered on Mount Werner Circle and Ski Time Square. U.S. 40 is known as Lincoln Avenue through the town of Steamboat, where it is crossed by 3rd through 13th streets. **Steamboat Springs Transit** (✆ **970/879-3717**) provides free rides throughout the area. Buses run approximately every 20 to 30 minutes during peak hours, less frequently at other times. **Alpine Taxi** (see above) provides local taxi service.

FAST FACTS The **Yampa Valley Medical Center,** 1024 Central Park Dr. (✆ **970/879-1322;** www.yvmc.org), provides 24-hour medical service, a child-care center, and a

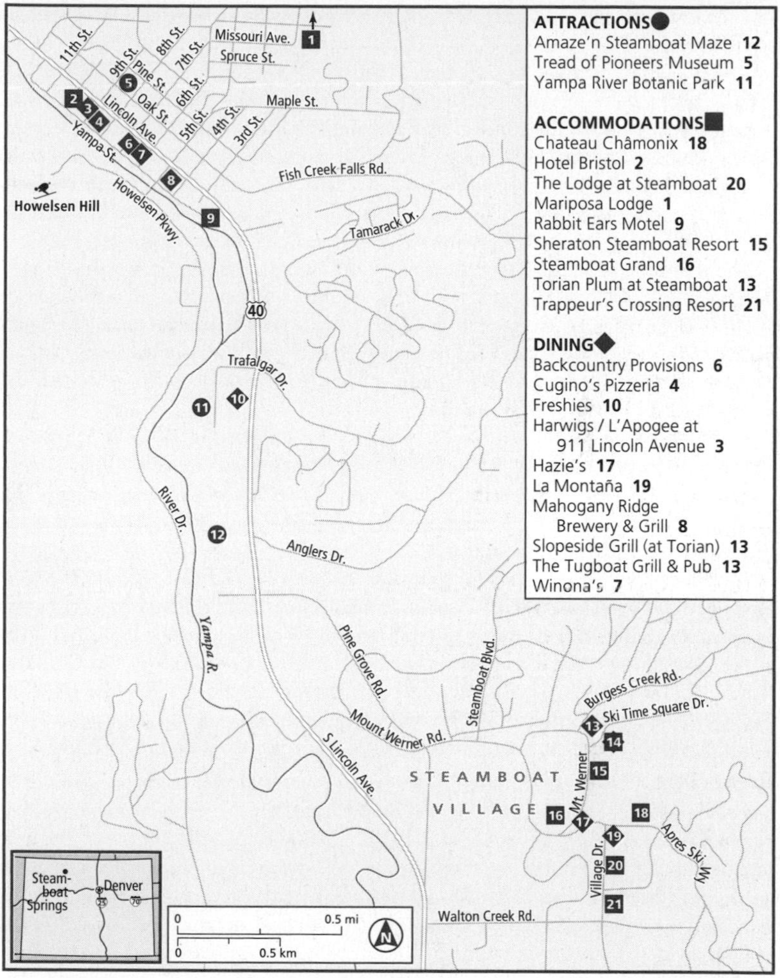

sports medicine center. The **post office** is at 200 Lincoln Ave. For hours and other information, contact the U.S. Postal Service (✆ **800/275-8777;** www.usps.com).

SPECIAL EVENTS Winter Carnival, early February; Steamboat Marathon, early June; Cowboy Roundup Days, Fourth of July weekend; Brewer's Festival, mid-September.

SKIING & OTHER WINTER ACTIVITIES

STEAMBOAT ★★ When devoted skiers talk about Steamboat, they invent new adjectives to describe its incredibly light powder.

Six peaks compose the ski area: Mount Werner, Christie, Storm, Sunshine, Pioneer Ridge, and Thunderhead. Christie Peak, the lower mountain area, is ideal for beginners. Thunderhead Peak, served by a high-speed detachable quad chairlift called the Thunderhead Express and the gondola, is great for intermediate and advanced skiers and riders. Arrowhead Glade provides an advanced playground for everybody. The Morningside Park lift accesses the extreme double black diamond terrain—chutes, advanced mogul runs, powder bowls, and one-of-a-kind tree skiing, all from the top of Mount Werner. Buddy's Run, one of the Rockies' great intermediate cruisers, is located on Storm Peak. The most famous tree runs—Shadows, Closet, and Twilight—are on Sunshine Peak, along with more bump runs and cruising slopes. Morningside Park includes 179 acres on the back of Storm Peak, with intermediate to advanced terrain served by a triple chair.

The vertical drop here is one of the highest in Colorado: 3,668 feet from the 10,568-foot summit. Skiable terrain of 2,965 acres includes 165 named runs, served by 23 lifts—an eight-passenger high-speed gondola, a high-speed six-person chair, five high-speed quad chairs, one conventional quad, six triple chairs, three double chairs, and six surface lifts. Trails are rated 14% beginner, 42% intermediate, and 44% advanced; the longest run is Why Not, at over 3 miles.

Lift tickets (3-day pass prices) cost $73 to $91 per day for adults, $57 to $73 for youth 13 to 17, $42 to $56 for children 6 to 12, $62 to $73 for seniors 65 to 69, $40 for seniors 70 and over, and free for children under 6. The rates are lowest at the beginning of the season, highest during the Christmas–New Year's holidays, and a bit lower the rest of the season. Lessons and rentals are available.

Steamboat is a great mountain for snowboarders, who especially love Mavericks Superpipe, which is 50 feet wide and 650 feet long, with 15-foot walls and a 17-foot transition!

Steamboat is usually open from the third week in November through mid-April, daily from 8:30am to 4pm. For further information, contact **Steamboat Ski & Resort Corporation,** 2305 Mt. Werner Circle, Steamboat Springs, CO 80487 (✆ **877/237-2628** or 970/879-0740 for reservations, 970/879-6111 for information; www.steamboat.com). For daily **ski reports,** check the resort's website (listed above) or dial ✆ **970/879-7300.**

HOWELSEN HILL ★ In addition to Steamboat, there's Howelsen Hill (✆ **970/879-8499;** www.steamboatsprings.net), which has remained open every winter since its first day in 1915, making it the oldest ski area in continuous use in Colorado. The first accredited public-school ski classes in North America were taught on this slope, which is operated by the city of Steamboat Springs. It offers both day and night skiing and snowboarding on its 30 acres of terrain served by a double chair, a Poma lift, a Magic Carpet, and a pony tow. There are 15 trails (the longest is 1 mile) and one half-pipe, and Howelsen Hill rises nearly 200 feet to a 7,136-foot summit elevation.

Tickets are $16 for adults and $11 for children 7 to 18 and seniors 60 and older, $6 for kids under 7, and $8 for everyone for night skiing (5–8pm Tues–Thurs). It's usually open from late November through late March Monday and Friday noon to 6pm, Tuesday and Thursday noon to 8pm, Wednesday 9am to 8pm, Saturday and Sunday 9am to 4pm.

Howelsen Hill has bred more North American skiers for international competition than any other ski resort—primarily because of its ski-jumping complex. The U.S. ski-jumping team trains each year on the 20m, 30m, 50m, 70m, and 90m jumps. Training and a variety of special events, including a Thursday night race series for adults and a Wednesday youth jumping series, are organized by the **Steamboat Springs Winter Sports Club** (✆ **970/879-0695** or 970/879-4300; www.sswsc.org), which was founded in 1914 and claims to be the oldest U.S. ski club west of the Mississippi River.

CROSS-COUNTRY SKIING, TELEMARK SKIING, & SNOWSHOEING Seasoned cross-country skiers swear by the **Steamboat Ski Touring Center** at the Sheraton Steamboat Resort (© **970/879-8180;** www.nordicski.net). Some 19 miles of groomed cross-country trails are set beside Fish Creek, near the foot of the mountain; there are also 6 miles of snowshoe trails. A full-day adult trail pass costs $16 a day; children 12 and under and seniors 65 and older pay $10. Gear rentals and lessons are available. Trails are open daily during ski season from 9am to 4pm. To get to the center, follow the signs off Mount Werner Road.

There are also cross-country trails at **Howelsen Hill** (see above). Popular cross-country ski trails in nearby national forest land include **Rabbit Ears Pass,** 25 miles east of Steamboat on U.S. 40, and **Dunkley Pass,** 25 miles south on Colo. 131. For trail maps and information, contact **Medicine Bow–Routt National Forest,** Hahns Peak/Bears Ears Ranger Station, 925 Weiss Dr., Steamboat Springs, CO 80487-9315 (© **970/879-1870;** www.fs.fed.us/r2).

Snowshoeing is gaining in popularity. There are numerous spots ideal for snowshoeing in the surrounding national forests, as well as at Steamboat Ski Touring Center (see above). Snowshoe and cross-country ski rentals are available at several outlets, including **Straightline Outdoor Sports** (see "Fishing," below).

ICE DRIVING ★ Okay all you NASCAR fans, you think you're great drivers? (Almost) any wimp can drive on dry pavement, but how good are you when your car's sliding down a sheet of ice? This is the place to find out. America's first (and only) school of ice driving is based at the foot of Mount Werner. Bridgestone Winter Driving School teaches safe winter driving the smartest way possible—hands-on, on a 1 mile circuit packed with frozen water and snow, and guarded by high snow banks. Classes combine instruction with on-track practice and are available for average drivers as well as professionals. Classes include a half-day introductory course ($270) and the most popular—a full-day course for $480. There's also a 2-day performance course for $1,550. The school is open daily from mid-December to early March, and reservations are recommended. Contact **Bridgestone Winter Driving School,** 1850 Ski Time Sq. Dr. (P.O. Box 774167), Steamboat Springs, CO 80477 (© **800/949-7543** or 970/879-6105; www.winterdrive.com).

ICE SKATING The **Howelsen Ice Arena,** 243 Howelsen Pkwy. (© **970/879-0341** or 970/879-4300; www.steamboatsprings.net), is an enclosed Olympic-size ice arena open year-round that has open skating hours, offers lessons in hockey and figure skating, and organizes various competitions. Admission is $6 adults, $5 youths 6 to 18, $3 for seniors 50 and older, and free for children 5 and younger. Skate rentals are $3 ($2 for seniors 50 and older). Call for the rink schedule.

SNOWMOBILING Snowmobilers consider the **Continental Divide Trail,** running over 50 miles from Buffalo Pass north of Steamboat to Gore Pass, west of Kremmling, to be one of the finest maintained trails in the Rockies, with some of the most spectacular scenery you'll see anywhere. For information, check with **Medicine Bow–Routt National Forest** (see "Cross-Country Skiing, Telemark Skiing, & Snowshoeing" above). Among those offering guided snowmobile tours is **High Mountain Tours,** P.O. Box 749, Clark, CO 80428 (© **877/879-6500** or 970/879-6500; www.steamboatsnowmobile.com). The cost is $115 for one person plus $65 for a passenger for a 2-hour ride, $165 for one person and $75 for a passenger for a half-day ride with lunch, $255 for one person plus $175 passenger for a full-day tour with lunch, with a four-machine minimum. Dinner rides and overnight trips are also offered.

WARM-WEATHER & YEAR-ROUND ACTIVITIES

Most outdoor recreation pursuits are enjoyed in 1.1-million-acre **Routt National Forest,** which virtually surrounds Steamboat Springs and offers opportunities for camping, hiking, backpacking, mountain biking, horseback riding, fishing, and hunting. For trail maps and information, contact **Medicine Bow–Routt National Forest,** Hahns Peak/Bears Ears Ranger Station, 925 Weiss Dr., Steamboat Springs, CO 80477 (© **970/879-1870;** www.fs.fed.us/r2).

Two wilderness areas in the forest are easily reached from Steamboat. Immediately north of town is the **Mount Zirkel Wilderness Area,** a region of rugged peaks approached through 10,800-foot Buffalo Pass, on Forest Road 60 off Strawberry Park Road via Seventh Street. Southwest of Stillwater Reservoir, some 40 miles south of Steamboat via Colo. 131 through Yampa, is the **Flat Tops Wilderness Area,** with picturesque alpine meadows and sheer volcanic cliffs. No motorized vehicles or mountain bikes are allowed in wilderness areas, although horses and dogs are permitted (dogs must be leashed in some areas).

Howelsen Hill (© **970/879-8499** or 970/879-4300; www.steamboatsprings.net) offers several warm-weather activities. You'll find a BMX and skateboard park, tennis, softball, volleyball, horseback riding, and mountain biking, plus the rodeo grounds (see below). In addition, an alpine slide, which operates daily from 10am until dusk during the summer, has a 2,400-foot dual track down the face of Howelsen Hill. For current rates and other information, contact the **Steamboat Springs Winter Sports Club** (© **970/879-0695;** www.sswsc.org).

The **Steamboat Ski Resort** doesn't go into hibernation after the snow melts; it just changes its focus, offering hiking, mountain biking, gondola rides, disc golf, and a multitude of other activities, including many that are great for kids. For information, check with **Steamboat Ski & Resort Corporation** (see "Skiing & Other Winter Activities," above).

Some 28 miles north of Steamboat Springs on C.R. 129 is **Steamboat Lake State Park** (© **970/879-3922;** www.parks.state.co.us), encompassing 1,053-acre Steamboat Lake. At an elevation of 8,000 feet, activities include summer camping (198 campsites with fees of $12–$18 plus the $6 park entrance fee; camping reservations are available through the state park website), picnicking, fishing, hunting, boating, swimming, canoeing, horseback riding, and nature walks. There's an attractive sandy beach (the sand was trucked in) and three boat-launching ramps. In winter, the park offers ice fishing, cross-country skiing, snowmobiling, and snowshoeing.

Steamboat Lake Marina (© **970/879-7019;** www.steamboatlakemarina.com), open year-round, has a small store with a deli—be sure to sample the especially good homemade fudge—plus groceries, fishing supplies, equipment rentals, boat fuel, and boat rentals. Canoes, kayaks, and paddleboats rent for $25 per hour; small fishing boats are $70 for 2 hours; 20-foot pontoon boats cost $125 for 2 hours; and 24-foot pontoon boats cost $160 for 2 hours. Pontoon boats either are outfitted for fishing or have barbecue grills. (Yes, you can fish from a boat with a grill—then you've got a grill for cooking your catch!) Rates for powerboats include fuel. Boat reservations are strongly recommended.

The marina has 10 cabins that have coffeemakers, small refrigerators, and a shared bathhouse. The nightly rate is $60 for two, and $5 for each additional person or pet.

Stagecoach State Park (© **970/736-2436;** www.parks.state.co.us), south of Steamboat Springs, offers camping, picnicking, fishing, boating, and other watersports. From Steamboat Springs, head 3 miles south on U.S. 40 to Colo. 131, turn southwest (right) and go about 6 miles to C.R. 14, and turn south (left) about 5 miles to the park entrance.

The main attraction here is a 780-acre reservoir, which is set among rolling hills, interspersed with forests and grasslands. The reservoir is fairly evenly divided for water-skiing and wakeless boating. The park has 92 campsites in four campgrounds, and two campgrounds have electric hookups. Camping fees are $8 to $18, plus the day-use fee of $6 per vehicle that everyone going to the park must pay. Camping reservations are available through the state park website (above). The elevation at the park is 7,250 feet.

Stagecoach Marina (© **970/736-8342**), usually open from mid-May through mid-September, has a store with fishing and camping supplies, plus boat fuel and boat rentals. Rates are highest Friday through Sunday, when canoes, kayaks, and paddleboats rent for $15 per hour; small fishing boats are $39 for 2 hours; 20-foot pontoon boats are $98 for 2 hours; and 24-foot pontoon boats cost $124 for 2 hours. There are discounts Monday through Thursday, and also discounts for longer time periods. Reservations are recommended.

The Steamboat Springs Chamber Resort Association produces a **trail map,** available at the information center on Lincoln Avenue, showing which trails are open to what sport: biking, horseback riding, hiking, 4WD, or ATVs. On the reverse side of the map are descriptions of several trails in the area.

ATV TOURS For a quick, fun, and relatively easy way to see this area's beautiful backcountry, consider a guided trip on an all-terrain vehicle. **Steamboat Lake Outfitters,** P.O. Box 749, Clark, CO 80428 (© **800/342-1889** or 970/879-4404; www.steamboatoutfitters.com), leads rides along old mining roads into the mountains, offering splendid views of the Continental Divide and Mount Zirkel Wilderness Area. Rates for a 2-hour ride are $85 for a one-person ATV or $150 for a two person machine, and half-day, full-day, and overnight rides are also offered.

BIKING & MOUNTAIN BIKING The 5-mile, dual-surface **Yampa River Trail** connects downtown Steamboat Springs with Steamboat Village, and links area parks and national forest trails. The **Mount Werner Trail** links the river to the ski area, which has numerous slopes open to mountain bikers in summer. **Spring Creek Trail** climbs from Yampa River Park into Routt National Forest. Touring enthusiasts can try their road bikes on the 110-mile loop over Rabbit Ears and Gore passes, rated one of the 10 most scenic rides in America by *Bicycling* magazine. Another option, especially for those of us who don't believe that sweating our way up the side of a mountain is fun, is to take the Silver Bullet Gondola (see "Gondola Rides," below) into the mountains and then ride the more than 40 upper mountain trails. Mountain bike rentals are available at the top of the gondola (© **970/871-5252**), with $55 rates for 3 hours for an adult bike and slightly less for kids' bikes. Diggler Mountain Scooters are also available for rent at the same rates. There is also a required mountain bike ticket (beyond the gondola ticket) that is $8 a day.

Rentals are available from **Ski Haus,** 1457 Pine Grove Rd. (© **800/932-3019** or 970/879-0385). Rentals of basic mountain bikes cost about $35 for a half-day and $50 for a full day. Town cruisers and road bikes are also available, as are repairs, gear, and advice.

CATTLE DRIVES ★★ The **Saddleback Ranch ★**, on C.R. 179 about 14 miles southwest of Steamboat Springs (© **970/879-3711;** www.saddlebackranch.net), is a working cattle ranch—not some Hollywood-style dude ranch—that offers a genuine Old West experience. The ranch has some 1,500 head of cattle on its 7,200 acres, and participants join working cowboys in moving cattle from pasture to pasture and performing other ranching tasks that are still done the old-fashioned way. Horses, tack, slickers, and snacks are provided, and cost for a half-day on the trail is $90 for those 10 and older. Children under 8 are not permitted on the rides. The cattle drives are held from June through mid-September.

FISHING The Steamboat Springs area, and particularly the Yampa River, has some of the best trout fishing in the state. There are nearly 150 lakes and reservoirs and almost 600 miles of streams in Routt County, which surrounds Steamboat Springs. Trout—rainbow, brown, brook, and cutthroat—are prolific, and the Yampa River and Stagecoach Reservoir are known for northern pike as well. Especially popular is the 5-mile stretch of the Yampa in downtown Steamboat Springs that is designated a catch-and-release trout stream; the Yampa's northern pike, whitefish, and small-mouth black crappy do not fall under the catch-and-release limitations.

Contact **Straightline Outdoor Sports,** 744 Lincoln Ave. (✆ **800/354-5463** or 970/879-7568; www.straightlinesports.com), for information, licenses, and either rental or purchase of equipment. Straightline also offers guide services (call for details).

GOLF The golf season here usually runs May through October, or as long as the snow isn't falling. The 18-hole municipal **Haymaker Golf Course,** at the intersection of U.S. 40 and Colo. 131, east of Steamboat Springs (✆ **970/870-1846;** www.haymakergolf.com), is a challenging links-style course with only 110 of its 233 acres used for fairways and greens. It conforms to the open-space philosophy of the Steamboat community, with native grasses, wetlands, and contours mimicking the surrounding valley and mountains. The greens fee during summer is $56 to $96 for 18 holes, and $54 to $69 at the beginning and end of the golfing season.

The **Steamboat Golf Club,** 6 miles west of downtown Steamboat Springs along U.S. 40 (✆ **970/879-4295;** www.steamboatgolfclub.com), is a picturesque 9-hole course along the Yampa River, with greens fees of $29 for 9 holes and $39 for 18 holes.

GONDOLA RIDES Summer visitors don't have to work hard to get up into the mountains above Steamboat—simply hop on the **Silver Bullet Gondola** (✆ **877/237-2628** or 970/879-0740; www.steamboat.com), which operates weekends in mid-June and mid-September, and daily from late June through early September. Prices for all-day passes are as follows: adults $18, seniors 65 and older $14, children 6 to 12 $8 (or $20 for one adult and one child 6–12), teens 13 to 17 $13 (or $25 for one adult and one teen 13–17), free for children 5 and younger. From the top of the gondola, hiking and mountain-biking trails can be accessed (see "Biking & Mountain Biking," above).

HIKING, BACKPACKING & MOUNTAINEERING There are numerous trails in the **Mount Zirkel Wilderness Area,** immediately north of Steamboat, and the **Flat Tops Wilderness Area,** 48 miles southwest. An especially scenic 4-hour hike in the Flat Tops area takes you from Stillwater Reservoir to the Devil's Causeway, with unforgettable views. Contact the U.S. Forest Service (p. 266) for information. There are also hiking trails at Steamboat Ski Area, which are easily reached on the Silver Bullet Gondola (see "Gondola Rides," above).

HORSEBACK RIDING Located behind the rodeo grounds in town (follow Fifth St. south from Lincoln Ave.) is **Sombrero Ranches** (✆ **970/879-2306;** www.sombrero.com), which offers 1- and 2-hour rides, breakfast rides, and special supervised rides for young children. Prices are $30 for an hour, $45 for the 2-hour and breakfast rides, and $20 for a half-hour lead-horse ride for kids.

Steamboat Lake Outfitters (see "ATV Tours," above) leads guided horseback tours at Steamboat Lake State Park, ranging from 1- and 2-hour rides ($35 and $55 per person, respectively) to half- and full-day rides, with lunch, for $100 and $195 per person, respectively. This company also offers breakfast and dinner rides plus pack trips and horseback fishing trips into nearby wilderness areas (call for details), and rents rooms and cabins (see "Where to Stay," below).

Dinner rides are offered during the summer by **Saddleback Ranch** (see "Cattle Drives," above), with a choice of New York strip steak, pork tenderloin, salmon, or barbecued chicken, plus all the extras. There's a 35-minute ride to the dinner site (transportation by hay wagon is also available), and the cost is $75 for adults and $65 for kids 6 to 12. Two-hour trail rides are $55 for those over 5.

HOT SPRINGS More than 150 mineral springs are located in and around the Steamboat Springs area. Several are located in city parks. Their healing and restorative qualities were recognized for centuries by Utes, and James Crawford, the area's first white settler, regularly bathed in Heart Spring and helped build the first log bathhouse over it in 1884.

Today Heart Spring is part of the new-and-improved **Old Town Hot Springs ★**, 136 Lincoln Ave. (**✆ 970/879-1828;** www.steamboathotsprings.org), in downtown Steamboat Springs. In addition to the man-made pools into which the spring's waters flow, there are a lap pool, water slide, spa, whirlpool, fitness center, tennis courts, and massage therapy. Pool admission is $12 for adults, $7 for youths 13 to 17 and seniors 65 and over, $4 for children under 3 to 12, and free for children under 3. Suit and towel rentals are available. The complex is open year-round Monday through Friday from 5:30am to 9:45pm, Saturday 7am to 8:45pm, and Sunday 8am to 8:45pm. The slide is open from noon to 6pm in summer and from 4 to 8pm in winter, and, in addition to the pool admission, costs $5 for five rides or $12 for unlimited rides.

The **Strawberry Park Hot Springs ★★**, 44200 C.R. 36 (**✆ 970/879-0342;** www.strawberryhotsprings.com), are 7 miles north of downtown (from Seventh St., follow the signs) up a rugged, rocky road navigable by regular cars in summer but requiring four-wheel-drive in winter; it's strongly recommended to ride the shuttle. (In summer, you can drive to the Hot Springs trail head off of C.R. 129 and hike 3 miles to the park.) The trip may be difficult, but it's a wonderful experience to spend a moonlit evening in a sandy-bottomed, rock-lined soaking pool, kept between 101° and 106°F (38°–41°C), with snow piled high around you. The hot springs are open Sunday through Thursday from 10am to 10:30pm (no entry after 9:30pm except to shuttles); Friday and Saturday 10am to midnight (no entry after 10:30pm except to shuttles). Admission costs $10 adults, $5 youths 13 to 17, and $3 children 3 to 12. After dark, children under 18 are not permitted and clothing is optional. Massages are available, and rustic cabins ($55–$65 a night) and tent sites ($50 a night) can be rented year-round, as well as a nifty caboose-turned-kitchenette ($105 a night). Overnighters get the pool all to themselves after-hours. There's a picnic area but no restaurant. Pets are not permitted.

RODEO The **Steamboat Springs PRCA Summer ProRodeo Series** (**✆ 970/879-1818;** www.steamboatrodeo.com) takes place each year from mid-June through mid-August at the Romick Rodeo Arena in Howelsen Park, at the corner of Fifth Street and Howelsen Parkway. Professional rodeo cowboys and cowgirls (or should that be cowpersons?) compete in bull riding, bareback and saddle bronc riding, steer wrestling, calf roping, team roping, and barrel racing. In the Calf Scramble, children are invited to try to pluck a ribbon from the tail of a calf. The rodeo takes place Friday and Saturday nights starting at 7:30pm. Admission costs $15 for adults, $8 for youths 7 to 15, and is free for children under 7.

SOME GREAT OUTDOOR AREAS

Fish Creek Falls Just 4 miles from downtown Steamboat in Routt National Forest, a footpath leads to a historic bridge at the base of this breathtaking 283-foot waterfall. There's also an overlook with a short .1-mile trail and ramp designed for those with disabilities, as well as a picnic area and hiking trails. Allow 1 to 2 hours.

Fish Creek Falls Rd. Information: Hahns Peak/Bears Ears Ranger Station, 925 Weiss Dr., Steamboat Springs, CO 80477. ✆ **970/879-1870.** www.fs.fed.us/r2. Free admission. Turn right off Lincoln Ave. onto 3rd St., go 1 block, and turn right again onto Fish Creek Falls Rd. Daily 24 hr.

Yampa River Botanic Park ★★ Finds For a pleasant and relaxing stroll among lovely gardens, stop at this botanic park along the Yampa River, between the ski mountain and downtown. Several picturesque ponds are set among low rolling hills, surrounded by a wide variety of flowering and nonflowering plants and trees of the Yampa River Basin plus many nonnative plants from many areas. A brochure describes the planted areas, with a map to help you navigate the many paths. There are wetlands on each side of the park, and the Yampa River Core trail connects to the park on its west side. The park is not wheelchair accessible, but tours for people with disabilities are offered by appointment. Allow at least an hour. From late June through August, the Strings in the Mountains Music Festival (see "Musical Mountains," below) presents free concerts at the park each Thursday at 12:15pm. Dogs and bikes are not permitted in the park.

1000 Pamela Lane (P.O. Box 776269, Steamboat Springs, CO 80477). ✆ **970/879-4300.** www.steamboat springs.net. Free admission, donations welcome. Dawn–dusk spring–Oct (or the first heavy snow). From U.S. 40, turn west toward the river on Trafalgar Dr. (the traffic light north of the Chamber Resort office light), then left on Pamela Lane, and go to the parking lot at the far end.

MORE TO SEE & DO

Amaze'n Steamboat Maze This intriguing puzzle lets you test your skills, or perhaps luck, in finding your way through a confusing maze. A free observation deck gives a bird's-eye view of the maze, allowing your quicker companions to point and laugh as you stumble into one dead end after another. In addition to the human maze, there is an 18-hole miniature golf course that uses items from Colorado's history, from a mine shaft to a Conestoga wagon, and a bumper car ride. Allow at least 1 hour.

1255 U.S. 40 (behind the chamber office.) ✆ **970/870-8682.** www.amazenmazes.com. Admission to the maze $6 adults, $5 children 5–12; golf $8 adults, $7 children; for both maze and golf $11 adults, $10 children; free for children 4 and under; other activity prices vary. Additional maze runs $3; additional rounds of golf $5. Memorial Day weekend to late Aug Sun–Thurs 10am–9pm, Fri–Sat 10am–9:30pm; weekends only thereafter, call for hours.

Tread of Pioneers Museum ★ This excellent museum combines two beautifully restored Victorian homes and a separate gallery. Two permanent displays are particularly interesting: "History of Skiing" (tracing the evolution of skiing from its roots as essential winter transportation to the multimillion-dollar recreational sport of today) and "History of Steamboat Springs" (showing the growth and changes in the county from the time of the Ute Indians through the agricultural and tourism growth of the last few decades). The museum also offers guided tours, kids' activities, and a gift shop. Allow about 1½ hours.

800 Oak St. ✆ **970/879-2214.** www.treadofpioneers.org. Admission $5 adults, $4 seniors 62 and older, $1 children 11 and under. Tues–Sat 11am–5pm.

Moments Musical Mountains

Summer is a musically magical time in Steamboat Springs. **Strings Music Festival** ★★★ offers an incredible array of musical programs, including classical, jazz, blues, and family-friendly music, in a beautiful new performance hall inspired by the lines of a string instrument.

If **chamber music** is your choice, don't miss the Wednesday and Saturday evening concerts. The choices are diverse: An evening might start with a gentle Chopin nocturne and move to a Schumann piano quartet, then finish off with Brahms. Instead of extensive program notes, nuggets of information about the music and/or composer are presented before each piece by a commentator.

Should **jazz, country, bluegrass,** or **pops** be the music that thrills your soul, Friday night is the night. The 2008 season included performances by Jessie Cook, the Nitty Gritty Dirt Band, and Natalie McMaster.

Don't forget to pack your lunch for Strings' **Music on the Green** at the new **Music Festival Park** at Yampa River Botanic Park—an inspiring location, the gardens a stirring backdrop—for a concert each Thursday at 12:15pm in the summer. It's a lovely way to spend your lunchtime—and many locals agree, so get there early to snag one of the free umbrellas to keep the scorching sun off your head. There's a cafe (5–9pm on Wed and Fri–Sat) that serves light fare and gourmet dinner specials.

What does all this cost, you ask? Surprisingly little for the quality and choices offered, including several free programs. Family-oriented concerts Tuesday or Thursday evenings, and youth concerts Tuesday morning, cost $10 for adults and just $1 for those 18 and under; the Wednesday Pre-Concert Talks are free, as are the Thursday Music on the Green lunchtime programs. Chamber music performances, Wednesday and Saturday evenings, cost $35 to $50; the Tuesday and Friday evening programs, which offer a variety of music, have widely varying prices, and there are several special events scattered throughout the summer and during the Christmas season (call for details). Strings also presents musical events at other times of the year, including a series of Christmas holiday concerts and a Winter Concert Series.

For additional information and a complete schedule, contact Strings Music Festival, P.O. Box 774627, Steamboat Springs, CO 80477 (✆ **970/879-5056;** www.stringsinthemountains.com).

SHOPPING

Lincoln Avenue, between Fifth and Ninth streets, is where most of the more interesting shops and galleries are located. Art lovers will enjoy **Artisans' Market of Steamboat,** 626 Lincoln Ave. (✆ **970/879-7512**), a nonprofit cooperative of local artists; and **Steamboat Art Company,** 903 Lincoln Ave. (✆ **800/553-7853** or 970/879-3383; www.steamboat-art.com), which offers an eclectic selection of limited-edition prints and other art, plus jewelry and crafts in wood, glass, and pottery. The **Homesteader**, 817 Lincoln Ave. (✆ **800/321-4702** or 970/879-5880), is a delightful kitchen shop with all manner of kitchen gadgets; salsa, chutney, and other Colorado-made food items; plus gourmet coffee beans and an espresso bar. If you forgot to pack your cowboy hat, there's a tremendous selection of Stetsons, plus just about everything else a Westerner wears, at **F.M. Light & Sons,** 830 Lincoln Ave. (✆ **970/879-1822;** www.fmlight.com), which has been in business since 1905 and has roadside signs advertising the place dotting the roadside for hundreds of miles. For books, head to **Epilogue Book Company,** 837 Lincoln Ave. (✆ **970/879-2665;** www.epiloguebookco.com). **Lyon's Corner Drug & Soda Fountain,** at the corner of Ninth and Lincoln (✆ **970/879-1114**), has an old-time soda fountain where you can get real malts, ice-cream sodas, egg creams, phosphates, sundaes, and fresh-squeezed lemonade.

WHERE TO STAY

As at all Colorado ski resorts, rates get progressively higher the closer you get to the slopes. You'll pay the highest rates during the Christmas holiday season (mid-Dec to New Year's Day). Next highest are the rates charged during February and March. Value season is usually January, and the low season runs from Thanksgiving to mid-December and from April until the ski areas close. Rates are normally much lower during the summer, from Memorial Day to mid-October. ***Note:*** Because vacancy rates are so high during shoulder seasons—April to May and October to November—many accommodations close at these times.

Steamboat Central Reservations (✆ **877/237-2628** or 970/879-0740; www.steamboat.com) can book your lodging and make virtually all of your travel arrangements. Be sure to ask about special packages and programs. **Resort Quest Steamboat,** 1855 Ski Time Sq. Dr., Steamboat Springs, CO 80487 (✆ **866/634-9618** or 970/879-8811; www.resortqueststeamboat.com), manages over 350 rental units spread among 15 properties. There are both condos and town homes, with accommodations for 4 to 12 persons; several of the properties are described below. **Steamboat Resorts,** 1847 Ski Time Sq. Dr., P.O. Box 772995, Steamboat Springs, CO 80477 (✆ **800/525-5502** or 970/879-8000; www.steamboatresorts.com), manages over 20 properties, offering a variety of possibilities, from small lodge rooms for two to condos that will accommodate up to 10. Several of the properties are described below. Room tax adds about 9.5% to lodging bills, and resort fees at properties at Steamboat Village add another 7.5%.

In addition to the properties discussed below, **Steamboat Lake Outfitters,** P.O. Box 749, Clark, CO 80428 (✆ **800/342-1889** or 970/879-4404; www.steamboatoutfitters.com), rents bunkhouse rooms and cabins in the mountains above Steamboat Lake State Park. Although rustic in decor, they have comfortable beds, kitchenettes, and indoor bathrooms, with rates for two starting at $89 per night in the bunkhouse rooms and $125 to $169 per night in the cabins. Call for details.

Very Expensive

Château Chamonix ★★ Made up of three condominium buildings just a few steps from the base of the Silver Bullet Gondola, this is one of the most convenient accommodations at Steamboat Village. Most units have two or three bedrooms—often with two king beds and two twins, with private decks, fireplaces, a whirlpool tub in the master bathroom, wet bars, and attractive wood furnishings. Each unit includes a washer and dryer plus a free high-speed Internet connection. During ski season, a free shuttle service into town is offered.

2340 Apres Ski Way, Steamboat Springs, CO 80487. ✆ **800/833-9877** or 970/879-7511. Fax 970/879-9321. www.chateau-chamonix.com. 48 units. 2-bedroom $185–$275 summer, $600–$1,100 winter;

3-bedroom $235–$335 summer, $750–$1,675 winter; 4-bedroom $300–$390 summer, $1,150–$1,875 winter; lower rates in spring and fall. AE, MC, V. Covered parking. **Amenities:** Outdoor heated pool; 2 outdoor hot tubs; exercise room; complimentary shuttle to town. *In room:* Cable TV/VCR, dataport w/ high-speed Internet, kitchen.

Steamboat Grand ★ Built in 2001, this is Steamboat's big, bold flagship property, a full-service hotel with plenty of bells and whistles. With upscale, understated interiors, the room configurations are set up to adjoin or not adjoin into one- to three-bedroom suites, as well as a few penthouse suites ranging from three to five bedrooms. Decorated with earth tones and a masculine sensibility, the rooms are some of the nicest and newest on the mountain. The list of amenities and facilities is long and comprehensive, including everything from make-up mirrors to private ski storage. Of special note are the two hot tubs: With maximum capacities of 35 and 45 people, they are said to be the largest in the entire state.

2300 Mt. Werner Circle, Steamboat Springs, CO 80847. ✆ **877/306-2628** or 970/871-5050. Fax 970/871-5559. 327 units. Studio to 3-bedroom units $174–$429 summer and early and late ski season; $285–$930 peak ski season; $115–$420 fall and spring. AE, DISC, MC, V. Underground parking. **Amenities:** 3 restaurants (American); 2 lounges; outdoor heated pool; exercise room; 2 outdoor hot tubs; sauna; children's programs; game room; concierge; courtesy shuttle; business center; shopping arcade; salon; room service; babysitting. *In room:* A/C, cable TV/DVD, wireless Internet access (free), kitchen, coffeemaker, hair dryer, iron, safe.

Torian Plum at Steamboat ★★ These slope-side ski-in/ski-out condominiums have handsome light-wood furnishings, a tile kitchen complete with microwave and dishwasher, washer/dryer, gas fireplace, private balcony, ski locker, and two phone lines with voice mail and a high-speed Internet connection. The Creekside Tower offers especially opulent master suites and handsome stone fireplaces. The property is scrupulously well maintained and attractive. Numerous free DVDs and a computer station are available.

1855 Ski Time Sq. Dr. (Resort Quest Steamboat, see above). ✆ **866/634-9618** or 970/879-8811. Fax 970/879-8485. www.resortqueststeamboat.com. 81 units. 1- to 6-bedroom units $155–$315 summer, $220–$1,095 early and late ski season, $460–$1,700 regular ski season, $725–$2,500 holiday season; lower rates available in spring and fall. AE, DISC, MC, V. Underground parking. **Amenities:** Outdoor heated pool; exercise room; 6 hot tubs (4 outdoor, 2 indoor); sauna; concierge; complimentary shuttle. *In room:* Cable TV/VCR/DVD player, wireless Internet access (free), kitchen.

Expensive

Sheraton Steamboat Resort ★★ Steamboat Springs's premier hotel is located in the heart of Ski Time Square, at the foot of the Silver Bullet Gondola. The Sheraton opens directly onto the ski slopes, and every room has a view of the mountain, valley, or slopes. There's a great cross-country ski course (p. 265), and in summer, avid golfers enjoy its golf club, one of the finest in the Rockies. Most units have one king or two queen beds, humidifiers, and a private balcony. You'll find outdoor hot tubs on a rooftop spa deck, retail shopping space, plus a 23-unit luxury suite tower. The resident eatery, Sevens, offers magnificent views of the mountain and the Headwall chairlift, along with meals three times a day. The hotel also offers après ski at the casual Western 3 Saddles Bar & Grill and massages and other treatments at the day spa.

2200 Village Inn Court, Steamboat Springs, CO 80477. ✆ **970/879-2220.** Fax 970/879-7686. www.sheraton.com/steamboat. 315 units, including 42 suites. Ski season and summer $219–$399; holiday rates higher; lower rates available in off season. AE, DISC, MC, V. Underground parking. Closed 1 month in spring and fall. **Amenities:** 3 restaurants; bar; outdoor heated pool; golf club (18-hole); health club; spa; 7 hot tubs; steam room; children's programs; game room; concierge; shopping arcade; room service (7am–10pm); massage; valet and coin-op laundry service. *In room:* A/C, cable TV/VCR, dataport w/high-speed Internet (fee), fridge, coffeemaker.

Moderate

Hotel Bristol ★ Among my favorites in Steamboat Springs, the Hotel Bristol offers lodging with character. Rooms are small (150 sq. ft.), in keeping with the heritage of this historic hotel, built in the 1940s. In fact, the reason this place is so great is because of the historic ambience—Zane Grey may not have stayed here, but if he had, he would have felt right at home. The standard rooms are sophisticated Old West, refined but not fancy, with solid dark-wood furnishings, lots of brass, Pendleton wool blankets, and reproduction 1940s-style phones. Rooms have one queen-size bed or two twins, and a bathroom with shower only (no tub). The former caretaker's unit has been converted into two suites with sleeper sofas in the living rooms. The family units, which accommodate four people, are two standard rooms with private baths.

917 Lincoln Ave. (P.O. Box 774927), Steamboat Springs, CO 80477. ✆ **800/851-0872** or 970/879-3083. Fax 970/879-8645. 18 units. Summer and ski season $109–$139 double, $149–$199 family unit; mid-Sept to mid-Nov $79 double, $109 family unit; rates higher during holidays. AE, DISC, MC, V. Closed mid-Apr to late May. **Amenities:** Restaurant (Italian); 6-person indoor whirlpool. *In room:* A/C, cable TV, wireless Internet access (free).

The Lodge at Steamboat ★ These well-maintained condominiums are just 600 feet from the Silver Bullet Gondola, and there's a free shuttle to take you to the mountain village, downtown, or shopping. The individually owned and decorated units have balconies, and upper-floor units have a cathedral ceiling with clerestory windows. A typical average-size unit is simply but pleasantly decorated in what might be termed mountain Western style, and includes an attractive brick fireplace, a sunny dining area, a counter island with high-stool seating between the kitchen and living area, a queen bed in the master bedroom, and twin beds in the second bedroom. Each unit boasts a fireplace and one bathroom per bedroom.

2700 Village Dr. (Steamboat Resorts, see above). ✆ **800/525-5502** or 970/879-8000. Fax 970/870-8061. 120 units. 1–3 bedrooms ski season $175–$825; summer $175–$270. AE, MC, V. **Amenities:** Outdoor heated pool; 2 tennis courts; 5 hot tubs (1 indoor, 4 outdoor); sauna; massage; babysitting; coin-op laundry; complimentary shuttle (winter only). *In room:* Cable TV/VCR (video rentals available), kitchen, wireless Internet access (free).

Trappeur's Crossing Resort (Value) Given its location 2 blocks from the slopes and its neat, well-maintained condo units, we consider Trappeur's Crossing an especially good value. There are actually five separate structures here, and as with most condominiums, these are individually owned and decorated; all have gas fireplaces, private balconies, washers and dryers, and kitchens. Many units also have private hot tubs.

2900 Village Dr. and Medicine Springs Rd. (ResortQuest Steamboat, see above). ✆ **866/634-9618** or 970/879-8811. Fax 970/879-8485. www.resortqueststeamboat.com. 102 units. 1- to 4-bedroom units summer and ski season $165–$400; $237–$640; $545–$1,200 holiday season. AE, DISC, MC, V. **Amenities:** 2 outdoor pools; indoor-outdoor pool; tennis courts (2 summer only); fitness center; 8 hot tubs (indoor, outdoor); sauna; concierge; ski shuttle. *In room:* Cable TV/VCR/DVD, wireless Internet access (free), kitchen, iron/ironing board.

Inexpensive

Mariposa Lodge ★★ (Finds) Located right on the pastoral edge of town, this modern, Pueblo-style bed-and-breakfast is a good value and perfectly cozy lodging any time of year. All four relatively small rooms have private baths, exposed log beams, and handmade quilts; the bear-themed Oso room is a bit larger, with a small sitting room, and Monarch is the largest and the only with a TV and jetted tub. Out back are a porch and small pond and access to Soda Creek, a nice spot to kick back and relax in the warmer months.

855 Grand St. (P.O. Box 771612), Steamboat Springs, CO 80477. ✆ **800/578-1467** or 970/879-1467. www.steamboatmariposa.com. 4 units. $129–$179 double. Rates include full breakfast. AE, DISC, MC, V. Closed Apr and Nov. *In room:* No phone.

Rabbit Ears Motel ★ Owned and operated by the Koehler family since 1970, this comfortable place features a vintage sign with the mug of a grinning bunny, a designated historic landmark that's served as Steamboat's welcome mat for more than a half-century. The original 10 rooms (and the sign) were built in 1952, with additional units added through 1991, some of which overlook the Yampa River. Renovated in 2008, all rooms are clean and comfortable. Even the smallest rooms (which are definitely tiny) have attractive cherry furnishings. The motel is conveniently located on the east end of the downtown shopping district, with Yampa River Park next door and the hot springs pool across the street (discount passes are available), and on the local free shuttle bus route. A good bargain for families is the meeting room, which doubles as a big suite (albeit a noisy one, being on the street), with a kitchen for $109 a night.

201 Lincoln Ave. (P.O. Box 770573), Steamboat Springs, CO 80477. ✆ **800/828-7702** or 970/879-1150. Fax 970/870-0483. www.rabbitearsmotel.com. 65 units. Summer and ski season $99–$179 double; higher holiday rates and lower off-season rates. Children 11 and under stay free in parent's room. Rates include continental breakfast. DISC, MC, V. Pets accepted ($15 one-time fee). **Amenities:** Coin-op laundry. *In room:* A/C, TV, wireless Internet access (free), fridge, coffeemaker, hair dryer, iron/ironing board, microwave.

A Guest Ranch

The Home Ranch ★★★ One of only two Relais & Châteaux properties in Colorado—the other is the Little Nell in Aspen—the Home Ranch effortlessly balances that French pedigree of culinary excellence with down-home Western hospitality. People come here for the horseback riding and the 90-horse-strong stable's revered custom program that allows guests to break free of the usual nose-to-tail rides and explore. In winter, riding gives way to cross-country skiing on-site, and the staff also provides transportation to the downhill slopes at Steamboat. The cabins and lodge rooms are beautifully done, with slick tiled bathrooms, wood-burning stoves, and a nice blend of rustic and comfortable that's perfect for the isolated locale. With 1,500 acres of aspen groves and idyllic woodland crisscrossed with trails, the setting is what ultimately defines Home Ranch, and it's one of the most sublime settings in the Rockies.

P.O. Box 822, Clark, CO 80428. ✆ **970/879-1780.** Fax 970/879-1795. www.homeranch.com. 14 units (8 cabins, 6 lodge rooms). Summer $5,110–$18,700 per room or cabin per week; winter $450–$1,445 per room or cabin per night. Rates include all meals and most activities AE, DISC, MC, V. **Amenities:** Restaurant; lounge; hot tub; sauna; horseback riding; cross-country skiing. *In room:* Wireless Internet access (free), fridge, coffeemaker, iron, no phone.

WHERE TO DINE

For a killer sandwich to eat on the premises or in the woods, **Backcountry Provisions,** 635 Lincoln Ave. (✆ **970/879-3617**), is the place, with creative offerings like the Sherpa (asiago cheese, roasted eggplant, tomato, red peppers, and more) and the Timberline (peanut butter, banana, and local honey). Midway between the slopes and downtown, **Freshies,** 595 S. Lincoln Ave. (✆ **970/879-8099**), is the local favorite for breakfast and lunch, with omelets, eggs "Benny," and a wide range of sandwiches and wraps. **Winona's,** 617 Lincoln Ave. (✆ **970/879-2483**), is a locally beloved downtown breakfast and lunch spot.

Many of the restaurants in Steamboat Springs cut back their hours or close completely in the slow seasons—primarily spring and fall—so if you're visiting at those times, it's best to call first to confirm hours.

Expensive

Harwigs/L'Apogée at 911 Lincoln Avenue ★★ Moments CONTEMPORARY FRENCH Located in downtown Steamboat Springs in an 1886 building that once housed the Harwigs saddle shop, this fine-dining establishment serves French cuisine with an Asian flair in a room featuring walls adorned with wine labels and crates. Owner-chef Jamie Jenny, who opened the eatery in 1979, keeps the menu fresh and diverse, but main courses might include selections such as seared Tasmanian salmon with grape tomato wild rice and rosé butter sauce, roasted duck with butternut squash and blueberry demi-glace, or cashew tofu cake on Napa cabbage with an Asian mushroom sauce. Small plates ($4–$10) include a delicious lamb slider with apple chutney and cheese. Service is superb, there's an award-winning wine cellar, and outdoor seating is available.

911 Lincoln Ave. ✆ **970/879-1919.** www.lapogee.com. Reservations recommended. Main courses $24–$36; steaks $6–$7 per oz. AE, MC, V. Daily 5–11pm.

Hazie's ★★ CREATIVE AMERICAN One of Steamboat Springs's most exciting dining experiences can be found at the top of the gondola, midway up Mount Werner. The views of the upper Yampa River valley are spectacular by day and romantic by night, as the lights of Steamboat Springs spread out at the foot of the mountain. Lunch features a variety of salads and sandwiches, plus a daily chef's special. But it's at dinner that Hazie's really excels. Start with an appetizer such as baked escargot strudel, then try the soup du jour or Hazie's house salad with lemon-parsley vinaigrette. Finally, choose from entrees like macadamia-crusted sea bass, grilled lamb served with goat cheese risotto, or a vegetarian portabella mushroom Wellington. In summer, you can enjoy Sunday brunch overlooking the lush greenery of the Yampa Valley.

Steamboat Ski Area, 2305 Mt. Werner Circle, Thunderbird Terminal, top of the Silver Bullet Gondola. ✆ **970/871-5150.** www.steamboat.com. Reservations recommended for lunch or brunch, required for dinner. Lunch main courses $12–$25; dinner 3-course meal $72–$80 winter, $47 summer; Sun brunch $39. Children 12 and under about half at brunch and dinner. AE, DISC, MC, V. Mid-Dec to early Apr daily 11:30am–2:30pm and 6–10pm; mid-June to Labor Day Fri–Sat 7–10pm; Sun 9:30am–1pm (brunch). Closed spring and fall.

La Montaña ★ SOUTHWESTERN/MEXICAN This isn't your everyday Mexican restaurant; it's a gourmet experience. The festive decor sets the mood, with greenhouse dining and handsome photos by owner Tom Garrett on the stuccoed walls. Southwestern dishes include unusual combinations such as grilled elk loin with a cilantro pesto crust and ancho chile demi-glace; the chef's award-winning dish of braided sausage, a mesquite-grilled combination of elk, lamb, and chorizo sausage; and enchiladas (which have been featured in *Gourmet* magazine) composed of blue corn tortillas, goat and Monterey Jack cheeses, roasted peppers, and onions.

2500 Village Dr. at Apres Ski Way. ✆ **970/879-5800.** www.la-montana.com. Reservations recommended. Main courses $14–$31. AE, DISC, MC, V. Daily 5–10pm (bar daily 4:30–10pm). Hours vary in spring, summer, and fall; call in advance.

Moderate

Mahogany Ridge Brewery & Grill ★ INTERNATIONAL This modern restaurant is one of Colorado's slickest, and more than a simple brewpub—it boasts a full bar with an extensive wine list in addition to its own microbrews, and the chef draws from all corners of the globe to offer a unique combination of flavors. Choose your entree—maybe maple-glazed chicken, or tandoori-spiced yellowfin tuna, or garlic-sage crusted buffalo; then choose two sauces, ranging from salsa to apple chutney to wasabi cream.

Once the order arrives, the dipping begins: The more the tastier, as sharing and double-dipping are encouraged. For the less adventuresome, Mahogany Ridge also offers several soups, salads, sandwiches, and burgers, plus fish and chips, fried chicken, an unusual and delicious chipotle chicken potpie, and even a kid's menu. Live music also plays on weekends (see "Performing Arts & Nightlife," below). There's really something for everyone here.

435 Lincoln Ave. (at Fifth St.). ✆ **970/879-3773.** www.myspace.com/mahoganysteamboat. Sandwiches and main courses $10–$19; dipping entrees $17–$33. DISC, MC, V. Daily 4–11pm.

Slopeside Grill ★ AMERICAN/ITALIAN This restaurant draws diners with its large portions—bring a big appetite—and views of the slopes. A large U-shaped light-colored wooden bar dominates the dining room, where eaters face the ski slopes through large windows and the walls are decorated with Western and early skiing memorabilia. When the weather cooperates, alfresco dining is popular on the patio under umbrellas. Grill options (available after 6pm) include the deservedly popular slow-roasted rack of ribs, and I recommend the fresh Gulf mahi blackened and served with raspberry–beurre blanc sauce. The pizza here is especially delicious, made in an Italian-style brick oven, with choices such as "The Chutes" (sweet and hot Italian sausage, fresh tomatoes, red onions, and mushrooms) and the "Vagabond" (garlic, feta cheese, sun-dried tomatoes, olive oil, and spinach). This dog-friendly place has Purina on the menu. There's a great happy hour from 9 to 11pm.

Ski Time Square in Torian Plum Plaza. ✆ **970/879-2916.** www.slopesidegrill.com. Reservations suggested. Pizza $10–$13; main courses $7–$21. AE, DISC, MC, V. Daily 11am–10pm; pizza oven open until midnight; bar open until 2am.

Inexpensive

Cugino's Pizzeria ★ Value ITALIAN Local families pack this restaurant in downtown Steamboat Springs, and with good reason—it offers great food, generous portions, and low prices. The extensive menu includes pizza, of course, plus hoagies and steak sandwiches, pasta, and calzones. Those with healthy appetites might want to try one of the strombolis—fresh-baked pizza dough stuffed with various ingredients such as mushrooms, onions, peppers, mozzarella and provolone cheeses, plus ham, Genoa salami, and capicola, or meatballs, pepperoni, and spicy sausage. A vegetarian version is also served. There is a full bar.

41 8th St. ✆ **970/879-5805.** www.cuginosrestaurant.com. Reservations not accepted. Pizzas from $6.75; sandwiches $5–$7; main courses $8–$17. MC, V. Daily 11am–10pm. Delivery available.

The Tugboat Grill & Pub AMERICAN Oak floors and rough barn-wood walls cloaked with game and fishing trophies, sports memorabilia, and celebrity photographs are the trademark of this foot-of-the-slopes establishment, which also boasts a sun deck for great people-watching. The hand-carved cherrywood bar, circa 1850, came from the Log Cabin Saloon in Baggs, Wyoming, a Butch Cassidy hangout; look for the bullet hole in one of the columns. The fare includes a variety of burgers, burritos, deli sandwiches, fish, soups, and huge salads throughout the day, and dinner entrees such as basil chicken, a lightly herbed chicken breast in a creamy vegetable sauce, with black olives, green onions, and tomatoes. Many folks sup on nachos, teriyaki wings, and other generous appetizer plates. There's also live music (see below).

1860 Ski Time Sq. ✆ **970/879-7070.** Reservations not accepted. Main courses $8–$23. AE, MC, V. Daily 11:30am–9:45pm. Bar open later.

PERFORMING ARTS & NIGHTLIFE

The music scene in Steamboat Springs is dominated by the **Strings in the Mountains Music Festival,** which offers a wide variety of musical events almost daily throughout the summer, and with lesser frequency at other times of the year. See the sidebar "Musical Mountains," earlier in this chapter.

The **bar scene** in Steamboat, while never dull, comes especially alive in winter. (Like Steamboat's restaurants, its nightlife ranges from quiet to nonexistent in spring.) One of the hottest new hangouts is **Level'z Nightclub,** at 1860 Ski Time Sq. (© **970/870-9090**), with live entertainment nightly, 20 beers on tap, pool tables, and video games, and some good happy hour specials. Other popular venues include the rustic **Tugboat Grill & Pub,** 1860 Ski Time Sq. (© **970/879-7070**), which attracts a noisy local crowd for a variety of live music and dancing, starting at about 9:30pm.

In downtown Steamboat, **The Tap House,** 729 Lincoln Ave. (© **970/879-2431**), has dozens of TVs (including a couple of huge ones) showing just about any sporting event you'd want to see. There are 21 beers on tap, good fajitas and chicken wings, pool tables, and a video arcade. A riverside bar and grill with New Orleans roots, **Sunpies,** 735 Yampa St. (© **970/870-3360**), is a hip young hangout specializing in po' boy sandwiches and potent rum "Slurricanes." **Mahogany Ridge Brewery & Grill,** 435 Lincoln Ave. (© **970/879-3773**), brews a nice selection of handcrafted ales and a wide variety of musicians grace its stage. **The Old Town Pub,** 600 Lincoln St. (© **970/879-2101**), is a local favorite, a low-key bar in a historic downtown building.

4 WINTER PARK

67 miles NW of Denver

Originally an Arapaho and Ute hunting ground, Winter Park was first settled by whites in the 1850s. The laying of a rail track over Rollins Pass in 1905 and the completion of the 6¼-mile Moffat Tunnel in 1928 opened forests here to logging, which long supported the economy while providing Denver with raw materials for its growth.

The birth of the Winter Park ski area in January 1940, at the west portal of the Moffat Tunnel, helped give impetus to the Colorado ski boom. Although it hasn't yet achieved the notoriety of Vail or Aspen, the tiny town of Winter Park—population around 700—still manages to attract a million skier visits per season. One of its draws is the Ski Train from Denver to Winter Park, the last of its kind in the West. Elevation here is about 9,400 feet.

ESSENTIALS

GETTING THERE **By Car** From Denver or other points east or west, take I-70 exit 232, at Empire, and climb 24 miles north on U.S. 40 over Berthoud Pass to Winter Park. U.S. 40 links Winter Park directly to Steamboat Springs, 101 miles northwest, and, via U.S. 34 (at Granby) through Rocky Mountain National Park, to Estes Park, 84 miles north.

By Plane Visitors fly into Denver International Airport and can continue to Winter Park with **Home James Transportation Services** (© **800/359-7503** or 970/726-4730; www.homejamestransportation.com); a one-way trip runs $60.

By Train Winter Park Resort is the only ski area in the western United States with rail service directly to the slopes. The dramatically scenic **Winter Park Ski Train ★★** (✆ **303/296-4754;** www.skitrain.com) has been making regular runs between Denver and Winter Park since 1940, stopping just 150 feet from the foot of the lifts. On its 2-hour run, the train climbs almost 4,000 feet and passes through 29 tunnels (including the 6¼-mile Moffat Tunnel). The train operates Saturdays and Sundays in December and January, plus Fridays in February and Thursdays in March, as well as Saturdays from late June to early August. Fees for coach seating are $49 for adults, $39 for seniors 62 and up and kids 3 to 13 (with an adult), and free for children 2 and younger. Rates for the upgraded club cars cost $74 per person and include a continental breakfast, après-ski snacks, and nonalcoholic beverages. ***Note:*** These are 2008 prices; 2009 could be higher because of increased fuel prices. Call for current information.

The **Amtrak California Zephyr** (✆ **800/USA-RAIL** [872-7245]; www.amtrak.com) stops twice daily (once in each direction) in Fraser, 2 miles north of Winter Park, on its Chicago–West Coast run.

VISITOR INFORMATION Main sources of visitor information are the **Winter Park–Fraser Valley Chamber of Commerce,** P.O. Box 3236, Winter Park, CO 80482 (✆ **800/903-7275** or 970/726-4118 for general information; www.playwinterpark.com), and the **Winter Park Resort,** P.O. Box 36, Winter Park, CO 80482 (✆ **866/722-5560** or 970/726-5514; www.skiwinterpark.com). The chamber of commerce's visitor center, on the east side of U.S. 40 in the center of town, is open year-round daily from 9am to 5pm.

GETTING AROUND U.S. 40 (Winter Park Dr.) runs almost directly north–south through the community. Vasquez Road, one of the few side roads with accommodations, is the first major left turn as you arrive from the south. Two miles north on U.S. 40 is Fraser, site of the Amtrak terminal and several condominium developments. **The Lift** (✆ **970/726-4163**), a free local shuttle service, runs between most accommodations and the ski area during the ski season, and from July 4th through Labor Day operates a free bus between Fraser and Winter Park. **Car rentals** are available from **Hertz** (✆ **970/726-8993**).

FAST FACTS The hospital, **Seven Mile Medical Clinic,** at 145 Parsenn Rd. in the Winter Park Resort (✆ **970/887-7470**), can handle most medical emergencies (call for hours). The **post office** is in the heart of Winter Park at 78490 U.S. 40. For hours and other information, contact the U.S. Postal Service (✆ **800/275-8777;** www.usps.com).

SPECIAL EVENTS Fat Tire Classic mountain biking and hiking event, late June; Jazz Festival, mid-July; High Country Stampede Rodeo, Saturday nights from early July through August; Rocky Mountain Wine, Beer, and Food Festival, early August.

SKIING & OTHER WINTER ACTIVITIES

Winter Park Resort ★★ is one of those rare resorts that seems to have something for everyone. Experts rave about the chutes and steep mogul runs on Mary Jane Mountain and the extreme skiing in the Vasquez Cirque, but intermediates and beginners are well served on other slopes. Moreover, Winter Park is noted for wide-ranging programs for children and those with disabilities.

The resort includes three interconnected mountain areas totaling 141 designated trails on 3,060 acres of skiable terrain. There are 25 lifts, including two high-speed six-passenger chairlifts, seven high-speed express quads, four triples, six double chairs, three surface lifts, and three Magic Carpets. In 2008, the resort opened a new open-air gondola connecting parking lots with the village. The resort rates its trails as 8% beginner, 17% intermediate, 19% advanced, 53% most difficult, and 3% expert only.

Winter Park Resort comprises several distinct areas. **Winter Park Mountain** has mostly beginner and intermediate terrain. **Discovery Park** encompasses more than 25 acres of prime beginner terrain. **Mary Jane Mountain** mainly offers intermediate, most difficult, and expert terrain, best known for its numerous mogul runs. **Vasquez Ridge,** the resort's third mountain area, has primarily intermediate and most difficult terrain. Fans of tree-line skiing will like **Parsenn Bowl,** more than 200 acres of open-bowl and gladed-tree skiing that fan out from the summit at North Cone and merge with Mary Jane's Backside. **Vasquez Cirque** is no place for beginners. It contains steep chutes and gladed pockets for advanced and expert skiers and snowboarders. The five terrain parks at Winter Park are cutting edge, and there is one for every skill level. **Rail Yard,** consisting of advanced terrain, is considered one of the nation's best.

Annual snowfall at Winter Park averages over 350 inches; this is one of the most consistently snowy resorts in the Rockies. The vertical drop is 3,060 feet, from the 12,060-foot summit off North Cone of Parsenn Bowl. There are about a dozen restaurants and several bars, including a mountaintop restaurant.

Winter Park's impressive **Kid's Adventure Junction** ★ includes a play area, rental shop, restrooms, and a children's instruction hill. The **National Sports Center for the Disabled** ★★, founded in 1970, is one of the largest programs of its kind in the world.

Daily lift tickets (2007–08 regular season prices) cost $86 for adults ages 13 to 64, $45 for children 6 to 12, $72 for seniors 65 to 69, and $35 for seniors 70 and older. Kids under 6 ski free. Full rental packages are available, as are lessons and snowshoe tours.

Winter Park is usually open for skiing from mid-November to mid-April. It's open for summer operations daily from early June until early September. For more information, contact **Winter Park Resort,** P.O. Box 36, Winter Park, CO 80482 (✆ **970/726-5514,** or 303/316-1564; www.skiwinterpark.com). For daily ski reports, call ✆ **970/726-7669** or 303/572-7669.

OTHER SKIING NEARBY Just 78 miles from Denver, **SolVista Basin at Granby Ranch,** 1000 Village Rd. (P.O. Box 1110), Granby, CO 80446 (✆ **888/850-4615** or 970/887-3384; www.solvista.com), has long been a favorite with parents and kids for its easy access, affordable prices, and family-friendly atmosphere.

The ski area comprises two separate but interconnected mountains. The resort contains 400 acres of skiable terrain, with 38 trails rated 30% beginner, 50% intermediate, and 20% advanced. The longest run is 1½ miles and the vertical drop is 1,000 feet from the top elevation of 9,202 feet. It's served by one high-speed quad, one fixed-grip quad, one triple, one double, and a surface lift. Average annual snowfall is 220 inches, and 60% of the terrain has snow-making, with top-to-bottom coverage on both mountains. Full-day lift tickets are $48 to $50 for adults, $26 to $30 for children 6 to 12, $34 to $36 for seniors 61 to 69, and free for those under 6 and over 69.

CROSS-COUNTRY SKIING & SNOWSHOEING The outstanding cross-country skiing in the Winter Park area is highlighted by what the *Denver Post* calls "the best touring center in Colorado." The **Devil's Thumb Nordic Country Center** ★★ at Devil's Thumb Ranch (✆ **970/726-8231;** www.devilsthumbranch.com) has more than 62 miles of groomed trails. Full rentals and instruction are available. Full-day passes are about $15, or free for those staying at the ranch.

Moments Totally Tubular

The **Fraser Snow Tubing Hill** (behind Kentucky Fried Chicken; ✆ **970/726-5954**) offers a return to childhood for many adults, as well as a lot of fun for kids (who must be 7 or older to ride alone). A lift pulls you and your big inner tube to the top of a steep hill, and then you slide down, sometimes reaching speeds of 45 mph. Hours Friday through Sunday are from 10am to 10pm, with slightly shorter hours Monday through Thursday, and the tubing hill is open November to April, snow permitting. Rides run about $15 an hour.

Snow Mountain Ranch–YMCA Nordic Center, on U.S. 40 between Winter Park and Grand Lake (✆ **970/887-2152;** www.ymcarockies.org), features 62 miles of groomed trails for all abilities, including a short section of lighted track for night skiing. Trail passes (2007–08 prices) cost $15 for adults, $8 for kids 6 to 12, and $7 seniors 61 to 69. Children under 6 and seniors over 69 ski free, and adults with YMCA membership receive $5 discounts. A 5-day adult trail pass costs $40.

All of the above provide **snowshoeing** opportunities, with rental equipment and guided tours. You can also rent snowshoes and get tips on where to go at **Winter Park Sports Shop** in Kings Crossing Shopping Center, at the intersection of Winter Park Drive and Kings Crossing Road (✆ **970/726-5554**).

WARM-WEATHER & YEAR-ROUND ACTIVITIES

There are plenty of recreational opportunities in the **Arapaho National Forest** and **Arapaho National Recreation Area.** Maps and brochures on hiking, mountain biking, and other activities are available at the **Sulphur Ranger District office,** P.O. Box 10, 9 Ten Mile Dr., off U.S. 40 about half a mile south of Granby, CO 80446 (✆ **970/887-4100;** www.fs.fed.us/r2). The **Devil's Thumb Ranch** (see "Where to Stay," below) is famous for its numerous recreation packages, including rafting, hiking, and fly-fishing.

ALPINE SLIDE Colorado's longest alpine slide, at 3,030 feet long and with 26 turns, cools summer visitors. Rates are $12 for adults, $10 for children 6 to 13 and for seniors 70 and older on Friday through Sunday. Kids under 6 get in free at all times and seniors 70 and older are admitted free Monday through Thursday. For information, contact the Winter Park Resort (see "Skiing & Other Winter Activities," above).

FISHING Fraser Valley and surrounding Grand County are renowned among anglers. Head to Williams Fork Reservoir and the Three Lakes District for kokanee salmon, lake trout, brookies, and browns. Fishing ponds stocked with various species are in Fraser, across from the Fraser Valley Center on U.S. 40. The upper pond is reserved for children and people in wheelchairs; the lower pond is open to everyone. Ponds are generally open and stocked by mid-May.

The fly shop at **Devil's Thumb Ranch** (see "Where to Stay," below) offers guided fly-fishing trips with rates of $375 for two people for a full day.

GOLF Local golf courses include the 27-hole **Pole Creek Golf Club,** 10 miles northwest of Winter Park on U.S. 40 (✆ **970/887-9195;** www.polecreekgolf.com), considered among the finest mountain courses in the state, with greens fees of $58 to $99 for 18 holes; and the **Headwaters Golf Course** (✆ **970/887-2709;** www.granbyranch.com), with fees of $40 to $80.

HIKING & BACKPACKING The nearby Arapaho National Forest and Arapaho National Recreation Area (see above) offer miles of hiking trails and plenty of backpacking opportunities. Beautiful Rocky Mountain National Park is less than an hour's drive north (see "Rocky Mountain National Park," earlier in this chapter).

MOUNTAIN BIKING Winter Park and the Fraser Valley have won national recognition for their expansive trail system and established race program. Many off-road bike trails connect to the more than 600 miles of backcountry roads and trails in the adjacent national forest. The King of the Rockies Off-Road Stage Race and Festival, held each year in August, is one of the top professional mountain-bike races in America; part of it is run on the 30-mile **Tipperary Creek Trail ★**, among Colorado's best mountain-bike trails. The Fat Tire Classic in late June is another big mountain-biking event and the single largest fundraiser for the American Red Cross. Entrants are recommended to be intermediate or advanced bikers or hikers.

For advice, information, and maps, talk to the knowledgeable folks at **Grand Sports Shop,** in downtown Winter Park at 78786 U.S. 40 (✆ **970/722-0484;** www.grandsports.net). The shop is open daily year-round, providing mountain sales, repairs, and very reasonably priced rentals (starting at $14 per half-day, $18 per day). Ask for a copy of the free trail map, also available from the **Winter Park–Fraser Valley Chamber of Commerce** (see "Visitor Information," above).

MORE TO SEE & DO

Amaze'n Winter Park A human maze by Amaze'n Colorado, this two-level labyrinth of twists and turns offers prizes to participants who can "beat the clock." The maze is constructed in such a way that it can be easily changed, which is done weekly to maintain interest for repeat customers. A free observation deck gives a bird's-eye view of the maze, as well as the surrounding scenery. Allow about 1 hour.

At the base of Winter Park Resort. ✆ **970/726-0214.** www.amazenmazes.com. Admission $10 adults, $7 children 6–12, free for children 5 and under. Additional maze runs $3. Daily Memorial Day weekend to Sept 10am–5:30pm.

Cozens Ranch House Museum This 1870s homestead is a National Historic Registry site and presents a glimpse into Colorado's pioneer past, with a restored and furnished family residence, small hotel, stagecoach stop, and the original Fraser Valley post office. There's also a replica of a stagecoach that traveled roads near here between 1875 and 1905, plus a small gift shop. Allow 30 minutes to an hour.

U.S. 40 btw. Winter Park and Fraser. ✆ **970/726-5488.** www.grandcountymuseum.com/CozensRanch.htm. Admission $4 adults, $3 seniors 62 and over, $2 students 6–18, free for children 5 and under. Memorial Day to Sept Tues–Sat 10am–5pm; rest of year Wed–Sat 10am–4pm.

WHERE TO STAY

There are more than 60 accommodations in the Fraser Valley, including hotels, condominiums, family-style mountain inns (serving breakfast and dinner daily), bed-and-breakfasts, lodges, and motels. Bookings can be made through **Winter Park Central Reservations** (✆ **800/729-5813;** www.skiwinterpark.com). The agency can also book air and rail tickets, rental cars, airport transfers, lift tickets, ski-school lessons, ski rentals, and other activities. Another option, for those interested in renting a private, upscale home, town house, or condo, is to contact **Destinations West** (✆ **800/545-9378;** www.mtnlodging.com).

Snow Mountain Ranch–YMCA of the Rockies, on U.S. 40 between Winter Park and Grand Lake, 1101 C.R. 53, Granby, CO 80446 (✆ **800/777-9622** or 970/887-2152; www.ymcarockies.org), offers a wide range of lodging possibilities, from economical lodge rooms to delightful Western-style cabins with up to five bedrooms. Rates are $74 to $144 double for the lodge rooms and $99 to $349 for cabins. The **Rocky Mountain Inn & Hostel,** U.S. 40, Fraser (✆ **866/467-8351** or 970/726-8256; www.therockymountaininn.com), is a solid budget option, clean and well maintained with a gorgeous valley view, with private rooms from $53 to $119 double and bunks from $19 to $28 a night, with higher holiday rates. Taxes add about 10% to lodging bills.

Devil's Thumb Ranch ★★★ Established in 1937 and reinvented for the new millennium, this guest ranch 8 miles north of Winter Park has become the standout property in the Fraser Valley, melding charming accommodations, an isolated location, and ecological consciousness into a wonderful whole. Bob and Suzanne Fanch bought the ranch and the 4,000 surrounding acres and rebuilt the cabins, then started on a new lodge inspired by the historic lodges of the national parks. The cabins, decorated with antiques in one of four themes (fishing, Nordic, Native American, or Western), are at once rustic, elegant, and cozy. The lodge, opened in late 2007, is a marvel, outdoing all expectations. Its "New West" trappings, hexagonal restaurant, and atmosphere are perfectly suited to the remote locale. It's also green—the lodge, cabins, and other ranch buildings utilize geothermal energy for heat—and has a terrific game room with candlepin bowling and other nonelectronic games. But Devil's Thumb Ranch is not all about the indoors: This is just the place to escape the modern world, and it is renowned for cross-country skiing and snowshoeing in winter and horseback riding, fly-fishing, and rafting in summer.

Grand County Rd. 83 (P.O. Box 750), Tabernash, CO 80478. ✆ **800/933-4339** or 970/726-5632. Fax 970/726-9038. www.devilsthumbranch.com. 68 units (52 lodge rooms, 16 cabins). $210–$565 double lodge room; $315–$895 cabin. Higher holiday rates. Minimum stay required for some accommodations. MC, V. **Amenities:** 2 restaurants (American); bar; indoor/outdoor pool; spa; whirlpool; sauna; fitness center; activities desk; business center; game room. *In room:* A/C, TV, wireless/wired Internet access (free), kitchens (cabins), fridge, iron, microwave.

The Vintage Resort Hotel and Conference Center The châteaulike Vintage rises five stories above the foot of Winter Park's ski slopes, not far from the Mary Jane base facilities. A full-service resort hotel, it offers convenient access to skiing, excellent dining and atmosphere, and luxury accommodations. The units range from average-size rooms with two queen beds to spacious two-bedroom suites with whirlpool tubs. Every room has a view of either the ski slopes or the Continental Divide, and many have kitchenettes and fireplaces. Some rooms also have high-speed Internet available. There are ski lockers and on-site ski rentals, mountain bike storage and work rooms, and a library with a pool table. The entire property is nonsmoking.

100 Winter Park Dr. (P.O. Box 3610), Winter Park, CO 80482. ✆ **800/472-7017** or 970/726-8801. Fax 970/726-9230. www.vintagehotel.com. 118 units. Summer $60–$105 double, $120–$220 suite; winter $111–$53 double, $218–$424 suite. Higher rates during holidays and special events. AE, DISC, MC, V. Pets accepted (one time fee of $25). **Amenities:** Restaurant (microbrewery); bar; outdoor heated pool; exercise room; outdoor hot tub; sauna; game room; shuttle service; business center; coin-op laundry. *In room:* Cable TV w/ pay movies, wireless Internet access (free), fridge (in some units), coffeemaker, hair dryer, iron.

Wild Horse Inn ★ Although the Wild Horse Inn was built in 1991, the pine logs used in it are over 400 years old, giving the place the feel of an 1800s mountain lodge. With rooms in the main house and a strip of adjacent one-bedroom cabins (with kitchenettes) to choose from, guests are treated to woodsy accommodations with pizzazz, complete with jetted tubs and balconies. Innkeepers Chris French and John Cribari are a gourmet chef and a licensed massage therapist, respectively, and both leverage their skills to their utmost: Chris oversees the gourmet breakfasts while John is the prime masseur in the inn's three massage rooms. The couple also owns the **Snowberry Bed & Breakfast** in Fraser (✆ **970/726-5974;** www.thesnowberry.com).

Grand County Rd. 83 (P.O. Box 609), Fraser, CO 80442. ✆ **970/726-0456.** Fax 970/726-9678. www.wildhorseinncolorado.com. 10 units (7 rooms, 3 cabins). $135–$235 double; $195–$285 cabin. Rates include full breakfast. Children 11 and under not accepted. AE, MC, V. **Amenities:** Outdoor hot tub; sauna; massage. *In room:* Cable TV/VCR or DVD player, wireless Internet access (free), kitchenette.

WHERE TO DINE

In addition to the restaurants discussed here, other local standbys include **Fontenot's,** 78711 U.S. 40, Winter Park (✆ **970/726-4021**), serving seafood and Cajun dishes; **Hernando's Pizza Pub,** 78199 U.S. 40, Winter Park (✆ **970/726-5409**), beloved for its pizzas and Italian fare; and, for a splurge, **Ranch House Restaurant** at Devil's Thumb Ranch (see "Where to Stay," above). I also like **Mirasol Cantina,** 74815 U.S. 40 (✆ **970/726-0280**), the only taco joint I've patronized with hummus and tofu tacos.

Deno's Mountain Bistro ★ CONTEMPORARY AMERICAN A favorite of locals and visitors alike, this bistro on Winter Park's main street has a casual atmosphere and impressive bar, with an extensive selection of national and international beers and an excellent wine list of more than 300 selections. The restaurant takes up two levels—the upstairs sports pub features copper-topped tables, while downstairs is casually elegant fine dining. Lunch here means sandwiches, burgers, and salads, as well as individual gourmet pizzas. The gourmet cuisine at dinner includes such dishes as angel hair pomodoro with fresh basil, garlic, grape tomatoes, and optional shrimp scampi for $5 more; braised pork shank with roasted apple, white wine, and thyme; and the absolute favorite of carnivores, the grilled New York strip steak, served with mashed potatoes and seasonal veggies.

78911 U.S. 40 (downtown, across from Copper Creek Sq.). ✆ **970/726-5332.** www.denosmountainbistro.com. Salads and most sandwiches $7–$16; main courses $13–$36. AE, DISC, MC, V. Daily 11:30am–11pm.

Untamed Southwest Grill ★ NEW AMERICAN/STEAK This large Western restaurant with 30-foot vaulted ceilings, exposed pine beams, and a handsome stone fireplace offers well-prepared and innovative cuisine. For lunch there are sandwiches and light entrees, and for dinner I suggest the coffee-spiced rib-eye or the cedar-plank rainbow trout (served with a tasty mango-tomatilla salsa). There's a nice selection of homemade Wild Creek microbeers, a good wine list, and specialty martinis.

78491 U.S. 40 (downtown). ✆ **970/726-1111.** www.wildcreekbrewingcompany.com. Main courses $14–$30. AE, DISC, MC, V. Sun–Thurs 11am–9pm; Fri–Sat 11–10pm. Bar until later.

5 BRECKENRIDGE & SUMMIT COUNTY ★★

67 miles W of Denver, 114 miles NW of Colorado Springs, 23 miles E of Vail

Breckenridge, founded in 1859, and its neighbors throughout Summit County comprise a major outdoor recreation center, with skiing in winter and fishing, hiking, and mountain biking in summer. But the area actually offers much more, with a number of historical attractions, good shopping opportunities, fine restaurants, and some interesting places to stay. The town of Breckenridge (elevation 9,603 ft.) is a good place to base yourself, as the

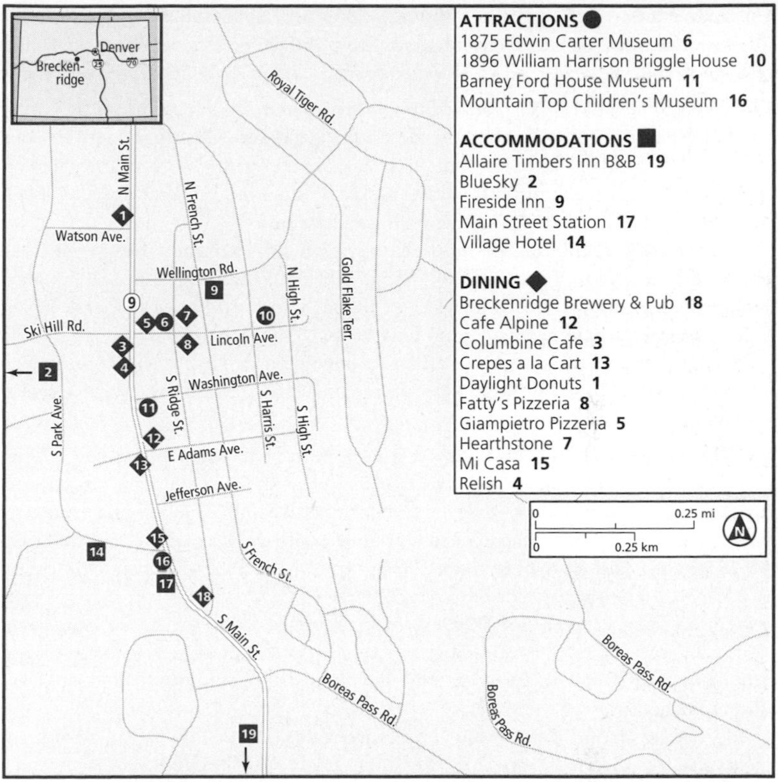

entire Victorian core of this 19th-century mining town has been carefully preserved, with colorfully painted shops and restaurants occupying the old buildings, most dating from the 1880s and 1890s.

Most of the mountain towns that surround the area's excellent ski resorts—Arapahoe Basin, Breckenridge, Copper, Keystone, and Loveland—were barely on the map in the 1880s, when the rest of the state was laying claim to its stake of history. Breckenridge, however, was a prosperous mining town in 1887 when the largest gold nugget ever found in Colorado, "Tom's Baby," was unearthed there. It weighed 13 pounds, 7 ounces, and is now in the Colorado History Museum in Denver. Today these communities are strictly in the tourism business and fill to capacity during peak seasons. Breckenridge, for example, has a year-round population of only 2,800 people, but swells to almost 34,000 during its top tourism times.

ESSENTIALS

GETTING THERE **By Car** I-70 runs through the middle of Summit County. For Keystone, exit on U.S. 6 at Dillon; the resort is 6 miles east of the interchange. For Breckenridge, exit on Colo. 9 at Frisco and head south 9 miles to the resort. Copper Mountain is right on I-70 at the Colo. 91 interchange.

 By Airport Shuttle Most visitors fly into Denver International or Colorado Springs and continue to Breckenridge, Frisco, Keystone, and/or Copper Mountain via shuttle. **Colorado Mountain Express** (✆ **800/525-6363** or 970/926-9800; www.cmex.com) offers shuttles; the cost from Denver starts at about $80 per person, one-way. (For listings of airlines servicing Denver and Colorado Springs, see chapters 6 and 9, respectively.)

VISITOR INFORMATION For additional information on Breckenridge and other parts of Summit County, contact the **Breckenridge Resort Chamber** at its welcome center at 203 S. Main St. (daily 9am–9pm summer and winter, with shorter hours in spring and fall), and administrative offices at 311 S. Ridge St., Breckenridge, CO 80424 (✆ **800/221-1091** or 970/453-2913; www.gobreck.com).

A source of visitor information for the entire region is the **Summit Chamber of Commerce,** P.O. Box 5450, Frisco, CO 80443 (✆ **800/530-3099** or 970/668-2051; www.summitchamber.org). The chamber has an information center in Silverthorne at 246 Rainbow Dr. Both are open daily from 9am to 5pm.

Parents traveling with kids can find all sorts of pointers in ***The Parents Handbook to Summit County*** (✆ **970/390-3533;** www.theparentshandbook.com), available free all over Summit County.

GETTING AROUND Dillon Reservoir is at the heart of Summit County, and I-70 lies along its northwestern shore, with Frisco at its west end, and Dillon and Silverthorne toward the east. From Dillon, take U.S. 6 about 5 miles east to Keystone and another 15 miles to Arapahoe. Breckenridge is about 10 miles south of Frisco on Colo. 9, and Copper Mountain is just south of I-70 exit 195 (Colo. 91). Loveland is just across the county line at exit 216 on the east side of the Eisenhower Tunnel.

Summit Stage (✆ **970/668-0999;** www.summitstage.com) provides free year-round service between Frisco, Dillon, Silverthorne, Keystone, Breckenridge, and Copper Mountain, daily from 6am to after midnight from late November to mid-April and shorter hours the rest of the year.

You can get around Breckenridge on the **free bus system** (✆ **970/547-3140**), and there's also **free shuttle service** at the Keystone Resort (✆ **970/496-4200**).

FAST FACTS Medical facilities here include the **Breckenridge Medical Center,** located in the Village at Breckenridge, 555 S. Park Ave.(✆ **970/453-1010**). **Post offices** are at 305 S. Ridge St., Breckenridge, and 35 W. Main St., Frisco. For hours and other information, contact the U.S. Postal Service (✆ **800/275-8777;** www.usps.com). For **weather** and **road conditions,** call ✆ **970/668-1090.**

SPECIAL EVENTS Ullr Fest, early January, in Breckenridge; International Snow Sculpture Championships, fourth week in January, in Breckenridge; Sunsation, early April, in Copper Mountain; Memorial Day Weekend Beach Party and Festival of the Brewpubs, Memorial Day weekend, in Arapahoe Basin; the Celtic Festival, late June, Keystone; Oktoberfest, mid-September, in Breckenridge. See also "The Festival Scene," later in this chapter.

SKIING & OTHER WINTER ACTIVITIES

Breckenridge and Keystone ski areas are now part of Vail Resorts, and any lift ticket purchased at Vail or Beaver Creek is valid without restriction at Breckenridge and Keystone (and Arapahoe Basin). However, only multiday lift tickets for 3 or more days purchased at Breckenridge or Keystone are also valid at Vail and Beaver Creek.

Beyond the major resorts listed below, snowboarders and beginners might want to check out **Echo Mountain Park,** near Idaho Springs (✆ **303/325-7347;** www.echomtn park.com), a dinky and inexpensive area with one lift and a focus on terrain parks.

Snowboarding is permitted at all local resorts.

ARAPAHOE BASIN Arapahoe Basin, 28194 U.S. 6, between Keystone and Loveland Pass, is one of Colorado's oldest ski areas, having opened in 1946. Several features make Arapahoe exceptional: Most of its 900 skiable acres are intermediate and expert terrain, much of it above timberline; it expanded to the new, wide-open slopes of Montezuma Bowl in January 2008; its longest run is 1$^1/_2$ miles; and it receives an average of 367 inches of snow a year and is frequently one of the last Colorado ski areas to close for the season—often not until mid-June. It usually opens in early November. Arapahoe offers a 2,270-foot vertical drop from its summit at 13,050 feet. It is served by two triple and three double chairs plus a conveyor. The mountain rates its 105 trails as 10% beginner, 30% intermediate, 37% advanced, and 23% expert.

Lift tickets during peak season cost $65 for adults, $52 for youths 15 to 19, $28 for children 6 to 14, $55 for seniors 60 to 69, $15 per day for seniors 70 and older, and free for children under 6. For information, including a snow report, contact Arapahoe Basin, P.O. Box 8787, Keystone, CO 80435 (✆ **888/272-7246** or 970/496-0718; www.arapahoebasin.com).

BRECKENRIDGE ★★ Spread across four large mountains on the west side of the town of Breckenridge, this area ranks third in size among Colorado's ski resorts. Once known for its wealth of open, groomed beginner and intermediate slopes, Breckenridge in recent years has expanded its acreage for expert skiers as well.

Peak 8, the original ski mountain, is the highest of the four at 12,998 feet and has the greatest variety. Peak 9, heavily geared to novices and intermediates, rises above the principal base area. Peak 10, served by a single high-speed quad chair, is predominantly expert territory. The vast bowls of Peak 8 and the North Face of Peak 9 are likewise advanced terrain. There are restaurants high on Peaks 8, 9, and 10 and three cafeterias at the base of the slopes. Peak 7 is a double black-diamond challenge on over 1,200 feet of vertical drop.

All told, the resort has 2,208 skiable acres, with 146 trails, including Four O'Clock, the longest, at 3$^1/_2$ miles! The resort rates its trails as 15% beginner, 33% intermediate, and 52% expert and advanced. There are 28 lifts—two high-speed six-passenger chairs, seven high-speed quads, one triple chair, six double chairs, four surface lifts, and eight carpet lifts. A gondola connecting the north side of town with Peak 7 and Peak 8 opened for the 2007–08 ski season. Vertical drop is 3,398 feet from a summit of 12,998 feet; average annual snowfall is 300 inches (25 ft.).

Lift tickets during peak season (2007–08 prices) cost $86 for adults, $45 for children 5 to 12, $76 for seniors 65 to 69, and are free for children 4 and younger and seniors 70 and older. Tickets purchased at Breckenridge are also valid at Keystone and Arapahoe Basin, and multiday tickets for 3 or more days are also valid at Vail and Beaver Creek.

Among Breckenridge's programs are its women's ski seminars, taught exclusively by women for women skiers of all abilities. Three- and four-day seminars are offered in January, February, March, and April. Women-only ski-school classes are available throughout the ski season. For more information, call ✆ **888/576-2754.** For snowboarders, the Breckenridge Superpipe is a delight. This half-pipe has a 15-degree slope, 15-foot-high walls, and 17-foot transitions.

Breckenridge is usually open from mid-November to mid-May daily from 8:30am to 4pm. For further information, contact **Breckenridge Ski Resort,** P.O. Box 1058, Breckenridge, CO 80424 (✆ **800/789-7669,** 970/453-5000, or 970/453-6118 for snow conditions; www.breckenridge.snow.com). From Memorial Day weekend to Labor Day, the alpine slide is in operation, and the trails are open to mountain bikers; minigolf is also available. Call for off-season hours and chairlift schedule.

COPPER MOUNTAIN From Copper Mountain village, the avalanche chutes on the west face of Ten Mile Mountain seem to spell out the word *ski*. Though this is a natural coincidence, locals like to say the mountain has terrain created for skiing.

Terrain is about half beginner and intermediate, with the rest ranging from advanced to "you'd better be really good." The area has a vertical drop of 2,601 feet from a peak elevation of 12,313 feet. There are 2,433 skiable acres and 125 trails served by 22 lifts—one high-speed six-person chair, four high-speed quads, five triple chairs, five double chairs, two surface lifts, four conveyors, and one tubing zone lift. Average annual snowfall is 280 inches. Copper Mountain has two terrain parks. Big floater jumps are spread out across an entire run, with proper takeoff and landing ramps; there's a regulation half-pipe, and several drainage and gladed runs have been thinned to provide challenging tree riding for more advanced snowboarders.

There are three restaurants on the mountain and several more in the base village. Also at the base are 16 miles of cross-country track, a tubing hill, and a full-service racquet and athletic club.

Lift tickets (2007–08 prices) during the peak season cost $69 for adults, $34 for children 6 to 13, and $59 for seniors 65 to 69. Tickets are free for seniors 70 and older and children 5 and under.

Copper Mountain is usually open from early November to mid-April, Monday through Friday from 9am to 4pm, Saturday and Sunday from 8:30am to 4pm. For information, contact **Copper Mountain Resort,** P.O. Box 3001, Copper Mountain, CO 80443 (✆ **866/841-2481;** www.coppercolorado.com). For **reservations,** call ✆ **888/219-2441;** for a **snow report,** call ✆ **800/789-7609.**

KEYSTONE Keystone is actually three separate mountains, offering a variety of terrain. And the resort is one of the best spots for night skiing in America, open daily from 8:30am until 8pm.

From its peak elevation of 12,200 feet, Keystone's vertical drop is 3,128 feet. It's three interconnected mountains offer 2,870 acres of skiing, 117 trails (17 open for night skiing), and 19 lifts—including two connecting high-speed gondolas, a high-speed six-person chair, five high-speed quads, one quad, one triple, four doubles, one surface lift, and four carpets. Average annual snowfall is 230 inches (about 19 ft.). Its trails are rated 12% beginner, 34% intermediate, and 54% expert and advanced.

For snowboarders, Keystone has 66 acres of terrain parks, including two half-pipes, which are lit for night riding.

Lift tickets during the peak season (2007–08 prices) cost $86 for adults, $45 for children 5 to 12, $76 for seniors 65 and older, and are free for children 4 and younger. Tickets purchased at Keystone are also valid at Breckenridge and Arapahoe Basin, and multiday tickets for 3 or more days are also valid at Vail and Beaver Creek.

Excellent on-mountain dining is available at the **Alpenglow Stube,** located in the Outpost, a log-and-stone lodge atop North Peak (elevation 11,444 ft.). Access is via two scenic gondola rides.

Keystone is usually open from early November through mid-April. For further information, contact **Keystone Resort,** P.O. Box 38, Keystone, CO 80435 (✆ **800/468-5004** or 970/496-4386; www.keystone.snow.com). For **snow reports,** call ✆ **800/404-3535** or 970/496-4111.

LOVELAND Just across the county line, on the east side of I-70's Eisenhower Memorial Tunnel, is **Loveland Ski Area,** P.O. Box 899, Georgetown, CO 80444 (✆ **800/736-3754** or 303/571-5580; www.skiloveland.com). Comprising Loveland Basin and Loveland Valley, it was created in the late 1930s by a Denver ski club wanting to take advantage of the area's heavy snowfall (400 in., more than 33 ft., annually). You can still see the original rope-tow cabins from 1942, when all-day tickets cost $2. Inflation (and the cost of many improvements) has taken a toll, but this is one of the best deals in the area. Today tickets during the skiing season cost $44 to $56 for adults, $42 for seniors 60 to 69, and $21 to $25 for children 6 to 14; children under 6 ski free, and seniors 70 and older are offered a season pass for $69.

There's good beginner-intermediate terrain on the 1,365 lift-served acres—13% and 41%, respectively, leaving 46% advanced. The vertical drop is 2,410 feet from a top elevation of 13,010 feet, and the longest run is 2 miles. Lifts include three quad chairs, two triples, three doubles, one surface lift, and one tow. Loveland's terrain parks offer natural half-pipes and big powder-filled bowls.

The resort usually opens in mid-October and remains open daily through May.

CROSS-COUNTRY SKIING & SNOWSHOEING The **Frisco Nordic Center,** at 18454 Colo. 9, south of Frisco (✆ **970/668-0866;** www.breckenridgenordic.com), sits on the shores of Dillon Reservoir. Its trail network includes 27 miles of groomed cross-country ski trails. The lodge has a snack bar and a shop with rentals and retail sales; instruction and backcountry and snowshoe tours are also offered. From the Frisco Nordic Center, you can ski to the **Breckenridge Nordic Center,** on Willow Lane near the foot of Peak 8 (✆ **970/453-6855;** www.breckenridgenordic.com), with its own series of 19 miles of groomed trails. The two operations share 12 miles of snowshoe trails and 3 miles of snowshoe trails where leashed dogs are welcome. One trail pass ($15 for adults, $10 for seniors and children) covers both Nordic centers, and rental equipment is available. The **Gold Run Nordic Center** at the Breckenridge Golf Club, 200 Club House Dr. (✆ **970/547-7889**), charges identical rates and features more than 14 miles of groomed trails, from beginner to advanced, in addition to backcountry and snowshoe trails, and also offers rental equipment.

For additional information on these and other cross-country skiing centers, check out **www.colorado-xc.org** on the Web. There are also numerous cross-country skiing possibilities in the area's national forests; contact the **Dillon Ranger District** (see below).

WARM-WEATHER & YEAR-ROUND ACTIVITIES

The **White River National Forest** encompasses the boundaries of Summit County. This recreational playground offers opportunities not only for downhill and cross-country skiing and snowmobiling in winter, but also for hiking and backpacking, horseback riding, boating, fishing, hunting, and bicycling in summer. White River National Forest includes the **Eagles Nest Wilderness Area** and **Green Mountain Reservoir,** both in the northern part of the county.

The **U.S. Forest Service's Dillon Ranger District,** located in the town of Silverthorne at 680 River Pkwy. (Colo. 9), Silverthorne, CO 80498, about half a mile north of I-70 exit 205 (✆ **970/468-5400;** www.fs.fed.us/r2), has an unusually good selection of information on outdoor recreation possibilities, including maps and guides to hiking and mountain-biking trails, jeep roads, cross-country skiing, snowmobiling, fishing, and camping. You can also get information on a wide variety of outdoor activities from the **Breckenridge Resort Chamber Welcome Center,** 203 S. Main St. (✆ **877/864-0868**).

BICYCLING There are more than 40 miles of paved bicycle paths in the county, including a path from Breckenridge (with a spur from Keystone) to Frisco and Copper Mountain, continuing across Vail Pass to Vail. This spectacularly beautiful two-lane path is off-limits to motorized vehicles. Also see "Mountain Biking," below.

BOATING Dillon Reservoir, a beautiful mountain lake along I-70 between Dillon and Frisco, is the place to go. Also called Lake Dillon, the 3,300-acre reservoir, which provides drinking water to Denver, is more than 200 feet deep in spots. At 9,017 feet elevation, it claims to have America's highest-altitude yacht club and holds colorful regattas most summer weekends. The popular Dillon Open, a huge sailboat race, occurs the first weekend in August. Swimming is not permitted.

The full-service **Dillon Marina,** 150 Marina Dr. (✆ **970/468-5100;** www.dillon marina.com), is open from the last weekend of May through the last weekend of October, offering boats for 2-hour, half-day, or full-day rentals; sailing instruction; and charter cruises. Half-day boat-rental fees run $170 for runabouts, $200 for 22-foot pontoon boats, and $380 for 25-foot pontoons. Fuel is extra. The half-day rate for 18- and 20-foot sailboats is $110, and more upscale 22-foot sailboats rent for $185 for a half-day. An 8-hour sailing class costs $275 per person, and the "sailing experience" 2-hour sailboat tour for novice sailors costs $60 per person. There are also a small store, repair shop, restaurant, and bar.

FISHING Major fishing rivers within an hour of Breckenridge include the South Platte, Arkansas, Eagle, Colorado, and Blue rivers, and for lake fishing, try Dillon Reservoir and Spinney Mountain Reservoir. The Blue River, from Lake Dillon Dam to its confluence with the Colorado River at Kremmling, is rated a gold-medal fishing stream. For tips on where they're biting, as well as supplies, fishing licenses, and all the rest, stop at **Mountain Angler ★**, 311 S. Main St., Breckenridge, in the Main Street Mall (✆ **800/453-4669** or 970/453-4665; www.mountainangler.com), which also offers year-round guide service. Guided fly-fishing wading trips, for two anglers, start at $265 for a half-day; $360 for a full day, including lunch. A full-day float-fishing guided trip for two anglers costs $400 to $450. Guided fly-fishing trips are also offered by **The Adventure Company** (✆ **800/497-7238;** www.theadventurecompany.com) at similar rates.

GOLF Among area golf courses, which all boast wonderful scenery, are the 27-hole **Breckenridge Golf Club,** 200 Clubhouse Dr., Breckenridge (✆ **970/453-9104;** www.breckenridgegolfclub.com), the only municipal course designed by Jack Nicklaus anywhere, with greens fee of $57 to $104 for 18 holes, cart not included; **Copper Creek Golf Club,** 104 Wheeler Place, Copper Mountain Resort (✆ **970/968-3333**), among the highest 18-hole courses in North America, at 9,752 feet, with fees of $39 to $99, including cart, for 18 holes; **Raven at Three Peaks,** 2929 N. Golden Eagle Rd., Silverthorne (✆ **970/262-3636**), new in 2008 and charging $35 to $149 for 18 holes, cart included; **Keystone Ranch Golf Course,** 1239 Keystone Ranch Rd., Keystone (✆ **970/496-4250**), charging $85 to $140, including a cart, for 18 holes; and the par-71 **River Course at Keystone,** 155 River Course Dr., Keystone (✆ **970/496-4444**), which also charges $85 to $140, including cart, for 18 holes.

HIKING & BACKPACKING The **Colorado Trail ★★** cuts a swath through Summit County. It enters from the east across Kenosha Pass, follows the Swan River to its confluence with the Blue River, then climbs over Ten Mile Mountain to Copper Mountain. The trail then turns south toward Tennessee Pass, north of Leadville. Contact the **Colorado Trail Foundation,** American Mountaineering Center, 710 10th St., #210, Golden, CO 80401 (✆ **303/384-3729;** www.coloradotrail.org).

In addition, there are myriad hiking opportunities in the national forests. Consult the U.S. Forest Service, the Breckenridge Resort Chamber Activity Center, or a visitor information center for maps and details.

HORSEBACK RIDING For some spectacular views of this area from atop a horse, take a ride with **Breckenridge Stables,** located just above the Beaver Run ski lift on Village Road (✆ **970/453-4438;** www.breckstables.com). The company offers rides of about 90 minutes, plus breakfast rides, for $55 per person (half-price for children 6 and under). Reservations should be made at least 1 day in advance.

MOUNTAIN BIKING Numerous trails are available for mountain bikers. Energetic fat-tire fans can try the Devil's Triangle, a difficult 80-mile loop that begins and ends in Frisco after climbing four mountain passes (including 11,318-ft. Fremont Pass). Check with the U.S. Forest Service or Breckenridge Resort Chamber Activity Center for directions and tips on other trails; for mountain bikers who prefer to not work so hard, check with the Breckenridge Resort Chamber Activity Center on times and costs for taking your bike up the mountain on the Breckenridge chairlift.

Clinics, including instructional guided rides, are offered by several local companies, including **Ripstoke Mountain Bike School** (✆ **303/818-3158;** www.ripstoke.com), **Colorado Ski and Bike Tours** (✆ **970/668-8900;** www.coloradobikeandski.com), and **Babes in the Backcountry** (✆ **970/453-4060;** www.babesinthebackcountry.com). One-day clinics usually run around $150.

Among the companies providing bike rentals and information is **Lone Star Sports,** at 200 W. Washington St., Breckenridge (✆ **800/621-9733** or 970/453-2003; www.ski lonestar.com), which charges full-day rates of $15 to $27.

RIVER RAFTING Trips through the white water of the Blue River—which runs through Breckenridge to Frisco—as well as longer journeys on the Colorado and Arkansas rivers, are offered by various companies, including **KODI Rafting** (✆ **877/747-7238;** www.white watercolorado.com), **Good Times Rafting Company** (✆ **800/808-0357;** www.good timesrafting.com), **Performance Tours Rafting** (✆ **800/328-7238;** www.performance tours.com), and **The Adventure Company** (✆ **800/497-7238;** www.theadventure company.com), all based in Breckenridge. Rates for half-day trips on the Blue River cost about $40 to $50 for adults and $30 to $40 for children. Full-day trips on other area rivers are about $75 to $100 for adults and $65 to $80 for kids.

THE FESTIVAL SCENE

The **Breckenridge Music Festival** presents dozens of classical and nonclassical music performances, with concerts in the Riverwalk Center from mid-June through mid-August. Adult tickets cost from $22 to $32; they're only $7 for students under 18. Contact the Breckenridge Music Festival, P.O. Box 1254, Breckenridge, CO 80424 (✆ **970/453-9142** or 970/547-3100 for the box office; www.breckenridgemusicfestival.com).

Genuine Jazz in Breckenridge, on the last weekend of June, showcases Colorado jazz ensembles with styles ranging from Dixieland to bebop to New Age. Local bars and nightclubs host Friday and Saturday night performances, and there are also free outdoor concerts. Contact **Peak Performances,** Box 57, Breckenridge, CO 80424 (✆ **866/464-2626** for tickets; www.genuinejazz.com).

The **Breckenridge Festival of Film,** held in early September, attracts Hollywood directors and actors to town to discuss some two dozen films in all genres. Films that have premiered here include *American Beauty, The Shawshank Redemption, Shark Tale,* and *L.A. Confidential.* For more information, contact the Breckenridge Festival of Film, P.O. Box 718, Breckenridge, CO 80424 (✆ **970/453-6200;** www.breckfilmfest.com).

MORE TO SEE & DO

Families traveling with kids might want to stop at the **Mountain Top Children's Museum,** 605 S. Park Ave. (✆ **970/453-7878;** www.mtntopmuseum.org), which has a number of exhibits open daily in summer and winter; children may also want to ride the kiddie train by **Breckenridge Train Company** at Main Street Station, 505 S. Main St. (✆ **970/453-2806**).

The **Arts District of Breckenridge,** Ridge Street and Washington Avenue, is a reclaimed series of old structures that offers workshops, programs, and a glimpse into working studios of visiting artists. Visit the town website at **www.townofbreckenridge.com** for further information.

Breckenridge National Historic District The entire Victorian core of this 19th-century mining town has been carefully preserved, and you can see it on your own (pick up a free walking-tour brochure at the Visitor Information Cabin), or during the summer on guided 1½-hour walking tours conducted by the Summit Historical Society. Colorfully painted shops and restaurants occupy the old buildings, most dating from the 1880s and 1890s. Most of the historic district focuses on Main Street and extends east on either side of Lincoln Avenue. Among the 254 historic buildings in the district are the **Barney Ford House Museum,** 111 E. Washington Ave.; the 1875 **Edwin Carter Museum,** 111 N. Ridge St.; and the 1896 **William Harrison Briggle House,** 104 N. Harris St., in Milne Park. The society also leads tours during the summer to the outskirts of town to visit the underground shaft of the hard-rock **Washington Gold Mine** and the gold-panning operation at **Lomax Placer Gulch.** Allow 2 to 4 hours.

Breckenridge. ✆ **970/453-9022.** www.summithistorical.org. Guided tours $3 per person. Tour tickets available at the Breckenridge Resort Chamber Welcome Center, 309 N. Main St. Historic district tours mid-June to Sept Tues–Sat; Edwin Carter Museum tours mid-June to Sept; museum open year-round, call for times. Free admission.

Country Boy Mine At this 100-year-old mine, you can take a guided tour 1,000 feet underground, pan for gold in Eureka Creek, explore the mining exhibit and the five-story 75-year-old mill, and listen to the legends. The mine is a constant 45°F (7°C) year-round, so take a jacket even in August. There are also a restored blacksmith shop, indoor gold panning in winter, and sleigh rides available in the snowy months (www.brecksleighrides.com). Burros also roam around, posing for pictures with children; every summer sees the addition of a baby burro. Tours start on the hour. Allow at least an hour.

0542 French Gulch Rd., P.O. Box 8569, Breckenridge. ✆ **970/453-4405.** www.countryboymine.com. Mine tour $19 adults, $13 children 4–12, free for kids 3 and under; dinner sleigh ride $53 adults, $43 children 4–10, free for kids 3 and under. Special rates and hours are available for families and groups. Summer daily 10am–4pm; winter by reservation. The hours have some other seasonal fluctuations, so call for details.

Dillon Schoolhouse Museum A one-room country school—built in 1883 and filled with such artifacts of early Colorado education as desks with inkwells, McGuffey readers, and scientific teaching apparatus—is the highlight of this historic park. Also on the site are the 1885 Lula Myers ranch house and the Depression-era Honeymoon Cabin. All buildings were moved from Old Dillon (now beneath the waters of the reservoir) or Keystone. Tours are also conducted (by appt.) of the 1884 Montezuma Schoolhouse, located at 10,400 feet elevation in the 1860s silver-mining camp of Montezuma. Allow about an hour.

403 LaBonte St., Dillon. ✆ **970/453-9022.** www.summithistorical.org. Admission/guided tour $6 adults, $3 children 12 and younger. Mid-June to Labor Day Tues–Sat 1–4pm or by appt.

Frisco Historic Park ★ Ten historic buildings—including the town's original 1881 jail, a one-room schoolhouse, a log chapel, and homes dating from the 1880s—make up this beautifully maintained historic park. The schoolhouse contains displays and artifacts from Frisco's early days, and a trapper's cabin has a hands-on exhibit of animal pelts. Artisans sell their wares in several buildings, and a variety of events are scheduled during the summer. A self-guided walking tour of historic Frisco can be obtained at the park. Allow 1 hour.

120 Main St. (at Second St.), Frisco. ✆ **970/668-3428.** www.townoffrisco.com. Free admission. Summer Tues–Sat 9am–5pm, Sun 9am–3pm; winter Tues–Sat 10am–4pm, Sun 10am–2pm.

SHOPPING

Breckenridge is the place to shop in Summit County, with a variety of shops and galleries in the historic buildings along Main Street.

For vintage snowboards, ski art, ski sweaters, and ski-themed home decor, check out **Vintage Snow,** 226 S. Main St. (✆ **970/453-2447**). Original Western paintings and bronzes, plus historic Navajo weavings and cowboy and Indian collectibles, can be found at **Paint Horse Gallery,** 226 S. Main St. (✆ **970/453-6813**). A cooperative managed by the Summit Arts Council, **Hamlet's,** 306 S. Main St. (✆ **970/453-8033**), is a fine bookstore in an old Victorian. If you're in the market for a unique hat—including some really hilarious ones—try the **Breckenridge Hat Company,** 411 S. Main St. (✆ **970/453-2737**). The **Silverthorne Factory Stores** (✆ **970/468-9440**) has about 80 outlet shops—from fashion and athletic wear to home accessories; take I-70 to exit 205. For all your outdoor gear needs, **Mountain Outfitters,** 112 S. Ridge St. (✆ **970/453-2201;** www.mtnoutfitters.com), is the place.

WHERE TO STAY

Thousands of rooms are available here at any given time. Even so, during peak seasons, finding accommodations may be difficult, and rates are dramatically higher from Christmas to New Year's. In many cases, it will be best to simply call one of the reservation services, tell them when you plan to visit and how much you want to spend, and ask for their suggestions. Throughout the county, condominiums prevail. While they often offer the best value, they're sometimes short on charm. If you're planning to spend much time in one, it pays to ask about views and fireplaces before booking. Local reservation services include **Wildernest Lodging** (✆ **800/554-2212;** www.skierlodging.com), **Breckenridge Central Reservations** (✆ **877/593-5260;** www.gobreck.com), and, in Keystone, **Key to the Rockies** (✆ **800/248-1942;** www.keytotherockies.com). **ResortQuest Breckenridge** (✆ **800/661-7604;** www.resortquestbreckenridge.com) has about 450 rooms spread across a number of properties, everything from simple studios to luxurious and spacious three-bedroom units and private luxury homes. Most have mountain views or are nestled among tall pines, have a fireplace, and are within easy strolling distance of historic Main Street, such as the Main Street Station hotel (see below). Many units are ski-in/ski-out. Double rates range from roughly $90 to $400 in summer and $120 to $2,500 in ski season.

In addition to the properties discussed below, there are the **Best Western Lake Dillon Lodge,** 1202 Summit Blvd., Frisco (✆ **800/727-0607** or 970/668-5094), charging $79 to $199 double; **Comfort Suites** in Dillon at I-70 exit 205 (✆ **800/424-6423** or 970/513-0300), with rates of $99 to $299 double; and **Super 8,** also at I-70 exit 205 (✆ **800/800-8000** or 970/468-8888), with double rates of $99 to $159 in ski season. For a hostel bunk or private bed-and-breakfast room, try the lively and eclectic **Fireside Inn,** 114 N. French St. (✆ **970/453-6456;** www.firesideinn.com), with 18 bunks ($28–$38) and four private rooms for $110 to $190 in ski season. Amenities include free Wi-Fi and one of the oldest hot tubs in Colorado.

Room taxes add about 10.7% to hotel bills; there are also often resort fees.

Allaire Timbers Inn Bed & Breakfast ★★ This romantic mountain hideaway is a lovely contemporary log lodge, with a stone fireplace in the living room and magnificent views of the mountains and town. All rooms are named for and decorated around the motif of a Colorado mountain pass. There are hand-painted tiled showers—no tubs—in standard rooms, but the two suites have hot tubs and river-rock gas-burning fireplaces. All units come with private decks, CD players, robes, and fuzzy fleece socks. The homemade gourmet breakfast includes a hot entree, plus fruit and muffins. In winter guests also enjoy complimentary après-ski drinks, including hot citrus cider (an old family recipe), and the beverage bar is available 24 hours. Located just outside the town limits, an easy path takes you right into town. The inn is also conveniently located on the free ski shuttle route; children 13 years and older are welcome. Neither smoking nor pets are allowed—the resident dog has prior claim.

9511 Colo. 9 (P.O. Box 4653), Breckenridge, CO 80424. ✆ **800/624-4904** or 970/453-7530. Fax 970/453-8699. www.allairetimbers.com. 10 units, including 2 suites. $149–$275 double; $255–$400 suite. Rates include full breakfast. AE, DISC, MC, V. **Amenities:** Outdoor hot tub. *In room:* TV, dataport.

BlueSky ★★ A posh condominium lodge with a classic, national-park-style look, BlueSky opened its doors in 2007 and the ski-in, ski-out lodge immediately became one of Breckenridge's toniest addresses. The New West–style design is at once attractive and elegant in the one- to four-bedroom units, featuring kitchens, balconies, resplendent views, and plenty in the way of luxury. Each unit has a balcony, washer-dryer, and other amenities. One of the biggest perks is the terrific year-round pool courtyard. There is also an adventure center with gear rentals.

42 Snowflake Dr., Breckenridge, CO 80424. ✆ **800/661-7604.** www.blueskybreckenridge.com. 52 condominium units. 1- to 4-bedroom condo winter $299–$1,389; summer $250–$350. Higher holiday rates. AE, DISC, MC, V. **Amenities:** Restaurant (American); lounge; outdoor pool; outdoor hot tub; bike rentals; spa; exercise room; game room; courtesy shuttle. *In room:* Cable TV, wireless Internet access (free), kitchen.

Main Street Station ★ The flagship property of ResortQuest Breckenridge (see above), the Hyatt-managed Main Street Station is in an enviable location, right on Maggie Pond (which becomes a skating rink in winter), 600 feet from the nearest lift, but also on Main Street right downtown. Built in 2001, the property offers an upscale ski lodge ambience and a selection of warmly decorated guest rooms with oversized bathrooms and one to three bedrooms. The units are full-service condos with kitchens, gas fireplaces, and plenty of room to spread out. The amenities list is long and comprehensive, including a shopping arcade, an outdoor Olympic-size pool, and a 24-seat state-of-the-art theater guests can reserve.

505 S. Main St. (P.O. Box 2738), Breckenridge, CO 80424. ✆ **800/506-7621** or 970/547-2700. Fax 970/453-0463. www.hyattmainstreetstation.com. 110 units. Summer $179–$299; winter $229–$599. AE, DISC, MC, V. Underground parking. **Amenities:** 2 restaurants; lounge; outdoor heated pool; fitness center; 7 outdoor hot tubs; concierge; courtesy shuttle. *In room:* Cable TV, Wi-Fi network, kitchen, hair dryer, iron.

Village Hotel ★ A slickly renovated slope-side property just a half-block off Main Street, the Village Hotel underwent a compete makeover in 2006 and now has a warm atmosphere befitting its enviable location just a few hundred feet from the chairlift at the base of Peak 9. A nice break from the separately owned condo units all over Summit County, the richly decorated rooms are identically done in earth tones, with small baths and a queen bed and a pullout sofa, or one king or two doubles. Perks include Starbucks coffee, MP3 player jacks in the clock radios, and humidifiers.

535 S. Park Ave. (P.O. Box 8329), Breckenridge, CO 80424. ✆ **888/400-8590** or 970/453-5192. Fax 970/453-5116. www.thevillagehotelbreck.com. 60 units. Winter $135–$295 double; summer $135–$205 double. AE, DC, DISC, MC, V. Pets accepted. **Amenities:** Restaurant (American); lounge; indoor and outdoor heated pools; fitness center; 4 outdoor hot tubs; sauna; courtesy shuttle. *In room:* Cable TV, wireless Internet access (free), coffeemaker, fridge, hair dryer, iron.

CAMPING

Tiger Run R.V. & Chalet Resort ★★ Named for a historic mine in the area, Tiger Run is both conveniently and beautifully located, with the Swan River running right through the property. Activities in winter include skiing, snowmobiling, cross-country skiing, and snowboarding; in summer there are wine-and-cheese parties, kids' s'mores night, and live music on Saturday. The clubhouse lodge, in the center of the park, is open year-round, with an indoor swimming pool, hot tubs, a game room, a TV room, laundry facilities, restrooms with showers, and telephones. There's a small no-food convenience store; tennis, volleyball, and basketball courts; a children's playground; and sports equipment available at the office. Pets are welcome in RV sites only. There are also 30 chalet-style cabins on the property, with rates of $77 to $172 for doubles ($15 per extra person). Tents and pop-up trailers are not accepted.

85 Tiger Run Rd. (3 miles north of Breckenridge off Colo. 9), Breckenridge, CO 80424. ✆ **800/895-9594** or 970/453-9690. Fax 970/453-6782. www.tigerrunresort.com. 250 sites. $47–$67. Rates include water, sewer, electric, and cable TV hookups. Weekly rates available. AE, DISC, MC, V.

WHERE TO DINE

Expensive

Cafe Alpine ★★ CONTEMPORARY AMERICAN With a refined, intimate atmosphere and a menu so creative it's a pleasure to read, Cafe Alpine is the best pick for a romantic dinner in Breckenridge. Sit in one of several small rooms, upstairs or down, or at the bar, and pick from a seasonally changing selection that combines traditions from near and far into slick dishes like crispy plantain soft-shell crabs with habanero-pineapple upside-down cake, or wasabi-crusted scallops. There is always a selection of fresh seafood and a vegetarian option. The inventive fare is matched by a terrific wine list, and there are tapas served on the deck here from 3pm daily in summer.

106 E. Adams Ave. ✆ **970/453-8218.** www.cafealpine.com. Reservations recommended. Main courses $16–$26. AE, DC, DISC, MC, V. Daily 5–10pm. Tapas from 3pm in summer.

Hearthstone ★ REGIONAL A favorite of locals because of its creative cuisine, the Hearthstone is in a historic home built in 1886. It has a rustic yet elegant interior, with fine mountain views from the upstairs lounge. Start with the house-smoked trout, a chile relleno, or crispy lobster, then choose from fresh seafood such as ginger-crusted scallops or ahi tuna. Other choices include the blackberry elk with a garlic-granola crust, Colorado lamb strip loin, and an 8-ounce beef tenderloin with a demi-glace and Yukon gold potatoes.

130 S. Ridge St. ✆ **970/453-1148.** www.stormrestaurants.com/hearthstone. Reservations recommended. Main courses $19–$38. AE, MC, V. Daily 5:30–10pm.

Keystone Ranch ★★ CREATIVE REGIONAL A working cattle ranch for more than 3 decades until 1972, the Keystone Ranch now boasts riding stables, a golf course, and this outstanding gourmet restaurant, located in a 1940s ranch house with a mountain-lodge decor. Among the area's best restaurants, the Keystone Ranch offers a six-course menu with a choice of appetizer, followed by soup, salad, and fruit sorbet. Main dishes, which vary seasonally, might include roasted rack of Colorado lamb, grilled duck breast, elk or other game, or fresh seafood. An extensive array of desserts is served in the living room in front of a handsome stone fireplace. There are valet parking and a full bar.

Keystone Ranch Rd., Keystone. ✆ **970/496-4386.** Reservations strongly recommended. 6-course dinner $95 adults, $60 children 12 and under. AE, DISC, MC, V. Summer and winter daily 5:30–8:45pm, 2 seatings; call for spring and fall hours.

Relish ★★ REGIONAL Located in a second-floor space above Blue River Plaza, Relish is a hip new addition to the Breckenridge dining scene. With pumpkin-hued walls, a cozy bar, and terrific views, the restaurant has an atmosphere that nicely balances social and intimate. Chef-owner Matt Fackler's menu focuses on regional approaches to classical preparations, with terrific results. The menu changes seasonally, but Fackler's creativity shines in starters like blue cornmeal-fried oysters and lemon-braised artichoke, and entrees like buffalo sirloin "steak Diane" with truffle-roasted garlic mashed potatoes, free-range veal meatloaf, or anise-grilled tofu with a bok choy–bamboo stir fry with pickled ginger and pineapple salsa.

137 S. Main St. ✆ **970/453-0989.** www.relishbreckenridge.com. Reservations recommended. Main courses $16–$32. AE, MC, V. Daily noon–2:15pm and 5–9:30pm. Bar opens 4pm.

Moderate & Inexpensive

For a quick meal on Main Street, try **Crepes a la Cart,** 307 S. Main St. (✆ **970/453-0622**), for crepes packed with everything from broccoli and chicken to ice cream and chocolate. **Fatty's Pizzeria,** 106 Ridge St. (✆ **970/453-9802**), is a local favorite with burgers, sandwiches, pizzas, pasta dinners, and a boisterous old barroom. For breakfast, the standbys are **Columbine Cafe,** 109 S. Main St. (✆ **970/547-4474**), and **Daylight Donuts,** 305N. Main St. (✆ **970/453-2548**).

Breckenridge Brewery and Pub ★ AMERICAN/BREWPUB This brewpub was designed around its brewery, giving diners a firsthand view of the brewing process. Of the award-winning beers, try the Trademark Pale or the Avalanche, a local favorite. Like many good brewpubs, lunch choices here include fish and chips, half-pound burgers, and soups and salads (try the mango spinach salad). But the menu also strives to be somewhat more interesting, offering items such as seared ahi tuna and grilled portobello mushroom sandwiches. The dinner menu adds tender tasty baby back ribs, the "Brewhouse Pork

Chops," buffalo meatloaf, and charbroiled fajitas for those who like it spicy. The desserts are homemade. Also see "Summit County After Dark," below.

600 S. Main St. ✆ **970/453-1550.** www.breckenridgebrewery.com. Reservations not accepted. Main courses $8–$21. AE, DISC, MC, V. Daily 11am–10pm; bar until later with limited menu.

Giampietro Pizzeria ★ Value ITALIAN Cozy, busy, and often with a long line out front (reservations are not accepted), Giampietro is worth the wait. The friendly service and red-and-white-checkered tablecloths make for a pleasant, casual atmosphere, but the Italian fare is what keeps people coming back. The pizza is excellent, as is the baked ziti, and the huge calzones—essentially a small pizza folded in half—are a meal that will satisfy just about any appetite, no matter how many miles biked or runs skied. There is a nice wine list, focused on Italian labels.

In Town Square Mall, Main and Lincoln sts. ✆ **970/453-7463.** www.giampietropizza.com. Reservations not accepted. Main courses $7–$15; pizzas from $13. MC, V. Daily 11am–10pm.

Mi Casa MEXICAN Mi Casa is Breckenridge's best Mexican restaurant. Its newly remodeled cantina is the locals' favorite spot for happy hour, and the margaritas are consistently voted the best in Summit County. In addition to the standard burritos, tostadas, and enchiladas, the restaurant is known for its homemade tamales and chile rellenos and its seafood dishes—fish tacos, chile-encrusted trout, snapper Vera Cruz, and spicy shrimp Diablo. The margaritas and tequila selection are both excellent.

600 Park Ave. ✆ **970/453-2071.** www.stormrestaurants.com. Reservations not accepted. Main courses $9–$18. AE, MC, V. Daily 11:30am–9pm.

SUMMIT COUNTY AFTER DARK

Though every community has its watering holes, Breckenridge has the best nightlife in the area.

In the Arts District of Breckenridge, the **Backstage Theatre,** 121 S. Ridge St., Breckenridge (✆ **970/453-0199;** www.backstagetheatre.org), has been presenting a variety of live theater since 1974. Recent productions have included Shakespeare's *Twelfth Night, The Vagina Monologues, The Hobbit, Cannibal! The Musical,* and *Reefer Madness.* Ticket prices vary, but most are $18 for adults and $10 for children under 12; reservations are strongly recommended.

Popular bars in Breckenridge include the **Breckenridge Brewery and Pub,** 600 S. Main St. (✆ **970/453-1550**), where the microbrews include Avalanche Ale, a full-bodied amber ale, and my favorite, Trademark Pale, an American-style pale ale loaded with hops. Also see "Where to Dine," above. The **Salt Creek Restaurant and Saloon,** 1101 E. Lincoln Ave. (✆ **970/453-4949**), is a popular live-music dance club where you'll hear practically everything but country. For everything from live blues to reggae, try **three-20south** (formerly **Sherpa & Yeti's**), 320 S. Main St. (✆ **970/547-5320;** www.three20south.com); and the young, hip **Downstairs at Eric's,** a lively bar and restaurant at 111 S. Main St. (✆ **970/453-1401;** www.downstairsaterics.com) that is popular with locals and the après-ski crowd alike and boasts 120 types of beer, including 22 on tap. **The Cellar,** 200 S. Ridge St. (✆ **970/453-4777**), is a slick wine and tapas bar with contemporary art and an attractive red granite bar. Established in the 1870s and said to be the longest continually operating bar west of the Mississippi (local lawmen were afraid to shut it down during Prohibition), the **Gold Pan,** 103 N. Main St. (✆ **970/453-5499**), is a rough-and-tumble, ornery place that's hard not to like.

6 VAIL & BEAVER CREEK ★

109 miles W of Denver, 150 miles E of Grand Junction

Consistently ranked the country's most popular ski resort by skiers and ski magazines almost since its inception, Vail is the big one. It's hard to imagine a more celebrated spot to schuss. Off the slopes, Vail is an incredibly compact replica of a Tyrolean village, full of restaurants, hotels, and shops frequented by almost as many Europeans as Americans. But the size of the mountain and the difficulty and excitement of many of its trails are still what draw the faithful.

Historically speaking, there is very little in the town's past to indicate that Vail would become the megadestination it is. Until U.S. 6 was built through Vail Pass in 1939, the only inhabitants were a handful of sheep ranchers. Dropping farther back into history, it's worth noting that the resort could never have been possible if it weren't for severe droughts in the 1850s and 1860s that resulted in numerous forest fires. The burnings created the wide-open ridges and back bowls that make skiers and snowboarders the world over quiver in their boots.

It was only when veterans of the 10th Mountain Division, who trained during World War II at Camp Hale, 23 miles south of the valley, returned in the 1950s that the reality of skiing was realized. One of them, Peter Siebert (1924–2002), urged development of this mountain land in the White River National Forest, and through his vision, Vail opened to skiers in December 1962, immediately becoming one of the largest ski areas in the United States. Additional ski-lift capacity made Vail America's largest ski resort by 1964.

Beaver Creek, built in 1980, has quickly garnered a reputation as an elegant (and pricey) vacation spot. Like Vail, it is a four-season resort that offers golf (the course was designed by Robert Trent Jones, Jr.), hot-air ballooning, mountain biking, fishing, and horseback riding, in addition to skiing. Its atmosphere is a bit more formal than the surrounding area, and its nightlife tends more toward refined piano bars than rowdy saloons, but the exclusivity of its après-ski spots isn't reflected on the slopes. At Beaver Creek, there's a trail for everyone. Experts are challenged but beginners aren't left out—they, too, can head straight to the top and then ski all the way down on a trail that matches their skill level.

ESSENTIALS

GETTING THERE **By Car** Vail is right on the I-70 corridor, so it's exceedingly easy to find. Just take exit 176, whether you're coming from the east (Denver) or the west (Grand Junction). A more direct route from the south is U.S. 24 through Leadville; this Tennessee Pass road joins I-70 5 miles west of Vail. Beaver Creek is located 12 miles west of Vail, off I-70 exit 167.

By Plane Year-round, visitors can fly directly into **Eagle County Airport,** 35 miles west of Vail between I-70 exits 140 and 147 (✆ **970/524-9490;** www.eaglecounty.us/airport), which is served by **American** (✆ 800/433-7300), **Continental** (✆ 800/523-3273), **Delta** (✆ 800/221-1212), **Northwest** (✆ 800/225-2525), **United/United Express** (✆ 800/864-8331), and **US Airways** (✆ 800/943-5436).

By Airport Shuttle Many visitors fly into Denver International Airport and continue to Vail and Beaver Creek aboard a shuttle service such as **Colorado Mountain Express** (✆ **800/525-6363** or 970/926-9800; www.cmex.com), with one-way rates starting at

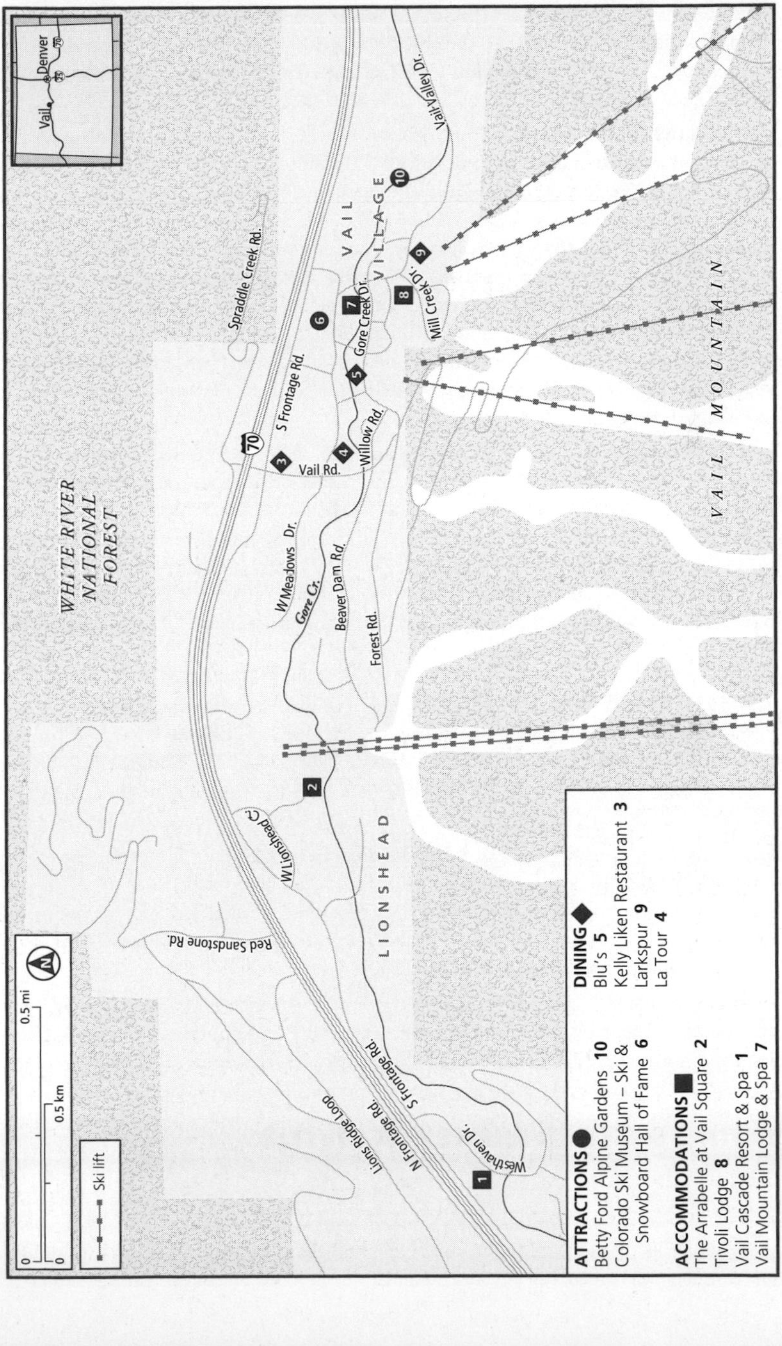
ATTRACTIONS
Betty Ford Alpine Gardens 10
Colorado Ski Museum – Ski & Snowboard Hall of Fame 6
ACCOMMODATIONS
The Arrabelle at Vail Square 2
Tivoli Lodge 8
Vail Cascade Resort & Spa 1
Vail Mountain Lodge & Spa 7
DINING
Blu's 5
Kelly Liken Restaurant 3
Larkspur 9
La Tour 4
Ski lift
0
0.5 mi
0.5 km
N
Vail
Denver
25
70
WHITE RIVER NATIONAL FOREST
VAIL MOUNTAIN
VAIL VILLAGE
LIONSHEAD
Spraddle Creek Rd.
S Frontage Rd.
N Frontage Rd.
Vail Rd.
Willow Rd.
Gore Creek Dr.
Mill Creek Dr.
Vail Valley Dr.
W Meadows Dr.
Gore Cr.
Beaver Dam Rd.
Forest Rd.
W Lionshead Cr.
Red Sandstone Rd.
Westhaven Dr.
Lions Ridge Loop

about $89 per person. There are also shuttle services from the Eagle County Airport to Vail and Beaver Creek; contact **High Mountain Taxi** (✆ **970/524-5555;** www.hmtaxi.com), which charges $125 to $150 for up to six passengers in a van and also provides regional shuttle services. Both of the above shuttle services offer online reservations. To save a bundle of money, take the **bus** (see "Getting Around," below). Also see **car rentals** under "Getting Around," below.

VISITOR INFORMATION For information or reservations in the Vail Valley, contact the **Vail Valley Partnership,** 113 Fawcett Rd. (P.O Box 1130, Vail, CO 81658), Ste. 201, in Avon (✆ **970/476-1000;** www.visitvailvalley.com); **Vail Mountain Resort,** P.O. Box 7, Vail, CO 81658 (✆ **877/204-7881** or 970/476-5601; www.vail.com); or **Beaver Creek Resort** (✆ **970/845-9090;** www.beavercreek.com). You can also get information on year-round activities and events by calling the **Resort Information and Activities Center** (✆ **970/476-9090**). Information centers are located at the parking structures in Vail and the Lionshead area on South Frontage Road.

Parents traveling with kids can find all sorts of pointers in ***The Parents Handbook to the Vail Valley*** (✆ **970/390-3533;** www.theparentshandbook.com), available free all over Eagle County.

GETTING AROUND Vail is one of only a few Colorado communities where you really don't need a car. The town of Vail runs the nation's largest **free shuttle-bus service** between 6am and 2am daily, although hours may be shorter in shoulder seasons. Shuttles in the Vail Village–Lionshead area run every 10 minutes, and there are regularly scheduled trips to West Vail and East Vail (✆ **970/479-2178;** www.vailgov.com). The **Eagle County Regional Transportation Authority,** known locally as ECO Transit (✆ **970/328-3520;** www.eaglecounty.us/ecotransit), runs shuttles between Vail and Beaver Creek, a 12-mile trip, plus regional bus service to Avon, Edwards, Minturn, Leadville, and the Eagle County Airport daily ($3–$5 each way). **High Mountain Taxi** (✆ **970/524-5555;** www.hmtaxi.com) operates throughout the area, around the clock.

Car rentals, including four-wheel-drive vehicles, are available at the Eagle County Airport: Call **Alamo** (✆ 970/524-2277), **Avis** (✆ 970/524-7571), **Budget** (✆ 970/524-8260), **Dollar** (✆ 970/524-9429), **Hertz** (✆ 970/524-7177), or **National** (✆ 970/524-2277).

FAST FACTS The hospital, **Vail Valley Medical Center,** with 24-hour emergency care, is at 181 W. Meadow Dr., between Vail Road and East Lionshead Circle (✆ **970/476-2451;** www.vvmc.org). The **post office** is at 1300 N. Frontage Rd. W.; for hours and other information, contact the U.S. Postal Service (✆ **800/275-8777;** www.usps.com). For **road conditions,** call ✆ **970/479-2226.**

SPECIAL EVENTS Taste of Vail, early April; Vail America Days, July 4th; Vail Arts Festival, mid-August; Beaver Creek Arts Festival, early August in Beaver Creek; Oktoberfest, mid-September in Vail; Vail Tannenbaum Festival, December; and New Year's Eve Celebration, December 31 in Beaver Creek. Also see "The Festival Scene," below.

SKIING & OTHER WINTER ACTIVITIES

VAIL ★★★ America's top ski resort by practically any standard, Vail is something that all serious skiers must experience at least once. It has fantastic snow, great runs, and everything is so convenient that skiers can concentrate solely on skiing. You can arrive at the base village, unload and park your car, and not have to drive again until it's time to go. Your lodging choices offer as much pampering as you want, or can afford. And you'll find all the shops, restaurants, and nightlife you could want within a short walk of your hotel or condominium.

In fact, the only real complaint about Vail (aside from the expense) is that it didn't exist before it became a ski resort, and so it lacks the historic ambience and Old West downtown area that you'll find in Aspen, Steamboat Springs, Telluride, Crested Butte, and a number of other Western ski centers. In fact, the village at times borders on Disney-esque.

Ski area boundaries stretch 7 miles from east to west along the ridge top, from Outer Mongolia to Game Creek Bowl, and the skiable terrain is measured at 5,289 acres. Virtually every lift on the front side of the mountain has runs for every level of skier, with 18% beginner terrain, 29% intermediate, and the remaining 53% expert and advanced. The seven legendary Back Bowls are strictly for advanced and expert skiers; snow and weather conditions determine just how expert you ought to be. One trip down the Slot or Rasputin's Revenge will give you a fair idea of just how good you are. Blue Sky Basin, on the next mountain south of Vail, is accessed by three high-speed quad chairlifts, and intermediate to advanced terrain offering backcountry-like conditions. There is a warming hut at the top of the basin with a basic snack bar, water, restroom facilities, and a pair of gas grills.

Vail has a vertical drop of 3,450 feet; average annual snowfall is 346 inches (nearly 29 ft.). All told, there are 193 conventional trails served by 31 lifts—a gondola, 16 high-speed quad chairs, 1 fixed-grip quad, 3 triple chairs, 1 double chair, 3 surface lifts, and 6 conveyors. There are also three terrain parks for snowboarders of all skill levels, and a unique log-rail park at Golden Peak.

There are about 20 **on-mountain restaurants** at Vail. **Game Creek Restaurant** (✆ **970/479-4275**), in a handsome European-style chalet, offers creative regional cuisine and splendid views from its perch overlooking Game Creek Bowl at the top of Vail Mountain. **Two Elk Restaurant** on the top of China Bowl offers Southwestern cuisine, pizza, and pasta, plus baked potato and salad bars. At **Buffalo's,** you'll find deli sandwiches, pizza, chile, soup, and a good variety of specialty coffees. **Wildwood** touts an eclectic selection of American dishes; at the Eagle's Nest atop the Eagle Bahn Gondola, **The Marketplace** serves various ethnic dishes in a cafeteria setting; and **Blue Moon Restaurant and Bar** offers a variety of dishes and a wide range of après-ski refreshments. Mid-Vail has two levels of food courts that serve breakfast, lunch, and après-ski drinks, including **Sarge's Shelter,** which offers great barbecue and burgers and a wonderful outdoor deck.

Vail also has a highly respected children's program, and there are daily NASTAR races where skiers can test their abilities on a standardized course that's available at resorts across the country.

Peak season daily lift tickets (2007–08) are $92 for adults, $82 seniors, $52 for children 5 to 12, and free for children 4 and younger. Any lift ticket purchased at Vail is also valid at Beaver Creek, Keystone, Arapahoe Basin, and Breckenridge ski areas. Vail is usually open from mid-November to late April daily from 9am to 3:30pm. For further information, contact **Vail Mountain,** P.O. Box 7, Vail, CO 81658 (✆ **877/204-7881,** 970/476-5601, or 970/476-4888 for snow report; www.vail.com or www.snow.com).

BEAVER CREEK ★★ Also owned by Vail Resorts, Beaver Creek is an outstanding resort in its own right, one with a more secluded atmosphere and maybe even more luxury than its better-known neighbor. Located in a valley 1½ miles off the I-70 corridor, Beaver Creek combines European château–style elegance in its base village with expansive slopes for novice and intermediate skiers. The Grouse Mountain, Birds of Prey, and Cinch lifts reach expert terrain.

The big news here is the opening in 2006 of the new Stone Creek Chutes, an expert terrain area with chutes up to 550 vertical feet long, with pitches up to 44 degrees. There's also a new gondola from Avon, which opened for the 2007–08 season. The gondola will connect a new Westin in Avon with the Lower Beaver Creek lift.

From Beaver Creek Village, the Centennial Express lift to Spruce Saddle and the Birds of Prey Express lift reach northwest-facing midmountain slopes and the Flattops beginners' area atop the mountain, offering a unique beginner's experience. Opposite, the Strawberry Park Express lift accesses Larkspur Bowl and the McCoy Park cross-country ski and snowshoe area at 9,840 feet. Three other lifts—Larkspur, Grouse Mountain, and Birds of Prey (serving the expert area of the same name, one of the steepest downhill slopes in the world) leave from Red-Tail Camp at midmountain. Arrowhead Mountain is also part of Beaver Creek. The two are connected through Bachelor Gulch, offering village-to-village skiing.

Beaver Creek's vertical drop is 4,040 feet from the 11,440-foot summit. There are 1,805 developed acres, though Vail Resorts is licensed to develop up to 5,600. Beginner terrain accounts for 19% of the acreage, with intermediate terrain at 43% and advanced and expert terrain at 38%. There are 17 lifts (2 gondolas, 10 high-speed quad chairs, 2 triple chairs, and 3 doubles) that serve 148 trails, and the average annual snowfall is 310 inches. There are three terrain parks and a half-pipe. The resort offers a unique **Talons Challenge** every day, awarding a lanyard, pin, and recognition on a "Wall of Fame" to skiers and snowboarders who complete 13 designated runs in one day, a total of 23,722 vertical feet.

There are seven **mountain restaurants,** including the highly praised **Beano's Cabin** (see "Where to Dine," later in this chapter). Among other on-mountain eateries are the **Spruce Saddle Lodge,** a dining court offering burgers, wraps, pizza, and salads; the upscale **Zach's Cabin,** which is reached for dinner via sleigh; the **Red Tail Camp,** a barbecue fast-food stop; and the **Broken Arrow Café,** serving burgers, sandwiches, pizzas, and soups.

Peak-season daily lift tickets (2007–08 prices) are $92 for adults, $82 seniors, $52 for children 5 to 12, and free for children 4 and younger. Any lift ticket purchased at Beaver Creek is also valid at Vail, Keystone, Arapahoe Basin, and Breckenridge ski areas.

Beaver Creek is open from mid-November to late April daily from 9am to 4pm, conditions permitting. For more information, contact **Beaver Creek Resort,** P.O. Box 7, Vail, CO 81658 (© **970/845-9090** or 800/427-8308 for snow reports; www.beavercreek.com).

BACKCOUNTRY SKI TOURS **Paragon Guides** (© **877/926-5299** or 970/926-5299; www.paragonguides.com) is one of the country's premier winter guide services, offering backcountry ski trips on the 10th Mountain Trail and Hut System between Vail and Aspen (see "Cross-Country Skiing," below). A variety of trips are available, lasting from 1 to 6 days and designed for all ability levels. Costs start around $400 for two people for the day trip and $1,000 per person for a 3-day expedition.

CROSS-COUNTRY SKIING Cross-country skiers won't feel left out here, with trails at both resorts as well as a system of trails through the surrounding mountains. **Vail Nordic Center** (© **970/476-8366;** www.vailnordiccenter.com) has 21 miles of trails, part of them on the Vail Golf Course, and offers guided tours, lessons, and snowshoeing. A day pass is $6. The **Beaver Creek Nordic Center** (© **970/845-5313**), at Beaver Creek

Resort, has a 20-mile mountaintop track system with a skating lane in 9,840-foot McCoy Park. Most of the high-altitude terrain here is intermediate, though there's some space for both beginner and advanced cross-country skiers; telemarking lessons are available. A day pass is $23 for adults, $13 for seniors, and kids under 13 ski free.

For general information on the network of backcountry trails in the Vail area, contact the **Holy Cross Ranger District Office,** White River National Forest, at 24747 U.S. 24, 2 miles north of Minturn, off I-70 exit 171, Minturn, CO 81645 (✆ **970/827-5715;** www.fs.fed.us/r2).

Of particular note is the system of trails known as the **10th Mountain Division Hut System,** 1280 Ute Ave., Ste. 21, Aspen, CO 81611 (✆ **970/925-5775;** www.huts.org). Generally following the World War II training network of the Camp Hale militia, the trails cover 350 miles and link Vail with Leadville and Aspen, with 29 huts along the way where cross-country skiers and hikers can find shelter for the night. Huts are basic, with bunk beds, but do have wood stoves, propane burners, photovoltaic lighting, kitchen equipment, mattresses, and pillows. A one-person bed in one of the huts owned by the 10th Mountain Division Hut Association costs $28 per night for adults; huts owned by others but booked through the association cost approximately $20 to $40 per adult, but some require the entire unit to be rented for upward of $300. Children under 13 are charged half-price.

WARM-WEATHER & OTHER YEAR-ROUND ACTIVITIES

Vail doesn't shut down once the skiers go home. Instead, visitors and locals alike trade their skis for mountain bikes and hiking boots, and hit the trails again. The resort closes parts of the mountain from early May to late June to protect elk-calving habitats, but other than that, warm-weather activities cover the mountains.

Nova Guides, in Vail (✆ **888/949-6682** or 719/486-2656; www.novaguides.com), offers guided fishing, mountain-bike, and off-road tours, plus paintball and white-water rafting. The **10th Mountain Division Hut System,** which runs for 350 miles, is open to hikers and mountain-bikers in the summer months (see "Cross-Country Skiing," above).

You'll find many of the companies listed below on the Internet at **www.visitvailvalley.com**; **www.vail.com** is also a good source for information on summer activities. For maps and information on the numerous activities in the White River National Forest, consult the **Holy Cross Ranger District Office** (see "Cross-Country Skiing," above).

FISHING The streams and mountain lakes surrounding Vail are rich with rainbow, brook, brown, and cutthroat trout, plus mountain whitefish. Gore Creek, which runs through the town of Vail, is a popular anglers' venue, especially toward evening from its banks along the Vail Golf Course. Other prime spots are the Eagle River, joined by Gore Creek 5 miles downstream near Minturn; the Black Lakes near the summit of Vail Pass; and 60-acre Piney Lake (see directions under "Mountain Biking," below). The **Lazy J Ranch** in Wolcott (✆ **970/926-3472;** www.lazyjranch.net) offers guided fly-fishing trips on 4 miles of private Eagle River frontage and stocked lakes; half-day guided wade or float trips cost $250 for one person, $325 for two.

Other fishing guides in the area with similar rates include **Nova Guides** (✆ **888/949-6682** or 719/486-2656; www.novaguides.com); **Gore Creek Fly Fisherman,** 193 E. Gore Creek Dr. (✆ **970/476-3296;** www.gorecreekflyfisherman.com); and **Fly Fishing Outfitters, Inc.** (✆ **800/595-8090** or 970/476-3474; www.flyfishingoutfitters.net), which also has a retail store with fishing supplies and outdoor clothing in Avon, across from the entrance to Beaver Creek.

GOLF Courses here are usually open from mid-May to mid-October. The **Vail Golf Club,** 1778 Vail Valley Dr., Vail (✆ **970/479-2260;** www.vailgolfclub.net), has greens fees of $45 to $80, cart not included; the **Eagle-Vail Golf Course,** 6 miles west of Vail at 431 Eagle Dr., Avon (✆ **970/949-5267;** www.eaglevailgolfclub.com), charges $57 to $98 for 18 holes, with the lowest rates coming after 3pm.

HIKING & BACKPACKING The surrounding White River National Forest has a plethora of trails leading to pristine lakes and spectacular panoramic views. The Holy Cross Wilderness Area, southwest of Vail, encompasses 14,005-foot Mount of the Holy Cross and is an awesome region with over 100 miles of trails. Eagle's Nest Wilderness Area lies to the north, in the impressive Gore Range. For information and maps for these and other hiking areas, consult the **Holy Cross Ranger District Office** (see "Cross-Country Skiing," above).

HORSEBACK RIDING & CATTLE ROUNDUPS One of the best ways to explore this beautiful and rugged mountain country is on the back of a horse. The **Ranch in Vail at Spraddle Creek,** 100 Spraddle Creek Rd. (✆ **970/476-6941;** www.ranchinvail.com), is open mid-May through September and is especially geared to families, with rides for beginners to experts. A 1½-hour ride costs $60. Also providing guided horseback rides is the **Lazy J Ranch** (see above); prices start at $65 for 2 hours. **Triple G Outfitters,** at 4 Eagle Ranch, 4 miles north of I-70 exit 157 (✆ **970/926-1234;** www.tripleg.net), charges $40 and up for horseback rides, and also offers half-day cattle roundups for about $100, lunch included. Triple G also offers combination riding-rafting "Saddles & Paddles" trips starting at $130.

LLAMA TREKKING **Paragon Guides** (see "Backcountry Ski Tours," above) offers llama-trekking trips, from 3 to 6 days, July through September. They are limited to eight persons for camping, or slightly larger groups for hut trips, and start around $1,100 per person for 3 days. Pricier custom treks are also available, from overnight to 1 week.

MOUNTAIN BIKING Summer visitors can take their bikes up the Eagle Bahn Gondola to Adventure Ridge on Vail Mountain (all-day passes are $30 for adults, $23 for children 5–12) and cruise downhill on a series of trails. There are many other choices for avid bikers, on both backcountry trails and road tours. A popular trip is the 13-mile Lost Lake Trail along Red Sandstone Road to Piney Lake. The 30-mile Vail Pass Bikeway goes to Frisco, with a climb from 8,460 feet up to 10,600 feet. Pick up a trail list (with map) at an information center.

Mountain-bike repairs and rentals are available at a number of shops, including **Vail Bike Tech,** 555 E. Lionshead Circle (✆ **800/525-5995** or 970/476-5995; www.vailbiketech.com), which also offers guided tours starting around $50 per rider; and **Wheel Base,** 610 W. Lionshead Circle (✆ **970/476-5799;** www.vailskibase.com). Rental rates are about $10 to $20 for a half-day, $20 to $65 for a full day, depending on the type of bike.

RIVER RAFTING The Eagle River, just a few miles west of Vail, offers thrilling white water, especially during the May-to-June thaw. Families can enjoy the relatively gentle (Class II–IV) lower Eagle, west of Minturn; the upper Eagle, above Minturn, is significantly rougher (Class IV–V rapids). Area rafting companies also take trips on the Colorado River, which they access about 35 miles northwest via Colo. 131, at State Bridge. Rafting companies here include **Timberline Tours** (✆ **800/831-1414** or 970/476-1414; www.timberlinetours.com), **Nova Guides** (see above), and **Lakota River Guides** (✆ **970/845-7238;** www.lakotariver.com). Rates run $69 to $100 per adult for a half-day trip, with slightly lower rates for youths. (Young children aren't usually permitted.)

THE FESTIVAL SCENE

The summer season's big cultural event is the **Bravo! Vail Valley Music Festival,** from late June through early August. Established in 1988, the festival features a variety of classical music, from orchestral to chamber music to vocal, with performers such as the New York Philharmonic, the Columbus Jazz Orchestra, and the Dallas Symphony. Tickets range from $23 to $84; contact the festival office at P.O. Box 2270, Vail, CO 81658 (✆ **877/812-5700** or 970/827-5700; www.vailmusicfestival.org).

The **Vail International Dance Festival** features both classes and performances. The World Masters Ballet Academy at Vail teaches the Russian style of artistic expression and other techniques, and presents a series of performances each summer. For information, contact the Vail International Dance Festival, P.O. Box 309, Vail, CO 81658 (✆ **888/920-2787** or 970/949-1999; www.vaildance.org). Tickets are $17 to $85. The Vail Valley Foundation also hosts **Hot Summer Nights,** free concerts of contemporary rock, jazz, or blues, on Tuesday evenings at 6:30pm from mid-June through early August at the Gerald R. Ford Amphitheatre near Betty Ford Alpine Gardens.

NEARBY MUSEUMS & OTHER ATTRACTIONS

Betty Ford Alpine Gardens ★ A wonderful place for a relaxing break from the rigors of an active vacation, these peaceful gardens offer a chance to see a variety of flowering alpine plants unique to the Rocky Mountains. At 8,200 feet, these are the highest public botanical gardens in North America. The alpine display, perennial garden, and mountain meditation garden together represent about 2,000 varieties of plants, demonstrating the wide range of choices to be grown at high altitudes. The gardens attract a variety of birds, and there is also a rock garden with a stunning 120-foot waterfall. Allow 1 to 3 hours.

Ford Park, east of Vail Village, Vail. ✆ **970/476-0103.** www.bettyfordalpinegardens.org. Free admission. Snowmelt to snowfall daily dawn–dusk.

Colorado Ski Museum—Ski & Snowboard Hall of Fame The history of more than a century of Colorado skiing—from the boards that mountain miners first strapped on their feet to the post–World War II resort boom, to Coloradans' success in international racing and the Olympics—is depicted in this popular showcase. Also included is the 40-year-plus evolution of snowboarding, plus the role of the U.S. Forest Service. There's one room devoted to the 10th Mountain Division, the only division of the military trained in ski warfare. A theater presents historical and current ski videos. The museum incorporates the Colorado Ski & Snowboard Hall of Fame, with plaques and photographs honoring Vail founder Peter Seibert, filmmaker Lowell Thomas, Olympic skier Buddy Werner, and others. Allow 1 hour.

Vail Transportation Center, Level 3. ✆ **970/476-1876.** www.skimuseum.net. Free admission. Daily 10am–6pm (until 8pm in ski season).

SHOPPING

There are a wide variety of shops and galleries in Vail and Beaver Creek, but this is not a place for bargain hunters. Among art galleries of note are **Vail Fine Art Gallery,** Vail Village Crossroads Center, 141 E. Meadow Dr. (✆ **970/476-2900**), with beautiful sculptures and fine paintings. **Currents Fine Jewelers,** 285 Bridge St. (✆ **970/476-3322**), offers original designs in platinum, gold, and silver jewelry plus fine Swiss watches. Other interesting shops include **Mountain Dog,** 100 E. Meadow Dr., #33 (✆ **970/479-8488**), with canine accessories of all kinds; and **Kitchen Collage,** at Riverwalk, the

 Crystal Building, Edwards (✆ **970/926-0400;** www.kitchencollage.com), which carries fine cookware, gourmet foods, linens, and a multitude of handy gadgets.

WHERE TO STAY

Like most of Colorado's ski resorts, Vail has an abundance of condominiums. Many are individually owned and available for rent when the owners aren't in town; you'll find that they have more individuality and homey touches than you'd often find in a hotel. Some of the better condominium developments are discussed below (along with other lodging choices), but there are scores more. Contact the **Vail Valley Partnership** (p. 300), which can provide additional lodging information or make your reservations for you, as well as provide information on skiing and other activities.

As in most ski areas, rates are highest during peak ski season, particularly Christmas, and can sometimes be halved after the lifts close. During ski season, you'll find the lowest rates at the very beginning, from opening to about December 20. Unless otherwise noted, parking is free. Room taxes add almost 12% to lodging bills.

Skiers on a tight budget can probably save a few dollars by staying in the town of Eagle, just south of I-70 exit 147, about 18 miles west of Beaver Creek and 29 miles west of Vail. Here there is a **Comfort Inn Vail Valley,** 285 Market St. (✆ **970/328-7878**), with rates of $99 to $199 double; and the **Best Western Eagle Lodge & Suites,** 200 Loren Lane (✆ **800/475-4824** or 970/328-6316), which charges rates of $130 double and $255 suite, with higher holiday rates.

In Vail

Expensive

The Arrabelle at Vail Square ★★★ The storybook-looking centerpiece of the reinvention of Lionshead Square, Arrabelle has a hand-stenciled, multiterraced facade that looks like several buildings straight from the Old Country, and includes a clock tower, glockenspiel, and other Bavarian touches. Best of all, it's Vail's only true ski-in, ski-out lodging, featuring a ski valet who warms up your skis and has them waiting lift-side on your command. Inside it's just as wondrous, from the happy bronze bear that inhabits the lustrous lobby to the spa (the signature treatment involves hot wine) to the guest rooms, which are the best in the village. The 32 units here feature canopied beds, original art, rich red color schemes, fireplaces, and private balconies. There is a splendid rooftop pool with a remarkable view of Eagle Bahn and an excellent French eatery, **Centre V.**

675 Lionshead Place, Vail, CO 81657. ✆ **866/662-7625** or 970/754-7777. www.arrabelle.rockresorts.com. 36 units, including 3 suites, plus 55 condos, some of which are in a rental pool. Winter $750–$3,000; summer $300–$2,000. Higher holiday rates, lower rates spring and fall. AE, DISC, MC, V. **Amenities:** Outdoor heated pool; exercise room; spa; 2 outdoor hot tubs; steam room and sauna; concierge; business center; coin-op laundry; dry cleaning. *In room:* Cable TV/DVD player, wireless Internet access (free), kitchen, fridge, hair dryer, iron.

Vail Cascade Resort & Spa ★★ A wonderful choice for those who love pampering, the Vail Cascade gets better every year. A recent $30-million renovation project has resulted in air-conditioning, new furnishings, and huge plasma TVs, as well as a rebuilt creek-side deck with an infinity pool. All units boast fabulous mountain or courtyard views; some units have outdoor balconies with tables and chairs. The courtyard entrance is beautifully landscaped, with tall Colorado blue spruce, aspens, and an abundance of flowers in the summer. There are elevators accessing the four floors, and interior corridors everywhere so you never have to go outside until you're ready to ski—and the Cascade Village chairlift is just outside the door. Of course, there is also a ski concierge on hand to assist.

And here is where the pampering gets really serious: The **Aria Spa & Club** is a 78,000-square-foot spa and athletic club, offering practically every treatment imaginable.

1300 Westhaven Dr., Vail, CO 81657. ✆ **800/420-2424** or 970/476-7111. Fax 970/479-7020. www.vailcascade.com. 292 rooms and suites, 72 condos and private residences. Winter $259–$619 double, $879–$1,300 suite, higher at Christmas; summer $129–$299 double, $750 suite. AE, DISC, MC, V. Free underground parking available (7-ft. height limit). Take I-70 exit 173 for West Vail, head east on South Frontage Rd. to Westhaven Dr., and turn right. **Amenities:** Restaurant (American/regional); bar; 2 heated outdoor pools; 7 tennis courts (4 indoor, 3 outdoor); state-of-the-art health club and spa; 3 hot tubs (2 outdoor, 1 indoor); sauna; concierge; shopping arcade, including sporting-goods stores w/rentals and apparel; 24-hr room service; massage; babysitting. *In room:* A/C, cable TV w/pay movies, wireless Internet access (free), minibar, coffeemaker, hair dryer, iron.

Moderate

Tivoli Lodge ★ The first shining ray of light from Vail's New Dawn, a billion-dollar makeover/redevelopment of the base village, the Tivoli Lodge was rebuilt from scratch by the race car–driving Lazier family, who built the original Tivoli on the same spot in 1968. Gone are the small, dated rooms, replaced by large (many are almost 500 sq. ft.) guest quarters decorated with a masculine feel; the corner suite has a commanding view of Vail Mountain from its private balcony. The new lobby, with quartzite floors that sport fossils, features a bar and a breakfast area. Located immediately east of the center of Vail Village, the property offers a great location for skiers and plenty of elbow room for families and large groups.

386 Hanson Ranch Rd., Vail, CO 81657. ✆ **800/451-4756** or 970/476-5615. Fax 970/476-6601. www.tivolilodge.com. 62 units, including 1 suite. Winter $229–$499 double, $799–$999 suite; rest of year $149–$250 double, $400–$500 suite. Higher holiday rates. Rates include full breakfast. AE, DISC, MC, V. **Amenities:** Outdoor heated pool; 2 outdoor hot tubs; concierge; dry cleaning. *In room:* Cable TV, wireless Internet access (free), fridge, coffeemaker, hair dryer, iron, microwave.

Vail Mountain Lodge & Spa ★★ Finds Nestled along Gore Creek, this property offers B&B intimacy and hotel service. While the property is relatively small, its 20 rooms are relatively large and feature a pleasant contemporary decor that doesn't get hung up on Western or ski themes. The property just underwent a $25-million upgrade, and it was money well spent. Located just a few steps from world-class skiing, dining, and shopping, all rooms have gas fireplaces, soaking tubs, and oh-so-comfy feather beds. Beyond the standard rooms, there are eight suites with two or three bedrooms, the latter of which measures a whopping 2,000 square feet. The facilities here are similarly first rate: **Terra Bistro,** the resident eatery, offers global fusion cuisine and some of the best tuna tartare in the Rockies; the health club features Vail's only indoor climbing wall; and the spa is frequented by local pros getting ready for ski season.

352 E. Meadow Dr., Vail, CO 81657. ✆ **866/476-0700** or 970/476-0700. Fax 970/476-6451. www.vailmountainlodge.com. 20 units. Winter $350–$600 double, $900–$2,300 suite; rest of year $149–$299 double, $235–$600 suite. Minimum stays required in ski season. Rates include continental breakfast. AE, DC, MC, V. **Amenities:** Restaurant (global fusion); lounge; health club; whirlpool (indoor); spa; concierge; massage; dry cleaning. *In room:* Cable TV, wireless Internet access (free), kitchen, coffeemaker, hair dryer, iron.

Beaver Creek & Edwards Area

Very Expensive

Park Hyatt Beaver Creek Resort and Spa ★★ An architecturally unique hotel at the foot of the Beaver Creek lifts, this luxurious ski-in/ski-out Park Hyatt blends features of medieval European alpine monasteries with Rocky Mountain styles and materials. The exterior is native stone, offset with stucco and rough timbers. The interior is of rough-hewn pine and sandstone; wall-size fireplaces enhance numerous cozy alcoves furnished with overstuffed chairs and sofas. Elk-antler chandeliers and works by contemporary artisans lend a Western ambience. Guest rooms have a European country elegance, with knotty-pine furnishings and TVs hidden in armoires. The raised beds have dust ruffles, pillow shams, and quilted comforters; the bathrooms feature marble-top vanities and heated towel racks; and most rooms have private balconies. Other amenities include high-speed Internet access, bathrobes and slippers, and refrigerators.

50 W. Thomas Place (P.O. Box 1595), Avon, CO 81620. ✆ **800/778-7477** or 970/949-1234. Fax 970/949-4164. www.parkhyattbeavercreek.com. 190 units. Winter $479–$1,179 double, $1,250–$6,000 suite; rest of year $139–$439 double, $350–$2,100 suite. AE, DISC, MC, V. Valet parking $20. **Amenities:** 3 restaurants (American, French, Southwestern); lounge; indoor/outdoor heated pool; health club; full-service spa; 5 outdoor whirlpools; sauna; children's programs; concierge; 24-hr. room service; massage; coin-op laundry; dry cleaning. *In room:* Cable TV w/pay movies, wireless Internet access (free), coffeemaker, hair dryer, iron, safe.

Ritz-Carlton, Bachelor Gulch ★★★ A stunning structure modeled after the grand national park lodges, the rock-and-log "parkitechture" exterior sheaths one of the most luxurious hotels in the West. While not your typical Ritz-Carlton at first glance, the property has style and comfort to spare (there are over 100 fireplaces) and a Rocky Mountain style that's all its own. For instance, the property has a "Loan-a-Lab" program for guests who want to hike with the hotel's yellow Labrador, Bachelor, and the staff includes a firepit concierge who tends the coals nightly at the outdoor pit. The rooms are also studies in New West glitz, complete with mountain and earth tones, decor inspired by wildlife and forests, and jaw-dropping views. The club level, which includes five courses a day and an open bar, is especially plush. Of the long list of amenities, the spa here is a national standout, featuring 19 treatment rooms centered on a rock-laden, candlelit grotto with an oversized coed hot tub. Also onsite is Wolfgang Puck's **Spago.**

0130 Daybreak Ridge (P.O. Box 9190), Avon, CO 81620. ✆ **800/241-3333** or 970/748-6200. Fax 970/343-1070. www.ritzcarlton.com. 237 units, including 29 suites. Winter $400–$1,800 double, $550–$9,140 suite; rest of year $195–$415 double, $340–$1,920 suite. AE, DC, DISC, MC, V. Valet parking $20. **Amenities:** 3 restaurants (contemporary eclectic/cafe/bar); lounge; outdoor heated pool; 4 outdoor tennis courts; health club; full-service spa; indoor and outdoor whirlpools; sauna; children's programs; concierge; babysitting; limited room service; massage; dry cleaning. *In room:* TV w/pay movies, dataport, coffeemaker, hair dryer, iron, safe.

Expensive

The Charter at Beaver Creek ★ This elegant European-style lodging offers the luxury of a world-class hotel and the convenience of condominiums, set in the magnificent Rocky Mountains. Lodge rooms, simply decorated, can accommodate up to four persons; most have two queen beds, though some have one king. All units have robes, and most have grand views of the valley or surrounding mountains. The one- to five-bedroom condominiums have a full kitchen, fireplace—some of lovely river rock—and balcony or patio. All are decorated by the owners—some in Western motif, some more traditional. The property is ski-in/ski-out, with ski valet service. And there are trails radiating from the property; a walking trail is just 5 minutes from the village center.

120 Offerson Rd. (P.O. Box 5310), Beaver Creek, CO 81620. ✆ **800/525-2139** or 970/949-6660. Fax 970/949-4667. www.thecharter.com. Winter $119–$500 double, $250–$3,200 condo; summer $119–$200 double, $225–$1,000 condo. AE, MC, V. Valet parking; underground parking (7-ft., 6-in. height limit). **Amenities:** 2 restaurants (Italian, American); indoor and outdoor (seasonal) heated pools; separate children's pool (seasonal); 18-hole golf course; large health club and spa; indoor and outdoor hot tubs; sauna; game room; concierge; full-service rental and retail sports shop; limited room service; coin-op laundry; valet laundry and dry cleaning;. *In room:* Cable TV/DVD, dataport (DSL), kitchen (in condos), fridge, coffeemaker, hair dryer, iron, safe.

The Lodge & Spa at Cordillera ★★ Reminiscent of a Belgium mountain-style château, this luxurious hideaway is nestled in 7,500 gated and secluded acres of private forest just 15 minutes west of Beaver Creek. Rocky Mountain timber and stone, along with elegant wrought iron, are prominent in the handsome, residential-style guest rooms. Most rooms feature a wood-burning or gas fireplace, all have king- or queen-size beds, and most have private balconies or decks with views of the Sawatch Range of the Rockies. Smoking is not permitted. The award-winning spa includes two dedicated facial rooms, a hydrotherapy room, a dedicated manicure and pedicure salon, a meditation room, and several multipurpose treatment rooms. The resort offers 15 miles of mountain biking/cross-country ski trails, horseback riding, a Nordic ski center, ski shuttles, and private clubs at both Vail and Beaver Creek. Cordillera is considered one of the premier golf communities in the state, and there are also private fly-fishing waters on-site.

2205 Cordillera Way (P.O. Box 1110), Edwards, CO 81632. ✆ **800/877-3529** or 970/926-2200. Fax 970/926-2486. www.cordilleralodge.com. 55 units, including 10 suites. $150–$400 double; $275–$750 suite. Extra person $25; children 11 and under stay free in parent's room. AE, MC, V. Self- and valet parking. **Amenities:** 2 restaurants (global, pub); 2 pools (outdoor, indoor lap); golf courses (3 18-hole and a 10-hole short course); 2 tennis courts; exercise room; full-service spa; indoor/outdoor whirlpool; steam room; sauna; bicycle rentals; concierge; limited room service (6:30am–10pm); massage; valet laundry and dry cleaning. *In room:* A/C, cable TV, coffeemaker, hair dryer, iron.

Inexpensive

Inn & Suites at Riverwalk (Value) Located 10 miles west of Vail at the posh Riverwalk, a retail/office/entertainment district in Edwards, this is a considerable value in comparison with your options right at the slopes, and access to both Beaver Creek and Vail Mountain is excellent. The rooms are nice, modern hotel rooms with bright colors and attractive spreads; the condos have balconies, gas fireplaces, Jacuzzi tubs, and full kitchens. There are dozens of restaurants and bars within walking distance, and, in the off season, they're typically bustling when the nightlife in Vail Village can be relatively sleepy.

27 Main St., Edwards, CO 81632. ✆ **888/926-0606** or 970/926-0606. Fax 970/926-0616. www.innandsuitesatriverwalk.com. 75 units, including 16 condos. Winter $140–$240 double, $320–$560 condo; rest of year $100–$130 double, $230–$370 condo. AE, DISC, MC, V. Take I-70 exit 163 to Edwards; the Riverwalk is just south. **Amenities:** Outdoor pool; outdoor hot tub; fitness center; coin-op washers and dryers. *In room:* Cable TV, dataport w/Internet access (free), kitchen (in condos), coffeemaker, hair dryer, iron.

Where to Dine

Vail and Beaver Creek have dozens of excellent restaurants, although few of them are what you would call bargains. In addition to the ones listed below, I also like **Blu's,** 193 E. Gore Creek Dr. (✆ **970/476-3113**), for its blueberry pancakes and killer creek-side patio; **eat! drink!,** 56 Edwards Village Blvd. at the Corner @ Edwards shopping center (✆ **970/926-1393**), an establishment with a wine shop on one side and a cafe serving wine, cheese, and small plates on the other; and **Larkburger,** 105 Edwards Village Blvd. (✆ **970/926-9336**), specializing in sublime burgers made of beef, turkey, and portabella mushroom, as well as salads and shakes.

Beano's Cabin ★★ AMERICAN CONTINENTAL A splurge that many Beaver Creek visitors consider one of the highlights of their stay is the sleigh-ride dinner trip (or, in summer, on horseback) to Beano's. This isn't the log homestead that Chicago lettuce farmer Frank "Beano" Bienkowski built on Beaver Creek Mountain in 1919—it's far more elegant. Diners board the 42-passenger, Sno-Cat–driven sleighs at the base of the Centennial Lift, arriving 20 minutes later for a candlelit five-course dinner around a crackling fire with musical entertainment. The menu varies, but entree choices might include selections such as grilled Colorado tenderloin of beef, balsamic-marinated ostrich, seared Rocky Mountain trout, wood-grilled venison loin chop, and herb-crusted rack of Colorado lamb. Vegetarian meals and a lower-priced children's menu are available.

Near Larkspur Bowl, Beaver Creek Resort. ✆ **970/949-9090.** Reservations required. Fixed-price meal $99 and up. AE, DC, DISC, MC, V. Departures from Beaver Creek Chophouse (at Centennial Lift) winter 4:15–9:15pm daily; summer Wed–Sun. Closed several months in spring and fall.

Kelly Liken Restaurant ★★★ SEASONAL AMERICAN This is my favorite eatery in Vail. Some local chefs grumbled when 20-something Kelly Liken slapped her name on the marquee here when the restaurant opened in 2004, but the fantastic food and stylish room are undeniably Colorado standouts. Liken, who graduated first in her class from the Culinary Institute of America, strove to "raise the bar" in Vail, and she succeeds with such dishes as her signature potato-crusted trout filets elk carpaccio with bulgur tabbouleh salad and mustard aioli. The menu changes with the season, using as much locally grown ingredients as possible. Any time of year, the creative fare is a feast for the senses, with contrasting flavors, sublime sauces, and sensational presentations. The wine list is terrific, the wait staff is sharp (and sharply dressed), and the desserts—especially the "can't be missed" sticky bun sundae—approach otherworldly.

12 Vail Rd., in the Gateway Bldg. ✆ **970/476-0175.** www.kellyliken.com. Reservations recommended. Main courses $30–$40 dinner. AE, DISC, MC, V. Daily 6–10pm. Bar open later.

La Tour ★★ CONTEMPORARY FRENCH La Tour opened in the 1970s, but it sprang to life when chef-owner Paul Ferzacca, known for his high-altitude skills, took it over in 1998. He gave both the room and the menu a needed jolt of creativity, adding contemporary European art and a new bright color scheme to the walls and implementing a metaphorically similar makeover to the menu. The preparations use French traditions as a starting point, but Ferzacca loves to mix and match ingredients and preparations from all corners of the globe. The menu changes seasonally but is heavy on seafood and steaks, and many dishes are unique. The soups and desserts are standouts.

122 E. Meadow Dr. ✆ **970/476-4403.** www.latour-vail.com. Reservations recommended. Main courses $28–$42. AE, DISC, MC, V. Daily 5–9:30pm.

Larkspur ★★ REGIONAL/ECLECTIC A grand, high-ceilinged room with plenty of space, large artworks, and an open kitchen in back, Larkspur is a good pick for couples and larger groups alike. With a superb, white-jacketed wait staff, white tablecloths, and subtly striped booths, the food takes center stage: starters like a frothy chilled corn soup with shrimp tempura or a delectably salty pork belly with contrasting Colorado and Asian peaches; entrees like Thai snapper with corn pudding, heirloom tomatoes, and lobster emulsion, or a rich Colorado rack of lamb with fava beans; and such heavenly desserts as buttermilk panna cotta with strawberry salad. I enjoyed everything at this upscale slopeside eatery. The wine cellar, 4,000 bottles deep, is excellent.

458 Vail Valley Dr. ✆ **970/476-8050.** www.larkspurvail.com. Reservations recommended. Main courses $27–$43. AE, MC, V. Winter daily 11am–10pm; summer daily 6–9pm.

Vail After Dark

Vail's greatest concentration of late-night haunts can be found in a 1½-block stretch of Bridge Street from Hanson Ranch Road north to the covered bridge over Gore Creek. From mountainside to creek, they include **The Club** (✆ **970/479-0556**), the **Red Lion**

A Float on the Wild Side: Rancho Del Rio

Rancho Del Rio is a former hippie commune that's now one of the last remaining river communities of its kind, a haven for oddballs and river rats who live in the assorted cabins and trailers here. The slow waters of the Upper Colorado River in this area are perfect for beginner rafters and families; even first-timers will be comfortable paddling the river solo. The **Colorado River Center** (✆ **888/888-7238** or 970/653-7238; www.coloradorivercenter.com) offers rentals, shuttles ($25 – $50), lessons, and guided rafting trips. I recommend renting a "duckie" (an inflatable kayak) and paddling it to State Bridge, and then getting a shuttle back to Rancho. A few other rafting companies run guided trips out of Rancho Del Rio.

After a river trip and a shuttle ride back, it's time for a bite and a beer at **K.K.'s BBQ,** also known as the "Center of the Universe." An outdoor bar and grill with jars of homemade pickles and pots of homemade sauce and slices of homemade pies, this is the most fun you can have at a meal in the Northern Rockies. Eponymous proprietor K. K. is quite the character and a one-woman act, cooking burgers, ribs, and sausages; making sundaes and change; telling jokes; and generally entertaining everyone within earshot. I can't resist the 4K, a burger with a split Italian sausage on top and a heap of fresh jalapenos under molten cheese, or the aptly named Little Beauty. K. K. fires up the grill at 11am and closes around 5pm Saturday and Sunday between Memorial Day and the last Sunday in September.

For more information, contact **Rancho Del Rio,** 4199 Trough Rd., Bond, CO 80423 (✆ **970/653-4431;** www.ranchodelrio.com). Beyond the rafting and barbecue, there is a campground ($3 per person per night), four rental cabins ($70–$80 a night), and fly-fishing guides. There is a day-use fee of $1 per person and $2 per vehicle.

(✆ **970/476-7676**), and **Vendetta's** (✆ **970/476-5070**), reportedly the hangout for Vail's ski patrollers. **The Tap Room,** 333 Bridge St. (✆ **970/479-0500**), not surprisingly, has an extensive selection of beers on tap, plus good pub grub and martinis. **Samana Lounge,** 228 Bridge St. (✆ **970/476-3433;** www.samanalounge.com), is a small, sophisticated dance club with a candlelit ambience and world-class DJs. The **George Restaurant & Pub,** 292 E. Meadow Dr. (✆ **970/476-2656**), has a laid-back vibe and is a great pick for an après-ski cocktail. **Garfinkel's,** 536 E. Lionshead Circle (✆ **970/476-3789**), keeps sports fans busy with tons of TVs and everybody else happy with a great deck at the foot of the Eagle Bahn gondola.

In nearby Minturn, the happy hour at the historic **Minturn Saloon,** 146 N. Main St. (✆ **970/827-5954**), attracts a party-hearty horde for Vail Valley's best margaritas. In summer, the place to be Friday night is the **Wolcott Yacht Club,** 15 miles west of Vail at 27190 U.S. 6, Wolcott (✆ **970/926-3444;** www.wolcottyachtclub.com), and its unbeatable back patio, complete with band shell and live band, not to mention pretty good grub.

7 LEADVILLE ★

38 miles S of Vail, 59 miles E of Aspen, 113 miles W of Denver

Not much more than a century ago, Leadville was the most important city between St. Louis and San Francisco. It was the stopping point for Easterners with nothing to lose and everything to gain from the promise of gold and silver. Today Leadville is one of the best places to rediscover the West's mining heritage.

Founded in 1860 on the gold that glimmered in prospectors' pans, Leadville and nearby Oro City quickly attracted 10,000 miners who dug $5 million in gold out of a 3-mile stretch of the California Gulch by 1865. When the riches were gone, Leadville was deserted, although a smaller lode of gold-bearing quartz kept Oro City alive for another decade. Then in 1875, two prospectors located the California Gulch's first paying silver lode. Over the next 2 decades, Leadville grew to an estimated 30,000 residents—among them "the Unsinkable" Molly Brown, whose husband made his fortune here before moving to Denver, where the family lived at the time of Molly's *Titanic* heroism.

Now an isolated mountain town (elevation 10,152 ft.) of about 2,700 residents, Leadville has managed to maintain its historic character. Many buildings of the silver boom (which produced $136 million in 1879–89) have been preserved in Leadville's National Historic Landmark District. So for those who want to take a break from playing outdoors to explore Colorado's frontier past, this is just the place to do it.

ESSENTIALS

GETTING THERE **By Car** Coming from Denver, leave I-70 at exit 195 (Copper Mountain) and proceed south 24 miles on Colo. 91. From Grand Junction, depart I-70 at exit 171 (Minturn) and continue south 33 miles on U.S. 24. From Aspen, in the summer take Colo. 82 east 44 miles over Independence Pass (closed in winter), then turn north on U.S. 24 for 15 miles. There's also easy access from the south via U.S. 24.

By Plane The nearest airport with commercial service is the **Eagle County Regional Airport,** which offers car rentals and bus service to Leadville (see "Essentials," under Vail, earlier in this chapter).

VISITOR INFORMATION Contact the **Leadville/Lake County Chamber of Commerce,** 809 Harrison Ave. (P.O. Box 861), Leadville, CO 80461 (✆ **888/532-3845** or 719/486-3900; www.leadvilleusa.com), which operates a visitor center that's usually open daily from 9am to 4pm in summer, and 10am to 4pm Tuesday through Saturday the rest of the year.

GETTING AROUND U.S. 24 is Leadville's main street. Entering Leadville from the north, it's named Poplar Street; then it turns west on Ninth Street for a block and then south on Harrison Avenue. The next 7 blocks south, to Second Street, are the heart of this historic town. A block north, Seventh Street climbs east to the historic train depot and 13,186-foot Mosquito Pass, among America's highest, open to four-wheel-drive vehicles after the snow melts, usually sometime in July.

Dee Hive Tours, 506 Harrison Ave. (✆ **719/486-2339**), offers **taxi** service.

FAST FACTS There's a 24-hour emergency room at **St. Vincent's General Hospital,** 822 W. Fourth St. (✆ **719/486-0230**). The **post office** is at 136 W. Fifth St.; for hours and other information, contact the U.S. Postal Service (✆ **800/275-8777;** www.usps.com). The sheriff's office (✆ **719/486-1249**) provides **road reports.**

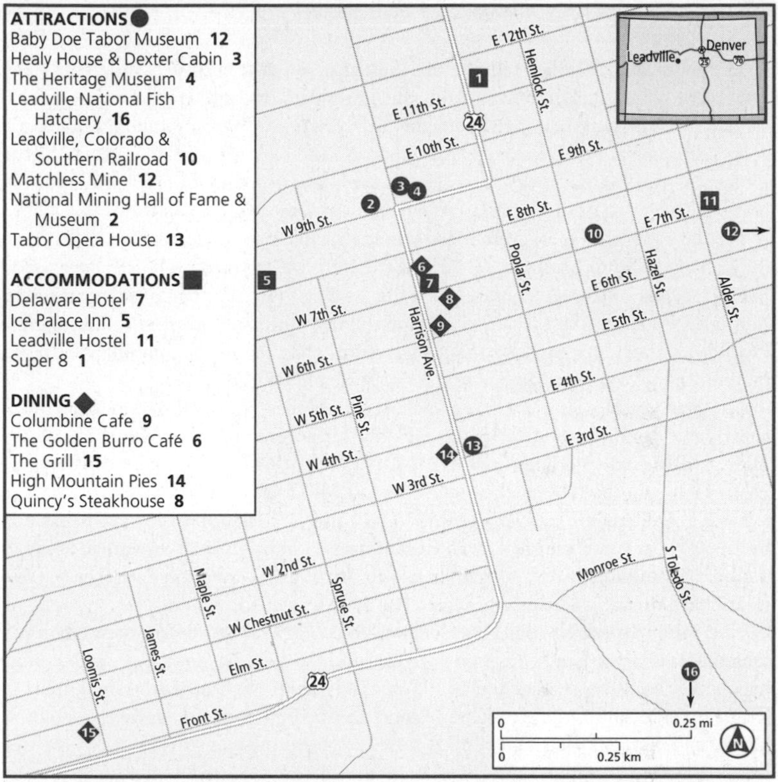

EXPERIENCING LEADVILLE'S PAST

A great many residences of successful mining operators, engineers, and financiers are preserved within the **Leadville National Historic Landmark District ★★**, which stretches along 7 blocks of Harrison Avenue and part of Chestnut Street, where it intersects Harrison at the south end of downtown. A self-guided walking tour of this district, with map, is available free at the visitor center. An informative 30-minute video, *The Earth Runs Silver: Early Leadville,* is shown at the visitor center (see "Visitor Information," above) for free on request, and it provides a good overview of Leadville's place in American mining history.

Leadville has numerous historic buildings open to the public; allow 30 minutes to an hour for each of the following.

You'll discover Leadville's colorful past at the **Heritage Museum,** corner of Ninth Street and Harrison Avenue (**© 719/486-1878**), a historical museum loaded with exhibits on and artifacts from Leadville's early days, from mining dioramas to a scale model of the ice palace that Leadville residents created in 1896. There's also an art gallery displaying the work of local artists (most of it is for sale), and a gift shop with a good selection of books and mining-related souvenirs. Admission costs $6 for adults, $5 for seniors 62 and older, $3 for students 6 to 16, and free for children under 6. It's open May through October daily from 10am to 6pm, with slightly shorter hours at the beginning and end of the season.

At the **National Mining Hall of Fame and Museum ★★**, 120 W. Ninth St. (✆ **719/486-1229;** www.mininghalloffame.org), you'll find walk-through replica mines, models of mining machinery, and dioramas depicting the history of Colorado mining from coal to gold. Admission is $7 for adults, $6 for seniors 62 and older, $4 for children 6 to 12, and it's free for children under 6. Open May through October daily from 9am to 5pm, and November through April Monday through Saturday from 10am to 4pm.

Peer into Horace Tabor's **Matchless Mine,** 1¼-mile east up Seventh Street, and tour the **Baby Doe Tabor Museum** (✆ **719/486-1229**), where you'll see how Tabor's widow, Baby Doe, spent the final 36 years of her life, hoping to strike it rich once more. Admission is $7 for adults, $6 for seniors, $4 for children 6 to 12, and free for kids under 6. Open Memorial Day to Labor Day daily from 9am to 5pm. Combination mining museum/mine tickets run $10 adults, $9 seniors, and $5 kids.

To get an up-close look at where a few fortunate miners were able to escape the rough-and-tumble atmosphere of the mines, if only for an evening, visit **Healy House and Dexter Cabin ★**, 912 Harrison Ave. (✆ **719/486-0487;** www.coloradohistory.org). Healy House was built by smelter owner August Meyer in 1878 and later converted into a lavish boardinghouse by Daniel Healy. The adjacent rough-hewn log cabin was built by James Dexter and furnished in an elegant style. Admission is $5 for adults, $4.50 for seniors 65 and older, $3.50 for children 6 to 16, and free for children under 6. Open Memorial Day weekend through September daily from 10am to 4:30pm.

The **Tabor Opera House,** 308 Harrison Ave. (✆ **719/486-8409;** www.taboroperahouse.net), is where Leadville's mining magnates and their wives kept up with cultural happenings back East. Opened in 1879, over the years it has hosted everything from the Ziegfeld Follies and the Metropolitan Opera to prizefighter Jack Dempsey (a Colorado native) and magician Harry Houdini (whose vanishing square is still evident on the stage floor). Visitors can explore the 880-seat theater, backstage, and the dressing rooms, or attend one of the musical or theater performances still held here. (Check the website for the current schedule and prices.) Admission to tour the opera house is $5 for adults, $4 for seniors 65 and older, and $2.50 for children under 13. Open Memorial Day to Labor Day Monday to Saturday from 10am to 5pm.

Although opera and the other refinements of a cultured society may have been on the minds of some early Leadville residents, others were more interested in "pleasures of the flesh," and in the 1870s and 1880s Leadville was a pretty wild place, with a hundred or more saloons and a busy red-light district.

MORE TO SEE & DO

Leadville, Colorado & Southern Railroad ★ This spectacularly scenic ride, in a 1955 diesel train, departs the 1893 C&S Depot, 3 blocks east of U.S. 24, and follows the old "high line" along the headwaters of the Arkansas River to a splendid view of Fremont Pass. The return takes you to the French Gulch water tower for a dramatic look at Mount Elbert, Colorado's tallest mountain (14,433 ft.). The ride lasts about 2½ hours, and because of the high elevations, jackets or sweaters are recommended even on the hottest summer days.

326 E. Seventh St. at Hazel St. ✆ **719/486-3936.** www.leadville-train.com. Admission $29 adults, $17 children 4–12, free for children 3 and under. Daily Memorial Day to late Sept; call for schedule.

Leadville National Fish Hatchery Established in 1889, this is the second-oldest hatchery operated by the U.S. Fish and Wildlife Service that's in existence today. Rainbow, brown, and cutthroat trout are raised here, at an elevation of 10,000 feet on the east side of Mount Massive. Visitors can also enjoy self-guided nature trails, with breathtaking views of the surrounding mountains and occasionally deer and elk. One trail passes by the remains of the Evergreen Hotel, a late-1800s resort, and several trails connect to the Colorado Trail. In winter, take cross-country skis or snowshoes. There are also picnic tables and two public fishing ponds. Allow 30 to 45 minutes.

2844 Colo. 300 (6 miles southwest of Leadville off U.S. 24). ✆ **719/486-0189.** http://leadville.fws.gov. Free admission. Daily 7am–4pm.

SPORTS & OUTDOOR ACTIVITIES

Much of the outdoor recreation in this area takes place in nearby national forest lands, and you can get information at the **San Isabel National Forest** office, 810 Front St. (✆ **719/486-0749;** www.fs.fed.us/r2), as well as the visitor center. **Bill's Sport Shop,** 225 Harrison Ave. (✆ **719/486-0739;** www.billsrentals.com), is a good source for gear (to rent or buy) and advice.

Adventurous **hikers** can attempt an ascent of Mount Elbert (14,440 ft.), Mount Sherman (14,036 ft.), or Mount Massive (14,428 ft.); all three can be climbed in a day without technical equipment, though altitude and abruptly changing weather conditions are factors that should be weighed. One popular trail for hiking, walking, and mountain biking is the **Mineral Belt Trail,** a 12-mile loop that circles Leadville, passing through the mining district and the mountains in the process. A good access point for it is near the recreation center at Sixth Street and McWethy Drive.

There's good trout and kokanee **fishing** at Turquoise Lake, Twin Lakes, and other small high-mountain lakes, as well as at beaver ponds located on side streams of the Arkansas River. There's also limited stream fishing in the area.

Golfers head to 9-hole **Mount Massive Golf Course,** 3 1/2 miles west of town at 259 C.R. 5 (✆ **719/486-2176;** www.mtmassivegolf.com), which claims to be North America's highest golf course, at 9,700 feet. Greens fees are $34 for 18 holes, not including a cart, and views of surrounding mountain peaks are magnificent.

If snow sports are more to your liking, **Ski Cooper,** P.O. Box 896, Leadville, CO 80461 (✆ **800/707-6114** or 719/486-3684, 719/486-2277 for snow reports; www.skicooper.com), is the place to go, with 400 acres of lift-served skiable terrain and another 2,400 acres accessible by snowcat. It began as a training center for 10th Mountain Division troops from Camp Hale during World War II. Located 10 miles north of Leadville on U.S. 24 near Tennessee Pass, it offers numerous intermediate and novice runs, and hosts backcountry Chicago Ridge Snowcat Tours for experts (call for details). Four lifts serve 26 runs—rated 30% beginner, 40% intermediate, and 30% expert—and the mountain has a 1,200-foot vertical drop from the peak of 11,700 feet. Full-day tickets cost $42 for adults, $23 for children 6 to 14, $31 for seniors 60 to 69, $18 for seniors 70 and older, and are free for kids under 6. The **Tennessee Pass Nordic Center** (✆ **719/486-1750;** www.tennesseepass.com), at the foot of the mountain, has 15 miles of groomed track and skating trails, plus rentals and lessons and a highly regarded restaurant, the Tennessee Pass Cookhouse. Trail passes cost $14 for adults, $10 for children and seniors.

WHERE TO STAY

In addition to the properties listed below, Leadville has a **Super 8,** 1128 U.S. 24 (✆ **800/800-8000** or 719/486-3637), with rates of $50 to $100 double. Taxes add just about 9% to lodging bills.

Delaware Hotel ★ Built in 1886, this hotel was restored in 1985 and is once again a Victorian gem. The lobby is beautiful in the style of grand old hotels, with a turn-of-the-20th-century player piano, crystal chandeliers, and magnificent Victorian furnishings. Guest rooms have brass or iron beds, quilts, and lace curtains. Rooms have private bathrooms with showers but no tubs; the four suites have full bathrooms with tub/shower combos. There's an eclectic antiques shop in the lobby. Smoking is not permitted.

700 Harrison Ave., Leadville, CO 80461. ✆ **800/748-2004** or 719/486-1418. Fax 719/486-2214. www.delawarehotel.com. 36 units. $70–$119 double; $139–$199 family room or suite. 10 and younger stay free. Rates include continental breakfast. AE, DC, DISC, MC, V. **Amenities:** Restaurant (American, breakfast only); whirlpool. *In room:* Cable TV, wireless Internet access (free), hair dryer.

Ice Palace Inn An 1899 Victorian named for the Ice Palace, the frozen palace/resort that prematurely thawed in March 1896, this inn was originally built from some of the leftover lumber from that ill-fated project and has since been lovingly restored. Featuring a turret and an artful, eclectic interior, the inn has five rooms in all, each named for a feature of the original Ice Palace. The largest and most lavish is the Grand Ballroom, located on the second floor of the turret with a canopied queen bed and an oversized hydro-massage tub; the Lady Leadville is the smallest but features the best mountain views.

813 Spruce St., Leadville, CO 80461. ✆ **800/754-8272** or 719/486-8272. www.icepalaceinn.com. 5 units. $105–$179 double. Rates include full breakfast. AE, DISC, MC, V. *In room:* Cable TV/VCR, wireless Internet access (free).

Leadville Hostel (Value) "Wild Bill" Clower and Cathy Hacking have made this hostel into one of the best in the West. With a convivial atmosphere, an eclectic style, and plenty of amenities (including shuttle service and a massage room), this is a great stopover for outdoors buffs in the midst of a great adventure or anybody looking for a good deal. The dorm rooms—divided into men's and women's—have four to eight bunks each; the more expensive bunk rooms have their own bathrooms. There are also couples rooms with shared bathrooms and family rooms with private bathrooms. There's a big-screen TV in the family room, a communal kitchen and dining area, and a picture-perfect backyard. Upkeep is great on this 1970s ranch house—it just gets better and better—and Cathy and Bill's personable service is second to none. All-you-can-eat breakfasts and dinner are available ($5–$10). It's popular with training athletes, so make reservations well in advance.

500 E. 7th Ave., Leadville, CO 80461. ✆ **719/486-9334.** www.leadvillehostel.com. 32 dorm beds, 5 private rooms (2 with private bathroom). $17–$23 double; $35–$50 private room. MC, V. **Amenities:** Exercise room; massage room; shuttle service; coin-op washers and dryers; wireless Internet access (free). *In room:* No phone.

WHERE TO DINE

Besides the establishments listed below, I also like **The Grill,** 715 Elm St. (✆ **719/486-9930**), for Mexican fare and tasty margaritas; and **High Mountain Pies,** 311 Harrison Ave. (✆ **719/486-5555**), for pizza, sandwiches, and ribs.

Columbine Cafe AMERICAN/VEGETARIAN This simple, colorful cafe is a local favorite and healthier than the norm. Breakfasts range from traditional eggs and pancakes to more exotic dishes such as malted Belgian waffles and eggs Benedict, which can be prepared with avocados and tomatoes instead of meat. Lunches are sandwiches, burgers, and vegetarian dishes, and down-home hearty specials, such as pot roast, fried chicken, and red beans and rice.

612 Harrison Ave. ✆ **719/486-3599.** Reservations not accepted. Main courses $6–$9 breakfast and lunch. AE, DISC, MC, V. Daily 7am–2pm. Closed in winter.

The Golden Burro Café AMERICAN People have been enjoying good food in a comfortable Western setting at the Golden Burro since it opened in 1938. Old photos and drawings hang on the white walls above the wainscoting, glass-and-brass chandeliers cast a warm glow, and the large front windows provide views of the mountains. The emphasis at the Burro is on food like Grandma used to make, such as a hot meatloaf sandwich (homemade meatloaf, served open-faced with brown gravy, mashed potatoes, and a vegetable), pork chops, chicken-fried steak, and liver and onions, plus burritos with your choice of red or green chile. The freshly baked cinnamon rolls are especially good.

710 Harrison Ave. ✆ **970/486-1239.** Main courses $5–$15. MC, V. Daily 6:30am–9pm, with shorter hours fall through spring. Bar open later.

Quincy's Steakhouse (Value) STEAKS Menus don't get much simpler than this: At Quincy's, it's filet mignon Sunday to Thursday and prime rib on Friday and Saturday. That's it. You get a baked potato, too, and bread and a salad, not to mention a helping of historic ambience. But the focus is on the beef, and while you don't have a choice of the kind of steak you want, you do have four sizes to choose from. This is one of the best values in the Northern Rockies, with 6-ounce filets running $7.95 and 8-ounce slices of prime rib for $9.95.

115 E. Seventh St. ✆ **719/486-9765.** Reservations accepted for parties for 6 or more only. Main courses $8–$18. MC, V. Daily 5–9:30pm.

LEADVILLE AFTER DARK

There's occasional entertainment at the **Tabor Opera House** (see "Experiencing Leadville's Past," above), and a handful of historic watering holes. My picks are the 1878 **Pastime Bar,** 120 W. 2nd St. (✆ **719/486-9434**), and the 1879 **Silver Dollar Saloon,** 315 Harrison Ave. (✆ **719/486-9914**), one-time haunts of Doc Holliday.

8 ASPEN

172 miles W of Denver, 130 miles E of Grand Junction

Like Vail, Aspen's reputation precedes it. It's more than likely to wind up in the tabloids when two celebrities—who are married to other people—are captured on film sharing a chairlift together; and, yes, plenty of Hollywood stars and wannabe stars hang out here.

However, if you take the time to dig beneath the media hype, you may be surprised by what you find. Aspen, at an elevation of 7,908 feet, is a real town with a fascinating history, some great old buildings, and spectacular mountain scenery. If you're a serious skier, you owe yourself at least a few days' worth of hitting the slopes (as if you need me to tell you that); but if you've never strapped on boards and you're thinking of visiting in summer, you'll be doubly pleased: Prices are significantly lower, and the crowds thin out. Many of the fabulous restaurants are still open, the surrounding forests are teeming with great trails for hiking, biking, and horseback riding, and it becomes one of the best destinations in the country for summer music and dance festivals.

Aspen was "discovered" when silver miners from nearby Leadville wandered a bit farther afield. When the Smuggler Mine produced the world's largest silver nugget (1,840 lb.), prospectors started heading to Aspen in droves. The city soon had 12,000 citizens—but just as quickly the population dwindled to one-tenth that number after the 1893 silver crash.

It took almost 50 years for Aspen to begin its comeback, which came as a result of another natural resource—snow. Shortly before World War II, a small ski area was established on the mountain now known as Ajax. During the war, 10th Mountain Division ski-soldiers training near Leadville spent weekends in Aspen and were enthralled with its possibilities. An infusion of money in 1945 by Chicago industrialist Walter Paepcke, who moved to Aspen with his wife, Elizabeth, resulted in the construction of what was then the world's longest chairlift. The Aspen Skiing Corporation (now Company) was founded the following year, and in 1950 Aspen hosted the alpine world skiing championships. Then came the opening in 1958 of Buttermilk Mountain and Highlands, and in 1967, the birth of Snowmass.

The Paepckes' vision of the resort was not exclusively commercial, however. They saw Aspen as a year-round intellectual and artistic community that would nourish the minds and spirits as well as the bodies of those who visited. Chief among their accomplishments was the establishment of the Aspen Music Festival. A love of ideas and high-minded discourse attracted the likes of Thornton Wilder and Albert Schweitzer to the community, and today a wide variety of intellectual types, artists, and writers (and yes, even those annoying Hollywood people) make this town of almost 6,000 their full- or part-time home.

ESSENTIALS

GETTING THERE **By Car** Aspen is located on Colo. 82, halfway between I-70 at Glenwood Springs (42 miles northwest) and U.S. 24 south of Leadville (44 miles east). In summer, it's a scenic 3½-hour drive from Denver: Leave I-70 West at exit 195 (Copper Mountain); follow Colo. 91 south to Leadville, where you pick up U.S. 24; turn west on Colo. 82 through Twin Lakes and over 12,095-foot Independence Pass. In winter, the Independence Pass road is closed, so you'll have to take I-70 to Glenwood Springs and head east on Colo. 82. In optimal driving conditions, it'll take about 4 hours from Denver by this route.

By Plane Visitors who wish to fly directly into Aspen can arrange to land at **Aspen/Pitkin County Airport,** 5 miles northwest of Aspen on Colo. 82 (✆ **970/920-5384;** www.aspenairport.com). Operating year-round flights are **United Airlines** (✆ 800/864-8331), **Delta** (✆ 800/221-1212), and **Frontier** (✆ 800/432-1359). **US Airways** (✆ 800/943-5436) also operates during ski season.

Another option is the **Eagle County Regional Airport** near Vail (✆ **970/524-9490;** www.eaglecounty.us/airport). See section 6, earlier in this chapter.

By Airport Shuttle **Colorado Mountain Express** (✆ **800/525-6363** or 970/926-9800; www.cmex.com) offers shuttle service from Denver International Airport starting at $104 per person, one-way.

ATTRACTIONS●
Aspen Art Museum **14**
Wheeler/Stallard House
 Museum **1**

ACCOMMODATIONS■
Hearthstone House **3**
Hotel Jerome **13**
Hotel Lenado **5**
Limelight Lodge **6**
The Little Nell **15**
The Mountain Chalet **7**
Sky Hotel **16**
St. Moritz Lodge &
 Condominiums **2**
St. Regis Resort, Aspen **8**

DINING◆
Gusto Ristorante **12**
Jimmy's **9**
Main Street
 Bakery & Cafe **4**
Piñons **11**
Social **10**

THE NORTHERN ROCKIES

11

ASPEN

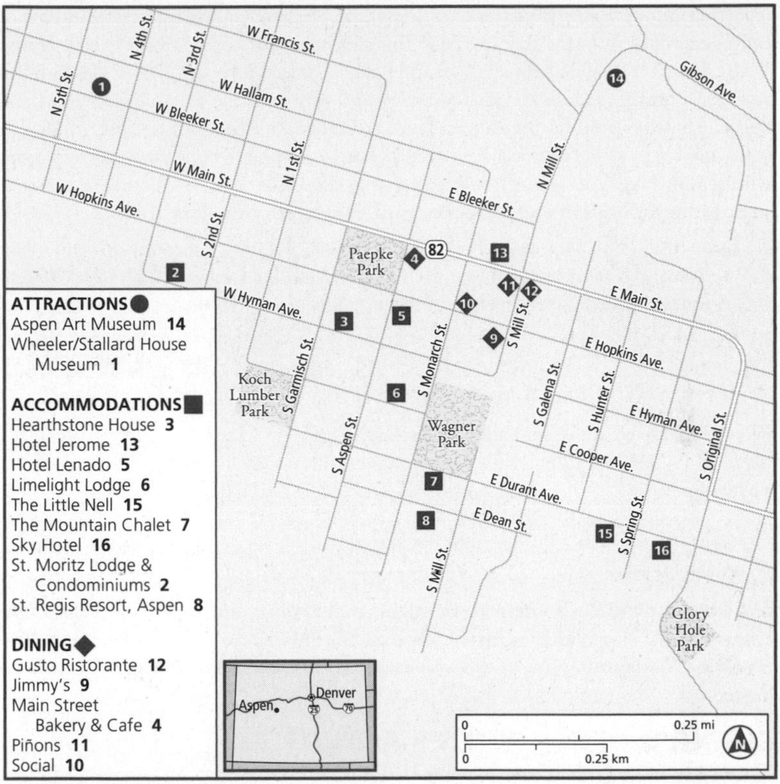

By Train Coming from the San Francisco area or Chicago, **Amtrak** (✆ **800/872-7245;** www.amtrak.com) stops in Glenwood Springs, 42 miles northwest of Aspen.

VISITOR INFORMATION For information, contact the **Aspen Chamber of Commerce and Resort Association,** 425 Rio Grande Place, Aspen, CO 81611 (✆ **800/670-0792** or 970/925-1940; www.aspenchamber.org), which operates a **visitor center** at the same location (Mon–Fri 8:30am–5pm), and another at the Wheeler Opera House, located at Hyman Avenue and Mill Street (usually daily 10am–6pm), as well as smaller locations at the Aspen/Pitkin County Airport and on the Cooper Avenue Mall. You can also get information from the **Snowmass Village Resort Association,** 130 Kearns Rd. (P.O. Box 5010), Snowmass Village, CO 81615 (✆ **800/766-9627;** www.snowmassvillage.com).

GETTING AROUND Entering town from the northwest on Colo. 82, the artery jogs right (south) 2 blocks on Seventh Street, then left (east) at Main Street. East and west street numbers are separated by Garmisch Street, the next cross street after First Street. Mill Street is the town's main north–south street. There are several pedestrian malls downtown, which throw a curve into the downtown traffic flow.

By Shuttle Bus Free bus service is available within the Aspen city limits and between Aspen and Snowmass Village, beyond which you can get connections west as far as Glenwood Springs, at reasonable rates, usually less than $5. Exact fare is required. Information can be obtained from the Roaring Fork Transportation Authority's **Rubey Park Transit Center,** Durant Avenue between Mill and Galena streets, in Aspen (✆ **970/925-8484;** www.rfta.com). Schedules, frequency, and routes vary with the seasons; services include free ski shuttles in winter between all four mountains, shuttles to the Aspen Music Festival, and tours to the Maroon Bells scenic area in summer. Free shuttle transportation within Snowmass Village is offered daily during ski season and on a limited schedule in summer, by the **Snowmass Transportation Department** (www.tosv.com).

By Taxi Call **High Mountain Taxi** (✆ **970/925-8294;** www.hmtaxi.com). For a more distinctive (and bizarre) experience, call Jon Barnes and the **Ultimate Taxi** (✆ **970/927-9239;** www.ultimatetaxi.com; also see "Riding in Style: The Ultimate Taxi," below).

By Rental Car Car-rental agencies at Aspen/Pitkin County Airport include **Alamo** (✆ 970/920-2603), **Avis** (✆ 970/920-2355), **Budget** (✆ 970/925-4693), **Dollar** (✆ 970/920-9008), **Enterprise** (✆ 970/544-3678), and **Hertz** (✆ 970/925-7368).

FAST FACTS The **Aspen Valley Hospital,** 401 Castle Creek Rd., near Aspen Highlands (✆ **970/925-1120;** www.aspenhospital.org), has a 24-hour emergency room. The **post office** is at 235 Puppy Smith St., off Mill Street north of Main; there's another in Snowmass and another in Woody Creek Center. For hours and other information, contact the U.S. Postal Service (✆ **800/275-8777;** www.usps.com). For **road reports,** call ✆ **970/920-5454.**

SPECIAL EVENTS Winterskől Carnival, mid-January, in Aspen and Snowmass; Aspen Gay Ski Week, mid-January; Snowmass Mardi Gras, early February; *Food & Wine* Magazine Classic, mid-June, in Aspen; Aspen Arts Festival, mid-July; Aspen Filmfest, late September.

SKIING & OTHER WINTER ACTIVITIES

Skiing Aspen ★★ really means skiing the four Aspen-area resorts—Aspen Mountain, Aspen Highlands, Buttermilk, and Snowmass. All are managed by Aspen Skiing Company, and one ticket gives access to all. Daily lift ticket prices (2007–08 prices) during peak season run $87 for adults 18 to 64, $78 for youths 13 to 17 and seniors 65 and older, and $55 for children 7 to 12. Children 6 and under ski free. You can get substantial savings by buying tickets by phone or online a week or more in advance, or buying for 3 days or more. For more information, contact **Aspen Skiing Company,** P.O. Box 1248, Aspen, CO 81612 (✆ **800/308-6935** or 970/925-1220; www.aspensnowmass.com). Call ✆ **888/277-3676** or 970/925-1221 for snow reports.

ASPEN MOUNTAIN Named for an old miner's claim, Aspen Mountain is not for the timid. This is the American West's original hard-core ski mountain, with no fewer than 23 of its runs named double diamond—for experts only. One-third of the mountain's runs are left forever ungroomed—sheer ecstasy for bump runners. There are mountain-long runs for intermediates as well as advanced skiers, but beginners should look to one of the other Aspen/Snowmass mountains.

From the **Sundeck** restaurant at the mountain's 11,212-foot summit, numerous intermediate runs extend on either side of Bell Mountain—through Copper Bowl and down Spar Gulch. To the east of the gulch, the knob of Bell offers a mecca for mogul mashers,

Moments Riding in Style: The Ultimate Taxi

Known in the Aspen Valley as the **Ultimate Taxi ★**, Jon Barnes's yellow cab is one of the most unusual vehicles on the planet: There's a rainbow of luminescent fiber optics on the ceiling, laser projectors, a webcam, a recording studio complete with keyboards and drum machines, a mirror ball, a roller-coaster simulator, and much, much more. Barnes has worked as a cabbie in Aspen since 1984, but started modifying his taxi in the early '90s. Today it's a blast for kids and partiers alike, with rides running $150 per group for a ride lasting about 40 minutes. Barnes even takes your picture and posts it on his website (www.ultimatetaxi.com) for posterity—check mine out from June 2006. Call Jon for reservations or a ride at ✆ **970/927-9239.**

with bump runs down its ridge and its east and west faces. To the west of the gulch, the face of Ruthie's is wonderful for intermediate cruisers, while more mogul runs drop off International. Ruthie's Run extends for over 2 miles down the west ridge of the mountain, with an extension via Magnifico Cut Off and Little Nell to the base, and is accessed by the unique Ruthie's high-speed double chair.

Aspen Mountain has a 3,267-foot vertical drop, with 76 trails on 673 skiable acres. The resort rates its trails as follows: none easiest, 48% more difficult, 26% most difficult, and 26% expert. There are eight lifts—a high-speed gondola, one high-speed quad chair, two quads, one high-speed double, and three double chairs. Average annual snowfall at the 11,212-foot summit is 300 inches (25 ft.). Aspen Mountain is usually open from late November to mid-April from 9am to 3:30pm. There are four restaurants.

ASPEN HIGHLANDS A favorite of locals for its expert and adventure terrain—Highland Bowl—Aspen Highlands also has a good mix of terrain, from novice to expert, with lots of intermediate slopes. It also offers absolutely splendid views of the famed Maroon Bells (see the box "Natural Attractions," below).

It takes two lifts to reach the 11,675-foot Loge Peak summit, where most of the advanced expert runs are found in the Steeplechase area and 199 acres of glades in the Olympic Bowl. Kandahar, Golden Horn, and Thunderbowl give the intermediate skier a long run from top to bottom, and novices are best served midmountain on trails like Red Onion and Apple Strudel. There are also some fantastic opportunities for experts at Highland Bowl, which is a short walk from the top of the Loge Peak lift.

Freestyle Friday, a tradition at Highlands for almost 3 decades, boasts some of the best freestyle-bump and big-air competitors in Colorado every Friday from early January to mid-April. In this technical head-to-head contest, competitors bump their way down Scarlett's Run and finish with a final jump that lands them within perfect view of lunchtime guests at the Merry-Go-Round Restaurant.

There are 118 trails on 1,028 acres, served by five lifts (three high-speed quads and two triple chairs). Trails are rated 18% easiest, 30% more difficult, 16% most difficult, and 36% expert.

There are six restaurants, including three on the mountain. Highlands is usually open from mid-December to early April, with lifts operating from 9am to 3:30pm.

BUTTERMILK MOUNTAIN Buttermilk is a premier beginners' mountain, one of the best places in America to learn how to ski. And it's also the home of the ESPN Winter X Games.

The smallest of Aspen's four mountains, it has 44 trails, which the resort rates at 35% easiest, 39% more difficult, 26% most difficult, and none expert, plus a great terrain park. There are nine lifts (two high-speed quads, three double chairs, two handle tows, and two school lifts) on 470 acres, with a 2,030-foot vertical drop. Average annual snowfall at the 9,900-foot summit is 200 inches (16 ft., 8 in.). There's a restaurant on top and a cafe at the base. Buttermilk is usually open from mid-December to early April, its lifts running from 9am to 3:30pm.

SNOWMASS A huge, mostly intermediate mountain with something for everyone, Snowmass has 33% more skiable acreage than the other three Aspen areas combined! Actually four distinct self-contained areas, each with its own lift system, its terrain varies from easy beginner runs to the pitches of the Cirque and the Hanging Valley Wall, the steepest in the Aspen area.

Big Burn, site of a 19th-century forest fire, boasts wide-open advanced and intermediate slopes and the expert drops of the Cirque. Atop the intermediate Alpine Springs trails is the advanced High Alpine Lift, from which experts can traverse to the formidable Hanging Valley Wall. Elk Camp is ideal for early intermediates who prefer long cruising runs. Sam's Knob has advanced upper trails diving through trees, and a variety of intermediate and novice runs around its northeast face and base. All areas meet in the scattered condominium developments that surround Snowmass Village Mall. All told, there are 3,132 skiable acres at Snowmass, with a 4,406-foot vertical drop from the 12,510-foot summit. The mountain has 91 trails, rated 6% easiest, 50% more difficult, 12% most difficult, and 32% expert. The longest trail is over 5 miles long. There are 21 lifts (one high-speed eight-passenger gondola, one high-speed six passenger, one six-passenger gondola, seven high-speed quad chairs, two quads, three double chairs, two platter pulls, and four ski/snowboard school lifts). Average annual snowfall at the summit is 300 inches (25 ft.).

The renowned Snowmass ski school has hundreds of instructors, as well as programs for children 18 months and older. The area also has three terrain parks, a superpipe, and a rail yard. There are 12 restaurants.

Snowmass is usually open from late November to mid-April from 8am to 3:30pm.

CROSS-COUNTRY SKIING The Aspen/Snowmass Nordic Council operates a free Nordic trail system with about 40 miles of groomed double track extending throughout the Aspen–Snowmass area, and incorporating summer bicycle paths. Instruction and rentals are offered along the trail at the **Aspen Cross-Country Center,** Colo. 82 between Aspen and Buttermilk (✆ **970/925-2145;** www.utemountaineer.com), and the **Snowmass Cross Country Center,** Snowmass Village (✆ **970/923-5700**), both of which provide daily condition reports and information regarding the entire trail system.

Independent backcountry skiers should consult **White River National Forest,** 806 W. Hallam St. (✆ **970/925-3445;** www.fs.fed.us/r2), and two hut systems provide shelter on multiday trips (see "Hiking & Mountaineering," below).

DOG SLEDDING For rides in winter or a kennel tour in summer, call **Krabloonik,** 4250 Divide Rd., Snowmass Village (✆ **970/923-4342;** www.krabloonik.com). Every day in winter, teams of Alaskan sled dogs pull guests into the Snowmass–Maroon Bells Wilderness Area. Half-day trips, at 8:30am and 12:30pm, include lunch at **Krabloonik**

Moments **Natural Attractions**

The two sheer, pyramidal peaks called **Maroon Bells,** on Maroon Creek Road 10 miles west of Aspen, are probably two of the most photographed mountains in the Rockies. During summer and into early fall, you can take a 20- to 30-minute narrated bus tour from Aspen Highlands up the Maroon Creek Valley (✆ **970/925-8484;** www.rfta.com/maroon). Cost for the bus trip is $6 adults, $3 for youths 6 to 16, $4 for seniors, and it's free for children under 6.

restaurant (see "Where to Dine," later in this chapter) and cost $265 per adult and $165 for children 3 to 8 years of age. Children under 3 are not permitted. There are also twilight rides that include dinner at 3:45pm for $340 adults, $270 kids. Kennel tours rare available in summer; contact Krabloonik for more information or an appointment.

WARM-WEATHER & YEAR-ROUND ACTIVITIES

Your best source for information on a wide variety of outdoor activities in the mountains around Aspen, including hiking, mountain biking, horseback riding, four-wheeling, fishing, and camping, is the **White River National Forest** (see "Cross-Country Skiing," above).

There's no lack of guides, outfitters, and sporting-goods shops in Aspen. Among the best one-stop outfitters is **Blazing Adventures** (✆ **800/282-7238** or 970/923-4544; www.blazingadventures.com), which offers rafting, mountain-biking, hiking, four-wheeling, hot-air ballooning, and horseback-riding excursions.

BICYCLING There are two bike paths of note. One connects Aspen with Snowmass Village; it covers 13 miles and begins at Seventh Street south of Hopkins Avenue, cuts through the forest to Colo. 82, then follows Owl Creek Road and Brush Creek Road to the Snowmass Mall. Extensions link it with Aspen High School and the Aspen Business Park. The Rio Grande Trail follows the Roaring Fork River from near the Aspen Post Office, on Puppy Smith Street, 2 miles west to Cemetery Lane. **Durrance Sports,** 414 E. Cooper Ave (✆ **970/429-0101;** www.durrancesports.com), rents comfort bikes, kids' bikes, and cruisers ($30 a day), as well as mountain bikes. See also "Mountain Biking," below.

FISHING Perhaps the best of a great deal of good trout fishing in the Aspen area is to be found in the Roaring Fork and Frying Pan rivers, both considered gold-medal streams. The Roaring Fork follows Colo. 82 through Aspen from Independence Pass; the Frying Pan starts near Tennessee Pass, northeast of Aspen, and joins the Roaring Fork at Basalt, 18 miles down valley.

Stop at **Aspen Fly Fishing** in the Gondola Plaza at 601 E. Dean St. (✆ **970/920-6886;** www.aspenflyfishing.com), for a guided fishing trip; two people wading for a half-day is $350. **Blazing Adventures** (see above) also offers fishing guide service.

GOLF Public 18-hole championship courses in the Aspen valley include **Aspen Golf Course,** 9461 Colo. 82, 1 mile west of Aspen (✆ **970/925-2145;** www.aspenrecreation.com), one of the longer courses in Colorado, at 7,165 yards, charging $53 to $105 for 18 holes plus $20 per person for the cart; and the **Snowmass Club,** 239 Snowmass Club Circle (✆ **970/923-5700;** www.snowmassclub.com), charging about $220 for 18 holes, including a cart and range balls. Carts are reserved for members until 1pm.

HIKING & MOUNTAINEERING Among the best ways to see the spectacular scenery here is on foot. You can get maps and tips on where to go from **White River National Forest** offices (see above). One popular trail is the route past the Maroon Bells to Crested Butte; the trek would take 175 miles by mountain road, but it's only about 30 miles by foot—14 miles from the end of Aspen's Maroon Creek Road.

Hikers can also make use of two hut systems for multiday trips—the 12-hut **10th Mountain Trail Association**'s system toward Vail, and the six-hut **Alfred A. Braun and Friends Hut System** (© **970/925-5775** for both; www.huts.org) toward Crested Butte. Huts are basic, with bunk beds, but do have wood-burning stoves, propane burners, photovoltaic lighting, kitchen equipment, mattresses, and pillows. A bed in one of the huts costs $28 per night. Offices are at 1280 Ute Ave., Ste. 21, in Aspen.

Those who would like a guide for their hiking or mountaineering excursion should contact **Aspen Expeditions,** 414 E. Cooper Ave. (© **970/925-7625;** www.aspenexpeditions.com), which offers guided trips up fourteeners and other mountains (about $300–$500 per person, depending on the size of the group), as well as less strenuous days of high-alpine trekking (about $100 per person). Aspen Expeditions also offers guided rock-climbing trips.

HORSEBACK RIDING Several stables in the Aspen valley offer a variety of rides, and some outfitters even package gourmet meals and country-and-western serenades with their expeditions. A wide variety of adventures are offered; rates for day trips usually run about $70 to $100 per person for a 2-hour ride or $150 to $200 for a half-day. Inquire at **Aspen Wilderness Outfitters** (© **970/963-0211;** www.aspenwilderness.com), **Capitol Peak Outfitters** (© **970/928-0723;** www.capitolpeak.com), or **OutWest Guides** (© **970/963-5525;** www.outwestguides.net).

MOUNTAIN BIKING There are hundreds of miles of trails through the White River National Forest that are perfect for mountain bikers, offering splendid views of the mountains, meadows, and valleys. Check with the Forest Service and local bike shops for tips on the best trails. Among full-service bike shops offering rentals are **Aspen Velo Bike Shop,** 465 N. Mill St. (© **970/925-1495;** www.aspenvelo.com), and **Durrance Sports,** 414 E. Cooper Ave (© **970/429-0101;** www.durrancesports.com). A full-day rental is typically $40 to $60.

RIVER RAFTING Rafting trips are offered on the Roaring Fork, Arkansas, and Colorado rivers with several companies, including **Colorado Riff Raft** (© **800/282-7238** or 970/923-4544; www.riffraft.com), **Up Tha Creek Expeditions** (© **877/982-7335** or 970/947-0030; www.upthacreek.com), and **Blazing Adventures** (see above). Rates are usually about $65 to $95 for a half-day.

MUSEUMS, ART CENTERS & HISTORIC SITES

The **Aspen Historical Society,** 620 W. Bleeker St. (© **970/925-3721;** www.aspenhistory.org), offers a variety of guided tours of Aspen and the surrounding mining camps during the summer. One 2-hour walking tour of Aspen covers about 1 mile and begins on the grounds of the Wheeler/Stallard House Museum (see below), explores the West End residential area, and ends in the lobby of the historic Hotel Jerome (see "Where to Stay," below). The cost is $12 per adult. **The History Coach** is a motorized electric vehicle that takes six guests at a time on 2-hour tours of town. Tours are offered Tuesday through Saturday for $25 per adult, $20 seniors, and free for kids under 12. Additionally, guided tours of Ashcroft and Independence **ghost towns** are available daily in summer for $3 adults. Call for reservations and specific times. Self-guided tour brochures are also available.

Aspen Music

Nestled in the picturesque Roaring Fork Valley is one of the top ski resorts in Colorado, and in summer, when the snows have (mostly) melted, the schussing of skis is replaced with the glorious sound of music.

The **Aspen Music Festival and School** originated in 1949 and is now considered one of America's top summer music programs. Lasting 9 weeks from mid-June to late August, it offers more than 350 events, including symphonic and chamber music, opera, choral, and children's programs. Most concerts take place in the state-of-the-art, 2,050-seat Benedict Music Tent and 500-seat Joan and Irving Harris Concert Hall, both at Third and Gillespie streets. The acoustics in the tent are very good, but in Harris Hall they're amazing.

During the season, ensembles-in-residence—the American and Emerson string quartets and the American Brass Quintet—give recitals; the Aspen Chamber Symphony and Aspen Festival Orchestra perform; and varied chamber groups are created from among the roster of professional musicians that make up the school's faculty. Plus, there are numerous open rehearsals and other programs offered. Events scheduled for 2008 included works by Brahms, Mozart, Beethoven, Sibelius, Tchaikovsky, and Christopher Rouse, to name a few.

On top of Aspen Mountain—you'll have to buy a ticket and ride the gondola—student groups perform free 1-hour concerts each Saturday at 1pm. This **Music on the Mountain** soars into the backdrop of the Elk Mountain range. The **family events** include several programs geared to youngsters under 10, such as storytelling and music at the Pitkin County Library (free; various times), plus the annual family picnic and concert of short, fun classical pieces. Certain **dress rehearsals** of the Aspen Chamber Symphony and Aspen Festival Orchestra are open to the public, giving visitors an inside look at how a concert is put together. And if you're a visiting musician, check out the master classes while you're in town.

Open rehearsals and master classes typically cost under $20, and most concert tickets run $20 to $70. Free programs include most of the family events, plus the popular Saturday Music on the Mountain concerts atop Aspen Mountain. **Free tours** of the tent and concert hall, a historic walking tour from the Hotel Jerome to the tent, and a tour of the music school campus are available. Parking is limited, but there is free bus service from many points in town, Snowmass Village, and down-valley (✆ **970/925-8484** for schedule information).

For additional information, contact **Aspen Music Festival and School,** 2 Music School Rd., Aspen, CO 81611 (✆ **970/925-9042** for the box office and 970/925-3254 for the office; www.aspenmusicfestival.com).

Aspen Art Museum ★★ This attractive museum presents rotating exhibits highlighting the work of nationally known contemporary artists, and hosts a biannual exhibit showcasing talent with local ties. Lectures and art education programs for adults and children are offered year-round, and there's a free wine-and-cheese reception the first Thursday of every month from 5 to 7pm. Allow 30 minutes.

 590 N. Mill St., Aspen. ✆ **970/925-8050.** www.aspenartmuseum.org. Free admission. Tues–Sat 10am–6pm (until 7pm Thurs); Sun noon–6pm.

Wheeler/Stallard House Museum Silver baron Jerome B. Wheeler had this three-story Queen Anne–style brick home built in 1888, and its steeply pitched roofs, dormers, and gables have made it a landmark in Aspen's West End neighborhood. A museum since 1969, the exterior of this handsome house has been restored to its appearance in the heady days of silver mining. Exhibits describe Aspen's history from Ute culture through the mining rush, and from railroads and ranching to the founding of the skiing industry. Allow an hour. Admission includes access to the **Holden/Marolt Mining and Ranching Museum,** 40180 Colo. 82, located on a former silver mill site that became a ranch in 1940.

620 W. Bleeker St., Aspen. ✆ **970/925-3721.** www.aspenhistory.org. Admission $6 adults, $5 seniors, free for children 11 and under. Tues–Sat 1–5pm.

SHOPPING

To truly appreciate the Aspen experience, one must shop Aspen. Note that I say "shop" (meaning browse) rather than buy, because if you're not careful, you just might blow next month's mortgage payment on some Western fashion accessory. No one ever brags about the great bargain they snagged last season in Aspen.

On the other hand, quality is usually tops, shop clerks are friendly, and your neighbor probably doesn't already have one. Having said all that, I suggest you lock up your credit cards, put on some good walking shoes, and spend a few hours exploring the galleries and shops of Aspen. The following are a few of my favorites, and several are grouped together in a minimall at 525 E. Cooper Ave. For **original art,** check out **Aspen Grove Fine Arts,** 525 E. Cooper Ave., upper level (✆ **970/925-5151;** www.aspengrovefineart.com), featuring paintings, graphics, and sculpture. When it's time to pick up a gift, **Chepita,** 525 E. Cooper Ave. (✆ **970/925-2871;** www.chepita.com), is an attractive store with jewelry, sculpture, and home accessories; and **Curious George Collectibles,** 426 E. Hyman Ave. (✆ **970/925-3315**), has silver buckles, belts, and Western artifacts that (allegedly) used to belong to notorious cowboys. For **clothing,** try **Kemo Sabe,** 434 E. Cooper Ave. (✆ **970/925-7878;** www.kemosabe.com), for wonderful hats and other Western wear; and **Gorsuch, Ltd.,** 611 E. Durant Ave. (✆ **800/525-9808** or 970/920-9388; www.gorsuchltd.com), for outdoor clothing.

WHERE TO STAY

Occupancy rates run 90% or higher during peak winter and summer seasons, so it's essential to make reservations as early as possible (or avoid peak seasons, as I try to do). The easiest way to book your lodgings is to call **Stay Aspen Snowmass** central reservations (✆ **888/649-5982;** www.stayaspensnowmass.com). You can also find lodging through **Aspen Resort Accommodations** (✆ **800/727-7369;** www.aspenreservations.net).

Many accommodations close during the spring and fall; if they're open, rates during those months are typically the lowest of any time during the year. Unless otherwise noted, parking is free. A tax of 9.6% is added to hotel bills.

Very Expensive

Hotel Jerome ★★ The historic ambience and superb service at the Hotel Jerome make it one of the best places to stay in Aspen—for those who can afford it. Jerome B.

Wheeler built the Jerome during the peak of the silver boom. It opened in 1889 as Colorado's first hotel with electricity and indoor plumbing, and the first west of the Mississippi River with an elevator. The silver crash of 1893 ended Aspen's prosperity and the glory years of the Hotel Jerome, but today its original splendor has been restored—and then some. Lovingly preserved and furnished with period antiques, the Jerome is now on the National Register of Historic Places. Each beautifully appointed guest room is spacious—even the smallest is more than 500 square feet—and unique, containing luxurious furnishings, desks, comfortable chairs, queen or king beds with down comforters, and plush robes. Bathrooms, finished with white marble and reproduction octagonal tiles, boast oversize tubs and separate showers. Resort fees of $15 to $30 cover parking, Internet, and other niceties.

330 E. Main St., Aspen, CO 81611. ✆ **800/331-7213** or 970/920-1000. Fax 970/925-2784. www.hoteljerome.com. 91 units. Summer and ski season $495–$675 double, $700–$1,700 suite; spring and fall $175–$420 double, $275–$520 suite. Higher holiday rates. AE, MC, V. Pets permitted ($75 fee). **Amenities:** 2 restaurants (American); 2 bars; heated outdoor pool; exercise room; 2 whirlpools; concierge; ski concierge; courtesy shuttle; secretarial services; 24-hr. room service; valet laundry. *In room:* A/C, TV/VCR or TV/DVD, wireless Internet access (included w/resort fee), minibar, hair dryer, iron, safe.

The Little Nell ★★★ Located just 17 paces (yes, it's been measured) from the base terminal of the Silver Queen Gondola, the ski-in, ski-out Little Nell boasts the virtues of an intimate country inn as well as the personalized service and amenities of a grand hotel. No two guest rooms are alike, but each has a gas fireplace, Belgian-wool carpeting, down-filled lounge chairs or sofa, oversized bed with down comforter, and marble-finished bathroom with two vanities, separate shower and tub, and high-end toiletries. Some suites have separate Jacuzzi tubs and steam showers. All rooms have a view of either the town or the mountain. The hotel's signature (and dog-friendly!) **Montagna** restaurant serves "farmhouse cooking" by acclaimed chef Ryan Hardy in an artsy atmosphere with large windows looking toward the hotel courtyard and Aspen Mountain. Both the famed living room and the bar were designed by David Easton, an interior designer of renown. The adjoining bar offers a more relaxed atmosphere.

675 E. Durant Ave., Aspen, CO 81611. ✆ **888/843-6355** or 970/920-4600. Fax 970/920-4670. www.thelittlenell.com. 92 units, plus 80 condominiums and suites. Ski season and summer $510–$995 double, $1,330–$5,775 condo or suite; spring and fall $330–$415 double, $730–$2,400 condo or suite. Call for holiday rates. AE, DISC, MC, V. Valet parking $21 per day. Pets accepted. **Amenities:** Restaurant (American regional); 2 bars; heated pool; health club and spa; outdoor whirlpool; concierge; shopping arcade; 24-hr. room service; massage; same-day valet laundry; courtesy shuttle. *In room:* A/C, TV/DVD player (video rental available), wireless Internet access (fee), minibar, coffeemaker, hair dryer, iron.

Sky Hotel ★★ One of the hippest hotels in Colorado, the Sky Hotel melds kitsch and class into one satisfying colorful whole. Located slopeside just steps from the Silver Queen Gondola in downtown Aspen, Kimpton Hotels renovated the old Aspen Club Lodge beyond recognition in 2002. The rooms are a study in color and animal prints, with perks like cordless phones, iPod docking stations, and humidifiers. The only complaint is that the rooms are pretty small—look elsewhere if you need space to spread out. The year-round pool features an outdoor bar, a waterfall, and a pair of fire pits. Walk inside to the ultrahip bar, **39 degrees,** with vibrant striped sofas and log walls, great burgers, and specialty cocktails like the Botox Martini. The fun and funky lobby features a 15-foot chandelier shaped like a bright red lampshade, stately wood columns, high-backed white chairs, and an assortment of proudly displayed board games like Sorry! and Yahtzee.

709 E. Durant Ave., Aspen, CO 81611. ✆ **800/882-2582** or 970/925-6760. Fax 970/925-6778. www.theskyhotel.com. 90 units, including 6 suites. Summer $179–$499 double, $299–$649 suite; winter $209–$629 double, $329–$779 suite. Lower rates spring and fall. Valet parking $25; self-parking $15. Pets accepted. AE, DISC, MC, V. **Amenities:** Restaurant/lounge; outdoor heated pool; exercise room; outdoor whirlpool; limited watersports rentals; courtesy car; business center; in-room massage; dry cleaning. *In room:* A/C, cable TV w/pay movies, wireless Internet access (free), minibar, coffeemaker, hair dryer, iron.

St. Regis Resort, Aspen ★★★ Located at the base of Aspen Mountain, between the gondola and Lift 1A, the St. Regis offers luxurious comfort in a casual but definitely upscale Western atmosphere. Decorated with rich wood, muted earth tones, and original paintings by 19th- and 20th-century artists, the lobby offers cozy seating, a large river-rock fireplace, and magnificent views of Aspen Mountain. Most rooms have views of either the mountains or town, and a few on the ground floor offer views of the flower-filled courtyard. Each unit features "contemporary alpine" decor, with overstuffed leather chairs, leather tabletops, and handsome marble bathrooms; all sport such amenities as bathrobes, Bose CD players, 30-inch flatscreen TVs, and portable phones. The Alpine Floor offers key-access service, a dedicated concierge, and five complimentary food and beverage servings throughout the day. The St. Regis recently added new units and constructed a large spa. In winter, a ski concierge coordinates ski rentals, lift tickets, and lessons.

315 E. Dean St., Aspen, CO 81611. ✆ **888/454-9005** or 970/920-3300. Fax 970/925-8998. www.stregisaspen.com. 179 units. Ski season $900–$1,500 double, $1,600–$2,000 suite; summer $500–$1,000 double, $1,600–$2,000 suite. Higher holiday rates; lower rates spring and fall. AE, DISC, MC, V. 24-hr. valet parking $26. **Amenities:** Restaurant (Mediterranean); bar; outdoor heated pool; fitness center and spa; 2 whirlpools (1 indoor, 1 outdoor); sauna; steam room; concierge; courtesy airport transportation; business center; 24-hr. room service, concierge-level rooms. *In room:* A/C, cable TV/DVD player, fax (in suites only), wireless Internet access (fee), minibar, hair dryer, iron, safe.

Expensive & Moderate

Hearthstone House ★ Value Small and sophisticated, the Hearthstone House is located just 2 blocks west of the Wheeler Opera House. Guests share a large, elegant living room with teak-and-leather furnishings and a wood-burning fireplace, a dining room with bright flowers, and an extensive library. Rooms are bright and homey, with queen-size or twin beds, and two rooms have a king-size bed. Four units feature whirlpool tubs. Smoking is not permitted.

134 E. Hyman Ave. (at Aspen St.), Aspen, CO 81611. ✆ **888/925-7632** or 970/925-7632. Fax 970/920-4450. www.hearthstonehouse.com. 16 units. Summer $229–$279 double; ski season $199–$399 double. Higher holiday rates; lower rates spring and fall. Rates include breakfast plus afternoon wine and cheese. AE, DC, DISC, MC, V. **Amenities:** Access to Aspen Club & Spa; outdoor Jacuzzi; bikes available (free); herbal steam room. *In room:* TV/VCR, wireless Internet access (free), fridge, coffeemaker.

Hotel Lenado ★ This small hotel—best described as a contemporary mountain lodge—feels right at home in this old mining town, with natural wood beams, wood floors, handsome wood furniture, and a comfortable but upscale feel. The Western-style rooms have a rustic appearance, with four-poster hickory or apple-wood beds, down comforters and pillows, excellent sound systems, shared balconies, and twice-daily maid service. Some units have wet bars, refrigerators, and wood-burning stoves. There's a red-rock-and-concrete fireplace in the lobby that stands 28 feet tall, a hot tub on a second-floor deck that offers a spectacular view of Aspen Mountain, ski storage, and a heated locker for ski boots. An excellent gourmet breakfast is served daily.

200 S. Aspen St., Aspen, CO 81611. ✆ **800/321-3457** or 970/925-6246. Fax 970/925-3840. www.hotel lenado.com. 19 units. Ski season and summer $285–$499; spring and fall $125–$150. Rates include full breakfast. AE, DC, MC, V. **Amenities:** Bar; hot tub; concierge; limited room service; in-room massage; valet laundry service. *In room:* A/C, TV/VCR or TV/DVD player, wireless Internet access (free), hair dryer.

Limelight Lodge ★★ Value I was distraught when I heard the old Limelight was falling to the bulldozer in 2006, but a new one went up in the same quiet spot near downtown Aspen. Reopened in 2008, the property traded its mom-and-pop looks for a slick classic-meets-contemporary facade, sheathing larger rooms spread over four stories. Dale Paas, whose family has owned the motel since 1958, has committed to sustainable design, and the new Limelight is a model of green architecture and design.

228 E. Cooper Ave. (at Monarch St.), Aspen, CO 81611. ✆ **800/433-0832** or 970/925-3025. Fax 970/925-5120. www.limelightlodge.com. 126 units. $200–$350 double; $300–$450 suite. Rates include continental breakfast and après-ski drinks and cake. AE, DISC, MC, V. Pets accepted. **Amenities:** Outdoor pool; 2 outdoor hot tubs; coin-op laundry. *In room:* A/C, cable TV, wireless Internet access (free), fridge, hair dryer, iron.

Inexpensive

In addition to the property discussed below, those on a budget might want to consider the **St. Moritz Lodge & Condominiums,** 334 W. Hyman Ave., Aspen, CO 81611 (✆ **800/817-2069** or 970/925-3220; www.stmoritzlodge.com), which is one of the best deals in Aspen; small double rooms with shared bathrooms start at $72 in spring and fall, $123 in summer, and $96 in ski season. There are also hostel beds ($36–$63 per person), plus pricier rooms with private bathrooms, units with kitchenettes, and one- and two-bedroom condominium units.

The Mountain Chalet You'll find a friendly ski-lodge atmosphere at this family-owned lodging, open since 1954 just 1½ blocks from the lifts. There's a TV in the lobby (where complimentary wine and hors d'oeuvres are served on Monday nights in winter) and a piano and game room on the lower level. Rooms are bright and well maintained, with wood furnishings and good-quality twin, double, queen, or king beds, plus a few trundle beds. There are even some bunk rooms with four beds, rented by the bed at greatly reduced rates in ski season. Most rooms have refrigerators; some have central air-conditioning. Ski lockers are available and there are guest computers in the lobby.

333 E. Durant Ave., Aspen, CO 81611. ✆ **888/503-9355** or 970/925-7797. Fax 970/925-7811. www.mountainchaletaspen.com. 59 units. Winter $105–$450 double, $565 apt., rates higher during holidays; summer $75–$265 double, $380 apt.; spring and fall $65–$150 double, $180 apt. Children 3 and under stay free. Rates include full breakfast in winter, continental breakfast in summer. DC, DISC, MC, V. Underground parking. **Amenities:** Outdoor heated pool; exercise room; large indoor whirlpool; sauna and steam room; game room; massage; coin-op laundry. *In room:* Cable TV, fridge, hair dryer.

WHERE TO DINE

Most restaurants in the Aspen–Snowmass area are open during the ski season (Thanksgiving to early Apr) and summer (mid-June to mid-Sept) seasons. Between seasons, however, some close their doors or limit hours. Call ahead if you're visiting at those times.

Expensive

Krabloonik ★★ Moments INTERNATIONAL There's something very wild, something that hearkens back to Jack London, perhaps, about sitting in a log cabin watching teams of sled dogs come and go as you bite into a tender caribou loin or wild-boar chop. That's part of the pleasure of Krabloonik. A venture of one of the largest sled-dog kennels in America's lower 48 states, this rustic restaurant has huge picture windows with mountain views and seating around a sunken fireplace. Skiers drop into the restaurant from the Campground Lift for lunch, and visitors can dine before or after an excursion on a dog sled (see "Dog Sledding," earlier in this section). For dinner there's Krabloonik smoked trout with creamy horseradish for starters and a wide variety of game, beef, and fish for the main course. Those with hearty appetites can choose a combination game plate with venison, caribou, and lamb. A fresh vegetable sampler is also available daily.

4250 Divide Rd., off Brush Creek Rd., Snowmass Village. ✆ **970/923-3953.** www.krabloonik.com. Reservations recommended at lunch, essential at dinner. Lunch main courses $14–$20; dinner main courses $22–$70. AE, DISC, MC, V. Winter Mon–Fri 11am–2pm and daily 5:30–9:30pm (Sat–Sun also 11am–2pm during Christmas holidays); summer Fri–Sat 6–9pm. Closed spring and fall.

Piñons ★★★ CONTEMPORARY REGIONAL The apex of the Aspen dining scene, Piñons has been one of Colorado's best restaurants since it opened its doors in 1988. The room, with chairs backed with thatched wood and contemporary touches, is casually elegant, with picture windows providing the ideal lens to gaze at Aspen Mountain over a truly splendid splurge of a meal. With starters as delectable as this—lobster strudel, anyone?—it's hard to make it to the entrees, but they are works of inventive culinary art, letting the fresh flavors shine in simple but timeless preparations. The menu changes several times a year, but you can't miss with herb-crusted ruby trout with spinach, crab, pancetta, and sweet corn purée; or pistachio-crusted rack of lamb with potato-rutabaga hash. A more casual option is a two-course prix-fixe dinner, available at the happening bar only, for $35 per person. The desserts include an unforgettable chocolate bread pudding and homemade ice cream.

105 S. Mill St. ✆ **970/920-2021.** www.pinons.net. Reservations recommended. Main courses $26–$46. AE, DISC, MC, V. Daily 5:30–10pm. Closed Apr to early June and Oct–Nov.

Moderate & Inexpensive

For breakfast and lunch, the homey **Main Street Bakery and Cafe,** 201 E. Main St. (✆ **970/925-6446**), is a local favorite, serving a menu of quiches, omelets, sandwiches, and salads from 7am to 4pm. The pumpkin muffins are absolutely scrumptious.

Gusto Ristorante ★ ITALIAN Locals love this place, and I do, too. Open year-round, the spare, sleek eatery is lively and social, delivering great Italian specialties and assured service from an international staff. The kitchen plates up such knockout dishes as *linguine con scampi, penne con prosciutto,* and *gnocchi masseria* (potato dumplings with sausage, mushrooms, and tomatoes in red wine sauce). There are also gourmet pizzas (lunch only), steaks and seafood dishes, and a nice list of mostly Italian wines.

415 E. Main St. ✆ **970/925-8222.** www.gustoristorante.com. Reservations accepted. Main courses $9–$19 lunch ($15 for a 2-course "Power Lunch"), $17–$38 dinner. AE, DISC, MC, V. Mon–Fri 11:30am–2:30pm; daily 5:30–10:30pm. Bar open later.

Jimmy's ★ SOUTHWESTERN Another local favorite, Jimmy's (subtitled "An American Restaurant & Bar") is known for its steaks and seafood, but loved for its luscious meatloaf. Proprietor Jimmy Yeager says it's "fierce American food," busting with flavor and prepared without fear. Other signature dishes include the crab cakes, Colorado rack of lamb, and the addictive homemade chocolate chip cookies. The BBQ sauce and salsas are also worth a taste. Jimmy's also prides itself upon its selection of tequilas and mezcal: At 145 labels, it's one of the nation's best.

205 S. Mill St. ✆ **970/925-6048.** www.social-aspen.com. Reservations accepted. Main courses $12–$45. MC, V. Daily 5:30–11:30pm. Bar open later.

Social ★ TAPAS/SMALL PLATES A colorful, modern atmosphere nicely complements the savory fare at this new restaurant by the same owners of the attached **Elevation.** The room features multihued chairs, and chic-meets-kitsch design, and the decidedly eclectic tapas menu spans the globe with such enticing dishes as wok-charred edamame, hummus, gnocchi, buffalo slides, and crispy snapper tacos. When the weather is nice, seating is available on a terrific patio.

304 E. Hopkins Ave. ✆ **970/925-9700.** www.jimmysaspen.com. Reservations accepted. Tapas and small plates $5–$15. AE, DISC, MC, V. Daily 5:30–10pm. Bar open later.

Woody Creek Tavern ★★ Finds AMERICAN/MEXICAN A funky rustic tavern with personality to spare, Woody Creek is a true local hangout, and a favorite of late gonzo journalist (and one-time local) Hunter S. Thompson. A century old and serving as a bar and grill since 1980, the tavern is now wallpapered with old photos, posters, news clippings, and other paraphernalia, plenty of it relating to Thompson. You'll find a good selection of well-prepared tavern food, including barbecued pork ribs, thick steaks, and burgers (made with low-fat Colorado limousine beef); plus fresh tilapia, organic salads, vegetarian (and organic when possible) soups, as well as excellent Mexican food, hot and spicy just like I like it, which goes well with the house-specialty drink—fresh-squeezed lime-juice margaritas made with 100% blue-agave tequila.

Upper River Rd., Woody Creek. ✆ **970/923-4585.** Reservations not accepted. Main courses $10–$18 lunch, $10–$25 dinner. No credit cards. Daily 11:30am–10pm; bar open later. Drive west on Colo. 82, 3/4 mile past the Snowmass Village turnoff, turn right on Smith Rd. into Woody Creek Canyon, turn left at the first fork, and continue 1 1/4 miles. Accessible by bus and bike. This road can be icy in winter.

ASPEN AFTER DARK

Aspen's major performing arts venue is the 1889 **Wheeler Opera House,** 320 E. Hyman Ave., at Mill Street (✆ **970/920-5770** box office; www.wheeleroperahouse.com). Built at the peak of the mining boom by silver baron Jerome B. Wheeler, this meticulously restored stage hosts a year-round program of music, theater, dance, film, and lectures. The building itself is worth a visit, with brass wall sconces, crystal chandeliers, gold trim and stencils on the dark-blue walls, rich wood, red carpeting, and red velvet seats. The box office is open daily from 10am to 6pm (until 5pm Sun).

Among Aspen's top nightspots, **Syzygy,** 520 E. Hyman Ave. (✆ **970/925-3700**), ranks high with young, high-energy types who live for the "Aspen scene." **Bentley's at the Wheeler,** 328 E. Hyman Ave. (✆ **970/920-2240**), is an elegant English-style pub, good for the older crowd. The **Lobby Lounge** at the St. Regis, at the base of Aspen Mountain (✆ **970/920-3300**), draws scores of après-skiers; and among my favorite Aspen bars is the quietly sophisticated and historic **J-Bar,** in the Hotel Jerome at Main and Mill streets (✆ **970/920-1000**). The rich, hip, and wasted flock to **39 degrees,** in the Sky Hotel at 709 E. Durant Ave. (✆ **970/925-6760**), for outer-limits specialty cocktails and the unbeatable slopeside pool, which you can use even if you're just a bar customer and not a guest. For the opposite side of the spectrum and the best burger deal in town, hit the casual, funky, and unpretentious **Cooper Street Pier,** 508 E. Cooper

 Ave. (✆ **970/925-7758**). Live rock, folk, and country concerts are the hallmark of **Belly Up,** 405 S. Galena St. (✆ **970/544-9800;** www.bellyupaspen.com). **Eric's Bar,** 408 E. Hyman Ave. (✆ **970/920-6707**), is four bars in one, with a cigar bar, pool hall, a Mexican eatery, and the bustling main bar. The **Double Dog Pub,** 303 E. Hopkins (✆ **970/544-5110**), is a comfortable basement pub lined with pictures of patrons' dogs, dog art, and acoustic music on Tuesday nights.

12

The Western Slope

Separated from Colorado's major cities by the mighty Rocky Mountains, the communities along the state's western edge are not only miles but also years away from the hustle and bustle of Denver and the California-style sophistication of Boulder. Even Grand Junction, the region's largest city, is an overgrown Western town, and the rugged canyons and stark rocky terrain make you feel like you've stepped into a John Ford movie. The lifeblood of this semidesert land is its rivers: The Colorado, Gunnison, and Yampa have not only brought water to the region, but over tens of thousands of years, their ceaseless energy has also gouged out stunning canyons that lure visitors from around the world. Colorado National Monument, west of Grand Junction, is remarkable for its land forms and prehistoric petroglyphs; Dinosaur National Monument, in the state's northwestern corner, preserves a wealth of dinosaur remains; and the Black Canyon of the Gunnison, a dark, narrow, and almost impenetrable chasm east of Montrose, challenges adventurous rock climbers and rafters.

But it's not all rocks and dinosaurs here. In and around the tiny community of Palisade, outside Grand Junction, is Colorado's wine country; and downtown Grand Junction boasts a continually changing and evolving outdoor art exhibit with its delightful Art on the Corner sculpture display.

1 GRAND JUNCTION

251 miles W of Denver, 169 miles N of Durango

Grand Junction is an excellent jumping-off point for those who want to drive or hike through the awe-inspiring red-rock canyons and sandstone monoliths of Colorado National Monument, explore the canyons at Dinosaur National Monument (about 2 hr. north), or sip and savor in the wine country of Palisade, just a short drive east.

Grand Junction is also the eastern entrance to one of the West's most scenic and challenging mountain-biking treks, Kokopelli's Trail, which ends in Moab, Utah. For the less athletically inclined, Grand Junction has an active visual-arts community, good museums, and a fine botanical garden.

Located at the confluence of the Gunnison and Colorado rivers at an elevation of 4,586 feet, the city was founded in 1882 where the spike was driven to connect Denver and Salt Lake City by rail. It quickly became the primary trade and distribution center between the two state capitals, and its mild climate, together with the fertile soil and irrigation potential of the river valleys, helped it grow into an important agricultural area. Soybeans, and later peaches and pears, were the most important crops. The city was also a center of the western Colorado uranium boom in the 1950s and the oil-shale boom in the late 1970s, and today is a fast-growing trade center serving practically all of western Colorado and eastern Utah.

ESSENTIALS

GETTING THERE **By Car** Grand Junction is located on I-70. U.S. 50 is the main artery from the south, connecting with Montrose and Durango.

By Plane On the north side of Grand Junction, **Walker Field,** 2828 Walker Field Dr. (© **970/244-9100;** fax 970/241-9103; www.walkerfield.com), is less than a mile off I-70's Horizon Drive exit. About 20 commercial flights connect Grand Junction with the West's major cities.

Airlines serving Walker Field include **Allegiant Air** (© 702/505-8888), **Delta Connection/SkyWest** (© 800/453-9417), **Frontier** (© 800/432-1359), **United Express/SkyWest** (© 800/241-6522), and **US Airways** (© 800/428-4322).

By Train **Amtrak** (© **800/USA-RAIL** [872-7245] or 970/241-2733; www.amtrak.com) has a passenger station at 337 S. First St. The California Zephyr stops twice daily, once in each direction, on its main route from San Francisco and Salt Lake City to Denver and Chicago.

VISITOR INFORMATION Contact the **Grand Junction Visitor & Convention Bureau,** 740 Horizon Dr., Grand Junction, CO 81506 (© **800/962-2547** or 970/244-1480; www.visitgrandjunction.com). There's a visitor center on Horizon Drive at I-70 exit 31 (open 8:30am–8pm in summer and 8:30am–5pm the rest of the year), and a Colorado Welcome Center at I-70 exit 19 for Fruita and Colorado National Monument (© **970/858-9335**), 12 miles west of Grand Junction, which is open daily from 8am to 6pm (until 5pm fall through spring).

GETTING AROUND Main Street and named avenues run east–west, and numbered streets and roads run north–south. Downtown Grand Junction lies south of I-70 and north of the Colorado River, encompassing 1 block on each side of Main Street between First and Seventh streets. There is metered street parking (free 2-hr. parking on Main Street between First and Seventh sts.), plus several public parking lots.

Car-rental agencies in the airport area include **Alamo** (© 970/243-3097), **Avis** (© 970/244-9170), **Hertz** (© 970/243-0747), and **National** (© 970/243-6626). **Sunshine Taxi** (© 970/245-8294) offers cab service, and **Grand Valley Transit** (© 970/256-7433; www.grandvalleytransit.com) operates buses in the Grand Junction area, including a shuttle service to and from Walker Field.

FAST FACTS There's a 24-hour emergency room at **St. Mary's Hospital,** Patterson Road and Seventh Street (© **970/244-2273**). The main **post office** is at 241 N. Fourth St.; contact the U.S. Postal Service (© **800/275-8777;** www.usps.com) for hours and other information. For **weather conditions,** call © **970/243-0914;** for **road conditions,** call © **877/315-7623.**

SPECIAL EVENTS Dinosaur Days, mid-June, Fruita; Downtown Art & Jazz Festival, mid-May; Mesa County Fair, late July; Palisade Peach Festival, mid-August, Palisade; Colorado Mountain Winefest, late September.

COLORADO NATIONAL MONUMENT ★★

Just minutes west of Grand Junction, this relatively undiscovered national monument is a delight, offering a colorful maze of steep-walled canyons filled with an array of naturally sculpted spires, pinnacles, and other impressive sandstone rock formations. Easy to get to and easy to see, in many ways it's a miniature Grand Canyon, only without the crowds. You can see much of the monument from your car on the 23-mile Rim Rock Drive, but

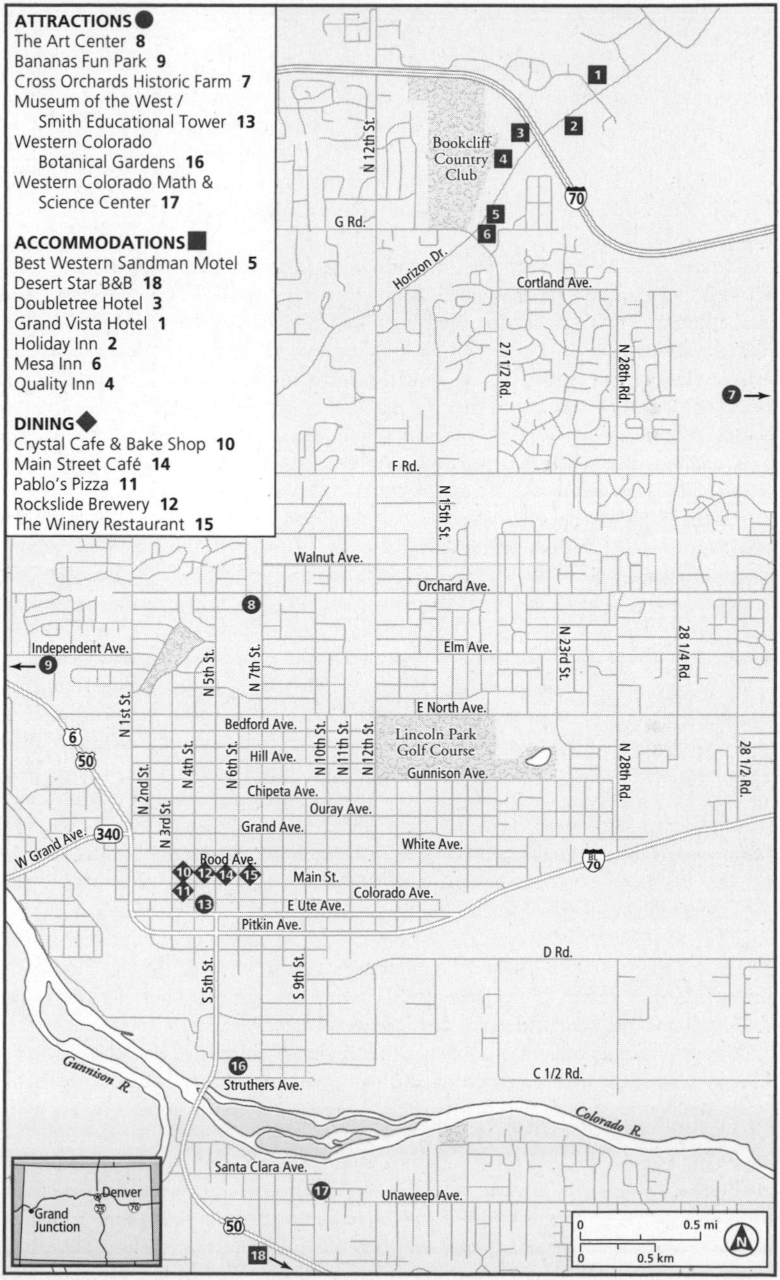
ATTRACTIONS
The Art Center 8
Bananas Fun Park 9
Cross Orchards Historic Farm 7
Museum of the West / Smith Educational Tower 13
Western Colorado Botanical Gardens 16
Western Colorado Math & Science Center 17
ACCOMMODATIONS
Best Western Sandman Motel 5
Desert Star B&B 18
Doubletree Hotel 3
Grand Vista Hotel 1
Holiday Inn 2
Mesa Inn 6
Quality Inn 4
DINING
Crystal Cafe & Bake Shop 10
Main Street Café 14
Pablo's Pizza 11
Rockslide Brewery 12
The Winery Restaurant 15
N 12th St.
Bookcliff Country Club
70
G Rd.
Horizon Dr.
Cortland Ave.
27 1/2 Rd.
N 28th Rd.
F Rd.
N 15th St.
Walnut Ave.
Orchard Ave.
Independent Ave.
N 5th St.
N 7th St.
Elm Ave.
N 23rd St.
28 1/4 Rd.
N 1st St.
E North Ave.
Bedford Ave.
N 10th St.
N 11th St.
N 12th St.
Lincoln Park Golf Course
6
50
N 2nd St.
N 4th St.
N 6th St.
Hill Ave.
Gunnison Ave.
28 1/2 Rd.
N 3rd St.
Chipeta Ave.
Ouray Ave.
Grand Ave.
W Grand Ave.
340
White Ave.
BL 70
Rood Ave.
Main St.
Colorado Ave.
E Ute Ave.
Pitkin Ave.
D Rd.
S 5th St.
S 9th St.
Struthers Ave.
C 1/2 Rd.
Gunnison R.
Colorado R.
Santa Clara Ave.
Unaweep Ave.
Denver
Grand Junction
25
0
0.5 mi
0.5 km
N

there are ample opportunities to hike, ride, and cross-country-ski the monument's many trails as well. Bighorn sheep, mountain lions, golden eagles, mule deer, and lizards are among the monument's residents. The monument ranges in elevation from 4,700 feet to 7,028 feet.

Carved by water and wind over millions of years, Colorado National Monument encompasses 32 square miles of red-rock canyons and sandstone monoliths, more than 1,000 feet above the Colorado River. A combination of upward lifts and erosion caused the chaos of formations here. Each layer visible in the striations of the canyon walls marks a time in the land's history. Fossils permit scientists to date these rocks back through the Mesozoic era of 225 million to 65 million years ago, and the Precambrian formation dates back 1.67 billion years.

The east entrance is only 5 miles west of Grand Junction, off Monument Road, but the best way to explore the monument is to follow the signs off I-70 from Fruita to the west entrance, 15 miles west of Grand Junction. It's here that **Rim Rock Drive,** built during the Great Depression, begins. Snaking up dramatic Fruita Canyon, it offers panoramic views of fanciful and bizarre natural stone monuments, as well as the cliffs and mesas beyond. At 4 miles, it reaches the national monument headquarters and **visitor center.** Exhibits on geology and history and an interactive video program introduce the park, and rangers can help you plan your visit. Guided walks and campfire programs are offered during the summer.

Rim Rock Drive—open to bicycles as well as motor vehicles—offers access to hiking trails varying in length from 400 yards to 8.5 miles. Many of the short, easy trails lead to spectacular canyon overlooks, while the longer backcountry trails head out across the mesas or down into the canyons. Strange formations such as Window Rock, the massive rounded Coke Ovens, the boulder-strewn Devils Kitchen, and the free-standing Independence Monument—all of which can be viewed from the road—are easily reached by foot.

If you're looking for an easy walk, try the 1-mile (round-trip) **Canyon Rim Trail,** which follows the edge of a cliff to spectacular views of the colorful rock formations in Wedding Canyon. Allow about an hour. Another shorter walk—the **Window Rock Trail**—also affords views of Wedding Canyon. Allow a half-hour for the .25-mile loop. Those who want to get down into the monument, rather than viewing it from above, should tackle one of the backcountry trails. The relatively difficult 12-mile round-trip **Monument Canyon Trail** drops 600 feet from the plateau into the canyon, through many of the monument's more dramatic rock formations, such as the aptly named Kissing Couple. The canyon is home to rattlesnakes and scorpions, so watch where you put your feet and hands. Also, it's hot and dry down there, so be sure to carry plenty of water. The **Black Ridge Trail,** the national monument's highest, offers panoramic views of the countryside that stretch to the canyons of Utah. Allow about 6 hours for the rugged 11-mile round-trip hike, and again, carry plenty of water.

Winter visitors may want to take their skis along. Among your best choices here is **Liberty Cap Trail,** which meanders across gently sloping Monument Mesa through a piñon-juniper forest and sagebrush flatlands. The trail is 14 miles round-trip, but cross-country skiers may want to turn back before the last 1.5 miles, which drop sharply into the Grand Valley.

While the monument is worth visiting at any time of year, the best time to go is fall, when the air is crisp but not cold, the cottonwood trees turn a brilliant gold, and the summer crowds have departed. Those visiting in May and June should carry insect repellent to combat the clouds of gnats that invade at this time.

The monument's **Saddlehorn Campground,** located in a piñon-juniper forest near the visitor center, has 80 sites, some shady, and restrooms but no showers or RV hookups. The cost is $10 per night. Like most areas administered by the National Park Service, pets must be leashed and are not allowed on trails or in the backcountry.

The national monument is open year-round. The day-use fee is $7 per vehicle or $4 per person for cyclists and pedestrians. The visitor center is open daily from 8am to 6pm in summer and 9am to 5pm the rest of the year. To obtain a brochure and other information, contact **Colorado National Monument,** Fruita, CO 81521 (© **970/858-3617;** www.nps.gov/colm). Those who want more in-depth information can order topographic maps, books, and other materials from the nonprofit Colorado National Monument Association at the monument's address and phone number above, or online at **www.coloradonma.org**.

DINOSAUR NATIONAL MONUMENT ★

This national monument, about 2 hours north of Grand Junction, is really two separate parks divided by the Utah–Colorado border. One side takes a close-up look at the world of dinosaurs, while the other opens onto a wonderland of colorful rock, deep river canyons, and a forest of Douglas firs.

About 150 million years ago, a river and sufficient vegetation made this region a suitable habitat for dinosaurs. Most of their skeletons decayed and disappeared, but in at least one spot they were preserved under a layer of sediment, when the river dried up and they died of thirst.

The **Dinosaur Quarry** and visitor center that provided access to it was closed in July 2006 and will remain closed indefinitely until much-needed structural repairs can be completed sometime around 2011. In the meantime, there is a **temporary visitor center** near the Jensen, Utah, entrance that has fossil displays, exhibits, films, and additional information. From Dinosaur, Colorado, head 20 miles west on U.S. 40 to Jensen, Utah, and then go 7 miles north into the park. This is the only place in the monument to see dinosaur bones.

However, even though exploration of the quarry area has been curtailed, there is still plenty to do here, especially on the Colorado side. Encompassing 325 square miles of stark canyons at the confluence of the Yampa and Green rivers in Colorado, the national monument also has hiking trails to explore, spectacular panoramic vistas, and the thrill of white-water rafting. Your first stop should be the **Canyon Area Visitor Center,** located about 2 miles east of the town of Dinosaur, Colorado, at the intersection of U.S. 40 and Harpers Corner Drive.

Allow about 4 hours for the scenic **Harpers Corner Drive.** This paved 62-mile round-trip drive has several overlooks offering panoramic views of the gorges carved by the Yampa and Green rivers, the derby-shaped Plug Hat Butte, and a variety of other colorful rock formations. The drive also offers access to the easy .25-mile loop that is the **Plug Hat Nature Trail** and the moderately difficult 2-mile round-trip **Harpers Corner Trail,** highly recommended for a magnificent view of the deep river canyons. In addition to several developed trails, experienced hikers with the appropriate maps can explore miles of unspoiled canyons and rock benches.

A superlative way to see this rugged country is on the river, crashing through thrilling white water and gliding over the smooth, silent stretches. One of the best authorized companies running the Yampa and Green rivers through the monument is **Hatch River Expeditions** (© **800/342-8243** or 435/789-4316; www.hatchriver.com). Prices start at

 $78 for adults, $68 for kids ages 6 through 14 for a 1-day trip; multiday trips over longer stretches are also available. The season generally runs from mid-May through mid-September, depending on water levels. A complete list of authorized river-running companies is available from monument headquarters.

The rivers here are not safe for swimming or wading; the water is cold, and the current is stronger than it may first appear.

Fishing in the Green and Yampa most often yields catfish, northern pike, and smallmouth bass, although there are also some trout. Several endangered species of fish—including the razorback sucker and humpback chub—must be returned unharmed to the water if caught. You'll need Utah and/or Colorado fishing licenses, depending on which side of the state line you're fishing.

There are **campgrounds** in both sections of the monument, but no showers or RV hookups, and camping fees range from $8 to $12 per night.

The national monument entrance near Dinosaur, Colorado, is about 110 miles north of Grand Junction. From Grand Junction, head west on I-70 about 12 miles to exit 15, turn right (north) onto Colo. 139, and go about 75 miles to Colo. 64; turn left and follow it west for 20 miles to the town of Dinosaur. Then turn right onto U.S. 40 and go east about 2 miles to the monument entrance. The monument is open around the clock, and the outdoor visitor center in Utah is open daily year-round, except Thanksgiving, Christmas, and New Year's Day. Hours in summer are 8:30am to 5:30pm, with shorter hours the rest of the year. The Canyon Area Visitor Center in Colorado is open daily May through late October 8:30am to 4:30pm but closed weekends in winter. The admission fee, charged only during summers on the Utah side, is $10 per vehicle and $5 per person for those on foot, motorcycles, or bicycles.

For information, contact **Dinosaur National Monument,** 4545 E. U.S. 40, Dinosaur, CO 81610-9724 (© **970/374-3000** or 435/781-7700; www.nps.gov/dino). In addition, the nonprofit **Intermountain Natural History Association,** 1291 E. U.S. 40, Vernal, UT 84078-2830 (© **800/845-3466;** www.inhaweb.com), offers numerous publications on the park's geology, wildlife, history, and dinosaur fossils.

SPORTS & OUTDOOR ACTIVITIES

In addition to activities in Colorado and Dinosaur national monuments, there are numerous opportunities for hiking, camping, mountain biking, off-roading, horseback riding, cross-country skiing, snowmobiling, and snowshoeing on other public lands administered by the federal government. Contact the **Bureau of Land Management,** 2815 H Rd., Grand Junction, CO 81506 (© **970/244-3000;** www.co.blm.gov), and the **Grand Valley Ranger District of Grand Mesa National Forest,** 2777 Crossroads Blvd., Ste. 1 (off Horizon Dr.), Grand Junction, CO 81506 (© **970/242-8211;** www.fs.fed.us/r2).

You'll also find plenty to do at **James M. Robb–Colorado River State Park** (© **970/434-3388;** www.parks.state.co.us), which has two main sections, both with campgrounds (see "Camping" under "Where to Stay," later in this section). **Island Acres** (© **970/464-0548**), on the east side of Grand Junction at I-70 exit 47, also offers hiking, picnicking, fishing, and just gazing out at the river. The **Fruita** section (© **970/858-9188**), located in the community of Fruita about 1/2-mile south of I-70 exit 19, covers 81 acres and has all of the above, plus boating and a swimming lagoon. Day-use fee at both sections is $6 per vehicle.

The Grand Junction **Parks and Recreation Department** (© **970/254-3842;** www.gjcity.org) manages more than 30 parks and other facilities, covering about 467 acres, which offer picnicking, hiking, tennis, playgrounds, swimming pools, softball, playing fields, horseshoe pits, and golf courses.

A busy local shop where you can get information on the best spots for outdoor recreation is **Summit Canyon Mountaineering,** 461 Main St. (© **800/254-6248** or 970/243-2847; www.summitcanyon.com). In addition to information, it stocks a wide variety of outdoor-sports equipment, plus travel and outdoor clothing.

GOLF My favorite course here, in large part because of the views—it's like golfing in the Grand Canyon—is the 18-hole **Golf Club at Redlands Mesa,** 2325 W. Ridges Blvd. (© **866/863-9270** or 970/263-9270; www.redlandsmesa.com), with greens fees of $48 for 9 holes and $84 for 18 holes. You'll also find great golfing and wonderful views at the 18-hole **Tiara Rado Golf Course,** 2057 S. Broadway (© **970/254-3830**), at the base of the Colorado National Monument canyons. Greens fees are $15 to $19 for 9 holes and $27 to $31 for 18 holes. The **Chipeta Golf Course,** an 18-hole executive course at 222 29 Rd. (© **970/245-7177;** www.chipetagolf.com), has greens fees of $12 to $14 for 9 holes and $20 to $24 for 18 holes. The 27-hole **Adobe Creek National Golf Course,** 876 18½ Rd., Fruita (© **970/858-0521;** www.adobecreekgolf.com), 9 miles west of Grand Junction, charges $23 to $31 for 18 holes.

HIKING Hikers and walkers who want to stay close to town can explore the trails in the Colorado Riverfront Project. Collectively known as the **Colorado River Trails,** the system includes almost 20 miles of paved trails that meander along the Colorado and Gunnison rivers, offering the chance to see ducks, geese, blue heron, deer, and rabbits. They are open to walkers and hikers, runners, bikers, in-line skaters, and horseback riders, but are closed to all motorized vehicles (except wheelchairs). Dogs are permitted if leashed. An excellent brochure with maps of the various river trails and directions to their trail heads is available free at the Grand Junction Visitor & Convention Bureau (see "Visitor Information," above). You'll also find hiking trails at **Colorado River State Park** (see the introduction to this section, above).

HORSEBACK RIDING Trail rides near the west entrance of Colorado National Monument are available through **Rimrock Adventures,** P.O. Box 608, Fruita, CO 81521 (© **888/712-9555** or 970/858-9555; www.rradventures.com). The stables are about a mile south of Fruita on Colo. 340. Rates for a 1-hour ride are $35 for adults and $25 for kids 5 to 12, and a half-day ride into the wilderness of Devil's Canyon costs $70 for adults and $60 for children. Kids' pony rides, running 15 minutes, cost $10.

MOUNTAIN BIKING Grand Junction has become important to mountain bikers as the eastern terminus of **Kokopelli's Trail** to Moab, Utah. Winding for 142 miles through sandstone and shale canyons, it has an elevation differential of about 4,200 feet. There are primitive campsites at intervals along the trail. The Colorado gateway is at the Loma Boat Launch, 15 miles west of Grand Junction off I-70.

For information on Kokopelli's Trail and several other area trails, contact the **Colorado Plateau Mountain-Bike Trail Association,** P.O. Box 4602, Grand Junction, CO 81502 (© **970/244-8877;** www.copmoba.com). There's also a bike route through and around Colorado National Monument (see earlier in this chapter). Covering 33 miles, it follows Rim Rock Drive through the park and 10 additional miles on rural South Camp Road and South Broadway at the base of the canyons. Rim Rock Drive does not have a separate bike lane or shoulders, so be alert for motor traffic. The national monument publishes a free brochure.

There are also several short mountain bike rides in the area. Inquire at the Visitor & Convention Bureau (see "Visitor Information," earlier in this chapter) for their brochures. You can also get information on area biking; rent mountain, road, and tandem bikes; and see some antique and unique bikes at **Brown Cycles,** 549 Main St. (✆ **970/245-7939;** www.browncycles.com). Bikes rent for $35 to $60 per day, and the shop's bicycle museum includes an 1885 high-wheeler, Schwinns from the 1920s and 1930s, and a human-powered bicycle airplane.

RIVER RAFTING For my money, one of the best ways to see this area's beautiful red sandstone canyons is from the river, in a big old rubber raft. Colorado River–rafting trips are provided by **Rimrock Adventures** (see "Horseback Riding," above). Cost for a 1½-hour trip about 5 miles down the Colorado is $28 for adults and $20 for children 12 and under; a 25-mile full-day float trip costs $100 per adult and $75 per child under 14. An exciting 17-mile white-water trip through Westwater Canyon costs $140 per person. The company also rents rafts ($65–$125 per day), canoes ($40 per day), and inflatable kayaks ($35–$45 per day), and offers shuttles for those who want to explore the river on their own.

Adventure Bound River Expeditions, 2392 H Rd., Grand Junction, CO 81505 (✆ **800/423-4668** or 970/245-5428; www.raft-colorado.com), offers 1- to 7-day trips. Rates for a 1-day trip through Westwater Canyon are $150 per adult and $135 for youths under 18. Two-day trips cost $335 per adult and $310 for youths under 18; call for additional rate information.

SKIING & SNOWBOARDING **Powderhorn Resort ★**, Colo. 65, 7 miles south of Mesa (✆ **970/268-5700;** www.powderhorn.com), is located 35 miles east of Grand Junction on the north face of the Grand Mesa. A favorite among local skiers and snowboarders of all ability levels, this pleasant resort offers 1,600 acres of skiable terrain with an average annual snowfall of 250 inches. Powderhorn has one quad lift and two doubles serving 27 trails, which are rated 20% beginner, 50% intermediate, 15% advanced, and 15% expert. Elevation at the top is 9,850 feet, and there's a vertical drop of 1,650 feet. Lift-ticket prices (highest Sat–Sun and holidays) are $46 to $53 for adults 19 to 59, $36 to $43 for youth 7 to 18 and seniors 60 to 69, $20 for those 70 and older, and $15 for children 6 and younger. The resort has a ski school, a rental shop, and a repair center. It is usually open from mid-December through late March. There is also a slope-side lodge, the **Inn at Wildewood** (✆ **970/268-5170**), with double rates in winter from $99 to $179.

SNOWMOBILING A trail connects Powderhorn Resort to Sunlight Mountain Resort, running 120 miles from Grand Junction's ski area to Glenwood Springs, the longest multiuse winter recreational trail in Colorado, traversing White River and Grand Mesa national forests. It is fully marked and continuously groomed. Other trails are accessed from parking areas along Colo. 65, between Mesa Lakes and Grand Mesa.

SWIMMING Centrally located **Lincoln Park,** at 12th Street and North Avenue, has an outdoor heated pool with a water slide. The **Orchard Mesa Pool,** 2736 C Rd., has an indoor pool, open year-round, with a diving area and shallow-water section. For hours, fees, and other specifics, contact the Grand Junction Parks and Recreation Department (✆ **970/254-3842;** www.gjcity.org).

THE MUSEUM OF WESTERN COLORADO ★★

For a huge step through time—from 150 million years ago all the way up to the present—you'll want to visit the various facilities of the **Museum of Western Colorado**

Wine Tasting & More Amid the Canyons

Colorado may not be the first location that comes to mind when winemaking is mentioned, but the state does have a growing wine industry, and the heart of it is here in the fertile Grand Valley. Area wineries welcome visitors for tastings and sometimes tours, and most have picnic areas, so bring your lunch. Organized tours by van or limousine are also available. Most wineries are located in the community of **Palisade,** about 12 miles east of Grand Junction, up the Grand Valley along U.S. 6 (I-70 exit 42).

The state's oldest existing winery, **Colorado Cellars Winery,** 3553 E Rd., Palisade (✆ **800/848-2812** or 970/464-7921; www.coloradocellars.com), produces an award-winning selection of chardonnays, merlots, Rieslings, fruit wines, and port. In summer, tasting room hours are Monday through Friday from 9am to 5pm, and Saturday from 10am to 5pm. **Carlson Vineyards,** 461 35 Rd., Palisade (✆ **888/464-5554** or 970/464-5554; www.carlsonvineyards.com), produces a variety of easy-drinking wines from Colorado fruit. Visitors are welcome year-round daily from 10am to 6pm. **Meadery of the Rockies,** 3701 G Rd., Palisade (✆ **970/464-7899;** www.meaderyoftherockies.com), produces honey wine—also known as mead, the "drink of the gods." Popular in medieval times, mead contains no grapes, but is made from orange-blossom honey. The tasting room is open daily 10am to 5pm.

Other Palisade wineries include **Grande River Vineyards,** 787 Elberta Ave. (✆ **970/464-5867;** www.granderiverwines.com); **Plum Creek Cellars,** 3708 G Rd. (✆ **970/464-7586;** www.plumcreekwinery.com); **Garfield Estates Winery,** located on a 100-year-old homestead at 3572 G Rd. (✆ **970/464-0941;** www.garfieldestates.com); **Canyon Wind Cellars,** 3907 N. River Rd. (✆ **970/464-0888;** www.canyonwindcellars.com); **St. Kathryn Cellars,** 785 Elberta Ave. (✆ **970/464-9288;** www.st-kathryn-cellars.com); **Debeque Canyon Winery,** 3943 U.S. 6 (✆ **970/464-0550;** www.debequecanyonwinery.com); and **Amber Ridge Vineyards,** 3820 G 1/4 Rd. (✆ **970/464-5314;** www.amberridgevineyards.com).

Wineries in Grand Junction include: **Two Rivers Winery,** 2087 Broadway (✆ **866/312-9463** or 970/255-1471; www.tworiverswinery.com), and **Whitewater Hill Vineyards,** 220 32 Rd. (✆ **970/434-6868;** www.whitewaterhill.com). South of Grand Junction about 7 miles is **Reeder Mesa Vineyards,** 7799 Reeder Mesa Rd., Whitewater (✆ **970/242-7468;** www.reedermesawines.com).

The **Colorado Wine Room,** 455 Kokopelli Blvd., Fruita, (✆ **877/858-6330** or 970/858-6330; www.coloradowineroom.com), is located near the Colorado Welcome Center just off I-70 exit 19 in Fruita, west of Grand Junction. It offers tastings and sales of over 25 Colorado wines. It's open Tuesday through Saturday from 10:30am to 5:30pm and Sunday from noon to 5pm. Maps to the wineries and additional information can be obtained from the Grand Junction Visitor & Convention Bureau (p. 334) and online at **www.coloradowinecountry.com**.

Palisade is just as famous for its fruit orchards as it is for its vineyards and wineries. Most fruit is picked between late June and mid-September, when it's available at roadside fruit stands. For a fruit directory, harvest schedule, and map, contact the **Palisade Chamber of Commerce,** 319 Main St., Palisade (P.O. Box 729), CO 81526 (✆ **970/464-7458;** www.palisadecoc.com).

 (© **888/488-3466** or 970/242-0971; www.wcmuseum.org). These include the **Museum of the West, Dinosaur Journey,** and **Cross Orchards Historic Farm** (each of which is discussed below). In addition, the Museum of Western Colorado manages three **natural resource areas,** where you can get a firsthand look at the geology and paleontology of western Colorado.

Combination admission tickets to the three facilities below, available at any of the sites, cost $12 adults, $10 seniors 60 and over, and $8 children 12 and under.

Cross Orchards Historic Farm With over 22,000 apple trees covering 243 acres, Cross Orchards was one of the largest apple orchards in western Colorado during the first quarter of the 20th century. Today the remaining 24 acres of the historic site preserve the feel of an old working farm and orchard, where blacksmiths and woodworkers continue to ply their trades, and visitors often smell ginger cookies baking in wood-burning stoves. Costumed guides lead tours through the original barn and packing house, workers' bunkhouse, and farm owner's gazebo. The site contains an extensive collection of vintage farm and road construction equipment, plus rail cars and a reconstructed depot. There's also a gift shop. Each year in mid-October visitors enjoy the **Apple Jubilee,** a harvest festival that includes plenty of fresh apple cider and other apple goodies. Allow 1½ to 2 hours.

3073 F Rd. © **970/434-9814** or 970/242-0971 (for event schedule). Admission $4 adults, $3 seniors 60 and over, $2.50 children 12 and under; immediate family rate $10. May–Oct Tues–Sat 9am–4pm. Closed Nov–Apr except for special events.

Dinosaur Journey Kids Enter a virtual time machine to journey back to the age of dinosaurs, where you'll encounter the 18-foot forelimb of a brachiosaurus. There are cast skeletons of dinosaurs such as allosaurus and stegosaurus, as well as real bones and robotic reconstructions. The cleverly designed and constructed full-size models move, bellow, and occasionally spit water. Hands-on, interactive exhibits allow kids of all ages to learn about and experience the forces that created the lands around us, and to feel the earth shake on an earthquake simulator. There is also a working paleontology lab, where you can see scientists prepare dinosaur bones for study. Visitors can join in a real dinosaur dig at one of the museum's quarries with advance registration. Allow 1 to 3 hours.

550 Jurassic Court, Fruita (just south of I-70 exit 19). © **970/858-7282** or 888/488-3466 (for dinosaur dig registration). www.dinosaurjourney.org. Admission $7 adults, $6 seniors 60 and over, $4 children 12 and under; family rate $20. Mon–Sat 10am–4pm; Sun noon–4pm.

Museum of the West This extensive museum offers a step back into the history of the American West, with "immersive" exhibits that remove the glass between visitor and exhibit, allowing you to literally step into history. Listen to the antique siren as you inspect the 1921 LaFrance fire truck, or examine a superb collection of Southwestern pottery in an adobe villa. You can explore an 1890s schoolhouse and a 1930s post office, as well as venture inside a full-size uranium mine, where the sounds of blasting and drilling continue to echo, and even "fly" a computer-controlled 1950 Cessna and learn about Colorado aviation history. The museum also boasts a display on the life of Alferd Packer, Colorado's notorious cannibal (p. 408). From the upper levels of the six-story Sterling T. Smith Education Tower, you'll get impressive 360-degree views of Grand Junction and the surrounding countryside. Connect to a wealth of historical, genealogical, and natural history materials in the Loyd Files Research Library. Allow 1½ to 3 hours.

462 Ute Ave. © **970/242-0971.** Admission $5.50 adults, $4.50 seniors 60 and over, $3 children 12 and under; family rate $16. Mon–Sat 9am–5pm; Sun noon–4pm.

MORE TO SEE & DO

The Art Center This fine gallery and museum has hundreds of works of art, many with Western themes, as well as traveling exhibits. The collection includes lithographs by Western artist Paul Pletka and more than 50 Navajo weavings dating from the early 1900s. There's also a gift shop featuring unique handcrafted items. Classes, changing exhibitions, and other events are scheduled throughout the year (call for a schedule). Allow at least an hour.

1803 N. Seventh St. ✆ **970/243-7337.** www.gjartcenter.org. Admission $3 adults, free for children 11 and under. Tues–Sat 9am–4pm.

Art on the Corner ★ This outdoor sculpture exhibit, with more than 100 works, helps make Grand Junction's downtown area a feast for the eyes. About half of the sculptures are on loan by the artists for 1 year, during which time they are for sale, and the rest are on permanent display. Keep an eye out for the whimsically rotund frog called *Puffed Up Prince,* the bronze pig named *Sir,* and *Greg La Rex,* a sculpture in steel that depicts a dinosaur skeleton atop a bicycle. The area has art galleries, antiques shops, restaurants, and a variety of retail stores, with wide, tree-lined pedestrian walkways. Allow at least an hour.

Main St., from Second to Seventh sts. ✆ **970/245-2926.** Free admission. Daily 24 hr., with shops and restaurants open usual business hours.

Bananas Fun Park Kids A fun place for kids of all ages (and the adults who are lucky enough to have their kids take them), this amusement park has a great miniature golf course—with waterfalls, fountains, and ponds—plus an arcade, go-karts, bumper boats, laser tag, batting cages, a playground, and a cafe. Allow 2 hours.

2469 River Rd. ✆ **970/243-0070.** www.bananasfunpark.com. Tickets for individual activities vary. Sun–Thurs 11am–9pm; Fri 11am–10pm; Sat 10am–11pm.

Western Colorado Botanical Gardens and Butterfly House ★★ Kids This botanical garden along the Colorado River offers a delightful escape into the natural world. Located on 15 acres, the facility includes a butterfly house, greenhouse with more than 600 exotic tropical plants, paved trails, and outdoor gardens and demonstration areas. In the butterfly house, visitors stroll through a lush forest of flowering plants, ferns, and ponds. But don't let the butterflies land on your palms—oil from your hands will clog their taste buds, which are located on their feet, and prevent them from finding food. The adjacent greenhouse contains hundreds of plants, including orchids and other colorful tropical varieties. Also in the greenhouse are fishponds and several whimsical metal sculptures. Walkways connect the botanical gardens with the Colorado River Trails system, which is discussed under "Hiking" on p. 339. Allow 2 to 4 hours.

641 Struthers Ave. ✆ **970/245-9030.** www.wcbotanic.org. Admission $5 adults, $3 students and seniors, $2 children 5–12, free for kids 4 and under. Tues–Sun 10am–4pm. Located at the south end of Seventh St.

Western Colorado Math & Science Center ★★ Kids This incredible hands-on facility is designed to "create enthusiasm and excitement for math and science" for kids of all ages—right on up to seniors. It's the brainchild of physicist John McConnell, who decided to turn from research to education and started a mentoring program in math and science for western Colorado students. With sophisticated experiments and interactive presentations packed in the trunk of his car, McConnell traveled from school to school; eventually, the popular program outgrew the car's trunk and morphed into the Western Colorado Math & Science Center. Somewhere along the way it acquired the acronym

Automobile Art

One of the best antique and classic car museums in the American West opened in 2006 in a highly unlikely spot: the tiny community of Gateway, in the middle of nowhere, about an hour's drive southwest of Grand Junction. Part of the Gateway Canyons resort, the **Gateway Colorado Auto Museum** has some four dozen beautifully restored automobiles—many of them luxury models of the day—that trace the history of American automotive design. The cars on display are part of the collection of John Hendricks, the founder and chairman of cable TV's Discovery Channel, who considers the cars as much pieces of art as transportation. The star of the collection is a one-of-a-kind 1954 Oldsmobile F-88 dream car, a fantastic piece of rolling sculpture that cost Hendricks $3.24 million when he bought it at auction specifically for the museum. Also on display are a 1906 Cadillac Model H Coupe, a 1913 Pierce Arrow, a 1939 Packard Darrin (a favorite of Hollywood stars), and a 1941 Lincoln V-12 Zephyr. There are also classics from the 1950s and 1960s, including muscle cars such as the 1967 Ford Mustang Shelby GT. All the vehicles are complete, in perfect running condition, and authentic. There are also exhibits on the automobile's influence on American life, from the assembly line to roadside diners to Hollywood glitter.

Gateway Colorado Auto Museum is located in Gateway Canyons resort, in the community of Gateway, on Colo. 141 near the Colorado–Utah border. It's open daily from 10am to 7pm, with the last ticket sold at 5pm. Admission costs $9 for adults, $7 for seniors 65 and older, $5 for children 6 to 12, and free for kids 5 and younger. The resort includes a restaurant, deli, store offering outdoor recreation gear and clothing, and lodging units. The address is 43224 Colo. 141, Gateway, CO 81522 (✆ **866/671-4733** or 970/931-2458; www.gateway automuseum.com).

SITHOK, or Science in the Hands of Kids. And that's it in a nutshell: The basic elements of science and math are presented with explanations, and kids (and adults) are invited to "touch, turn, look, listen, feel, pull, adjust, try out, and question." The staff of volunteers is continually adding and changing exhibits. Be sure to schedule your visit around school hours, since schools from a 160-mile radius make field trips to the center. Allow 1 to 4 hours.

2660 Unaweep Ave. ✆ **970/254-1626.** www.sithok.org. Admission $1. Wed–Sat 10am–4pm.

SHOPPING

For Colorado's most artful shopping experience, head to Grand Junction's **Downtown Shopping Park,** where you'll find a variety of shops, art galleries, and restaurants set amid an outdoor sculpture garden that runs some 7 blocks along Main Street. (See "Art on the Corner," above.)

One of the best galleries in the Downtown Shopping Park is **Working Artists Gallery and Studio,** 520 Main St. (✆ **970/256-9952**), with a wonderful variety of large—and expensive—wondrous things and quite affordable smaller items, including hand-thrown pottery, delightful sculptures, weavings, and wind chimes. In addition, there is an area in the back where you can usually watch an artist at work. There's also a resident cat, though he doesn't always show himself. Another not-to-be-missed stop here is **Monument Art Glass,** 428 Main St. (✆ **970/245-6800**), a galley and studio specializing in handblown glass. You can often watch a glass blower at work, or browse the fascinating and colorful glass objects, ranging from Christmas ornaments to bowls to paperweights, lamps, and bottles.

The western slope's largest indoor shopping mall, **Mesa Mall,** is located at 2424 U.S. 6 and 50 (✆ **970/242-0009;** www.shopmesamall.com). It's anchored by Sears, JCPenney, Target, and Herberger's.

WHERE TO STAY

Major chains offering reasonably priced lodging in Grand Junction are all conveniently lined up along Horizon Drive, include **Doubletree Hotel,** 743 Horizon Dr., Grand Junction, CO 81506 (✆ **970/245-8198**), with rates of $99 to $219; **Best Western Sandman Motel,** 708 Horizon Dr., Grand Junction, CO 81506 (✆ **970/243-4150**), with rates of $65 to $130; **Holiday Inn,** 755 Horizon Dr., Grand Junction, CO 81506 (✆ **888/489-9796** or 970/243-6790), with rates of $89 to $109; and **Quality Inn,** 733 Horizon Dr., Grand Junction, CO 81506 (✆ **800/329-7466** or 970/424-6423), with rates of $79 to $129. All rates listed above are for two people, with the highest rates during the summer. Room tax adds almost 11% to lodging bills.

Desert Star B&B ★ This beautiful 1898 Victorian faced demolition a century after its first occupancy but was saved from the path of the wrecking ball. It was instead moved across town to the foot of the starkly beautiful Gunnison Bluffs and near the gentle Gunnison River, where it has been restored into a delightful B&B with contemporary, sunny public areas, and geothermal heating and cooling. The guest rooms have queen beds (one of them has additional twins; both rooms feature a jetted tub); guest horses are welcome in the on-premises stables.

4000 U.S. 50 S., Whitewater, CO 81527. ✆ **970/254-8588.** www.desertstarbandb.info. 2 units. $85–$100 double. Well-behaved dogs and horses accepted. Rates include full breakfast. No credit cards. Located about 9 miles south of Grand Junction. *In room:* A/C, cable TV, no phone.

Grand Vista Hotel ★★ The aptly named Grand Vista does indeed have grand views, especially from the upper floors of its six stories. On the south side of the building you'll be looking out over Colorado National Monument, with its majestic canyons, while guests on the building's north side see the Book Cliffs and Grand Mesa. Units here are very quiet, with good lighting, comfortable seating, and solid wood furnishings. The minisuites are especially spacious and come with a king bed, recliner, modem dataport, and whirlpool tub. All king rooms have pillow-top mattresses. **Oliver's Restaurant & Bakery** serves buffets at every meal, and **Bailey's Lounge** is a handsome Old English–style pub with great deals on drinks and appetizers on weekday evenings. Golf and rafting packages are available. Four floors are designated completely nonsmoking.

2790 Crossroads Blvd., Grand Junction, CO 81506. ✆ **800/800-7796** or 970/241-8411. Fax 970/241-1077. www.grandvistahotel.com. 158 units. Apr–Oct $85–$95 double, lower at other times. AE, DC, DISC, MC, V. Pets accepted for a $10 per night fee. **Amenities:** Restaurant (American); bar; large 24-hr. heated indoor pool; use of a nearby full-service health club; indoor hot tub; complimentary airport/train/bus shuttle; business center. *In room:* A/C, TV w/on-demand movies and video games, wireless Internet access (free), coffeemaker, hair dryer, iron.

Mesa Inn A comfortable and reasonably priced alternative to the numerous chain motels in the vicinity, Mesa Inn offers everything you would expect in a modern American motel. Rooms have one or two queen-size beds, and the business units are especially nice, with well-lighted desks. Microwaves and refrigerators are available.

704 Horizon Dr., Grand Junction, CO 81506. ✆ **888/955-3080** or 970/245-3080. www.mesainngrandjunction.com. 123 units. $59–$99 double. Rates include continental breakfast. AE, DC, DISC, MC, V. Pets accepted for a $10 per night fee. **Amenities:** Heated outdoor pool; airport transportation; coin-op washers and dryers. *In room:* A/C, cable TV, wireless Internet access (free) coffeemaker.

Camping

In addition to campgrounds at **Colorado National Monument** (see earlier in this chapter), **James M. Robb–Colorado River State Park** (www.parks.state.co.us) has two campgrounds. The **Island Acres** unit (✆ **970/464-0548**), 10 miles east of Grand Junction off I-70 exit 47, has 80 campsites, and the **Fruita** unit ★★ (✆ **970/858-9188**), off I-70 exit 19 and about 10 miles west of Grand Junction, has 57 campsites. Rates at both are $14 for tents, $18 for RV sites with electricity, and $22 for full RV hookups. These fees are in addition to the $5 per vehicle day-use fee. Reservations for both campgrounds are available from March through October for an $8 reservation fee; call ✆ **800/678-2267** or go to the park's website (see above). The Fruita campground is the top camping choice in the Grand Junction area—it's well laid out and conveniently located just a few miles from the west entrance of Colorado National Monument. Both campgrounds have showers and laundry facilities, a playground, naturalist programs, picnicking, fishing, and hiking. The Fruita unit also boasts a swimming lagoon and boating.

Of the commercial campgrounds in the Grand Junction area, the pick is **Junction West R.V. Park,** 793 22 Rd., Grand Junction (✆ **970/245-8531**), which has clean bathhouses; 66 large, somewhat shaded sites; a store; coin-operated laundry; a game room; a dump station; and wireless Internet. Rates are $35 for RVs and $25 for tents. To get there, take U.S. 6 and 50 to 22 Road (or I-70 exit 26), and go north half a mile.

WHERE TO DINE

Expensive & Moderate

The Winery Restaurant ★★ STEAK/SEAFOOD Fine dining in an atmosphere of Western elegance is what you'll experience at the Winery, which is one of the best restaurants in Grand Junction. Tucked behind a gas-lit entry in an alley off Main, the dining room is housed in a historic firehouse, all redbrick and weathered wood and decorated with lots of plants, stained glass, and wine barrels and bottles. It's hard to go wrong here. The prime rib is especially enjoyable (get there early—it often sells out), as is the grilled salmon with herb butter. The salmon and catch of the day are always fresh. Also recommended is the filet Oscar—filet mignon and asparagus, covered in a lobster/crab Newburg sauce. You can get a variety of steaks, steak and seafood combos, a rack of lamb, or a center-cut pork chop as well. For dessert, try the homemade apple crisp with streusel topping, or the Palisade, the restaurant's signature dessert that is much too complicated to try to describe here.

642 Main St. ✆ **970/242-4100.** www.winery-restaurant.com. Reservations recommended. Main courses $16–$48. AE, DISC, MC, V. Sun–Thurs 5–9pm; Fri–Sat 5–10pm. Closed major holidays.

Rockslide Brewery ★ MICROBREWERY Featuring a brick-walled dining room and a mug-clad bar, the comfortable atmosphere of the Rockslide nicely complements the better-than-average pub grub on its menu: plump calzones, a stellar fish and chips, mahimahi tacos, and a long list of specialty burgers. I also am quite fond of the beers, especially the Widowmaker Wheat and the Big Bear Stout. There is a second location in nearby Fruita.

401 Main St. ✆ **970/245-2111.** Main courses $9–$12. AE, DISC, MC, V. Sun 8am–10pm; Mon–Wed 11am–10pm; Thurs–Sat 11am–10pm. Bar open later.

Inexpensive

Crystal Cafe and Bake Shop (Finds) AMERICAN You may have to wait for a table at this local favorite, especially for breakfast and lunch, but the food here is worth waiting for. The simple, modern decor includes hardwood tables and bentwood cafe-style chairs, with woven place mats and napkins. Selections are mostly innovative variations on standard American dishes, highlighted by the cafe's own fresh-baked breads, rolls, pastries, and desserts. For breakfast there's a variety of pancakes, as well as egg dishes that include a Greek omelet—a two-egg omelet with fresh tomatoes, black olives, red onions, oregano, and feta cheese. Lunch and dinner items include plenty of salads, hot and cold sandwiches, and a quiche of the day. Sandwiches often include uniquely seasoned mayonnaise. I particularly enjoy the smoked turkey with red onion and basil mayonnaise. Dinner hours can be sporadic.

314 Main St. ✆ **970/242-8843.** Breakfast $5–$10; lunch and dinner main courses $6–$12. AE, DISC, MC, V. Mon 7am–2pm; Tues–Fri 7am–2pm and 5–9pm; Sat–Sun 8am–noon and 5–9pm.

Main Street Café AMERICAN The '50s are back at the Main Street Café, with an old-fashioned soda fountain (there's also seating at tables and booths), photos of Marilyn and Elvis, and 45-rpm records. In addition to the shot of nostalgia, you'll find good diner food at reasonable prices. Breakfasts include bacon and eggs, pancakes, and, for the more adventurous, several spicy combinations. For lunch there are vegetarian items, numerous sandwiches and salads, excellent hand-packed cooked-to-order Black Angus burgers, and blue-plate specials including Italian-style meat loaf, brisket, and chicken-fried steak, all with real mashed potatoes and fresh vegetables. Leave room for the praiseworthy banana split or hot-fudge sundae.

504 Main St. ✆ **970/242-7225.** Breakfast $3.50–$8; lunch main courses $3.50–$12. AE, DISC, MC, V. Mon–Sat 7am–4pm; Sun 7am–3pm.

Pablo's Pizza ★ (Kids) PIZZA Inspired by Pablo Picasso, who forever changed the art world with his revolutionary creations, Pablo's Pizza strives for the same sort of impact on the taste buds. And it succeeds. For purists, the simple pepperoni pizza is delicious. But for the adventuresome spirit, step off the beaten path with specialty pizzas such as Dracula's Nemesis (garlic white sauce, roasted garlic, roasted red onion, chicken, green onions, and cheese) or Big Daddy's Rajun Cajun (spicy hot tomato sauce, andouille sausage, shrimp, red and green bell peppers, and cheese). Or you can build your own, beginning with one of their eight sauces and adding cheese, meats, vegetables, and even fruits. You can watch them make your pizza, from the tossing of the crust to when they take it from the oven on a wooden paddle. The redbrick-and-white walls are decorated with Picasso-style original artwork, and the ceiling is of pressed tin. All in all, the place has a 1960s Greenwich Village–coffeehouse atmosphere. Pablo's also offers panini sandwiches, soups, salads, and desserts, plus has takeout and delivery service.

319 Main St. ✆ **970/255-8879.** www.pablospizza.com. Pizza $7.75–$24; by the slice $1.95–$2.80. AE, DISC, MC, V. Sun–Thurs 11am–8:30pm; Fri–Sat 11am–9pm.

2 GLENWOOD SPRINGS

84 miles E of Grand Junction, 41 miles NW of Aspen, 169 miles W of Denver

Scenic beauty and hot mineral water are the big lures here. Members of the Ute tribe visited the Yampah mineral springs on the banks of the Colorado River for centuries. Calling it "big medicine," they came from miles around to heal their wounds or use nearby vapor caves as natural saunas. But it wasn't until the 1880s that the springs were commercially developed. The three Devereux brothers, who made a small fortune in silver at Aspen, built the largest hot-springs pool in the world, then added a red-sandstone bathhouse and built the Hotel Colorado. Soon everyone from European royalty to movie stars to President Theodore Roosevelt was stopping in Glenwood Springs.

The springs supported the town until the Great Depression and World War II caused a decline in business. After the war, with the growth of the ski industry at nearby Aspen, Glenwood Springs began to reemerge as a resort town, but on a smaller scale. Today this city of about 8,500, at an elevation of 5,746 feet, is a popular recreational center. The hot-springs complex underwent a total renovation in the 1970s, and additional improvements were made in 1993 as it celebrated its centennial.

Also completed that year was a 12-year, $490-million project to build a four-lane interstate through the 18-mile Glenwood Canyon. One of the most expensive roadways ever built—as well as one of the most beautiful interstate highway drives in America—the road offers a number of trail heads and raft-launching areas, as well as viewpoints from which travelers can safely gaze at the Colorado River and its spectacular canyon.

ESSENTIALS

GETTING THERE **By Car** I-70 follows the Colorado River through Glenwood Springs. Colo. 82 (the Aspen Hwy.) links the city with Aspen, 42 miles southeast.

By Bus **Roaring Fork Transportation Agency** (✆ **970/925-8484;** www.rfta.com) offers service between Glenwood Springs and Aspen, with numerous stops along the route daily, at a cost of $6 each way, less for intermediate stops.

By Shuttle Van Transportation from Denver to Glenwood Springs is provided by **Colorado Mountain Express** (✆ **800/525-6363** or 970/926-9800; www.cmex.com), at about $90 per person one-way.

By Train There's **Amtrak** service (✆ **800/USA-RAIL** [872-7245]; www.amtrak.com) to Glenwood Springs daily aboard the California Zephyr, direct from Denver and Salt Lake City. The depot is at Seventh Street and Cooper Avenue.

VISITOR INFORMATION The **Glenwood Springs Chamber Resort Association,** 1102 Grand Ave., Glenwood Springs, CO 81601 (✆ **970/945-6589;** www.visitglenwood.com), maintains a visitor center on the south side of downtown, on the southeast corner of 11th and Grand. Brochures are available 24 hours a day.

GETTING AROUND The confluence of the Roaring Fork and Colorado rivers forms a T in the heart of Glenwood Springs, and streets follow the valleys carved by the two streams. Downtown Glenwood is south of the Colorado and east of the Roaring Fork. The city-run bus service, **Ride Glenwood Springs** (✆ **970/384-6400;** www.ci.glenwood-springs.co.us/transpo/1a-1.htm), operates daily, providing free rides to and from hotels, motels, restaurants, shopping areas, and the Glenwood Hot Springs Pool. Schedules are available at the Chamber Resort Association office (see above).

Underground Fantasy & Above-Ground Thrills

Glenwood Caverns Adventure Park ★★ has something for everyone, from magnificent historic caves to a thrilling tram ride, plus horseback and mechanical bull rides, an alpine coaster (sort of like a roller-coaster ride through the mountains), a giant swing, a climbing wall, and chuck-wagon dinner shows. The centerpiece of this park is the historic **Fairy Caves,** which were a major tourist attraction in the late 1890s and early 1900s. The caves were a sight to see—numerous stalactites and stalagmites, needles, gypsum flowers, bacon, soda straws, and other delicate and colorful formations, illuminated by electric lights—all for the 1897 price of 50¢. Visitors would either walk to the caves' entrance or ride a burro.

Closed since the outbreak of World War I in 1917, the Fairy Caves were reopened to the public in 1999, along with a section of the caves that remained undiscovered until more recent times. The cave temperature remains a constant 52°F (11°C) year-round, so you'll probably want a light jacket even on the hottest summer day. Since you'll also be traversing some 127 stairs, be sure to wear comfortable walking shoes. New trails, hand rails, and lighting have been installed for the 1-hour guided **Cave Tour,** which covers a half-mile and costs $20 for adults, $18 for seniors 65 and older, and $15 for children 3 to 12.

Most of the caves have been left in as natural a state as possible for the guided 3- to 4-hour **Wild Tour,** which is for small groups of physically fit individuals who don't mind crawling on their stomachs through dirty narrow passages wearing knee pads and helmet lights. Participants must be at least 13 years old, and a parent or guardian must accompany each youth from 13 to 17. Reservations are required. Cost is $60 per person.

Eight six-person gondolas rise 1,400 feet from the valley floor up the side of Iron Mountain. The **tram ride** provides panoramic views all the way to the top, where there are a visitor center, gift shop, moderately difficult nature trail, good food, plus Discovery Rock (extra fee)—a place for kids to pan for jewels and unearth fossils. Tram rides cost $10 for adults, $9 for seniors 65 and up, and $7 for kids 3 to 12, and a tram ride is included in the cave tours.

Now a variety of other family activities has been added, including horseback riding (summer only), mechanical bull riding, an alpine coaster and various other rides, and rock climbing. There are a restaurant and gift shop, and chuck-wagon dinner shows during the summer. For details, including the current schedule and all activity fees, contact Glenwood Caverns Adventure Park, 51000 Two Rivers Plaza Rd., Glenwood Springs, CO 81601 (✆ **800/530-1635** or 970/945-4228; www.glenwoodcaverns.com).

FAST FACTS **Valley View Hospital,** providing 24-hour emergency care, is at 1906 Blake Ave. (✆ **970/945-6535;** www.vvh.org). The **post office** is at 113 Ninth St.; contact the U.S. Postal Service (✆ **800/275-8777;** www.usps.com) for hours and additional information.

SPECIAL EVENTS Glenwood Downtown Market, Tuesday June through September; Summer of Jazz, June and July; Strawberry Days Festival, mid-June; Vintage Baseball Game, late June; Fall Arts Festival, late September; Historic Ghost Walk, late October; and the Day of Infamy Snowshoe Race, early December.

SPORTS & OUTDOOR ACTIVITIES

There are plenty of outdoor recreation opportunities in and around Glenwood Springs. Stop at the **chamber** office (see "Visitor Information," above) or contact the **White River National Forest,** 900 Grand Ave. (✆ **970/945-2521;** www.fs.fed.us/r2/whiteriver), or the **Bureau of Land Management,** 50629 U.S. 6 and U.S. 24 (✆ **970/947-2800;** www.co.blm.gov), for maps and other information.

A busy local shop where you can get information on the best spots for hiking, mountain climbing, rock climbing, kayaking, camping, and cross-country skiing is **Summit Canyon Mountaineering,** 732 Grand Ave. (✆ **800/360-6994** or 970/945-6994; www.summitcanyon.com), which also sells and rents cross-country ski gear, tents, sleeping bags, and backpacks.

BICYCLING Biking options abound here. The new 44-mile **Rio Grande Trail** connects Glenwood Springs and Aspen, a paved bike trail runs from the Yampah Vapor Caves into Glenwood Canyon, and trails and four-wheel-drive roads in the adjacent White River National Forest are ideal for mountain bikers (see "Hiking," below). You'll find bike rentals (about $20–$50 per day) in town at **Canyon Bikes,** at the Hotel Colorado, 526 Pine St. (✆ **800/439-3043** or 970/945-8904; www.canyonbikes.com), which also offers a shuttle service, and **Sunlight Mountain Ski & Bike Shop,** 309 Ninth St. (✆ **970/945-9425;** www.sunlightmtn.com), which also offers repairs.

FISHING Brown and rainbow trout are caught in the Roaring Fork and Colorado rivers, and fishing for rainbow and brook trout is often good in the Crystal River above the community of Redstone. Get licenses, equipment, and advice from **Roaring Fork Anglers,** 2114 B Grand Ave. (✆ **800/781-8120** or 970/945-0180; www.rfanglers.com), who have offered guided fly-fishing trips since 1975. Rates for one or two people on a full-day float trip are $435, including lunch; a full-day wading trip, including lunch, is $295 for one and $360 for two. Half-day trips are available, and Roaring Fork also has 4 miles of private waters.

GOLF **Glenwood Springs Golf Club,** 193 Sunny Acres Rd. (✆ **970/945-7086;** www.glenwoodgolf.com), is a 9-hole course, with fees of $22 for 9 holes and $37 for 18 holes. Some 27 miles west of Glenwood Springs, near Rifle, is the championship 18-hole **Rifle Creek Golf Club,** at 3004 Colo. 325, off I-70 exit 90 (✆ **970/625-1093**), which charges $23 for 9 holes and $41 for 18 holes, not including cart rental.

Fans of miniature golf will discover two beautifully landscaped 18-hole water-obstacle courses at **Johnson Park Miniature Golf,** 51579 U.S. 6 and U.S. 24, in West Glenwood Springs (✆ **970/945-9608**). Open April through October, rates for 18 holes are $6 for adults and $5 for children under 12 and seniors over 60. The **Glenwood Hot Springs** resort (see "Taking the Waters," below) also has a miniature golf course, with rates of $6 for adults and $4 for kids under 12.

HIKING There are plenty of hiking opportunities in the area. Ask the national forest office (see above) for free **Recreational Opportunity Guide (ROG)** sheets for many local trails. The **Glenwood Springs Chamber Resort Association** offers a free map showing a variety of trails in the area, with trail heads marked.

One popular trek is the **Doc Holliday Trail ★★**, a .5-mile climb from 13th and Bennett streets to an old cemetery that contains the grave of notorious gunslinger Doc Holliday (see "Exploring Glenwood Springs's Frontier Past," below). Hikers will also find numerous trail heads along the **Glenwood Canyon Recreation Trail ★** in Glenwood Canyon, with some of the best scenery in the area. Among them, **Hanging Lake Trail ★★**, 9 miles east of Glenwood Springs off I-70, is especially popular. The trail head is accessible from eastbound I-70; westbound travelers must make a U-turn and backtrack a few miles to reach the parking area. The trail climbs 1,000 feet in 1 mile—allow several hours for the round-trip—and just beyond Hanging Lake is Spouting Rock, with an underground spring shooting out of a hole in the limestone cliff. Dogs, swimming, and fishing are forbidden. The **Grizzly Creek Trail** is in the Grizzly Creek Rest Area, along I-70 in Glenwood Canyon, where there is also a launching area for rafts and kayaks. The trail climbs along the creek, past wildflowers and dogwood trees.

JEEP TOURS Explore the high country around Glenwood Springs in an open-air jeep. The knowledgeable and friendly guides at **Rock Gardens** (✆ **800/958-6737** or 970/945-6737; www.rockgardens.com) will show you some breathtaking views—don't forget your camera—and share with you some of the history and wildlife of the area. Half-day trips cost $49 to $55 per person.

RIVER RAFTING Bouncing down the rapids through magnificent **Glenwood Canyon ★★** is certainly one of the best ways to see this spectacular country. Companies offering raft trips include **Blue Sky Adventures,** with offices in the Hotel Colorado (✆ **877/945-6605** or 970/945-6605; www.blueskyadventure.com), which offers rafting on the Colorado and Roaring Fork rivers. A half-day trip costs $47 for adults, $35 for youths 15 and under; the half-day "Mild" trip costs $35 and $28 respectively. A popular full-day trip through the white water of Shoshone Rapids costs $75 and $55, respectively, including a hot barbecue lunch. Other good bets for raft trips are **Rock Gardens Rafting,** 1308 C.R. 129, at I-70 exit 119 (✆ **800/958-6737** or 970/945-6737; www.rockgardens.com), and **Colorado Whitewater Rafting,** P.O. Box 2462, Glenwood Springs, CO 81602 (✆ **800/993-7238** or 970/945-8477; www.coloradowhitewaterrafting.com), with similar rates. In town on the river is the new **Glenwood Springs Whitewater Park** (www.glenwoodwhitewaterpark.org), at the Midland Avenue Bridge.

SKIING & SNOWBOARDING **Sunlight Mountain Resort,** 10901 C.R. 117, Glenwood Springs, CO 81601 (✆ **800/445-7931** or 970/945-7491; www.sunlightmtn.com), is located 10 miles south of Glenwood Springs in the White River National Forest. Geared toward families, Sunlight has 470 skiable acres and a 2,010-foot vertical drop from its 9,895-foot summit; it's served by one triple and two double chairlifts and a ski-school surface lift. There are 67 runs, rated 20% beginner, 55% intermediate, 20% advanced, and 5% expert. The ski area is usually open from early December to early April daily from 9am to 4pm. A full-day lift ticket runs $50 for adults, $40 for children 6 to 12 and seniors 60 to 69, and $10 for kids under 6 and seniors 70 and over. There are also a terrain park and 10 miles of groomed Nordic trails; the latter is accessible free of charge. For equipment rentals and repairs, see the **Sunlight Mountain Ski & Bike Shop,** 309 Ninth St., in downtown Glenwood Springs (✆ **970/945-9425**). Information and equipment are also available at **Summit Canyon Mountaineering,** 732 Grand Ave. (✆ **800/360-6994** or 970/945-6994; www.summitcanyon.com).

SNOWMOBILING The **Sunlight to Powderhorn Trail,** running 120 miles from Glenwood's local ski area to Grand Junction's, on the Grand Mesa, is the longest multiuse winter recreational trail in Colorado, traversing White River and Grand Mesa national forests. It is fully marked and continuously groomed. Other trails can be accessed from the end of C.R. 11, 2 miles beyond Sunlight Mountain Resort and 12 miles south of Glenwood Springs. For information and rentals, contact the resort.

TAKING THE WATERS

There may be no better or more luxurious way to rejuvenate the dusty, tired traveler than by soaking in a natural hot spring. In Glenwood Springs, there are two places to experience this ancient therapy.

Glenwood Hot Springs Pool ★★ Named Yampah Springs—meaning "Big Medicine"—by the Utes, this pool was created in 1888 when enterprising developers diverted the course of the Colorado River and built a stone bathhouse. The springs flow at a rate of 3$^1/_2$-million gallons per day, and, with a temperature of 122°F (50°C), they're one of the world's hottest springs. The content is predominantly sodium chloride, but there are significant quantities of calcium sulfate, potassium sulfate, calcium bicarbonate, and magnesium bicarbonate, plus traces of other therapeutic minerals.

The two open-air pools together are nearly 2 city blocks in length. The larger pool, 405 feet by 100 feet, holds more than a million gallons of water and is maintained at 90°F (32°C). The smaller pool, 100 feet long, is kept at 104°F (40°C). There's also a children's pool with water slides, plus a deli, sport shop, and miniature golf course. The red-sandstone administration building overlooking the pools was the Hot Springs Lodge until 1986, when the new Glenwood Hot Springs Lodge (see "Where to Stay," below) and bathhouse complex were built, and an athletic club opened (day passes are $30). Suit and towel rentals and coin-operated lockers are available. The new-for-2008 **Spa of the Rockies** offers massages and a full menu of other treatments. Allow from 1 to 4 hours.

401 N. River Rd. ✆ **800/537-7946** or 970/945-6571. www.hotspringspool.com. Admission summer $17–$18 adults, $11 children 3–12; rest of year $13 adults, $9.25 children 3–12; free for children 2 and under year-round. Reduced evening rates. Water slide summer $5.25 for 4 rides or $7.50 for 8 rides; rest of year $4.25 and $6, respectively. Summer daily 7:30am–10pm; rest of year daily 9am–10pm.

Yampah Spa and Vapor Caves The hot Yampah Spring water flows through the floor of nearby caves, creating natural underground steam baths. Once used by Utes for their curative powers, today the cave has an adjacent spa where such treatments as massages, facials, herbal wraps, body muds, and salt glow rubs are offered. There's also a full-service beauty salon on the premises. Allow at least 1 hour.

709 E. Sixth St. ✆ **970/945-0667.** www.yampahspa.com. Admission to caves $12; spa treatments vary; a full-body massage is $79. Daily 9am–9pm.

EXPLORING GLENWOOD SPRINGS'S FRONTIER PAST

Although most Colorado visitors tend to think of Telluride or Cripple Creek when the subject of the Wild West comes up, Glenwood Springs had its share of desperados and frontier justice. The Ute tribe first inhabited the area, using it as a base for hunting and fishing, and also making use of its mineral hot springs. By the mid- to late 1800s, Defiance—as it was then called—had grown into a prospector community, though it was still little more than a muddy street lined with saloons, brothels, and boardinghouses, where miners from nearby Aspen and Leadville could be relieved of their newfound wealth. The hot springs began to attract mine owners and other prominent businessmen to Defiance, and in 1885 the town's name was changed to the more refined Glenwood Springs. However, it wasn't until 1886 that civilization finally arrived, along with the railroad. The following year, notorious gunfighter Doc Holliday came to town, and although he is said to have practiced his card-playing skills (and even a bit of dentistry), there is no record that he was involved in any gunplay in the town. By 1888, the lavish Hot Springs Pool opened, followed in 1893 by the majestic Hotel Colorado, and Glenwood Springs—now dubbed the "Spa in the Rockies"—began to attract the rich and famous.

Much of the grandeur of Glenwood Springs in the late 19th and early 20th centuries remains and can be seen on a walk through the downtown area. The self-guided **Historic Walking Tour** guide and map is available at the Chamber Resort Association's visitor center (see earlier in this chapter) and the Frontier Historical Museum (see below). The guide describes more than 40 historic buildings and sites, including the 1884 Mirror Saloon, the oldest existing building in downtown Glenwood Springs; the site of the 1884 Hotel Glenwood (only a small portion remains), where Doc Holliday died; the 1893 Hotel Colorado, which was used by President Theodore Roosevelt as his "Western White House" in the early 1900s; and the 1885 Kamm Building, where gangster Al Capone is said to have been a jewelry customer in the 1920s.

Doc Holliday's Grave After the famous shootout at the OK Corral, Doc Holliday began a final search for relief from his advanced tuberculosis. But even the mineral-rich waters of Glenwood Springs could not dissipate the ravages of hard drinking and disease, and Doc died in 1887 at the Hotel Glenwood. Although the exact location of Doc's grave is not known, it is believed he was buried in or near the Linwood Cemetery, on Lookout Mountain overlooking the city. Also in the cemetery are the graves of other early citizens of Glenwood.

From the chamber office on Grand Avenue, walk or drive uphill on 11th to Bennett and turn right. Not far on the left is the sign marking the trail to the cemetery. The trail is a .5-mile uphill hike, and you'll have a grand view of the city along the way. In the cemetery, near the flagpole, is a tombstone with the inscription, DOC HOLLIDAY 1852–1887: HE DIED IN BED; in front of that is another monument that reads, THIS MEMORIAL DEDICATED TO DOC HOLLIDAY WHO IS BURIED SOMEPLACE IN THE CEMETERY. Allow about a half-hour.

Linwood Cemetery, off Bennett St. No phone. Free admission. Open dawn to dusk.

Frontier Historical Museum Highlights of this museum, which occupies a late-Victorian home, include the original bedroom furniture of Colorado legends Horace and Baby Doe Tabor, brought here from Leadville. The collection also includes displays on famed dentist-turned-gunfighter Doc Holliday, plus other pioneer home furnishings, including a complete kitchen. There are also toys, historic photos and maps, American Indian artifacts, and a mining and minerals display. The museum contains an extensive archive of historic documents and photographs from the early days of Glenwood Springs. Allow an hour.

1001 Colorado Ave. ✆ **970/945-4448.** www.glenwoodhistory.com. Admission $3 adults, $2 seniors 60 and older, $1 for children 3–12, free for children 2 and under. May–Sept Mon–Sat 11am–4pm; Oct–Apr Mon and Thurs–Sat 1–4pm.

WHERE TO STAY

Rates are usually highest in summer, although busy ski times, such as Christmas week, can also be high. You can get additional information and reserve a room from the **Glenwood Springs Central Reservations** (✆ **888/445-3696;** www.visitglenwood.com).

Among the reliable moderately priced chains and franchises are the **America's Best Value Inn,** 51871 U.S. 6 and U.S. 24, at I-25 exit 114 (✆ **888/315-2378** or 970/945-6279), with rates of $69 to $159; the **Best Western Antlers,** 171 W. Sixth Ave. (✆ **800/626-0609** or 970/945-8535), with rates from $80 to $250; the **Hampton Inn,** 401 W. First St. (✆ **800/426-7866** or 970/947-9400), charging $99 to $250; the **Holiday Inn Express,** 501 W. First St. (✆ **800/465-4329** or 970/928-7800), charging from $129 to $169; and **Ramada Inn & Suites,** 124 W. Sixth St. (✆ **800/332-1472** or 970/945-2500), with rates from $99 to $169. All the above are in Glenwood Springs, zip 81601, and rates for all of the hotels are for two people; taxes add about 11.5% to lodging bills.

Expensive

Glenwood Hot Springs Lodge ★ Heated by the springs that bubble through the hillside beneath it, this handsome five-story hotel overlooks the Glenwood Hot Springs Pool complex. Three-quarters of the rooms have private balconies or patios. Rooms are spacious, with one king or two queen beds, and cherry- or lightwood furnishings; some have hide-a-beds, refrigerators, and double vanities.

415 Sixth St. (P.O. Box 308), Glenwood Springs, CO 81602. ✆ **800/537-7946** or 970/945-6571. Fax 970/947-2950. www.hotspringspool.com. 107 units. Mid-Mar to Sept and holidays $186–$314 double; rest of year $130–$289 double. Rates include continental breakfast. AE, DISC, MC, V. **Amenities:** Unlimited admission to the hot springs pool (see "Taking the Waters," above); basic business center; coin-op washers and dryers. *In room:* A/C, TV, wireless Internet access (free), coffeemaker, hair dryer, safe.

Hotel Colorado ★ The stately Hotel Colorado, constructed of sandstone and Roman brick in 1893, was modeled after Italy's Villa de Medici. Among the most impressive Western hotels of its day, it attracted all the VIPs of the era. Two American presidents—William Howard Taft and Theodore Roosevelt—spoke to crowds gathered beneath the orators' balcony here. There are claims (disputed by some) that this is the birthplace of the teddy bear: Roosevelt allegedly returned to the hotel disappointed in May 1905 after an unsuccessful bear hunt, so maids crafted him a small bear from scraps of cloth, and the president's daughter Alyce named it Teddy. The attractive guest rooms are individually decorated, most with firm double beds and the usual hotel furnishings; suites are more spacious, with upgraded decor and period antiques. Two bell-tower suites, reached by stairs only, have double Jacuzzis and private balconies, as well as private staircases into the bell towers, where 19th-century graffiti can still be deciphered.

526 Pine St., Glenwood Springs, CO 81601. ✆ **800/544-3998** or 970/945-6511. Fax 970/945-5437. www.hotelcolorado.com. 126 units. $164–$199 double; $209–$725 suite. AE, DISC, MC, V. Pets accepted with a $15 fee. **Amenities:** Restaurant; bar; exercise room; spa; massage. *In room:* TV, wireless Internet access (free), coffeemaker, hair dryer, iron.

Moderate

Four Mile Creek Bed & Breakfast ★★ The historic log home was the headquarters of the Four Mile Ranch, homesteaded in 1885 and listed on the National Registry of Historic Places, and the surrounding grounds boast aspen groves and gardens of herbs and flowers, a handsome red barn-turned-theater built in 1919, and a variety of animals, including llamas and goats. In the main log house is a cozy living room with an imposing rock fireplace and an inviting sunroom overlooking the creek. The two rooms in the main house share a bathroom: The Blackbird Room has wrought-iron blackbirds perched on the queen bed and elegant furnishings; the nearby Star Room sets a totally different mood, with whimsical folk art and celestial symbols. The two cabins, with kitchens and private bathrooms, can accommodate up to four persons each. The charming Creekside Cabin is so named because Four Mile Creek gurgles by right outside.

6471 C.R. 117, Glenwood Springs, CO 81601. ✆ **970/945-4004.** Fax 970/945-2820. www.fourmilecreek.com. 4 units, 2 with private bathroom. Room $85–$95 double with shared bath; cabin $140–$160 (up to 4 people). Rates include evening refreshments and full breakfast. AE, MC, V. *In room:* Wireless Internet access (free); no phone.

Inexpensive

Glenwood Springs Hostel ★ Full of personality, this brightly painted and recently renovated Victorian house has been one of the best hostels in the Rockies for 2 decades. There are a large record library (2,000 meticulously organized albums) and two fully equipped kitchens for guests' use. Like most hostels, there are dormitory bunks, common toilets and showers, guest laundry, and other common areas. Linens are available ($2), and it's just a 5-minute walk from the train and bus. The individual rooms are great for couples and others who prefer more privacy, although they still share bathrooms.

1021 Grand Ave., Glenwood Springs, CO 81601. ✆ **800/946-7835** or 970/945-8545. www.hostelcolorado.com. 42 beds, including dorm and 5 private rooms. Dorms $16 per person per night (or $48 for 4 nights); private rooms $25 single, $33 double. No private bathrooms. Rates include tax. AE, MC, V. *In room:* Wireless Internet access (free), no phone.

Red Mountain Inn (Value) This cheery motel lives up to its advertising as "Glenwood's best value." Rooms are spacious, with better-than-average lighting, firm mattresses, and comfortable seating. Some have 10-foot ceilings. The dozen cabins are essentially larger motel units, with separate bedrooms and room for up to eight, plus complete kitchens. Some cabins have fireplaces, while a few have private patios with picnic tables. There's a delightful shaded grassy picnic area away from the road, and several restaurants and a miniature golf course are within easy walking distance.

51637 U.S. 6 and U.S. 24, Glenwood Springs, CO 81601. ✆ **800/748-2565** or 970/945-6353. www.redmountaininn.com. 40 units. Summer $89–$117 motel units, $118–$235 cabins; winter $62–$82 motel units, $89–$175 cabins. Holiday rates higher. AE, DISC, MC, V. On I-70 north Frontage Rd. btw. exits 114 and 116. Pets accepted with a $10 fee. **Amenities:** Outdoor heated pool (seasonal); outdoor hot tub (year-round); coin-op laundry. *In room:* A/C, cable TV, wireless Internet access (free), kitchen.

WHERE TO STAY IN NEARBY REDSTONE

Crystal Dreams Bed & Breakfast and Spa ★★ Located about 30 miles south of Glenwood Springs in the picturesque community of Redstone, this delightful B&B is the perfect spot for a romantic getaway or a base for exploring the mountains and streams in the surrounding White River National Forest—there's even fly-fishing right out the back door. The handsome house, built in country Victorian style in 1994, sits along the banks of the Crystal River, with splendid views of nearby red-rock cliffs and Elk Mountain. The three guest rooms are decorated in Victorian style, with Western touches such as the "twig" bed—the headboard and footboard are made of tree branches. I like the Mount Casa Room, named for its fine mountain view, with a queen bed, a separate twin bed, and a bathroom with a large shower.

0475 Redstone Blvd., Redstone, CO 81623. ✆ **970/963-8240.** www.crystaldreamsgetaway.com. 3 units. May–Oct $130 double Fri–Sun and holidays, $120 double Mon–Thurs; Nov–Apr $115 double. Rates include full breakfast. 2-night minimum weekends June–Oct. No credit cards. Suitable for children 13 and older. **Amenities:** Spa. *In room:* Wireless Internet access (free), no phone.

The Bayou CAJUN/CREOLE This delightful New Orleans–style eatery might not be the best choice for those who take themselves very seriously, but if you're looking for a good time along with excellent food, the Bayou is a solid choice. Located in a historic building in downtown Glenwood Springs, the decor is fun and funky, with harlequin masks on the walls. Come for Cajun cuisine—such as seafood gumbo, chicken étouffée, or swamp and moo (redfish and rib-eye)—and stay for the staff-provided entertainment, including "dumb server tricks" and the Frog Leg Revue. The Bayou has the largest selection of hot sauces in the valley, from "spicy" to "hurt me." There are also a few vegetarian dishes.

919 Grand Ave. ✆ **970/945-1047.** Main courses $7–$20. AE, DISC, MC, V. Sun–Thurs 4–10pm; Fri–Sat 4pm–11pm.

Daily Bread Cafe & Bakery CAFE/BAKERY Try not to be in a hurry when you go to the Daily Bread—the service isn't slow, but this is such a popular spot that you're likely to find yourself waiting behind a line of locals for your table or booth. Decor here is strictly American cafe: storefront windows with lace curtains, a high ceiling, oak floor, and local art on the walls. For breakfast you might try one of the many egg dishes, such as Terry's Delight (an English muffin topped with eggs, shaved ham, and melted cheese) or perhaps the healthful Fresh Fruit Special (a half cantaloupe stuffed with fresh fruit, covered with fat-free vanilla yogurt and granola). The lunch menu lists dozens of sandwiches, burgers, and salads.

729 Grand Ave. ✆ **970/945-6253.** Main courses $4–$12. MC, V. Mon–Sat 7am–2pm; Sun 7am–noon.

Glenwood Canyon Brewing Company ★ BREWPUB A varied and interesting menu along with some really good beer makes this a good spot for a hearty lunch or dinner. The decor is standard brewpub: brick walls, historic photos, wood tables, TVs with sporting events, and a view of the brewing equipment. The lunch menu, also available at dinner, includes a selection of half-pound burgers, sandwiches (such as a hot smoked-turkey Philly), salads, pasta, and bread bowls filled with soup or stew. Dinner entrees are a bit more elaborate and include fresh fish, baby back ribs, and chicken enchiladas. There are usually eight handcrafted beers on tap—I would suggest the Red Mountain ESB—and half-gallon growler jugs are available for takeout. The brewpub also has regulation-size billiards tables.

402 Seventh St. (in the Hotel Denver). ✆ **970/945-1276.** www.glenwoodcanyon.com. Main courses $7.50–$22. AE, MC, V. Daily 11am–10pm. Bar open later.

Italian Underground ★ **Value** ITALIAN A favorite of locals, the Italian Underground offers good Italian food at excellent prices. Get here early and expect to wait, especially on weekends. Located in a basement along busy Grand Avenue, the restaurant has stone walls, brick floors, red-and-white-checkered tablecloths, candlelight, and exceedingly generous portions of fine food. Try the lasagna, linguine with pesto, or spaghetti with tomato and basil sauce. All entrees come with salad and bread—and ice cream. There's an excellent selection of Italian wines by the glass and a full bar; espresso and cappuccino are also served.

715 Grand Ave. ✆ **970/945-6422.** Reservations not accepted. Main courses $11–$15; pizzas $10–$16. AE, DISC, MC, V. Daily 5–10pm.

Riviera ★★ CONTEMPORARY/ECLECTIC Reopening in early 2006 in a space long defined by its unmistakable neon sign, the Riviera has been reinvented under the guidance of owner Colleen Stuart. The creative design, featuring original contemporary art, blond wood, and a picture window looking out to the green riverbank of the Colorado, is a good match for the inventive fare. My appetizer of choice was the crisp and creamy *spanakopita* (spinach pastry); the house salad with bacon and gorgonzola is another dazzler. Entrees include shrimp with gnocchi, steaks, and a wide range of changing specialties. There is a full bar.

702 Grand Ave. ✆ **970/945-7692.** Reservations recommended. Main courses $16–$28. AE, MC, V. Sun–Thurs 5–9:30pm; Fri–Sat 5–10pm.

3 MONTROSE: GATEWAY TO THE BLACK CANYON

61 miles S of Grand Junction, 108 miles N of Durango

Although at first glance this quiet city of about 16,000 residents is little more than a commercial center for area ranchers and farmers, Montrose is rapidly being discovered as an ideal base camp for hikers, mountain bikers, anglers, and others who want to explore western Colorado. Located at an elevation of 5,794 feet, Montrose is surrounded by national forests, within a short drive of Black Canyon of the Gunnison National Park and Curecanti National Recreation Area.

Ute Chief Ouray and his wife, Chipeta, ranched in the Uncompahgre Valley here until the government forced the tribe to migrate to Utah in 1881. Once the Utes were gone, settlers founded the town of Pomona, named for the Roman goddess of fruit. Later the town's name was changed to Montrose, for a character in a Sir Walter Scott novel. The railroad arrived in 1882, providing relatively reliable transportation and a means to ship out potatoes, beets, and other crops; and Montrose began in earnest its role as a center for some of Colorado's major food producers, a role it still plays today.

ESSENTIALS

GETTING THERE **By Car** Montrose is an hour's drive southeast of Grand Junction via U.S. 50, a 2½-hour drive north of Durango via U.S. 550, and a 5½-hour drive west of Colorado Springs via U.S. 50 through Salida and Gunnison.

By Plane The **Montrose Regional Airport,** 2100 Airport Rd. (✆ **970/249-3203;** www.co.montrose.co.us), is off U.S. 50, 2 miles northwest of town. Regional airlines serving the town include **American** (✆ 800/433-7300), **Continental** (✆ 800/525-0280), **Delta** (✆ 800/221-1212), and **United** (✆ 800/241-6522).

GETTING AROUND Montrose lies along the east bank of the Uncompahgre River. Townsend Avenue (U.S. 50 and U.S. 550) parallels the stream; Main Street (U.S. 50 and Colo. 90) crosses Townsend in the center of town. Numbered streets extend north and south from Main.

Montrose Taxi (✆ **970/275-8965**) provides local cab service. Car-rental agencies with outlets at the airport include **Dollar** (✆ 970/249-3770), **Hertz** (✆ 970/240-8464), **National** (✆ 970/252-8898), and **Thrifty** (✆ 970/249-8741).

VISITOR INFORMATION Contact or stop at the **Montrose Visitors and Convention Bureau,** 1519 E. Main St. (P.O. Box 335), Montrose, CO 81402 (✆ **800/873-0244** or 970/252-0505; www.visitmontrose.net), or stop at the **visitor center** in the **Ute Indian Museum** (see "What to See & Do," below).

FAST FACTS **Montrose Memorial Hospital,** with a 24-hour emergency room, is at 800 S. Third St. (✆ **970/249-2211;** www.montrosehospital.com). The **post office** is at 321 S. First St. Call the U.S. Postal Service (✆ **800/275-8777;** www.usps.com) for hours and other information. For **road conditions,** call ✆ **970/249-6282.**

WHAT TO SEE & DO

Those wanting to step back into Montrose's past should ask at the visitor center, Visitors and Convention Bureau, or city hall (433 S. First St.) for a free copy of the self-guided **Historic Montrose Downtown Walking Tour** brochure. It contains a map to help you locate numerous historic buildings and interpretative signs.

Montrose County Historical Museum Pioneer life in western Colorado is highlighted at this museum, housed in a historic Denver & Rio Grande Railroad Western Depot. The museum features a furnished 1890s homesteader's cabin, a log cowboy cabin, railroad memorabilia including a Union Pacific caboose, farm equipment, antique dolls and toys, old musical instruments, a country store, and American Indian artifacts. Historical photos and Montrose newspapers from 1896 to 1940 depict the town's history. Allow at least an hour.

21 N. Rio Grande Ave. ✆ **970/249-2085.** Admission $6 adults, $4 seniors over 55, $2 students. Mid-May through early Oct Mon–Sat 10am–4pm.

Ute Indian Museum ★ Located on the site of the final residence of southern Ute Chief Ouray and his wife, Chipeta, the Ute Indian Museum offers one of Colorado's most complete exhibitions of Ute traditional and ceremonial artifacts, including clothing, baskets, and household items. Several dioramas depict mid-19th-century lifestyles, and historic photos are displayed. Also on the grounds are Chipeta's grave, bubbling Ouray Springs, a native-plant garden, and an outdoor display on Spanish explorers who passed this way in 1776. The museum sponsors various festivals and programs throughout the year (call for details). It also has a store that specializes in Ute pottery and other handcrafted American Indian arts and crafts, and houses the Montrose Visitor Center. Allow about 1½ hours.

17253 Chipeta Dr. ✆ **970/249-3098.** www.coloradohistory.org. Admission $3.50 adults, $3 seniors over 65, $1.50 children 6–16, free for children 5 and under. Located 3 miles south of downtown at the intersection of U.S. 550 and Chipeta Dr. Mid-May to mid-Oct Mon–Sat 9am–4:30pm, Sun 11am–4:30pm; mid-Oct to mid-May Mon–Sat 8:30am–5pm.

SPORTS & OUTDOOR ACTIVITIES

In addition to boating and other outdoor recreational activities available in Black Canyon of the Gunnison National Park (discussed below) and nearby Curecanti National Recreation Area (see "Gunnison & Curecanti National Recreation Area," in chapter 14), there are plenty of opportunities for hiking, mountain biking, horseback riding, off-roading, fishing, camping, cross-country skiing, and snowmobiling on other federal lands in the area. Information is available at the **Public Lands Center,** 2505 S. Townsend Ave. (✆ **970/240-5300**). For camping and fishing gear, bike rentals and repairs, outdoor clothing, and other outdoor recreation items and sporting goods, stop at **Jeans Westerner,** 147 N. Townsend Ave. (✆ **970/249-3600;** www.jeanswesterner.com), with the entrance to its bike facilities around back at 120 N. Selig Ave.

BIKING There are more than 9 miles of paved off-street walking and biking trails in Montrose, plus numerous areas for mountain biking in nearby lands administered by the U.S. Forest Service and Bureau of Land Management. A free map of **city trails** is available at the visitor center; stop at the Public Lands Center (see above) for information on where to ride on Bureau of Land Management and Forest Service lands. You can also obtain maps, information, bike repairs, and accessories at **Cascade Bicycles,** 21 N. Cascade Ave. (✆ **970/249-7375**), and **Jeans Westerner** (see intro to this section, above), which also rents basic mountain bikes at $29 per day.

The Tabeguache Trail—which runs 142 miles from Shavano Valley near Montrose to No Thoroughfare Canyon near the Colorado National Monument west of Grand Junction—is a popular and challenging route for mountain bikers. For information, contact the **Colorado Plateau Mountain-Bike Trail Association,** P.O. Box 4602, Grand Junction, CO 81502 (✆ **970/244-8877;** www.copmoba.org). Bikers can also use the **Uncompahgre RiverWay;** it's eventually scheduled to connect Montrose with Delta (21 miles north) and Ouray (37 miles south).

FISHING For starters, you can drop a line into the Uncompahgre River from **Riverbottom Park,** reached via Apollo Road off Rio Grande Avenue. Most anglers seek rainbow trout here and at **Chipeta Lake,** behind the Ute Indian Museum, south of Montrose. About 20 miles east via U.S. 50 is the Gunnison River, which produces trophy-class brown and rainbow trout.

GOLF The 18-hole **Black Canyon Golf Club,** 1350 Birch St. (✆ **970/249-4653**), is open year-round, weather permitting. Greens fees are $22 to $30 for 18 holes. The **Links at Cobble Creek,** 669 Cobble Dr., off Chipeta Drive (✆ **970/240-9542**), is another 18-hole course with fees of $35 to $37 for 18 holes.

HIKING The best hiking in the area is in the **Black Canyon of the Gunnison National Park** (p. 360), but there are also paved paths in town (see "Biking," above) and plenty of trails on nearby national forest and Bureau of Land Management parklands. These include the 4.5-mile Ute Trail along the Gunnison River, 20 miles northeast of Montrose; and the 17-mile Alpine Trail from Silver Jack Reservoir in Uncompahgre National Forest, 35 miles southeast of Montrose via Cimarron on U.S. 50. Contact the Public Lands Center (see above) for information.

WHERE TO STAY

Chains include a **Best Western Red Arrow Motor Inn,** 1702 E. Main St. (✆ **800/468-9323** or 970/249-9641), with rates for two from $65 to $130; **Comfort Inn,** 2100 E. Main St. (✆ **800/424-6423** or 970/240-8000), with double rates from $69 to $129; **Holiday Inn Express Hotel & Suites,** 1391 S. Townsend Ave. (✆ **800/550-9252** or 970/240-1800), with rates for two from $129 to $139; and **Quality Inn & Suites,** 2751 Commercial Way (✆ **800/424-6423** or 970/249-1011), with double rates from $79 to $139. Rates here are usually highest in July and August, and lowest November through April. Room tax is about 8.5%.

Country Lodge (Value) A well-kept mom-and-pop motel with reasonable rates and an unexpectedly quiet setting is what you'll find at Country Lodge. Rooms vary, from two double beds in a cozy standard room to a larger kitchenette, to a three-bedroom cabin, and several options in between, including king and queen units. The rooms are attractively furnished with quilts and plenty of woodsy charm. The courtyard pool and hot tub are perfect for hot summer days.

1624 E. Main St., Montrose, CO 81401. ✆ **970/249-4567.** Fax 970/249-3082. www.coundtryldg.com. 22 units. Summer $85–$95 double; off-season $50–$65 double. Rates include continental breakfast. MC, V. **Amenities:** Outdoor pool and hot tub. *In room:* Cable TV, wireless Internet access (free), fridge, kitchen.

CAMPING

In addition to the campgrounds in Black Canyon of the Gunnison National Park discussed below, I recommend the **Hangin' Tree R.V. Park** at 17250 U.S. 550 S. (✆ **970/252-7191**), with rates from $18 (tent) to $21 (RVs). Conveniently located within walking distance of Chipeta Lakes and open year-round, the Hangin' Tree has a store and very clean bathhouses.

DINING

A good bet for those seeking groceries, deli sandwiches, a bakery, or a pharmacy is one of the two **City Market** grocery stores in Montrose. There's one at 16400 S. Townsend Ave. (✆ **970/249-3236**), which is open daily from 5am to 11pm; and another at 128 S. Townsend Ave. (✆ **970/249-3405**). For a sit-down breakfast or lunch, try the **Daily Bread Bakery,** 346 E. Main St. (✆ **970/249-8444**), a diner that dishes up good breakfast burritos, French toast, and lunch specials. Come dinner, the Montrose location of Gunnison standby **Garlic Mike's,** 103 Rose Lane (✆ **970/249-4381**), is an excellent Italian restaurant.

4 THE BLACK CANYON OF THE GUNNISON

The **Black Canyon of the Gunnison ★★**, which had been a national monument since 1933, became a national park on October 21, 1999. In a statement issued after the bill-signing ceremony, President Bill Clinton called the Black Canyon a "true natural treasure" and added, "Its nearly vertical walls, rising a half-mile high, harbor one of the most spectacular stretches of wild river in America."

The canyon was avoided by early American Indians and later Utes and Anglo explorers, who believed that no human could survive a trip to its depths. The entire thing measures 48 miles long, and the 14 miles that are included in the national park (which, at 30,385 acres, is among America's smallest) range in depth from 1,730 to 2,700 feet. Its width at the narrowest point (cleverly called "the Narrows") is only 40 feet. This deep slash in the earth was created by 2 million years of erosion, a process that's still going on—albeit slowed by the damming of the Gunnison River above the park.

Most visitors view the canyon from the South Rim Road, site of the visitor center, or the lesser-used North Rim Road. Short paths branching off both roads lead to splendid viewpoints with signs explaining the canyon's unique geology.

The park also has hiking trails along both rims, backcountry-hiking routes down into the canyon, and excellent trout fishing for ambitious anglers willing to make the trek to the canyon floor. It also provides an abundance of thrills for the experienced rock climbers who challenge its sheer canyon walls. In winter, much of the park is closed to motor vehicles, but that only makes for a peaceful delight for cross-country skiers and snowshoers.

The Black Canyon shares a portion of its south boundary with Curecanti National Recreation Area (p. 404), which offers boating and fishing on three reservoirs, as well as hiking and camping.

FAST FACTS

Entry Points

The park is located northeast of Montrose. To reach the south rim, head east on U.S. 50 for 8 miles to the well-marked turnoff to the entrance, where you will turn north (left)

Impressions

No other canyon in North America combines the depth, narrowness, sheerness, and somber countenance of the Black Canyon.

—Wallace Hansen, geologist who mapped the canyon in the 1950s

onto Colo. 347 for 6 miles. To reach the north rim from Montrose, drive north 21 miles on U.S. 50 to Delta, east 31 miles on Colo. 92 to Crawford, then south on the 11-mile access road.

Fees & Regulations

Admission for up to 7 days costs $15 per vehicle or $7 for those on foot or two wheels. Required backcountry permits are free. Visitors are warned not to throw anything from the rim into the canyon, since even a single small stone thrown or kicked from the rim could be fatal to people below; and to supervise children very carefully because many sections of the rim have no guardrails or fences. Unlike at many national parks, leashed pets are permitted on several trails (check with rangers), but they are specifically prohibited from wilderness areas.

Visitor Centers & Information

The **South Rim Visitor Center** is open daily year-round, except winter federal holidays, with hours from 8am to 6pm in summer and from 8:30am to 4pm the rest of the year. For information on both the national park and the adjacent Curecanti National Recreation Area (discussed in chapter 14, "The Southern Rockies"), contact **Black Canyon of the Gunnison National Park/Curecanti National Recreation Area,** Park Headquarters, 102 Elk Creek, Gunnison, CO 81230 (✆ **970/641-2337;** www.nps.gov/blca).

Seasons

Temperatures and weather conditions often vary greatly between the canyon rim and the canyon floor, and it gets progressively hotter as you descend into the canyon. Average summer temperatures range from highs of 60° to 100°F (16°–38°C), with summer lows dropping to 30° to 50°F (–1° to –10°C). During winter, highs range from 20° to 40°F (–7°C to –4°C), with lows from –10° to 20°F (–23° to –7°C). Brief afternoon thunderstorms are fairly common in the summer. The South Rim Road usually remains open to the visitor center through the winter, but the North Rim Road is often closed by snow between December and March. The elevation at the South Rim Campground is 8,320 feet.

Ranger Programs

Ranger-conducted **nature walks, geology talks,** and **astronomy programs** are presented daily from Memorial Day through late September on the South Rim. (A schedule is posted at the visitor center.) During the winter, guided **snowshoe walks** and **cross-country ski tours** are sometimes offered on the South Rim. (Stop at the visitor center or call ahead for information and reservations.)

Seeing the Highlights

It's fairly easy to see a great deal here in a short amount of time, especially if you stick to the South Rim. First stop at the visitor center to see the exhibits and get an understanding of how this phenomenal canyon was created. Then drive the 7-mile (one-way) **South Rim Drive,** stopping at the overlooks. There are about a dozen overlooks along the drive, and in most cases you'll be walking from 140 feet to about 700 feet to reach the viewpoints from your vehicle. Among the not-to-be-missed overlooks are **Gunnison Point,** behind the visitor center, which offers stunning views of the seemingly endless walls of dark rock; and the **Pulpit Rock Overlook,** which provides a splendid view of the rock walls and about 1½ miles of the Gunnison River, some 1,770 feet down. Farther along the drive is **Chasm View,** where you can see the incredible power of water, which here cuts through over 1,800 feet of solid rock. Near the end of the drive, be sure to stop at **Sunset View,** where there's a picnic area and a short (140-ft.) walk to a viewpoint, which offers distant views beyond the canyon, as well as of the river, now 2,430 feet below your feet. And if your timing is right, you might be treated to a classic Western sunset, in all its red and orange glory. Finally, take off on one of the **rim hiking trails,** such as the easy Cedar Point Nature Trail or the somewhat more challenging Warner Point Nature Trail (see "Hiking & Backpacking," below). If you'll be camping in the park or staying nearby, you might plan to attend the evening ranger program.

SPORTS & OUTDOOR ACTIVITIES

CLIMBING The sheer vertical walls and scenic beauty of the Black Canyon make it an ideal and popular destination for rock climbers, but—and this cannot be emphasized too strongly—this is no place for on-the-job training. These cliffs, known for crumbling rock, dizzying heights, and very few places to put protective gear, require a great deal of experience and the best equipment. Free permits are required, but prospective climbers should discuss their plans first with park rangers.

FISHING Dedicated anglers can make their way to the Gunnison River at the bottom of the canyon in a quest for brown and rainbow trout. The Gunnison within the park has been designated as Gold Medal Waters. Only artificial lures are permitted, and other special rules apply (check with park rangers). A Colorado fishing license is required.

HIKING & BACKPACKING Trails on the park's rims range from short, easy walks to moderate-to-strenuous hikes of several miles. Hiking below the rim is mostly difficult and not recommended for those with a fear of heights. Permits are not needed for hiking rim trails, but are required for all treks below the rim.

Trails along the **South Rim** include the easy **Cedar Point Nature Trail.** From the Cedar Point trail head, along South Rim Road, this .7-mile round-trip walk has signs along the way describing the plants you'll see and provides breathtaking views of the Gunnison River, 2,000 feet down, at the end. The moderately rated **Rim Rock Nature Trail,** which is 1 mile round-trip, is accessed near the entrance to the campground's Loop C. Following the rim along a relatively flat path, this trail leads to an overlook, providing good views of the Gunnison River and the canyon's sheer rock walls. A pamphlet available at the trail head describes geology, plant life, and other points of interest.

The moderate **Warner Point Nature Trail** begins at High Point Overlook at the end of South Rim Road. It's 1.5 miles round-trip and offers a multitude of things to see, from flora such as mountain mahogany, piñon pine, and Utah juniper, to distant mountains and valleys, as well as the Black Canyon and its creator, the Gunnison River. A trail guide is available at the trail head. The trail head for the 2-mile round-trip **Oak Flat Loop Trail,** rated moderate to strenuous, is near the visitor center. Dropping slightly below the rim, this trail offers excellent views into the canyon, while also taking you through a grove of aspen, past Gambel oak, and finally through a forest of aspen, Gambel oak, and Douglas fir. Be aware that the trail is narrow in spots and a bit close to steep drop-offs.

Trails along the **North Rim** include the moderate **Chasm View Nature Trail** (.3 miles, round-trip), with a trail head at the end of the North Rim campground loop. Beginning in a piñon-juniper forest, this trail heads to the rim for good views of the canyon and the river; you'll also have a good chance of seeing swallows, swifts, and raptors here.

A longer North Rim trail is the 5-mile round-trip **Deadhorse Trail,** rated easy to moderate, which begins at the Kneeling Camel Overlook. Actually an old service road, this trail offers a good chance of seeing various birds, plus views of Deadhorse Gulch and the East Portal area at the southeast end of the park. The 7-mile **North Vista Trail,** which begins at the North Rim Ranger Station, is moderate to strenuous. It offers some of the best views into the Black Canyon and also rewards hikers with a good chance of seeing such birds as red-tailed hawks, white-throated swifts, Clark's nutcrackers, and ravens.

Experienced **backcountry hikers** in excellent physical condition may want to hike down into the canyon. Although there are no maintained or marked trails, there are several routes that rangers can help you find. Free permits are required. There are also a limited number of campsites available for backpackers. The most popular inner canyon hike is the strenuous **Gunnison Route,** which branches off the South Rim's Oak Flat Trail and heads down to the river. Eighty feet of chain help keep you from falling on a stretch about a third of the way down. This hike has a vertical drop of 1,800 feet and takes 4 to 5 hours.

WATERSPORTS Although the river may look tempting, my advice for watersports enthusiasts is: **Don't do it!** The Gunnison River through the park is **extremely dangerous,** for both swimmers and rafters. (It's considered **unraftable.**) There are sections of the river west of the park that are more suitable; information is available from the **Public Lands Center,** 2505 S. Townsend Ave., Montrose, CO 81401 (✆ **970/240-5300**). The only exception is for **experienced kayakers,** who find the river an exhilarating challenge. Free permits are required.

WILDLIFE VIEWING The park is home to a variety of wildlife, and you're likely to see chipmunks, ground squirrels, badgers, marmots, and mule deer. Although not frequently seen, there are also black bears, cougars, and bobcats; and you'll probably hear the lonesome high-pitched call of coyotes at night. Peregrine falcons can sometimes be spotted along the cliffs, and you may also see red-tailed hawks, turkey vultures, golden eagles, and white-throated swifts.

WINTER SPORTS When the South Rim Road is closed by winter snows, the park service plows only to the South Rim Visitor Center, leaving the road a perfect cross-country ski trail. There are also several areas in the park that are good for snowshoeing; get directions at the visitor center.

CAMPING

There are campgrounds on both rims, with pit toilets and no showers, but there are electric hookups available on Loop B of South Rim Campground. Cost per site is $12, $18 with electric hookups. The **South Rim Campground,** which is open year-round and is rarely full, has 88 sites, but the **North Rim Campground,** open from spring through fall and with only 13 sites, only occasionally fills up. Reservations can be made for some sites in the South Rim Campground from late May through early September through the park website or **www.recreation.gov**, or by phone (✆ **877/444-6777**).

5 PAONIA: COLORADO'S FRUIT COUNTRY

69 miles SE of Grand Junction, 51 miles NE of Montrose

Named by founder Samuel Wade for the Latin spelling of the peony flower, Paonia is enjoying a renaissance in recent years thanks to an enviable location in a fertile valley surrounded by a rugged mountain wilderness. Lined with trees and surrounded by orchards in the picturesque North Fork Valley, Paonia was settled by white pioneers who pushed out the Ute Indians in 1881. The economy has long been based almost exclusively on agriculture and coal mining, but it has grown increasingly diverse as young people priced out of the exclusive real-estate markets in the nearby resort towns have made Paonia their home in recent years. Today downtown Paonia is a vibrant place (the environmental-oriented publication *High Country News* calls it home, as do a number of interesting retailers), and easy access to outdoor recreation and a mild climate continue to attract newcomers. Tourism has also been growing, with the emergence of "agritourism" proving an especially good fit here.

ESSENTIALS

GETTING THERE **By Car** Paonia is an 1½-hour drive southeast of Grand Junction via U.S. 50 and Colo. 92 and Colo. 133, a 2½-hour drive north of Durango via U.S. 550 and Colo. 92 and Colo. 133, and a 4½-hour drive southwest of Colorado Springs via I-70 and other highways through Glenwood Springs and Redstone.

By Plane The closest airports with commercial service are in Montrose and Grand Junction (see above).

GETTING AROUND Paonia is situated on Colorado's shortest state highway, Colo. 187, which becomes Grand Avenue downtown, just south of Colo. 133 between Hotchkiss and Somerset. It's a relatively small town, with the 2-block downtown centered on 2nd Street and Grand Avenue.

VISITOR INFORMATION Contact the **Paonia Chamber of Commerce,** P.O. Box 366, Paonia, CO 81428 (✆ **970/527-3886;** www.paoniachamber.com). **Delta County Tourism** (✆ **970/874-2100;** www.westerncolorado.org) is another good resource for the area.

FAST FACTS **Delta County Memorial Hospital,** with a 24-hour emergency room, is at 1501 E. Third St. in Delta, 30 miles west of Paonia (✆ **970/874-7681;** www.deltahospital.com). The **post office** is at 125 Grand Ave. Call the U.S. Postal Service (✆ **800/275-8777;** www.usps.com) for hours and other information.

WHAT TO SEE & DO

There are three big draws for tourists in the Paonia area: fruit and farming, wine and wineries, and the outdoors. Of the first one, a great destination is **Delicious Orchards,** on Colo. 133 just west of Paonia (✆ **970/527-1110**), a combination market/farm with 16 acres of orchards where visitors can go out and pick their own fruit, including apricots, nectarines, pears, and apples, or shop the aisles for locally grown produce and other regional products. The store is the retail face of a locally produced brand of juice, Big B's, and the best place to try some. There is also local wine to be tasted and other locally made products. For more information on Delicious and the rest of the valley's farms—a good many of which welcome visitors—a useful resource is the **Valley Organic Growers Association**

Directory. Contact the association (www.vogaco.org) or the chamber (see above) for more information.

As far as the vino, there are about 10 wineries in Paonia and Hotchkiss, including **Terror Creek Winery,** 17445 Garvin Mesa Rd., Paonia (✆ **970/527-3484**), with daily tastings in summer 11am to 5pm; **Stone Cottage Cellars,** 41716 Reds Rd. (✆ **970/527-3444;** www.stonecottagecellars.com), with daily tours and tastings 11am to 6pm Memorial Day through October; and **Leroux Creek Vineyards,** 12388 3100 Rd., Hotchkiss (✆ **970/872-4746;** www.lerouxcreekvineyards.com), a winery with a bed-and-breakfast on-site and tasting-room hours of 11am to 5pm from May through November. For a full list of all wineries in Paonia and adjacent communities, contact the **Colorado Wine Industry Development Board** (✆ **720/304-3406;** www.coloradowine.org).

SPORTS & OUTDOOR ACTIVITIES

Contact the Paonia Ranger District of the **Gunnison National Forest,** 423 N. Rio Grande Ave. (✆ **970/527-4131**) for additional information on outdoor recreation in the area.

HIKING Some of the best hiking in the area is on the north rim of the **Black Canyon of the Gunnison National Park** (p. 360), but there are also canal-side paths in town and plenty of trails on nearby national forest and other public lands. A good trail for a day hike is the Inter-Ocean Pass Trail, a moderate to strenuous 8-mile round-trip hike that gains 2,500 feet in altitude. Contact the Paonia Ranger District (see above) for information.

FISHING & BOATING The North Fork of the Gunnison River is the favored destination for anglers as well as tubers and paddlers. Contact the Paonia Ranger District (see above) for information.

GOLF Set amidst the stark landscape of high desert badlands, the acclaimed **Devil's Thumb Golf Club,** 30 miles west of Paonia in Delta (✆ **970/874-6262;** www.deltagolf.org), charges $35 to $42 for 18 holes and $18 to $22 for 9 holes.

WHERE TO STAY

The **Rocky Mountain Inn,** 304 Niagara Ave. (✆ **970/527-0300**), is a clean, well-maintained mom-and-pop motel right in town, with rates of $65 to $105 double. Some rooms have kitchens, and bike rentals are included in the rate.

Bross Hotel ★ The 1906 Bross Hotel has been nicely restored and has plenty of charm and historic ambiance. Perhaps it's too comfortable: Mother Bross's spirit is said to have checked in for a long stay in room 2. Just a block from downtown Paonia, the grand old building, with triple-thick brick walls, a balcony and porch with apt rockers, and vibrantly blooming gardens, offers small but serviceable rooms, featuring quilts, small private bathrooms, and antique furnishings.

312 Onarga Ave. (P.O. Box 85), Paonia, CO 81428. ✆ **970/527-6776.** www.paonia-inn.com. 10 units. $115–$125 double. Rates include full breakfast. MC, V. **Amenities:** Outdoor pool and hot tub. *In room:* Wireless Internet access (free).

Fresh and Wyld Farmhouse Inn B&B ★ Finds A century after it was built in 1908—and after stints as a farmhouse, B&B, and apartments—Dava Parr bought the blue two-story place on the outskirts of Paonia and turned it back into a one-of-a-kind B&B. With hammocks and swings and a trail leading to the top of nearby Jumbo Peak, the inn's pastoral setting a little over a mile from the center of town melts into farmland,

and Parr even tends a small plot on-site in partnership with the Kampe Foundation (www.kampefoundation.org), where she sources many ingredients for her scrumptious breakfasts, such as fingerling potatoes, squash, and even eggs from the adjacent coop. There are six guest rooms, all outfitted with quilts, rockers, organic cotton sheets, and other eco-friendly perks. The rooms in the farmhouse have whimsical names (Queen Beet, Broccoli Forest, Sunflower Honeycomb) and appropriately painted doors by a local artist. A former personal chef in Aspen, Parr also offers Saturday suppers and Sunday brunches for nonguests and a Wednesday cooking class ($60).

1978 Harding Rd., Paonia, CO 81428. ✆ **970/527-4389.** www.freshandwyld.com. 6 units. Summer $85–$95 double; off season $90–$125 double. Rates include continental breakfast. DISC, MC, V. **Amenities:** Massage. *In room:* Wireless Internet access (free), no phone.

WHERE TO DINE

For a pizza and a beer (and some local color), it's hard to beat **Louie's,** 202 Grand Ave. (✆ **970/527-3265**), with a pie-oriented menu—try the Border to Border (Canadian bacon and jalapeno)—that also features a wide range of calzones, salads, and sandwiches. The taps above the bar pour plenty of good microbrew from Colorado and beyond.

Flying Fork ★★ The best restaurant in the North Fork Valley, the Flying Fork is tucked around the corner from the main drag and a world away, its leafy entry leading to a big patio and a diminutive restaurant. The kitchen, under the direction of owner-chef Kelly Steinmetz, does a great job with pasta dishes like linguine with garlic, kalamata olives, Italian parsley, and extra-virgin olive oil; or gemelli with applewood-smoked chicken, basil pesto, sun-dried tomatoes, and fresh mozzarella. There are also steaks on the menu, as well as entrees like *antrata* (grilled duck with sweet mushroom marsala sauce and sautéed gnocchi), braised Colorado lamb shank, vegetarian lasagna, and a daily fresh fish special. Lunches are sandwiches and salads, and the attached bakery offers a wide array of baked goods.

3rd and Main sts. ✆ **970/527-3203.** www.flyingforkcafe.com. Reservations recommended. Main courses $6–$8 lunch, $8–$22 dinner. AE, DISC, MC, V. Tues–Sun 11:30am–2:30pm and 5:30–9pm. Closed Mon.

13 Southwestern Colorado

A land apart from the rest of the state, southwestern Colorado is set off by the spectacular mountain wall of the San Juan Range. The Ancestral Puebloans (also called the Anasazi) who once lived here created cliff dwellings that more closely resemble structures found in New Mexico and Arizona than anything you might expect to see in Colorado. The ancient cliff dwellings of Mesa Verde National Park are a case in point, and there are similar but less well-known sites throughout the area, primarily around Cortez.

Durango is the area's major city. Its vintage main street (ca. 1880) and narrow-gauge railroad hearken back to the Old West days of the late 19th century, when it boomed as a transportation center for the region's silver and gold mines. Telluride, at the end of a box canyon surrounded by 14,000-foot peaks, has capitalized on its still-evident mining heritage in its evolution into an increasingly posh ski and summer resort. And those who drive the Million Dollar Highway—down U.S. 550 from Ouray, over 11,008-foot Red Mountain Pass through Silverton, and on to Durango—can't miss the remains of turn-of-the-20th-century mines scattered over the mountainsides.

1 DURANGO

332 miles SW of Denver, 169 miles S of Grand Junction, 50 miles N of Farmington, New Mexico

Born as a railroad town more than a century ago, Durango remains a railroad town to this day, as thousands of visitors take a journey back in time aboard the Durango & Silverton Narrow Gauge Railroad. Durango was founded in 1880 when the Denver & Rio Grande Railroad line was extended to Silverton to haul precious metals from high-country mines. Within a year, 2,000 new residents had turned the town into a smelting and transportation center. Although more than $300 million worth of silver, gold, and other minerals rode along the route over the years, the unstable nature of the mining business gave the town many ups and downs. (One of the "ups" occurred in 1915, when southern Colorado boy Jack Dempsey, then 20, won $50 in a 10-round boxing match. Dempsey went on to become the world heavyweight champion.)

Durango remained a center for ranching and mining into the 1960s. In 1965, with the opening of the Purgatory ski resort (now Durango Mountain Resort), 25 miles north of Durango, a tourism boom began. When the railroad abandoned its tracks from Antonito, Colorado, to Durango in the late 1960s, leaving only the Durango–Silverton spur, the town panicked. But from that potential economic disaster blossomed a savior: The Durango & Silverton Narrow Gauge Railroad is now Durango's biggest attraction, hauling more than 200,000 passengers each summer. Durango also attracts mountain-biking enthusiasts from all over the country—in fact, opportunities abound for outdoor activities of all kinds, from river rafting to trout fishing.

ESSENTIALS

GETTING THERE **By Car** Durango is located at the crossroads of east–west U.S. 160 and north–south U.S. 550.

By Plane **Durango/La Plata County Airport,** 14 miles southeast of Durango off Colo. 172 (© **970/247-8143;** www.flydurango.com), has direct daily nonstop service from Denver, Salt Lake City, and Phoenix, with connections to cities throughout North America. The airport is served by **Delta** (© 800/221-1212), **Frontier** (© 800/432-1359), **United Express** (© 800/864-8331), and **U.S. Airways** (© 800/428-4322).

VISITOR INFORMATION Contact the **Durango Area Tourism Office,** 111 S. Camino del Rio, Durango, CO 81302 (© **800/463-8726;** www.durango.org). The **Durango Visitor Center** is just south of downtown, on U.S. 160/550. June through October, it's open Monday through Saturday from 8am to 5pm, and Sunday from 10am to 4pm; the rest of the year, hours are from 8am to 5pm Monday through Friday.

GETTING AROUND The city is on the banks of the Animas River. U.S. 160 lies along the southern edge and is joined by U.S. 550 about 5 miles east of Durango. Just before U.S. 160 crosses the river, U.S. 550 branches north as Camino del Rio and junctions with Main Avenue at 14th Street. Downtown Durango is built around Main Avenue from 14th Street south to Fifth Street. College Drive (Sixth St.) is the principal downtown cross street.

Transportation throughout Durango is provided by the **Durango Lift** (© **970/259-5438;** www.durangogov.org). The **city bus** has three fixed-route loops that operate weekdays, from about 7am to 7pm, year-round (but not on major public holidays), and there are also some evening schedules, including late-night transportation Friday and Saturday. The fare is $1 per ride one-way. Also part of the Durango Lift is the **Durango Trolley,** which runs along Main Avenue every 20 minutes, from 7am to 10:40pm in summer and until 7:40pm the rest of the year. Cost is 50¢. Bus and trolley schedules and route maps are available at the visitor center (see above), and all are fully accessible for travelers with limited mobility.

Taxi service is provided 24 hours a day by **Durango Transportation** (© 970/259-4818). Car-rental agencies include **Budget** (© 970/259-1841), **Dollar** (© 970/259-3012), **Enterprise** (© 970/385-8648), **Hertz** (© 970/247-5288), and **National** (© 970/259-0068).

FAST FACTS There's a 24-hour emergency room at **Mercy Regional Medical Center,** 1010 Three Springs Blvd. (© **800/345-2516** or 970/247-4311; www.mercydurango.org). The **post office** is at 3465 Main Ave.; contact the U.S. Postal Service (© **800/275-8777;** www.usps.com) for hours and additional information. For **road conditions** (winter only), call © **877/315-7623.**

SPECIAL EVENTS Snowdown Winter Festival, late January or early February; Iron Horse Bicycle Classic, Memorial Day weekend; Animas River Days, early June; Music in the Mountains, at Durango Mountain Resort, mid- to late July; La Plata County Fair, early August; the Main Avenue Arts Festival, mid-August; the Durango & Silverton Narrow Gauge Railroad Railfest, late August; the Durango Cowboy Gathering, late September or early October; and the Durango Christmas Tree Lighting Ceremony, November.

THE TOP ATTRACTION

The Durango & Silverton Narrow Gauge Railroad ★★★ Colorado's most famous train has been in continual operation since 1881. In all that time, its route has never varied: up the Río de las Animas Perdidas (River of Lost Souls), through 45 miles of mountain and San Juan National Forest wilderness to the historic mining town of Silverton, and back. The coal-fired steam locomotives pull strings of gold-colored Victorian

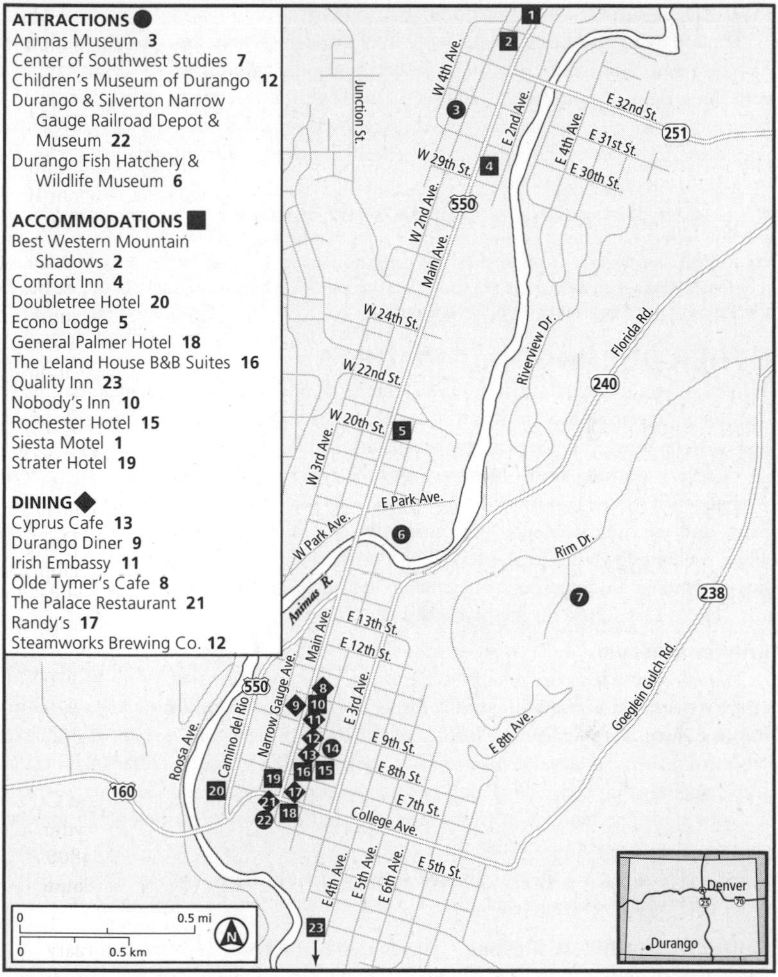

coaches on the 3,000-foot climb, past relics of mining and railroad activity from the last century.

A summer trip takes 3¼ hours each way, with a 2-hour stopover in the picturesque town of Silverton before the return trip. You can also overnight in Silverton and return to Durango the following day. (For information on what to see and do during your layover, see "A Side Trip to Silverton," later in this chapter.) Stops are made for water, and also for hikers and fishermen at remote trail heads inaccessible by road. Refreshments and snacks are available on all trains. Also available is Silver Vista Class, the opportunity to ride in a replica of a historic glass-domed pen-air gondola. The Alamosa Parlor Car, another special car, has a bar, and the most luxurious car is the Cinco Animas, which oozes Victorian splendor. Several private cars are available for charter, including an 1886 caboose and the 1878 *Nomad*—believed to be the oldest operating private railroad car in the world, host of U.S. presidents from Taft to Ford.

The summer schedule runs from early May through October, making the full trip to Silverton and back to Durango, with several trains daily during the peak season, from early June through mid-August, and fewer trains at other times. From the last week in November through early May (except Christmas), there's a daily train to Cascade Canyon and back, 52 miles round-trip. Call or check the website for information on special excursions and events.

479 Main Ave., Durango, CO 81301. ✆ **888/872-4607** or 970/247-2733. www.durangotrain.com. Advance reservations advised. Summer round-trip fare $75 adults, $45 children 5–11, $139 for the Vista Class car (minimum age 16), $139 for the parlor car (minimum age 21), $159 for the Cinco Animas (minimum age 21); winter round-trip fare $75 adults, $45 children 5–11. Bus rides available for either leg of the trip. Parking $7 per day per car, $9 for RVs and buses.

OTHER DURANGO HIGHLIGHTS

While taking a steam-train trip on the Durango & Silverton Narrow Gauge Railroad is undeniably the area's top attraction, there are other things to do here. Those interested in a close-up view of the city's numerous historic buildings will want to pick up free copies of several **walking-tour** brochures from the visitor center (see above). Along Main Avenue you'll see the handsome **Strater Hotel,** the building that housed the region's first bank, and the sites of saloons and other businesses of the late 1800s and early 1900s; while walking down Third Avenue you'll pass several stone churches and some of the finest homes in Durango from the same period, including the house where silent movie star Harold Lloyd lived during part of his childhood.

Animas Museum A 1904 stone schoolhouse in north Durango is the home of the La Plata County Historical Society museum, so it's appropriate that a turn-of-the-20th-century classroom is one of its central displays. The museum, which makes a good first stop for those interested in the history of the area, also contains a restored 1870s log cabin from the early days of Animas City, the town that predated Durango. There are also changing exhibits depicting local history, American Indians, and the American West. The museum shop has a good selection of new and used books on regional history and culture. Allow a minimum of 1 hour.

31st St. and W. Second Ave. ✆ **970/259-2402.** www.animasmuseum.org. Admission $3 adults, $1 children 7–12, free for children 6 and under. May–Oct Mon–Sat 10am–6pm; Nov–Apr Tues–Sat 10am–4pm.

Center of Southwest Studies This museum and research facility, located on the Fort Lewis College campus northeast of downtown Durango, contains a variety of Southwestern artifacts, including excellent exhibits of textiles, woven over 800 years by Navajo, Puebloan, and Hispanic weavers. Allow 45 minutes.

1000 Rim Dr., Fort Lewis College. ✆ **970/247-7494.** http://swcenter.fortlewis.edu. Free admission. Mon–Fri 1–4pm (until 7pm Thurs) and by appt.

Children's Museum of Durango (Kids) Hands-on activities for children from preschool through preteen make a nice break for vacationing kids who have seen a few too many Victorian homes. Parents stay with and supervise their children while the kids enjoy the changing exhibits, which might include a wood shop, mini grocery store, puppet theater, dress-up area, and a variety of physics demonstrations with items such as magnets and optical illusions. There are also computer games, arts and crafts, and an

Southwestern Colorado on the Silver Screen

This is John Wayne country, where the Duke slugged it out, shot it out, and sometimes yelled it out as he tamed the American West on movie screens from the late 1920s through the 1970s. This bigger-than-life symbol of American manhood made numerous films in and around Gunnison, Ridgway, Delta, Durango, and Pagosa Springs, where you can still find the exact spots certain scenes were filmed.

The classic, if bleak, 1956 John Ford film ***The Searchers,*** with Wayne, Jeffrey Hunter, Vera Miles, and Ward Bond, used a ranch near Gunnison as a military outpost. To reach the ranch, go north from Gunnison for 3 miles on Colo. 135, then turn left onto Ohio Creek Road and drive for about 8 miles, where you'll see a barn and several other buildings off to the left. Ford's later Western ***How the West Was Won*** (which, to the great disappointment of Wayne fans, didn't include the Duke) shows a wagon train crossing the Gunnison River west of Delta along 1800 Road, as well as scenes of the Durango & Silverton Narrow Gauge Railroad.

As real John Wayne aficionados know, in 1969 he teamed with Glen Campbell and Kim Darby to make one of his most famous films, ***True Grit.*** The town of Ridgway becomes Fort Smith in the movie, and nearby is the ranch where Wayne jumps his horse over a river. ***The Cowboys,*** filmed in 1972 outside Pagosa Springs, finds Wayne as a cattleman who hires a group of schoolboys to drive his herd of 1,500 cattle after the gold rush lures away his crew. There are several location shoots from this film in the area; ask for directions at the Pagosa Springs Chamber of Commerce.

But Wayne wasn't the only one shooting up Colorado's southwest corner. It also hosted ***City Slickers,*** the 1991 comedy starring Billy Crystal as a hapless city dweller on an Old West–style cattle drive. And several movie companies have made use of the classic Durango & Silverton Narrow Gauge Railroad. The best train scene on film has to be the one in the multi-Oscar-winning 1969 hit ***Butch Cassidy and the Sundance Kid,*** where Butch (Paul Newman), Sundance (Robert Redford), and their gang attempt to blow open the train's safe and instead blow up the entire mail car, sending money flying in all directions. Reportedly, the extent of this explosion was a surprise to everyone, even the special-effects technicians who apparently were a bit too liberal with their use of black powder. You can see the train at the depot at 479 Main Ave. in Durango, or in summer hop aboard for a ride to Silverton and back. There's a plaque commemorating the filming about 10 miles east of Durango; ask at the chamber of commerce for directions.

The **Colorado Film Commission,** 1625 Broadway, Ste. 950, Denver, CO 80202 (© **800/726-8887** or 303/592-4065; www.coloradofilm.org), works to bring filmmakers to the state and also has information for those who want to work in the film industry, possibly as extras, and others interested in movie production. The book *Hollywood in the Rockies,* by Frederic Wildfang, proprietor of Durango's Rochester Hotel, is widely available in town and is an excellent source for those who want to delve deeper into the area's film history.

archaeology section. Allow 2 hours. ***Note:*** A move to a new location is scheduled for 2009, so call first.

802 E. Second Ave., upstairs at the Durango Arts Center. ✆ **970/259-9234.** www.childsmuseum.org. Admission $4 adults and children, free for grandparents and children 2 and under. Wed–Fri 10am–5pm; Sat–Sun 1–5pm.

Durango Fish Hatchery and Wildlife Museum (Kids) A pleasant change from the usual attractions, this fish hatchery offers an opportunity to see and feed trout and also see mounted birds and other wildlife native to Southwestern Colorado. The hatchery, operated by the Colorado Division of Wildlife, also has a short video presentation on fish hatchery operation. Allow 1 hour.

151 E. 16th St. ✆ **970/375-6766** or 970/247-0855. Free admission. Open mid-May to mid-Sept Mon–Sat 10am–4:30pm; Sun 11am–3pm.

Durango & Silverton Narrow Gauge Railroad Museum The glory days of steam trains come alive here, where you can climb up into a full-size locomotive, a caboose, parlor car, and other rolling stock to get a close-up view. The large museum, located in the Durango & Silverton rail yard, also houses a vast amount of railroad memorabilia, from conductors' uniforms, watches, and belt buckles to lanterns, railroad art, and historic photos. Allow 1 hour.

479 Main Ave. ✆ **888/872-4607** or 970/247-2733. Admission $5 adults, $2.50 children 11 and under; free with a train ticket. Summer daily 8am–6pm; call for off-season hours.

SPORTS & OUTDOOR ACTIVITIES

In addition to contacting the various companies listed below, you can get additional information and even book some activities through the **Durango Area Tourism Office** (see "Visitor Information," above).

Durango is surrounded by public land, with numerous opportunities for hiking, mountain biking, fishing, and winter sports. For information, contact the **San Juan Public Lands Center,** at 15 Burnett Court (✆ **970/247-4874**), off U.S. 160 west in the Durango Tech Center, which offers information on activities in the **San Juan National Forest** (www.fs.fed.us/r2/sanjuan) and on lands administered by the **Bureau of Land Management** (www.co.blm.gov). The center is open Monday through Friday from 8am to 5pm.

The **Durango Parks and Recreation Department** (✆ **970/375-7300;** www.durango gov.org) operates about 20 parks throughout the city, where you'll find picnic areas, free tennis courts, and other facilities. The department operates (and has its administrative offices in) the **Durango Community Recreation Center,** 2700 Main Ave., which has an indoor swimming pool, climbing wall, weights and other workout equipment, an indoor track, and other facilities. A recreation center day pass, which includes all the facilities at the center, costs $4.75 for adults 18 to 59, $3.75 for kids 4 to 17 and adults 60 and up, and is free with a paying adult for children under 4.

Durango Mountain Resort, some 25 miles north of Durango on U.S. 550 (✆ **800/ 982-6103** or 970/247-9000; www.durangomountainresort.com), doesn't close down—or even slow down—after the winter's snows are gone. Summer activities here include the popular Alpine Slide, scenic chairlift rides, a climbing wall, miniature golf, disc golf, and bungee trampolines. Individual activities cost from $3 for a chairlift ride to $8 for the alpine slide or the bungee trampoline, but the best deal is the Total Adventure Ticket—a 4-hour pass for $29 or a full-day pass for $49, providing a shot at everything including unlimited alpine slide and chairlift rides, and disc and miniature golf. Durango Mountain Resort also offers free guided naturalist hikes; call ✆ **970/385-1256** for times and registration.

FISHING Six-mile-long **Vallecito Lake,** 23 miles northeast of Durango via C.R. 240 and C.R. 501, is a prime spot for rainbow trout, brown trout, kokanee salmon, and northern pike; for information, contact the Vallecito Lake Chamber of Commerce, P.O. Box 804, Bayfield, CO 81122 (✆ **970/247-1573;** www.vallecitolakechamber.com). There are also numerous streams in the Durango area. To buy Colorado fishing licenses and supplies, get information on the best fishing holes, rent equipment, or arrange for a guided fly-fishing trip, stop in at **Duranglers,** 923 Main Ave. (✆ **888/347-4346** or 970/385-4081; www.duranglers.com). Full-day float trips for two people cost $375; wading trips for two cost $350. Lunch is included.

GLIDER RIDES For a quiet, airborne look at Durango and the San Juan Mountains, take a glider ride with **Durango Soaring Club** (✆ **970/247-9037;** www.soardurango.com), located 3 miles north of Durango on U.S. 550. Rides are conducted daily from 9am to 6pm from mid-May through mid-October; soaring is smoother in the morning, but there is greater thermal activity, offering the opportunity for longer rides, in the afternoon. Rates for one person are $100 for 10 to 15 minutes and $150 for 30 to 35 minutes, and $170 and $230 for similar trips for two, but the total weight of both passengers must be less than 300 pounds.

GOLF Two public 18-hole golf courses open in early spring, weather permitting, in Durango. There's **Hillcrest Golf Club,** 2300 Rim Dr., adjacent to Fort Lewis College (✆ **970/247-1499;** www.golfhillcrest.com), with fees of $36 for 18 holes and $18 for 9 holes, not including cart rental; and **Dalton Ranch and Golf Club,** 589 Trimble Lane (C.R. 252), 6 miles north of Durango via U.S. 550 (✆ **970/247-8774;** www.daltonranch.com), charging $49 to $89 for 18 holes, including a cart.

HIKING & BACKPACKING The **Animas Mountain Trail** is a 5-mile loop with terrific views of the entire valley, accessible via a trail head in the northwest corner of town near 32nd Street and 4th Avenue. Durango is at the western end of the 500-mile **Colorado Trail** (www.coloradotrail.org) to Denver. The trail head is 3½ miles up Junction Creek Road, an extension of 25th Street west of Main Avenue. There are numerous other trails in the Durango area, including several that delve into the Weminuche Wilderness Area via the Durango & Silverton railroad. For information on area trails, contact the San Juan Public Lands Center (see above).

HORSEBACK RIDING & CATTLE DRIVES To see this spectacular country as the pioneers did, arrange for a short horseback ride or a 2- to 6-day expedition into the San Juan National Forest or Weminuche Wilderness. My choice for a licensed outfitter here is **Rapp Corral,** located on the east side of U.S. 550 about 20 miles north of Durango at 51 Haviland Lake Rd. (✆ **970/247-8454;** www.rappcorral.com). Riders go into the San Juan National Forest, and rides start at $35 for a 1-hour ride. A 2-hour ride to a natural cave costs $65, and a 4- to 5-hour trip into southern Colorado's high country costs $150. Reservations are required, and payment should be made with personal or traveler's checks or cash; credit cards are not accepted. During winter, Rapp Corral offers sleigh rides for $30 per person, $27 for kids 6 to 12, and free for kids under 6, or $90 for a private sleigh for two.

LLAMA TREKKING Guided llama trips, overnight pack trips, and llama leasing are the specialty of **Buckhorn Llama Co.** (✆ **970/667-7411;** www.llamapack.com).

Guided pack trips for one to three people cost $350 per person per day and include all equipment, meals, and necessary supplies, except for sleeping bags.

MOUNTAIN BIKING The varied terrain and myriad trails of San Juan National Forest have made Durango a nationally known mountain-biking center. The Colorado Trail (see "Hiking & Backpacking," above), Hermosa Creek Trail (beginning 11 miles north of Durango off U.S. 550), and La Plata Canyon Road (beginning 11 miles west of Durango off U.S. 160) are among my favorites. For information, contact the Public Lands Center (see above). You can also get information and rent mountain bikes at **Hassle Free Sports,** 2615 Main Ave. (© **800/835-3800** or 970/259-3874; www.hasslefreesports.com), which rents full suspension mountain bikes for $35 per half-day or $45 for a full day.

MOUNTAINEERING & ROCK CLIMBING A variety of terrain offers mountaineering and rock-climbing opportunities exists for beginners as well as advanced climbers. Guided tours and instruction are offered by **SouthWest Adventure Guides** (see "Mountain Biking," above), with rates starting at $150 for a group half-day rock-climbing course and $350 per day for one-on-one private instruction, $150 per additional person.

RIVER RAFTING The three stages of the Animas River provide excitement for rafters of all experience and ability levels. The churning Class IV and V rapids of the upper Animas mark its rapid descent from the San Juan Range. The 6 miles from Trimble Hot Springs into downtown Durango are an easy, gently rolling rush. Downstream from Durango, the river is mainly Classes II and III, promising a few thrills but mostly relaxation.

Most of the many outfitters in Durango offer a wide variety of rafting excursions, such as 2- to 4-hour raft trips that cost $25 to $45 for adults and $15 to $30 for kids, and full-day river trips, which include lunch, costing $70 to $80 for adults and $60 to $70 for kids. Trips in inflatable kayaks are also offered at slightly higher rates. Among my favorite companies here are **Durango Rivertrippers** (© **800/292-2885** or 970/259-0289; www.durangorivertrippers.com), **Mild to Wild Rafting** (© **800/567-6745** or 970/247-4789; www.mild2wildrafting.com), and **Mountain Waters Rafting** (© **800/585-8243** or 970/259-4191; www.durangorafting.com).

RODEO From late June through the third weekend in July, the **Durango Pro Rodeo** series takes place most Friday and Saturday nights starting at 6pm at the La Plata County Fairgrounds, Main Avenue and 25th Street (© **970/739-3851**). Admission costs $10 for adults and $5 for kids 12 and under.

SWIMMING & MINERAL BATHS **Trimble Hot Springs ★**, 7 miles north of Durango just off U.S. 550 (© **970/247-0111;** www.trimblehotsprings.com), at the junction of C.R. 203 and Trimble Lane, is a National Historic Site more than 100 years old, where you'll often find Mom and Dad relaxing in the soothing mineral pools or getting a massage while the kids have fun in the adjacent swimming pool. Facilities include two natural hot-springs therapy pools, a separate Olympic-size swimming pool (heated by the hot springs but not containing hot-springs water), massage and therapy rooms, a snack bar, a picnic area, and gardens. Water from the natural hot springs comes out of the ground at 118° to 120°F (48°–49°C), and the therapy pools are kept at a more comfortable temperature of 102° to 108°F (39°–42°C). The swimming pool is usually about 85°F (29°C). The complex is open daily from 8am to 10pm (weekdays) or 11pm (Fri–Sun) in summer, and in winter from 9am to 10pm Sunday through Thursday and until 11pm

Soaring Tree Top Adventures: A Bird's-Eye View of the Forest

Dubbed a "Canopy Tour," **Soaring Tree Top Adventures ★★** offers visitors a chance to ride a one-of-a-kind zip-line course through the trees north of Durango. The course is accessible only by the Durango & Silverton train and consists of over a mile of zip-line spans ranging in length from 50 feet to 1,400 feet, many of them crossing over the Animas River. The zip lines connect a number of stainless-steel platforms that grip their host trees without harming them, some of them 100 feet above the forest floor. The attraction opened in 2004 and has won scads of accolades since.

After an exhilarating day confronting acrophobia and learning to keep facing forward, I found it to be well worth the somewhat high price ($339 a person for the full day, lunch and train included) and a great time for all ages. You have to just take a step and let gravity and technology do the rest—the harnesses are state-of-the-art and the staff make sure you're connected properly every span of the way—and you're literally flying through the treetops at speeds pushing 30 miles an hour, gliding to a stop thanks to the resort's patented braking system.

For more information, contact Soaring Tree Top Adventures (✆ **970/769-2357;** www.soaringcolorado.com).

Friday and Saturday. Day passes cost $13 for adults and $8.50 for children under 13, and cover use of the therapy mineral pools and the swimming pool. The **Trimble Hot Springs Spa** (✆ **970/247-0212**) is open daily from 9am to 9pm year-round, providing expanded body treatments and a quiet, relaxing atmosphere for therapeutic massage, herbal oil wraps, face and scalp treatments, dry body brush, and radiant salt glow. Massages start at about $55 for a half-hour or $75 for an hour. Reservations are recommended, but walk-ins are welcome.

WINTER SPORTS Some 25 miles north of Durango on U.S. 550, **Durango Mountain Resort ★★**, 1 Skier Place, Durango, CO 81301 (✆ **800/982-6103** or 970/247-9000; www.durangomountainresort.com), has bragging rights to more sunshine than any other Colorado resort. Surprisingly, the sun doesn't come at the expense of snow—average annual snowfall is 260 inches—so you really get the best of both snow and sun. The resort, which has a laid-back, friendly atmosphere that I particularly enjoy, contains 1,200 acres of skiable terrain, with 85 trails rated 23% beginner, 51% intermediate, and 26% advanced, and 10 lifts (one high-speed six, one high-speed quad, four triples, three doubles, and one Magic Carpet). The mountain has a vertical drop of 2,029 feet from a summit elevation of 10,822 feet.

Snowboarders are welcome on all lifts and trails, and two snowboard parks offer jumps, slides, and a half-pipe. The Durango Nordic Center has 10 miles of trails for Nordic skiers for both classic and skate skiing, and charges $12 for a trail pass.

Three on-mountain restaurants complement the facilities, which include a hotel, condominiums, several restaurants and taverns, shops, and equipment rentals. All-day lift tickets (2007–08 prices) are $60 for adults, $32 for children 6 to 12, $44 for seniors 62 to 69 and students, $20 for seniors 70 and older, and free for kids 5 and younger, with considerable discounts in the spring. The resort is usually open from late November or early December to early April, daily from 9am to 4pm.

SHOPPING

You'll find some of your best shopping opportunities in southwest Colorado in downtown Durango, along Main Avenue from the Durango & Silverton Railroad Depot north to 10th Street. Here, interspersed among restaurants and historic hotels, are shops selling a wide variety of items—ranging from custom-made Western hats to kitchen gizmos to fine porcelain and imported gifts. And yes, there are plenty of tacky T-shirts as well.

Those seeking the region's premier art gallery will have to leave Main Avenue, but it's not far to the **Toh-Atin Gallery,** 145 W. Ninth St. (✆ **800/525-0384** or 970/247-8277; www.toh-atin.com). Specializing in original Southwestern and American Indian art, the gallery stocks Navajo weavings, bronze and alabaster sculptures, original paintings, pueblo pottery, and handcrafted jewelry.

WHERE TO STAY

Durango has a definite lodging season. When the Durango & Silverton Narrow Gauge Railroad runs most of its trains in midsummer, expect to pay top dollar for your room, and expect higher rates during the Christmas holidays and in peak ski seasons as well. But go in the off season—late spring and fall—and you'll find much more reasonable rates. An easy way to book accommodations is to contact **Durango Central Reservations** (✆ **866/294-5187;** www.durangoreservations.org). Room taxes add almost 10% to lodging bills.

Among chain and franchise motels offering moderately priced rooms are the **Best Western Mountain Shadows,** 3255 N. Main Ave. (✆ **800/521-5218** or 970/247-5200), charging $114 to $179 double in high season; the **Comfort Inn,** 2930 N. Main Ave. (✆ **800/424-6423** or 970/259-5373), with rates for two from $69 to $149 year-round; the recommended **Doubletree Hotel,** 501 Camino Del Rio (✆ **970/259-6580**), charging $175 to $250 double (the best rooms are right above the Animas River); and **Quality Inn,** 455 S. Camino del Rio (✆ **800/424-6423** or 970/259-7900), with rates for two from $79 to $149. An interesting staff-free downtown lodging is **Nobody's Inn,** 920 Main Ave. (www.nobodysinn.com), with eclectically decorated historic rooms for $99 to $179 for two people. You reserve the room online and get a key code, and never see an employee face to face. All are in Durango, CO 81301.

Very Expensive

The Wit's End Guest Ranch & Resort ★★ Kids A delightful dude ranch some 24 miles northeast of Durango at 8,000 feet elevation, the Wit's End is located on 550 acres in a narrow valley at the head of Vallecito Lake. Surrounded by the 12,000- to 14,000-foot peaks of the Weminuche Wilderness, the Wit's End offers a unique combination of rustic outdoors and sophisticated luxury, with numerous activities ranging from guided horseback rides and boating to a summer kids' program. The one- to four-bedroom log cabins, some dating from the 1870s, have retained their rustic outer appearance, but the knotty-pine interiors have been fully renovated. All have stone fireplaces, queen beds, full bathrooms with tub/shower combos, robes, porches (with porch swings), and striking views. Most meals are served in the beautiful 1870s log lodge with a huge stone fireplace. Filet mignon, roast duckling, and other hearty dishes are served, with fine dining 3 evenings each week and outdoor Western cookouts the other nights.

254 C.R. 500, Bayfield, CO 81122. ✆ **800/236-9483** or 970/884-4113. Fax 970/884-3261. www.witsendranch.com. 32 cabins. Memorial Day to Labor Day $2,549 per guest per week per cabin for up to 7 people per cabin; $1,125 per week for children 3–11 and nannies; $2,049 per week for teens and additional adults. Rates include all meals and activities. Other plans also available. Off-season cabin-only rates available. AE, DISC, MC, V. **Amenities:** Restaurant (Western/American); bar; large outdoor pool (summer only); 2 outdoor tennis courts; exercise room; spa; mountain biking; extensive summer children's program for ages 4–17; game room; airport transportation; limited room service; horseback riding (private lessons available); fishing (Orvis-endorsed instruction available); hiking; boating; trap shooting; winter-sports equipment. *In room:* TV/VCR (videos available), kitchen.

Expensive

Strater Hotel ★★★ Durango's most famous hotel is a wonderful place to relax and soak up the ambience of the Old West—at least, the Old West for those who had money. An exceptional example of American Victorian architecture, the four-story redbrick Strater was built in 1887 by Henry H. Strater, a prominent druggist of the mining-boom era. It boasts the original ornamental brickwork and white-stone cornices, embossed ceiling designs, and intricately carved columns. Spread throughout the guest rooms is one of the world's largest collections of American Victorian walnut antiques, and even the wallpaper is authentic to the 1880s. One of the most popular units is no. 222, a corner room directly over the Diamond Belle Saloon, where prolific author Louis L'Amour gave life to many of his Western heroes. The bathrooms are modern, with tub/shower combos in most but not all units. The hotel also boasts a Victorian-style hot tub, which is free for guests but available by reservation only.

699 Main Ave., Durango, CO 81301. ✆ **800/247-4431** or 970/247-4431. Fax 970/259-2208. www.strater.com. 93 units. Early May to mid-Oct and Christmas holidays $175–$265 double; mid-Oct to early May $105–$185 double. Rates include continental breakfast. AE, DISC, MC, V. **Amenities:** Restaurant (contemporary American); 2 bars; hot tub; concierge; limited room service; valet laundry. *In room:* A/C, cable TV, wireless Internet access (free).

Moderate

General Palmer Hotel ★ Named for one of Durango's founding fathers who established the hotel in 1898, the charming General Palmer offers historic ambiance and a terrific location right between the train depot and downtown. Fronted by wraparound patio decks, the brick structure has an antique elevator, Victorian furnishings, and little perks like teddy bears on every bed. Most rooms have one or two queens, but some family units have as many as three beds. The fresh-baked cookies are addictive.

561 Main Ave., Durango, CO 81301. ✆ **800/523-3358** or 970/247-4747. www.generalpalmer.com. 39 units. Summer $120–$295 double; off season $98–$295 double. Rates include continental breakfast. AE, DISC, MC, V. *In room:* A/C, cable TV, wireless Internet access (free).

The Leland House Bed & Breakfast Suites ★★ Built as an apartment house in 1927 and handsomely restored in 1993, the Leland House offers an intriguing mix of lodging types in a comfortable inn with early-20th-century decor. Owned by the Komick family, who also own the historic Rochester Hotel across the street (see below), the Leland House contains six suites with sitting rooms and full kitchens, plus four studios with kitchenettes. All have private bathrooms with showers (no tubs) and are decorated with a compatible combination of good-quality beds, antiques, near-antiques, and contemporary furniture. The Pittman Suite is a large family suite with two full bedrooms, two bathrooms, a full kitchen, and a balcony. Rooms are named for historic figures associated with the Leland House and its neighbors, such as Max Baer, world heavyweight boxing champion in the 1930s. Throughout the house are photos, memorabilia, and framed biographies of these individuals, many of whom played significant roles in the development of early Durango.

721 E. Second Ave., Durango, CO 81301. ✆ **800/664-1920** or 970/385-1920. Fax 970/385-1967. www.leland-house.com. 10 units. $119–$159 studio; $169–$209 1-bedroom suite; $299–$349 2-bedroom suite. Rates include full breakfast. AE, DISC, MC, V. **Amenities:** Complimentary bike rentals. *In room:* A/C, cable TV, wireless Internet access (free).

Rochester Hotel ★★ Among my favorite places to stay in Durango, the 1892 Rochester retains the feel of an Old West hotel with high ceilings, original trim and hardware, antiques, historic photos and original Western art, and 1890s-style furnishings. Completely renovated in the mid-1990s, the hotel offers 15 spacious rooms, each with its own bathroom (two have whirlpool tubs with showers, and the rest have large walk-in showers). Rooms have good, firm queen or king beds; one unit has a king bed and a kitchen, and another, a king and a separate living room. The hotel's hallways are lined with posters and photos from many of the films shot in the area, including *City Slickers, Butch Cassidy and the Sundance Kid, How the West Was Won,* and *The Cowboys.*

726 E. Second Ave. (write to 721 E. Second Ave.), Durango, CO 81301. ✆ **800/664-1920** or 970/385-1920. Fax 970/385-1967. www.rochesterhotel.com. 15 units. $129–$219 double; $199–$249 suite (called King Deluxe). Rates include full breakfast. AE, DISC, MC, V. Pets accepted in 2 units with $20 per pet per night charge. **Amenities:** Complimentary bike rentals. *In room:* A/C, cable TV, wireless Internet access (free).

Inexpensive

Siesta Motel ★ Value A vintage 1950s-era roadside motel owned and operated by the same family since 1975, the Siesta Motel has a cactus-shaped neon sign and a sign proclaiming "Free Rooms, Just Kidding" as a rib to the less honest advertisements on Main Avenue. But make no mistake: This is the best value in Durango, featuring clean, well-kept motel rooms with a king bed or two queens or doubles, and a Mexican theme and a hot tub in the courtyard gazebo.

3475 Main Ave., Durango, CO 81301. ✆ **877/314-0741** or 970/247-0741. Fax 970/247-0941. www.durangosiestamotel.com. 22 units, including 2 suites. $82–$156 double; $98–$174 suite. Lower off-season rates. AE, DISC, MC, V. Pets accepted ($10 fee). **Amenities:** Indoor hot tub. *In room:* A/C, cable TV, wireless Internet access (free), coffeemaker.

WHERE TO DINE

Expensive

Cyprus Cafe ★★ MEDITERRANEAN This tiny restaurant a block from Durango's busy Main Avenue offers a delightful alternative to the basic American and Southwestern cuisine that dominates southwestern Colorado; it's where I go when I'm feeling adventurous. The dining room has a simple cafe atmosphere, with 10 wood tables, a stained-glass window, and a few pieces of original art. In summer, there's also plentiful outdoor patio seating. The emphasis is on freshness, with produce from local farms when available. The menu changes seasonally, but dinner entrees might include spanakopita (spinach and feta cheese wrapped in phyllo dough), Colorado beef and lamb, fresh seafood, and at least one vegetarian item. Those new to Mediterranean cuisine might try the combination appetizer plate that includes hummus, baba ganouj, olives, feta, spanakopita, and grilled pita, which can easily serve several people as an appetizer or one for dinner.

725 E. Second Ave. ✆ **970/385-6884.** www.cypruscafe.com. Lunch $8.50–$15; dinner $14–$28. AE, DISC, MC, V. Mid-May to Sept daily 11:30am–3pm, 5–10pm; Oct to mid-May Mon–Sat 11:30am–2:30pm, 5–9pm.

The Palace Restaurant STEAK/SEAFOOD/PASTA Adjacent to the Durango & Silverton Narrow Gauge Railroad terminal, the Palace Restaurant has a Victorian drawing-room atmosphere, with Tiffany lamps hanging over the tables, historical photos and classic oil paintings on the walls, and a large fireplace. At dinner, try the slow-roasted duck in a honey-almond sauce or the steak McMahon—a 12-ounce New York cut served on crisp hash browns with a roasted-garlic sauce. The resident Quiet Lady Tavern is named for the headless female sculpture at its entrance.

505 Main Ave. ✆ **970/247-2018.** www.palacerestaurants.com. Main courses $9–$15 lunch, $15–$37 dinner. AE, MC, V. Mon–Sat 11am–10pm. Closed Easter, Christmas, and New Year's Day.

Randy's ★★ CONTEMPORARY AMERICAN My favorite eatery in Durango, Randy's is a dim and intimate room with an adult vibe, just a block from the hustle and bustle of the throngs of families on Main Avenue. Featuring comfortable booths and walls clad in contemporary art, Randy's, named for owner-chef Randy Burton, who opened the restaurant in 1986, consistently delivers inventive and rich flair, from the seared ahi (when available) to robust Colorado lamb, to wasabi-crusted scallops. The house-made soups are also recommended, as are the desserts.

152 E. College Dr. ✆ **970/247-9083.** www.randysrestaurant.com. Main courses $11–$26. AE, DISC, MC, V. Daily 5–9:30pm. Closed Easter, Christmas, and New Year's Day.

Moderate

Irish Embassy ★★ IRISH PUB An authentic Irish pub from the bar to the stonework to the art—everything was shipped over from the Emerald Isle—the Irish Embassy emerged as a local favorite as soon as it opened its doors in summer 2008. And the menu is just as traditional, with Irish standbys like bangers and mash, pub steak, lasagna, and, of course, fish and chips. The starters show a little more worldliness—such as baked goat cheese dip and salmon fingers—but this is a pub that proudly exudes a friendly vibe in a comfortable space just like a good Irish pub should.

900 Main Ave. ✆ **970/403-1200.** www.theirishembassypub.com. Main courses $8–$16. AE, DISC, MC, V. Mon–Wed 10:30am–midnight; Thurs–Sun 10:30am–2am. Pub menu only after 10pm.

Steamworks Brewing Co. BREWPUB Situated in a 1920s building, formerly a car dealership, this brewpub has made the most of the funky, warehouselike structure with huge wooden rafters and pipes of all sizes running in all directions. There's also patio dining. The food matches the decor: large, substantial portions to satisfy any appetite, and with an emphasis on spicy. Half-pound burgers come in a variety of choices, such as Southwestern, with green chile, pepper jack cheese, and a chipotle sauce. There's also a spicy buffalo chicken sandwich and a grilled Reuben. Entrees include burritos, steak, chicken, and a Cajun boil ($20 per person). The tasty side salad with Italian vinaigrette dressing practically overflows the plate, and along with a pizza is a perfect (and inexpensive) dinner for two. Close to a dozen of the brewer's beers are usually on tap, including an excellent bitter pale ale.

801 E. Second Ave. at Eighth St. ✆ **970/259-9200.** www.steamworksbrewing.com. Main courses $8.50–$22; pizza $8.50–$13 (serves 1 or 2). AE, DISC, MC, V. Daily 11am–10pm; bar open later.

Inexpensive

Durango Diner AMERICAN Locally famous for good basic grub at reasonable prices, the Durango Diner has been going strong since 1965. Serving breakfast and lunch only, the diner is a skinny storefront with a long counter and a table or two looking out on busy Main Avenue. Breakfasts include standard American egg choices, huge hotcakes, and a variety of specials such as excellent homemade green chile, chile rellenos, and breakfast burritos. Lunch here means sandwiches and burgers—the half-pound burger with Swiss cheese and green chile is great—plus turkey and roast beef dinners. The Durango Diner also does a booming business selling its green chile, salsa, and enchilada sauce by the pint, quart, and gallon.

957 Main Ave. ✆ **970/247-9889.** www.durangodiner.com. Most items $3–$8. No credit cards. Mon–Sat 6am–2pm; Sun 6am–1pm.

Olde Tymer's Cafe AMERICAN This popular local hangout is a busy, noisy place in a historic building, complete with the original tin ceiling and decorated with antique bottles and tins from the early-20th-century drugstore that was once located here. The food is primarily burgers, sandwiches, and finger food—the 8-ounce burger in an onion roll is especially good. The menu also features homemade chile, nachos, and hearty salads such as the chicken salad and Cobb salad, and there are daily specials. Service is fast, friendly, and efficient. The patio out back, open in warm weather, is especially pleasant (and quieter than inside).

1000 Main Ave. (at 10th St.) ✆ **970/259-2990.** Reservations not accepted. Most items $3.50–$9. AE, DISC, MC, V. Daily 11am–10pm.

DURANGO AFTER DARK

During summer, the highly acclaimed **Diamond Circle Melodrama,** at the Durango Arts Center, 802 E. 2nd Ave. (✆ **970/247-3400;** www.diamondcirclemelodrama.com), presents authentic late-1800s melodrama—hiss the evil villain and cheer the beautiful heroine—plus a vaudeville review of singing, dancing, and comedy from early June through late September on Wednesday through Monday evenings at 7:45pm, plus several Saturday matinees in midsummer. Tickets are $10 to $24.

You'll get a tasty meal and a live Western stage show at **Bar D Chuckwagon Suppers,** 8080 C.R. 250 (✆ **970/247-5753;** www.bardchuckwagon.com), 9 miles north of Durango via U.S. 550 and Trimble Lane (C.R. 252). Open from Memorial Day weekend through Labor Day weekend, Bar D offers a traditional chuck-wagon-style meal with a tasty choice of roast beef, barbecued chicken breast, or flame-broiled 12-ounce rib-eye steak, served with all of the fixings. The ranch complex, which includes an Old West town of shops and a miniature train, opens at 5:30pm. By 7:30pm you should be in the chow line for your grub, piled onto big metal plates, before taking your seat at a long picnic table. After dinner comes the show: Western music with fiddle, flatpick guitar, mandolin, bass, and great singers, plus some really hokey comedy. Reservations are required. Cost includes supper and show, and is $18 to $38 for those 9 and older and $9 for children under 9 for the beef or chicken supper.

Durango being a college and tourist town, the bar scene is especially lively. Stalwarts include **El Rancho Tavern,** 975 Main Ave. (✆ **970/259-8111**), a historic local favorite with pool tables and TVs; and **Lady Falconburgh's Barley Exchange,** 640 Main Ave (✆ **970/382-9664**), with superlative pub grub and over 140 beers on tap; as well as **Steamworks Brewing Co.** and the **Irish Embassy** (see "Where to Dine," earlier in this chapter) and the **Diamond Belle Saloon** at the Strater Hotel (see "Where to Stay," earlier in this chapter). A prime live music venue is the **Henry Strater Theatre,** 699 Main Ave. (✆ **970/375-7160;** www.stratertheatre.com).

A SIDE TRIP TO SILVERTON

For a look at the real Old West, without the need for a time machine, head to the town of Silverton. At an elevation of 9,318 feet at the northern terminus of the Durango & Silverton Narrow Gauge Railroad, the town has a year-round population of about 500 and plenty of things to see and do for the more than 250,000 people who visit each year.

Founded on silver production in 1871, today the entire town is a National Historic Landmark District. In its heyday, Blair Street was such a notorious area of saloons and brothels that no less a character than Bat Masterson, fresh from taming Dodge City, Kansas, was imported to subdue the criminal elements. Today the original false-fronted buildings remain—some in better shape than others—but they now house restaurants and galleries, and are occasionally used as Old West movie sets. There are some fascinating shops and galleries here, along with plenty of places to buy tacky T-shirts, and I strongly recommend that you spend at least an hour just wandering around.

From Memorial Day through Labor Day, the Silverton Gunfighters Association stages gunfights at the corner of 12th and Blair streets Thursday, Friday, Saturday, and holidays at 5:30pm. On Sunday from June through September, the Silverton Brass Band performs at 6pm on one of Silverton's street corners—don't worry, you won't have any trouble finding them; just follow the music and the crowds.

You can get walking-tour maps of the historic downtown area; information on local shops, restaurants, and lodgings; plus details on the numerous outdoor activities in the surrounding mountains from the **Silverton Chamber of Commerce,** at the intersection of Colo. 110 and U.S. 550 (P.O. Box 565), Silverton, CO 81433 (✆ **800/752-4494** or 970/387-5654; www.silvertoncolorado.com). From July through September the chamber's visitor center is open daily 9am to 6pm; in May, June, and October it's open daily 9am to 5pm; and from November through April it's open daily from 10am to 4pm. (It's closed Easter, Thanksgiving, Christmas, and New Year's Day.)

For a step back into Silverton's Wild West days, head for the **San Juan County Historical Society Museum,** in the 1902 county jail at Greene and 15th streets (✆ **970/387-5838;** www.silvertonhistoricsociety.org). Here you'll see memorabilia of Silverton's boom days, including lots of railroad stuff and a collection of Derringer handguns. Altogether, there are three floors of historic displays, including the most popular stop—the original jail cells, a good place to snap a photo of that would-be convict you're traveling with. From this building, a tunnel leads to the mining museum next door, which recreates the feeling of being deep in a mine, with displays of mining machinery, ore cars, and other mining memorabilia. There's also a shop that sells books on area history. The museum is open daily, from Memorial Day weekend through September from 9am to 5pm, and from 10am to 3pm from October 1 to 15. Admission is $5 for adults and free for children 12 and under. The adjacent **San Juan County Courthouse** has a gold-domed clock tower, and the restoration of the **Town Hall,** at 14th and Greene streets, after a devastating 1993 fire, has won national recognition.

The **Old Hundred Gold Mine** (✆ **800/872-3009** or 970/387-5444; www.minetour.com) is located about 5 miles east of Silverton via Colo. 110, offering an underground guided tour that takes 45 to 50 minutes and starts with a ride 1,500 feet underground in an electric mine train. The tour continues with a walk through lighted tunnels, where you see drilling and mucking demonstrations. There's gold panning aboveground, plus a gift shop, snack bar, and picnic area. Cost is $17 for adults 13 to 59, $8 for children 5 to 12 (children under 5 held on a lap are free), and $15 for seniors 60 and older. Reservations are not necessary; the temperature in the mine is about 48°F (9°C), so a sweater or jacket is recommended. The mine is open from early May through mid-October daily from 10am to 4pm, with tours on the hour.

Expert and advanced skiers and snowboarders have discovered Silverton's newest attraction, **Silverton Mountain Ski Area,** which opened in early 2002 and has been booked solid ever since. Located almost 7 miles north of Silverton, the ski area has one double chairlift that accesses more powder than most skiers have ever seen. The base is at 10,400 feet, with a peak lift-served elevation of 12,300 feet and a fairly easy hike to 13,300 feet elevation. The area's steepest run is 55 degrees and its easiest runs are 25 to 30 degrees—what most other ski areas call a really steep run. In summer, the area offers scenic chairlift rides and a difficult mountain bike trail for experienced riders. Both guided and unguided skiing is available (guided-only skiing from mid-January through March), and the season usually runs from Thanksgiving through April. The day rate for unguided skiing is $49, and rates for guided group skiing are $99 to $129. Private guided skiing is also available. For current hours, required equipment, and other details, contact **Silverton Mountain,** P.O. Box 654, Silverton, CO 81433 (✆ **970/387-5706;** www.silvertonmountain.com).

Where to Stay

The Wyman Hotel & Inn ★★ My top choice for overnight lodging in Silverton, the Wyman fits in beautifully with the historic ambience of this Old West mining town, but, then, it ought to—the hotel's been here almost as long as the town. Built in 1902 and now listed on the National Register of Historic Places, this handsome red-sandstone building has arched windows, high ceilings, Victorian-style wallpaper, and rooms and common areas furnished with antiques dating from the 1870s to the early 1900s—mostly Renaissance and East Lake styles. Rooms are individually decorated and range in size. The hotel also offers a two-room suite, a three-room suite, and a very large family room. In addition to the rooms in the hotel, a Southern Pacific Railroad caboose has been converted into a honeymoon suite, with a hand-carved antique bed from Spain and a two-person whirlpool tub. (Four other units also have two-person whirlpool tubs.) Ten rooms have showers only, and all have top-quality king- or queen-size feather beds with down pillows and down duvets. Although the rooms are wonderful, it would be well worth coming here simply for the food, which is truly a gourmet experience.

1371 Greene St., Silverton, CO 81433. ✆ **800/609-7845** or 970/387-5372. Fax 970/387-5745. www.thewyman.com. 17 units. B&B rates $145–$165 double; $175–$300 suite or caboose. AE, DISC, MC, V. Rates include full breakfast and afternoon wine and cheese or tea and homemade cookies. **Amenities:** Guest computer. *In room:* TV/VCR, wireless Internet access (free), hair dryer.

2 THE SAN JUAN SKYWAY

The **San Juan Skyway ★★**, a 233-mile circuit, crosses five mountain passes and takes in the magnificent San Juan Mountains, as well as the cities and towns of the region. It can be accomplished in a single all-day drive from Durango or divided into several days, incorporating stops in Cortez, Telluride, and Ouray—all of which are discussed later in this chapter. Check for closed passes in winter and early spring.

The route can be driven either clockwise (heading west from Durango on U.S. 160) or counterclockwise (heading north from Durango on U.S. 550). I'll describe the clockwise route.

Eleven miles west of Durango you'll pass through the village of Hesperus, from which a county road runs 10 miles north into **La Plata Canyon,** with its mining ruins and ghost towns.

Farther west, U.S. 160 passes the entrance road to **Mesa Verde National Park.** About 45 miles west of Durango, just before Cortez, turn north on Colo. 145, which traverses the historic town of Dolores, site of the **Anasazi Heritage Center** (see section 4 of this chapter), then proceeds up the **Dolores River Valley,** a favorite of trout fishermen.

Sixty miles from Cortez, the route crosses 10,222-foot **Lizard Head Pass,** named for a startling rock spire looming above the roadside alpine meadows. It then descends 13 miles to the resort town of **Telluride,** set in a beautiful box canyon 4 miles off the main road.

Follow Colo. 145 west from Telluride down the San Miguel River valley to **Placerville.** Then turn north on Colo. 62, across 8,970-foot Dallas Divide, to Ridgway, a historic railroad town and home of **Ridgway State Park** (✆ **970/626-5822;** www.parks.state.co.us), with a sparkling mountain reservoir, trout fishing, boating (there's a marina), swimming, hiking, mountain biking, horseback riding, and camping. There are also three yurts available for overnight rentals ($60).

From Ridgway, turn south and follow U.S. 550 to the scenic and historic town of **Ouray.** Here begins the remarkable **Million Dollar Highway,** so named for all the mineral wealth that passed over it.

The 23 miles from Ouray over 11,008-foot **Red Mountain Pass** to Silverton is an unforgettable drive. It shimmies up the sheer sides of the Uncompahgre Gorge, through tunnels and past cascading waterfalls, then follows a historic toll road built in the 19th century. Mining equipment and log cabins are in evidence on the slopes of the iron-colored mountains, many of them over 14,000 feet in elevation. Along this route you'll pass a monument to snowplow operators who died trying to keep the road open during winter storms.

From Silverton, U.S. 550 climbs over the Molas Divide (elevation 10,910 ft.), then more or less parallels the track of the Durango & Silverton Narrow Gauge Railroad as it follows the Animas River south to Durango, passing the **Durango Mountain Resort** (p. 375) en route.

3 CORTEZ

45 miles W of Durango, 203 miles S of Grand Junction

An important archaeological center, Cortez is surrounded by a vast complex of ancient villages that dominated the Four Corners region—where Colorado, New Mexico, Arizona, and Utah's borders meet—1,000 years ago. Mesa Verde National Park, 10 miles east, is certainly the most prominent nearby attraction, drawing hundreds of thousands of visitors annually (see section 4 of this chapter). In addition, archaeological sites such as those at Canyons of the Ancients and Hovenweep national monuments, as well as Ute Mountain Tribal Park, are an easy drive from the city. San Juan National Forest, just to the north, offers a wide variety of recreational opportunities. The community of Cortez provides lodging, food, and supplies, making it the best spot to use as a home base when visiting these sites. Elevation is 6,200 feet.

ESSENTIALS

GETTING THERE **By Car** Cortez is located at the junction of north–south U.S. 491 and east–west U.S. 160.

As it enters Cortez from the east, U.S. 160 crosses Dolores Road (Colo. 145, which goes north to Telluride and Grand Junction), then runs due west through town for about 2 miles as Main Street. The city's main thoroughfare, Main Street intersects U.S. 491 (Broadway) at the west end of town.

By Plane **Cortez Airport,** off U.S. 160 and 491, southwest of town (✆ **970/565-7458;** www.cityofcortez.com), is served by **Great Lakes Airlines** (✆ **800/554-5111** or 970/565-9510), with direct daily flights to Denver.

Budget (✆ **970/564-9012**) and **Hertz** (✆ **970/565-2001**) provide car rentals at the airport.

VISITOR INFORMATION Stop at the **Colorado Welcome Center at Cortez/Cortez Area Chamber of Commerce,** 928 E. Main St. (✆ **970/565-4048** or 970/565-3414; www.cortezchamber.org), open daily from 8am to 6pm in summer and from 8am to 5pm the rest of the year; or contact the **Mesa Verde Country Visitor Information Bureau** (✆ **800/253-1616;** www.mesaverdecountry.com).

FAST FACTS The local hospital is **Southwest Memorial Hospital,** 1311 N. Mildred Rd. (✆ **970/565-6666**), which has a 24-hour emergency room. The **post office** is at 35 S. Beech St.; contact the U.S. Postal Service (✆ **800/275-8777;** www.usps.com) for hours and additional information.

SPECIAL EVENTS American Indian Dances and Cultural Programs, mid-May to late August; Indian Arts and Culture Festival, Memorial Day Weekend; Ute Mountain Roundup Rodeo, Montezuma County Fair, late July; Food, Wine & Art Festival, late August.

WHAT TO SEE & DO

In addition to the area's excellent archaeological sites, discussed in section 4 of this chapter, attractions here include the **Four Corners Monument,** the only place in the United States where you can stand in four states at once. Operated by the **Navajo Parks and Recreation Department** (✆ **928/871-6647;** www.navajonationparks.org), there's a flat monument marking where Utah, Colorado, New Mexico, and Arizona meet, and visitors perch for photos. The official seals of the four states are displayed, along with the motto "Four states here meet in freedom under God." Surrounding the monument are the states' flags, flags of the Navajo Nation and Ute tribe, and the U.S. flag.

A visitor center has crafts demonstrations by Navajo artisans, and jewelry, pottery, sand paintings, and other crafts are for sale. In addition, traditional Navajo food, such as fry bread, is available. The monument is located half a mile northwest of U.S. 160, about 40 miles southwest of Cortez. It's open daily from 7am to 8pm in summer and 8am to 5pm the rest of the year. Admission costs $3 per person. Allow 30 minutes.

WHERE TO STAY

Summer is the busy season here, and that's when you'll pay the highest lodging rates. Among the major chains providing comfortable, reasonably priced lodging in Cortez (zip code 81321) are **Best Western Turquoise Inn & Suites,** 535 E. Main St. (✆ **800/547-3376** or

970/565-3778), with rates for two from $79 to $159; **Econo Lodge,** 2020 E. Main St. (✆ **800/553-2666** or 970/565-3474), with double rates of $59 to $139 in peak season and $39 to $89 the rest of the year; **Holiday Inn Express,** 2121 E. Main St. (✆ **888/465-4329** or 970/565-6000), with double rates from $99 to $159; and **Super 8,** 505 E. Main St. (✆ **800/800-8000** or 970/565-8888), with rates of $50 to $85 double. Room tax adds about 8% to lodging bills.

Mesa Verde Inn This colorful, well-kept motel offers spacious Southwest-decorated rooms with either one king-size bed or two queens; many of the ground-floor rooms have patios. There are also a sand volleyball court, horseshoe pits, a short walking trail, and free shuttle service to downtown.

640 S. Broadway, Cortez, CO 81321. ✆ **800/972-6232** or 970/565-3773. Fax 970/565-1027. www.mesa-verdeinn.com. 87 units. $59–$81 double. AE, DC, DISC, MC, V. Pets accepted. **Amenities:** Restaurant (barbecue); outdoor heated pool; outdoor hot tub. *In room:* A/C, cable TV, wireless Internet access (free).

WHERE TO DINE

Main St. Brewery and Restaurant ★ AMERICAN Fans slice the air under a stamped-tin ceiling, and fanciful murals splash color above subdued wood paneling. The pleasant contrasts found in the decor carry over to the menu. In addition to brewpub staples such as fish and chips, pizza, and bratwurst, this brewery and restaurant offers steaks and prime rib—dry-aged Angus beef from its own herd of Angus cattle, raised with no artificial growth stimulants or antibiotics—plus a vegetarian stir-fry plate and Rocky Mountain trout. The beers brewed here go well with everything. I especially recommend the hoppy, slightly bitter Pale Export and the Munich-style Pale Bock.

21 E. Main St. ✆ **970/564-9112.** Main courses $7–$26. AE, MC, V. Daily 3:30pm–close.

Nero's ★★ ITALIAN/AMERICAN My top choice in this area when I'm craving something a bit different. The innovative entrees, prepared by Culinary Institute of America chef Richard Gurd, include house specialties such as the Cowboy Steak (a charbroiled 12-oz. sirloin seasoned with a spicy rub and served with pasta or fries); my favorite, the mushroom ravioli served with an Alfredo sauce, sautéed spinach, sun-dried tomatoes, and pecans; and shrimp Alfredo—sautéed shrimp with spinach served over fettuccine with Alfredo sauce and Romano cheese. There's an excellent selection of beef, plus seafood, fowl, pork, veal, and lots of homemade pasta. A small, homey restaurant with a Southwestern art-gallery decor, Nero's also offers pleasant outdoor seating in warm weather. Value hunters, take note: There is an early bird special served from 5 to 6pm that costs $8 to $10.

303 W. Main St. ✆ **970/565-7366.** http://subee.com/neros/home.html. Reservations recommended. Main courses $11–$25. AE, MC, V. Wed–Sun 5–9:30pm.

Pippo's Cafe AMERICAN This friendly down-home cafe is an easy place to like, especially if you like a casual atmosphere, good basic American cooking, and reasonable prices. Located along busy Main Street, Pippo's serves lunch and dinner, but the specialty is breakfast, served during all open hours. I especially like the omelets and the homemade hash browns, but then I wouldn't turn down the steak and eggs either. The lunch menu includes the usual burger and fries, along with homemade soups, Navajo tacos, and fried chicken with mashed potatoes and gravy; dinner brings hearty plates like hot beef, pork chops, and steaks, as well as Navajo tacos and green and red chile.

100 W. Main St. ✆ **970/565-6039.** Most main courses $3–$10. AE, DISC, MC, V. Mon–Sat 6:30am–8:30pm; Sun 6:30am–2pm.

MESA VERDE NATIONAL PARK

Mesa Verde is the largest archaeological preserve in the United States, with some 4,000 known sites dating from A.D. 600 to 1300, including the most impressive cliff dwellings in the Southwest.

The earliest known inhabitants of Mesa Verde (Spanish for "green table") built subterranean pit houses on the mesa tops. During the 13th century they moved into shallow caves and constructed complex cliff dwellings. Although a massive construction project, these homes were only occupied for about a century; their residents left in about 1300 for reasons as yet undetermined.

The area was little known until ranchers Charles and Richard Wetherill chanced upon it in 1888. Looting of artifacts followed their discovery until a Denver newspaper reporter's stories aroused national interest in protecting the site. The 52,000-acre site was declared a national park in 1906—it's the only U.S. national park devoted entirely to the works of humans.

Fires have plagued the park in recent years, and burned, dead trees and blackened ground are very evident today. Two lightning-induced fires blackened about 40% of the park during the summer of 2000, closing the whole thing for about 3 weeks. Officials said that although the park's piñon-juniper forests were severely burned, none of the major archaeological sites were damaged, and in fact the fires revealed some sites that they were not aware existed. Then a lightning-induced fire struck again in the summer of 2002, closing the park for about 10 days. Officials said that the only damage to archaeological sites was the scorching of the wall of one ruin.

JUST THE FACTS

ENTRY The park entrance is located on U.S. 160, 10 miles east of Cortez and 6 miles west of Mancos.

FEES & REGULATIONS Admission to the park for up to 1 week costs $15 per vehicle in spring and summer, $10 fall and winter. Motorcyclists, bicyclists, and pedestrians must pay $8 in spring and summer, $5 in fall and winter. Tours of Cliff Palace, Balcony House, and Long House are $3; ranger-guided tours of other areas are free. To protect the many archaeological sites, the Park Service has outlawed backcountry camping and off-trail hiking. It's also illegal to enter cliff dwellings without a ranger present. The Wetherill Mesa Road cannot accommodate vehicles longer than 25 feet. Cyclists must have lights to pedal through the tunnel on the entrance road.

VISITOR CENTERS & INFORMATION **Chapin Mesa,** site of the park headquarters, museum, and a post office, is 20 miles from the park entrance on U.S. 160. The **Far View Visitor Center,** site of Far View Lodge, a restaurant, gift shop, and other facilities, is 15 miles off U.S. 160. For a park brochure, contact Mesa Verde National Park, P.O. Box 8, Mesa Verde, CO 81330 (✆ **970/529-4465;** www.nps.gov/meve).

HOURS & SEASONS The park is open daily year-round, but full interpretive services are available only from mid-June to Labor Day. In winter, the Mesa Top Road and museum remain open, but many other facilities are closed. The **Far View Visitor Center** is open from mid-April through mid-October only, from 8am to 5pm daily. The **Chapin Mesa Archeological Museum** is open daily from 8am to 6:30pm from early April through early October, daily from 8am to 5pm the rest of the year.

Tips Keeping Fido Safe & Happy

While there's plenty to do for human visitors to Mesa Verde National Park, the U.S. Park Service is not very welcoming to canine friends and prohibits them on all trails. (The only exceptions are for service dogs, such as Seeing Eye dogs.) This means that if you want to explore the park, you'll need to leave your dogs behind. Fortunately, there are several kennels in the area, including **The Dog Hotel,** 33350 Colo. 184, Mancos (✆ **970/882-5416**), which is a well-run facility, open 7 days a week, that also offers accommodations for cats. Appointments are necessary, and pet owners must have proof of current vaccinations.

AVOIDING THE CROWDS With close to half a million visitors annually, Mesa Verde seems packed at times, but the numbers are much lower just before and after the summer rush, usually from June 15 to August 15. Another way to beat the crowds is to make the 12-mile drive to Wetherill Mesa, which attracts only a small percentage of park visitors.

RANGER PROGRAMS In addition to guided tours to the cliff dwellings (see below), rangers give nightly campfire programs at Morefield Campground in summer.

SEEING THE HIGHLIGHTS IN A DAY

If you have only a day to spend at the park, stop first at the Far View Visitor Center to buy tickets for a late-afternoon tour of either Cliff House or Balcony House—visitors are not allowed to tour both on the same day. Then travel to the Chapin Mesa archeological museum for a look at the history behind the sites you're about to see. From there, walk down the trail behind the museum to Spruce Tree House. Then drive the Mesa Top Loop Road. Cap your day with the guided tour.

EXPLORING THE PARK

The **Cliff Palace,** the park's largest and best-known site, is a four-story apartment complex with stepped-back roofs forming porches for the dwellings above. Accessible by guided tour only, it is reached by a quarter-mile downhill path. Its towers, walls, and kivas (large circular rooms used for ceremonies) are all set back beneath the rim of a cliff. Another ranger-led tour takes visitors up a 32-foot ladder to explore the interior of **Balcony House.** Each of these tours is given only in summer and into fall (call for exact dates). Guided tours are also offered by Far View Lodge (see "Where to Stay & Dine in the Park," below).

Two other important sites—**Step House** and **Long House,** both on Wetherill Mesa—can be visited in summer only. Rangers lead free tours to **Spruce Tree House,** another of the major cliff-dwelling complexes, only in winter, when other park facilities are closed. Visitors can also explore Spruce Tree House on their own at any time.

Although none of the trails to the Mesa Verde sites is strenuous, the 7,000-foot elevation can make the treks tiring for visitors who aren't used to the altitude. For those who want to avoid hiking and climbing, the 12-mile **Mesa Top Road** makes a number of pit houses and cliff-side overlooks easily accessible by car. **Chapin Mesa Archeological Museum** houses artifacts and specimens related to the history of the area, including other nearby sites.

OUTDOOR ACTIVITIES Although this isn't an outdoor recreation park, per se—the reason to come here is to see the cliff dwellings and other archaeological sites—you'll find yourself hiking and climbing to get to the sites. Several longer hikes into scenic Spruce

Canyon let you stretch your legs and get away from the crowds. Hikers must register at the ranger's office before setting out.

CAMPING Open from early May to early October, **Morefield Campground** (✆ **800/449-2288** or 970/529-4421; www.visitmesaverde.com), 4 miles south of the park entrance, has 435 sites, including 15 with full RV hookups. The campground is set in rolling hills in a grassy area with scrub oak and brush. The attractive sites are fairly well spaced and are mostly separated by trees and other foliage. Facilities include modern restrooms, coin-operated showers (not within easy walking distance of most campsites), picnic tables, grills, and an RV dump station. Programs on the area's human and natural history and other subjects are presented nightly at the campground amphitheater from Memorial Day weekend through Labor Day weekend. Campsites cost $20, $25 with hookups. If you're hoping to snare one of the 15 full hookup sites, try getting to the park by late morning; there are almost always nonhookup sites available. There is also a "base camping" option where the campground provides you with tents, cots, and a lantern for $39 to $49 per night. There are also several commercial campgrounds along U.S. 160, just outside the park entrance.

Where to Stay & Dine in the Park

I like to be where the action is and recommend staying overnight at either the Morefield Campground (see "Camping," above) or the Far View Lodge (see below); both are operated by park concessionaire Aramark, which also operates several restaurants in the park. There are numerous lodging and dining possibilities in Cortez, too (see "Cortez," above).

Far View Lodge ★ Located in the heart of Mesa Verde National Park, Far View Lodge offers not only the most convenient location for visiting the park, but also the best views. The facility lodges guests in 17 separate buildings spread across a hilltop. Rooms aren't fancy and they're a bit on the small side, but they are well maintained and more than adequate, with Southwestern decor. Most standard rooms have one queen-size bed or two doubles, although a variety of bed combinations is available. I prefer the rooms with one bed—they seem less cramped than rooms with two beds. There are no TVs, but each unit has a private balcony, and the views are magnificent in all directions. Half-day guided tours of Cliff Palace and a few Chapin Mesa sites jump off from the lodge in summer ($49 adults, $38 children 5–11, and free for children under 5).

Mesa Verde National Park (P.O. Box 277), Mancos, CO 81328. ✆ **800/449-2288** or 970/529-4421. www.visitmesaverde.com. 150 units. Open late Apr through late Oct only. $116–$143 double. AE, DC, DISC, MC, V. Pets accepted with a deposit. **Amenities:** 2 restaurants (Southwestern American). *In room:* Coffeemaker.

NEARBY ARCHAEOLOGICAL SITES

Cortez Cultural Center

The Cortez Cultural Center, 25 N. Market St., Cortez (✆ **970/565-1151;** www.cortezculturalcenter.org), includes a museum with exhibits on both prehistoric and modern American Indians, an art gallery with displays of regional art, a good gift shop offering crafts by local tribal members, and a variety of programs including American Indian dances during the summer. From June through August, the center is open Monday through Saturday from 10am to 10pm, and the rest of the year it is open Monday through Saturday from 10am to 5pm. Admission is free and you should plan to spend at least an hour. Call or check the website for the schedule of Indian dances and other programs, which are also free.

Fun Facts What's in a Name?

The prehistoric inhabitants of the ancient villages of the Four Corners region have long been known as the Anasazi. That word is being phased out, however, in favor of "Ancestral Puebloans" or "ancient Pueblo people," because modern American Indians who trace their roots to the **Ancestral Puebloans** consider the word Anasazi demeaning. "Anasazi" is a Navajo word meaning "enemy of my people," as the Navajos considered the Ancestral Puebloans their enemies.

Ute Mountain Tribal Park ★★

If you liked Mesa Verde but would have enjoyed it more without the company of so many fellow tourists, you'll *love* the Ute Mountain Tribal Park, P.O. Box 109, Towaoc, CO 81334 (✆ **800/847-5485** or 970/565-3751 ext. 330; www.utemountainute.com/tribalpark.htm). Set aside by the Ute Mountain tribe to preserve its heritage, the 125,000-acre park—which abuts Mesa Verde National Park—includes ancient pictographs and petroglyphs as well as hundreds of surface sites and cliff dwellings that are similar in size and complexity to those in Mesa Verde.

Access to the park is strictly limited to guided tours. Full- and half-day tours begin at the Ute Mountain Museum and Visitor Center at the junction of U.S. 491 and U.S. 160, 20 miles south of Cortez. Mountain-biking and backpacking trips are also offered. No food, water, lodging, gasoline, or other services are available within the park. Some climbing of ladders is necessary on the full-day tour. There's one primitive **campground** ($12 per vehicle; reservations required).

Charges for tours in your vehicle start at $24 per person for a half-day, $44 for a full day; it's $9 per person extra to go in the tour guide's vehicle, and reservations are required.

Anasazi Heritage Center

When the Dolores River was dammed and the McPhee Reservoir was created in 1985, some 1,600 ancient archaeological sites were threatened. Four percent of the project costs were set aside for archaeological work, and over two million artifacts and other prehistoric items were rescued. Most are displayed in this museum. Located 10 miles north of Cortez, it is set into a hillside near the remains of 12th-century sites.

Operated by the Bureau of Land Management, the Anasazi Heritage Center emphasizes visitor involvement. Children and adults are invited to examine corn-grinding implements, a loom and other weaving materials, and a re-created pit house. You can touch artifacts 1,000 to 2,000 years old, examine samples through microscopes, use interactive computer programs, and engage in video lessons in archaeological techniques.

A half-mile trail leads from the museum to the **Dominguez Pueblo Ruins,** atop a low hill, with a beautiful view across the Montezuma Valley.

The center also serves as the visitor center for Canyons of the Ancients National Monument (see below). It is located at 27501 Colo. 184, Dolores (✆ **970/882-5600;** www.co.blm.gov/ahc). It's open March through October daily from 9am to 5pm; November through February daily from 10am to 4pm; and closed Thanksgiving, Christmas, and New Year's Day. An admission fee of $3 for adults is charged March through October only; admission is free for those 17 and under. Allow 2 hours.

Canyons of the Ancients National Monument

Among the country's newest national monuments, Canyons of the Ancients was created by presidential proclamation in June 2000. The 164,000-acre national monument, located west of Cortez, contains thousands of archaeological sites—what some claim is the highest density of archaeological sites in the United States—including the remains of villages, cliff dwellings, sweat lodges, and petroglyphs at least 700 years old, and possibly as much as 10,000 years old.

Canyons of the Ancients includes **Lowry Pueblo,** an excavated 12th-century village that is located 26 miles from Cortez via U.S. 491, on C.R. CC, 9 miles west of Pleasant View. This pueblo, which was likely abandoned by 1200, is believed to have housed about 100 people. It has standing walls from 40 rooms plus 9 kivas (circular underground ceremonial chambers). A short, self-guided interpretive trail leads past a kiva and continues to the remains of a great kiva, which, at 54 feet in diameter, is among the largest ever found. There are also a picnic area, drinking water, and toilets.

Canyons of the Ancients is managed by the Bureau of Land Management and as yet has no on-site visitor center or even a contact station. Those wishing to explore the monument are strongly advised to contact or, preferably, stop first at the visitor center located at Anasazi Heritage Center (see above) for information, especially current road conditions and directions. Information is also available online at **www.co.blm.gov/canm** and from the Welcome Center in Cortez (see the Cortez section, earlier). Allow at least 2 hours.

Hovenweep National Monument

Preserving some of the most striking and isolated archaeological sites in the Four Corners area, this national monument straddles the Colorado–Utah border, 40 miles west of Cortez.

Hovenweep is the Ute word for "deserted valley," appropriate because its inhabitants apparently left around 1300. The monument contains six separate sites and is noted for mysterious 20-foot-high sandstone towers, some square, others oval, circular, or D-shaped. Archaeologists have suggested possible functions: everything from guard or signal towers, celestial observatories, and ceremonial structures to water towers or granaries.

A ranger station, with exhibits, restrooms, and drinking water, is located at the **Square Tower Site,** in the Utah section of the monument, the most impressive and best preserved of the sites. The **Hovenweep Campground,** with 30 sites, is open year-round. Sites are fairly small—most appropriate for tents or small pickup truck campers—but a few sites can accommodate RVs up to 25 feet long. The campground has flush toilets, drinking water, picnic tables, and fire pits, but no showers or RV hookups. Cost is $10 per night; reservations are not accepted, but the campground rarely fills.

From Cortez, take U.S. 160 south to C.R. G (McElmo Canyon Rd.) and follow signs into Utah and the monument. The other five sites are difficult to find, and you'll need to obtain detailed driving directions and check on current road conditions before setting out. Summer temperatures can reach over 100°F (38°C), and water supplies are limited—so take your own and carry a canteen, even on short walks. Bug repellent is advised, as gnats can be a nuisance in late spring.

The visitor center/ranger station is open daily from 8am to 6pm from April through September and 8am to 5pm the rest of the year; it's closed Thanksgiving, Christmas, and New Year's Day. Trails are open from sunrise to sunset. Admission for up to a week costs $6 per vehicle or $3 per person on bike or foot. For advance information, contact

Hovenweep National Monument, McElmo Route, Cortez, CO 81321 (© **970/562-4282;** www.nps.gov/hove).

Crow Canyon Archaeological Center

The Crow Canyon Archaeological Center focuses on the rich history of the Anasazi. Crow Canyon's campus-based programs allow visitors to participate in actual research in both the field and laboratory. Offerings open to the public include digs with pro archaeologists, family programs that cover a gamut of archaeological skills, and summer camps for teens. Programs have been developed with help from American Indians.

Crow Canyon Archaeological Center, located just a few miles north of Cortez at 23390 Rd. K, is based out of a 170-acre campus (complete with labs, classrooms, a dormitory, and 10 rustic cabins inspired by Navajo hogans); classes range from a $50 day tour to programs that last a week or more starting at about $1,000 a student. Contact the Center (© **800/422-8975** or 970/565-8975; www.crowcanyon.org), for a course catalog or other information.

5 TELLURIDE

126 miles N of Durango, 127 miles S of Grand Junction

This was one seriously rowdy town a century ago—in fact, this is where Butch Cassidy robbed his first bank, in 1889. Incorporated with the boring name of Columbia in 1878, the mining town assumed its present name the following decade. Some say the name came from tellurium, a gold-bearing ore, while others insist the name really means "to hell you ride," referring to the town's boisterous nature.

Telluride became a National Historic District in 1964, and in 1968 entrepreneur Joe Zoline set to work on a "winter recreation area second to none." The Telluride Ski Company opened its first runs in 1972, and Telluride was a boomtown again. Telluride's first summer festivals (bluegrass in June, film in Sept) were celebrated the following year. Today the resort, at 8,745 feet elevation, is a year-round destination for mountain bikers, skiers, anglers, and hikers. Funky has mostly given way to chic these days, but the surrounding natural beauty remains unforgettable.

ESSENTIALS

GETTING THERE **By Car** Telluride is located on Colo. 145. From Cortez, follow Colo. 145 northeast for 73 miles. From the north (Montrose), turn west off U.S. 550 at Ridgway, onto Colo. 62. Proceed 25 miles to Placerville and turn left (southeast) onto Colo. 145. Thirteen miles ahead is a junction—a right turn will take you to Cortez, but for Telluride, continue straight ahead 4 miles to the end of a box canyon. From Durango, in summer take U.S. 550 north to Colo. 62 and follow the directions above; in winter it's best to take the route through Cortez and avoid Red Mountain Pass above Silverton.

By Plane **Telluride Regional Airport** (© **970/728-5313;** www.tellurideairport.com), 5 miles west of Telluride atop a plateau at 9,078 feet, is served year-round by **Great Lakes Airline** (© 800/554-5111) from Denver. During ski season, flights from various cities are available from **Frontier** (© 800/432-1359), **US Airways** (© 800/428-4322), and **United** (© 800/241-6522).

VISITOR INFORMATION Contact **Telluride Tourism Board,** 630 W. Colorado Ave. (P.O. Box 1009), Telluride, CO 81435 (✆ **888/605-2578;** www.visittelluride.com). The **Telluride Visitor Information Center,** open daily from 9am to 6pm, can be found at the corner of West Colorado Avenue and Davis Street, on the west side of town.

GETTING AROUND The city is located on the San Miguel River, where it flows out of a box canyon formed by the 14,000-foot peaks of the San Juan Mountains. Colo. 145 enters town from the west and becomes Colorado Avenue, the main street.

With restaurants, shops, and attractions within easy walking distance of most lodging facilities, many visitors leave their cars parked and use their feet. However, if you do want to ride, there's a free town shuttle in winter and summer. Telluride Mountain Village, at 9,500 feet, can be reached in winter and summer by a free gondola, operating daily from 7am to midnight. Motorists can take Mountain Village Boulevard off Colo. 145, a mile south of the Telluride junction.

Budget (✆ **970/728-4642**) and **Alamo** (✆ **970/728-9380**) provide car rentals, including vans and four-wheel-drive vehicles, at the airport, and **Dollar** (✆ **970/369-0020**) has an outlet in Telluride. Two- and four-seat electric cars are available from **Go Green** (✆ **970/708-4023;** www.gogreentelluride.com); charging and parking are included in the rental price.

FAST FACTS The hospital, **Telluride Medical Center,** with a 24-hour emergency room, is at 500 W. Pacific Ave. (✆ **970/728-3848;** www.tellmed.org). The **post office** is at 150 S. Willow St.; call the U.S. Postal Service (✆ **800/275-8777;** www.usps.com) for hours and other information.

SPECIAL EVENTS Telluride Wine Festival, late June; Chamber Music Festival, mid-August; Culinary and Art Festival, late August; Mushroom Festival, late August; Imogene Pass Run, early September; Oktoberfest, early October. See also "The Festival Scene," below.

DOWNHILL SKIING & SNOWBOARDING

The elegant European-style Mountain Village, built in 1987, offers a fascinating contrast to the laid-back community of artists, shopkeepers, and dropouts in the 1870s Victorian mining town of Telluride below. Located midmountain at an elevation of 9,450 feet, the Mountain Village offers ski-in/ski-out accommodations, a variety of slope-side restaurants, and great skiing.

The mountain's **South Face,** which drops sharply from the summit to the town of Telluride, is characterized by steep moguls, tree-and-glade skiing, and challenging groomed pitches for experts and advanced intermediates. **Lift 4,** which rises from the Mountain Village Resort, caters to intermediate skiers. The broad, gentle slopes of the **Meadows** stretch to the foot of Sunshine Peak. This part of the mountain, with trails over 2½ miles long devoted entirely to novice skiers, is served by a high-speed quad chair. Average annual snowfall is 300 inches (25 ft.). The gently rolling slopes of **Ute Park** (Lift 11) serve as the beginner training area, while **Prospect** (Lift 12) accesses intermediate and expert terrain. **Gold Hill** (Lift 14) offers intermediate and expert skiers an expanse of steep terrain, as well as breathtaking views.

In all, Telluride offers more than 1,700 acres of skiable terrain. The lift-served vertical drop is an impressive 3,845 feet from the 12,570-foot summit. The mountain has over 100 trails served by 18 lifts (two high-speed gondolas, seven high-speed quads, one quad, two triples, two doubles, two surface lifts, and two Magic Carpets). Of the trails, 24% are rated for beginners, 38% for intermediates, and 38% for experts. The longest run here, at 4½ miles, is **Galloping Goose,** but for some of the most spectacular views in Colorado, ski the aptly named run **See Forever.** Telluride also has one of the top **snowboarding parks** in Colorado, offering more than 13 acres of terrain.

Full-day lift tickets during the regular season cost $92 for adults, $56 for children 6 to 12, $82 for seniors 65 and older, and are free for children under 6. Rates over the Christmas holidays are higher, and rates at the very beginning of the season are lower. Ski and snowboarding lessons are offered, along with childcare. The resort is usually open daily from 9am to 4pm from Thanksgiving to early April.

For additional information, contact **Telluride Ski and Golf Company,** 565 Mountain Village Blvd., Telluride, CO 81435 (✆ **800/801-4832** or 970/728-6900; www.tellurideskiresort.com).

OTHER WINTER ACTIVITIES

In addition to skiing at Telluride Ski Resort, there are plenty of opportunities for other cold-weather adventures in the Telluride area. Many of them take place at **Town Park,** at the east end of town (✆ **970/728-3071;** www.telluride-co.gov), where there are groomed cross-country trails, daytime sledding and tubing at Firecracker Hill, and free ice skating. There's also free ice skating at the outdoor rink in the Mountain Village. Skate rentals are available at local sporting-goods stores.

The **River Corridor Trail** follows the San Miguel River from Town Park to the valley floor. Popular with bikers and hikers in warm weather, it's perfect for cross-country skiing and skate-skiing after the snow falls. The Mountain Village at Telluride Ski Resort (see above) has 19 miles of **Nordic trails,** which connect with 12 miles of groomed trails at Town Park and River Corridor Trail, giving cross-country skiers a total of 31 miles.

Guided snowmobile tours ranging from 2 hours to all day, with rates starting at about $150 for one rider on one machine, are offered by several local companies, including **Dave's Mountain Tours** (✆ **970/728-9749;** www.telluridetours.com). Those who want to (and can afford to) take a helicopter to some of the best powder skiing available should contact **Telluride Helitrax** (✆ **866/435-4754** or 970/728-8377; www.helitrax.net), with rates for a 6-run day of $1,350 per person.

WARM-WEATHER & YEAR-ROUND ACTIVITIES

Telluride isn't just a ski town—there's a wide variety of year-round outdoor activities. **Town Park** (see above) is home to the community's various festivals. It also has a public outdoor pool, open in summer, plus tennis courts, sand volleyball courts, a small outdoor basketball court, a skateboarding ramp, playing fields, picnic area, and fishing pond (see "Fishing," below). A first-come, first-served campground for tent and car campers, open from May 15 to October 15, has 34 sites and showers ($2 in quarters only), but no RV hookups, and costs $12 to $16 per night.

There are a number of outfitting companies in the Telluride area, including **Telluride Outside,** 121 W. Colorado Ave. (✆ **800/831-6230** or 970/728-3895; www.tellurideoutside.com), which offers a wide range of guided adventures. Equipment rentals are available throughout Telluride and Mountain Village. You'll find mountain bikes, fishing gear, camping equipment, and inflatable kayaks at **Telluride Sports,** 150 W. Colorado Ave. (✆ **800/828-7547** or 970/728-4477; www.telluridesports.com).

FISHING There's excellent fishing in the San Miguel River through Telluride, but it's even better in nearby alpine lakes, including Silver Lake, reached by foot in Bridal Veil Basin, and Trout and Priest lakes, about 12 miles south via Colo. 145. At Town Park there's the Kids Fishin' Pond for children 12 and under, which is stocked Memorial Day to Labor Day. Recommended guides include Telluride Outside (see above) and **San Miguel Anglers** (✆ **970/728-4477;** www.sanmiguelanglers.com), with prices around $350 to $400 for a full-day wade trip for two people on the San Miguel or Upper Dolores.

FOUR-WHEELING To see old ghost towns, mining camps, and spectacular mountain scenery from the relative comfort of a bouncing four-wheel-drive vehicle, join Telluride Outside (see above) or Dave's Mountain Tours (see "Other Winter Activities," above). A variety of trips is offered, including rides over the 13,000-foot Imogene Pass jeep road, with prices for full-day trips about $125 for adults and $105 for children 12 and younger. Half-day trips are about $80 and $70, respectively.

GOLF The 18-hole par-71 **Telluride Golf Course** is located at Telluride Mountain Village (✆ **970/728-6366** or 970/728-6157; www.tellurideskiresort.com). Greens fees with the required cart are $160 from July through Labor Day, lower at other times.

HIKING & MOUNTAINEERING The mountains around Telluride offer innumerable opportunities for hiking, mountaineering, and backpacking. Sporting goods stores and the visitor center have maps of trails in the Telluride area. Especially popular are the easy 4-mile (round-trip) **Bear Creek Canyon Trail ★**, which starts at the end of South Pine Street and leads to a picturesque waterfall; the **Jud Wiebe Trail** that begins at the north end of Aspen Street and does a 2.7-mile loop above the town, offering views of Bridal Veil Falls, the town, and ski area; and the 1.8-mile (one-way) hike to the top of **Bridal Veil Falls,** which starts at the east end of Telluride Canyon.

HORSEBACK RIDING One of the best ways to see this spectacular country is by horse. **Telluride Horseback Adventures** (✆ **970/728-9611;** www.ridewithroudy.com) has "gentle horses for gentle people and fast horses for fast people, and for people who don't like to ride, horses that don't like to be rode." Another good company is **Many Ponies Outfit** (✆ **970/728-6278;** www.manyponiesoutfit.com). Rates are about $90 for a 2-hour ride, $150 for a half-day ride, and $190 for a full day in the saddle.

MOUNTAIN BIKING Telluride is a major mountain-biking center. The **San Juan Hut System** links Telluride with Moab, Utah, via a 206-mile-long network of backcountry dirt roads. Every 35 miles is a primitive cabin, with bunks, a wood stove, propane cooking stove, and cooking gear. The route, open to mountain bikers from June through September (and cross-country skiers and snowshoers in snow season), is appropriate for intermediate-level riders in good physical condition, and an advanced technical single track is found near the huts for more experienced cyclists. Cost for riders who plan to make the whole trip is about $750, which includes use of the six huts, three meals daily, sleeping bags at each hut, and maps and trail descriptions. Shorter trips, guide services, and vehicle shuttles are also available. For information, contact San Juan Hut System, P.O. Box 773, Ridgway, CO 81432 (✆ **970/626-3033;** www.sanjuanhuts.com). Mountain bike rentals are available from **Telluride Sports** (see above) for $35 to $50 per day.

SEEING THE SIGHTS

The best way to see the Telluride National Historic District, examine its hundreds of historic buildings, and get a feel for the West of the late 1800s is to take to the streets. Either follow the **walking tour** described in the ***Telluride Visitor's Guide,*** available at the Telluride Visitor Information Center (see "Visitor Information," above), or rent a mini disk player with a disk and accompanying map at the Telluride Historical Museum (see below) for one of the recorded **audio walking tours** of Telluride. Cost of the audio tour rental is $10, and there are five tours available, each concentrating on a different part of the community.

Among the buildings you'll see are the **San Miguel County Courthouse,** Colorado Avenue at Oak Street, built in 1887 and still in use today. A block north and west, at Columbia Avenue and Aspen Street, is the **L. L. Nunn House,** home of the late-19th-century mining engineer who created the first high-voltage alternating-current power plant in the world. Two blocks east of Fir Street, on Galena Avenue at Spruce Street, is **St. Patrick's Catholic Church,** built in 1895, whose wooden Stations of the Cross figures were carved in Austria's Tyrol region. Perhaps Telluride's most famous landmark is the **New Sheridan Hotel** and the **Sheridan Opera House,** opposite the county courthouse at Colorado and Oak. The hotel, built in 1895, rivaled Denver's famed Brown Palace Hotel in service and cuisine in its early days. The exquisite opera house, added in 1914, boasts a Venetian scene painted on its roll curtain.

Colorado's highest waterfall (365 ft.) can be seen from the east end of Colorado Avenue. **Bridal Veil Falls** freezes in winter, then slowly melts in early spring, creating a dramatic effect. Perched at the top edge of the falls is a National Historic Landmark, a hydroelectric power plant that served area mines in the late 1800s. Recently restored and once again supplying power to the community, it's accessible by hiking or driving a switchback, four-wheel-drive road.

Telluride Historical Museum ★★ This fine museum should be the first stop in Telluride for anyone interested in learning about the history of this Wild West town. Built in 1896 as the community hospital, this beautifully restored facility contains a collection of some 9,000 artifacts and 1,400 historic photos that show what Telluride was like when the likes of Butch Cassidy stalked the streets. Exhibits include hard rock mining, with displays of mining equipment and models of mines and mills; the narrow-gauge railroad; the area's Ute Indian heritage; the history of medical facilities and treatments in Telluride (this was the town hospital, after all); and the development of the town's AC electric power—the world's first AC-generating plant was built here in the 1890s by Nikola Tesla. There is also a replica of a local mining family's cabin in the early 1900s, plus exhibits on the town's Victorian architecture and Telluride's emergence as a major outdoor recreation destination. You'll learn about train and bank robber Cassidy and other historic figures from Telluride's past, and see some of the fancy dresses worn by Big Billie, one of the community's leading madams during the town's red-light days. The museum store is a good source for books on the area's history—an especially good local read is *Tomboy Bride* by Harriet Backus—and you can rent equipment for a self-guided audio tour of Telluride (see above). Allow 1 to 2 hours.

201 W. Gregory Ave., at the top of Fir St. ✆ **970/728-3344.** www.telluridemuseum.com. Admission $5 adults, $3 seniors and students 6–17, free for children 4 and under. Summer Tues–Sat 11am–5pm (Thurs until 7pm), Sun 1–5pm; the rest of the year Tues–Sat 11am–5pm.

THE FESTIVAL SCENE

Telluride must be the most festival-happy town in America, and visitors come from around the world to see the finest new films, hear the best musicians, and even pick the most exotic mushrooms. In addition to the phone numbers listed, you can get additional details and often tickets from the Telluride Tourism Board (see "Visitor Information," above).

The **Telluride Film Festival ★★** (✆ **510/665-9494;** www.telluridefilmfestival.org), an influential festival within the film industry that takes place over Labor Day weekend, has premiered some of the finest films produced in recent years (*Brokeback Mountain* and *Juno* are just a couple examples). What truly sets it apart, however, is the casual interaction between stars and attendees. Open-air films and seminars are free to all.

Mountainfilm (✆ **970/728-4123;** www.mountainfilm.org), which takes place every Memorial Day weekend, brings together filmmakers, writers, and outdoor enthusiasts to celebrate mountains, adventure, and the environment. Four days are filled with films, seminars, and presentations.

The **Telluride Bluegrass Festival ★★** (✆ **800/624-2422;** www.bluegrass.com/telluride) is one of the most intense and renowned bluegrass, folk, and country jam sessions in the United States. Held over 4 days during mid- to late June in conjunction with the Bluegrass Academy, recent lineups have featured Mary Chapin Carpenter, Bela Fleck, Ani DiFranco, and Ryan Adams.

The **Telluride Jazz Celebration** (✆ **970/728-7009;** www.telluridejazz.org), a 3-day event in early June, is marked by day concerts in Town Park and evening happenings in downtown saloons. Recent performers have included Dr. John, the Neville Brothers, Stanley Jordan, and Bettye LeVette.

Nothing Fest (www.telluridenothingfestival.com), a non-event begun in the early 1990s, is just that—nothing special happens, and it doesn't happen all over town. It's usually scheduled in mid-July. When founder Dennis Wrestler was asked how long the festival would continue, he responded, "How can you cancel something that doesn't happen?" Admission is free, and you can get all the noninformation you need from the Telluride Tourism Board (see above, or don't).

WHERE TO STAY

Telluride's lodging rates probably have more different "seasons" than anywhere else in Colorado. Generally speaking, you'll pay top dollar for a room over the Christmas holidays, during the film and bluegrass festivals, and at certain other peak times. Nonholiday skiing is a bit cheaper, summertime lodging (except for festival times) is cheaper yet, and you may find some real bargains in spring and fall. The key to finding inexpensive lodging and avoiding crowds is timing; unless you particularly want to attend the Bluegrass Festival, plan your trip another time. You're also much more likely to find attractive package deals on skiing and other activities if you go during quieter times, and not on weekends.

Telluride has a wide variety of lodging options, including B&Bs, hotels, private homes, and in my opinion, a few too many condominiums. Many are managed by **ResortQuest Telluride** (✆ **866/538-7731;** www.resortquesttelluride.com). Perhaps the best way to book lodging, however, is with the **Telluride Central Reservations** (✆ **888/605-2578;** www.visittelluride.com). Room tax adds a bit over 12%.

In Mountain Village—a 15-minute gondola ride from downtown but in the middle of the action come wintertime—I like the condos and luxury cabins at **Mountain Lodge,** atop the gondola above the village center at 457 Mountain Village Blvd. (✆ **866/368-6867;** www.mountainlodgetelluride.com), featuring such amenities as gas fireplaces and cozy robes along with superlative views; in ski season, double rates are $299 to $389 for a studio and $409 to $1,379 for a one- to four-bedroom condo (lower rates the rest of the year). Also recommended is the slick and colorful **Lumière** (✆ **866/530-9466;** www.lumierehotels.com), a new-for-2008 LEED-certified ski-in/ski-out hotel at the base of the lifts with double rates of $375 to over $1,000 a night in ski season and lower rates the rest of the year.

Expensive

Camel's Garden Resort Hotel ★ This property, with 30 rooms and suites plus six condo units, has a perfect location—it's ski-in/ski-out, only steps from the town gondola, and also within 2 short blocks of the main shopping and dining section of historic Telluride. The hotel rooms—even the smallest, least expensive ones—are spacious, with the feel of upscale condo units, and all have cherry-oak furnishings, Italian marble bathrooms with oversized tubs, CD players, and gas fireplaces. Most units have balconies, with views of either the town or mountains, and king beds on pedestals. The simple but tasteful decor includes attractive black-and-white photos of the area. The one-, two-, three-, and four-bedroom condos are huge, with complete kitchens, washer/dryers, jetted tubs and showers, and heated towel racks. Other amenities include a 25-foot outdoor jetted hot tub that offers great views of the nearby mountains, a sporting-goods store, and ski storage and ski valet services. The entire property is nonsmoking.

250 W. San Juan Ave. (P.O. Box 4145), Telluride, CO 81435. ✆ **888/772-2635** or 970/728-9300. Fax 970/728-0433. www.camelsgarden.com. 36 units. Ski season and festivals $375–$675 double hotel room and suite, $725–$2,500 condo; other times $180–$495 double hotel room and suite, $460–$900 condo. Rates include continental breakfast and afternoon refreshments in ski season. AE, DC, DISC, MC, V. Free underground heated parking (6-ft., 4-in. height limit); outside parking available for larger vehicles. **Amenities:** Restaurant (continental); spa; Jacuzzi; steam room; laundry. *In room:* Cable TV/DVD player, wireless Internet access (free), safe deposit boxes available on request.

Moderate

Hotel Telluride ★★ Finds This thoroughly modern luxury hotel's gas-lit entry belies its young age, and its guest rooms are among the best you'll find in town. The stately, somewhat masculine decor, rife with earth tones, dark wood, and granite counters, is rich and organic to Telluride's historic vibe, but the superlative square footage and modern conveniences are sure to please 21st-century travelers. The location is northwest of the town center, a few blocks' walk to restaurants or the gondola, but the place's high style and well-thought-out comfort are worth it.

199 N. Cornet St., Telluride, CO 81435. ✆ **970/369-1188.** Fax 970/369-1292. www.thehoteltelluride.com. 59 units, including 2 suites. Ski season and summer $219–$259 double, $419–$479 suite; festivals and holidays $479–$499 double, $649–$729 suite; off season $169 double, $350–$450 suite. Underground parking ($15 per night). Rates include full breakfast. AE, DISC, MC, V. Pets accepted ($100 one-time fee). **Amenities:** Restaurant; bar; concierge; complimentary bike rentals; exercise room; business center; massage. *In room:* A/C, cable TV, wireless Internet access (free), coffeemaker, fridge, microwave/toaster oven, hair dryer, iron, safe.

Ice House Lodge and Condominiums A full-service lodge just half a block from the Oak Street chairlift, the Ice House offers casual and comfortable accommodations in European alpine style. Stairs and an elevator ascend from the ground-floor entrance to the lobby, which is furnished with simple Southwestern pieces. The decor carries to the guest rooms, which contain king-size beds and sleeper sofas or two full-size beds, European comforters, custom-made light wood furniture, and great mountain views from private decks. Thirty-nine of the rooms have shower/tub combos with oversized tubs; three rooms have showers only. The one-, two-, and three-bedroom condominium units have full kitchens, washers and dryers, two bathrooms, and a large deck. Guests also have access to a nearby spa.

310 S. Fir St. (P.O. Box 2909), Telluride, CO 81435. ✆ **800/544-3436** or 970/728-6300. Fax 970/728-6358. www.icehouselodge.com. 42 units. Ski season and festivals $245–$650 double lodge room and suite, $450–$1,149 condo; other times $155–$425 double lodge room and suite, $375–$875 condo. Rates

include continental breakfast and afternoon refreshments. AE, DC, DISC, MC, V. **Amenities:** Pool (half indoors and half outdoors); hot tub; steam room; limited room service; massage; laundry service. *In room:* TV, minibar.

Inexpensive

The Victorian Inn ★ Value Built in 1976, but in keeping with the turn-of-the-20th-century flavor of the town, the well-maintained and service-oriented Victorian offers a pleasant alternative to the seemingly hundreds of condos that populate Telluride. The spacious rooms, decorated with Victorian-style furnishings, are fully carpeted and have individually controlled heating, one or two queen beds, and refrigerators. Two units have kitchenettes, and there is also a honeymoon suite and a cottage. The continental breakfast includes pastries, coffee, juice, teas, and hot cocoa. The inn is located a half-block from Main Street, the free gondola, and ski lift no. 8.

401 W. Pacific Ave. (P.O. Box 217), Telluride, CO 81435. ✆ **800/611-9893** or 970/728-6601. Fax 970/728-3233. www.tellurideinn.com. 32 units. Ski season and festivals $159–$249 double; summer and off season $99–$119. Children 12 and under stay free in parent's room. Rates include continental breakfast. AE, DC, DISC, MC, V. **Amenities:** Hot tub; dry sauna; coin-op laundry. *In room:* Cable TV, wireless Internet access (free), fridge, coffeemaker, hair dryer.

WHERE TO DINE

Telluride lives by its seasons, and some restaurants will close for a few weeks in the slow seasons, generally spring and fall.

Expensive

Cosmopolitan ★★ CREATIVE AMERICAN An elegant fine-dining restaurant, the Cosmopolitan is also casual enough for a relaxing meal after a hard day on the slopes. The decor is modern and comfortable, and there's a delightful enclosed patio. The dinner menu includes a variety of dishes—beef, fish, lamb, duck, and vegetarian—all prepared with an innovative flair by chef-owner Chad Scothorn. Recommended dishes are the sesame grilled wild king salmon with shoestring sweet potatoes, sesame vegetables, and seaweed; and the all-natural Colorado lamb loin with polenta, grilled eggplant, and roasted red pepper rouille. The wine list—there are more than 200 wines—has received the Award of Excellence from *Wine Spectator* magazine.

300 W. San Juan Ave., in the Hotel Columbia ✆ **970/728-1292.** www.cosmotelluride.com. Reservations recommended. Main courses $19–$35. AE, MC, V. Daily 5–9:30pm.

Moderate

Las Montañas ★ MEXICAN A stylish and upscale Mexican joint with a social bar and a long and varied margarita list (try a Purple Haze), Las Montañas offers a New West–style spin on traditional Mexican and Latin American dishes like fajitas, rellenos, and burritos, as well as more adventurous specials that might explore the cuisine of the Southwest to South America. The house-made salsa is fantastic, as is the tapas menu. The front room is centered on an attractive granite bar, and there are tables on the street (in summer) and in the colorful dining room in the back.

122 S. Oak St. ✆ **970/728-3985.** Reservations not accepted. Main courses $11–$15. AE, MC, V. Daily 8am–10pm.

Inexpensive

Cornerhouse Grille Value AMERICAN A bit ornery but efficient—and the best deal in town—the Cornerhouse is housed in a historic building, not too surprisingly, on a corner just a block off the main drag. The kid-friendly bar and grill (the former being topped with copper and lined with TVs) specializes in sandwiches. (The house specialty is the Big Willy: turkey, tomato, guacamole, and cheddar on sourdough.) There are also burgers and salads on the menu, which is displayed on a chalkboard across from the bartender/cashier, and a number of beers on tap.

131 N. Fir St. © **970/728-6207.** Reservations not accepted. Main courses $6–$11. MC, V. Daily 11am–10pm.

Maggie's Bakery & Cafe AMERICAN The atmosphere here is simple, with oak tables and antique cookie jars, and the cuisine is geared toward those who appreciate home-baked breads and pastries, and hearty sandwiches. Breakfast dishes include traditional bacon and eggs with potatoes and fresh-baked bread, pancakes, biscuits with sausage gravy, and fresh fruit. Lunch possibilities include large burgers on home-baked buns, a variety of deli and vegetarian sandwiches, pizzas, and soups. Coffee drinks are also available.

217 E. Colorado Ave. © **970/728-3334.** Reservations not accepted. Breakfast and lunch $4–$8. No credit cards. Daily 7:30am–3pm.

6 OURAY

73 miles N of Durango, 96 miles S of Grand Junction

Named for the greatest chief of the southern Ute tribe, whose homeland was in this area, Ouray, at an elevation of 7,760 feet, got its start in 1876 as a gold- and silver-mining camp. Within 10 years it had 1,200 residents, a school, a hospital, dozens of saloons and brothels, and even a few churches. Today Ouray retains much of its 19th-century charm, with many of its original buildings still standing. It offers visitors a restful getaway while serving as home base for exploring the beautiful San Juan Mountains, with peaks rising to over 14,000 feet.

ESSENTIALS

GETTING THERE **By Car** U.S. 550 runs through the heart of Ouray, paralleling the Uncompahgre River and connecting it with Durango to the south and Montrose to the north. As you enter town from the north, the highway becomes Main Street. Above Third Avenue, U.S. 550 begins its climb up switchbacks to the Million Dollar Highway.

VISITOR INFORMATION Stop at the **Ouray Visitor Center** beside the Ouray Hot Springs Pool, on U.S. 550 at the north end of town, open from 9am to 5pm Monday through Wednesday, 9am to 7pm Thursday through Saturday, and 10am to 4pm Sunday; or contact the **Ouray Chamber Resort Association,** P.O. Box 145, Ouray, CO 81427 (© **800/228-1876** or 970/325-4746; www.ouraycolorado.com).

FAST FACTS The **post office** is at 620 Main St.; contact the U.S. Postal Service (© **800/275-8777;** www.usps.com) for hours and additional information.

SPECIAL EVENTS Ouray Ice Festival, mid-January; the Artists' Alpine Holiday, August; Oktoberfest, early October.

WHAT TO SEE & DO

The main summertime outdoor activity here is exploring the spectacularly beautiful mountains and forests by foot, mountain bike, horse, or four-wheel-drive vehicle. My favorite local outfitter, which can arrange for a variety of outdoor adventures, is **Switzerland of America,** 226 Seventh Ave. (© **866/990-5337** or 970/325-4484; www.soajeep.com), which also rents four-wheel-drive jeeps for about $135 per day. The company leads jeep tours into the high country ($60 for a half-day, $120 for a full day) and arranges horseback rides (starting at $60 per person for 2 hr.), raft rides ($65 for a half-day on the San Miguel River), and balloon rides ($275). Children 12 and under are charged about half.

At the southwest corner of Ouray, at Oak Street above Third Avenue, the **Box Canyon Falls & Park ★★** (✆ **970/325-4464**) features some of the most impressive waterfalls in the Rockies. The Uncompahgre River tumbles 285 feet through—not over, *through*—a cliff: It's easy to get a feeling of vertigo as you study the spectacle. The trail to the bottom of the falls is easy; to the top it is moderate to strenuous. Admission to the area is $3 for adults, $2.50 for seniors 65 and older, and $1.50 for children 5 to 12. It's open daily 8am to 8pm or dark, whichever comes first.

Winter visitors will likely be basing themselves in Ouray to ski at Telluride or head out into the mountains on cross-country skis or snowshoes, but Ouray's main claim to winter fame is the **Ouray Ice Park,** located in the southwest corner of town off U.S. 550 (✆ **970/325-4288;** www.ourayicepark.com). Ouray folks claim it is the world's first park devoted exclusively to the sport of ice climbing. Climbing in the park is free and it's open at any time during the winter. Ice-climbing courses are offered by **San Juan Mountain Guides** (✆ **970/325-4925;** www.ourayclimbing.com); a 2-day basic ice-climbing course costs $320 and includes all equipment.

Bachelor-Syracuse Mine Tour ★★ For a fun time while actually learning something, I heartily recommend this trip into the underworld. A mine train takes visitors 1,800 feet inside Gold Hill, to see where some $8 million in gold, $90 million in silver, and $5 million in other minerals have been mined since silver was discovered here in 1884. Guides, many of them former miners, explain the mining process and equipment and recount the various legends of the mine. Also on the property is an operating blacksmith shop, plus streams where you can learn the technique of gold panning ($4 extra). The mine temperature is a cool 50°F (10°C), so jackets are recommended, even in summer. Allow about 1½ hours.

2 miles from Ouray via C.R. 14. ✆ **888/227-4585** or 970/325-0220. www.bachelorsyracusemine.com. Admission $17 adults, $8.95 children 4–11, free for children 3 and under. Mid-May to mid-Sept 9am–5pm; shorter hours at the beginning and end of this period. Closed July 4 and mid-Sept to mid-May. Reservations recommended, especially July–Aug.

Ouray County Museum Lodged in the original Miners' Hospital, which was completed in 1887 and operated by the Sisters of Mercy, this large three-story museum is packed to the rafters with fascinating exhibits from Ouray's past. There are more than two dozen exhibit rooms, each having a different theme, plus many small displays and changing exhibits. You'll see pioneer and mining-era relics, items relating to railroad and other transportation modes of the 19th century, ranch artifacts, memorabilia of Chief Ouray and the Utes, early hospital equipment including some scary-looking medical devices, Victorian artifacts, and historic photos. Allow about an hour, and ask here for a walking-tour guide to the town's many historic buildings.

420 Sixth Ave. ✆ **970/325-4576.** www.ouraycountyhistoricalsociety.org. Admission $5 adults, $3.50 seniors 60 and older, $1 children 12 and under. Summer Mon–Sat 10am–4pm, Sun noon–4pm; shorter hours spring and fall. Closed Dec–Apr.

Ouray Hot Springs Pool & Fitness Center This oval outdoor pool, 120 feet by 150 feet, holds nearly a million gallons of odorless mineral water. Spring water is cooled from 150°F (66°C) and there are three separate soaking sections, with temperatures ranging from 88° to 105°F (31°–41°C). Also on the property are a waterslide and a fitness center with aerobic exercise equipment, including treadmills, a stair climber, a stationary bicycle, free weights, leg-press machines, and an abdominal board. There's a picnic area and playground in an adjacent municipal park. Allow 1 to 2 hours.

U.S. 550, at the north end of Ouray. ✆ **970/325-7073.** Pool only $10 adults, $8 students 7–12 and seniors 62 and over, $5 children 3–6, free children 2 and under; fitness center only $10 for all ages; both pool and fitness center $15 all ages. Memorial Day through Labor Day daily 10am–9:45pm; the rest of the year daily noon–9pm.

WHERE TO STAY

Rates here are highest during summer and winter holidays. A good chain motel is the **Comfort Inn,** 191 Fifth Ave. (P.O. Box 771), Ouray, CO 81427 (✆ **800/424-6423** or 970/325-7203), with rates for two from $69 to $159 in summer. Room tax is 6.9% plus $2 per night.

Beaumont Hotel ★★ Originally opened in 1887—and reopened in 2003 after decades of neglect—the Beaumont Hotel is once again the finest lodging in Ouray. Once known as the "Flagship of the San Juans" and playing host to luminaries like Sarah Bernhardt and Theodore Roosevelt, the opulently restored version of the hostelry is again first class from the lobby to the tower, the latter of which houses the aptly named Tower Room, featuring cathedral ceilings and 600 square feet of living space. All of the rooms have period furnishings, many of them restored originals, and the junior suites have sitting areas and more room, and such perks as cozy bathrobes and nightly turndown service.

505 Main St. (P.O. Box 1119), Ouray, CO 81427. ✆ **888/447-3255** or 970/325-7000. www.beaumonthotel.com. 12 units. $165–$250 double; $350–$375 suite. AE, DISC, MC, V. Pets not accepted. **Amenities:** 2 restaurants (American); bar; spa; shops. *In room:* A/C, cable TV/DVD player, wireless Internet access (free), coffeemaker.

Box Canyon Lodge and Hot Springs ★ (Finds) Tucked into a serene corner near Box Canyon Falls, this excellent motel has its own natural hot springs–fed soaking pools, on a forested property surrounded by pristine mountainsides. The scenery outside is spectacular, but the rooms here are top drawer, too, located in several different buildings but all featuring understated Western design and several different layouts, some of which include kitchens and fireplaces.

45 Third Ave. (P.O. Box 439), Ouray, CO 81427. ✆ **800/327-5080** or 970/325-4981. www.boxcanyonouray.com. 39 units, including 5 suites. $75–$135 double; $110–$270 suite. Rates include continental breakfast. AE, DISC, MC, V. **Amenities:** Outdoor natural springs hot tubs. *In room:* Cable TV, wireless Internet access (free), kitchen, fridge, coffeemaker, microwave, hair dryer, iron.

WHERE TO DINE

For a festive outdoor atmosphere, reasonable prices, and plenty of German beer, **Billy Goat Gruff's Biergarten,** 400 Main St. (✆ **970/325-4370;** www.billygoatsouray.com), serves burgers and brats. There's more upscale, more expensive food ($13–$26) in the adjacent Bistro at Billy Goat Gruff's.

Bon Ton Restaurant ★★ STEAK/ITALIAN A fixture in Ouray for more than a century—it was in another location before moving into the St. Elmo Hotel basement in 1898—the Bon Ton is one of Ouray's finest restaurants. With stone outer walls, hardwood floors, and reproduction antique furnishings, it carries a Western Victorian appeal. The menu includes a variety of pasta dishes, such as my choice, the lasagna Luciano—a classic seven-layer, four-cheese lasagna with spinach and either marinara or meat sauce. I also recommend the charbroiled 8-ounce beef tenderloin wrapped in bacon and served with a Bordelaise sauce and herb butter. There's an exceptionally good wine list, and an elaborate brunch is offered each Sunday.

In the St. Elmo Hotel, 426 Main St. ✆ **970/325-4951.** www.stelmohotel.com. Reservations recommended. Main courses dinner $12–$37, brunch $11–$14. AE, DC, DISC, MC, V. Sun 9:30am–1pm and 5:30–9:30pm; Mon–Sat 5:30–9:30pm.

7 WOLF CREEK SKI AREA

75 miles E of Durango, 65 miles W of Alamosa

Wolf Creek is famous throughout Colorado as the area that consistently has the most natural snow in the state—an annual average of 465 inches (almost 39 ft.)!

One of the state's oldest ski areas, Wolf Creek has terrain for skiers of all ability levels, but especially intermediates. Expert skiers often leave the lift-served slopes to dive down the powder of the Water Fall area. The Alberta Peak area offers extremely steep skiing and one of the most spectacular views of the peaks and pristine wilderness. Slopes are rated 20% beginner, 35% intermediate, 25% advanced, and 20% expert. Snowboarders are welcome in all areas of the resort.

In all, the area has 1,600 acres of terrain with 50 miles of trails, and a vertical drop of 1,604 feet from the 11,904-foot summit. The mountain has 50 trails served by seven lifts—one quad, one detachable quad, two triple chairs, one double, a high-speed Poma, and a Magic Carpet. Wolf Creek Lodge is a day lodge with restaurant and bar service. The Sports Center offers ski sales, rentals, and lessons.

Contact **Wolf Creek Ski Area,** P.O. Box 2800, Pagosa Springs, CO 81147 (✆ **970/264-5639** or 800/754-9653 for the ski report; www.wolfcreekski.com). Lift tickets cost $52 for adults, $28 for children 12 and under and seniors 65 and over. The resort is usually open from early November through mid-April daily from 8:30am to 4pm.

WHERE TO STAY Among nearby communities with lodging, dining, and other services are Pagosa Springs, 25 miles southwest of the ski area via U.S. 160, and South Fork, 20 miles northeast of Wolf Creek. For information, consult the **Pagosa Springs Area Chamber of Commerce,** P.O. Box 787, Pagosa Springs, CO 81147 (✆ **800/252-2204** or 970/264-2360; www.pagosaspringschamber.com), or the **South Fork Visitor Center and Chamber of Commerce** (✆ **719/873-5512;** www.southforkcolorado.org).

14

The Southern Rockies

If Colorado is the rooftop of America, then the southern Rockies are the peak of that roof. Some 30 of Colorado's fourteeners—14,000-plus-foot peaks—ring the area, and from Monarch Pass, at 11,312 feet, rivers flow in three directions.

Isolated from the rest of Colorado by the fourteeners and rugged canyons, this region has historically bred proud, independent-minded people. In the 18th century, settlers came from Taos, New Mexico, and built some of the region's striking Spanish architecture.

Today these mountain and river towns are renowned as recreational capitals: Gunnison for fishing and hunting, Crested Butte for skiing and mountain biking, and Salida and Buena Vista for white-water rafting. Alamosa is within easy reach of numerous attractions, including the remarkable Great Sand Dunes National Park and Preserve. In the foothills of the San Juan Range are the historic mining towns of Creede and Lake City, and in the tiny community of Antonito you can hop a narrow-gauge steam train for a trip back to a simpler (though smokier) time. This is rugged and sparsely populated land, with numerous opportunities for seeing the wilds of mountain America at their best.

1 GUNNISON & CURECANTI

196 miles SW of Denver, 161 miles W of Pueblo, 65 miles E of Montrose

A rough-and-ready Western town, Gunnison is a good central base for the outdoor recreation and natural attractions that abound in the Southern Rockies, whether it's hiking, boating, or hunting in the rugged mountains and canyons in the surrounding area. It's more blue-collar community than resort town, but that works to the benefit of budget-conscious travelers looking for a good meal and a place to hang their hat for the night after a wilderness expedition or day sightseeing.

Utes began hunting here about 1650, and although Spanish explorers probably never penetrated this isolated region, mountain men, who were pursuing pelts, arrived by the 1830s. First mapped by U.S. Army Capt. John Gunnison in 1853, the town was established in 1874, soon growing into a ranching center and transportation hub for nearby silver and gold mines. Established in 1911, Western State College now has an enrollment of 2,400 and was the first college in the United States with a certified technical-evaluation mountain-rescue team. Ninety percent of the all-volunteer team is made up of college students, with the remainder coming from the community. Gunnison sits at an elevation of 7,681 feet and its population is about 5,000.

ESSENTIALS

GETTING THERE **By Car** Gunnison is located on U.S. 50, midway between Montrose and Salida. From Denver, the most direct route is U.S. 285 southwest to Poncha Springs, then west on U.S. 50. From Grand Junction, follow U.S. 50 through Montrose.

By Plane The **Gunnison–Crested Butte Airport,** 711 Rio Grande Ave. (✆ **970/641-2304**), is just off U.S. 50, a few blocks south of downtown Gunnison. **American** (✆ **800/433-7300**) and **Delta** (✆ **800/221-1212**) provide air service during ski season and **United Express** (✆ **800/241-6522**) provides daily year-round service from Denver.

VISITOR INFORMATION Contact the **Gunnison Country Chamber of Commerce,** 500 E. Tomichi Ave., Gunnison, CO 81230 (✆ **800/851-0482** or 970/641-1501; www.gunnisoncrestedbutte.com), which operates a visitor center at the same location, open Monday through Friday from 8am to 5pm.

GETTING AROUND The town lies along the southeast bank of the west-flowing Gunnison River. Tomichi Avenue (U.S. 50) runs east–west through town. Main Street (Colo. 135) intersects Tomichi Avenue in the center of town and proceeds north to Crested Butte.

Car-rental agencies include **Avis** (✆ 970/641-0263), **Budget** (✆ 970/641-4403), **Dollar** (✆ 970/642-0199), and **Hertz** (✆ 970/641-2881).

FAST FACTS **Gunnison Valley Hospital,** with a 24-hour emergency room, is at 711 N. Taylor St. (✆ **970/641-1456**), 2 blocks east of Main Street and 6 blocks north of U.S. 50. The **post office** is located at 200 N. Wisconsin St. at Virginia Avenue; for hours and other information, contact the U.S. Postal Service (✆ **800/275-8777;** www.usps.com). For **road conditions** (winter only), call ✆ **877/315-7623** (in-state only).

SPECIAL EVENTS Winter Carnival, early February; Cattlemen's Days, Colorado's longest-running rodeo, late July; Art in the Park, mid-July; Classic and Custom Car Show, late August; and the Night of Lights, early December.

CURECANTI NATIONAL RECREATION AREA

Dams on the Gunnison River, just below Gunnison, have created a series of three very different reservoirs, extending 35 miles to the mouth of the Black Canyon of the Gunnison (see "Black Canyon of the Gunnison National Park," in chapter 12). **Blue Mesa Lake** (elevation 7,519 ft.), the easternmost (beginning 9 miles west of Gunnison), is the largest lake in Colorado when filled to capacity, and a watersports paradise popular for fishing, motorboating, sailboating, board sailing, and other activities. Fjordlike **Morrow Point Lake** (elevation 7,160 ft.) and **Crystal Lake** (elevation 6,755 ft.) fill long, serpentine canyons accessible only by precipitous trails and thus are limited to use by hand-carried boats. These lakes offer some of Colorado's best boating. (Permits cost $4 for 2 days, $10 for 14.)

There are two full-service marinas, both under the same management, offering fuel, supplies, boat rentals, and guided fishing trips. **Elk Creek Marina** is on Blue Mesa Lake, 16 miles west of Gunnison off U.S. 50 (✆ **970/641-0707**); and **Lake Fork Marina** (✆ **970/641-3048**) is 25 miles west of Gunnison, at the reservoir's west end. Contact either marina for current boat rental and guide rates. There's also a restaurant, Pappy's, at Elk Creek Marina, serving three meals daily.

A boat tour, offered by the park service, leaves the Pine Creek Trail boat dock on Morrow Point Lake at 10am and 12:30pm daily except Tuesday, Memorial Day through mid-September, to explore the Upper Black Canyon of the Gunnison. ***Warning:*** There is a .8-mile hike followed by 232 steps down to get to the dock, all of which has to be repeated in reverse after the boat ride. Rates are $15 adults, $7.50 children under 13. Reservations are required; stop at the Elk Creek Visitor Center or call (✆ **970/641-2337,** ext. 205).

Star Parties

The brand-new **Gunnison Valley Observatory,** 2 miles southwest of Gunnison on Yucca Court (✆ **970/642-1111;** www.coloradoskies.org), is home to a 30-inch telescope open to the public most Friday nights. It also plays host to some Saturday night lectures on astronomical topics of all kinds. Contact the Observatory or consult the website for the current calendar.

Hikers will find a variety of trails, often with splendid views of the lakes. Those who want to see birds can't go wrong with the **Neversink Trail,** a mile-long round-trip hike on the north shore of the Gunnison River, near a great blue heron rookery. Also watch for warblers, redwing blackbirds, and great horned owls, plus an occasional mule deer among the cottonwoods and willows that shade the river. The trail is flat and relatively easy, and also provides fishing access. A moderately strenuous hike where you might see a golden eagle or two, and possibly some bighorn sheep, is the 4-mile round-trip **Dillon Pinnacles Trail,** which is open to horseback riders as well as hikers. It provides spectacular views of the strangely eroded volcanic formations called the Dillon Pinnacles. The visitor center has a free brochure that describes these and several other hikes.

Anglers visit Curecanti year-round—there's ice fishing in winter—but the main season is May to October, when rainbow, brown, and Mackinaw trout and kokanee salmon are caught in large numbers. **Hunting,** especially for elk and deer, is popular in the adjacent West Elk Mountains.

The recreation area has 10 developed **campgrounds,** with about 350 sites. Showers are available for a small fee at Elk Creek (160 campsites) and Lake Fork (90 campsites). Elk Creek is open year-round, but water is turned off in winter. The other campgrounds are open spring through fall. Camping costs $12 per night, $18 with electric. Reservations are available from late May through early September through the recreation area's website or **www.recreation.gov**, or by phone (✆ **877/444-6777**). Several campgrounds have marinas, boat ramps, and RV dump stations; Loop D at Elk Creek has electric hookups. Backcountry and boat-in camping is also permitted, at no charge; check with rangers.

The **Elk Creek Visitor Center,** 16 miles west of Gunnison off U.S. 50, has exhibits and audiovisual programs, as well as maps and publications. It's open daily 8am to 6pm in summer, and Monday through Friday from 8:30am to 4pm the rest of the year, except for federal holidays in winter. Nature hikes and evening campground programs are presented throughout the summer. At **Cimarron,** 35 miles west of Gunnison, there's a visitor center open intermittently from mid-May through September, with a historic train exhibit, book sales, and a road to **Morrow Point Dam** power plant. The **Lake Fork Visitor Center,** 25 miles west of Gunnison off U.S. 50, near Blue Mesa Dam, is open daily from mid-May through September.

Admission to the recreation area is free except for those entering via the East Portal, where a $15 fee is charged. For a brochure and other information before your trip, contact **Curecanti National Recreation Area,** 102 Elk Creek, Gunnison, CO 81230 (✆ **970/641-2337;** www.nps.gov/cure).

OTHER SPORTS & OUTDOOR ACTIVITIES

In addition to activities in the recreation area, there are opportunities for hiking, mountain biking, hunting, fishing, camping, and four-wheeling on other nearby public lands under the jurisdiction of the U.S. Forest Service and Bureau of Land Management. For maps and other information, contact the offices of the **Gunnison Ranger District** and the **Bureau of Land Management Resource Area** at 216 N. Colorado St. (© **970/641-0471;** www.fs.fed.us/r2 or www.co.blm.gov).

A good base for exploring this area is **Three Rivers Resort and Outfitting,** 11 miles north of Gunnison at 130 C.R. 742 (P.O. Box 339), Almont, CO 81210 (© **888/761-3474** or 970/641-1303; www.3riversoutfitting.com). Located between Gunnison and Crested Butte, close to the national forest, Three Rivers offers fishing and rafting trips (see below), and also has fully equipped and furnished cabins and lodge rooms ($65 to $200).

FISHING The Gunnison River, both above and below town, and the tributary Taylor River, which joins the Gunnison at Almont, 11 miles north of town, are outstanding trout streams. In addition, the region's lakes are rich in fish. **Willowfly Anglers,** located at Three Rivers Resort, Almont (© **970/641-1303;** www.willowflyanglers.com), offers fly-fishing instruction, rentals, and guide service. Full-day float fishing trips cost $265 for one person and $315 for two, and walking trips are also available, starting at $155 for one person, half-day.

GOLF The 18-hole **Dos Rios Golf Club,** off U.S. 50 about 2 miles west of town (© **970/641-1482**), charges $65 for 18 holes and $40 for 9, including a cart.

HORSEBACK RIDING One of the best ways to see this beautiful area is from a saddle. **Ferro's Blue Mesa Lake Ranch,** P.O. Box 853, Gunnison, CO 81230 (© **800/617-4671** or 970/641-4671; www.coloradodirectory.com/ferrosbluemesa), offers horseback rides into remote areas of Curecanti National Recreation Area and to nearby national forests. Rates start at about $20 for 1 hour, and half- and full-day rates are also available. Also contact Ferro's about multiday pack trips. Ferro's is located on Soap Creek Road, about 26 miles west of Gunnison, overlooking Blue Mesa Reservoir. In addition to horseback rides, Ferro's has a general store with fishing licenses and supplies, plus several historic cabins, with rates from $40 to $85. There are also campsites starting at $10. Another recommended horseback-riding guide service is **Tenderfoot Outfitters** (© **800/641-0504** or 970/641-0504; www.tenderfoot-outfitters.com), with half-day rides starting at $70 for adults, $50 for kids 6 to 12.

RIVER RAFTING & KAYAKING For trips on the Taylor and other rivers, check with **Three Rivers Resort and Outfitting** (see above) or **Scenic River Tours,** 703 W. Tomichi Ave. (© **970/641-3131;** www.scenicrivertours.com). Rates for 3-hour raft trips over relatively calm stretches are about $30 for adults and $25 for children under 12. Both companies also offer guided white-water trips with rates from $55 per person. For paddlers of all kinds, the new **Gunnison Whitewater Park,** just west of town off U.S. 50 on the Gunnison River, is a series of rock structures along a few hundred feet of the river that make it an ideal course.

SKIING The two major winter-sports centers in the area are **Crested Butte,** 32 miles north on Colo. 135 (see section 2 of this chapter), and **Monarch,** 44 miles east on U.S. 50 (see section 3 of this chapter).

DISCOVERING GUNNISON'S PAST

Founded in the 1870s, the town of Gunnison has a number of historic buildings, ranging from log cabins to fancy 1880s homes—many in Gothic revival and Italianate styles—plus the 1882 stone Episcopal Church. A free walking-tour brochure is available at the chamber of commerce visitor center (see above).

Gunnison Pioneer Museum A Denver & Rio Grande narrow-gauge steam train and depot are highlights at this museum, which includes a dozen buildings from the area's past. There's an emphasis on ranching and homemaking equipment from the late 1800s and early 1900s, and exhibits include a rural schoolhouse (ca. 1905), a home with 19th-century furnishings, a dairy barn (ca. 1880), minerals and arrowheads, wagons, toys, and Gunnison's first post office (1876), plus over 50 antique and classic motor vehicles on display, from a Model A Ford tanker truck to an old Cadillac hearse. Allow 2 hours.

803 E. Tomichi Ave. ✆ **970/641-4530.** Admission $7 adults, $1 children 6–12, free for children 5 and under. Memorial Day to mid-Sept Mon–Sat 9am–5pm; Sun 1–5pm.

WHERE TO STAY

Lodging rates are at their highest in Gunnison in summer and at Christmas. You'll usually find the lowest rates in late winter and early spring. Major chain and franchise motels that provide reasonably priced lodging in Gunnison include the **Comfort Inn,** 911 N. Main St. (✆ **800/424-6423** or 970/642-1000), with rates of $80 to $120 double in summer and $70 to $100 at other times; and **Quality Inn,** 400 E. Tomichi Ave. (✆ **800/424-6423** or 970/641-1237), with double rates from $75 to $149 in summer and $55 to $89 at other times. Room tax adds just over 11% to lodging bills.

Water Wheel Inn ★ Kids A clean and well-kept roadside motel that's so quiet it's hard to hear any traffic at night, the Water Wheel Inn is a diamond in the rough. The "rough" is literal: The fringe of Dos Rios Golf Club is the backyard. Besides its convenient location next to the golf course and a restaurant 2 miles west of the center of Gunnison, the Water Wheel Inn also has a nice range of amenities, but alas no water wheel—a new one is in the works. However, the resident ponds are teeming with fish (fish food is for sale in the lobby) and there's a play area for canine guests. Usually sporting one or two queen beds or a king, the rooms are standard motel rooms with patios and balconies; the suites have full kitchens and sleep four.

U.S. 50 (P.O. Box 882), Gunnison, CO 81230. ✆ **800/642-1650** or 970/641-1650. www.waterwheelinnatgunnison.com. 52 units, including 3 suites. $65–$105 double; $120–$150 suite. Rates include continental breakfast. AE, DISC, MC, V. Pets accepted ($5 per night). From downtown, go west about 2 miles on U.S. 50; the Water Wheel Inn is on the south side of the road. **Amenities:** Outdoor hot tub; exercise room; massage. *In room:* Cable TV, wireless Internet access (free), kitchen, coffeemaker, hair dryer, iron.

Wildwood Resort Built in 1928 as a summer refuge for members of the Chicago underworld, the Wildwood is today a favorite hideaway for budget-conscious outdoor sports lovers. The rooms are quaint, quiet, and cozy, and all have a full kitchen. Several units were recently remodeled with all new soft goods, upgraded plumbing, flooring, and kitchens. Five units have shower/tub combos and the rest have showers only. Additionally, there are six cabins, with two or three bedrooms, two bathrooms, washers and dryers, and private decks. The property also boasts several shady picnic tables, a fish-cleaning station, and two duck ponds that are stocked with rainbow trout.

1312 W. Tomichi Ave., Gunnison, CO 81230. ✆ **866/770-1663** or 970/641-1663. www.wildwoodmotel.net. 25 units, including 7 cabins. $75–$85 double; $175–$235 cabin. Fishing, hunting, and ski packages

The Bizarre Tale of Alferd Packer

The winter of 1873 to 1874 was bad in southwest Colorado's San Juan Mountains—deep snow, staggeringly strong winds, and below-zero temperatures. But among the many miners who found themselves there, drawn by the hope of staking a claim among the region's newly discovered silver deposits, the temptation to change their fortunes in a day was just too powerful to resist. In February, six eager miners, led by Alferd Packer, set out from a Ute encampment near the present-day town of Delta, ignoring warnings from Ouray, chief of the Ute people. They took only 10 days' worth of food and weren't heard from for over 2 months, until Packer arrived alone at Los Piños Indian Agency, about 25 miles south of the present town of Gunnison.

Packer told Indian Agency officials that after he became ill, his companions abandoned him, and he survived on roots and bushes while making his way through the mountains. Curiously, he refused food upon his arrival. After resting, Packer traveled to the nearby community of Saguache, where he went on a drinking binge, paying with money from several wallets.

Since Packer had been penniless when the six men left the Ute encampment, and was the only one to return, Indian Agency officials became suspicious. When strips of what appeared to be human flesh were discovered along the path Packer had taken, he changed his story, claiming that others in the party had killed their companions one by one, until only he and fellow miner Wilson Bell remained. Finally Packer was forced to kill Bell in self-defense. After admitting to eating the remains of his companions, Packer was arrested and jailed.

Packer escaped from jail that August, at just about the time that five partially decomposed bodies were discovered along the northeast side of Lake San

available. MC, V. From downtown, continue straight on Tomichi Ave. when U.S. 50 curves to the left and you see the motel's blue sign; from the west turn left on New York Ave. (1st traffic light), then right on 8th and left onto Tomichi. The motel is ahead on the right. **Amenities:** Laundry. *In room:* Cable TV, kitchen.

Camping

In addition to the campgrounds in Curecanti National Recreation Area (see above), you'll find dozens of sites scattered throughout the Gunnison National Forest and lands administered by the Bureau of Land Management (✆ **970/641-0471**). Wildwood Resort (see above) also offers RV sites.

Mesa RV Resort A good base camp for fishing, hunting, or sightseeing trips, this campground caters mostly to RVs. The campground has large pull-through sites to accommodate big RVs, and 50-amp electric service is available. Facilities include clean bathhouses with plenty of hot water, a dump station, self-service laundry, gas pumps, wireless Internet access, and a store with propane and a limited selection of groceries and RV supplies. The more expensive sites have private hot tubs and privacy fences.

36128 W. U.S. 50, Gunnison, CO 81230. ✆ **800/482-8384** or 970/641-3186. www.mesarvresort.com. 135 sites. $32–$75. DISC, MC, V. Closed mid-Oct through mid-Apr. Located 3 miles west of Gunnison.

Cristobal, a few miles south of the present town of Lake City. Four of the men had apparently been murdered in their sleep, their heads split open with an ax, while a fifth had been shot. Chunks of flesh had been cut from at least two of the men's chests and thighs, and one was decapitated.

The search was now on in earnest, but Packer was nowhere to be found. About 9 years later, he was discovered living in Wyoming, using the name John Schwartz. He was arrested, and in April 1883 was convicted of premeditated murder and sentenced to hang. That should have been the end of Packer, but the trial was declared unconstitutional on a technicality.

Retried in 1886, Packer was convicted on five counts of manslaughter and sentenced to 45 years in prison. However, due to poor health, he was pardoned by Gov. Charles Thomas after only 5 years behind bars. Packer died of natural causes (and allegedly as a vegetarian) in the Denver area in 1907, at the age of 64, and was buried in the Littleton Cemetery. As an interesting aside, all through his life, Packer's first name, Alferd, had been misspelled. Apparently, it was a problem that followed him into death, since today the name "Alfred" is prominently displayed on his tombstone.

Though many at the time considered it an open-and-shut case, some have questioned whether Packer was really guilty of murder, or if he was simply convicted because of the public's revulsion at his admission of cannibalism. In 1989, the bodies were exhumed, and it was determined that they had likely been victims of cannibalism—but no evidence has shown definitively that Packer killed them. The site where the bodies were found, near the town of Lake City (see "A Side Trip to Lake City," below), is now known as Cannibal Plateau.

WHERE TO DINE

Besides Garlic Mike's (below), Gunnison has a number of good restaurants. The **Ol' Miner Steakhouse,** 139 N. Main St. (✆ **970/641-5153**), serves three hearty meals a day, with an emphasis on beef. For local suds and color and good pub grub, head across the street to the **Gunnison Brewery,** 138 N. Main St. (✆ **970/641-2739**). Or if you're looking for spicy Mexican food, the **Blue Iguana,** 303 E. Tomichi (✆ **970/641-3403**), serves more-than-respectable chimichangas and other traditional dishes.

Garlic Mike's ★★ ITALIAN Featuring a rustic dining room with red-and-white checkered tablecloths and an imposing fireplace, Garlic Mike's also has a great back patio within sight of the green banks of the Gunnison River. But besides the comfortable tables inside and out, the food is the town's best, and an entire wall of awards from the local paper serves as proof. The cream of mushroom soup is hard to get out of your head after consuming a cup, as are many of owner-chef Mike Busse's recipes. Most everything on the menu is quite good—and often quite garlicky—and caters to a range of tastes, from pasta dishes like the meatless lasagna verdure to steaks and gourmet pizzas.

2674 N. Colo. 135. ✆ **970/641-2493.** www.garlicmikes.com. Reservations recommended. Main courses $11–$27. AE, MC, V. Daily 5–9:30pm summer; daily 5–9pm winter.

A SIDE TRIP TO LAKE CITY ★★

The historic mining town of Lake City is 55 miles southwest via Colo. 149 (turn south off U.S. 50, 9 miles west of Gunnison). Founded in 1874, this former silver and gold town is set at 8,671 feet elevation against a backdrop of 14,000-plus-foot peaks in three different national forests—the Gunnison, Uncompahgre, and Rio Grande. Although the year-round population is a bit under 400, that figure quintuples in summer.

One of Colorado's largest national historic districts, Lake City has more than 75 buildings that date from the 19th century. Visit the renovated **Hinsdale County Courthouse,** 317 N. Henson St., built in 1877 and still the home of county government. You'll see exhibits on the trial of the notorious Alferd Packer and the courtroom where his trial took place (see "The Bizarre Tale of Alferd Packer," above).

History buffs will also enjoy the **Hinsdale County Museum,** 130 N. Silver St. (✆ **970/944-2050** in summer, or 970/944-2515 at other times; www.lakecitymuseum.com), with exhibits about the Packer trial, of course, plus the area's silver-mining heritage and other aspects of Lake City's history. There's also a Denver & Rio Grande Western caboose and a delightful Victorian garden with a sitting area. Next door is the 1870s **Smith-Grantham House,** a small, furnished Victorian home where you can see how people here lived in the late 1800s. The museum and Smith-Grantham House are open from mid-June until Labor Day, Monday through Saturday from 10am to 5pm and Sunday from 1 to 4:30pm; and irregular hours the rest of the year. Admission, which includes both the museum and the Smith-Grantham House, costs $3 for adults, $1 for children 8 to 12, and is free for children 7 and younger. The museum leads historic walking tours, home tours, cemetery tours, and ghost tours; call for the current schedule and prices.

For those intrigued with mining, visit the **Hard Tack Mine Tours & Museum,** about 3 miles west of town, via C.R. 20 (✆ **970/944-2506;** www.hardtackmine.com). George and Beth Hurd of Lake City own the property and, with the help of their daughter Buffy, developed the tour and museum. The 40-minute tour through the state-inspected mine takes you back more than 100 years and shows you how the miners lived and worked, and you'll also see all sorts of mining equipment and an excellent display of crystals in the museum. Be aware that the temperature underground is a constant 45°F (7°C), so take a jacket even on the hottest summer day. There's also a gift shop, and gold panning is also offered (call for times and rates). It's open Tuesday through Saturday from 10am to 5pm, from Memorial Day to Labor Day. The cost is $11 for adults and $7 for youths 14 and under.

Surrounded by some 600,000 acres of public land, Lake City is an important recreational center, offering hiking, mountain biking, horseback riding, jeep rides, camping, and fishing in summer; and ice fishing, cross-country skiing, snowshoeing, and snowmobiling in winter. Lake San Cristobal, just south of town via C.R. 30, is Colorado's second-largest natural lake and is particularly popular with fishermen. Also nearby you'll find several ghost towns and historic sites, most of which will require a four-wheel-drive vehicle, horse, mountain bike, or a good pair of hiking boots.

For information, including lists of boat and jeep rentals, outfitters, stables, accommodations, and restaurants, contact the **Lake City/Hinsdale County Chamber of Commerce,** P.O. Box 430, Lake City, CO 81235 (✆ **800/569-1874** or 970/944-2527; www.lakecity.com). The chamber operates a visitor information center at 800 N. Gunnison Ave., on the north side of town, which is usually open from 9am to 6pm Monday through Friday, 9am to 5pm Saturday, and from 1am to 5pm Sunday.

2 CRESTED BUTTE ★★

28 miles N of Gunnison, 224 miles SW of Denver

A delightful little gem of a town, Crested Butte is a year-round destination resort, with wonderful skiing in winter, and hiking, mountain biking, and other outdoor recreational activities in warmer weather. In fact, Crested Butte has the best mountain biking in the state, and boasts of having some of the most colorful displays of wildflowers you'll see anywhere.

The town of Crested Butte was born in 1880 as the Denver & Rio Grande line laid a narrow-gauge rail track from Gunnison to serve the gold and silver mines in the area. But it was coal, not the more precious minerals, which sustained the town from the late 1880s until 1952, when the last of the mines closed. The economy then languished until Mt. Crested Butte ski area was developed in 1961.

An influx of newcomers began renovating the old buildings in the 1970s, and in 1974 the entire town was designated a National Historic District—one of the largest in Colorado. In 1976, local riders started bicycling off-road; they were integral in the birth of the sport of mountain biking. Crested Butte is quite different from many of Colorado's resorts in that it's not overdeveloped (at least, not yet) and its funky personality still outshines the Western chic.

ESSENTIALS

GETTING THERE **By Car** Crested Butte is 28 miles north of Gunnison on Colo. 135, the only year-round access. In summer, the gravel-surface Kebler Pass Road links Crested Butte with Colo. 133 at Paonia Reservoir, to the west.

By Plane The **Gunnison–Crested Butte Airport,** 711 Rio Grande Ave. (✆ **970/641-2304**), is just off U.S. 50, a few blocks south of downtown Gunnison. **American** (✆ **800/433-7300**) and **Delta** (✆ **800/221-1212**) provide air service during ski season and **United Express** (✆ **800/241-6522**) provides daily year-round service from Denver.

Alpine Express (✆ **800/822-4844** or 970/641-5074; www.alpineexpressshuttle.com) provides shuttle service from the airport to Crested Butte frequently in ski season; call to check on availability at other times. Reservations are required. Adults are $34 per person one-way and kids under 13 are $23.

VISITOR INFORMATION Consult the **Crested Butte–Mt. Crested Butte Chamber of Commerce** (✆ **800/851-0482** or 970/349-6438; www.gunnisoncrestedbutte.com). An **information center** is located downtown at the four-way stop at the corner of Elk Avenue and Sixth Street.

GETTING AROUND There are actually two separate communities here: the old mining town of Crested Butte and the modern resort village of Mt. Crested Butte, 3 miles away. Colo. 135 enters Crested Butte from the south and is intersected by Elk Avenue, which runs east–west as the town's main street.

Free transportation throughout Crested Butte and the ski resort is provided by **Mountain Express** (✆ **970/349-7318;** www.crestedbutte-co.gov).

FAST FACTS The **Crested Butte Medical Center,** in the Ore Bucket Building in downtown Crested Butte (✆ **970/349-0321;** www.cbmedicalcenter.com), can handle most health needs; the medical center also operates a clinic at the ski area during winter (✆ **970/349-4370**). The **post office** is on the north side of Elk Avenue between Second and Third streets; contact the U.S. Postal Service (✆ **800/275-8777;** www.usps.com) for hours and other information.

SPECIAL EVENTS Fat Tire Bike Week, June; Crested Butte Music Festival, early July; Wildflower Festival, July; Wine and Food Festival, late July; Festival of the Arts, early August; Wild Mushroom Festival, early August; Vinotok Fall Festival, September.

SKIING & OTHER WINTER SPORTS

Crested Butte may be Colorado's best-kept secret. Situated at the intersection of two overlapping winter storm tracks, it's guaranteed to have outstanding snow. Offering abundant opportunities for beginners and intermediate skiers, Crested Butte also has what many experts consider the most challenging runs in the Rockies.

The resort has 1,167 acres of skiable terrain. Altogether, trails are rated 23% beginner, 57% intermediate, and 20% advanced. The vertical drop is 3,062 feet from a summit of 12,162 feet. There are 121 trails served by 16 lifts (four high-speed quads, two fixed-grip quads, two triples, three doubles, three surface lifts, and two Magic Carpet rolling conveyors). Average annual snowfall is 240 inches, and there's snow making on trails served by all but two of the resort's lifts. The resort also has an easily accessible snowboard terrain park and superpipe, and offers snowboarding lessons.

Crested Butte offers both a ski and snowboard program (plus year-round recreation) for visitors with disabilities, with specially trained and certified instructors, at the Adaptive Sports Center, located at the base of the ski area in the Treasury Center Building. The resort's Kid's Ski & Snowboard World provides lessons, day care, and nursery services. (Don't forget to keep an eye out for Bubba and Betty Bear, the beloved mascots of Crested Butte Mountain Resort, who will gladly stop for a warm, fuzzy hug and a picture.) Private and group lessons are available in half- or all-day packages. The resort offers rentals of skis, snowboards, helmets, snowshoes, ski boards, and telemark equipment, in single and multiday prices, with overnight storage included. A full-service repair shop is available also. All children 12 and under who participate in lessons are required to wear a helmet (included in the lesson price and available at the rental shop). Equipment rental is also available at several other shops in the base area and around town.

For more information, contact **Crested Butte Mountain Resort,** 12 Snowmass Rd. (P.O. Box 5700), Mt. Crested Butte, CO 81225 (✆ **800/810-7669** or 970/349-2222, 888/442-8883 or 970/349-2323 for snow reports; www.skicb.com). Full-day regular-season lift tickets are $82 for adults, $47 for seniors 65 and older, $74 for youths 13 to 17, and $41 for children 7 to 12. Early-season lift tickets are less; kids under 7 are free all season long. The resort is usually open from mid-November to early April daily from 9am to 4pm.

CROSS-COUNTRY SKIING, SNOWSHOEING, SLEDDING & ICE SKATING The **Crested Butte Nordic Center,** based at Big Mine Park, Second Street and Whiterock Avenue in downtown Crested Butte (P.O. Box 1269), CO 81224 (✆ **970/349-1707;** www.cbnordic.org), maintains 26 miles of marked and groomed trails and organizes backcountry tours over more than 100 miles of wilderness trails. It's open in winter daily from 9am to 4pm. A 1-day trail pass costs about $15, with discounts for children and seniors. Nordic ski rentals (skis, boots, and poles) cost $20 per day for adults and $15 for children. The center also maintains several warming huts, a free lighted ice-skating rink, and a free sledding hill, plus skate and sled rentals. In addition, it offers snowshoe tours and rentals.

WARM-WEATHER SPORTS & OUTDOOR ACTIVITIES

This is rugged country, surrounded by **Gunnison National Forest,** three wilderness areas, and towering 12,000- to 14,000-foot peaks. For maps and tips on the many activities available, contact the Gunnison Ranger District office at 216 N. Colorado St. in Gunnison (✆ **970/641-0471;** www.fs.fed.us/r2).

The lifts at Crested Butte Mountain Resort don't stop just because the snow's gone, but operate daily from late June through early September for hikers or those who simply want to enjoy the beautiful mountain scenery without effort. Single trips cost $15 for adults, $8 for children 7 to 17 and seniors 65 and older; all-day passes cost $20 and $12, respectively. Kids 6 and younger ride free.

GOLF The 18-hole course at **The Club at Crested Butte,** 2 miles south of Crested Butte off Colo. 135 (✆ **970/349-6131;** www.crestedbutte.com), is one of Colorado's best mountain courses. It's usually open from mid-May through October. The fee for 18 holes, including the mandatory cart, is $95 to $135 in summer, lower in the off season.

HIKING There are practically unlimited opportunities for hiking and backpacking in the Crested Butte area. Some of the best are in the **Maroon Bells–Snowmass Wilderness Area,** accessible from a trail head at Gothic, above Mt. Crested Butte, where you can hike to Aspen if properly motivated. Another good trail is located off Cement Creek Road: The **Farris Creek Trail** (aka the Caves Trail) takes hikers up to a great vantage point of some cavelike geological formations and a great view of the area's original and long-closed ski resort. Ask the chamber of commerce for other trail suggestions, or contact the Gunnison National Forest office (see above).

HORSEBACK RIDING Guided rides are offered year-round by **Fantasy Ranch Horseback Adventures,** P.O. Box 236, Crested Butte, CO 81224 (✆ **888/688-3488** or 970/349-5425; www.fantasyranchoutfitters.com), ranging from 1½ hours to weeklong pack trips. Trips go into three different mountain wilderness areas, at elevations from 7,000 feet to 12,700 feet, including the incredibly beautiful Maroon Bells (p. 323). Prices per person are $55 for the 1½-hour ride and $85 for a 3-hour ride.

MOUNTAIN BIKING One of the towns that lays claim to the sport's invention, **Crested Butte** has established a firm reputation as the place to mountain-bike in Colorado. From single-track trails to jeep roads, there's something here to please every ability level. Among local shops where you can get trail information, maps, and mountain-bike rentals (from about $40 per day), I recommend **Flatiron Sports** (✆ **800/821-4331** or 970/349-6656; www.flatironsports.net), in the Treasury Center at Mt. Crested Butte, as well as **Crested Butte Sports** (✆ **800/301-9169** or 970/349-7516; www.crestedbuttesports.com) and **The Alpineer** (✆ **800/847-0244** or 970/349-5210; www.alpineer.com), in the town of Crested Butte.

Popular choices include the **Strand Hill** route, which runs for 18 miles and is considered intermediate. It climbs to 10,255 feet elevation, through wooded areas, and includes several miles on downhill single-track. Advanced mountain bikers will love **Trail No. 401,** one of the best trails in the area. This 26-mile round-trip route climbs to 11,500 feet and offers incredible mountain scenery, including views of the magnificent Maroon Bells (p. 323), as it passes through aspen groves and meadows of wildflowers.

Guided mountain-bike tours are offered by **Crested Butte Mountain Guides,** 416 Sopris Ave. (✆ **877/455-2307** or 970/349-5430; www.crestedbutteguides.com), which charges $260 for two riders for a 6-hour guided ride, not including bike rental.

OTHER HIGHLIGHTS

The chamber of commerce provides a free brochure on a **self-guided walking tour** of more than three dozen historic buildings in Crested Butte, including the picturesque 1883 Town Hall, 1881 railroad depot, numerous saloons and homes, and a unique two-story outhouse. Downtown Crested Butte is also home to a half-dozen or so **art galleries,** mostly along or just off Elk Avenue. The **Paragon Galley,** at the corner of Second Street and Elk Avenue (✆ **970/349-6484**), is a cooperative, displaying the works of more than a dozen local artists and craftspersons.

Crested Butte Mountain Heritage Museum & Mountain Bike Hall of Fame This interesting museum, located in an 1883 building, concentrates on the area's mining, ranching, and skiing heritage, with interactive exhibits, historical photos, and a wide array of memorabilia from local settlers' cabins. The Mountain Bike Hall of Fame covers the compelling story of the "clunkers"—no-frills, fat-tire beach cruisers—that took perhaps the world's first mountain bikers over Pearl Pass to Aspen in 1976; other exhibits cover inductees, technological innovation, and other landmark moments in the sport. You can pick up a free copy of the Crested Butte walking-tour map here, and there is a well-stocked gift shop, to boot. Allow about an hour.

331 Elk Ave. ✆ **970/349-1880.** Admission $3, children 12 and under free. Winter daily noon–6pm; summer daily 10am–8pm; by appt. spring and fall.

WHERE TO STAY

Lodging properties listed below with Mt. Crested Butte addresses are at or near the ski slopes, while those in Crested Butte are about 3 miles away. However, free transportation from Crested Butte to the slopes is available with the Mountain Express (see "Getting Around," above). Rates are usually highest during ski season and lowest in what locals call "mud season," after the ski area closes and before summer—known in other parts of the country as spring.

Slopeside in Mt. Crested Butte, the luxury property is **WestWall Lodge,** on Hunter Hill Rd. (✆ **888/349-1280** or 970/349-1280; www.westwalllodge.com), at the foot of the eponymous WestWall lift (yes, it has its own lift), which has a wide array of luxury condos (studios to four bedrooms) with nightly rates in the $300 to $600 range; **Elevation,** 500 Gothic Rd. (✆ **800/8107669;** www.elevationhotel.com), is similarly swank, just a step down the luxury ladder, with rates of $150 to $450 double; the **Grand Lodge,** 6 Emmons Loop (✆ **970/349-8000;** www.grandlodgecondos.com), is the recommended midrange option, with double rates of $125 to $235 during ski season and much less the rest of the year; the budget pick is the **Nordic Inn** (see below).

Crested Butte International Lodge & Hostel ★ This handsome, three-story hostel is among the nicest you'll find in Colorado, and it's just 100 feet from the free ski shuttle. Dorm rooms have four, six, or eight single beds, so a family can have a private room by renting all its beds. Of course, in the hosteling tradition, they'll share the large bathrooms and other facilities. Each bunk has its own reading light and a lockable drawer, and all rooms have a desk. Sleeping bags, sheets, and towels can be rented. The large shared living room has a stone fireplace and comfortable sitting areas, and guests have use of a fully equipped kitchen. Ski and other outdoor recreation packages are available. There are three private rooms for two, a family room that sleeps five, and an apartment that sleeps six; linens are provided for these. The hostel offers the use of copy and fax machines. Smoking and alcoholic beverages are not permitted.

615 Teocalli Ave. (P.O. Box 1332), Crested Butte, CO 81224. ✆ **888/389-0588** or 970/349-0588. www.crestedbuttehostel.com. 50 total beds; 4 private rooms; 1 apt. All but one private room share bathrooms. Bunk rooms $25–$39 per bed; private rooms $65–$99 double; $184–$205 apt. (a 3-night minimum may apply in ski season). AE, DISC, MC, V. **Amenities:** Coin-op washers and dryers. *In room:* Wireless Internet access (free), no phone.

Elk Mountain Lodge ★ Built in 1919 as a miners' hotel, this historic three-story lodge has been nicely renovated for the tourist crowd. Now warm and unpretentious, the lodging is a good choice for those seeking both a good night's sleep and a bit of historic ambience. Located near the center of town, it offers individually decorated basic rooms with twin, queen, or king beds. Third-floor units have spectacular views of the town and surrounding mountains, and many have balconies. The hot breakfast is quite good; there's also ski storage.

Second St. and Gothic Ave. Crested Butte, CO 81224. ✆ **800/374-6521** or 970/349-7533. Fax 970/349-5114. www.elkmountainlodge.net. 19 units. $120–$160 double. Rates include full breakfast. AE, DISC, MC, V. **Amenities:** Bar; indoor hot tub; complimentary bike rentals. *In room:* TV, dataport, wireless Internet access (free), hair dryer.

The Historic Pioneer Guest Cabins (Finds) Located 10 minutes from the Crested Butte ski area, the Pioneer is a great escape for those seeking a rustic (but not too rustic) log cabin in the woods. Although these historic cabins lack TVs and in-room phones, they have modern bathrooms (with showers only), fully equipped kitchens, handmade wood furniture, and cozy down comforters on the beds. In addition to propane heaters, the cabins have either fireplaces or wood-burning stoves, and outside each is a fire pit and picnic table. With two beds apiece, the four small cabins were built as part of a historic ski resort that closed in the early 1950s. The four larger cabins, built in the late 1960s and early 1970s, have three beds and more of a modern feel than the historic cabins. Located in the Gunnison National Forest, the cabins provide easy access to a full slate of outdoor adventures. All units are nonsmoking.

Cement Creek Rd., Crested Butte, CO 81224. ✆ **970/349-5517.** Fax 970/349-9697. www.thepioneer.net. 8 units. $139–$229 double. Free for children 4 and under. MC, V. Most breeds of dogs accepted for $15 per dog per night fee (maximum 2 dogs per unit) at management discretion. From Crested Butte, take Colo. 135 south 7 miles to Cement Creek Rd., turn left and go 2 miles. *In room:* Kitchen, no phone.

The Nordic Inn (Kids) Among the first lodges built at the foot of the Crested Butte ski slopes, this well-kept, family-owned inn is still going strong. The big fireplace in the lobby is the focus of attention at breakfast, and the whirlpool tub on the sun deck is open year-round. Guest rooms have Scandinavian decor; most have two double beds, although a few contain either one king- or two queen-size beds. Each also has a bathroom with a tub/shower combo and a separate vanity. Especially good for families are the adjacent guesthouses, which sleep from six to eight people and feature knockout views and plenty of room to romp around. The entire inn is nonsmoking.

14 Treasury Rd. (P.O. Box 939, Crested Butte, CO 81224), Mt. Crested Butte, CO 81225. ✆ **800/542-7669** (reservations only) or 970/349-5542. Fax 970/349-6487. www.nordicinncb.com. 29 units, including two guesthouses. $82–$180 double; $155–$345 guesthouse with a 3- to 5-night minimum in peak season. Rates include continental breakfast. AE, MC, V. Closed from the end of ski season through May. **Amenities:** Whirlpool tub. *In room:* Cable TV, wireless Internet access (free), kitchen, hair dryer.

WHERE TO DINE

Beyond the favorites listed below, **McGill's,** 228 Elk Ave. (✆ **970/349-5240**), is a solid breakfast or lunch pick, located in a converted historic general store and specializing in milkshakes, big salads, "scromelettes" (scrambled omelets), and gourmet sandwiches. For a Mexican dinner, mountain bikers and ski bums alike swear by **Donita's Cantina,** 330 Elk Ave. (✆ **970/349-6674**), and its homemade salsa and terrific fajitas. And it's hard to beat a couple of slices or a calzone at **Brick Oven Pizza,** 223 Elk Ave. (✆ **970/349-5044**), with a terrific patio and outdoor bar in the summer months.

Le Bosquet ★★ COUNTRY FRENCH Green plants peek through the lace curtains of this popular restaurant, which is my choice for a quiet, intimate dinner. Under the same ownership since 1978, the restaurant's menu changes seasonally but always includes fresh seafood, beef, lamb, and vegetarian entrees. Typical entrees might include a roast rack of lamb in a red-wine and garlic-butter sauce; fresh tilapia in an apple-leek-dill ragout; and the 10-ounce all-natural range-fed New York strip steak served with mashed new red potatoes. Available from 5:30 to 6:30pm only, the Twilight Menu offers soup or salad, a choice of several entrees such as tofu or chicken picatta or grilled rack of pork, and a choice of desserts, all for $20. There are also an excellent wine list and a popular menu of small plates ($6–$12) like fondue and lobster ravioli.

Sixth St. at Belleview Ave. (in Majestic Plaza). ✆ **970/349-5808.** Reservations recommended. Entrees $18–$36. AE, DISC, MC, V. Daily 5:30–10pm. May be closed 1 month in spring and 2 weeks in fall.

The Slogar Bar & Restaurant ★ Kids AMERICAN If you do something right, why mess around with anything else? That's the way the Slogar feels about its skillet-fried chicken, and I couldn't agree more. The fixed-price menu offers chicken every night—the best in the region—accompanied by tangy coleslaw, mashed potatoes and gravy, biscuits with honey butter, creamed corn, and ice cream. Also available is a family-style steak dinner, which is fine, but I still prefer the chicken. The atmosphere here is 1880s Victorian, somewhat elegant but not so highbrow as to scare off families.

517 Second St., at Whiterock Ave. ✆ **970/349-5765.** Reservations recommended. Fixed-price dinner $16–$27. AE, MC, V. Daily 5–9pm.

3 WHITE-WATER RAFTING SALIDA

138 miles SW of Denver, 96 miles W of Pueblo, 82 miles N of Alamosa

With a strategic location on the upper Arkansas River, it was natural that Salida (elevation 7,080 ft.) should become an important farming, ranching, and transportation center in its early days, and a major river-rafting and kayaking center today. Zebulon Pike opened the area for Americans in the early 19th century; he was followed by trappers, then miners after the discovery of gold in 1859. When Leadville boomed on silver in the late 1870s, the Denver & Rio Grande Railroad built a line up the Arkansas from Pueblo, and the town of Salida was founded at a key point on the line. The downtown core has kept its historic ambience alive, and now has a growing arts community while it serves as a base camp for outdoor recreation enthusiasts, namely river rats. About 25 miles north, Buena Vista is another rafting center on the Arkansas.

ESSENTIALS

GETTING THERE **By Car** U.S. 50 connects Salida with Gunnison, 66 miles west, and Pueblo, 96 miles east on I-25. Colo. 291 heads north from Salida, providing a vital 9-mile link between U.S. 50 and U.S. 285, which runs north–south 5 miles west of

Salida (through Poncha Springs), connecting Alamosa with Buena Vista and eventually Denver.

By Plane The nearest airport with commercial service is at **Gunnison,** 65 miles west (see "Gunnison & Curecanti National Recreation Area," earlier in this chapter).

VISITOR INFORMATION Consult the **Heart of the Rockies Chamber of Commerce,** 406 W. Rainbow Blvd. (U.S. 50), Salida, CO 81201 (✆ **877/772-5432** or 719/539-2068; www.salidachamber.org), which operates an information center Monday through Friday from 9am to 5pm.

GETTING AROUND Salida sits on the southwestern bank of the Arkansas River, just above its confluence with the South Arkansas. U.S. 50 (Rainbow Blvd.), which follows the north bank of the South Arkansas, marks the southern edge of town. At the eastern city limit, Colo. 291 (Oak St.) turns north off U.S. 50, and 6 blocks later turns northwest as First Street through the historic downtown area.

FAST FACTS The **Medical Clinics,** 550 W. U.S. 50 (✆ **719/530-2000**), provide 24-hour emergency care. The **post office** is at 310 D St. Contact the U.S. Postal Service (✆ **800/275-8777;** www.usps.com) for hours and other information.

SPECIAL EVENTS Second Saturday Art Events, year-round; Continental Divide Auto Hill Climb, early June; FIBArk Whitewater Festival, mid-June; Art Walk, late June; Colorado Brewers Rendezvous, early July; Crest Crank Mountain Bike Ride, late August; Banana Belt Bicycle Weekend, mid-September; Lighting of Christmas Mountain USA, Thanksgiving weekend, late November.

RIVER RAFTING

Considered the white-water rafting center of the Rockies, Salida is the perfect base for enjoying the **Arkansas Headwaters Recreation Area,** a 148-mile stretch of river from Leadville to Pueblo Lake. With headquarters off Colo. 291 in downtown Salida at 307 W. Sackett Ave., Salida, CO 81201 (✆ **719/539-7289;** www.parks.state.co.us), the recreation area includes about 20 developed sites along the river, offering raft and kayak access, fishing, hiking, camping, and picnicking. There are also undeveloped areas that offer access to the river, but be careful not to trespass on private property. User fees are $6 per vehicle per day, $3 walk-in, plus $14 per night for camping.

The busiest stretch of the river is Browns Canyon, a granite wilderness between Buena Vista and Salida, with Class III and IV rapids (moderately difficult to difficult) along a 10-mile stretch of river from Nathrop to Stone Bridge.

Most people explore Colorado's rivers with experienced rafting companies, which provide trips on stretches of river that range from practically calm and suitable for everyone to extremely difficult, with long, violent rapids that are recommended only for skilled white-water boaters. Leading outfitters in the Salida and Buena Vista area include **Dvorak Expeditions** (✆ **800/824-3795** or 719/539-6851; www.dvorakexpeditions.com), **Wilderness Aware** (✆ **800/462-7238** or 719/395-2112; www.inaraft.com), **KODI Rafting** (✆ **877/747-7238;** www.whiewatercolorado.com), **River Runners** (✆ **800/332-9100;** www.riverrunnersltd.com), and **American Adventure Expeditions** (✆ **800/288-0675** or 719/395-2409; www.americanadventure.com). Generally, adult rates for half-day raft trips are $50 to $70; full-day trips including lunch are in the $100 to $150 range, and multiday excursions start at about $250. Prices for children are about 20% less. For a full listing of dozens of rafting companies approved to run the Arkansas, contact the recreation area office (see above).

For kayaking classes, duckie (inflatable kayak) rentals and tours, and other clinics and rafting-related needs, the **Rocky Mountain Outdoor Center,** 228 N. F St. (✆ **800/255-5784;** www.rmoc.com), is the spot. Two-day group lessons for beginning and intermediate paddlers cost $220, duckies rent for $50 a day, and guided full-day trips are $100. Rock climbing instruction is also offered. North of town, **Independent Whitewater,** 10830 C.R. 165 (✆ **800/428-1479** or 719/538-7737; www.independentrafting.com), offers similar services.

For practice, the **Arkansas River Whitewater Park** is located on the river downtown.

OTHER SPORTS & OUTDOOR ACTIVITIES

FISHING The Arkansas River is considered by many to be the finest fishing river in Colorado. There's also trout fishing in numerous alpine lakes, including Cottonwood Lake, Twin Lakes, and O'Haver Lake. For tips on the best fishing spots, plus licenses, supplies, and equipment sales and rentals, stop at **Arkansas River Fly Shop,** 7500 W. U.S. 50, Salida (✆ **719/539-3474;** www.arkanglers.com), which also offers a guide service. Cost for a guided half-day wading trip for one person is $175, and a half-day float-fishing trip on the Arkansas River for two costs $250. The company also offers fly-fishing and fly-tying lessons and has locations in Pueblo and Buena Vista.

GOLF The **Salida Golf Club,** a municipal course that opened in 1926, is at Crestone Avenue and Grant Street (✆ **719/539-1060**). Greens fees are $26 to $28 for 18 holes, $16 to $18 for 9.

HIKING There are outstanding trails for all experience levels throughout the region, particularly in the San Isabel National Forest, along the eastern slope of the Continental Divide west of Salida. Of particular interest are hikes into the Collegiate Range (mts. Harvard, Columbia, Yale, Princeton, and Oxford) off Cottonwood Creek Road west of Buena Vista, and trips from the ghost town of St. Elmo up Chalk Creek Road from Mount Princeton Hot Springs. For maps and other information, stop at the **Salida Ranger District** office, 325 W. Rainbow Blvd. (✆ **719/539-3591;** www.fs.fed.us/r2).

MOUNTAIN BIKING There are numerous trails suitable for mountain biking throughout the area, and they provide stupendous views of the surrounding 14,000-plus-foot peaks. Many locals undertake the short but steep ride up **"S" Mountain** for their daily exercise. Attached to Bongo Billy's Salida Café, a great breakfast spot and acoustic venue, **Absolute Bikes,** 330 W. Sackett St. (✆ **888/539-9295** or 719/539-9295; www.absolutebikes.com), rents, sells, and services mountain bikes and can provide information and maps on nearby trails. Rentals—from three-speed townies to full-suspension, plus kid bikes, tandems, and road bikes—are available. Prices start at $40 per day for mountain bikes, $15 for kid bikes and adult's town cruisers.

SKIING & SNOWBOARDING Among the finest of Colorado's small ski resorts, **Monarch Mountain ★★**, 20 miles west of Salida at Monarch Pass on U.S. 50, serves all levels of ability with 63 trails, with 14% rated beginner, 28% intermediate, 27% advanced, and 31% expert. The longest run is 1 mile.

Covering 800 acres, the mountain has a vertical drop of 1,162 feet from its summit of 11,952 feet. It gets about 350 inches of snow annually and has no snow-making equipment. It has one fixed quad and four double chairs. All-day tickets are $54 for adults, $32 for youths 13 to 15, $20 for juniors 7 to 12, $29 for seniors 62 to 68, and free for those under 7 or over 68. The area is usually open daily from late November to mid-April from 9am to 4pm. For information, contact the resort at 1 Powder Place, Monarch, CO

81227 (✆ **888/996-7669** or 719/539-3573; www.monarchmountainlodge.com). The closest accommodations are at **Monarch Mountain Lodge,** 22720 W. U.S. 50, Monarch, CO 81227 (✆ **888/996-7669** or 719/530-5000; www.monarchmountainlodge.com), with double rates of $98 to $200 in ski season, but I recommend heading down the mountain and staying in Salida.

SEEING THE SIGHTS

Monarch Crest Tram Climbing from 11,312-foot Monarch Pass to the Continental Divide at an altitude of 12,012 feet, this tram offers views of five mountain ranges—up to 150 miles away—when skies are clear. The tram includes six four-passenger gondolas. At the top is a gift shop. Pets are welcome. Allow about 2 hours.

Monarch Pass, U.S. 50, 22 miles west of Salida. ✆ **719/539-4091.** Admission $7 adults, $6 seniors over 55, $4 children 4–12, and free for children 3 and under. Mid-May to mid-Sept, weather permitting, daily 8:30am–5:30pm.

Mt. Shavano Fish Hatchery This state-run fish hatchery, about a half-mile northwest of town off Colo. 291, produces some two million trout each year, used to stock Colorado's numerous streams and lakes. Visitors can see how the hatchery operates, walk among the fish raceways and ponds, and feed the fish (food provided from coin-operated machines). Guided tours are provided daily 10am to 4pm from June until Labor Day, and self-guided tours are available at other times. Allow 30 minutes to an hour.

7725 C.R. 154. ✆ **719/539-6877.** Free admission. Daily 7:30am–4pm.

Salida Hot Springs Colorado's largest indoor hot springs have been in commercial operation since 1937, when the Works Progress Administration built the pools as a Depression-era project. Ute tribes considered the mineral waters, rich in bicarbonate, sodium, and sulfate, to be sacred and medicinal. Today the main 25m (82-ft.) pool, with two lap lanes available at all times, is kept at a refreshing 82°F (28°C), and a 4-foot-deep leisure pool, with a ramp entrance, is kept at about 100°F (38°C). Allow 1 to 3 hours.

410 W. Rainbow Blvd. (U.S. 50). ✆ **719/539-6738.** www.salidapool.com. Admission $11 adults, $9 seniors 60 and older, $5 children 6–17, $3 children 5 and under. Memorial Day to Labor Day Mon–Fri 1–8pm, Sat–Sun noon–8pm; call or check website for winter hours.

Salida Museum The Salida Museum provides a look at the history of this part of Colorado, with a wide selection of pioneer, mining, and railroad exhibits, plus displays on the lives of the American Indians who lived here. You'll see lots of arrowheads, plus exhibits that explain how baskets and pots were made. The museum also contains rocks, fossils, and shells from the area, plus petrified wood and dinosaur bones and teeth. You can learn about Laura Evans, a local madam who operated a brothel in Salida from the late 1800s until 1953, and see a replica of a lady's bedroom of the late 1800s, bizarre-looking medical equipment, and bone baskets—used to transport corpses in the late 1800s. Allow 30 minutes.

406 W. Rainbow Blvd. (U.S. 50). ✆ **719/539-7483.** www.salidachamber.org/museum. Admission $3 adults, $1 children 6–12, free for kids 5 and under. Memorial Day to Labor Day daily 10am–4pm; Labor Day to Memorial Day by appt. Located just behind the chamber of commerce.

WHERE TO STAY

Rates are highest here during summer and lowest in late winter and early spring (before rafting season begins). Among reliable chain motels in the area are the **Comfort Inn,** 315 E. Rainbow Blvd./U.S. 50 (✆ **800/424-6423** or 719/539-5000), with rates from $109 to $169 for two in peak summer season and lower rates the rest of the year; **Holiday Inn Express,** 407 E. Rainbow Blvd./U.S. 50 (✆ **800/356-3584** or 719/539-8500), with double rates from $89 to $199; **Super 8,** 525 W. Rainbow Blvd./U.S. 50 (✆ **800/800-8000** or 719/539-6689), with rates of $109 to $149 for two in peak summer season, lower the rest of the year; and the **Travelodge,** 7310 U.S. 50 (✆ **800/234-1077** or 719/539-2528), with double rates from $89 to $109 in peak summer season, lower the rest of the year.

New in 2008, the **Simple Lodge & Hostel,** 224 E. 1st St. (✆ **719/650-7381;** www.simploelodge.com), is the best value in town, offering bunks for $21 a night and private rooms for $50 a night in a slickly restored 1883 railroad boardinghouse just 2 blocks from the town center.

Room tax adds 8.8% to lodging bills; at press time, a proposal to add a $5 nightly fee was on the fall 2008 ballot.

River Run Inn ★★ Built by Chaffee County in 1895 as a home for the indigent, this large, stately building—about 3 miles northwest of town—served that purpose for half a century. Since 1983, however, it has functioned as a charming bed-and-breakfast, and is listed on the National Register of Historic Places. A wide front porch leads into a large sitting room and library, and the back porch looks out over the Arkansas River and the mountains beyond. Inside, the lovely guest rooms, most with mountain views, are decorated with period furnishings, including brass or four-poster beds; they have either all-new showers or tubs (not both). The dormitory, available to parties of 5 to 13 people, covers the entire third floor (with a shared bathroom). Full breakfasts include a hot entree, baked goods, and fruit. The grounds include a section of the river with private fishing access. (A Colorado fishing license is required.)

8495 C.R. 160, Salida, CO 81201. ✆ **800/385-6925** or 719/539-3818. Fax 801/659-1878. www.riverruninn.com. 6 units (5 with private bathroom). $100–$145 double with private bathroom; $40 per person for dormitory ($200 minimum). Rates include full breakfast. AE, MC, V. Children over 12 welcome. Closed Nov to mid-Apr. *In room:* Wireless Internet access (free), no phone.

Woodland Motel ★ (Value Owned and operated by the Borbas family since 1976, this small independent motel within easy walking distance of downtown has a friendly feel and some of the cleanest rooms I've seen in the Rockies. There are 10 different room layouts here, many with kitchens, a few with microwaves and fridges, and several with neither. The closets are large, designed to accommodate ski gear. The place is especially dog friendly: Freshly laundered doggie beds are available, and there is a jar of treats on the counter in the lobby. An amazing 70% of guests are repeat customers here, and it's easy to see why.

903 W. 1st St., Salida, CO 81201. ✆ **800/488-0456** for reservations or 719/539-4980. www.woodlandmotel.com. 18 units, including 3 condos. $68–$120 double; $120–$134 condo. AE, DISC, MC, V. Pets accepted. **Amenities:** 2 outdoor hot tubs. *In room:* A/C, cable TV, dataport w/high-speed Internet, kitchen, coffeemaker, hair dryer.

WHERE TO DINE

Salida's tried-and-true breakfast and lunch standby is the **First Street Café,** 137 E. First St. (✆ **719/539-4759**), which churns out consistently good American fare.

BoatHouse Cantina ★ MEXICAN/AMERICAN The only place in Salida for a bite right on the Arkansas River, this immediately became the restaurant with the best location in town when it opened in 2008. With garage-door-style windows that open in summer and provide a near bird's-eye view of passing paddlers, the people-watching is fantastic. The food's pretty good, too, from the taco plates to vegetarian or pork green chile to tasty chile rellenos, as well as burgers and other sandwiches. There is a full bar and a number of specialty margaritas on the menu.

228 F St. on the Arkansas River. ✆ **719/539-5004.** www.boathousecantina.com. Main courses $5–$11. MC, V. Mon–Sat 11am–10pm; Sun 11am–9pm.

Laughing Ladies Restaurant ★★ CONTEMPORARY AMERICAN Jeff Schweitzer, the amiable chef-owner of Laughing Ladies, opened his vibrant downtown eatery in 1996 and is still waiting for the Salida culinary scene to fully catch up. His creative, regularly changing menu is a delight, from starters like grilled balsamic quail or house-smoked salmon to such tantalizing entrees as orange roasted free-range chicken with almond quinoa or yogurt-marinated Atlantic salmon with sticky rice and cucumber-jalapeno salsa. There is a full bar and a short but well-chosen wine list.

128 W. 1st St. ✆ **719/539-6209.** www.laughingladiesrestaurant.com. Reservations recommended. Main courses lunch and brunch $7–$10; dinner $19–$29. DISC, MC, V. Thurs–Sat 11am–3pm; Sun 8am–2pm; Thurs–Sun 5–8:30pm. Closed Tues–Wed.

4 ALAMOSA & THE GREAT SAND DUNES

212 miles SW of Denver, 149 miles E of Durango, 173 miles N of Santa Fe, New Mexico

Founded in 1878 with the extension of the Denver & Rio Grande Railroad into the San Luis Valley, Alamosa was named for the cottonwood (*álamo* in Spanish) trees that lined the banks of the Rio Grande. Soon rails spread out in all directions from the community, and it became a thriving transportation center for farmers and a supply depot for miners. Farming remains important today, but Alamosa is also an educational center with Adams State College, a 4-year institution founded in 1921. And if you're looking for Colorado's largest sandbox, here it is: Just 35 miles from Alamosa are the tallest sand dunes in North America, the Great Sand Dunes. Elevation is 7,544 feet, and the population is almost 9,000.

ESSENTIALS

GETTING THERE **By Car** Alamosa is at the junction of U.S. 160, which runs east 73 miles to I-25 at Walsenburg and west to Durango; and U.S. 285, which extends south to Santa Fe, New Mexico, and north to Denver. Because of a jog in U.S. 285, however, a more direct route into the city from the north is to take Colo. 17 the last 50 miles.

By Plane The **San Luis Valley Regional Airport** (✆ **719/589-9446**), 2500 State St., 3 miles off U.S. 285 South, has service to and from Denver with **Great Lakes Airlines** (✆ **800/554-5111**).

VISITOR INFORMATION The **Alamosa Convention & Visitors Bureau,** 601 State Ave., Alamosa, CO 81101 (✆ **800/258-7597** or 719/589-4840; www.alamosa.org), operates a visitor information center, with summer hours from 8am to 6pm daily year-round, except holidays.

FAST FACTS The **San Luis Valley Regional Medical Center,** with a 24-hour emergency room, is at 106 Blanca Ave. (✆ **719/589-2511;** www.slvrmc.org). The **post office** is at 505 Third St., off State Avenue. Contact the U.S. Postal Service (✆ **800/275-8777;** www.usps.com) for hours and other information.

SPECIAL EVENTS Crane Festival, early to mid-March, in Monte Vista; Rodeo, late June; Farm and Ranch Heritage Days, early July, Monte Vista; Early Iron Festival (classic cars and hot rods), Labor Day weekend.

GREAT SAND DUNES NATIONAL PARK & PRESERVE ★★

Just 35 miles northeast of Alamosa, on Colo. 150, is Colorado's fourth—and newest—national park. Since 2000, when Congress passed the law approving park status pending the acquisition of "sufficient land having a sufficient diversity of resources," Coloradoans had been waiting for this moment. It came in 2004, when the U.S. secretary of the interior arrived to publicly announce the designation of Great Sand Dunes National Park and Preserve. The necessary property was acquired with the help of the Nature Conservancy.

Far from any sea or major desert, this 39-square-mile expanse of sand seems incongruous here. The dunes are the tallest on the continent, piled nearly 750 feet high against the western edge of the Sangre de Cristo Mountains—a startling sight. The dunes were created over thousands of years by southwesterly winds blowing across the valley. They formed when streams of water from melting glaciers carried rocks, gravel, and silt down from the mountains. In addition, as the Rio Grande changed its course, it left behind sand, silt, and debris.

Even today the winds are changing the face of the dunes. So-called "reversing winds" from the mountains pile the dunes back upon themselves, building them higher and higher. Though it's physically impossible for sand to be piled steeper than 34 degrees, the dunes often appear sheerer because of deceptive shadows and colors that change with the light: gold, pink, tan, even bluish. Climbing dunes is fun, and the view from the top is one of the best in the state, but it can be tiring at this 8,200-foot altitude. And be careful: The sand's surface can reach 140°F (60°C) in summer.

Among the specialized animals that survive in this harsh environment are the Ord's kangaroo rat, a creature that never drinks water, plus four insects found nowhere else on Earth: the Great Sand Dunes tiger beetle and three other beetle varieties. These animals and the flora of the adjacent mountain foothills are discussed in evening programs and guided walks during summer.

For orientation, walk the easy .5-mile self-guided nature trail that begins at the visitor center. If you want more of a challenge, hike the dunes—you can get to the top of a 750-foot dune and back in about 90 minutes. Those who make it all the way to the top are rewarded with spectacular views of the dunes and the surrounding mountains.

Pinyon Flats Campground, with 88 sites, is open year-round. It has picnic tables, fire grates, flush toilets, and drinking water, but no showers or RV hookups. Campsites are assigned on a first-come, first-served basis, and cost $14 per night. Admission to the monument for up to a week is $3 per person (free for those under 17). The **visitor center** (© **719/378-6399**) is open daily year-round (closed on winter holidays). For further information, contact Great Sand Dunes National Park and Preserve, 11999 Colo. 150, Mosca, CO 81146 (© **719/378-6300;** www.nps.gov/grsa).

From Alamosa, there are two main routes to Great Sand Dunes: east 14 miles on U.S. 160, then north on Colo. 150; or north 14 miles on Colo. 17 to Mosca, then east on Six Mile Lane to the junction of Colo. 150.

SPORTS & OUTDOOR ACTIVITIES

Many of the best outdoor activities in this part of the state take place in the **Rio Grande National Forest,** with the Supervisor's Office at 1803 W. U.S. 160, Monte Vista (© **719/852-5941;** www.fs.fed.us/r2). For equipment for a variety of outdoor activities (including

Moments The Cumbres & Toltec Scenic Railroad

This is my idea of the best way to see this country. Built in 1880 to serve remote mining camps, the **Cumbres & Toltec Scenic Railroad ★★** follows a spectacular 64-mile path through the San Juan Mountains from Antonito, Colorado, to Chama, New Mexico. This narrow-gauge steam railroad weaves through groves of pine and aspen and past strange rock formations before ascending into the spectacular Toltec Gorge of the Los Piños River. At the rail-junction community of Osier, passengers enjoy lunch while the *Colorado Limited* exchanges engines with the *New Mexico Express.* Round-trip passengers return to their starting point in Antonito, while onward passengers continue a climb through tunnels and trestles to the summit of 10,015-foot Cumbres Pass, then drop down a precipitous 4% grade to Chama. A joint venture by the states of Colorado and New Mexico, the train is a registered National Historic Site.

A trip from Antonito to Chama (or vice versa), traveling there by train and returning by bus, costs $74 for adults, $37 for children under 12. A regular round-trip to Osier is $65 for adults and $33 for children under 12, but this omits either the gorge or the pass. Either way, it's an all-day adventure, leaving between 8 and 10:30am, and returning between 4:30 and 6:30pm. All fares include lunch at Osier. The train runs daily from Memorial Day weekend to mid-October. For reservations and information, contact the Cumbres & Toltec Scenic Railroad, P.O. Box 1057, Chama, NM 87520 (✆ **888/286-2737** or 719/376-5483 for the Antonito Depot; www.cumbrestoltec.com). The depot is 28 miles south of Alamosa, just off U.S. 285.

mountain bike and ski rentals), visit **Kristi Mountain Sports,** Villa Mall, 3217 Main St., Alamosa (✆ **719/589-9759**).

FISHING The Rio Grande is an outstanding stream for trout, walleye, and catfish; there are also numerous high mountain lakes and streams throughout the Rio Grande National Forest where you're apt to catch rainbow, brown, brook, cutthroat, and Rio Grande cutthroat trout. For information, contact the Forest Service office (see above). You can get licenses, tackle, and advice at **Wal-Mart,** 3333 Clark St., off U.S. 160 about 3 miles east of downtown Alamosa (✆ **719/589-9071**).

GOLF The **Cattails Golf Club,** 6615 N. River Rd. (✆ **719/589-9515**), is an 18-hole course along the Rio Grande on the north side of Alamosa. Generally open March through November, the cost is $33 for 18 holes. The 9-hole **Monte Vista Country Club,** at 101 Country Club Dr. in the town of Monte Vista (✆ **719/852-4906**), 17 miles west of Alamosa, is a particularly challenging course due to its small greens. Open April through October, the course is on the migratory path of sandhill and whooping cranes. The fee is $16 for 9 holes, $23 for 18.

HIKING The best opportunities in the region are found in the surrounding **Rio Grande National Forest,** with nearly 2 million acres. One of the most popular hikes, with easy access, is **Zapata Falls,** reached off Colo. 150, about 20 miles northeast of Alamosa and south of Great Sand Dunes. This cavernous waterfall on the northwest flank of 14,345-foot Mount Blanca freezes in winter, turning its cave into a natural icebox that often remains frozen well into summer. More challenging hikes include trails into the **Wheeler Geologic Area,** known for its unique rock formations. Obtain directions from the Forest Service (see above).

MOUNTAIN BIKING There are plenty of opportunities for mountain biking on local federal lands. Stop at the visitor center to pick up a copy of the ***San Luis Valley Mountain Bike Guide.*** Get additional information from the Forest Service (see above), or stop at Kristi Mountain Sports (see above) for tips on the best places to go, rentals (starting around $30 per day), repairs, and accessories.

OTHER HIGHLIGHTS

Adams State College–Luther E. Bean Museum Located on the second floor of Richardson Hall in room 256, this museum has an excellent fine-arts gallery featuring works by local artists. Also on display is the Woodard Collection, a sampling of artifacts from around the world. Allow about an hour.

208 Edgemont Blvd. © **719/587-7151.** www.adams.edu/lutherbean. Free admission. Summer Tues–Fri 8am–4:30pm; fall through spring Tues–Fri 8am–5pm. Closed Dec 23–Jan 1 and other major holidays.

Colorado Gators ★ Kids Alligators in Colorado? Strangely enough, yes. Geothermal wells keep the temperature a cozy 87°F (31°C) at this alligator farm located 17 miles north of Alamosa off Colo. 17. There are more than 400 gators—some 11 feet long and weighing 600 pounds. Kids should love watching the alligator feedings, which happen several times each day. The farm also raises fish and has a reptile refuge populated with desert tortoises, turtles, and iguanas. Brave souls can pose for a picture with a baby gator in their hands; braver souls can fork over $100 for a 3-hour alligator-handling class. Early August brings Gatorfest, featuring a gator-wrestling competition. Allow about an hour.

9162 C.R. 9 N., Mosca. © **719/378-2612.** www.gatorfarm.com. Admission $13 adults, $6.25 children 6–12 and seniors 65–79, free for those 5 and under and over 80. Memorial Day through Labor Day daily 9am–7pm; rest of year daily 9am–5pm. Closed Thanksgiving and Christmas.

Rio Grande Scenic Railroad ★ Over routes more than a hundred years old, the diesel locomotives of the Rio Grande Scenic Railroad haul classic Pullman passenger railcars through the mountains and valleys of southern Colorado. There are several trips available: Typical is the half-day round-trip excursion between Alamosa and Antonito, connecting with the Cumbres & Toltec Scenic Railroad (see sidebar earlier in this chapter), but the railroad also connects Alamosa and the mountain community of La Veta to the east and the town of Monte Vista to the northwest. The passenger cars are climate controlled with comfortable seating, and the trains have snack bars and open-air observation cars. Allow at least a half-day.

601 State St. © **877/726-7245.** www.alamosatrain.com. $12–$58 adults, $10–$48 seniors, $8–$43 children 2–12, 1 and under free round-trip. Train operates from late May to mid-Oct; call for current schedule.

NATURAL HIGHLIGHTS

The **Alamosa–Monte Vista National Wildlife Refuges** (© **719/589-4021;** http://alamosa.fws.gov) together have preserved nearly 25,000 acres of vital land for a variety of marsh birds and waterfowl, including many migrating and wintering species. Sandhill and whooping cranes visit in early to mid-October and early March; at other times of the year there may be egrets, herons, avocets, bitterns, and other species. A wide variety of ducks are year-round residents, with waterfowl numbers at their peak March through

May. The refuges have self-guided driving tours with a number of viewpoints, and also several hiking trails. To get to the Alamosa refuge, which contains the refuge headquarters, go 4 miles east of Alamosa on U.S. 160 and then south 3 miles on El Rancho Lane. The Monte Vista refuge is located 6 miles south of the community of Monte Vista on Colo. 15. Admission is free. The refuges are open daily from sunrise to sunset.

WHERE TO STAY & DINE

In Alamosa, some reliable chain properties include the **Best Western Alamosa Inn,** 2005 Main St. (✆ **800/459-5123** or 719/589-2567), with double rates of $70 to $105; **Comfort Inn,** 6301 U.S. 160 (✆ **800/424-6423** or 719/587-9000), charging $75 to $119 double; and **Super 8,** 2505 W. Main St. (✆ **800/800-8000** or 719/589-6447), with double rates of $66 to $73. Room tax adds about 11% to lodging bills.

You'll find a number of restaurants along Alamosa's Main Street, many of them chains but also a few good independents. I especially like the Mexican food at **Cavillo's,** 400 Main St. (✆ **719/587-5500**).

5 A SIDE TRIP TO CREEDE

Among the best preserved of all 19th-century Colorado mining towns, Creede had a population of 10,000 in 1892 when a balladeer wrote, "It's day all day in the daytime, and there is no night in Creede." Over $1 million in silver was mined every day, but the Silver Panic of 1893 eclipsed Creede's rising star. For most of the next century, area mines produced just enough silver and other minerals to sustain the community until the 1960s, when tourism and outdoor recreation became paramount. Today this mountain town, at an elevation of 8,838 feet, has a population of about 400. It's fairly easy to see most of the town in a day; be sure to include a stop at the Creede Museum, drive the Bachelor Historic Tour route, and if at all possible attend a show at the Creede Repertory Theatre.

To get to Creede from Alamosa, drive west on U.S. 160 about 48 miles to South Fork, and turn north on Colo. 149, which follows the Rio Grande about 23 miles to Creede.

You can obtain information on what to see and do, as well as lodging and dining options, from the **Creede & Mineral County Chamber of Commerce,** in the County Annex building at the north end of Main Street (P.O. Box 580), Creede, CO 81130 (✆ **800/327-2102** or 719/658-2374; www.creede.com). The office is staffed Monday through Friday from 9am to 5pm, and brochures and other information are available on a self-serve basis 24 hours daily. There's also a visitor information booth on Main Street in the middle of town, open daily from 9am to 5pm from Memorial Day to mid-September. Another good source for information is the **Divide Ranger District office** of the U.S. Forest Service, located at the corner of 3rd Street and Creede Avenue (✆ **719/658-2556;** www.fs.fed.us/r2), which can provide maps and information on hiking, mountain biking, horseback riding, four-wheeling, fishing, cross-country skiing, and all sorts of other outdoor activities in the nearby San Juan and Rio Grande national forests. Ask for directions to the **Wheeler Geologic Area,** a region of volcanic rock formations accessible only by jeep, horseback, or a 5-hour hike; or **North Creede Canyon,** where remnants of the old town of Creede still stand near the **Commodore Mine,** whose workings seem to keep a ghostly vigil over the canyon.

There's plenty to do in Creede, but for my money the absolutely best way to spend some time here is to take in a production by the **Creede Repertory Theatre ★★**, 124 N. Main St. (✆ **866/658-2540** or 719/658-2540; www.creederep.org). Established in 1966 by a small troupe of young actors from the University of Kansas, this theater company is now nationally acclaimed, and offers matinee and evening performances from late May through September in its 243-seat main theater and a separate 90-seat theater. The company usually presents four full-length productions, a family show, and sometimes shorter plays, in repertory. Productions vary but might be musicals, comedies, or contemporary or classic dramas. Recent productions have included Rupert Holmes's loony musical *The Mystery of Edwin Drood,* Neil Simon's *Fools,* and a family show based on fables by Aesop and La Fontaine. Tickets for full-length productions run from $15 to $30, and family shows are $7 to $15. In addition to its repertory theater productions, the company presents a variety of concerts and other special events year-round. Advance reservations are strongly recommended.

The former Denver & Rio Grande Railroad depot is now the **Creede Museum,** behind City Park (✆ **719/658-2004**), which tells the story of the town's wild-and-woolly heyday. There were dozens of saloons and gambling tables, and shootouts were not uncommon. Bob Ford, the killer of Jesse James, was murdered in his own saloon, and Bat Masterson and "Poker Alice" Tubbs were other notorious residents. Photographs and exhibits on gambling and other activities, as well as a horse-drawn hearse, are included in the museum's collection. It's usually open Monday through Saturday from 10am to 4pm, Sunday 1 to 4pm in summer, with $2 admission for adults, $1 for seniors, and free for children.

The **Underground Mining Museum,** on the north edge of town (✆ **719/658-0811**), is contained in a series of rooms and tunnels blasted into a cliff face. Inside this subterranean world are exhibits that trace the history of mining, along with displays of mining memorabilia and gemstones. It's always 51°F (11°C) down here, so bring a jacket. Guided tours are offered at 10am year-round, as well as 3pm in summer ($15, reservations recommended), and there's also a gift shop. The museum is open daily from 10am to 4pm in summer and 10am to 3pm Monday through Friday the rest of the year. Admission costs $7 for adults, $6 for seniors 60 and over, and $5 for children 12 and under.

The 17-mile **Bachelor Historic Tour** is described in a booklet available from the chamber of commerce ($1). The route follows a Forest Service road through the mountains, past abandoned mines, mining equipment, the original Creede cemetery, and 19th-century town sites. The road is fine for passenger cars in dry weather but may be closed by winter snow. Allow 1 to 2 hours.

Southeastern Colorado

Colorado's southeastern quadrant owes its life to the Arkansas River, which forges one of the world's most spectacular canyons—the deep, narrow Royal Gorge. On the river's trek through Pueblo, it not only supplies water for a major steel industry, but also provides a delightful riverfront park, walkway, and shopping area with a reason for being. From Pueblo, the river rolls across the Great Plains, providing life-giving water to an arid but soil-rich region that produces a wide variety of vegetables and fruits. Bent's Old Fort, a national historic site that has re-created one of the West's most important frontier trading posts, also rests beside the river, east of the community of La Junta. South of Pueblo, the town of Trinidad is the center of a century-old coal-mining district, boasting a number of handsome old Victorian-style buildings.

1 PUEBLO

111 miles S of Denver, 42 miles S of Colorado Springs, 317 miles N of Albuquerque, New Mexico

Don't trust your first impressions. As you drive through Pueblo along the interstate, it might appear that this bland but industrious city—with its railroad tracks, warehouses, and factories—doesn't warrant a stop. But take the time to get off the superslab and discover the real Pueblo. You'll find handsome historic homes, fine Western art, a well-run zoo, a delightful riverfront park, and a number of outdoor recreational opportunities.

Although Zebulon Pike and his U.S. Army exploratory expedition camped at the future site of Pueblo in 1806, there were no white settlements here until 1842, when El Pueblo Fort was constructed as a fur-trading outpost. It was abandoned following a Ute massacre in late 1854, but when the Colorado gold rush began 5 years later, the town of Pueblo was born on the site of the former fort.

In the early 20th century, the city grew as a major center for coal mining and steel production. Job opportunities attracted large numbers of immigrants, especially from Mexico and eastern Europe. Pueblo today is home to high-tech industries as well as the University of Southern Colorado. As the largest city (pop. a bit over 100,000) in southeastern Colorado, it is the market center for a 15-county region extending to the borders of New Mexico, Oklahoma, and Kansas. Elevation is 4,695 feet.

ESSENTIALS

GETTING THERE **By Car** I-25 links Pueblo directly with Colorado Springs, Denver, and points north; and Santa Fe, Albuquerque, and other New Mexico cities to the south. U.S. 50 runs east to La Junta and west to Cañon City, Gunnison, and Montrose.

By Plane **Pueblo Memorial Airport,** 31201 Bryan Circle, Keeler Parkway off U.S. 50 East (✆ **719/553-2760;** www.pueblo.us), is served by **Great Lakes Airlines** (✆ **800/554-5111;** www.greatlakesav.com), with daily flights to Denver as a United partner. Agencies providing rental cars at the airport include **Avis** (✆ **800/331-1212** or 719/948-9665) and **Hertz** (✆ **800/654-3131** or 719/948-3345).

VISITOR INFORMATION Contact the **Greater Pueblo Chamber of Commerce,** 302 N. Santa Fe Ave. (P.O. Box 697), Pueblo, CO 81003 (✆ **800/233-3446** or 719/542-1704; www.pueblochamber.org and www.destinationpueblo.com), for most travel-related needs. The **Visitor Information Center** is located at the chamber office, which is open year-round Monday through Friday from 8am to 5pm, and some Saturdays from 10am to 2pm.

GETTING AROUND Pueblo lies on the eastward-flowing Arkansas River at its confluence with Fountain Creek. The downtown core is located north of the Arkansas and west of the Fountain, immediately west of I-25. Santa Fe Avenue and Main Street, 1 block west, are the principal north–south thoroughfares; the cross streets are numbered (counting northward), with Fourth and Eighth streets the most important. Pueblo Boulevard circles the city on the south and west, with spurs leading to the nature center and Lake Pueblo State Park.

Public transportation is provided by **Pueblo Transit** (✆ **719/553-2725;** www.pueblo.us). For taxi service, call **City Cab** (✆ **719/543-2525**). In addition to the rental-car agencies at the airport (see above), there is an outlet for **Enterprise** in Pueblo (✆ **719/542-6100**).

FAST FACTS Medical services, including emergency services, are provided by **Parkview Medical Center,** 400 W. 16th St. (✆ **719/584-4000;** www.parkviewmc.com), and **St. Mary-Corwin Medical Center,** 1008 Minnequa Ave. (✆ **719/557-4000;** www.stmarycorwin.org). The main **post office** is located at 1022 Fontino Blvd.; call the U.S. Postal Service (✆ **800/275-8777;** www.usps.com) for hours and locations of other post offices.

SPECIAL EVENTS Bluegrass Festival, at the Greenway & Nature Center, early June; Boats, Blues & BBQ on the Historic Arkansas Riverwalk, mid-June; Rocky Mountain Street Rod Nationals, late June; National Little Britches Rodeo Finals, mid-July; Colorado State Fair, late August into early September; the Chile and Frijoles Festival, late September; Veterans Day Parade, early November; and the Christmas Art Show and Parade of Lights, late November.

WHAT TO SEE & DO

Historic Pueblo runs along Union Avenue north from the Arkansas River to First Street, a distance of about 5 blocks. More than 40 buildings in the **Union Avenue Historic District** (www.seepueblo.com) are listed on the National Register of Historic Places, including the **Vail Hotel** (217 S. Grand Ave.), headquarters of the **Pueblo County Historical Society** museum and library (✆ **719/543-6772;** www.pueblohistory.org), with railroad memorabilia, locally made saddles, and some 8,000 books, historical maps, and photographs depicting Pueblo's history. **Union Depot,** with its mosaic-tile floors and beautiful stained-glass windows, houses retail stores and offices, yet still serves rail freight lines. **Walking-tour maps** can be obtained at the Visitor Information Center (see "Visitor Information," above), as well as from Union Avenue businesses.

Located in a historic fire station built in 1881 is **Hose Company #3—Pueblo's Fire Museum,** 116 Broadway Ave. (✆ **719/553-2830;** www.pueblofire.org). Open for guided tours by appointment only (free, donations encouraged), the museum contains antique fire engines, firefighting equipment, photographs, and other firefighting-related displays.

El Pueblo History Museum ★★ This beautiful museum is a splendid introduction to this region. Located at the intersection of West First Street, Union Avenue, and Grand

ACCOMMODATIONS ■
Abriendo Inn **5**
Best Western Eagle Ridge Inn & Suites **3**
Comfort Inn **3**
Hampton Inn **3**

DINING ◆
La Renaissance **6**
Patti's Restaurant **12**
Star Bar & Lunch **15**

ATTRACTIONS ●
El Pueblo History Museum **11**
Hose Company #3 **7**
Infozone News Museum **8**
The Nature & Raptor Center **1**
Pueblo Weisbrod Aircraft Museum **14**
Pueblo Zoo **2**
Rosemount Museum **4**
Sangre de Cristo Arts & Conference Center **13**
Southeastern Colorado Heritage Center **9**
Steelworks Museum of Industry & Culture **16**
Vail Hotel **10**

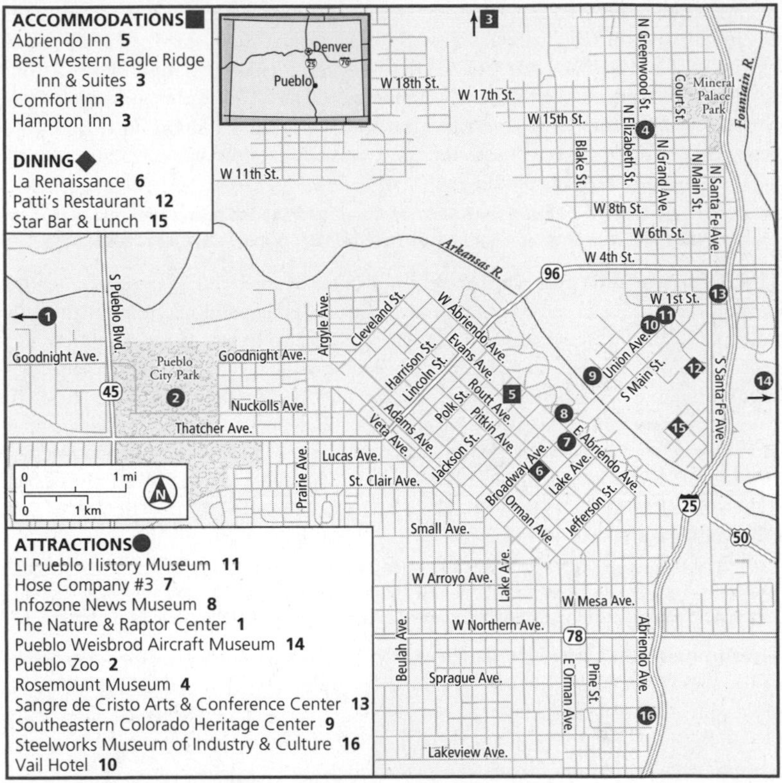

Avenue, the museum also serves as the Scenic Byways Visitor Center and as a gateway to the Arkansas Riverwalk (see "Outdoor Activities," below) and the historic district.

Evocative of a mid-1800s trading post, the museum's design replicates a square adobe building with a central plaza, reminiscent of Bent's Old Fort. The museum showcases the traditions of the numerous cultural and ethnic groups in the area, utilizing maps and photos plus displays specific to each era. It begins with such items as beaded garments, pouches, American-Indian baskets, and stonework; then it moves into the Spanish, French, and American exploration of the area, highlighting the fur traders and Bent's Fort. The founding of the city through farming, ranching, and the early steel and mining industries is next, followed by early-20th-century labor issues.

The museum also explores the area's continued industrial expansion, which brought a tremendous influx of immigrants, resulting in a rich cultural mix. Other exhibits explain how outdoor activities drew visitors to the area in the 20th century, and will likely tempt visitors outside to explore the Riverwalk. Allow at least an hour and a half.

301 N. Union Ave. ℂ **719/583-0453.** www.coloradohistory.org. Admission $4 adults; $3 seniors 65 and older, students with IDs, and children 6–12; free for children 5 and under; free for children 12 and under on Sat. Tues–Sat 10am–4pm.

Infozone News Museum (Kids) Say whatever you want about this museum—one of its primary goals is to increase visitors' knowledge and understanding of American rights to freedom of speech and freedom of the press. Located on the fourth floor of the public library, the state-of-the-art facility also provides a look at the history of Pueblo and its newspapers, and has hands-on activities that youths will especially enjoy. There's a working Linotype typesetting machine to examine, as well as a 100-seat movie theater where a variety of films are shown. Interactive touch-screen computer kiosks turn visitors into reporters as they go on assignment, interview those close to the action, and then see the story in print. Allow 45 minutes.

Robert Hoag Rawlings Public Library, 100 E. Abriendo Ave. ✆ **719/562-5604.** www.infozonenewsmuseum.com. Free admission. Mon–Thurs 9am–9pm; Fri–Sat 9am–6pm; Sun 1–5pm. Closed major holidays.

The Nature and Raptor Center ★ A major recreation and education center, this area provides access to more than 36 miles of paved biking and hiking trails along the Arkansas River and around Lake Pueblo. There are also volleyball courts, a 150-foot fishing dock, horseshoe pits, an amphitheater, nature trails, picnic areas, and a large children's playground. Boats and canoes can be put into the Arkansas River here. An interpretive center displays exhibits on the flora and fauna of the area, there are demonstration gardens along the river, and the **Cafe del Rio** serves American and Southwestern dishes. At the Raptor Center, injured eagles, owls, and other birds of prey are nursed back to health and released into the wild. The center also houses several resident birds of prey. Allow at least an hour.

5200 Nature Center Rd., via W. 11th St. ✆ **719/549-2414** main office or 719/549-2327 Raptor Center. www.gncp.org. Free admission, but donations welcome. On-site parking $3. Grounds daily sunrise–sunset; Raptor Center Tues–Sun 11am–4pm; Interpretive Center and gift shop Tues–Sat 9am–5pm.

Pueblo Weisbrod Aircraft Museum The place to come to see some fascinating old airplanes, this museum has more than two dozen historic aircraft—World War II and postwar—on display, as well as numerous exhibits and photographs depicting the B-24 bomber and its role in World War II. It's hard to miss the restored Boeing B-29 Superfortress, with its 141-foot wingspan, which dominates a large hangar. Also on display are a Douglas A-26 Invader, a Grumman F-9 Cougar, a Douglas C-47 Skytrain (or, as the GIs dubbed it, a Gooney Bird), an RA5C Vigilante, and a McDonnell Douglas F-101A Voodoo. There's a well-stocked souvenir shop, offering hard-to-find military and general aviation-related items. Allow 1 to 2 hours.

31001 Magnuson Ave. ✆ **719/948-9219.** www.pwam.org. Admission $7, free for children 9 and under. Mon–Sat 10am–4pm; Sun 1–4pm. At Pueblo Memorial Airport, 6 miles east of downtown via U.S. 50.

Pueblo Zoo (Kids) More than 400 animals representing some 130 species live in this 25-acre zoo, which is listed on the National Register of Historic Places because of several buildings and other structures (including a moat) that were constructed of native sandstone during the Depression by WPA workers. Attractions include a northern river otter exhibit, a tropical rainforest, and a black-footed penguin underwater exhibit. You'll find all sorts of reptiles and insects in the herpetarium; kangaroos and emus in the Australia Station; an excellent African lion exhibit; and endangered species such as cotton-top tamarins, prehensile tail skinks, and maned wolves. You'll also see zebras, Malayan sun bears, and Lar gibbons. Kids in a participatory mood should flock to Pioneer Farm, where they can feed a variety of rare domesticated animals, and to the Discovery Room, which features hands-on exhibits for all ages. Stop by the Watering Hole snack bar or the

Wild Things gift shop, which boasts a better-than-average selection of animal-related items, if you need a rest between exhibits. Allow 2 to 4 hours.

City Park, 3455 Nuckolls Ave. ✆ **719/561-1452.** www.pueblozoo.org. Admission $7.50 adults, $6.50 seniors 65 and older, $5 children 3–12, free for children 2 and under. Memorial Day weekend through Labor Day daily 9am–5pm; rest of year Mon–Sat 9am–4pm, Sun noon–4pm. Closed from noon on the day before Thanksgiving, Christmas, and New Year's, and all day on those 3 holidays.

Rosemount Museum ★ Were you a rich and sophisticated Westerner in a previous life? Then you probably lived in an elegant home like this. Completed in 1893 for the pioneer Thatcher family, this 37-room mansion is one of the finest surviving examples of late-19th-century architecture and decoration in North America. The three-story, 24,000-square-foot home was built entirely of pink rhyolite stone. Inside you'll find handsome oak, maple, and mahogany woodwork; remarkable works of stained glass; hand-decorated ceilings; exquisite Tiffany lighting fixtures; period furniture; and 10 fireplaces. Allow 1 hour for the guided tour.

419 W. 14th St. (at Grand Ave.). ✆ **719/545-5290.** www.rosemount.org. Admission $6 adults, $5 seniors 60 and over, $4 youths 6–18, free for children 5 and under. Tues–Sat 10am–4pm (last tour begins at 3:30pm). Closed major holidays and Jan. Take the I-25 exit for 13th St.

Sangre de Cristo Arts & Conference Center ★ Kids Pueblo's cultural hub is a three-building complex that houses a 500-seat theater, two dance studios, four art galleries (including one with a fine collection of Western art), a gift shop, a restaurant, and the state-of-the-art Buell Children's Museum, which covers 12,000 square feet with a wide variety of hands-on arts and science exhibits. The center also hosts concerts and other performing arts events, including a children's theater program (call for details). Allow 2 to 3 hours.

210 N. Santa Fe Ave. ✆ **719/295-7200.** www.sdc-arts.org. $4 adults, $3 children 15 and under. Galleries and children's museum Tues–Sat 11am–4pm, restaurant Tues–Sat 11am–2pm.

Southeastern Colorado Heritage Center Located across the street from the historic Union Depot train station, this facility includes exhibits on southeastern Colorado's pioneer days, including a mid-1800s store and early communications equipment. There are also railroad exhibits, presented in cooperation with the Pueblo Railway Museum, which also maintains the outdoor exhibits of locomotives, passenger cars, and freight cars just west of the depot at 132 W. B St. (www.pueblorailway.org). Allow at least 1 hour for the museum and railyard.

201 W. B St. ✆ **719/295-1517.** www.theheritagecenter.us. Free admission. Tues–Sat 10am–4pm.

Steelworks Museum of Industry & Culture New in 2007, this facility focuses on the history and impact of the Colorado Fuel and Iron Corporation, which began in the 1870s to provide steel rails for the region's railroads and grew to include mining and steel and iron production, and then merged with a fuel company. At one time it operated mines and quarries throughout the West, and the company was the single largest private landowner in Colorado.

Housed in a historic medical dispensary building, the museum's exhibits examine the history of mining and steel production, including the company's sometimes-violent labor relations, plus railroading and general history of the area. Among displays are a one-of-a-kind mine rescue railcar and exhibits on industrial medicine. There is also a gift shop. Allow 1 hour.

1612 E. Abriendo Ave. ✆ **719/564-9086.** www.cfisteel.org. Admission $5 adults, $3 children 3–11, and free for children 2 and under. Mon–Sat 10am–4pm, in summer also Sun noon–4pm.

One Big Artwork

Designated the world's largest mural by *Guinness World Records,* the **Pueblo Mural Project** makes a canvas of a concrete wall that fronts the Arkansas River Levee for about 2 miles near downtown Pueblo. From its bohemian beginnings in the 1970s, the project was soon legitimized and encouraged, and today there are hundreds of different oversized works of art depicting everything from political slogans to rock stars to cartoon animals. Contact the Greater Pueblo Chamber of Commerce (✆ **800/233-3446**) for more information.

OUTDOOR ACTIVITIES

Pueblo's mild climate makes it a popular destination for boating, fishing, and other outdoor recreation, with several major stops for the region's outdoor enthusiasts.

Watersport aficionados are drawn to **Lake Pueblo State Park** ★ (also called Pueblo Reservoir), which boasts some 4,500 surface acres of water and 60 miles of shoreline. The lake is popular among **anglers** trying for rainbow trout, brown trout, crappie, black bass, and channel catfish, and there's a free fish-cleaning station.

It's also a huge attraction for boaters, who come from all over southern Colorado, and the park offers swimming, hiking, and biking. The park's **North Shore Marina** (✆ **719/547-3880;** www.noshoremarina.com) provides a gas dock, boating and fishing supplies, groceries, and a restaurant. The **South Marina** (✆ **719/564-1043;** www.thesouthshoremarina.com) provides the same services and also rents pontoon boats ($135–$175 for 4 hr. and $240–$320 for 9 hr., plus fuel) April through October.

The **Rock Canyon Swim Beach** (✆ **719/564-0065**) at the east end of the park is open daily from Memorial Day to Labor Day Thursday to Monday 11am to 7pm and has lifeguards on duty. There's a five-story, three-flume **water slide** ($1.75 per ride or $10 all day), plus rentals of paddle boats ($6 per half-hour) and a snack bar. Entrance to the beach costs only $1. These fees are in addition to the $6 general park admission fee.

The park has about 400 **campsites,** some with electric and water hookups. A dump station and showers are available, and camping rates are $14 to $18 May 1 through Labor Day; $12 to $20 the rest of the year. Camping reservations are available for an extra charge of $8 by calling ✆ **800/678-2267** or through the state parks website listed below. Day use costs $6 per vehicle, and campers must pay this in addition to camping fees.

From Pueblo, take U.S. 50 west for 4 miles, turn south onto Pueblo Boulevard and go another 4 miles to Thatcher Avenue, then turn west, and go 6 miles to the park. For information, contact the park office at ✆ **719/561-9320,** or go to **www.parks.state.co.us**.

The **Historic Arkansas Riverwalk of Pueblo** ★★ is a beautifully landscaped waterfront park that covers some 26 acres and offers pedestrian and bike paths, benches, sculptures, gardens, and natural areas that provide good wildlife-viewing opportunities. Pedal-boat rentals are available from early April to late September on a small lake along the Riverwalk (weekends only in Apr and daily the rest of the season). Rates are $6 per half-hour for a one-person boat and $10 per half-hour for a two- to four-seat boat. Excursion boat rides along the Arkansas take place on weekends in April and operate daily from May to late September. Rates for the narrated 25-minute tours are $5 for adults, $4 for seniors and members of the military, and $3 for children 3 to 12. Hours for both pedal-boat rentals and the excursion-boat rides vary throughout the season; call the boathouse (© **719/595-1589**) for the schedule. The Riverwalk is located near the south end of the Union Avenue Historic District (see "What to See & Do," above) and is easily accessed via Main Street. For information, contact Historic Arkansas Riverwalk of Pueblo Authority, 200 W. First St., Ste. 303, Pueblo, CO 81003 (© **719/595-0242;** www.puebloharp.com).

Also in town, stop at **City Park,** northeast of the intersection of Pueblo Boulevard (Colo. 45) and Thatcher Avenue. The park, home to the Pueblo Zoo (see above), covers some 200 acres and offers two fishing lakes, tennis courts, a swimming pool (open in summer), and playgrounds. There's also a beautiful hand-carved antique carousel built in 1911, with music provided by a 1920 Wurlitzer Military Band Organ. The carousel is open evenings and Sunday afternoons in summer; the park is open daily year-round. For information, call the Pueblo Parks and Recreation Department (© **719/553-2790;** www.pueblo.us).

There are plenty of opportunities for hiking, backpacking, mountain biking, fishing, and camping nearby in lands under the jurisdiction of the U.S. Forest Service. For information, contact the headquarters of the **Pike and San Isabel National Forests and Comanche and Cimarron National Grasslands,** 2840 Kachina Dr., Pueblo, CO 81008 (© **719/553-1400;** www.fs.fed.us/r2).

Local **golf courses** open to the public include **Walking Stick,** 1301 Walking Stick Blvd. (© **719/553-1180**), at the northwest corner of the University of Southern Colorado. Rated among Colorado's best courses and best values, this 18-hole course has a driving range and charges $28 to $30 for 18 holes and $11 for a cart. Other local courses include **Elmwood** at City Park, 3900 Thatcher Ave. (© **719/561-4946**), with an 18-hole regulation course plus executive 9-hole course. Greens fees for 18 holes are $22. **Desert Hawk Golf Course at Pueblo West,** 251 S. McCulloch Blvd. (© **719/547-2280**), is an 18-hole regulation course with greens fees for 18 holes from $26 to $28.

SPECTATOR SPORTS

MOTOR SPORTS Stock-car races are held every Saturday evening from April to September at **I-25 Speedway,** off I-25 at exit 108 (© **303/798-4387;** www.i25speedway.com). Nationally sanctioned drag racing, Sports Car Club of America road racing, and other motor sports take place at the **Pueblo Motorsports Park,** U.S. 50 and Pueblo Boulevard in Pueblo West (© **719/583-0907;** www.pueblomotorsportspark.com) April through September.

RODEO Those visiting Pueblo from mid-August to early September can take in the **Colorado State Fair** (© **800/876-4567** or 719/561-8484; www.coloradostatefair.com), which includes a professional rodeo, carnival rides, food booths, industrial displays, horse shows, animal exhibits, and household-name entertainers.

WHERE TO STAY

There are numerous lodging possibilities in Pueblo, with many of the national chains represented. Rates are highest in summer, and highest of all during the State Fair (mid-Aug to early Sept). Among the reliable major chains are the **Best Western Eagle Ridge Inn & Suites,** 4727 N. Elizabeth St. (© **800/WESTERN** [937-8376] or 719/543-4644), with double rates of $85 to $150; **Comfort Inn,** 4645 N. Freeway (© **800/424-6423** or 719/542-6868), charging $69 to $119 double; and **Hampton Inn,** 4703 N. Freeway, just west of I-25, exit 102 (© **800/972-0165** or 719/544-4700), with double rates from $119 to $159. Room tax adds just under 12%.

Abriendo Inn ★★ This delightful B&B, built in 1906 as a mansion for brewing magnate Martin Walter, his wife, and their eight children, is the best place to stay for those who want to soak up some of the region's history without sacrificing modern comforts and conveniences. A traditional foursquare-style house listed on the National Register of Historic Places, the Abriendo Inn has won a deserved number of awards. It's also very conveniently located in Pueblo's historic district, close to shops, the Riverwalk, and other attractions.

The comfortable guest rooms are decorated with antique furniture and period reproductions, plus king- or queen-size brass or four-poster beds. Four units have showers only; the rest have tub/shower combos or whirlpool tubs for two. Delicious homemade breakfasts, which might include egg-sausage soufflé or baked apricot French toast, are served in the oak-wainscoted dining room or on the outdoor patio. Smoking is permitted on the veranda only.

300 W. Abriendo Ave., Pueblo, CO 81004. ✆ **719/544-2703.** Fax 719/542-6544. www.abriendoinn.com. 10 units. $98–$155 double. Rates include full breakfast and 24-hr. refreshments. AE, MC, V. *In room:* A/C, cable TV, complimentary wireless Internet access, fridge (some), hair dryer.

Camping

There are two Kampgrounds of America (KOA) campgrounds in the Pueblo area, both open year-round and with all the usual commercial campground amenities, including seasonal swimming pools. The **Pueblo KOA** is 5 miles north of the city at I-25, exit 108 (✆ **800/562-7453** for reservations, or 719/542-2273; www.koa.com), and charges $25 to $29 for tent sites and $33 to $39 for RV hookup sites. The **Pueblo South KOA,** about 20 miles south of Pueblo at I-25, exit 74 (✆ **800/562-8646** for reservations, or 719/676-3376; www.koa.com), charges $24 for tent sites and $35 to $42 for RV hookup sites. Both also have camping cabins (you share the bathhouse with campers), with rates in the $45 to $50 range. There are also some 400 campsites at **Lake Pueblo State Park** (see "Outdoor Activities," above).

WHERE TO DINE

For a comfortable, down-home dining experience, I like the American and Italian food served for breakfast, lunch, and dinner at **Patti's Restaurant,** 241 S. Santa Fe Ave. (✆ **719/543-2371**). Located on the Riverwalk, in the same location since 1936, Patti's offers American favorites, including sandwiches, burgers, steak, and seafood, plus Italian specialties, in a relaxed, family-friendly atmosphere. You'll find more in the way of local color and local delicacies at the venerable **Star Bar & Lunch,** 300 Spring St. (✆ **719/542-9718**). The house special is the green chile slopper, an aptly named dish comprised of a hamburger submerged in a bowl of green chile.

La Renaissance ★★ STEAK/SEAFOOD Housed in a historic 1880s Presbyterian church, La Renaissance, a favorite of locals since it opened in 1974, offers casually elegant dining in a unique atmosphere. The decor includes stained-glass windows, high vaulted ceilings, and oak pews, which provide some of the seating. Dinners begin with a tureen of soup and finish with dessert—maybe the delightful cream puffs. Although the menu changes periodically, entrees might include the tender slow-roasted prime rib, steamed Alaskan king crab legs, rack of lamb in a rosemary glaze, baby back pork ribs, or breast of chicken with sautéed mushrooms. There's a wide variety of domestic and imported wine and beer, and service is attentive and friendly.

217 E. Routt Ave. ✆ **719/543-6367.** Reservations recommended. 5-course dinner $12–$36. AE, DC, DISC, MC, V. Mon–Sat 5–9pm. From I-25 exit 97B, take Abriendo Ave. northwest for 4 blocks, turn left onto Michigan St., and go 2 blocks to the restaurant.

2 ROYAL GORGE & CAÑON CITY

The Royal Gorge, one of the most impressive natural attractions in the state, lies 8 miles west of Cañon City off U.S. 50, at the head of the Arkansas River valley.

This narrow 1,053-foot-deep canyon was cut through solid granite by 3 million years of water and wind erosion. When Zebulon Pike saw the gorge in 1806, he predicted that man would never conquer it. But by 1877, the Denver & Rio Grande Railroad had laid a route through the canyon and it soon became a major tourist attraction.

The gorge is spanned by what is said to be the world's highest suspension bridge and an aerial tramway, built for no other reason than to thrill tourists. The quarter-mile-long bridge was constructed in 1929, suspended from two 300-ton cables, and reinforced in 1983. An incline railway, believed to be the world's steepest, was completed in 1931; it plunges from the rim of the gorge 1,550 feet to the floor at a 45-degree angle, giving passengers a view from the bottom as well as the top. Added in 1968, the 35-passenger tram provides views of the gorge and the bridge from a height of 1,178 feet above the Arkansas River.

Owned by Cañon City, the park also includes a 260-seat multimedia theater (where visitors can see a video presentation on the area's history and construction of the bridge), miniature railway, trolley, old-fashioned carousel, various thrill rides and children's attractions, restaurants, gift shops, a petting zoo with free burro rides, and herds of tame mule deer. Live entertainment and a variety of special events take place throughout the year.

The bridge is open year-round daily from 7 or 8am to dusk; the rest of the park is open daily late April through October from 10am until 5 to 7pm. Admission—$22 for adults, $19 for seniors, $17 for children 4 to 11, free for children under 4—includes crossing the bridge and all other park rides and attractions. For information, contact **Royal Gorge Bridge & Park,** P.O. Box 549, Cañon City, CO 81215 (✆ **888/333-5597** or 719/275-7507; www.royalgorgebridge.com).

An interesting way to view the canyon is from the **Royal Gorge Route Railroad,** 401 Water St. (south of U.S. 50 on 3rd St.), Cañon City, CO 81212 (✆ **888/724-5748** or 303/569-1000; www.royalgorgeroute.com). The train takes passengers on a 2-hour, 24-mile trip through the canyon. From early May to early October, the train departs daily at 9:30am and 12:30pm; there are also 3:30pm departures in summer and 7pm dinner rides on select evenings. Coach tickets cost $33 for adults, $22 for children 3 to 12, and are free for children under 3 who sit on a guardian's lap. Reservations are recommended. Observation dome tickets are $25 more and dinner rides are $85 a person ($110 in the observation dome).

To see this beautiful gorge looking up from the river while also enjoying some thrills, consider a raft trip. Rates for adults run $100 to $120 for a full-day trip, including lunch; a half-day trip is about $50 to $65. Most Royal Gorge raft trips include rough whitewater stretches of the river; those preferring calmer sections should inquire with local rafting companies. Major outfitters include **Arkansas River Tours** (✆ **800/321-4352** or 719/942-4362; www.arkansasrivertours.com), **Echo Canyon River Expeditions** (✆ **800/748-2953;** www.raftecho.com), and **Wilderness Aware Rafting** (✆ **800/462-7238** or 719/395-2112; www.inaraft.com).

OTHER AREA ATTRACTIONS

Cañon City was a popular setting for filmmakers during the industry's early days, and it was a special favorite of silent screen actor Tom Mix, who reputedly worked as a cowboy in the area before becoming a film star. The drowning death of a prominent actress temporarily discouraged film companies from coming here, but the area's beautiful scenery and Old West heritage lured them back in the late 1950s with the creation of Buckskin Joe, a Western theme park and movie set. Dozens of films have been shot there since, including *How the West Was Won, True Grit, Cat Ballou,* and *Lightning Jack.*

Although movies are rarely shot here nowadays, **Buckskin Joe Frontier Town & Railway** (**© 719/275-5149;** www.buckskinjoe.com), about 8 miles west of Cañon City on U.S. 50, remains a popular tourist attraction. The authentic-looking Old West town was created from genuine 19th-century buildings relocated from across the state. Visitors can watch gunfights, pan for gold, see a magic show, ride horseback (or in a horse-drawn trolley), and wander through a Western maze. The **Scenic Railway** (**© 719/275-5485**) offers a 30-minute trip through rugged Royal Gorge country, where you're likely to see deer and other wildlife, to the rim of the Royal Gorge for a panoramic view of the canyon and bridge.

Frontier Town is open May through September and mid-October to Halloween. Hours are 10am to 5pm daily in May, 9:30am to 6pm daily from June to August, and 10am to 5pm Thursday to Monday in September. The railway runs from March to December. Hours from Memorial Day to Labor Day are 9am to 7pm; call for hours at other times. Combination admission tickets, which include the Scenic Railway, a horse-drawn trolley, and all the Frontier Town attractions and entertainment, are $18 for adults, $14 for children 4 to 11, and free for children under 4. Tickets for the railway only are $11 for adults and $10 for children; tickets for Frontier Town only are $14 adults and $12 children. Expect to spend 2 to 4 hours here.

Other Cañon City attractions include the **Museum of Colorado Prisons ★**, 201 N. 1st St. (**© 719/269-3015;** www.prisonmuseum.org), especially interesting for those with an appreciation of the macabre. Housed in the state's former women's prison, just outside the walls of the original territorial prison that opened in 1871, it contains an actual gas chamber, historic photos of life behind bars, weapons confiscated from inmates, the last hangman's noose used legally in the state, a simulation of a lethal-injection system and of the "Old Gray Mare" (a cruel apparatus used to punish misbehaving prisoners), and other artifacts and exhibits. There's also a gift shop selling arts and crafts made by inmates at a medium-security prison next door. The museum is open May through September daily from 8:30am to 6pm, October through April Friday through Sunday from 10am to 5pm. Admission is $7 for adults, $6 for seniors 65 and older, $5 for youths 6 to 12, and free for children under 6. Allow about an hour.

Those interested in Colorado history might also enjoy stopping at the **Royal Gorge Regional Museum and History Center,** 612 Royal Gorge Blvd. (**© 719/276-5279**), which holds displays of American-Indian artifacts, guns, gems, minerals, wild-game trophies, historic photos, old dolls, pioneer household items, and other memorabilia. These are pretty much the kinds of things you'll find in most small-town museums in the American West, but what sets this museum apart somewhat are several renovated and authentically furnished buildings out back. The 1860 log cabin built by Anson Rudd, local blacksmith and first warden of the Colorado Territorial Prison, is one. The museum is typically open from 10am to 4pm Wednesday through Saturday. It's closed December 24 plus all state and federal holidays. Admission is free. Allow a half-hour.

Another local attraction, especially fascinating for young would-be dinosaur hunters, is **Dinosaur Depot ★**, 330 Royal Gorge Blvd. (**© 800/987-6379** or 719/269-7150; www.dinosaurdepot.com). The depot's main claim to fame is the dinosaur lab, where paleontologists are working to remove various dinosaur fossils from the rock that has encased them for the past 150 million years. There are also several interpretive exhibits, including fossilized bones that visitors can hold, a fossilized tree, a children's Discovery Room with plenty of hands-on exhibits, and a gift shop. Dinosaur Depot also sells brochures for self-guided tours of the internationally renowned **Garden Park Fossil Area** just north of town, which is the source of many of the museum's exhibits, and to see some 90-million-year-old dinosaur tracks nearby. The museum is open daily from 9am to 5pm late May to mid-August, shorter hours the rest of the year. Admission is $4 for adults, $2 for children 4 to 12, and free for children under 4. Allow 45 minutes at Dinosaur Depot, and another 1 to 2 hours at Garden Park Fossil Area.

WHERE TO STAY & DINE

Cañon City has several midpriced lodging options, including the **Best Western Royal Gorge Motel,** 1925 Fremont Dr., Cañon City, CO 81212 (✆ **800/231-7317** or 719/275-3377), with double rates ranging from $69 to $109 in summer. A more off-the-beaten-path option is **The Orchard Bed & Breakfast,** 1824 Pinion Ave., Brookside, CO 81212 (✆ **877/212-0497** or 719/275-0072; www.theorchardbandb.com), tucked away in an agricultural area on the edge of an apple orchard south of town. Double rooms are $90, full breakfast included. **Merlino's Belvedere,** 1330 Elm Ave. (✆ **719/275-5558;** www.belvedererestaurant.com), which serves gourmet Italian cuisine, steaks, and seafood at lunch and dinner daily, is my pick for a meal. Most dinner main courses run $15 to $35.

For more information on where to stay and eat, a walking tour of historic downtown Cañon City, and details on scenic drives and other attractions, contact the **Cañon City Chamber of Commerce,** 403 Royal Gorge Blvd., Cañon City, CO 81212 (✆ **800/876-7922** or 719/275-2331; www.canoncitychamber.com).

3 TRINIDAD

197 miles S of Denver, 247 miles N of Albuquerque, New Mexico

Western history and art are two good reasons to stop in Trinidad when traveling along I-25 through southern Colorado. Bat Masterson was sheriff in the 1880s, Wyatt Earp drove the stage, Kit Carson helped open the trade routes, and even Billy the Kid passed through. Many historic buildings—handsome structures of brick and sandstone—survive from this era. Plains tribes roamed the area for centuries before the 17th- and 18th-century forays by Spanish explorers and settlers. Later, traders and trappers made this an important stop on the northern branch of the Santa Fe Trail.

German, Irish, Italian, Jewish, Polish, and Slavic immigrants were drawn to the area starting in the late 1800s for jobs at area coal mines and cattle ranches, and agriculture and railroading were also important economic factors. Ranching remains a cornerstone of the economy today, and the tourism industry is growing. Today the population is slightly above 9,000; elevation is 6,019 feet.

ESSENTIALS

GETTING THERE **By Car** If you're traveling from north or south, take I-25: Trinidad straddles the interstate, halfway between Denver and Santa Fe, New Mexico. From the east, take U.S. 50 into La Junta, then turn southwest for 80 miles on U.S. 350; or from southern Kansas follow U.S. 160 to Trinidad. From Durango and points west, follow U.S. 160 to Walsenburg, then travel south 37 miles on I-25.

By Train The **Amtrak** Southwest Chief passes through Trinidad twice daily—once eastbound, once westbound—on a run between Chicago and Los Angeles. The depot is at 110 W. Pine St. just off North Commercial Street (✆ **800/872-7245;** www.amtrak.com).

VISITOR INFORMATION The **Colorado Welcome Center,** 309 N. Nevada Ave. (I-25 exit 14A), Trinidad, CO 81082 (✆ **719/846-9512**), open daily from 8am to 5pm in winter and from 8am to 6pm in summer, has information not only on Trinidad and southeastern Colorado, but also on the entire state. Information before your trip can be obtained from the **Trinidad & Las Animas County Chamber of Commerce,** 309 Nevada Ave., Trinidad, CO 81082 (✆ **866/480-4750** or 719/846-9285; www.historictrinidad.com or www.trinidadchamber.com).

GETTING AROUND Main Street (U.S. 160/350) parallels El Rio de Las Animas en Purgatorio ("The River of Lost Souls in Purgatory"), better known as the Purgatoire River, which flows south to north through the center of town. The historic downtown area is focused around Main and Commercial streets on the south side of the river. Main Street joins I-25 on the west side of downtown.

Car rentals are available from **J&J Motors** (✆ **719/846-3318**) and **Pioneer Motors** (✆ **719/846-4100**).

The **Trinidad Trolley,** operating Memorial Day to Labor Day, provides an excellent—and free—way to see this historic city. Running daily from 10am to 3pm, you can board the trolley at the Colorado Welcome Center (see above), and get on and off at the various museums and other attractions. Pick up a schedule at the Welcome Center.

FAST FACTS Medical services, including a 24-hour emergency room, are provided at **Mt. San Rafael Hospital,** 410 S. Benedicta Ave. off Main Street (✆ **719/846-9213;** www.msrhc.org). The **post office** is at 301 E. Main St. Contact the U.S. Postal Service (✆ **800/275-8777;** www.usps.com) for hours and other information.

SPECIAL EVENTS Santa Fe Trail Days, in June; fireworks display over Trinidad Lake on the Fourth of July; Trinidaddio Bluesfest, late August; Las Animas County Fair and Rodeo, Labor Day weekend.

WHAT TO SEE & DO

Main Street was once part of the Mountain Route of the Santa Fe Trail, and many of the streets that cross it are paved with locally made redbrick. The Trinidad Historical Society distributes a booklet titled ***A Walk Through the History of Trinidad,*** available at local shops and museums. Among the buildings it singles out for special attention are the Trinidad Opera House (1883) and Columbian Hotel (1879), which are across from each other on Main Street, as well as the Trinidad Water Works (1879), on Cedar Street at the Purgatoire River.

A. R. Mitchell Memorial Museum of Western Art ★ The Old West is alive and well here, at least on canvas and photographic paper. More than 350 paintings and illustrations by Western artist Arthur Roy Mitchell (1889–1977) are displayed, along with works by other nationally recognized artists and a collection of early Hispanic folk art, including bultos, retablos, and tinwork, plus Penitente artifacts. The museum also contains a historic collection of photographs taken by Oliver E. Aultman, Benjamin Wittick, and Almerod Newman from the late 1800s through much of the 20th century, as well as early cameras, darkroom equipment, and studio props. The museum gift shop sells a

Map legend:

ACCOMMODATIONS ■
Best Western Trinidad Inn **9**
Budget Host Derrick Motel **10**
Quality Inn **10**
The Stone Mansion B&B **8**
Super 8 **3**

DINING ◆
El Capitan Restaurant & Lounge **1**
Nana & Nano Monteleone's Deli & Pasta House **7**

ATTRACTIONS ●
A.R. Mitchell Memorial Museum of Western Art **5**
Louden-Henritze Archaeology Museum **2**
Old Firehouse No. 1 Children's Museum **4**
Trinidad History Museum **6**

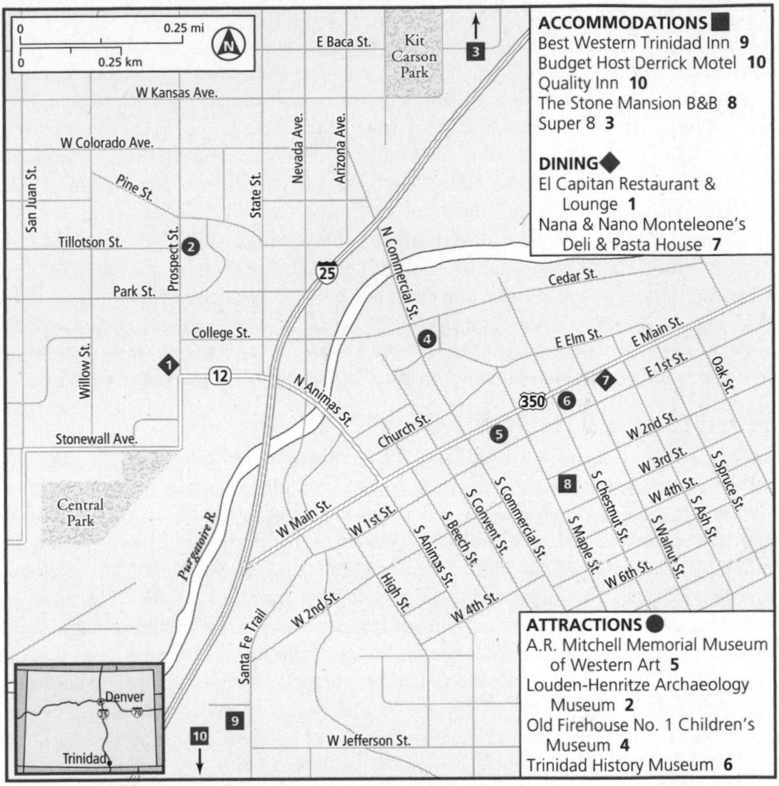

wide variety of jewelry, pottery, prints, and some original works of art, at fairly reasonable prices. The huge building, originally a department store, is a 1906 Western-style structure with the original pressed-tin ceiling, wood floors, and a horseshoe-shaped mezzanine. Allow 1 to 1¹/₂ hours.

150 E. Main St. ℂ **719/846-4224.** www.armitchell.org. Admission $3 adults, free for children 12 and under, free admission Sun. May to early Oct Tues–Sat 10am–4pm; Sun 11–4pm; off season by appt.

Louden-Henritze Archaeology Museum Millions of years of southern Colorado history are displayed here, including fossils, casts of dinosaur tracks, arrowheads, pottery, petroglyphs, and other prehistoric-man artifacts discovered during area excavations. Watch for the fossilized partial skeleton of a mosasaur (a sea reptile) that lived in the area some 80 million years ago. There's also a gift shop. Allow 1 to 2 hours.

Freudenthal Memorial Library, Trinidad State Junior College, near the intersection of Park and Prospect sts. ℂ **719/846-5508.** www.trinidadstate.edu/museum. Free admission. May–Sept Mon–Fri 10am–3pm; call for off-season hours.

Trinidad History Museum ★★ Trinidad has a rich and interesting history, and this is the best place to find out about it. Together, the Baca House, Bloom Mansion, and

Santa Fe Trail Museum, along with historic gardens, are known collectively as the Trinidad History Museum and rank as Trinidad's principal attraction. The 1870 Baca House, along the Mountain Route of the Santa Fe Trail, is a two-story Greek Revival–style adobe. Originally owned by sheep rancher Felipe Baca, the house contains some of the Baca family's original furnishings. Nearby stands the 1882 Bloom Mansion, a Second Empire–style Victorian manor embellished with fancy woodcarving and ornate ironwork. The Colorado Historical Society operates both homes as well as the Santa Fe Trail Museum, located behind the homes in a building that was originally living quarters for Baca's hired help. Both the Baca House and Santa Fe Trail Museum are certified sites on the Santa Fe National Historic Trail.

On the grounds are shade trees and gardens of hollyhocks, grapevines, and cacti. The museum bookstore offers a good selection of books on local history, the Santa Fe Trail, Hispanic culture, area recreation, and children's books. Allow 2 to 3 hours.

312 E. Main St. ✆ **719/846-7217.** www.coloradohistory.org. Admission $6 adults, $5 seniors 65 and older, $3 children 6–16 and students, free for children 5 and under. May–Sept daily 10am–4pm; off season Santa Fe Trail Museum Mon–Fri 10am–2pm; Baca House and Bloom Mansion by appt. only.

SPORTS & OUTDOOR ACTIVITIES

Located 3 miles west of town on Colo. 12, **Trinidad Lake State Park** (✆ **719/846-6951;** www.parks.state.co.us) is the place to go for all sorts of outdoor recreational possibilities, and it's also a good base for campers who want to explore southern Colorado and northern New Mexico. Its 800-acre reservoir on the Purgatoire River is popular for powerboating, water-skiing, sailboating, and sailboarding. Swimming is prohibited, however. There's a boat ramp and dock, but no boat rentals or supplies. Fishermen go after largemouth bass, rainbow and brown trout, channel catfish, walleye, crappie, and bluegills. Ten miles of hiking and mountain-biking trails here include the Levsa Canyon Nature Trail, a 1-mile self-guided loop that also branches off for another 4 miles to the historic town of Cokedale (see "A Drive Along the Scenic Highway of Legends," below). For those with their own horses, there are 4 miles of equestrian trails on the south side of the lake. The Long's Canyon Watchable Wildlife Area offers viewing blinds in a wetlands area. Commonly seen in the park are great blue herons, Canada geese, red-tailed hawks, great horned owls, hummingbirds, mule deer, cottontail rabbits, and ground squirrels. An attractive 62-unit campground has some electric hookups, a dump station, and coin-operated showers; a basic campground with 10 sites on the south shore opened in 2008. Nightly camping fees are $14 to $18. Reservations are available for an extra charge of $8 through the state parks website (see above) or by calling ✆ **800/678-2267.** Day-use admission costs $6 per vehicle, which is also tacked onto camping fees. During the winter there's cross-country skiing, ice skating, and ice fishing.

BICYCLING, ROLLERBLADING & SKATEBOARDING The **Trinidad Skate Park★** covers 15,000 square feet and offers a terrific layout with the snake leading into the two bowls, offering long runs with plenty of speed and opportunity for tricks. Use of safety equipment (helmets, knee and elbow pads, wrist supports, and proper shoes) is required at all times, and users are responsible for the proper maintenance of their gear. Summer hours are daily 8am to 10pm, and admission is free. For additional information, contact the City of Trinidad (✆ **719/846-9843**) or the chamber of commerce (✆ **719/846-9285**). From I-25, take exit 13B onto Main Street east, turn right (south) onto Santa Fe Trail Drive, then left onto Jefferson Street. Take the second right (follow the community center sign) and continue straight to the park.

GOLF The 9-hole **Trinidad Golf Course,** 1417 Nolan Dr. off the Santa Fe Trail adjacent to I-25 at exit 13A (© **719/846-4015;** www.trinidadgc.com), is considered among the best 9-hole courses in the state, with fees of $16 to $18 for 9 holes and $21 to $23 for 18 holes.

WHERE TO STAY

Several national chains provide most of the lodging in Trinidad (zip code 81082). Rates here are for two people in summer; rates at other times are usually 10% to 20% lower. Among your choices are the **Best Western Trinidad Inn,** 900 W. Adams St., I-25 exit 13A (© **800/955-2215** or 719/846-2215), charging $99 to $109 double; **Budget Host Derrick Motel,** just off I-25 exit 11 at 10301 Santa Fe Trail (© **800/283-4678** or 719/846-3307), with double rates of $79 to $99; **Quality Inn,** 3125 Toupal Dr., I-25 exit 11 (© **800/424-6423** or 719/846-4491), charging $90 to $120 double; and **Super 8,** 1924 Freedom Rd., I-25 exit 15 (© **800/800-8000** or 719/846-8280), charging $65 to $90 double. Taxes totaling about 10% are added to lodging bills.

Those looking for lodging with more character, along with a bit of pampering and a really good full breakfast, should consider **The Stone Mansion Bed and Breakfast ★,** 212 E. Second St., Trinidad, CO 81082 (© **877/264-4279** or 719/845-1625; www.stonemansionbb.com), an elegant home built in 1904 that combines Victorian and Arts and Crafts styles. Located 2 blocks from downtown, the inn has three rooms, decorated with mostly Victorian antiques. Summer rates for two, which include a full breakfast with entrees such as peach puff pancakes, are $115 to $125; November through April rates are lower. Smoking is not permitted inside, and children 8 and older are welcome.

WHERE TO DINE

El Capitan Restaurant & Lounge MEXICAN/ITALIAN/AMERICAN This attractive but simply decorated restaurant with a relaxing, comfortable atmosphere serves some of the best margaritas in southern Colorado. It's known for its Mexican and Italian dishes, although you can also get steaks, seafood, barbecued ribs, burgers, and sandwiches. Mexican items include green or red chile, bean or beef burritos, and enchiladas. On the Italian side of the menu you'll find gnocchi, beef ravioli, and spaghetti with meatballs, meat sauce, or sausage. There are a number of vegetarian items, including vegetable fajitas and pasta with olive oil, garlic, and vegetables. Best of all might be the tasty fried ice cream for dessert.

321 State St. © **719/846-9903.** Breakfast dishes and a la carte Mexican items $3–$7; dinners $6–$18. AE, DISC, MC, V. Mon–Fri 5–9pm; Sat 4:30–9pm; Sun 8am–2pm.

Nana & Nano Monteleone's Deli & Pasta House ITALIAN The Monteleone family takes pride in the Italian specialties served here, each cooked to order and served with salad, bread, and butter. Daily specials include rigatoni, spaghetti, and ravioli, and the regular menu offers a good selection of pasta, sandwiches, and fish. Many pasta selections are available with a choice of meatballs or Italian sausage, and there is also a "Smaller Appetite" menu for all ages. Monteleone's Deli, located in the restaurant, offers traditional deli sandwiches to eat in or take out, plus deli meats and cheeses by the pound.

418 E. Main St. © **719/846-2696.** Main courses $6–$12; deli sandwiches $5–$6. AE, DISC, MC, V. Wed–Sat 10:30am–7:30pm.

4 THE SCENIC HIGHWAY OF LEGENDS

Unquestionably the most fascinating day trip from Trinidad is the appropriately named Scenic Highway of Legends, which runs some 80 miles west, north, and then northeast, mostly on Colo. 12, from Trinidad to Walsenburg.

Traveling west about 7 miles from Trinidad, past Trinidad Lake State Park, the first site of special note is **Cokedale,** just north of the highway. The best existing example of a coal camp in Colorado, **Cokedale** was founded in 1907 by the American Smelting and Refining Co. as a self-contained company town, and by 1909 was a thriving community of 1,500. When the mine closed in 1947, residents were offered the company-owned homes at $100 per room and $50 per lot. Some stayed, incorporating in 1948, and in 1984 Cokedale was placed on the National Register of Historic Places. Many of today's 125 or so residents are descendants of those miners, or retired miners themselves. As you drive in, you'll see some of the 350 coke ovens, used to convert coal to hotter-burning coke, for which the town was named. Walking through the community, you'll see the icehouse, schoolhouse, mining office, Sacred Heart of Jesus and Mary Church, Gottlieb Mercantile Company, and other buildings, including a boardinghouse where bachelors could get room and board for $25 a month.

Proceeding west, you'll pass several old coal towns, including Segundo, Weston, and Vigil, and two coal mines—the Golden Eagle, where underground mining is still done, and New Elk Mine, now a processing plant—before entering **Stonewall Valley,** 33 miles west of Trinidad. Named for a striking rock formation—a vertical bed of lithified sandstone—Stonewall is both the site of a small timber industry and the location of many vacation homes.

From Stonewall, Colo. 12 turns north past **Monument Lake,** part of Trinidad's water-supply system, named for a rock formation in the middle of the lake that some say resembles two American Indian chiefs. Several miles past Monument Lake is **North Lake,** a state wildlife area and home to rainbow, cutthroat, kokanee, and brown trout.

The highway continues north across 9,941-foot **Cucharas Pass.** Overlooking the pass are the **Spanish Peaks,** eroded remnants of a 20-million-year-old volcano. The native Arapaho believed them to be the home of the gods, and they served as guideposts to early travelers. Legends persist about the existence of a treasure of gold in this area, but none has been found. Several miles north of Cucharas Pass is **Cucharas River Recreation Area,** home of Blue Lake, named for its spectacular color.

Numerous geologic features become prominent as the road descends toward Walsenburg. Among them are the **Devil's Stairsteps,** one of a series of erosion-resistant igneous dikes that radiate out like spokes from the Spanish Peaks; **Dakota Wall,** a layer of pressed sandstone thrust vertically from the earth; and **Goemmer Butte,** sometimes called "Sore Thumb Butte," a volcanic plug rising 500 feet from the valley floor. At this point, about 65 miles from Trinidad, is the foothills village of **La Veta** (pop. about 900), founded in 1862 by Col. John M. Francisco, who reportedly said after seeing the pretty valley, "This is paradise enough for me."

Continuing east, Colo. 12 joins U.S. 160, which goes by **Lathrop State Park** (✆ **719/738-2376;** www.parks.state.co.us), the state's oldest state park, with two lakes for boating (no rentals), swimming, and fishing (rainbow trout, channel catfish, tiger muskie, bass, walleye, bluegill, and crappie). There's also a 3-mile paved trail around the lake for hikers and bikers, plus the 2-mile Hogback Trail, a self-guided nature hike (free brochures available at the visitor center). Also available at the visitor center are lists of birds sighted in Lathrop and the wildflowers found here, with descriptions and blooming times noted. In winter, there's cross-country skiing, ice skating, and ice fishing. There are 103 campsites, about 40 with electric hookups, plus showers and a dump station. Camping costs $14 to $18 per night, and reservations are available for an extra charge of $8 by calling ✆ **800/678-2267** or through the state park website (see above). The park's day-use fee is $6 per vehicle, which is also added to camping fees. Located at the park but managed independently is the 9-hole **Walsenburg Golf Course** (✆ **719/738-2730;** www.thewgc.com), with a fee of $15 for 9 holes and $20 to $21 for 18 holes.

From the park it's about 2 miles to Walsenburg on U.S. 160, and then just under 40 miles south down I-25 to return to Trinidad.

5 LA JUNTA

81 miles NE of Trinidad, 64 miles E of Pueblo, 274 miles NW of Amarillo, Texas

Situated in one of Colorado's fruit-growing pockets, this busy little town has several surprises for visitors, including some of the best American Indian art in the country and a nearby handsome reconstruction of a historic fort.

Once the hunting and fishing grounds of the Arapaho, Cheyenne, and Ute tribes, and visited briefly by Spanish soldiers in the 17th and 18th centuries, this area did not become known to white Americans until Zebulon Pike led his exploratory expedition into the Arkansas River valley in 1806. Trappers and traders followed, creating the Santa Fe Trail, and brothers William and Charles Bent built Bent's Fort in 1833 as a trading post and the first American settlement in the region.

La Junta was founded in 1875 as a railroad camp, and named La Junta—Spanish for "the junction"—on completion of rail links to Pueblo and Trinidad in 1877. The town flourished as a farming and ranching center. Today it produces a wide variety of fruits, vegetables, and wheat. The population is a bit over 7,500, and the town sits at an elevation of 4,052 feet.

ESSENTIALS

GETTING THERE **By Car** La Junta is easily reached via U.S. 50, which comes into town from Kansas in the east and continues west to I-25 at Pueblo. From New Mexico, exit I-25 at Trinidad and take U.S. 350; from Durango and southwestern Colorado, take U.S. 160 to Walsenburg, and continue on Colo. 10 to La Junta.

By Train Passenger service is available aboard **Amtrak** (✆ **800/872-7245;** www.amtrak.com), with a depot on First Street at Colorado Avenue. The Southwest Chief passes through twice daily (once in each direction) on the main line between Chicago and Los Angeles.

VISITOR INFORMATION Contact the **La Junta Chamber of Commerce,** 110 Santa Fe Ave., La Junta, CO 81050 (✆ **719/384-7411;** www.lajuntachamber.com). The chamber is open Monday through Friday 8:30am to 12:30pm and 1:30 to 5pm.

GETTING AROUND La Junta is located on the Arkansas River, and U.S. 50, which runs through town as First Street, follows the river's south bank. Highways from Trinidad and Walsenburg join it just west of town. The downtown core focuses on First, Second, and Third streets, crossed by north–south Colorado and Santa Fe avenues. At the east edge of town, Colo. 109 (Adams Ave.) crosses the Arkansas into north La Junta (where it becomes Main St.); 6 blocks past the river, Colo. 194 (Trail Rd.) forks to the right and leads 5 miles to Bent's Old Fort.

FAST FACTS Health services are provided by the **Arkansas Valley Regional Medical Center,** 1100 Carson Ave., at 10th Street (✆ **719/384-5412;** www.avrmc.org), which has a 24-hour emergency room. The **post office** is located at 324 Colorado Ave. (at Fourth St.); contact the U.S. Postal Service (✆ **800/275-8777;** www.usps.com) for hours and other information.

SPECIAL EVENTS Santa Fe Trail Caravan, starting at Bent's Old Fort, May; Kids Rodeo, early August; Early Settlers Day, mid-September; Santa Fe Trail Encampment, at Bent's Old Fort, early October; Traditional Holiday Celebration, at Bent's Old Fort, early December.

WHAT TO SEE & DO

To see a number of buildings from the late 1800s and early 1900s that are listed on the National Register of Historic Places, take the self-guided Historic Homes of La Junta walking/driving tour, described in a free packet available from the La Junta Chamber of Commerce (see "Visitor Information," above).

Bent's Old Fort National Historic Site ★★ Once the most important settlement on the Santa Fe Trail between Missouri and New Mexico, Bent's Old Fort has been reconstructed as it was during its reign as a major trading post from 1833 to 1849. Located 7 miles east of modern La Junta, this adobe fort on the Arkansas River was built by brothers Charles and William Bent and partner Ceran St. Vrain. It was the hub of trade for Eastern U.S. merchants, Rocky Mountain fur trappers, and plains tribes (mainly Cheyenne, but also Arapaho, Ute, Apache, Kiowa, and Comanche).

As American settlement increased, driving off the buffalo that were the lifeblood of the tribes, the Bents were caught between two cultures. Serious hostilities began in 1847, and trade rapidly declined during a cholera epidemic in 1849. Part of the fort burned that year and was not rebuilt until modern times. Reproductions furnish the 33 rooms, which include a kitchen with adjoining pantry, a cook's room, and a dining room; a trade room with robes, pelts, and blankets; blacksmith and carpenter shops; William Bent's office and bedroom; quarters for Mexican laborers, trappers, and soldiers; a billiards room; and the quarters of a merchant's wife (who kept a meticulous diary).

It's a quarter-mile walk on a paved path from the historic site's entry station to the fort itself, where hosts in period costume greet visitors during the summer. You'll see demonstrations of frontier life, such as blacksmithing, adobe making, trapping, cooking, and medical and survival skills. You can tour the fort on your own or take a guided tour. Tours are offered at 10:30am and 1pm from September through May and more frequently in summer; call for the current times. A 20-minute film on the fort is shown year-round. There's also a gift and bookshop. Allow 1 to 4 hours.

35110 Colo. 194 E. ✆ **719/383-5010.** www.nps.gov/beol. Admission (including optional guided tour) $3 adults, $2 children 6–12, free for children 5 and under. June–Aug daily 8am–5:30pm; Sept–May daily 9am–4pm. Closed Thanksgiving, Christmas, and New Year's Day.

Koshare Indian Museum and Kiva ★★★ American Indian art—featuring Pueblo and plains tribal members both as artists and subjects—is the focus of this excellent museum, which gets my vote as a must-see for anyone even remotely interested in the arts and crafts of American Indians and art depicting the American West. On display

In Search of Dinosaur Tracks

Dinosaur tracks from the Jurassic period, about 150 million years ago, are a highlight of the **Comanche National Grassland,** and more than 1,300 prints in about 100 separate trackways make this the largest known dinosaur track site in North America. The grassland, a 442,000-acre area south of La Junta, also draws bird-watchers, hunters, anglers, and hikers. Access to Picket Wire Canyonlands, where the dinosaur tracks are located, is limited to those hiking or on mountain bikes or horseback, and by taking a guided tour.

The tracks are believed to be from dinosaurs in the Sauropodmorpha "lizard feet" and Theropoda "beast feet" families, who lived here when the area was a savanna—a tropical grassland with a few scattered trees. There was plenty of food for the sauropods, who were plant eaters, making them all the more tempting to their enemies, the meat-eating theropods. The sauropods, particularly the brontosaurus, grew to about 14 feet tall and weighed up to 33 tons. Theropods grew up to 16 feet tall, but were not as long and generally weighed much less. Still, with their sharp claws, they would attack the sauropods whenever given the chance.

You can see the dinosaur tracks on your own on a strenuous hike or on a ride by mountain bike or horse—get maps and other details from the Comanche National Grassland office (see below)—but the best way to see them is on a U.S. Forest Service–guided tour. The tours, which are scheduled by appointment on Saturdays in May, June, September, and October, cost $15 for adults and $7.50 for children, and those taking the tours need to provide their own high-clearance four-wheel-drive vehicle.

Information is available from the Comanche National Grassland office, 1420 E. Third St., La Junta, CO 81050 (✆ **719/384-2181;** www.fs.fed.us/r2/psicc/coma). Also contact the office for information on other attractions in the grasslands, including its wildlife—such as the threatened lesser prairie chicken—and rock art that's hundreds of years old.

are authentic American Indian clothing, jewelry, pottery, and baskets. There are also Western paintings and sculptures, including one of the finest collections of works by early Taos, New Mexico, artists I've seen—watch for the painting *Relics of His Ancestors,* considered one of the best works by Bert Phillips, one of the founding artists of the Taos art colony in 1898. In operation since 1949, the museum is housed in an adobe-style building resembling a northern New Mexico pueblo.

The Koshare Dancers, a nationally acclaimed troop of Boy Scouts, have been honing their dancing skills since 1933. They perform an average of 60 times a year, primarily in their own great kiva, a circular chamber traditionally used for religious rites by Southwestern tribes. Dances are held frequently in summer (call or check the website for the current schedule), and the Koshare Winter Ceremonials are a December tradition. Allow at least 2 hours for a museum visit, longer for a museum visit and the dances together.

Otero Junior College, 115 W. 18th St. ✆ **719/384-4411.** www.koshare.org. Museum admission $5 adults, $3 seniors 55 and older and students 7–17, free for children 6 and under; dance performance and museum admission $8 adults, $5 youths 17 and younger. Daily 10am–5pm (until 9pm on dance nights); extended hours during ceremonials. Located 1 block west of Colorado Ave.

Otero Museum (Finds) One of the more interesting small-town museums I've run across, this museum complex—there are several historic buildings—provides a look at what life was like in eastern Colorado between the 1870s and 1940s. Although lighting could be a bit better and exhibits tend to be a bit dusty, there's a good collection here, and anyone who likes old stuff is bound to find something of interest. There's a genuine 1865 Concord stagecoach, an 1880s-type reaper, a well-stocked grocery store from the early 20th century, a fully restored and working windmill, an early-1900s blacksmith shop, a replica of the community's first school, railroad equipment and memorabilia, and items from World Wars I and II plus the Civil War. Being a fan of classic cars, I especially like the 1905 Reo Sidewinder and the 1954 fire engine, purchased by the Rural Fire Department after its formation in 1953. Allow 1½ to 2 hours.

Third and Anderson sts. ✆ **719/384-7500.** www.coloradoplains.com/otero/museum. Free admission, donations welcome. June–Sept Mon–Sat 1–5pm; off-season tours by appt.

OUTDOOR ACTIVITIES

Among Colorado's newest state parks, **John Martin Reservoir★★** (✆ **719/829-1801;** www.parks.state.co.us) is a welcome oasis in the plains of southeastern Colorado. The entrance is off C.R. 24 out of Hasty, about 35 miles east of La Junta, although the reservoir stretches along the south side of U.S. 50 for some 10 miles before you reach it. That's just to whet your appetite for the many recreational opportunities that await you.

The park's namesake is very popular with those who love to windsurf, water-ski, or zip around in personal watercraft. You can swim, go birding, and do some great fishing, plus there are three boat ramps, picnic areas scattered about, and two campgrounds.

On the back side of the dam that forms John Martin Reservoir is the much smaller Lake Hasty, where only small watercraft with electric motors—no gas—are permitted. Lake Hasty also boasts a wheelchair-accessible fishing pier and small swimming area, plus there are several picnic areas and the developed Hasty Campground lies on its north side. You'll find coin-op showers, laundry facilities, and a dump station there; all sites have electric hookups. The many cottonwood and Russian olive trees provide shade and shelter numerous birds—I saw about a dozen turkey vultures resting in a group of trees not far from my campsite—and you'll see cottontail and jack rabbits all over the place. Point Campground is on a peninsula on the north side of the reservoir, with vault toilets, no electricity or water, but stupendous views of the reservoir and surrounding plains. It's closed in winter.

Anglers try for walleye, wiper, large- and small-mouth bass, crappie, catfish, bluegill, and perch in the main reservoir. Lake Hasty has those plus rainbow and cutthroat trout, and nearby is a fish-cleaning station. A portion of the reservoir is usually closed to all public access from November through mid-March. That's the nesting and brooding season of the threatened piping plover and endangered interior least tern, and the shores of the reservoir are one of their few remaining nesting areas in Colorado. The bald eagle also likes to winter here, in the large trees in Hasty Campground, so some of the campsites there are closed from November through March.

The 4.5-mile **Red Shin Hiking Trail** circles Lake Hasty and leads to a Santa Fe Trail Marker overlooking the reservoir.

There are 109 electric sites in Hasty Campground and 104 basic sites in the Point. Camping rates are $14 to $18; reservations are available for an extra charge of $8 by calling ✆ **800/678-2267,** or through the state parks website (listed above). Day use costs $6 per vehicle, and campers must pay this in addition to camping fees. From La Junta, take U.S. 50 east for 35 miles, then turn south on C.R. 24 to the park.

WHERE TO STAY

Besides the campgrounds listed above, there are a few national chain motels in the area. In La Junta is the **Holiday Inn Express,** 27994 U.S. 50 Frontage Rd., La Junta, CO 81050 (✆ **800/465-4329** or 719/384-2900), with rates from $109 to $129 double. In Las Animas, about 20 miles east of La Junta, there is the **Best Western Bent's Fort Inn,** 10950 E. U.S. 50 (P.O. Box 108), Las Animas, CO 81054 (✆ **877/236-8738** or 719/456-0011), with rates of $65 to $85 double. Room tax of about 8% is added to lodging bills.

Hotel Ordway (Finds) Dinky Ordway's eponymous historic hotel is located across from a park in a shady nook of the city center (about 25 miles northwest of La Junta). The 1903 redbrick has the frilly and flowery feel of a B&B but operates more like a motel and also offers bare-bones "Plain Jane" rooms with shared baths for bicyclists halfway across the cross-country route. Next door under the same ownership is a restaurant, **Beans 2 Go.**

132 Colorado Ave., Ordway, CO 81063. ✆ **719/267-3541.** www.hotelordway.com. 20 units. $35 double for "Plain Jane" rooms with shared bath; $55 double with private bath. AE, DISC, MC, V. **Amenities:** Restaurant. *In room:* A/C, cable TV, wireless Internet access (free), coffeemaker, hair dryer, iron.

Mid-Town Motel ★ (Value) A great little mom and pop motel off the main highway, the Mid-Town offers clean, quiet, and comfortable rooms with good-quality beds and linens, and standard, well-kept bathrooms. Rooms have desks and one or two beds; several have couches or love seats, and the rooms with one bed also have recliners. The friendly staff is an invaluable source of information for area visitors.

215 E. Third St., La Junta, CO 81050. ✆ **719/384-7741.** Fax 719/384-7323. 24 units. $42–$50 double. AE, DISC, MC, V. Pets accepted ($10 per pet one-time fee). *In room:* A/C, cable TV, wireless Internet access (free), coffeemaker.

Appendix: Fast Facts, Toll-Free Numbers & Websites

1 FAST FACTS: COLORADO

AMERICAN EXPRESS The American Express travel agency, 555 17th St., Denver (✆ **303/383-5050**), is open Monday through Friday from 8am to 5pm. It offers full member services and currency exchange.

AREA CODES In the Denver and Boulder area, the telephone area codes are **303** and **720.** In the south-central and southeast (Colorado Springs), the area code is **719.** In the north and west, the area code is **970.**

ATM NETWORKS/CASHPOINTS See "Money & Costs," p. 38.

AUTOMOBILE ORGANIZATIONS The **American Automobile Association (AAA)** is the major auto club in the United States. If you belong to a motor club in your home country, inquire about AAA reciprocity before you leave. You may be able to join AAA even if you're not a member of a reciprocal club; to inquire, call AAA (✆ **800/222-4357;** www.aaa.com). AAA is actually an organization of regional motor clubs, so look under "AAA Automobile Club" in the White Pages of the telephone directory. AAA has a nationwide emergency road service telephone number (✆ **800/AAA-HELP** [222-4357]).

BUSINESS HOURS Generally, businesses are open weekdays from 9am to 5pm and government offices are open from 8am until 4:30 or 5pm. Stores are open 6 days a week, with many also open on Sunday; department stores usually stay open until 9pm at least 1 day a week. Discount stores and supermarkets are often open later than other stores, and some supermarkets are open 24 hours a day. Banks are usually open weekdays from 9am to 5pm, occasionally a bit later on Friday, and sometimes on Saturday. There's 24-hour access to automated teller machines (ATMs) at most banks, plus in many shopping centers and other outlets.

CAR RENTALS See "Toll-Free Numbers & Websites," p. 454.

DRINKING LAWS The legal age for purchase and consumption of alcoholic beverages is 21; proof of age is required and often requested at bars, nightclubs, and restaurants, so it's always a good idea to bring ID when you go out.

Do not carry open containers of alcohol in your car or any public area that isn't zoned for alcohol consumption. The police can fine you on the spot. And nothing will ruin your trip faster than getting a citation for DUI ("driving under the influence"), so don't even think about driving while intoxicated.

In 2008, Colorado retracted its "blue laws" banning the sale of hard alcohol and beer over 3.2% alcohol content on Sundays.

DRIVING RULES See "Getting There & Getting Around," in chapter 3.

ELECTRICITY Like Canada, the United States uses 110–120 volts AC (60 cycles), compared to 220–240 volts AC (50 cycles) in most of Europe, Australia, and New Zealand. Downward converters that change 220–240 volts to 110–120 volts are difficult to find in the United States, so bring one with you.

EMBASSIES & CONSULATES All embassies are located in the nation's capital, Washington, D.C. Some consulates are located in major U.S. cities, and most nations have a mission to the United Nations in New York City. If your country isn't listed below, call for directory information in Washington, D.C. (✆ **202/555-1212**), or check **www.embassy.org/embassies**.

The consulate of **Australia** is at 2629 Main St., Ste. 190, Littleton, CO 80120-4643 (✆ **303/321-2234;** www.austemb.org).

The consulate of **Canada** is at 1625 Broadway, Ste. 2600, Denver, CO 80202 (✆ **303/626-0640;** www.canadianembassy.org).

The embassy of **Ireland** is at 2234 Massachusetts Ave. NW, Washington, D.C. 20008 (✆ **202/462-3939;** www.irelandemb.org). Irish consulates are in Boston, Chicago, New York, San Francisco, and other cities.

The embassy of **New Zealand** is at 37 Observatory Circle NW, Washington, D.C. 20008 (✆ **202/328-4800;** www.nzembassy.com). New Zealand consulates are in Los Angeles, Salt Lake City, San Francisco, and Seattle.

The consulate of the **United Kingdom** is at 1675 Broadway, Ste. 1030, Denver, CO 80202 (✆ **303/592-5200;** www.britainusa.com).

EMERGENCIES In case of emergency, call ✆ **911.** For the **Colorado Poison Center,** call ✆ **303/739-1123.** For the **Rape Crisis and Domestic Violence Hotline,** call ✆ **303/318-9989.**

GASOLINE (PETROL) At press time, in the U.S., the cost of gasoline (also known as gas, but never petrol) was about $2 a gallon in Denver and the vicinity. Taxes are already included in the printed price. One U.S. gallon equals 3.8 liters or .85 imperial gallons. Fill-up locations are known as gas or service stations.

HOLIDAYS Banks, government offices, post offices, and many stores, restaurants, and museums are closed on the following legal national holidays: January 1 (New Year's Day), the third Monday in January (Martin Luther King, Jr., Day), the third Monday in February (Presidents' Day), the last Monday in May (Memorial Day), July 4 (Independence Day), the first Monday in September (Labor Day), the second Monday in October (Columbus Day), November 11 (Veterans' Day/Armistice Day), the fourth Thursday in November (Thanksgiving Day), and December 25 (Christmas). The Tuesday after the first Monday in November is Election Day, a federal government holiday in presidential-election years (held every 4 years, and next in 2012).

HOSPITALS See the "Fast Facts" sections in chapters 6 to 15.

INSURANCE Medical Insurance Although it's not required of travelers, health insurance is highly recommended. Most health insurance policies cover you if you get sick away from home—but check your coverage before you leave.

International visitors to the U.S. should note that, unlike many European countries, the United States does not usually offer free or low-cost medical care to its citizens or visitors. Doctors and hospitals are expensive and, in most cases will require advance payment or proof of coverage before they render their services. Good policies will cover the costs of an accident, repatriation, or death. Packages such as **Europ Assistance's Worldwide Healthcare Plan** are sold by European automobile clubs and travel agencies at attractive rates. **Worldwide Assistance Services, Inc.** (✆ **800/777-8710;** www.worldwideassistance.com) is the agent for Europ Assistance in the United States.

Though lack of health insurance may prevent you from being admitted to a hospital in non-emergencies, don't worry about being left on a street corner to die: The American way is to fix you now and bill the daylights out of you later.

If you're ever hospitalized more than 150 miles from home, **MedJetAssist** (✆ **800/527-7478;** www.medjetassistance.com) will pick you up and fly you to the hospital of your choice in a medically equipped and staffed aircraft 24 hours day, 7 days a week. Annual memberships are $225 individual, $350 family; you can also purchase short-term memberships.

Canadians should check with their provincial health plan offices or call **Health Canada** (✆ **866/225-0709;** www.hc-sc.gc.ca) to find out the extent of their coverage and what documentation and receipts they must take home in case they are treated in the United States.

Travelers from the U.K. should carry their **European Health Insurance Card** (EHIC), which replaced the E111 form as proof of entitlement to free/reduced-cost medical treatment abroad (✆ **0845/606-2030;** www.ehic.org.uk). Note, however, that the EHIC only covers "necessary medical treatment," and for repatriation costs, lost money, baggage, or cancellation, travel insurance from a reputable company should always be sought (www.travelinsuranceweb.com).

Travel Insurance The cost of travel insurance varies widely, depending on the destination, the cost and length of your trip, your age and health, and the type of trip you're taking—but expect to pay between 5% and 8% of the vacation itself. You can get estimates from various providers through **InsureMyTrip.com**. Enter your trip cost and dates, your age, and other information, for prices from more than a dozen companies.

U.K. citizens and their families who make more than one trip abroad per year may find an annual travel insurance policy works out cheaper. Check **www.moneysupermarket.com**, which compares prices across a wide range of providers for single- and multitrip policies.

Most big travel agents offer their own insurance and will probably try to sell you their package when you book a holiday. Think before you sign. **Britain's Consumers' Association** recommends that you insist on seeing the policy and reading the fine print before buying travel insurance. The **Association of British Insurers** (✆ **020/7600-3333;** www.abi.org.uk) gives advice by phone and publishes *Holiday Insurance,* a free guide to policy provisions and prices. You might also shop around for better deals: Try **Columbus Direct** (✆ **0870/033-9988;** www.columbusdirect.net).

Trip Cancellation Insurance Trip-cancellation insurance will help retrieve your money if you have to back out of a trip or depart early, or if your travel supplier goes bankrupt. Trip cancellation traditionally covers such events as sickness, natural disasters, and State Department advisories. The latest news in trip-cancellation insurance is the availability of **expanded hurricane coverage** and the **"any-reason"** cancellation coverage—which costs more but covers cancellations made for any reason. You won't get back 100% of your prepaid trip cost, but you'll be refunded a substantial portion. **TravelSafe** (✆ **888/885-7233;** www.travelsafe.com) offers both types of coverage. Expedia also offers any-reason cancellation coverage for its air-hotel packages. For details, contact one of the following recommended insurers: **Access America** (✆ 866/807-3982; www.accessamerica.com), **Travel Guard International** (✆ 800/826-4919; www.travelguard.com), **Travel Insured International**

(✆ 800/243-3174; www.travelinsured.com), and **Travelex Insurance Services** (✆ 888/457-4602; www.travelex-insurance.com).

INTERNET ACCESS Coffee shops, libraries, FedEx Office locations, and most hotels offer Internet access on Colorado's Front Range. Also see "Staying Connected," in chapter 3.

LAUNDROMATS There are numerous laundromats in Denver, Boulder, Colorado Springs, and the rest of Colorado; consult local phone books.

LEGAL AID If you are "pulled over" for a minor infraction (such as speeding), never attempt to pay the fine directly to a police officer; this could be construed as attempted bribery, a much more serious crime. Pay fines by mail or directly into the hands of the clerk of the court. If accused of a more serious offense, say and do nothing before consulting a lawyer. Here the burden is on the state to prove a person's guilt beyond a reasonable doubt, and everyone has the right to remain silent, whether he or she is suspected of a crime or actually arrested. Once arrested, a person can make one telephone call to a party of his or her choice. International visitors should call their embassy or consulate.

LOST & FOUND Be sure to tell all of your credit card companies the minute you discover your wallet has been lost or stolen and file a report at the nearest police precinct. Your credit card company or insurer may require a police report number or record of the loss. Most credit card companies have an emergency toll-free number to call if your card is lost or stolen; they may be able to wire you a cash advance immediately or deliver an emergency credit card in a day or two. **Visa**'s U.S. emergency number is ✆ **800/847-2911** or 410/581-9994. **American Express** cardholders and traveler's check holders should call ✆ **800/221-7282. MasterCard** holders should call ✆ **800/307-7309** or 636/722-7111. For other credit cards, call the toll-free number directory at ✆ **800/555-1212.**

If you need emergency cash over the weekend when all banks and American Express offices are closed, you can have money wired to you via **Western Union** (✆ **800/325-6000;** www.westernunion.com).

MAIL At press time, domestic postage rates were 26¢ for a postcard and 42¢ for a letter. For international mail, a first-class letter of up to 1 ounce costs 90¢ (69¢ to Canada and Mexico); a first-class postcard costs the same as a letter. For more information go to **www.usps.com** and click on "Calculate Postage."

If you aren't sure what your address will be in the United States, mail can be sent to you, in your name, c/o General Delivery at the main post office of the city or region where you expect to be. (Call ✆ **800/275-8777** for information on the nearest post office.) The addressee must pick up mail in person and must produce proof of identity (driver's license, passport, and so on). Most post offices will hold your mail for up to 1 month and are open Monday to Friday from 8am to 6pm, and Saturday from 9am to 3pm.

Always include zip codes when mailing items in the U.S. If you don't know your zip code, visit **www.usps.com/zip4**.

MAPS The region's best map store, **Mapsco Map and Travel Center,** 800 Lincoln St., Denver, CO 80203 (✆ **800/456-8703** or 303/830-2373; www.mapsco.com), offers USGS and recreation maps, state maps and travel guides, raised relief maps, and globes.

MEDICAL CONDITIONS If you have a medical condition that requires **syringe-administered medications,** carry a valid signed prescription from your physician; syringes in carry-on baggage will be inspected. Insulin in any form should have the proper pharmaceutical documentation.

If you have a disease that requires treatment with **narcotics,** you should also carry documented proof with you—smuggling narcotics aboard a plane carries severe penalties in the U.S.

For **HIV-positive visitors,** requirements for entering the United States are somewhat vague and change frequently. For up-to-the-minute information, contact **AIDSinfo** (✆ **800/448-0440** or 301/519-6616 outside the U.S.; www.aidsinfo.nih.gov) or the **Gay Men's Health Crisis** (✆ **212/367-1000;** www.gmhc.org).

NEWSPAPERS & MAGAZINES The ***Denver Post*** (www.denverpost.com) is Colorado's largest daily newspaper, with coverage of the Denver metropolitan area plus news of the state. The ***Rocky Mountain News*** (www.rockymountainnews.com) also covers the metropolitan area. Each publishes a weekday edition; only the *News* prints on Saturday, and only the *Post* appears on Sunday. A widely read free weekly, ***Westword*** (www.westword.com), is known as much for its controversial jabs at local politicians and celebrities as for its entertainment listings. In Boulder and Colorado Springs, the daily newspapers are the ***Daily Camera*** and ***The Gazette,*** respectively.

PASSPORTS The websites listed below provide downloadable passport applications as well as the current fees for processing applications. For an up-to-date, country-by-country listing of passport requirements around the world, go to the "International Travel" tab of the U.S. State Department website at **http://travel.state.gov**. International visitors to the U.S. can obtain a visa application at the same website. ***Note:*** Children are required to present a passport when entering the United States at airports. More information on obtaining a passport for a minor can be found at http://travel.state.gov. Allow plenty of time before your trip to apply for a passport; processing normally takes 4 to 6 weeks (3 weeks for expedited service) but can take longer during busy periods (especially spring). And keep in mind that if you need a passport in a hurry, you'll pay a higher processing fee.

For Residents of Australia You can pick up an application from your local post office or any branch of Passports Australia, but you must schedule an interview at the passport office to present your application materials. Call the **Australian Passport Information Service** at ✆ **13/12-32,** or visit the government website at **www.passports.gov.au**.

For Residents of Canada Passport applications are available at travel agencies throughout Canada or from the central **Passport Office,** Department of Foreign Affairs and International Trade, Ottawa, ON K1A 0G3 (✆ **800/567-6868;** www.ppt.gc.ca). ***Note:*** Canadian children who travel must have their own passports. However, if you hold a valid Canadian passport issued before December 11, 2001, that bears the name of your child, the passport remains valid for you and your child until it expires.

For Residents of Ireland You can apply for a 10-year passport at the **Passport Office,** Setanta Centre, Molesworth Street, Dublin 2 (✆ **01/671-1633;** www.irlgov.ie/iveagh). Those under age 18 and over 65 must apply for a 3-year passport. You can also apply at 1A South Mall, Cork (✆ **21/494-4700**), or at most main post offices.

For Residents of New Zealand You can pick up a passport application at any New Zealand Passports Office or download a copy from the website. Contact the **Passports Office** at ✆ **0800/225-050** in New Zealand or 04/474-8100, or log on to **www.passports.govt.nz**.

For Residents of the United Kingdom To pick up an application for a standard 10-year passport (5-yr. passport for children under 16), visit your nearest passport office, major post office, or travel agency, or contact the **United Kingdom Passport Service** (✆ **0870/521-0410;** www.ukpa.gov.uk).

POLICE Call ✆ **911** for emergencies.

SMOKING As of 2006, smoking was banned in all public places in Colorado, including restaurants and bars.

TAXES Colorado has a 2.9% state sales tax; local jurisdictions often add another 4% or 5%. Lodging tax is typically 10% to 15%. The United States has no value-added tax (VAT) or other indirect tax at the national level. Every state, county, and city may levy its own local tax on all purchases, including hotel and restaurant checks and airline tickets. These taxes will not appear on price tags.

TELEGRAPH, TELEX & FAX **Telegraph and telex services** are provided primarily by **Western Union** (✆ **800/325-6000;** www.westernunion.com). You can telegraph (wire) money, or have it telegraphed to you, very quickly over the Western Union system, but this can cost 15% to 20% of the amount sent.

Most hotels have **fax machines** available for use (be sure to ask about the charge to use them). Many hotel rooms are wired for guests' fax machines. A less expensive way to send and receive faxes may be at stores such as the **UPS Store.**

TELEPHONES Many groceries and packaging services sell **prepaid calling cards** in denominations up to $50; for international visitors these can be the least expensive way to call home. Many public pay phones now accept American Express, MasterCard, and Visa credit cards. **Local calls** made from pay phones in most locales cost either 25¢ or 35¢ (no pennies, please). Most long-distance and international calls can be dialed directly from any phone. **For calls within the United States and to Canada,** dial 1 followed by the area code and the seven-digit number. **For other international calls,** dial 011 followed by the country code, city code, and the number you are calling.

Calls to area codes **800, 888, 877,** and **866** are toll free. However, calls to area codes **700** and **900** can be very expensive—usually a charge of 95¢ to $3 or more per minute, and they sometimes have minimum charges that can run as high as $15 or more.

For **reversed-charge or collect calls,** and for **person-to-person calls,** dial the number 0, then the area code and number; an operator will come on the line, and you should specify whether you are calling collect, person-to-person, or both. If your operator-assisted call is international, ask for the overseas operator.

For **local directory assistance** ("information"), dial ✆ **411;** for long-distance information, dial 1, then the appropriate area code and 555-1212.

TIME All of Colorado is in the **Mountain Standard Time Zone.** The continental United States is divided into **four time zones:** Eastern Standard Time (EST), Central Standard Time (CST), Mountain Standard Time (MST), and Pacific Standard Time (PST). Alaska and Hawaii have their own zones. When it's 9am in Los Angeles (PST), it's 7am in Honolulu (HST), 10am in Denver (MST), 11am in Chicago (CST), noon in New York City (EST), 5pm in London (GMT), and 2am the next day in Sydney.

Daylight saving time is in effect from 1am on the second Sunday in March to 1am on the first Sunday in November, except in Arizona, Hawaii, the U.S. Virgin Islands, and Puerto Rico. Daylight saving time moves the clock 1 hour ahead of standard time.

TIPPING In Colorado, tips are a very important part of certain workers' income, and gratuities are the standard way of showing appreciation for services provided. (Tipping is certainly not compulsory if the service is poor!) In hotels, tip

bellhops at least $1 per bag ($2–$3 if you have a lot of luggage) and tip the **chamber staff** $1 to $2 per day (more if you've left a disaster area for him or her to clean up). Tip the **doorman** or **concierge** only if he or she has provided you with some specific service (for example, calling a cab for you or obtaining difficult-to-get theater tickets). Tip the **valet-parking attendant** $1 every time you get your car.

In restaurants, bars, and nightclubs, tip **service staff** 15% to 20% of the check, tip **bartenders** 10% to 15%, tip **checkroom attendants** $1 per garment, and tip **valet-parking attendants** $1 per vehicle.

As for other service personnel, tip **cab drivers** 15% of the fare; tip **skycaps** at airports at least $1 per bag ($2–$3 if you have a lot of luggage); and tip **hairdressers** and **barbers** 15% to 20%.

TOILETS You won't find public toilets or "restrooms" on the streets in most U.S. cities, but they can be found in hotel lobbies, bars, restaurants, museums, department stores, railway and bus stations, and service stations. Restaurants and bars in resorts or heavily visited areas may reserve their restrooms for patrons.

USEFUL PHONE NUMBERS **City of Denver** (non-emergency): ✆ 311. **Colorado Road Conditions:** ✆ 303/639-1111. **U.S. Dept. of State Travel Advisory:** ✆ 202/647-5225 (manned 24 hr.). **U.S. Passport Agency:** ✆ 202/647-0518. **U.S. Centers for Disease Control International Traveler's Hotline:** ✆ 404/332-4559.

VISAS For information about U.S. visas, go to **http://travel.state.gov** and click on "Visas," or see below for information.

Australian citizens can obtain up-to-date visa information from the **U.S. Embassy Canberra,** Moonah Place, Yarralumla, ACT 2600 (✆ **02/6214-5600;** http://usembassy-australia.state.gov/consular).

British subjects can obtain up-to-date visa information by calling the **U.S. Embassy Visa Information Line** (✆ **0891/200-290;** www.usembassy.org.uk).

Irish citizens can obtain up-to-date visa information through the **Embassy of the USA Dublin,** 42 Elgin Rd., Dublin 4, Ireland (✆ **3531/668-8777;** http://dublin.usembassy.gov).

Citizens of **New Zealand** can obtain up-to-date visa information by contacting the **U.S. Embassy New Zealand,** 29 Fitzherbert Terrace, Thorndon, Wellington (✆ **644/472-2068;** http://wellington.usembassy.gov).

2 TOLL-FREE NUMBERS & WEBSITES

MAJOR U.S. AIRLINES

(*flies internationally as well)

Alaska Airlines/Horizon Air
✆ 800/252/7522
www.alaskaair.com

American Airlines*
✆ 800/433-7300 (in U.S. and Canada)
✆ 020/7365-0777 (in U.K.)
www.aa.com

ATA Airlines
✆ 800/435-9282
www.ata.com

Continental Airlines*
✆ 800/523-3273 (in U.S. and Canada)
✆ 084/5607-6760 (in U.K.)
www.continental.com

Delta Air Lines*
✆ 800/221-1212 (in U.S. and Canada)
✆ 084/5600-0950 (in U.K.)
www.delta.com

Frontier Airlines
✆ 800/432-1359
www.frontierairlines.com

jetBlue Airways
✆ 800/538-2583 (in U.S.)
✆ 080/1365-2525 (in U.K. and Canada)
www.jetblue.com

Midwest Airlines
✆ 800/452-2022
www.midwestairlines.com

Northwest Airlines*
✆ 800/225-2525 (in U.S.)
✆ 870/0507-4074 (in U.K.)
www.flynaa.com

Southwest Airlines
✆ 800/435-9792
www.southwest.com

United Airlines*
✆ 800/864-8331 (in U.S. and Canada)
✆ 084/5844-4777 (in U.K.)
www.united.com

US Airways*
✆ 800/428-4322 (in U.S. and Canada)
✆ 084/5600-3300 (in U.K.)
www.usairways.com

MAJOR INTERNATIONAL AIRLINES

Aeroméxico
✆ 800/237-6639 (in U.S.)
✆ 020/7801-6234 (in U.K., information only)
www.aeromexico.com

Air France
✆ 800/237-2747 (in U.S.)
✆ 800/375-8723 (in U.S. and Canada)
✆ 087/0142-4343 (in U.K.)
www.airfrance.com

Air India
✆ 212/407-1371 (in U.S.)
✆ 9122/2279-6666 (in India)
✆ 020/8745-1000 (in U.K.)
www.airindia.com

Air Jamaica
✆ 800/523-5585 (in U.S. and Canada)
✆ 208/570-7999 (in Jamaica)
www.airjamaica.com

Air New Zealand
✆ 800/262-1234 (in U.S.)
✆ 800/663-5494 (in Canada)
✆ 0800/028-4149 (in U.K.)
www.airnewzealand.com

Alitalia
✆ 800/223-5730 (in U.S.)
✆ 800/361-8336 (in Canada)
✆ 087/0608-6003 (in U.K.)
www.alitalia.com

American Airlines
✆ 800/433-7300 (in U.S. and Canada)
✆ 020/7365-0777 (in U.K.)
www.aa.com

British Airways
✆ 800/247-9297 (in U.S. and Canada)
✆ 087/0850-9850 (in U.K.)
www.british-airways.com

China Airlines
✆ 800/227-5118 (in U.S.)
✆ 022/715-1212 (in Taiwan)
www.china-airlines.com

Continental Airlines
✆ 800/523-3273 (in U.S. and Canada)
✆ 084/5607-6760 (in U.K.)
www.continental.com

Delta Air Lines
✆ 800/221-1212 (in U.S. and Canada)
✆ 084/5600-0950 (in U.K.)
www.delta.com

EgyptAir
✆ 212/581-5600 (in U.S.)
✆ 020/7734-2343 (in U.K.)
✆ 09/007-0000 (in Egypt)
www.egyptair.com

El Al Airlines
✆ 972/3977-1111 (outside Israel)
✆ *2250 (in Israel)
www.el.co.il

Emirates Airlines
© 800/777-3999 (in U.S.)
© 087/0243-2222 (in U.K.)
www.emirates.com

Finnair
© 800/950-5000 (in U.S. and Canada)
© 087/0241-4411 (in U.K.)
www.finnair.com

Iberia Airlines
© 800/722-4642 (in U.S. and Canada)
© 087/0609-0500 (in U.K.)
www.iberia.com

Icelandair
© 800/223-5500 (in U.S. and Canada)
© 084/5758-1111 (in U.K.)
www.icelandair.com

Israir Airlines
© 877/477-2471 (in U.S. and Canada)
© 700/505-777 (in Israel)
www.israirairlines.com

Japan Airlines
© 012/025-5931 (international)
www.jal.co.jp

Korean Air
© 800/438-5000 (in U.S. and Canada)
© 0800/413-000 (in U.K.)
www.koreanair.com

Lan Airlines
© 866/435-9526 (in U.S.)
© 305/670-9999 (in other countries)
www.lanchile.com

Lufthansa
© 800/399-5838 (in U.S.)
© 800/563-5954 (in Canada)
© 087/0837-7747 (in U.K.)
www.lufthansa.com

North American Airlines
© 800/359-6222 (in U.S. and Canada)
www.flynaa.com

Olympic Airlines
© 800/223-1226 (in U.S.)
© 514/878-9691 (in Canada)
© 087/0606-0460 (in U.K.)
www.olympicairlines.com

Philippine Airlines
© 800/IFLY-PAL (435-9725)
(in U.S. and Canada)
© 632/855-8888 (in Philippines)
www.philippineairlines.com

Quantas Airways
© 800/227-4500 (in U.S.)
© 084/5774-7767 (in U.K.)
© 13 13 13 (in Australia)
www.quantas.com

South African Airways
© 271/1978-5313 (international)
© 0861/FLY-SAA (086/135-9122) (in South Africa)
www.flysaa.com

Swiss Air
© 877/359-7947 (in U.S. and Canada)
© 084/5601-0956 (in U.K.)
www.swiss.com

TACA
© 800/535-8780 (in U.S.)
© 800/722-TACA (722-8222)
(in Canada)
© 087/0241-0340 (in U.K.)
© 503/2267-8222 (in El Salvador)
www.taca.com

Thai Airways International
© 212/949-8424 (in U.S.)
© 020/7491-7953 (in U.K.)
www.thaiair.com

Turkish Airlines
© 90212/444-0849 (in Turkey)
www.thy.com

United Airlines
© 800/864-8331 (in U.S. and Canada)
© 084/5844-4777 (in U.K.)
www.united.com

US Airways
© 800/428-4322 (in U.S. and Canada)
© 084/5600-3300 (in U.K.)
www.usairways.com

Virgin Atlantic Airways
© 800/821-5438 (in U.S. and Canada)
© 087/0574-7747 (in U.K.)
www.virgin-atlantic.com

CAR RENTAL AGENCIES

Advantage
✆ 800/777-5500 (in U.S.)
✆ 021/0344-4712 (outside of U.S.)
www.advantagerentacar.com

Alamo
✆ 800/GO-ALAMO (462-5266) (in U.S.)
www.alamo.com

Avis
✆ 800/331-1212 (in U.S. and Canada)
✆ 084/4581-8181 (in U.K.)
www.avis.com

Budget
✆ 800/527-0700 (in U.S.)
✆ 800/268-8900 (in Canada)
✆ 087/0156-5656 (in U.K.)
www.budget.com

Dollar
✆ 800/800-4000 (in U.S.)
✆ 800/848-8268 (in Canada)
✆ 080/8234-7524 (in U.K.)
www.dollar.com

Enterprise
✆ 800/261-7331 (in U.S.)
✆ 514/355-4028 (in Canada)
✆ 012/9360-9090 (in U.K.)
www.enterprise.com

Hertz
✆ 800/645-3131 (in U.S.)
✆ 800/654-3001 (for international reservations)
www.hertz.com

National
✆ 800/CAR-RENT (227-7368) (in U.S.)
www.nationalcar.com

Payless
✆ 800/PAYLESS (729-5377) (in U.S.)
www.paylesscarrental.com

Rent-A-Wreck
✆ 800/535-1391 (in U.S.)
www.rentawreck.com

Thrifty
✆ 800/367-2277 (in U.S.)
✆ 918/669-2168 (international)
www.thrifty.com

MAJOR HOTEL & MOTEL CHAINS

Best Western International
✆ 800/780-7234 (in U.S. and Canada)
✆ 0800/393-130 (in U.K.)
www.bestwestern.com

Clarion Hotels
✆ 800/CLARION (252-7466) or 877/424-6423 (in U.S. and Canada)
✆ 0800/444-444 (in U.K.)
www.choicehotels.com

Comfort Inns
✆ 800/228-5150 (in U.S.)
✆ 0800/444-444 (in U.K.)
www.comfortinn.com

Courtyard by Marriott
✆ 888/236-2427 (in U.S.)
✆ 0800/221-222 (in U.K.)
www.marriott.com/courtyard

Crowne Plaza Hotels
✆ 888/303-1746 (in U.S.)
www.ichotelsgroup.com/crowneplaza

Days Inn
✆ 800/329-7466 (in U.S.)
✆ 0800/280-400 (in U.K.)
www.daysinn.com

Doubletree Hotels
✆ 800/222-TREE (222-8733) in U.S. and Canada)
✆ 087/0590-9090 (in U.K.)
www.doubletree.com

Econo Lodges
✆ 800/55-ECONO (553-2666) (in U.S.)
www.choicehotels.com

Embassy Suites
© 800/EMBASSY (362-2779) (in U.S.)
http://embassysuites1.hilton.com

Fairfield Inn by Marriott
© 800/228-2800 (in U.S. and Canada)
© 0800/221-222 (in U.K.)
www.marriott.com/fairfieldinn

Four Seasons
© 800/819-5053 (in U.S. and Canada)
© 0800/6488-6488 (in U.K.)
www.fourseasons.com

Hampton Inn
© 800/HAMPTON (426-4766) (in U.S.)
www.hamptoninn.com

Hilton Hotels
© 800/HILTONS (445-8667) (in U.S. and Canada)
© 087/0590-9090 (in U.K.)
www.hilton.com

Holiday Inn
© 800/315-2621 (in U.S. and Canada)
© 0800/405-060 (in U.K.)
www.holidayinn.com

Howard Johnson
© 800/446-4656 (in U.S. and Canada)
www.hojo.com

Hyatt
© 888/591-1234 (in U.S. and Canada)
© 084/5888-1234 (in U.K.)
www.hyatt.com

InterContinental Hotels & Resorts
© 800/424-6835 (in U.S. and Canada)
© 0800/1800-1800 (in U.K.)
www.ichotelsgroup.com

La Quinta Inns and Suites
© 800/642-4271 (in U.S. and Canada)
www.lq.com

Loews Hotels
© 800/23LOEWS (235-6397) (in U.S.)
www.loewshotels.com

Marriott
© 877/236-2427 (in U.S. and Canada)
© 0800/221-222 (in U.K.)
www.marriott.com

Motel 6
© 800/4MOTEL6 (466-8356) (in U.S.)
www.motel6.com

Omni Hotels
© 888/444-OMNI (444-6664) (in U.S.)
www.omnihotels.com

Quality
© 877/424-6423 (in U.S. and Canada)
© 0800/444-444 (in U.K.)
www.QualityInn.ChoiceHotels.com

Radisson Hotels & Resorts
© 888/201-1718 (in U.S. and Canada)
© 0800/374-411 (in U.K.)
www.radisson.com

Ramada Worldwide
© 888/2-RAMADA (272-6232) (in U.S. and Canada)
© 080/8100-0783 (in U.K.)
www.ramada.com

Red Carpet Inns
© 800/251-1962 (in U.S.)
www.bookroomsnow.com

Red Lion Hotels
© 800/RED-LION (733-5466) (in U.S.)
www.redlion.rdln.com

Red Roof Inns
© 866/686-4335 (in U.S. and Canada)
© 614/601-4075 (international)
www.redroof.com

Renaissance
© 888/236-2427 (in U.S.)
www.renaissance.com

Residence Inn by Marriott
© 800/331-3131 (in U.S.)
© 800/221-222 (in U.K.)
www.marriott.com/residenceinn

Rodeway Inns
© 877/424-6423 (in U.S.)
www.RodewayInn.com

Sheraton Hotels & Resorts
© 800/325-3535 (in U.S.)
© 800/543-4300 (in Canada)
© 0800/3253-5353 (in U.K.)
www.starwoodhotels.com/sheraton

Super 8 Motels
✆ 800/800-8000 (in U.S.)
www.super8.com

Travelodge
✆ 800/578-7878 (in U.S.)
www.travelodge.com

Westin Hotels & Resorts
✆ 800/937-8461 (in U.S. and Canada)
✆ 0800/3259-5959 (in U.K.)
www.starwoodhotels.com/westin

Wyndham Hotels & Resorts
✆ 877/999-3223 (in U.S. and Canada)
✆ 050/6638-4899 (in U.K.)
www.wyndham.com

INDEX